The American
Corporation Today

The American Corporation Today

Edited by
CARL KAYSEN

New York   Oxford
OXFORD UNIVERSITY PRESS
1996

Oxford University Press

Oxford   New York
Athens   Auckland   Bangkok   Bombay
Calcutta   Cape Town   Dar es Salaam   Delhi
Florence   Hong Kong   Istanbul   Karachi
Kuala Lumpur   Madras   Madrid   Melbourne
Mexico City   Nairobi   Paris   Singapore
Taipei   Tokyo   Toronto

and associated companies in
Berlin   Ibadan

Library of Congress Cataloging-in-Publication Data
Kaysen, Carl.
The American corporation today / edited by Carl Kaysen.
p.   cm.   Includes bibliographical references and index.
ISBN 0-19-510492-7
1. Corporations—United States.   I. Title.
HD2785.K34   1996   338.7'0973—dc20   96-26549

9 8 7 6 5 4 3 2 1

Printed in the United States of America
on acid-free paper

Contents

Foreword

For most of its existence the Sloan Foundation has been headed by a leader from the corporate world. From 1934 until his death in 1966, Alfred P. Sloan, Jr. was in charge. Since 1989, former IBM Senior Vice-President Ralph E. Gomory has been the president. (During the intervening years the Foundation was headed by former academic administrators.) This kind of leadership is unique among the large general-purpose foundations and helps to explain the Foundation's sponsership of this volume of essays. A deep understanding of the importance of corporations to American society is built into the Sloan Foundation's history.

That historical understanding, however, does not necessarily provide a basis for prescribing about the role of the corporation in today's world. But it certainly leads to questions. Does focus on efficiency of operations and shareholder return produce the best societal outcomes? Are societal outcomes a corporation's business? Are two decades of declining real wages for most of the U.S. labor force and significant growth in inequality of incomes the corporation's concerns?

The Archer Daniels Midland Company (ADM) runs an ad on television identifying itself with President John F. Kennedy's exhortation at his inaugural address: "Ask *not* what your country can do for you; ask what you can do for your country." Is that admonition a practical policy for the corporation? If American corporations, in the aggregate, shared that philosophy, how would they act differently? Or does pursuing the goals of efficiency and shareholder return serve the public interest most effectively? These are some of the questions that prompted the Sloan Foundation to undertake this project.

Harvard professor Edward S. Mason and others examined the role of the corporation in 1959 in the book *The Corporation in Modern Society*. But in the three and a half decades since that book appeared, a new and very different world has evolved. When Sloan determined that a fresh inquiry was needed, Carl Kaysen was the only person we considered to direct it. Not only was he a contributor to the 1960 Mason volume, but a large part of his professional life has been concerned with matters that bear on the corporation and society. To our great good fortune he accepted our invitation. We are proud of what he and his collaborators have achieved here, and hope it will stimulate discussion and debate in both the academic and corporate communities.

ARTHUR L. SINGER, JR.
Vice-President (retired)
Alfred P. Sloan Foundation

Contributors

GREGORY ACS
Senior Research Associate
The Urban Institute

JANET BERCOVITZ
Ph.D. candidate
Haas School of Business
University of California, Berkeley

BARBARA BERGMANN
Professor of Economics
American University

CHARLES W. CALOMIRIS
Paul M. Montrone Professor of
Private Enterprise
Division of Finance
and Economics
Graduate School of Business
Columbia University

DAVIS DYER
The Winthrop Group, Inc.

NEIL HARRIS
Professor of History
University of Chicago

CARL KAYSEN
David W. Skinner Professor
of Political Economy, Emeritus
Massachusetts Institute
of Technology

THOMAS KOCHAN
George Maverick Bunker Professor
of Management
Massachusetts Institute
of Technology

DAVID MOWERY
Professor of Business
and Public Policy
Haas School of Business
University of California, Berkeley
& Canadian Institute
for Advanced Research

RICHARD R. NELSON
Professor of Public Policy
Columbia University

CARLOS RAMIREZ
Professor of Economics
George Mason University

MARK ROE
Milton Handler Professor
of Business Regulation
Columbia University Law School

GEORGE SMITH
President, Winthrop Group, Inc.,
and Clinical Professor
of Economics
Stern School of Business
New York University

EUGENE STEUERLE
Senior Fellow
The Urban Institute

LESTER THUROW
Jerome and Dorothy Lemelson
Professor of Managemant
and Economics
Massachusetts Institute of
Technology

MICHAEL USEEM
Karen and Gary Rose Term
Professor of Sociology
and Management
University of Pennsylvania

RAYMOND VERNON
Clarence Dillon Professor
of International Affairs, Emeritus
Kennedy School of Government
Harvard University

OLIVER E. WILLIAMSON
Edgar F. Kaiser Professor
of Business Administration
University of California, Berkeley

JAMES Q. WILSON
Professor of Political Science
University of California,
Los Angeles

*The American
Corporation Today*

1

Introduction and Overview

✦

CARL KAYSEN

"The business of America is business." So said President Calvin Coolidge in 1925 in one of his few memorable utterances, spoken at the height of the post–World War I economic boom. This would hardly have been an appropriate epigraph for the following two decades, when the business of the United States was first socioeconomic experiment in the face of the Great Depression, with business in low repute, and then worldwide war.

In the long post–World War II boom, when the success of the U.S. economy won the admiration and envy of most of the rest of the world, the slogan might well have been revived. The president of General Motors may or may not have been echoing Coolidge when he said, "What's good for our country is good for General Motors, and vice versa."[1] But at that moment, another slogan could have claimed equal time: "The business of the United States is containing communism."

Today, it could be justly said that the business of the whole world is business. More and more of the world's nations are organizing their economies, and increasingly their polities and societies, around the institutions of the market, a market that is rapidly becoming global. What for more than half a century was a vigorous ideological competitor and for some of that period seemed a viable alternative—the centrally planned economy—has collapsed in practice and lost its force as an idea. Though the subsistence village economy still provides the livelihoods—poor as they are—for a fifth to a third of the world's people, it is everywhere in rapid retreat before the market economy. The characteristic institution of today's market economies is the large business corporation. It is the vehicle for the

3

technologies of production and distribution and the organizational arrangements that underlie urban industrial and so-called postindustrial society.

The essays here collected examine various aspects of the current American version of the large business corporation. The volume has its genesis in a broad comparison of the large American corporation today with its predecessor of a generation ago. In 1959 Edward S. Mason of Harvard edited a collection of essays on *The Corporation in Modern Society*. Although two of its fourteen chapters were comparative, the volume was focused on the American corporation. It was written in the context of the (brief) "American Century," when the United States was in the middle of more than two decades of sustained economic growth and dominated half the world economically and politically. The premise of the volume was that the large American business corporation was a uniquely powerful institution with largely unchecked power in the hands of its managers, and many of the essays asked to what purpose and for what interest the power was used. In particular, how did management use its power vis-à-vis stockholders, workers, consumers, and governments at the local and national level? The power of the large corporation was seen as resting in part on its size, on the sheer scale of resources at the command of managements. But it was also a function of the lack of constraint, either by competitors, since a few large corporations dominated many of the markets in which they sold and bought, or by the capital markets through which they received financing. Internal finance in the form of retained earnings and other cash flow was important; stockholders were, or were becoming, functionless rentiers. These views, in turn, grew out of Berle and Means's classic: *The Modern Corporation and Private Property* (1932).[2]

The context in which the large American corporation now operates thirty-five years later has changed radically. Most important is the globalization of markets, so that international competition, unimportant in the late 1950s, has become crucial, especially in manufacturing. The disappearance of the dominance of the U.S.—and world—automobile markets by the big three U.S. manufacturers is emblematic of the change. In finance, communications, and some areas of business services, there has also been increased global competition, though not to the same degree. Here in the United States, deregulation has led to a substantial increase in competition in the transportation and telecommunication industries, and in some parts of the markets of gas and electric public utilities. Further, the degree to which U.S. markets are dominated by a few domestic producers who treat each other as oligopolistic cooperators as much as rivals has declined substantially even apart from the increasing importance of international competition. Together these sets of changes have led to a more competitive economy. (See the appendix to this chapter, part 1, for further discussion.)

As a result, corporate power no longer lies at the center of the inquiry; efficiency gets at least an equal place. One of the thirteen essays that follow, that by Williamson and Bercovitz (chapter 10), presents a formal analysis of the corporation as an efficiency instrument; in two others, efficiency questions are salient and questions of power largely absent: Roe on legal regulation (chapter 4), and Calomiris and Ramirez on financing (chapter 5). Nelson and Mowery's discussion of technical progress (chapter 6) also focuses on efficiency rather than power, but the efficiency of a system which combines market and equally important nonmarket elements. In the chapters on the corporation as an employer—Kochan's (chapter 7) and Bergmann's (chapter 8)—power issues remain important; they also are central to Wilson's discussion of the corporation as a political actor (chapter 13).

Five essays deal with topics not treated in the first collection: Vernon, on the degree to which American corporations are indeed American (chapter 3), Useem on training and education in the corporation (chapter 9), Steuerle and Acs on the corporation as a dispenser of welfare and security (chapter 11), Thurow on income distribution (chapter 12), and Harris on the corporation as a patron of architecture (chapter 14). Smith and Dyer's overview of American corporate history (chapter 2) completes the set. Vernon and Thurow also touch on corporate power, the former more centrally.

Earlier, the large corporation was described as the characteristic institution of our market economy. So it is, but it is hardly the representative one: the typical business is not organized as a corporation, but rather as an individual proprietorship or partnership. In 1990, the latest year for which statistics are published, a total of 20.0 million nonfarm businesses reported to the tax authorities: 16.3 million proprietorships and partnerships, 3.7 million corporations. The corporations accounted for 90 percent of the sales and receipts reported by all business firms. There were some seven thousand corporations with assets of $250 million or more, the largest class demarcated. These accounted for more than half (51 percent) of the total sales and receipts of all businesses. Large corporations were most dominant in manufacturing (2,602 with 74 percent of sales), utilities and transportation (716 with 76 percent of sales), and finance and real estate (1,503 with 71 percent of sales).[3]

The importance of large corporations was called to wide public attention outside the circle of academic economists by *Fortune* magazine, which

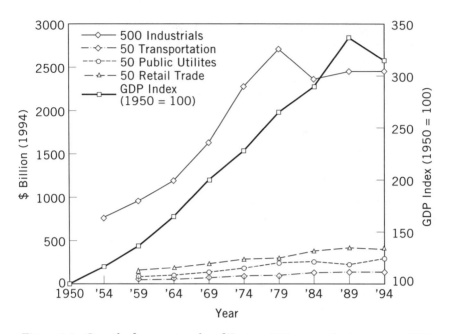

Figure 1.1. Growth of aggregate sales of Fortune 500 companies in constant 1994 dollars by industry group in five-year intervals compared with the growth of gross domestic product: 1950–1994.

has published lists of the very largest corporations annually since 1954. The initial list comprised the five hundred largest industrial corporations, almost all in manufacturing and mining, ranked by total sales. Soon after, the fifty largest trade, transportation, and utilities were added, and more recently, the one hundred largest service companies. This relative handful of corporations accounted for more than half, and in some years as much as two-thirds, of the sales of all corporations. These shares fluctuated over time, but no strong trends, either up or down, appear. Figures 1.1 and 1.2, respectively, show the total sales of the *Fortune* companies in 1994 dollars, and their share of the sales of all corporations, by industry group, plotted at five-year intervals. The first chart shows that the aggregate sales of the five hundred largest industrial companies grew fairly steadily, with one blip, from 1954 to 1979, at a rate that was somewhat higher than the growth of the gross domestic product. After a drop in 1984, the figure rose only a little in the last decade. The growth of aggregate sales of the fifty largest retail trade, public utility, and transportation companies, respectively, was much lower. The second chart shows that the share of the five hundred largest industrial corporations in the total sales of all industrial corporations increased steadily from 1954 to 1979, dropped slightly between 1979 and 1984 and then turned up sharply in the last quinquennium. In contrast, the shares of the fifty largest transportation and retailer components showed little trend, and that of the fifty largest utilities, a decline.[4] More detail on the *Fortune* companies and their shares of total corporate activity, as well as other measures of the importance of large corporations, is contained in the appendix to this chapter, part 2.

These static measures of concentration—the shares of the few very largest corporations in the industry aggregates, and their trends over time—give one measure of the importance and potential power of large corporations. Another and perhaps more significant measure is the dynamics of turnover. To what extent are the same corporations in the same position at the top of the heap year after year? Over the whole period 1955–1994, a total of 1,318 companies appeared on the list, or an average of 21 new companies per year. The total turnover was 2.64, or 7 percent per year. For the period 1955–1980, 932 companies appeared on the list, including the original 500, an average 17 new companies per year. In the most recent fourteen-year period, 1981–1994, 407 new companies appeared, for a substantially higher average turnover of 29 per year.

This striking increase in turnover is explained by the merger wave of the

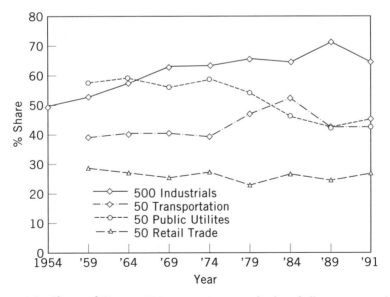

Figure 1.2. Shares of Fortune 500 companies in total sales of all corporations by industry group in five-year intervals: 1954–1991.

middle and late eighties, in which 143 companies disappeared from the list; at the earlier turnover rate, that figure would have been 90. Forty-seven of the disappearances resulted from mergers into other *Fortune* 500 companies; twenty resulted from mergers into large foreign firms. The merger wave, which had subsided by 1990, was stimulated by the economic expansion, the invention and wide use of high-yield (junk) bonds to finance mergers and acquisitions, and the lax antitrust policy of the Reagan administration. The antitrust authorities permitted, without objection, mergers that would earlier have been at least the object of inquiry if not suit, for example, the acquisition of Gulf Oil by Chevron, or Getty by Texaco. By the end of the decade the market for junk bonds dried up; abuses in their use had been exposed, the flow of profits was smaller, and the stimuli to an extraordinary wave of mergers gone.[5]

This is certainly not a picture of stasis. In the absence of an obvious "natural" base of comparison, it is difficult to characterize the observed turnover as "high" or "low." What can be said is that membership in the set of corporate giants at any one time is not, in itself, a guarantee of continuig status in the group: very large firms move up and down in relative size, and many disappear altogether. These changes are driven by shifts in technologies and markets. Some firms anticipate or lead such shifts, some adapt to them quickly. Those that fail to do so, for whatever reason, decline and even disappear.

Turnover figures are more relevant to the Schumpeterian competition of the new—new technologies, new markets, frequently new firms—than to measures of market share or even changes in these measures over time. Yet the question of the relation of one set of measures to the other remains puzzling. In their paper Nelson and Mowery engage the puzzle without resolving it. The relation of the broader question of what makes an economy as a whole dynamic to either measure of the degree of competition is equally unclear. The underlying concept that the desired quantitative index would measure is the adaptability of an economy in the face of change—in technology, in the scope of markets, in the preferences and expectations of workers, capitalists, and consumers. Broadly viewed, modern economic history—from the eighteenth century forward—teaches that competition promotes adaptability. But the economic literature provides no persuasive and widely accepted elaboration of this thesis with enough detail to define and specify measures of competition that have predictive power. Over the same period in which the static measure of competition increased substantially, and measures of large firm turnover increased, the adaptive powers of many large firms in the face of competition from new rivals abroad appeared low—particularly in the steel and automobile industries.

What is clear is that very large firms have substantial time to react. Their command of large absolute amounts of resources, and the probably high costs of takeovers or nonconsensual changes in their management gives them protection from the immediate pressures of competition. It is in this sense that the instinctive reaction of the noneconomist that size does confer power points to something real, and is not merely the illusion or confusion of the inexpert.

Viewed in this light, it is clear that the managements of these firms do have power, in the sense of a range of discretionary choice, the outcome of which is important. The firm is more than the mere register of market forces it is in the classic competitive model of the economist. It conforms more to what could be termed the "business school" view which sees the active role of managers as central to the behavior of the firm.[6] Managements' strategic choices of what technologies to develop and what markets to cultivate shape the way the economy develops. If competition corrects "wrong" choices, it does so only over substantial time, and the path not taken may not necessarily be available at a later time.

The changes over the last several decades in the environment of the large corporation are discussed in Smith and Dyer's broad historical survey, Vernon's examination of the increasing internationalization of American business, and Roe's review of the legal and regulatory surround. Smith and Dyer see both a more competitive environment, internationally and domestically, and more professionalized managements that are more responsive to external constituencies: stockholders; consumers concerned with the safety and quality of the products they buy; employees worrying about health and safety as well as their more traditional concerns about wages, hours, work rules, and job security; and the broader public's interests in environmental protection.

Vernon sees the increasing globalization of business as the most significant change in the corporate environment over the last decades. Net income of U.S. corporations from sales and operations outside the United States is currently reaching nearly half of that from domestic operations; in the fifties, the proportion was closer to one-tenth. Thus, the fundamental question for the corporation is how it maintains and implements a coherent business strategy while it is increasingly subject to the often conflicting rules, regulations, demands, and expectations of different sovereignties. In Vernon's words:

> A global economy that is populated by multinational enterprises has yet to come to terms with a world organized by nation states. In a global system organized by nation states, a [corporate] network made up of units of different na-

tionalities that respond to a common strategy bustles with latent contradictions. Until some measures are taken to blunt the contradictions, the multinational enterprise faces an environment...which will be constantly placing impediments in the way of its efficient functioning and exacerbating relations
between governments.

Vernon exemplifies the problems by discussing the struggles among
competing national sovereigns for tax revenue, for the location of activities
such as research or high-technology manufacture because they are thought
to be particularly beneficial to the economy as a whole, or implicated in national security or both. He sees the resolution of such conflicts as requiring
the creation of internationally accepted rules, and mechanisms to secure
their observance, but sees little prospect of this happening. In the meantime, American corporations will respond to the pressures of other jurisdictions and thus become less responsive to demands from the United States,
in part because the United States, more than other jurisdictions, tends to
deal with each issue separately through a different bureaucratic institution
and lacks an overall view.

Roe points to a shift in the focus of legal constraint of the corporation
from the restraint of anticompetitive behavior through the antitrust laws to
the scrutiny of corporate governance arrangements affecting the roles of
management, directors, and stockholders. The shift in the law's focus paralleled the shift in the environment of the large corporation. The firms that
in the fifties faced only the competition of their fellow American oligopolists, in the nineties faced and were seen to face worldwide competition.
The law accordingly moved from concern with controlling business power
through the antitrust laws to other, primarily efficiency, concerns. Roe,
along with Calomiris and Ramirez, sees the growing importance of financial
intermediaries and pension funds as shareholders as a source of pressure on
boards and managements toward more efficient performance.

Calomiris and Ramirez go further, finding in the set of legal constraints
on financial institutions that prevent them from being providers of the full
range of business financing from short-term debt to equity the major barrier to efficient financial arrangements. These constraints, growing out of
the deep-seated populist hostility to large financial institutions throughout
much of American history, have resulted in a fragmented structure of financial institutions as opposed to the "universal banks" à la Germany and
Japan that efficiency would dictate. Such universal banks would offer businesses a menu of financial choices from which to select an appropriate balance of costs and risks. Further, and equally important, well-informed eq-

uity holders with intimate knowledge of their client firms, especially ones who also hold debts of the same clients, would provide a critical check on management decisions and, when necessary, pressure to change managements failing in the competitive struggle.

In the late forties and fifties, large corporations financed themselves primarily through retained earnings. In the sixties there was a shift to private placements of debt, and in the seventies and eighties increasingly to public offerings of securities. This change was a further constraint on the power of corporate managers as the equity market grew in importance and institutional investors, such as pension funds, held an increasing share of equities. The outside institutional sources of finance could and did scrutinize management performance and were able to exercise pressures both by selling and more directly.

The essays by Roe and by Calomiris and Ramirez address the efficiency of the market for corporate control, as evidenced in the wave of mergers, hostile takeovers, and leveraged buyouts of the eighties. Many were financed through the issue of high-yield junk bonds. The scandals connected with the sales techniques used in promoting these issues by a few leading investment firms aroused public concern, as did the layoffs and plant closings that often followed. Both essays conclude that, by and large, these actions were efficiency-promoting. Their summaries of the research in the field accept the equation of increases in stock prices of the reorganized firms over the next two to three years following the reorganization as an appropriate measure of social benefit, although Roe cites at least one skeptical study.

Nelson and Mowery's examination of the role of the large corporation in technical progress—the often interlinked activities of creating and bringing to market new products and discovering or inventing and applying new production technologies—emphasizes that the corporation is part of a larger system that includes the activities of small new start-up firms and the extramarket support of both basic and applied research, chiefly by the federal government, carried on in universities, other nonprofit institutions, and government laboratories. The flow of scientists and engineers from the universities is also an essential part of the system, and one again that operates chiefly through nonmarket institutions, though clearly within the domain of market incentives for most of the people in the stream. The "output" of technical progress is a product of the whole system.

Historically, the very large corporation has been the leading locus of organized industrial research, and many of the most important industrial laboratories were created by large firms. In more recent years, small start-up firms have assumed greater importance, and in several areas of technology, have equaled or overshadowed the contributions of the giants, especially in biotechnology and computer software. The evolution of a sophisticated and flexible market for venture capital for high-risk operations made these developments possible, a change from the situation in which only large firms had long enough time horizons and large enough resources to permit investments in radically new technologies, the payoffs from which were highly uncertain and distant.

The authors are agnostic as to the optimum balance—if it indeed exists—between large and small new firm activity in producing technical progress. The globalization of research and development activity—as well as manufacturing—further changes the picture, and often lessens the dominant role of the giant corporation.

Williamson and Bercovitz's discussion of the corporation as an instrument of economic efficiency presents the size and shape of the large corporation as the result of a process of contracting that appropriately distributes the rewards and risks of the contracting parties and comes as near as possible to efficiency. They offer a qualification to this conclusion, recognizing that managements have superior access to contract-relevant information to that of stockholders and employees. They reject as distorting the contracting process and thus inefficient the notion of participatory management in which other stakeholders than stockholders are represented on corporate boards. Instead, they suggest that the creation of an oversight board, with access to information and the right to comment on and criticize management decisions but no powers of decision, might provide a remedy for the possibility of management's using its superior information to the disadvantage of employees and shareholders.

Another view of the corporation, more historical and sociological, less analytic, sees it as a learning organization, a respository of knowledge and a corporate culture or style, and a training institution that socializes its new recruits to management into this culture and passes onto them the organizational knowledge it has accumulated. The plan for this volume included an essay on this way of looking at the corporation, but unfortunately it fell by the wayside.

The essays that deal with the relation between the large business corporation and its employees emphasize power as much as or more than efficiency. Kochan describes the substantial decline in union strength over the last three decades. Part of it has arisen from changes in the location of and industrial composition of economic activity, part from the changing administration of the laws setting the framework for union activities—moving away from the pro-union framework of earlier years, and the vigorous exploitation of this change by managements eager to limit union strength and, if possible, eliminate unions. Yet the consequence has not been to increase management power over employees and the work situation to the same degree that unions have lost it. Federal regulation in the areas of health and safety, nondiscrimination, and management and funding of pension plans have constrained managers in new ways. Kochan looks to changes in both corporate behavior and the government framework of employer-employee relations to achieve the better power balance that he sees is necessary to achieve a more productive workforce in a more competitive world.

Like Kochan, Bergmann emphasizes the range of management discretion in dealing with issues of race and gender discrimination. She finds the results of the exercise of that discretion in the past badly wanting, and argues it would have been even worse without the pressure of legislation and the federal rule-making and enforcement efforts it generated. Nevertheless, she looks largely to a positive exercise of managerial discretion in the pursuit of a long-run, broad societal interest in ending race and gender discrimination in the workplace which, on an enlightened view, business interests share.

Useem's examination of the corporation's provision of training and education to the workforce deals with an activity of long standing but one that has become more salient recently. It is not narrowly an issue of management power but is certainly one in which management discretion is large and direct competitive constraints small. Useem's assessment of the needs and opportunities of the large corporation to invest in training and education of its workforce and its responses to them reaches a mixed verdict, but one leaning to the conclusion that corporations have done less than they might, and less than the changing work situation and labor force may require.

In the story of the growing inequality of incomes in the United States—and probably other modern market economies as well—Thurow sees the corporation, driven by competition, as primarily a register and transmitter of underlying economic forces: the globalization of the labor market through both the internationalization of production and increasing immigration; the consequent increase in the supply of labor relative to capital; the differential effects of changing technologies on the skill spectrum of the demand for labor; and the corporate pursuit of cost reduction under the pressures of competition. Only in two areas does he see the exercise of managerial discretion as contributing significantly to the results he presents. First is the successful campaign to reduce union presence and power, with its consequent increase in the inequality of labor incomes. Second is the substantial increase in the pay of top corporate executives relative to the average pay of workers.

Whatever the importance of discretionary choice in producing this change in the income distribution, Thurow raises the question of the political sustainability of the result. Can a modern democratic society tolerate a system in which almost all the fruits of economic progress go to the few and still remain democratic? Further, to the extent that the business community as a whole, and the large corporations that are its most visible symbols, vigorously and successfully oppose government redistributive measures to alter significantly market outcomes in the distribution of income, the question becomes even sharper.

Wilson squarely engages the issue of corporate power in his essay on the corporation as a political actor. In comparison with what he pictures as the high point of both broad public approval and a supportive government stance in the Eisenhower years, he sees significant change in both. Business leaders and business itself are now substantially less highly esteemed by the public. The political system is more fragmented, especially the Congress, now consisting of more individualistic, more entrepreneurial members less committed to party and less ruled by powerful committee chairmen. The Congress treats business as one interest group among many. In response to these changes and the increasing constraints of "process regulation" for environmental, health, and safety reasons, large firms, in turn, have changed their style of political action. They rely less on broad inclusive organizations such as the National Association of Manufacturers and the U.S. Camber of Commerce, and more on their own individual efforts, or ad hoc coalitions on particular issues. There is less effort addressed to broad ideological issues and more to specifics. Most large firms now typically maintain Washington offices; far fewer did in the fifties. They are organized to deal with both Congress and the executive agencies on the specific details of legislation and rule making, offering information as well as argument—information in sufficient detail and specificity to be helpful. But business corporations are one interest group among many, and the degree to which they prevail in any particular political contest is determined by the balance of forces in that specific contest, rather than by any overarching exercise of business power.

Wilson observes that although business-government relations in the United States are adversarial rather than cooperative, the market system and the business enterprise are seen as fundamentally legitimate across almost all of the American political spectrum. There is no more than fringe support for any alternative. In contrast, in Western Europe business-government relations are much less adversarial, but the legitimacy of the market system is in question for a substantial part of the political spectrum.

Steuerle and Acs trace the evolution of the large role of the business corporation as a tax collector for public social insurance, as well as dispenser of such private goods as health care and pensions. The expansion of Social Security, the efficiency of the corporation as a tax collector and record keeper, its advantages as a large buyer, and the tax advantages that were offered to private health and pension plans operated through the corporation led to an enormous growth in the coverage and scale of both. Increasing demand for insurance, whether public or private, was also a major impetus for growth. There is some indication that this growth may have stabilized in recent years. Steuerle and Acs see the system as now under strain, in terms of both the demands it places on the corporation and its limitations in a changing labor market. Yet they see no realistic prospect of eliminating the corporate role in the provision of health insurance and pension plans by a move either to individual responsibility outside the employment nexus or to total public provision through government. The recent (1994) struggle over changing the health care system well illustrates the problems that Steuerle and Acs discuss.

The final contribution—Neil Harris's essay on the corporation as a patron of architecture—stands outside the largely economic framework of the rest of the volume. Harris has produced a pioneering effort at a historical survey and synthesis, looking chiefly at corporate headquarters buildings, but touching briefly on factories and distribution sites as well. Corporate choices have set the dominant tone for public building in recent decades, certainly from the fifties on. They spread the International Style in the fifties and sixties. In more recent decades they have been the leading bearers of postmodernism, as earlier they had brought the skyscraper to the urban landscape. Harris sees their choices as the embodiment of broader social rhythms. Asserting the impossibility of an overall evaluation of the merits of American corporate architecture as compared with the choices of other kinds of patrons, Harris goes on to say:

> certainly in terms of popular sentiment and nostalgic memory the collective power of the Chrysler, Woolworth, Empire State, New York Times, Metropolitan Life, and Grand Central Station buildings in New York, John Hancock, Chicago Tribune, and Wrigley in Chicago, Smith Tower in Seattle, Esperson and Gulf in Houston, and Candler in Atlanta, to single out just a handful among many hundreds, is difficult to challenge. A society that measures time by

changing commercial jingles and television theme music will not undervalue a building's function as billboard, or insist upon civic and religious structures as the only appropriate collective symbols. Corporate architecture is to our physical landscape what civil religion is to our politics: an instrument of social integration.

Thirty-five years ago, Edward Mason drew as the broad lesson from his examination of the corporate role in American society the blurring of the distinction between public and private. The managements of business corporations served broader interests than maximizing the wealth of their shareholders. Governments used the instrument of the business corporation to serve many government purposes from national defense to economic development in third world countries. Some mixture of market constraints, managerial choice, and government regulation guided the results. Among the contributors to the Mason volume, only Rostow urged a complete reliance on the market; Lintner came close to that position. The others by and large accepted the inevitability or desirability of the mixture. The essayists offered no explicit or consistent view as to how nearly optimum the balance among the elements was, but showed an inclination, by and large, to seek more external regulation.

The contributors to the present volume are more divided. Only one essay (Kochan's) calls even by implication for government action to address a problem: in this case, labor-management relations. The authors of four put efficiency first among the criteria for judging the corporation, and, for three, the market is the instrument that will best push toward its attainment. Those who address the issue of corporate power appear to rely on management choice more than on formal regulation to guide the appropriate use of that power; "What's good for the United States is good for General Motors" might be their slogan.

If the quadrivium of socioeconomic virtue is Efficiency, Progress, Stability, and Equity, then the contributors as a whole give the large corporation a high grade on the first two, and either a lower grade on the second two, or conclude they are not an appropriate part of the examination. Thurow, focusing on Equity, gives the corporation a low grade but also—to change the metaphor—offers a defense of diminished responsibility. Useem, and to a lesser degree Kochan and Roe, acknowledge that a more competitive world for the corporation is a less stable one for its employees over most of the range from entry-level worker to high-level manager. They only touch on the question of whether anything can be done to ameliorate these effects. Only Bergmann, assigning the corporation at best a marginal pass on the score of equity among genders and races, attributes most of the achievements to government action.

What accounts for this shift of perspective? Among the contributors to the present volume, Vernon and Kaysen wrote in the earlier one. The rest are outstanding representatives of their professional disciplines and specialties, in general at the middle of their careers, as were their counterparts a generation ago. Perhaps the most important factor in the change is the shift in attitude—one might almost say ideology—in the economics profession in respect to the virtues and shortcomings of the market as a master institution for organizing economic activity. In the fifties, economists and political scientists concerned with government's role in the economy on the whole emphasized the shortcomings of the market and the need for government action to correct them, even while acknowledging the market's virtues. Many markets were not naturally competitive; business firms strove to make them less so, and continuing government action was needed to prevent the firms from succeeding. Neither equity nor macroeconomic stability was assured even by well-functioning competitive markets, and again, government action was needed to better achieve these goals.

Today, the virtues of the market and the shortcomings of government action are the baseline of discussion. Advocates of the new political economy in both economics and political science, emphasizing the self-interested motivations of bureaucrats seeking to expand their power and politicians seeking perpetual reelection to office, mistrust or even scorn the idea of government action in the public interest. These views are widely reflected in the media.

There is certainly empirical support for the negative assessments of the governmental process, but new learning does not account for the whole story. At a deeper level, it is not only government as an instrument that is widely seen as inherently flawed; it is the idea of social interests and social goals that are other than the resultant of essentially self-referential individual choices that is widely suspect. This view is more widespread among the broader public than in the community of academic social scientists. It is often cast in populist terms: any effort to define social goals beyond the aggregate of individual desires is termed "elitist" and attacked accordingly.

The contributors to the present volume are not proponents of the strong antigovernment view. Most would acknowledge that many elements of government regulatory action are justified and, with all their imperfections, necessary for a healthy economy. Yet overall they are, at most, mildly critical of existing institutions, and thus evince little impulse to suggest significant change, either imposed through the political process, or evolved through the leadership of managements, or both.

In the narrower circles of academic economics and political science, another force is at work. Ideas about the public good and the desirable society are vague and fuzzy. The puzzles of working out in full detail the way markets might operate under varying hypotheses about the preferences and knowledge of the individuals who constitute them are intellectually challenging. In disciplines where formal analysis is dominant, as in economics, or becoming increasingly important, as in political science, the drive to deal with those problems that are susceptible to formal modeling and make those assumptions that lead to definite solutions is strong, and has a strong effect in shaping the kind of work that is done. "The market" answers these needs; "the public good" does not. This observation is not offered as a specific characterization of the contributors to this volume but rather as a broad feature of the intellectual atmosphere in which we all work. So it is that this set of essays on the corporation is as much about the market as it is about the corporation.

Leaving aside the centrally important issues of macroeconomic efficiency and stability—which fall outside the scope of this volume—there are at least two significant issues within its scope on which I believe that strong skepticism of the power of the market to produce socially acceptable results is warranted. One is a question of efficiency, the other a question of equity. Current conventional wisdom sees the market for corporate control as essentially the ultimate constraint on management, forcing it to operate efficiently or be displaced, as argued both by Roe and by Calomiris and Ramirez. The same line of argument leads to the conclusion that there is no significance in the separation of stockholder ownership from management control in most large corporations. The current institutions and operations of financial markets offer just as much or more reason to believe the opposite. The stock market operates on a rather short time horizon—two or three years. This is especially true for the large share of equities held by pension funds, mutual funds, and other fiduciaries whose decisions are sensitive to short-term fluctuations in the value of their portfolios. At the same time, banks and distributors of high-risk, high-yield bonds stand ready to finance buyers in the takeover market. A newly installed corporate management has a wide margin of discretion to increase short-run cash flow to creditors and stockholders at the expense of longer-term investments in technological and market development. The modest two- to three-year increases in stock prices that on the average have followed takeovers and leveraged buyouts are not good predictors of long-term performance.

The Calomiris and Ramirez proposal for a large role for "universal banks" as shareholders provides some prospect for significant stakes by investors with both a long-term perspective and a well-informed basis of judgment. But it is far from clear that they will outweigh the mutual funds and pension funds with their focus on short-term fluctuations. All in all, the current interactions of financial markets seem to contribute as much to instability as to efficiency in the operation of large publicly-owned corporations.

As Thurow has forcefully urged, the workings of the market currently tend to drive the distribution of income in the direction of greater inequality. Management choices in the large corporate sector reinforce that tendency, especially in the way that rewards for the top managers of large corporations are determined. This process is largely one of emulative comparison in which professional compensation consultants play a strong role. The system as a whole looks much more like the setting of status-appropriate rewards than the functioning of a competitive market.[7] And the same is broadly true at the intermediate levels of management, although the mechanism that produces the result is somewhat different.

The large firm typically (but not universally) shows a distribution of status and deference that parallels the distribution of economic rewards within it, and is perhaps even sharper the larger the enterprise. At the moment of writing, talk of flattening hierarchies and "empowerment" of employees at all levels is highly fashionable in the business literature. It is too early to see what, if anything, the results will be. The current situation in both the monetary and the status dimensions is not one that is in accord with the temper of a democratic society.

Both the efficiency and the equity questions call for some response beyond reliance on the market. How much the political process will produce appropriate response, how much managerial initiatives will try to anticipate such responses and successfully shape them in ways more acceptable to business is impossible to predict. Thirty-five years ago, Mason observed a blurring of the distinction between the private and public realms, insofar as the functioning of the corporation went. Yet now the dichotomy is being sharpened, at least rhetorically. The Smith and Dyer essay that immediately follows this introduction sees a historical dialectic, making the corporation more responsive to a wider array of constituencies and interests: employees, suppliers, and customers, local communities, and the broader "general public." Perhaps because I am a relic of an earlier era, I project into the future a history in which pressures from the side of political institutions, as well as the market, have been an indispensable element in shaping the evolution of corporate structure and behavior and moving it in a more socially desirable direction.

Appendix

1. Changes in the Extent of Competition in the American Economy

There are no precise measures of the extent of competition or its converse, monopoly power, in the markets of an economy, but quantitative indicators that can be compared over time do exist.[1] The most widely available important measure is the concentration ratio, which measures the degree to which a small number of firms (four or eight) dominate a market. A high concentration ratio is not itself a measure of monopoly power, but a low one is a more certain sign of competition.[2]

The most recent comprehensive set of measures of the trend in monopoly and competition in U.S. markets was made by W. G. Shepherd.[3] His findings are summarized in Tables 1.1 and 1.2. They show a small increase in the share of economic activity accounted for by competitive markets in the U.S. economy between 1939 and 1958, and a substantial increase between 1958 and 1980. Shepherd explains the change as the result of three forces: increased import competition, antitrust action, and deregulation. The interplay of the last two was hard to disentangle; together they outweighed the changes due to import competition. A more recent study, carrying the measures forward to 1987, shows a slight increase in the share of concentrated industries, but not enough to suggest a reversal of the broad trend.[4]

2. The Relative Importance of Large Corporations in Economic Activity

Several sets of data show the size and industrial distribution of business firms in the United States. One major source of data on the activities of businesses distributed by size is the *Statistics of Income*, based on income tax returns. In 1990, the most recent year for which complete data are available, 20 million business firms filed income tax returns.[5] Table 1.3 shows the distribution of these firms by industry group, form of organization, and

Table 1.1. Shares of National Income in Competitive vs. Noncompetitive Markets

Year	1939	1958	1980
Effectively competitive	52	56	77
Noncompetitive	48	44	23

size class. Four industry groups are dominated by large corporations, the receipts of which accounted for more than 70 percent of the total receipts of all corporations in manufacturing, public utilities and transportation, and finance. The share of large corporations in total receipts for the other industry groups is under 30 percent.

A somewhat more detailed look at the small end of the size distribution of business firms is provided by the census data published in the series of *Enterprise Statistics*, most recently available for 1987. In that year the census recorded 15.6 million business firms with 84.5 million paid employees. Slightly more than two-thirds of these—10.9 million—were truly mom-and-pop businesses, with no paid employees. A subset constituting 3.9 million of the 4.7 million enterprises with paid employees was analyzed in detail. These accounted for 81percent of all paid employees. Tables 1.4 and 1.5 present some highlights of this analysis with respect to the relative importance of enterprises of different sizes. Table 1.4 shows the distribution of numbers of enterprises with and without paid employees by major industrial groups.

Table 1.2. Share of National Income in Effectively Competitive Markets, by Industrial Sectors

	Percent of output in competitive markets		
Sector	1939	1959	1980
Agriculture	92	85	86
Mining	87	92	96
Construction	28	56	80
Manufacturing	52	56	69
Transportation and utilities	9	26	39
Trade	58	61	93
Finance, insurance, real estate	62	64	94
Services	54	54	78

Table 1.3. U.S. Business Firms, 1990: Number of Businesses and Receipts, by Form of Organization, Industry and Size

	Number of firms (1,000)			Total receipts ($B)			Large corporations > assets $250m Total Receipts		
	Proprietorships & Partnerships	Corporations	% Corporations	Proprietorships & Partnerships	Corporations	% Corporations	Number	$ Billions	% of all firms
All Nonagricultural	16,337	3,717	19	1,273	10,914	90	7,139	6,258	51
Mining	173	40	15	27	97	78	89	59	27
Construction	1,841	407	18	130	523	80	45	47	7
Manufacturing	408	302	43	87	3,434	98	1,090	2,602	74
Utilities and transport	640	160	20	63	874	93	368	716	76
Trade	2,825	1,023	27	344	3,217	88	415	1,077	29
Finance and real estate	2,153	609	22	171	1,956	92	3,364	1,503	71
Services (including agricultural services)	8,090	1,135	12	440	808	65	238	208	17

Table 1.4. Enterprises With and Without Paid Employees, by Major Industry Groups, 1987

	All Companies	
Industry group	Number (1000)	Employees (1000)
All Industries	15,623	84,481
With paid employees	4,743	84,481
Without paid employees	10,880	
Minerals	158	446
With paid employees	25	446
Without paid employees	133	
Construction	1,590	5,097
With paid employees	529	5,097
Without paid employees	1,061	
Manufacturing	572	20,846
With paid employees	306	20,846
Without paid employees	226	20,846
Transportation and public utilities	633	5,348
With paid employees	165	5,348
Without paid employees	468	
Wholesale trade	640	4,979
With paid employees	355	4,979
Without paid employees	295	
Retail trade	2,460	18,513
With paid employees	1,069	18,513
Without paid employees	1,391	
Finance, insurance, real estate	1,435	6,092
With paid employees	402	6,902
Without paid employees	1,033	
Services	7,031	
With paid employees	1,644	21,673
Without paid employees	5,387	
Unclassified	781	
With paid employees	172	253
Without paid employees	609	

Table 1.5. Shares on Total Receipts of Very Large and Small Enterprises, by Major Industry Groups, 1987

Industry group	Number of companies	Share of total sales and receipts
All	3,879,000	100%
Very large (> 1.0 billion)	608	32
Small (< 10 million)	3,809,000	31
Mineral	25,000	100%
> 500 million	23	34
< 10 million	24,000	20
Construction		
All	529,000	100%
> 1.0 billion	11	5
< 10 million	523,000	60
Manufacturing		
All	307,000	100%
> 2.5 billion	153	43
< 10 million	290,000	12
Wholesale trade	355,000	100%
> 1 billion	86	18
< 10 million	332,000	32
Retail trade		
All	1,070,000	100%
> 500 million	193	33
< 10 million	1,054,000	37
Services		
All	1,467,000	100%
> 500 million	82	14
< 10 million	1,461,000	61

Table 1.5, covering only the subset of 3.9 million enterprises studied in detail, shows the number of very large and very small enterprises, classified by size of sales and receipts, and their respective shares in total sales and receipts for each major industry group.

Table 1.6 shows the growth over 5-year intervals of the sales of the *Fortune* companies by major industry groups in 1993 dollars, and their relative shares of the sales of all corporations in those industries, as shown in *Statistics of Income.*

The drop in aggregate sales of the industrials between 1979 and 1984 reflected the sharp appreciation of the dollar over that period, leading to a decline in the dollar value of foreign sales, which are important to most of them.

Table 1.6. Aggregate Sales of *Fortune* Companies and Shares of Sales of All Corporations by Industry Group, Five-Year Intervals

	500 Industrials		50 Transportation		50 Public utilities		50 Retail trade	
Year	$ billion sales	% of sales of all corporations	$ billion sales	% of sales of all corporations	$ billion sales	% of sales of all corporations	$ billion sales	% of sales of all corporations
1954	778	49	—	—	—	—	—	—
1959	972	53	58	39	92	58	169	29
1964	1213	57	66	40	117	59	206	27
1969	1679	63	84	40	141	56	257	26
1974	2342	63	101	39	202	59	313	27
1979	2781	66	121	47	268	54	338	23
1984	2436	65	148	52	280	46	412	27
1989	2515	71	159	43	272	43	451	24
1991	—	65	—	43	—	45	—	26
1994	2515	—	182	—	371	—	520	—

These are the figures plotted in Figures 1.1 and 1.2 in the text.

Table 1.7. Global Top 50 Industrial Firms 1956–93 at Five-Year Intervals

	National distribution of firms in top 50				United States firms, share of total sales
Year	United States	European	Japanese	Other	%
1956	42	8	—	—	81
1959	44	6	—	—	87
1964	37	13	—	—	79
1969	37	12	1	—	80
1974	24	20	4	2	57
1979	22	20	6	2	54
1984	22	18	6	4	45
1989	17	21	10	2	42
1993	15	19	13	3	37

The changing role of large U.S. corporations in the increasingly global economy is shown in Table 1.7, which shows the numbers and share of total sales of the fifty largest global companies. *Fortune* began publication of data on the fifty largest non-U.S. companies in 1956; the figures come from the combination of these data with those on the five hundred largest U.S. industrials to construct a list of the fifty largest global companies. Over the period, the position of U.S. firms goes from more than four out of five of the fifty world's largest firms with more than 80 percent of their aggregate sales in 1956 to less than half that number and less than half that share. But they are still disproportionately the largest companies, with half of the first ten, along with two European and three Japanese companies; these have nearly 60 percent of the total sales of the ten largest.

Notes

1. The context of this statement was the hearing before the Senate Committee in the Armed Services on Wilson's confirmation as secretary of defense in January 1952. When Wilson was asked whether there was a possible conflict of interest between his new responsibilities and his past position with General Motors, he replied, "I cannot conceive of one because for years I thought that what is good for our country is good for General Motors, and vice-versa." Precisely what "vice-versa" referred to is not clear, but on its face it appears to mean "what is good for General Motors is good for the country." This statement in this form is often incorrectly attributed to Wilson. I owe the reference and the accurate version of Wilson's statement to Professor Marina Whitman of the University of Michigan.

2. Adolph A. Berle and Gardiner C. Means. *The Modern Corporation and Private Property* (New York: Commerce Clearing House, 1932). At the time of writing, Berle was a lecturer in law at Columbia University and had been working for some years on the legal questions of corporate managements' responsibilities to stockholders. In 1972 he received funding from the Social Science Research Council to broaden his research, whereupon he hired Means, who had just received an M.A. in economics from Harvard after a variety of nonacademic experiences, as an economic researcher. Means received a Ph.D. from Harvard in 1933 based on the work he had done in the collaboration. Means published an elaborated version of his thesis in 1962 under the title *The Corporate Revolution in America* (New York: Crowill-Collier Press). See Frederic S. Lee and Warren J. Samuels, eds., *The Heterodox Economics of Gardiner C. Means* (Armonk, N.Y.: M. E. Sharpe, 1992), for a full discussion of Means's work.

3. See Tables 833 and 842, *Statistical Abstract of the United States* (Washington, D.C.: U.S. Department of Commerce, 1995), p. 539 ff. The data are compiled from tax returns and originally published by the Internal Revenue Service in the *Statistics of Income.*

4. These data are taken from the respective annual issues of *Fortune*.

5. The May 5, 1980, issue of *Fortune* contained the turnover statistics for 1955–1980; the more recent ones were compiled from the annual *Fortune* lists. For the merger wave of the eighties, see "A New Era of Rapid Rise and Run," Fortune, April 24, 1989, p. 77 ff. The broader background is shown in the FTC records of mergers in which acquiring companies had assets of at least one million dollars (in current dollars). There were 11,532 such mergers in the decade 1960–1969, 11,239 in the following decade, and 20,251 in the decade 1980–1989. See *Statistical Abstract of the United States*, various years.

6. This view is not unrepresented in the writings of mainstream economists but is distinctly not the dominant one. See, e.g., Sidney G. Winter, "On Coase, Competence, and the Corporation," in *The Nature of the Firm, Origins, Evolution, and Development,* ed. Oliver E. Williamson and Sidney G. Winter (New York: Oxford University Press, 1991), and the literature cited therein.

7. See Derek Bok, *The Cost of Talent* (New York: Free Press, 1995), chap. 5, and Graef S. Crystal, *In Search of Excess* (New York: Norton, 1991).

Appendix

1. Madeline S. Zavodny, a doctoral candidate in economics, compiled the data presented in this appendix, including searching the literature for measurements of changes in concentration in specific markets. I am grateful for her thorough, careful, energetic, and cheerful assistance.

2. See Carl Kaysen and Donald F. Turner, *Antitrust Policy, Legal and Economic Analysis* (Cambridge, Mass.: Harvard University Press,1959), chap. 2, and the statistical appendix.

3. See William G. Shepherd, "Causes of Increased Competition in the U.S. Economy, 1939–1980," *Review of Economics and Statistics* 64/4 (1982): 613–26.

4. F. M. Scherer, *Industry Structure, Strategy and Public Policy* (New York: HarperCollins, 1995).

5. See *Statistical Abstract of the United States* (1994), tables 833 and 842, p. 539 ff.

2

The Rise and Transformation of the American Corporation

✦

GEORGE DAVID SMITH

DAVIS DYER

"The joint-stock companies, which are established for the public spirited purpose of promoting some particular manufacture," the great champion of free enterprise Adam Smith warned in 1776, "can...scarce ever fail to do more harm than good."[1] We have come a long way from the pristine, agrarian world of small traders and craftspeople in which buyers and sellers could meet and satisfy one another's needs with scarcely little more coordination than that provided by the "invisible hand" of the free market. Today, even in the freest of markets, the production and exchange of goods and services are highly managed, rigorously planned, and controlled by the heir to the joint stock company: the modern corporation.

The corporation has become the fundamental organizing unit of the capitalist economy, the institutional basis for bringing capital and labor together in a common enterprise. The textbook definition of the corporation as a privately owned "person," endowed with potentially perpetual life and limited liability for its investors, overlooks the fact that its most important attribute today is its capacity for managing, especially those large-scale processes required for the conversion of raw materials and energy into mass-produced and widely distributed goods and services to consumers. As Peter Drucker noted in a famous essay written at the end of World War II, the complex corporate form, even where shorn of its private ownership, had become central to the development of noncapitalist societies as well, as the principal means of organizing production and distribution.[2]

In the United States, the nature and legal status of corporate owner-ship is a highly significant matter. The tension between the natural inter-ests of "owners and managers," perhaps even more than that between "cap-ital and labor," has helped shape the American corporation in very specific ways. Nowhere else in the world, except possibly in Great Britain, do the claims of owners—often no more than a fragmented group of remote share-holders—weigh on the corporation as heavily as they do in the United States. So, too, has a peculiarly adversarial tension between American pri-vate enterprise and the U.S. government shaped the corporation. Yet within the context of these pressures has emerged a remarkably innovative, adap-tive entity: the large, complex business corporation in its manifold guises and functions.

Consider that in its early American setting, the corporation was rarely employed for undertaking even small-scale enterprise. By the late nine-teenth century, however, it had become essential to conducting virtually any business on a large scale. The first transregional corporations were not merely small companies writ large, even though they remained essentially "unitary" enterprises, companies that concentrated on providing a single product, or closely related set of products, or on providing a single service. Even the greatest of the turn-of-the-century corporate giants—United States Steel, American Tobacco, Standard Oil, the Pennsylvania Railroad, and American Telephone and Telegraph—remained unitary at their core, although many had merged, or "integrated," their basic manufacturing or service operations backward into supplies or forward into distribution. Most of them, with a few notable exceptions, such as International Harvester, Singer Sewing Machine, or United Fruit, conducted almost all of their business within the confines of the continental United States.

Compare this with the manifold types of large-scale corporate enter-prise in evidence today. Big public corporations include such holding and investment companies as Berkshire Hathaway as well as such multipronged financial companies as American Express, Citicorp, or Merrill Lynch. There are "conglomerate" organizations of loosely related, or even unre-lated, businesses, such as General Electric and Allied Signal, which have long since expanded from their original core businesses into diversified manufacturing and service enterprises, while such protean holding compa-nies as Harcourt General or Textron have undergone almost complete transformation in nature as the result of acquisition and divestiture activ-ity. There remain "focused" manufacturing corporations like Intel or Kellogg's or highly diversified manufacturing consortiums, such as Emerson Electric or Dover Corporation. Most big corporations (except public utilities) derive a significant fraction—sometimes the majority—of their sales from overseas. (It is important to note what this sampling excludes—although many of the trends and factors described in the following apply to other entities. For example, many foreign corporations have U.S.-based subsidiaries that, were they included in rankings by sales, employment, or assets, would number among the biggest corporations in the country. Finally, the United States fostered growth of some very big, very powerful, private financial firms like Kohlberg Kravis Roberts (KKR), the Marmon Group, and investment vehicles for wealthy families (such as the Hafts, the Hillmans, the Bass brothers), and many others, whose buying and selling of assets during the 1980s were influential in reshaping the environment for and the conduct of business.)

Another pertinent historical comparison concerns the change in the relationship between the corporation and the larger economy. When the large corporation emerged, its most important task was to guide the transformation of an agrarian society of island communities into a manufacturing nation. All that happened within a half century, from roughly the 1870s to 1920, when the United States became an urban nation (meaning that more Americans lived in urban than in rural areas) and established itself as the wealthiest, most productive economy in the world, with a manufacturing output more than that of the next three largest powers combined. During much of that time the business environment for corporations resembled a Darwinian world of unregulated, free-market capitalism. None of the infrastructure industries, with the exception of the postal service, were state-owned, and unlike any other industrializing country (except perhaps for Great Britain), the American corporation did not become an instrument of national economic policy.

Gradually, however, the rise of the large corporation prompted the rise of other large institutions, some of them complementary—in education, for example—while others were explicitly countervailing to corporate power: in government, in organized labor, and, finally, in the emergence of well-organized interest groups. Again, none of this was the result of a coherent national strategy. The long-term consequence was that competing, as well as complementary, corporate and other interests came to form a tangled administrative jumble of private and public institutions.

Since 1945 the business environment has become progressively more complex. Not only have modern corporations been obliged to deal with other big institutional agents, but they also have had to cope with periods of wage and price controls, energy shortages, inflation, stagflation, and (since 1973), the floating value of the dollar. They have had to respond to legal, political, and increasing social demands. Degrees of inflation, exchange rates fluctuations, and changes and amendments to the tax code caused shifts in investment preferences. Changing approaches to enforcing the antitrust laws had an impact on the number and types of mergers and acquisitions within any given period, as did innovations in the financial markets.

All these developments occurred within the larger context of a long-term shift in the basic structure of economic activity, as the manufacturing-based economy of the early postwar era became, by the late twentieth century, something else—a so-called postindustrial economy. One manifestation of this trend has been a change in where people go to work. By World War II, large-scale, complex corporations were already to be found even in most nonindustrial centers of the economy. The managerial and organizational regimes of what came to be known as "big business" already embraced what Fritz Machlup and others identified as the broad spectrum of industries engaged in "the production and distribution of knowledge"— communications media, education, research and development, computing machines, and financial and real estate services.[3]

By the 1970s this broad band of "information" enterprises would account for as much as 40 percent of GNP, and by 1980 would employ more than 40 percent of the civilian workforce. Conversely, the manufacturing sector, which had employed more than 40 percent of all civilians at the beginning of World War II, accounted for about half that forty years later. Meanwhile, so efficient was that most traditional form of economic activity, agriculture, which benefited from the productive applications of new biological and management "sciences" alike, that huge surpluses of the low-cost foodstuffs so essential to sustaining economic progress could ultimately be produced by less than 2 percent of the nation's workforce. (Great multinational agricultural combines had long since joined the ranks of big business.) The remaining service sectors of the economy accounted for the rest, which had increased from about 22 percent in 1940 to about 29 percent forty years later.[4]

Just as the railroad and the telegraph knit local agrarian economies into regional ones and then a national economy in the late nineteenth century, we are witnessing today the emergence of a more global economy. Commercial air transportation and communications satellites have compressed time and space, making possible the more efficient expansion of corporate enterprise worldwide. Quantum advances in computer hardware and software have led to more instantaneous and widespread access to information and its control worldwide. These technologies, even more than the railroad and telegraph in the nineteenth century, have improved the prospects for more efficient multinational enterprise. Technology has increased the competitive pressures in a world also characterized by a gradual loosening, since World War II, of regional and national trade barriers in countries that have been hard at work on improving their own corporate capabilities.

At the same time large corporations in virtually every sector of the economy grew ever more elaborate in their strategies and structures. Many, looking to find new outlets for investment as older markets matured, expanded operations overseas and pursued more diverse strategies, giving rise to "conglomerate" organizations of loosely related, or even unrelated, businesses, justified on the grounds of improved "synergies" in finance, technology, and management. Following the shift in economic activity, complex organizations spread from the manufacturing "center" of the economy into mass retailing, financial services, and virtually any other industry in which companies strove for scale and breadth of operations. Today the American corporation supervises virtually all the activities of a postindustrial economy.

Finally, there are crosscurrents that leave the social status of the American corporation in a state of uncertainty. On the one hand, the emergence of a market for corporate control restored shareholder influence that had been in eclipse for decades. On the other hand, corporate management has even greater obligations to other stakeholders in the corporation, having taken on social responsibilities that none of the pioneers of big business in the nineteenth century could have foreseen. And the emergence of new and highly focused interest-group coalitions, cutting across private and public sectors of the economy, constrains corporate choices affecting both market and "nonmarket" arenas. Today the pluralistic and often contradictory character of the nation's political and legal process has come to weigh more heavily than ever on corporate management. These conflicting pressures on the managements of corporations are related to the question of whether or to what degree corporate managers should seek to transcend their obligations to their owners to serve the public welfare.

The Historians' Perspective

History is very largely what historians say it is, and so it is useful to review the prevailing interpretation of the rise of the modern corporation. We have learned a lot about the subject since 1959, when *The Corporation in Modern Society* was first published. That same year, by coincidence, Alfred

D. Chandler Jr. published his pathbreaking essay "The Beginnings of 'Big Business' in American Industry" just as a spate of scholarship on entrepreneurship and its impact on large-scale business enterprise seemed to have reached its explanatory limits. Chandler's essay, which most certainly did not arise in a scholarly vacuum, owed as much to the sociology of Max Weber and Talcott Parsons as it did to accumulating historical research on business. It was the first of an impressive series of studies that would form the dominant interpretation of how the modern corporation emerged and developed in the United States during the period between the Civil War and the 1920s. At the center of the story were unsung heroes, organization builders such as the railroad executives Daniel McCallum and Charles Perkins, General Robert Wood of Sears, Roebuck, and Alfred Sloan of General Motors. These were the pioneers of the modern, complex corporation, or what Chandler dubbed the "managerial hierarchy."[5]

The Chandlerian dynamic was as simple as it was profound. Companies, particularly those in capital-intensive businesses, had to grow to great scale and scope if they were to capture the efficiencies inherent in their technologies of production. Given the high fixed costs of their operations, such companies not only had to produce on a large scale but also to take control of their inputs and distribution channels in order to keep their plants running steady and full. Coordinating the "throughput," from sourcing to distribution, over wider and wider territory, resulted in considerable operating complexities. As a consequence, big companies began to employ increasingly specialized teams of managers, supervisors, and laborers. In time their executive managers turned to outside sources of capital to support further growth, and virtually all adopted the corporate legal form of ownership and control. Quite unlike the more traditional small proprietorships, big corporations acquired the capabilities to expand and sustain large-scale enterprise production through the systematic management of complex organizations. It was by virtue of these managerial capabilities that big corporations became the indispensable vehicles for progress at the heart of the industrializing (and nationalizing) American economy.

Within this dynamic, two of the complex corporation's evolving social characteristics proved profoundly important. Management *within* the corporation became a profession of specialized functionaries, as corporate executives replaced the "invisible hand" of the traditional marketplace with the "visible hand" of administrative coordination. Management *of* the corporation became progressively separated from ownership.

Most of the elements of the modern corporation were in place by the 1920s. Key to the success of the large-scale enterprise was the dynamic relationship between corporate strategy and administrative structure. In

Chandlerian terms, corporations pursued strategies that were successful over the long run if, and only if, the appropriate form for administering those strategies were fashioned. Successful managers were those who developed the right strategy for the technology and then devised the best administrative means to implement the strategy. It was no accident that so many of the great pioneers in complex corporate administration were engineers by training or experience.[6] This simple formulation of the dynamics of strategy and structure—a formulation that seemed to imply that the best outcomes were technologically determined—would have enormous appeal among management and engineering experts, who were attracted to what Chandler revealed as justifiable, predictable, and reproducible patterns of corporate development.

Chandler's account of the managerial revolution, including the careful and methodical reasoning and the mountainous store of evidence that seemed to support it, proved so compelling that few historians of business and technology took issue with it. Since the 1960s a profusion of institutionally focused studies has followed this basic outline in rendering the history of modern American enterprise as the product of a "second industrial revolution," a concatenation of powerful forces: new technologies of mass production and mass marketing; the rise of infrastructure technologies in transportation and telecommunications; the discovery and exploitation of economies of scale and scope; and the creation of large-scale business bureaucracies. Surrounded by these larger technological and economic forces, the corporate manager—an increasingly specialized expert on how to administer the organization of big business—brought them to harness.

There were dissenters, however. Neo-Marxists, for instance, saw more sinister forces lurking in the unfolding story of big business. Others took issue with Chandler's apparent approbation of the rise of big business and corporate bureaucracy. But all who sought to explain the nature of postindustrial American culture had to concur with the broader implication of his argument: that, as its economic development came increasingly under the control of large corporations, the United States became a managerial society. Virtually everyone had to recognize that while the broad developments described by Chandler were by no means unique to the American context, the rapid rise and unprecedented influence of the big public corporation were historical forces to be reckoned with.

Today most historians of business take Chandler's work as a point of departure. But the literature has expanded in recent years, widening the scope of inquiry to include broader currents of politics and ideology, social values, law and regulation, and human (including labor) relations. Some historians returned to biography, reemphasizing the fortuitous role of idiosyncratic personalities in economic progress, including that of the kind of organizational entrepreneurs favored by Chandlerians. Others widened their inquiry into those nonmanufacturing sectors of the economy, including finance, to which Chandler had paid scant attention. And still others began to consider how business related to the aspirations of the larger society and to the policy aims, such as they were, of the nation-state.[7]

The Emergence of the Managerial Corporation

The rise of the managerial corporation in the nineteenth century was a truly remarkable, transforming phenomenon, especially when we consider that its emergence occurred in a nation that was still predominantly agrarian and self-sufficient, in which most commerce and industry took place locally, on a small scale, in island communities. In the United States, markets for manufactured goods were fragmented, factories were small and their financial requirements modest. Even though a handful of companies in the textile and machinery industries employed basic techniques of mass production, most goods in the United States were still crafted by hand using traditional small-scale methods. Although it was abundantly endowed with natural resources—food, navigable waterways, cotton, coal, iron, oil, and other material prerequisites for rapid industrial development—the country was fragmented in ways that presented considerable obstacles to the growth of large-scale enterprise. Disjointed networks of transportation, poor distribution networks, as yet untapped sources of energy, and limited financial resources constrained businesses seeking to grow beyond their local environs. State laws impeded incorporation of private enterprise. Large-scale enterprise was also handicapped by an abiding cultural and ideological aversion to concentrations of wealth and power that had strong roots in the radical strains of British political thought that inspired the founding fathers. By the end of the nineteenth century, even as the United States became the great incubator of big business, Americans displayed a peculiar hostility, by world standards, to institutions of great size and power.

Nonetheless, there were important developments in the infrastructure during the early years of the nation's history—the postal service (the nation's one state-owned enterprise), the canal, the railroad, and the telegraph all had their origins in the Antebellum era. Otherwise, as Alexis de Tocqueville saw it, "productive industry" was characterized "not so much by the marvelous grandeur of some undertakings, as the innumerable multitudes of small ones."[8] Business in the young United States was vibrant: a high degree of entrepreneurship combined with a lust for individual fortune in a highly mobile society that was relatively free of Old World class structures, political authoritarianism, and constraints on property ownership. The American citizenry was also blessed with a high degree of literacy and a continuing influx of ambitious immigrants in search of opportunity. These factors would bode well for rapid industrial development. But the history of business from the Revolution until the Civil War was dominated by the artisan-inventor and the small entrepreneur—figures like Eli Whitney, Samuel F. B. Morse, Elias Howe, Elisha Graves Otis—whose longer-term impact on industrial society was barely, if at all, discernible. Some just invented, some just organized, but even the most creative and important of these entrepreneurs were by modern standards little more than tradesmen operating what were essentially family firms, owner-managed with few employees and little administrative overhead, and organized, for the most part, as unincorporated proprietorships or partnerships.

An important precondition for large-scale enterprise was a corporate organizational structure, which in turn required the development of an accommodating corporate legal structure. Today in the United States it is a simple matter to charter a corporation. For a small fee, papers can be filed with any state government for a charter that allows an individual or group of investors to form an enterprise that exists independently of its individual proprietors. The liability of investors in a corporation is limited to that of the amount of money they have placed in the business. As a legal "person," the corporation can borrow, issue stock, sue and be sued, and own other businesses. It has proven over time to be a marvelously adaptive vehicle not only for spreading the risk of investment but also for applying investment at great scale over huge distances. But that was not always the case. What is now accepted as commonplace was rare; what is now a matter of every citizen's right was once a matter of privilege.

The traditional corporation under Anglo-Saxon law had been a grant of entitlement from the sovereign to a private group of citizens. Eleemosynary and religious corporations aside, the corporate charter for business provided a monopoly incentive for carrying out business that the state deemed useful. In the mercantilist era of the seventeenth century, businesses that were strictly private in nature, and that made their money purely from market transactions, did not incorporate. After 1776 the power to incorporate passed from the Crown to American legislatures, but it would take decades, under the pressures of industrialization, before the corporation became more a private right than a grant from the state, and achieved its recognizably modern form.[9]

While the federal Constitution had always supported interstate commerce and the sanctity of contracts, and while most states had developed relatively liberal bankruptcy codes early in the century, laws accommodating large-scale business incorporation were slower to develop. In the early nineteenth century the business corporation was still a somewhat tainted device; corporations granted by the several state legislatures were generally limited to municipalities, churches, charitable institutions, and banks. It was a cumbersome procedure for a private entrepreneur to apply for a charter, which almost always implied currying for political favor in addition to demonstrating that the enterprise in question served some public purpose. The few incorporated businesses (other than banks, which numbered in the hundreds) were mainly public works projects that were often granted monopoly rights and even subsidies under the assumption that they were vital for economic growth. Even more remarkable in retrospect is that limited liability for shareholders was in most states not yet embedded in corporate law.

With the emergence of mass manufacturing, there was an increasing demand on the part of private investors for corporate status. By the 1830s the impulses of Jacksonian democracy were working their way through both the federal courts and state legislatures, rapidly eroding the traditional state-sanctioned monopoly privileges associated with incorporation and shielding the corporation itself from tampering by the state with its basic contractual rights, even loosening restrictions on the ability of a "foreign," that is, out-of-state, company to do interstate business. "[T]he conviction that the individual was the *raison d'être* of civil society and the agent of national progress" became increasingly embedded in the law."[10] Under this doctrine, the right to incorporate became generally available, along with a growing body of other rights that protected property and the sanctity of contracts. In 1899 New Jersey liberalized its already permissive corporation law so that "the conduct and conditions of [a corporation's] . . . business are treated as private and not public affairs."

This separation of private from public interests involved nothing less than a wholesale shift in the underlying theory of economic growth. As a key part of the evolution of private rights, the right to incorporate did two things: for investors it substantially reduced uncertainties as to personal liability and the long-term legal status of the enterprise, even as it left their business more open to competition from other private concerns. The net effect of the liberalization of corporate law and competitive ideology was to stimulate the formation of thousands of business firms on a scale far larger than the traditional family firm.

For instance, by 1860 the State of New York was in the vanguard of these trends, having already provided for the perpetual life of corporations and for the limited liability for fully paid-in shareholders. A general act of incorporation for manufacturers had been enacted in 1848, based on a new constitutional provision prohibiting the state from giving or lending its credit to private parties, while at the same time making it possible to incorporate without undergoing the cumbersome process of lobbying the legislature. With the promise of perpetual life for their business and limited liability for its prospective shareholders, entrepreneurs could now fuse, in effect, the interests of a wider network of creditors and stockholders in an enterprise that would absorb far more capital than they themselves could provide. While there remained limits to what could be achieved (New York law limited the total capitalization of manufacturing corporations to two million dollars before 1890), no one could yet have imagined the scale some businesses would achieve late in the century.

Indirectly, but importantly, competition also stimulated more liberal laws for incorporation. Companies in capital-intensive industries struggled to find ways to limit "ruinous competition" in times of overcapacity. The railroads, in the spirit of mutual preservation, had tried pooling arrangements with little success, so tempting was it for members to cut rates in hard times. Likewise, cartel associations of manufacturing companies that formed in the wake of the depression of 1873 had limited success; they lacked the necessary legal enforcement powers, for one thing, as they were of doubtful legitimacy under both state and common law. The German immigrant-cum–railroad magnate, Albert Fink, proclaimed to Congress in 1880 that nothing could be more American than the well-administered cartel, but he was wrong.[11] Neither American consumers (in this case, smaller businessmen and shippers of agricultural commodities) nor the law would tolerate it. In the end the railroads would consolidate into huge systems, which then engendered extraordinary demands for sophisticated administrative management.

Emerging large-scale manufacturers also saw the logic of system building to achieve efficiencies (and therefore cost advantages) that derive from scale economies. But the legal barriers remained high. In addition to growing misgivings about cartels, even those state governments that permitted some measure of "free" incorporation continued to set limits on capitalization and to restrict the ability of firms to hold stock in other companies. To avoid the legal barriers to cartels and interstate corporations, John D. Rockefeller's rapidly expanding Standard Oil Company devised a "trust" where, as trustee, it could exchange its certificates for the common stock of participating companies, a device used by but a handful of other industries in the 1880s.[12] At the end of the decade New Jersey and Delaware enacted general incorporation laws, whereby holding companies could purchase stock in other corporations on a more or less unrestricted basis. This, then, after the passage of the Sherman Act, which definitively outlawed cartels, cleared away the legal impediments to the consolidation of large, national enterprises, one of the more ironic outcomes of the clash between American ideology and economic forces. Holding companies, initially established for ownership control, soon evolved into more elaborate offices for corporate governance.

All told, big business came of age with astonishing speed. The rise and consolidation of most capital-intensive industries occurred within the span of a quarter century, running roughly from the mid-1870s to the turn of the century, culminating in history's first "merger wave" between 1895 and 1904.[13] During that era organizational innovators, such as Rockefeller, Andrew Carnegie, Theodore Vail, and J. P. Morgan found ways to enable small companies employing capital-intensive technologies to grow into huge manufacturing, distribution, and utility complexes.

Strategy, Structure, and Management

The large-scale corporation had antecedents in an antebellum development, the railroad and its fellow traveler, the telegraph. With their potential for compressing time and space and their elaborate system requirements, the railroad and telegraph not only triggered the rise of big business but also set the pattern for its financing and management. The enormous capital requirements and geographic reach of the railroads put them beyond the investment means of even the wealthiest individuals or families. Premodern capital markets emerged and evolved in large measure to finance this new form of infrastructure, very largely with foreign funds. At the same time the logistical problems of building and operating the main line, or trunk, rails called into being specialized experts to oversee and manage them. By the 1870s large systems had developed recognizably modern, functionally organized administrative organizations and practices. Borrowing from the military chain of command, these companies distinguished between line operations and staff support, and they organized activities around such specialized departments as finance, purchasing, traffic (logistics and scheduling), sales, real estate, engineering, and law. They fashioned policy manuals, organization charts, administrative bulletins, and other aids to standardize and routinize operations. They developed and adopted new accounting methods to prepare budgets, to track costs, to improve the flow of materials through production and distribution, and to measure results.

The railroad and telegraph made possible the combination of technologies of mass production with sales into far-flung markets. As large manufacturing companies emerged to take advantage of this opportunity, what had been learned on the railroad spread to other forms of capital-intensive enterprise. The first companies to grow large and then adopt managerial hierarchies enjoyed powerful "first-mover" advantages. Many of the largest industrial corporations that emerged in those years remain dominant competitors today: AT&T, General Electric, General Motors, Du Pont, Coca-Cola, Standard Oil, Alcoa, to name but a few. Even those that have struggled, disappeared, or merged into bigger combines—Swift, Armour, U.S. Steel, Otis Elevator, Singer, International Harvester—bequeathed organizational forms and strategies that were to become characteristic of their industries, first, in the United States and eventually worldwide.

The myriad variants of large-scale administration that evolved into the twentieth century can be grouped into two general types: functional and multidivisional organizations, with each of these being responsive sequentially to the evolution of strategies. First came strategies for expanding the markets for a single product. Such "horizontal" growth occurred often simply by combining, or integrating, once competing companies, to achieve desired economies of scale and to limit competition. Horizontal growth was sooner or later followed by some degree of "vertical integration." To ensure that their productive capacities would be utilized as fully as possible, companies often had to acquire or develop the capabilities of their suppliers and/or customers. Vertical integration called for the development of specialized departments with specialized "middle managers" who could manage such distinct functions as purchasing, production, and sales and distribution. Corporate offices became more specialized, with centralized staff departments for treasury, legal, engineering, and other functions that supported the enterprise as a whole.[14]

This sequence of strategies, from horizontal to vertical integration, was exemplified by Carnegie Steel. Andrew Carnegie had originally exploited economies of scale to put smaller, less efficient iron producers out of business. To keep his furnaces filled, Carnegie integrated backward into mining and processing of ore. For the same reason, he developed downstream capabilities in fabricating rails and other structural shapes from raw steel. In the 1880s he stole a march on other large steelmakers when he adopted the open-hearth furnace that displaced the more traditional Bessemer process. Carnegie sold his business in what by some measures remains the biggest merger in history, the 1901 formation of U.S. Steel, a transaction financed by J. P. Morgan to combine the largest steelmakers in the country into a giant entity that controlled nearly two-thirds of the market.[15]

Creative bankers helped arrange and finance other consolidations in a long wave of merger activity that billowed between 1897 and 1904, when some 4,227 companies merged into 257 corporations. By the end of this period, 318 corporations controlled as much as two-fifths of the country's manufacturing assets. Those industries amenable to continuous-process or large-batch production benefited from improved economies of scale and operation. This trend toward concentration continued, accelerating in another merger wave led by utilities companies in the 1920s, so that by 1930 the vital center of the business economy had become a cluster of oligopolies.[16]

As Carnegie had shown, large corporations did not merely apply technology, they improved it. They continuously brought out new products while striving for more efficient ways of making them. "Scientific methods" of management, propounded by Frederick W. Taylor and other consultants and academicians, greatly improved the organization and techniques of production, which were then transformed through the constant application of breakthrough and incremental engineering improvements. In the 1910s, when Henry Ford demonstrated the efficacy of the assembly line, which brought the prices of automobiles within reach of his labor force, his competitors hastened to adopt the new process. This had the effect of putting the automotive industry, with all its vital linkages to other productive sectors, in the very center of the booming industrial economy after World War I. (In 1929 the United States produced more than 4.5 million automobiles, or about nine times as many as Britain, France, and Germany combined.) Such innovation—both the initiation and the rapid copying—was becoming a normal part of the corporate dynamic.[17]

In high-technology industries based on electricity and chemistry, companies not only innovated, they went so far as to establish expensive overhead functions in research and development. By 1920 some 350 companies claimed to have research and development (R&D) programs. Dominant companies like AT&T, General Electric, and Du Pont had established world-renowned research laboratories staffed by highly paid scientists and engineers who were charged to explore the fundamentals of their disciplines, as well as their applications. Like other vertical strategies, corporate R&D arose largely from defensive concerns: it helped large, science-based corporations protect their massive investments and leading market positions from outside forces of "creative destruction." Still, even as industrial science was subordinated to corporate strategy, it had larger social benefits. The aluminum monopoly, Alcoa, developed knowledge on the structure and composition of metals that might not have happened elsewhere for years to come. R&D also supported corporate growth through improvements in existing products and through the development of new products.[18]

After World War I, growth was also achieved through strategies of diversification. Such companies as U.S. Steel, Standard Oil, American Tobacco, and the Pennsylvania Railroad had achieved dominance in their industries on the basis of a single product or service. For many companies, however, growth had limits. Bound by high fixed costs and fearing excess productive capacity, a few pioneering manufacturers began to expand into multiple products or services. It usually took a crisis, or at least the perception of one, to move a corporation to diversify. Diversification strategies, though often ingenious, were relatively easy to conceive; organizing their implementation was hard. Once corporations began to expand beyond a single product line, centralized operating structures designed to cope with vertical integration proved inadequate to the increasing complexity of sourcing, production, and distribution problems. The most appropriate form for administering complex, diversified corporations, as it turned out, was the "multidivisional" corporation.

The chemical giant Du Pont, primarily a maker of explosives before World War I, worried that its business would fall off sharply in a peacetime economy. Its leaders pushed the company to develop business that could make alternative uses of its employees and assets by diversifying into two areas that depended upon chemical technologies somewhat similar to explosives: celluloid (plastic) products and protective coatings such as paints and varnishes. These new businesses, however, proved truly successful under common ownership only after Pierre du Pont recognized that the markets for these product lines were separate and distinct, with each requiring general management attention. Accordingly, in the 1920s he devised a new decentralized structure composed of distinctly different units to plan and administer the company's separate businesses. Each unit, or division, had its own executive management, its own productive and marketing organizations, its own more or less complete set of functional capabilities. In this configuration of businesses within a business, the corporate office and its executives, no longer preoccupied with operational details, took on a new, more rarefied, set of roles: allocating resources to the various businesses; deciding which business to enter and exit; providing common services to the various divisions.

During the 1920s multidivisional structures were adopted by other chemical companies (Hercules Powder and Allied Chemical) and beyond, into diversified manufacturing combines (General Electric and Westinghouse), even retailing (Sears, Roebuck) and automobiles. At General Motors (where Pierre du Pont was chairman), the adoption of multidivisional management enabled Alfred Sloan to implement a product differentiation strategy that within just a few years would reduce the once-dominant, single-product Ford Motor Company to a distant second in the automotive marketplace. Sloan's General Motors had general office capabilities for forecasting market conditions, allocating resources among product lines, and providing support for executives of semiautonomous operating divisions. Henry Ford was a brilliant entrepreneur, but he was also an arbitrary, controlling, and unsophisticated owner-manager, and was virtually helpless to respond.[19]

The rise of the multidivisional corporation in the aftermath of World War I was the final, critical step in the creation of the modern, *efficient* corporate bureaucracy. Even more elaborate, modern configurations of large-scale enterprise—the multinational corporation and the conglomerate—are but variants of the basic multidivisional principle. And yet, while the multidivisional structure made it possible to grow and coordinate diversified enterprise over vast geographic expanses, it was hard to master and was fraught with questions about which functions to centralize and which to decentralize (and thereby risk duplication and loss of control). Consequently, the multidivisional organization spread slowly, and not until after World War II did it become commonplace in the United States.[20] When it did, American business—with its array of organizational capabilities—became the fear and envy of the world.

Managers, Owners, and Other Stakeholders

What Sloan and Ford (by contrary example) demonstrated was that big corporations required a highly developed "technic of administration." The trend was for salaried executive managers to succeed owners and entrepreneurs who lacked strategic and administrative skills. As management became increasingly systematic in linking the problems of production to the social and economic realities of the national (in some cases, international) marketplace, big business came increasingly to rely on people with professional training. Schools of engineering and business administration emerged to supply companies with more formally trained technicians and functionaries, with functions and interests that were distinct from those of "capital" and "labor."

Management triumphed not only because of its expertise, but also because shareholdings in corporations dispersed, as large enterprises went increasingly to the capital markets to finance their marginal requirements for funds. Unlike Germany or Japan, there was no process in the United States by which corporations and banks could affiliate in stable relationships. Finance capitalism, in which bankers, on behalf of creditors and shareholders, became intimately involved in the governance of large combines that they had helped to organize, was a fleeting phenomenon in American corporate development, one that lasted from about the turn of the century to 1912. By World War I the professional manager had effectively replaced the financial capitalist, who, in turn, had displaced the family owner as the controlling agent of the large corporation.

This transfer of power to management in large corporations was analyzed by Adolf Berle and Gardiner Means in a famous 1932 book, in which they argued that when the owners of an enterprise also managed and controlled it, their interest in maximizing their personal wealth and income was congruent with the efficient administration of the enterprise. But as ownership became divorced from control, this identity of personal and business interests could easily disappear.[21] It was not simply that executives tended to favor retained earnings over dividends (a classic tension in the stories of high-growth, nineteenth-century companies). The managerial corporation posed what more modern economists call a "principal-agent problem": managers had incentives to exploit corporate assets opportunistically in their personal interests rather than in the interests of the owners.

The doctrine that business must operate first and foremost in the interests of its shareholders remained a staple in the teaching of corporate law, but the reality was quite different. It was a fact of life that on a day-to-day basis managers tended increasingly to worry about a *wider* range of constituents—bankers, suppliers, customers, workers, the communities in which they did business, and the government. This view of the corporate manager's responsibilities received respectable support from intellectual bastions like the Harvard Business School, and it became *de rigueur,* as Edward Mason observed in 1959, for managers "to deny . . . exclusive preoccupation with profits and to assert that [they] are really concerned with the equitable sharing of corporate gains" among broader constituencies.

But, he pointed out, "If equity rather than profits is the corporate objective, one of the traditional distinctions between the private and public sectors disappears."[22]

The distinction between "private" and "public" sectors in the economy had already been blurred to some extent. The prosperous, urban economy of the twentieth-century United States owes much to the presence of big business. Between 1870 and 1930, the U.S. population increased from fewer than 40 million to 123 million, including 30 million immigrants who came in search of fortune created by America's industrial boom. Per capita gross income more than tripled in real terms during the same period, while the nation's labor pool quadrupled, from 12.5 million to 48.8 million.[23] After World War I, better-managed companies and more efficient production brought once luxurious technologies into more common household use, as the automobile, electricity, the telephone, the radio, and kitchen appliances began to transform the very patterns of everyday life. As the United States became more of a consumer's economy, increasing numbers of Americans accumulated savings and invested them in corporate bonds and stocks, through which they hoped to benefit from the sale as well as the purchase of goods and services.

Moreover, big business, as authoritarian as it might be in its administrative structure, carried within it the seeds of a more egalitarian society. The complex corporation was increasingly dependent, after all, on expertise—managerial and engineering—which opened up avenues for individual achievement. Corporations were also hospitable to the great leveler of traditional privilege based on social class, family ties, and inherited wealth: the ability to make money. In this respect, at least, the corporation, as a social mechanism, had progressively meritocratic tendencies.

Yet if big business corporations were engines of plenty and sources of individual opportunity, they were also worrisome creatures. The early giants were bigger than state governments. They wielded power, but, unlike governments, they did so in secrecy. They were associated with the rise of urban squalor, gloomy factories, and the degradation of labor. Even before the turn of the century, cynical manipulations of stocks and bonds in railroads and utilities, extortionate practices in the consolidation of the oil and tobacco industries, the production and distribution of unhealthy products in the food and drug industries, and the ill-concealed bribery of public officials formed a litany of horrors in newspapers, magazines, and popular books. The development of efficient bureaucratic hierarchies within the corporations, along with the emergence of scientific management, only added to the general discomfort. As concentrations of wealth and power, large corporations deeply disturbed American individualistic and democratic sensibilities that had been honed in a simpler, Jeffersonian world of quiet and familiar communities and small enterprises.

Attacks on big business came from farmers, urban populists, progressive reformers, intellectuals, labor organizers, and small businessmen. Cutting through the more generalized fears about size and power was an economic argument: large corporations drove out smaller producers, exercised extraordinary control over prices and wages, and closed off opportunities for entrepreneurs of modest means. The issue of the "trusts" dominated political debate from the 1880s to World War I, as the focus of business regulation widened from cities and states to the federal government, laying the foundation for the modern "administrative state." The Interstate Commerce Commission was established in 1887, in the first of a series of actions taken to control rate making and to stem other market abuses associated with monopoly power in transportation and telecommunications. In 1914 the Federal Trade Commission was set up with powers to demand information from corporations, to issue cease and desist orders, and to bring offending companies to trial. In between, other federal agencies and commissions were empowered to monitor activities in corporations, mostly with respect to pricing issues but also, as was the case with the Food and Drug Administration, to ensure the public safety.[24]

Equally important, and distinctively American, was the Sherman Antitrust Act of 1890, enacted in a climate of growing hostility toward monopolies. At first the courts did little to apply the law against large corporations. As noted earlier, the statute did not prevent large-scale mergers, but it did serve as a brake on bald efforts to monopolize industries or markets. A series of Supreme Court decisions between 1897 and 1903 dampened combinations in the railroad industry, but the full force of the law was not felt by big monopolistic manufacturing concerns until 1911, when the Supreme Court ordered the dissolution of the American Tobacco Company and Standard Oil. The tide against large corporations reached a peak in 1914 with the passage of the Federal Trade Commission Act and the Clayton Antitrust Act. Antitrust was unevenly applied over subsequent decades, and was often brought to bear more on small business combinations than on large corporations, but the mere existence of the law served as a salutary warning to leaders of big business.[25]

Finance was the one key sector of the American corporate economy that would remain remarkably fragmented, by world standards. Here, again, uniquely American factors in both government regulation and ideology played a role. Fear and mistrust of big banks dates to the beginnings of the

Republic (the first banking corporation in the emerging nation was established to help finance the Revolution). Andrew Jackson's veto of the rechartering of the Second Bank of the United States in 1832 put an end to quasi-central banking in this country until 1913. State laws universally prohibited interstate branch banking and, in some cases, branch banking at all, resulting in a jumble of commercial and savings banks (as well as unchartered private banks, many of which developed investment banking functions). In 1906 the State of New York forbade insurance companies from underwriting securities and owning banks and trust companies, putting an end to efforts to centralize a full range of financial services.

Even before then, by World War I, the great investment and commercial banking houses, under congressional and public pressure, had already more or less voluntarily withdrawn from their once active roles in the governance of large corporate combines they had financed since the turn of the century. In a world of financial capitalism, the solution to the principal-agent problem posed by Berle and Means, in theory at least, was to have bankers ensure that corporate managers were acting in the interests of the creditors and the shareholders to whom the bankers had sold the corporation's securities. But the bankers were in retreat, and were unlikely to reassert their power. The result of all these developments was that nothing like the more "universal banking" systems of Germany or Japan would develop in the United States, nor would corporate governance become subject to the kind of close, "insider" systems of governance that existed in the alliance between particular banks and industrial concerns in most other major capitalist countries.[26]

The manager was a beneficiary of the profound ambivalence toward corporations. On the one hand were the champions of small business, who, like the corporate lawyer Louis Brandeis, inveighed against the unholy alliance between finance and management. In "Other People's Money," an influential series of magazine articles, Brandeis condemned the nation's monied oligarchy and warned the general public about the perils of big business, the evils of interlocking directorates, and the crass spectacle of greedy financiers who conspired with their corporate allies in secrecy and who took large underwriting fees while contributing little to the welfare of society. Brandeis simply feared large-scale enterprise and feigned not to understand why the market structure of the oil industry should be any different from that of the shoe industry. Though he most likely grasped the efficiencies of large-scale enterprise, he stood for a more traditional economy, one based on small-scale enterprise and competitive individualism.

On the other hand, a rising generation of intellectuals like the young

Walter Lippmann no longer equated size and power with greed. "The real news about business," he wrote in 1914, was "that it is being managed by men who are not profiteers. The managers are on salary, divorced from ownership and from bargaining . . . . The motive of profit is not their motive. That is an astounding change." What Lippmann and other commentators on public affairs were beginning to appreciate was that professional management might deal effectively with large organizations with positive results for society. Perception of this change reached the Supreme Court in 1920, when it declared in dismissing an antitrust action against U.S. Steel: "The law does not make mere size an offense." Perhaps Woodrow Wilson best summed up the nation's feeling toward corporate enterprise when he declared: "I am for Big Business, and I am against the trusts."[27]

America's entry into World War I was supported by a command economy in which the railroads were nationalized, production rationed to the ends of war, and more cooperative relations between industrial leaders and government officials prevailed. But this set of circumstances, along with the notion that business should serve the goals of the state, was short-lived. When the war ended, controls were lifted, railways were returned to their private owners, and the Roaring Twenties became halcyon days for corporate capitalism. The business of America, as Calvin Coolidge proclaimed, was business, and if the state had a role to play, it was to free up the constraints on private enterprise. That was eminently plausible public policy at a time when the corporation achieved a positive stature in public opinion that it has not enjoyed since.

But the onset and long duration of the Great Depression brought such overwhelming discredit to the workings of the business system that there emerged a broad political consensus for more business regulation, including the regulation of securities, which went a long way toward making the financial activities of American corporations the most transparent in the world. Attempts by commercial or investment banks to develop "financial department stores" in the 1920s were stopped cold by the Banking Act of 1933 (the "Glass-Steagall Act"), which separated commercial from investment banking, and banks generally were restricted from holding securities in nonfinancial companies. A wave of antitrust prosecutions began in 1937, and the hearings of the Temporary National Economic Committee kept the spotlight on actual and potential abuses of market power.[28]

In the meantime, organized labor, after decades of struggle, finally managed to unionize the shop floors of big business. The American Federation of Labor (AFL) had dominated the labor movement for nearly half a century, but as an association of craft unions it was ill equipped to organize the growing mass of semiskilled industrial laborers in the nation's center industries. The result was that before World War I, industrial labor was an ill-managed commodity. Workers' compensation, employment security, and work conditions were largely subject to an employer's arbitrary will. The brief success that organized labor enjoyed during World War I, when the National War Labor Board compelled companies to bargain collectively with workers through their chosen representatives, faded rapidly in the ensuing peace. Public fears of "Bolshevism" and rising prosperity enabled companies to break the power of the labor movement, as trade union membership declined precipitously during the 1920s, when managerial paternalism held sway in the more progressive of the nation's large corporations. Fosered by a number of business leaders, such as General Electric's Gerard Swope and Bethlehem Steel's Charles Schwab, business academics, and a new breed of professional personnel directors, "welfare capitalism"—with its emphasis on more enlightened shop-floor management, improved working (and, in some cases, living) conditions, and job security—became a powerful counterforce to unionism.

When the Great Depression struck, however, the implicit promise of job security that had grown out of the boom years of the 1920s was shattered. No amount of paternalistic goodwill could stanch the bleeding. As management lost credibility both inside and outside the corporation, the New Deal Congress enacted a positive legal basis for mass labor organization and collective bargaining. The most important of a series of laws was the National Labor Relations (Wagner) Act of 1935, which affirmed the rights of employees to organize, outlawed the imposition of company unions, and explicitly forbade employer interference, coercion, or influence on organizing efforts. A new national labor federation, the Congress of Industrial Organization (CIO), mounted a series of successful organizing drives in the steel and auto industries, which goaded the AFL into action. Companies resisted, often violently, and the two national unions fought fiercely with each other over jurisdiction. But despite the turmoil, labor unions gained a strong foothold in all the important mass-production sectors of the economy.

The war, which for the second time in the century brought big business directly into the service of the state, provided an umbrella under which unions could consolidate their gains. No company could afford to have a strike. Wages were frozen, and so labor concentrated on wrenching from management other concessions: the dues checkoff, seniority rights, and substantial control over working conditions. As a rule-bound "internal labor market" formed within the larger corporate structure, the relationship between salaried shop-floor managers and hourly paid workers became subject to well-defined contracts, principles, and procedures.

When peace returned, companies in most major industries sought to achieve stability on the production lines and predictable patterns of bargaining by negotiating master labor contracts on a routine and periodic basis. Unlike their counterparts in Europe, American unions forswore direct involvement in managerial decision making or boards of directors, concentrating instead on enforcing terms of the master agreements. As a result, organized labor become yet another big bureaucratic entity, one that coexisted in adversarial equipoise with the business corporation in a more or less predictable routine of bargaining sessions, punctuated by occasional disputes and strikes. Managers managed and workers grieved.[29]

Thus did big business, with all its potential for scale, power over people, and tendencies toward monopoly and managerial oligarchy, meet countervailing forces, first in big government, then in big labor. By the end of World War II, a broad principle of government regulation was well established. The national government had assumed authority to regulate business in order to check the market power of large corporations, to prevent pricing abuses, to ensure the public safety, and to prevent conflicts of interest and improve the quality of information in the financial markets. A pattern for carrying out these goals was also well established: regulatory agencies and congressional committees, increasingly populated with lawyers, exercised their oversight functions as an adversary process. Big government and big business became chronic antagonists.

From Stability to Crisis

World War II provided an immense boost to American business. Its onset had brought to a close a decade of depressed business conditions, rapidly absorbing all the excess capacity in the economy. Its progress stimulated the growth of new science-based industries in electronics, communications, chemistry, and what came to be aerospace; removed debt from the balance sheets of most big companies; provided them with modern facilities at cut-rate prices; and introduced and publicized new management techniques in planning and operations research. Its ending opened world markets for the rebuilding of devastated economies. With the advent of the cold war between competing capitalist and socialist economic systems, the United States assumed global responsibilities it had theretofore avoided, and with those responsibilities came the rise of what President Eisenhower called a new "military-industrial complex," the one arena in which business and government found common ground. As virtually all the advanced European and Asian economies were in disarray, American corporations had come to possess such apparent strength relative to the rest of the world that the nation seemed destined to lead the "free world" in business as well as military might.

During the quarter century after the war, the nation's GNP more than doubled while per capita GNP increased by nearly 60 percent (in real, inflation-adjusted, terms). Facing little competition from abroad, the United States enjoyed an unparalleled period of prosperity—a "golden age" some called it—while serving as the engine for the growth of the noncommunist world.[30] Strategically, at the center of the economy, the big capital-intensive industries operated as stable oligopolies. As some once highly fragmented industries (e.g., beer, retailing) became more managerially sophisticated, they consolidated. From the other end of the spectrum, once nearly monopolistic industries (e.g., steel, oil) became more populated, but they too settled into patterns of nonprice competition. For example, in 1945 Alcoa's nearly absolute control over primary aluminum production came to an end after a federal court ruled it to be an illegal monopoly. The postwar emergence of Reynolds and Kaiser as fully integrated producers resulted in a relatively benign pattern of competition in which the major North American companies (including Canada's Aluminium Limited) tended to compete on product innovation, promotion, and service rather than on price. For years, as the low-cost producer, Alcoa could not afford to undercut its new domestic rivals (for legal reasons). And indeed, for Alcoa, typical of most leading enterprises, adversarial relationships with government and labor were accepted as costs of doing business.[31]

During the 1950s and '60s, most leading U.S. industrials held their dominant positions in domestic markets without substantial price competition. Foreign companies could not enter and perform effectively in the United States unless they could acquire the necessary capital and demonstrate that they could make products not only at substantial cost advantages but also of better quality than those of domestic producers. In the meantime an increasing number of U.S. multinationals, on the basis of technological and cost advantages, spread around the world, casting a large, and to many an ominous, shadow. In 1967 John Kenneth Galbraith published *The New Industrial State*, in which he warned of the immense power of the American corporation, arguing that it threatened the ability of society to control it. The view from abroad was captured by the French journalist Jean-Jacques Servan-Schreiber, who in *The American Challenge* (1968) forecast the day when U.S. corporations, by dint of their superior organizational capabilities, would conquer world markets.[32] The organizational capabilities of large American corporations that Alfred Chandler chronicled in *The Visible Hand* (1977) seemed remarkably enduring. Companies that had been first movers in developing organizational capabilities around capital-intensive technologies in the pre–World War II era had continued to lead their industries. At home, as well as overseas, U.S. corporations not only seemed dominant but also had an air of permanence about them.

Ironically, just as commentators began to agree on the strength of American business, forces were at work that ultimately revealed its weakness and vulnerabilities. As events unfolded from the 1970s forward, the environment for American corporations took a very different shape. Once Europe and Asia had fully recovered from their devastation in World War II, their revived industrial economies would constitute a new challenge to American economic preeminence. Latent during the 1950s and '60s, the challenge arrived full force in the 1970s, when the United States was beset by the social turmoil and costs of the Vietnam War, as well as an alarming surge in inflation, accelerated by two "oil shocks," and the new and less predictable effects of exchange rates after the United States abandoned the gold standard. A long, progressive movement toward freer international trade hastened this trend, as many "bedrock" U.S. industries lost their comparative advantages to enterprises overseas. U.S. textile manufacturers, for example, found it harder to compete with foreign producers who had lower labor costs. Others, in aluminum or in civilian aircraft manufacture, ran up against "unfair" competition from government-subsidized producers or foreign cartels.

The apparent vibrancy of many U.S. multinationals contrasted with the performance of big corporations in the center of the industrial economy. In some industries, such as chemicals, U.S. companies sustained their leading positions through innovative technologies and alert management. But in other major sectors of the industrial economy, traditional American leadership withered under competition from more efficient production systems and more effective administration, which, especially in the case of the Japanese, were bolstered by hard-nosed trading policies and a system of government supports to strategic industries. The American automobile industry was revealed to be bloated, excessively bureaucratic, inefficient, lagging in production techniques, and unresponsive to changing consumer needs. The U.S. consumer electronics industry, based mainly on American inventions, was pushed nearly to extinction. Once seemingly invincible companies like U.S. Steel, International Harvester, Sears, Singer Sewing Machine, Baldwin Piano, Houdaille (machine tools), Chrysler, and RCA fell on hard times, merged with other companies, declared bankruptcy, or simply disappeared.

The steel industry was a particularly dramatic example of the problem. In 1950 American steel producers were the biggest and best in the world. Yet within a decade the vertically integrated producers of raw steel and various semifinished products had became technologically obsolete and grossly inefficient by rising world standards. Conditioned by their experience in the Great Depression, American steel company executives were reluctant after World War II to invest in new plant and technology, and did so only after the government provided incentives to do so. Very little of the expansion resulted in technological upgrading, which would have made American steel plants more productive and less costly to operate. The result of all this was a kind of self-fulfilling prophecy. As capacity utilization became more difficult to manage, there was less incentive to invest, which in turn made the integrated steelmakers more vulnerable to competition. By 1960 American steel companies were operating at just two-thirds of capacity. Their costs were high, and the quality of their products low by world standards. Acrimonious labor relations had resulted in higher wages and benefits without gains in worker productivity. As American steel executives' fears of excess capacity mounted, the United States became a net importer of steel. Despite shipping costs and tariffs (and notwithstanding accusations that foreign producers were "dumping"), steel made in Japan and Europe was less costly than domestic steel to produce and deliver. Only belatedly did the integrated producers make the conversion from old, open-hearth furnace technology to more modern, basic oxygen furnace technology. They were also tardy in the adoption of continuous casting methods for turning raw steel into semifinished shapes, and their R&D expenditures remained the lowest for any major industry, except textiles.

The rise of the Japanese steel industry exposed these weaknesses. Japanese steelmakers benefited from a combination of fortuitous factors: a high-growth (rebuilding) domestic market, new plant and equipment, flexible and low-cost labor, managerial optimism, protection against foreign competition, and effective government "administrative guidance," which worked in ways that were hard to imagine in the United States. Through protectionism, the careful management of foreign reserves, and targeted capacity allocation, Japanese bureaucrats stimulated fierce domestic rivalry in steel, which honed the skills of the strongest producers. These produc-

ers built huge greenfield plants in order to seize new advantages in technological innovation and production economies. Japanese steel enjoyed not
only superior scale economies (new furnace and casting technologies
had increased minimum efficient plant scale) but also better layouts, computerized production processes, and a more disciplined workforce. While
Japanese companies pursued short-term, scrap-and-build strategies for
long-term returns, U.S. producers remained obsessed with minimizing
losses. As Japan demonstrated a successful formula for steel, Korea and
other less-developed countries joined the fray.

By 1978 the integrated U.S. Steel companies were in dire straits. By
some accounts more than half the nation's steel capacity was idled, and the
industry's net income plunged well below break-even costs. Yet American
steel executives tended to follow the logic that had guided them during the
entire postwar period, seeking political protection against foreign imports
and relief from environmental laws, even as they embarked on a massive redeployment of assets into other lines of business, ranging from oil and
chemicals to financial services. In the mid-1980s the major American steel
companies were spiraling toward what U.S. Steel's David Roderick called a
"state of accelerating liquidation." That, as much as anything else going on
at the time, spurred public outrage and fueled an emerging crisis of confidence in American industry.[33]

Variants of the steel story occurred in a number of U.S. industries
where complacent executives shied away from building or innovating in
their core businesses, allowed organizational capabilities to erode, and
then, like a headless herd, moved headlong into uncertain territory. Across
the industrial landscape, serious management failures became apparent.
As foreign competition began to erode U.S. companies' market shares at
home and abroad, there were terrible dislocations in major manufacturing
centers. Once-great industrial cities along the crescent that ran from
Pittsburgh to Chicago came to be known as the Rust Belt.[34] Even the most
pretigious corporations were eventually affected. IBM, for example, under-
estimated the strategic significance of microprocessors and the growing importance of software relative to hardware, and posted a series of huge financial losses that led to a wrenching restructuring.

Finance Capitalism and the Claims of Owners

As the cumulative effects of underinvestment in innovation, executive
timidity, wasteful empire building, and inefficient administration became

clear in the 1970s corporate raiders moved into the breach. Even if they did not succeed in mounting a full-fledged takeover, they could, by exacting "greenmail" or simply by bidding up the price of targeted stocks, push share prices up while forcing managers to cut costs. Although hostile takeovers were actually outnumbered by more "friendly" transactions to which sitting managers of target firms agreed, the raiders received most of the publicity and, by their very existence, had a powerful behavioral effect across the broad spectrum of industry. The raiders, and their financial backers, moreover, plied their trade in the name of the near-forgotten stockholder, taking comfort in the support of a legal system that was becoming more sympathetic to shareholder suits and a new wave of academic analysis on the problems of principals and agents.[35]

By the mid-1980s a new merger wave—the century's fourth—formed around a variety of transactions ranging from mergers between competing companies (in a relaxed antitrust environment), to internal management buyouts, to takeovers led by third parties.[36] All the activity was characterized by an extraordinary use of debt financing, including the new application of high-yield, "junk" securities, placed largely by one firm, Drexel Burnham Lambert, and its impresario, Michael Milken, who had originally developed the securities to finance low-rated, undercapitalized businesses. Leveraged management buyouts were perfected by financial firms like KKR, Forstmann-Little, and Clayton and Dubilier, who borrowed most of the money to finance the transactions, while ensuring that the managers of bought-out properties had large personal equity stakes in the enterprise. Meanwhile, corporate raiders such as T. Boone Pickens and Carl Icahn continued their assaults. KKR's buyout of the gigantic and egregiously mismanaged RJR Nabisco in 1988 demonstrated that even the largest corporations were not immune to takeovers. The net effect of all this activity—which in a decade resulted in some thirty thousand transactions with a value in excess of $1 trillion, yielding, by one estimate, some $650 in additional value to shareholders—was further to shock corporate managers throughout the economy into actively pursuing more profitable strategies while streamlining their operations. The tactics of financial entrepreneurs were widely criticized in Congress and in the media. All this activity ran against the tide of public opinion, swelled by a proliferation of exposés alleging that while the financiers enriched themselves, the target companies were too often subjected to post-buyout mismanagement, or even downright plundering, as healthy operations were dismantled or run down simply to pay off excessive debt.[37]

Nonetheless, there is substantial agreement among serious students of the subject that leveraged buyouts—those transactions that had received the worst publicity in the popular press—generally resulted directly and/or indirectly in more efficient, and even more innovative, companies in virtually every sector of the private economy. As for more conventional mergers—whether horizontal, vertical, or conglomerate—a mounting body of critical scholarship seemed to show that after shareholders of selling companies reaped short-term benefits, it was hard to show that the longer-term performances of merged corporations resulted in more profitable enterprises. If anything, the evidence seemed to point the other way, casting doubt on more conventional management wisdom about the strategic value of mergers, or the prospects for achieving better-operating economies and synergies through mergers.[38] Many of the diversified companies that grew out of the so-called conglomerate wave of the late 1960s and early '70s proved to be little more than the unwieldy products of opportunistic financial engineers who sought to avoid antitrust problems, exploit tax loopholes, or indulge in accounting games by suddenly raising the price-earnings ratios of combined firms. Some of the largest combinations, such as Ling-Temco-Vaught (LTV), ITT, and Litton Industries proved to be too difficult to manage and fell quickly into decline. Others, like Beatrice, stumbled into the path of takeover specialists, who proved that the parts were often far more valuable than the whole.[39] Scholars and industry analysts alike began to ask why executives of cash-rich companies or of companies in mature or declining markets attempted to expand their managerial empires rather than return profits to shareholders.[40] Were the more durable conglomerates like General Electric or United Technologies simply too big or too complicated to administer effectively? Were attempts to secure sources of supply or distribution channels by telecommunications and media companies (e.g., Time Warner) simply doomed to a future of bureaucratic confusion and subpar performance?

In any case, institutional investors, especially state pension funds, began to assert more active interest in corporate policies (even though the mass of their constituent shareholders remained indifferent). In 1993 the spirit of shareholder activism penetrated some of the more quiescent boards of directors. The unprecedented ouster of chief executives in four of the nation's largest firms—IBM, General Motors, Eastman Kodak, and American Express, all once thought to have been impenetrable bastions of managerial control—sent shock waves through corporate boardrooms everywhere. The old tension between ownership and management thus surfaced in a new form, as shareholders effectively reasserted their rights.

By the 1990s one thing above all else became clear: the relatively stable postwar American corporate universe had come undone. The gales of
creative destruction were gathering force and coming from every direction:
not only from new technologies but also from global competition in mature
ones; not only from new forms of corporate organization but also from
more fundamental economic forces connected to the longer-term shift in
the U.S. economy from manufacturing- to service-based enterprise.

Under these circumstances, American corporations pursued restructurings (including mergers and divestitures); downsizing (eliminating layers
of management and laying off personnel); outsourcing (reducing internal
functions in favor of buying them in the marketplace); moving production
"offshore" (in cases where U.S. wage rates were deemed too high by world
standards); forming strategic alliances with customers and even competitors; and implementing new, and sometimes radical, "leaner" production
methods, while bargaining for concessions from organized labor. The companies that were not quick to recognize shifting trends or to capitalize on
the latest improvements in management and technology were subject to
sharp reversals of fortune. It also meant that managers who were not perceived to be performing were more likely to be ousted by their owners, or,
to be more precise, by those acting on behalf of shareholder interests.

The reality was that revived claims of owners did not displace those of
other stakeholders. If anything, the claims of other stakeholders continued
to pile up. Powerful interests organized around mounting concerns for consumer protection, equal employment opportunities, workplace safety and
conduct, and environmental controls. The liabilities of the corporation expanded with new regulatory controls and lawsuits that went far beyond
more traditional concerns to protect the interests of equity holders, debtors,
the bargaining rights of workers, and the contractual rights of suppliers and
customers. Corporate managers found themselves under increasing pressure to take on "social responsibilities," based on a growing sense that business had a positive duty to advance, if not the broader aims of society, at
least the moral and economic aims of many of its constituencies.

Institutional Responses

The growing complexity of the corporate environment prompted new forms
of administration as well as new or greatly expanded functions within the
corporation. The emergence of these new functions corresponded with im-

proved capabilities for transferring learning across the corporate economy, which, despite the apparent crisis, greatly improved capabilities for managing under more pressured social and competitive circumstances.

At the top of the corporation the response was to expand the office and divide the duties of the chief executive. In most big companies the chairman of the board served as the CEO, but increasingly focused on relations with external constituencies. A new position, that of the chief operating officer (often the president) was concerned with administrative and operating matters. From there, "chiefs" began to proliferate. By the 1980s the office of the chief executive had come to include as many as half a dozen officers, including vice chairmen, chief financial officers, chief administrative officers, and even chief information officers. The specialization at the top paralleled increasing functional specialization at lower levels. Examples of new or expanded functions included human resource management, public affairs, strategic planning, marketing, and information systems. These functions either had not existed or were considered unimportant in the prewar period.[41]

Human resources management embraces in part what used to go by the names of personnel or "employee" or "industrial relations." The big American corporations of the nineteenth and early twentieth centuries carried out the function, usually through an employment office and foremen or first-level supervisors. In the 1930s and '40s, however, how big employers understood and organized the function began to change under the pressures of the Great Depression, the rise of industrial unions, and—the biggest boost—the imperative to staff up and train people quickly during the World War II defense mobilization. These years saw the rise of personnel management as a profession—as distinct from an activity carried out by people with little training or interest—with corporate vice presidents in charge; an enormous expansion of interest in the subject and the formation (or rapid growth) of organizations like the American Management Association, the National Association of Manufacturers, and the Industrial Relations Research Association; and an explosion of research on the subject at such places as the Harvard Business School, Cornell University, MIT, the University of Michigan, and other leading universities. By the 1990s, human resource and related functions had not yet achieved the status in American companies that they enjoyed in Germany or Japan, but their importance to the health of American business was increasing.[42]

This development reflected broader trends in society. In the 1960s the Great Society's call to end poverty and discrimination found expression in specific legislation, as did increasing public pressure on government to provide for employee welfare. As corporations increased their efforts to ensure workplace safety, equal opportunity, pensions, medical, and other benefits, the personnel function gained increasing importance. Charged with accommodating the growing diversity of the workforce, many corporations provided basic education to employees, responding in part to a growing crisis in the quality of public education. Employees—especially but not exclusively managers—had to become more sophisticated in technology, cross-functional integration, and cross-border competition and cooperation. And as economic activity worldwide expanded beyond its traditional manufacturing base into "knowledge-based industries," the potential strength of American corporations came to depend far less on advantageous access to natural resource endowments and capital (access to which is becoming progressively easier everywhere) and far more on the quality of its human resources.

Concurrently, the nature of corporate employment in the United States became less predictable than during the halcyon years after World War II. As institutional stability gave way to restructuring and organizational experimentation, the nation's large companies shed thousands, even tens of thousands, of employees. In the 1980s net new job creation came mainly from small business, many of them start-up ventures.[43] At the same time, as the ranks of traditional blue-collar workers decreased relative to office and technical personnel, big labor lost much of its bargaining power. This trend occurred in a darkening political environment for labor, and as competitive pressures encouraged management to harden its resistance to wage-cost pressures. The result was the most severe dislocation in patterns of employment since the 1930s, albeit in a different form. The problem now was how to redeploy and restructure the workforce.

By the 1990s, corporations had to confront the fact that the larger society could not provide the means to retrain and relocate redundant personnel. Thus many began to assume more responsibility for providing generous severance packages and outplacement services. Meanwhile, broad social pressures for more flexible working conditions, the increasing entry of women and minorities into the workforce, and the spread of low-cost methods of computer processing and networked telecommunications appeared to be leading to a radical reordering of workplace relationships and conditions. Companies began to respond with "flextime," "job sharing," "secretaryless offices," "telecommuting," and increasing use of temporary workers. By the 1990s, corporate managers were contemplating a future that might partly reverse one of the great social transformations of the Industrial Revolution—that people leave their isolated dwellings to go live and work in a central location.

Expanding emphasis on public relations, governmental affairs, and legal functions resulted from many of the same pressures. So much corporate activity had become regulated or otherwise subject to public scrutiny that most big companies developed large public relations staffs—or made liberal use of public relations firms and consultants—and provided extensive financial and managerial support to industry trade associations that sought to influence not only industry-specific legislation but also general economic policy. During the 1960s and '70s, many companies, particularly among those in regulated industries or those that sold to the government (such as aerospace or computer and information services), opened offices in Washington, D.C. The corporate officers for public relations and public affairs acquired professional training, joined professional associations, and found their advice and counsel heeded in boardrooms and executive suites. Likewise, corporate lawyers played a more prominent role in executive management in response to increasing regulation and pressures arising from litigation, especially related to product problems, environmental damage, and workplace misconduct.[44]

The emergence of corporate planning was a response to competitive pressures in increasingly complex markets. In the prewar era, CEOs and a handful of top managers typically projected growth based on certain trends or assumptions that were seldom rigorously tested. For the most part, the quality of such plans did not matter, given that most companies sold into high-growth markets. Major strategic studies were mounted on a sporadic basis, usually in response to a real or perceived crisis. Most big companies based planning on short-term considerations such as inventory levels and the amount of activity in their distribution channels. Occasionally, in special circumstances, senior executives in some companies met as a group to weigh some options for diversification. During or immediately after World War I, for example, several munitions suppliers, including Du Pont and Hercules Powder Company, held management conferences to consider how to redeploy personnel and assets necessary for wartime production. While these conferences led to diversification efforts, the process to support long-term planning was neither sustained nor institutionalized.

Several factors caused companies to give more weight to long-term planning. One was the experience gained in running multidivisional corporations, which delegated operational decision making to divisional managers, leaving senior managers free to focus on "the big picture." Gradually, and in part because they had to focus on the long-term issues of R&D, top executives began to appreciate the value of long-term projections. The logistical challenges posed by mobilizing for defense production during World War II provided still another impetus to long-term planning. In the military, in their own companies, and as "dollar-a-year men" working for the government, business executives came to understand intimately the value of planning and coordinating activities to achieve specific objectives.

Companies like Du Pont and General Electric pioneered highly systematic planning techniques after the war, when they and other big, diversified concerns began to hold regular management conferences during which they discussed long-term initiatives as well as short-term operating issues. At Thompson Products (now part of TRW Inc.) and Emerson Electric Co. these conferences became annual events during which divisional managers presented three- to five-year plans, which were then consolidated into an overall corporate plan. Both corporate and division managers were then at least partly evaluated according to how well actual performance corresponded to the plan.

Strategic planning as a formal exercise became generalized in the late 1960s, when companies were coming to terms with rapid diversification via acquisition—the conglomerate mergers—as well as perceived "limits to growth" in the U.S. market. The advent of the computer enabled companies more quickly to model different scenarios of the future with a high degree of quantitative, as well as qualitative, sophistication. Strategy and policy courses in business schools helped spread the concept, and most big American companies also made liberal use of professional strategy consultants who transferred planning techniques and insights, first within the United States and then abroad. By the 1980s, corporate planning was no longer a top executive staff activity, but rather one that engaged operating executives at all levels.[45]

The modern marketing function evolved out of the traditional functions of sales, advertising, and, to some extent, traffic or logistics as they applied to distribution channels. Consumer product companies had already developed sophisticated understandings of their customers, but marketing did not formally become a corporate function distinct from sales until the 1950s, when it took hold in other sectors of the economy. Distinct from merchandising, marketing became the systematic effort to discover what customers want as an input to developing products and services to offer them. The spread and professionalization of marketing signified an important transition in the larger economy toward consumption. Within the corporation engineering and manufacturing functions, which had once driven

corporate strategies, became increasingly subordinated to marketing. Most
big companies came to place a premium on marketing and invested heavily
to collect basic information, analyze it, and use it in planning new offerings
and other business moves. Marketing then moved beyond a support staff
function (many marketing managers now lead cross-functional product or
service development teams). This was true not only in industries such as
consumer products, where it might be expected, but also in traditional manufacturing and continuous processing industries.[46]

Finally, the growing adoption of computers and other new information
technology in big corporations swelled to the point that many companies
developed management information systems that were distinct from traditional accounting and control systems. Originally a tool for automating
back-office functions such as bookkeeping and order processing, information technology came to pervade nearly every aspect of corporate life. It also
become a competitive weapon (American Airlines' vaunted "SABRE" reser-
vations system is a well-known example) and a force for streamlining activities inside companies and between companies, their suppliers, and their
customers.[47]

The increase in functions and the adoption of computerized information systems both encouraged and enhanced more decentralized decision
making, whether or not companies diversified their lines of business. There
was a marked trend after 1970 toward decentralization, and the breakup of
large units into smaller, more entrepreneurial organizations. It is important
to bear in mind that decentralization, like many corporate trends, moved, if
not in cycles, in spurts, and was reversible. In the aftermath of the conglomerate merger wave of the late 1960s, for example, many diversified
businesses divested many units that they had so recently acquired to "refo-
cus" on core businesses, even while other companies diversified.[48] To an extent, this pattern played out again during the late 1980s and early 1990s,
when many U.S.-based companies restructured—some to improve market
share through merger, some to seek new growth prospects through diversification, and others to improve profitability or eliminate waste by "returning
to their knitting."

All these restructurings were stimulated by a commonly perceived set
of experiences, including increased awareness of successful strategies of diversification and managing diversified organizations; new possibilities and
economies arising from computerized and high-speed information technologies; intense competitive pressure on costs; and widely publicized examples of successful companies based in Europe and Japan. In recent

years, companies once touted for their degree and tightness of vertical integration or the vast scale of their operations—Kodak, USX, AT&T, Caterpillar—reorganized away from structures based on facilities, technologies, or operations toward "market units" based on customer segments. For instance, Caterpillar, which once organized itself around two or three types of construction equipment that it sold around the world, now has more than a score of market units, each attentive to different segments in different regions. Even the phone companies (the Regional Bell Operating Companies spun off from AT&T), which for decades epitomized a monolithic bureaucracy based on the engineering challenges of providing universal access and serving a vast, undifferentiated base of customers, restructured around discrete market units that focus on particular groups of customers, such as big and small businesses, cellular phone users, and consumers of various "value-added" information services.

A notable feature of the postwar American corporation—one that truly cut across all sizes and industries—was the development of a common language, which in turn was based on shared goals, philosophies, and techniques. Within each corporation there were highly specialized disciplines with their own common languages and techniques, which likewise cut across corporate boundaries. Much of this was due to the expansion of the business press and specialized consultancies. The postwar period saw an enormous expansion of business education, which enabled companies to recruit entry-level managers with similar background and training. The American habit of high turnover among executives—fed by waves of mergers and acquisitions as well as by the rise of "headhunter" firms—also served to transfer corporate knowledge and skills, even at the expense of creating short-term instabilities in corporate leadership. In recent years it has become commonplace for even the most inbred companies to look outside for chief executive officers—at IBM, Kodak, Allied-Signal, Owens-Corning, and Merck, among others.

Accordingly, most American companies learned to proclaim similar goals in similar ways, usually expressed as growth rates, share of market, or value of the stock price. Corporations not only learned to think and talk in similar ways, they were more likely to move, if not in tandem, at least in similar directions, to adopt similar organizational structures and management policies. At worst, corporate mimicry became a substitute for creative problem solving and sometimes obscured the significant differences among firms.[49] In general, business school education and consulting expertise, by their very nature as fonts of received learning, tended to disseminate *con-*

ventions, and thus did not necessarily foster what in particular industry or corporate circumstances was often most needed: creative responses to new problems. At best, the availability and transfer of common knowledge encouraged the adoption of better practices.

As of the mid-1990s the institutional responses of many American companies were effective in slowing, even reversing, the impact of the crises of the preceding decades. Although some industries, such as machine tools and electronics, remained in disarray, others manifested marked improvement. After years of struggle, for example, Ford and Chrysler regained some of the market share they had lost and once again became highly profitable. In the steel industry, after a decade of downsizing, investment in new technology, divestiture of underperforming and unrelated assets, and internal management changes, USX, Bethlehem, and other big integrated producers returned to profitable growth. The rubber industry, which endured a crisis like that of the steel and auto industries in the 1970s and '80s, regained health by adapting their basic technologies to new markets, focusing on high-value-added products such as polymers, elastomers, and other specialty materials and chemicals.

In still other industries, American companies continued to display the vibrancy that had been their hallmark for more than a century. During the past two decades big new companies arose in such mundane but venerable businesses as mass retailing (Wal-Mart) and package delivery (Federal Express). Young American corporations have established leadership positions in high-technology areas, including microprocessors (Intel), software (Microsoft), spacecraft (Orbital Sciences), and biotechnology (Genzyme). Amid the heightened financial activity of the 1980s, many other promising ventures were spawned along the cutting edges of telecommunications, mass media, financial services, and consumer products.

Yet there can be no question that the era of world dominance for American corporations is gone. The postwar Japanese and German "miracles," the development of the European Community, the emergence of new economic powers in Asia, and the cultivation of market economies in erstwhile communist nations all portended a more competitive global economy.

History and Prospect

As corporate managers confront the future, they might pause to consider where they stand in the flux of history. Over time the American corporation has had to learn to operate in a progressively more complex economic and technological environment. It has also had to learn to conduct its business amid the more complicated demands of competing social and political interests. As it struggles to cope with these demands, the modern American corporation, whatever its claims to "privacy," remains true to its historical and legal origins as a public concern, inextricably woven into the larger community.

On the one hand, the complexity of corporate relationships exists within a larger context of recurrent challenges posed by the peculiar character of American society. For example, the chronically adversarial nature of business-government relations will no doubt continue to weigh heavily on American corporate managers, as will the mounting claims of overlapping constituencies—women and minorities, consumer and environmental groups, not to mention more assertive shareholders, debtors, suppliers, and employees. Indeed, what is new is that more explicit social and ethical responsibilities are now vested in American corporations than ever were before.

On the other hand, the globalization of markets brings the American corporation into comparative perspective. With the end of the cold war it has become more apparent than ever that varieties of capitalism exist along a continuum, on which the American model occupies one extreme.[50] In many countries corporations find it easier (and arguably more economical) to transact business along the vertical supply chain by virtue of social customs and legal systems that support intercompany cooperation. Neither the resurgent emphasis on shareholder rights nor the sharp line drawn between business and government policy-making in the United States has a parallel elsewhere in the strongest or emerging economic powers. In countries such as Germany, Japan, France, and Italy—or, for that matter, Brazil, Mexico, Korea and China—enterprise systems place much greater emphasis on communitarian principles of business organization, as well as on the relationship of business to the welfare of the nation.

In recent years there have been many signs of convergence in policy and practice among nations in the conduct of business. Large European corporations have successfully mimicked American forms of organization, just as Americans have learned from the Japanese about lean manufacturing methods.[51] Once cartelized, industries in Europe have become increasingly characterized by interfirm competition, just as the United States eases the enforcement of its antitrust laws. Financial markets in Japan are opening up to foreign firms, even as the United States removes restrictions on the scaling up and integration of financial institutions. As erstwhile communist countries experiment with free markets, American policy makers seek grounds for better cooperation between big government and big business to enhance the nation's position in global arenas. Even developing countries, like Brazil and India, have been abandoning policies of import substitution and protection, privatizing government-owned companies, and opening up their capital markets—edging ever closer to "Anglo-American" ideals of free enterprise. An important point, however, is that these and numerous other tendencies toward convergence will not significantly erode the sovereignty of the nation-state, at least for the foreseeable future. Nations will continue to wield peculiar, often dominant, influences over their corporations' business policy, organization, and conduct. In many advanced economies corporations will continue to work explicitly in the service of national goals, just as nations will work to enhance corporate goals.

In that regard, the American nation's sense of corporate purpose (in the largest sense of the term) has never been a match for that of other leading economic powers. This could become a problem in a world that relies as much on cooperation as it does on competition to succeed—cooperation in balancing the corporation's own business objectives with the needs of nation-states. The ability of American corporations to conduct business in other parts of the world—which occurs increasingly through joint ventures with local firms—will require more cosmopolitan appreciation among its managers for cultural and ideological differences over the very nature and purpose of enterprise.

And yet the American corporation has its undeniable strengths. The United States has always been blessed with a striving entrepreneurial culture, one that gradually came to realize its creative ambitions quite effectively through corporate means. By the mid–twentieth century the large American corporation, for all its shortcomings, had become an indispensable agent for financing, engineering, and commercializing new ideas and for allocating resources to progressively better uses. Can it continue to play that role effectively in the future? We think it can.

Through its continuous transformations since the nineteenth century, the American corporation has proven to be remarkably progressive, dynamic, elastic, and resilient. As the pace of change in the business environment has picked up, so have the adaptive responses. Despite unceasing pressure from global competitors, new information technologies, and other forces, the American corporation of the mid-1990s is leaner and more focused than its earlier incarnations, far better prepared to do business at home and around the world. If the past is any indication, there is good reason to expect that the American corporation will thrive in the global economy of the twenty-first century.

Notes

1. Adam Smith, *An Inquiry into the Nature and Causes of the Wealth of Nations* (New York: Modern Library, 1965), bk. 5, pp. 715–16. Throughout this chapter, in addition to citing sources for quoted materials or references for statistical data, we offer suggestive, rather than comprehensive, sources for the general reader who may want to read further. For the more contemporary history we provide references only for works that probe more deeply than mass media reports.

2. Peter Drucker, *The Concept of the Corporation* (New York: John Day Co., 1946).

3. Fritz Machlup, *The Production and Distribution of Knowledge in the United States* (Princeton, N.J.: Princeton University Press, 1962).

4. James R. Beniger, *The Control Revolution: Technological and Economic Origins of the Information Society* (Cambridge, Mass.: Harvard University Press, 1988), pp. 22ff., provides a good summary of the data and the literature. On agricultural combines see the detailed corporate history by Wayne G. Broehl Jr., *Cargill: Trading the World's Grain* (Hanover, N.H.: University Press of New England, 1992).

5. The best introduction to Chandler's work is Thomas K. McCraw, ed., *The Essential Alfred Chandler* (Boston: Harvard Business School Press, 1988). This collection includes the 1959 essay "The Beginnings of 'Big Business' in American Industry," which had originally appeared in the *Business History Review*. The main body of Chandler's work is subsumed in his books *The Visible Hand: The Managerial Revolution in American Business* (Cambridge, Mass.: Harvard University Press, 1977) and *Scale and Scope* (Cambridge, Mass.: Harvard University Press, 1992).

6. See Chandler's *Strategy and Structure: Chapters in the History of Industrial Enterprise* (Cambridge: MIT Press, 1962), esp. chap. 1.

7. Several key works that have expanded the literature on corporations will be cited in subsequent notes to relevant passages, although two worth noting here are David Noble, *America by Design: Science, Technology, and the Rise of Corporate Capitalism* (New York: Alfred Knopf, 1977) and Jonathan Hughes, *The Vital Few: The Entrepreneur & American Economic Progress*, expanded edition (New York: Oxford University Press, 1986). Noble's book, which appeared in the same year as Chandler's *Visible Hand*,was a neo-Marxist critique of corporate capitalism, which focused on the nexus of the engineering profession, institutions of higher education, and large-scale corporate development. Hughes's book, which embraces ten biographical sketches, is an engaging attempt to link the entrepreneurial activity of individuals to larger economic forces in a celebration of free enterprise. Chandler himself continued to study the nexus between technology and bureaucracy—in works that, as his biographer put it, ran "narrow and deep" (see the introduction to *The Essential Alfred Chandler*). He, along with scholars from around the world, became interested in the comparative history of bureaucratic enterprise in the United

States and other industrialized countries. More recently he has been at work trying to decipher the patterns of change in the modern, post–World War II era, which his main corpus of work does not address.

8. Alexis de Tocqueville, *Democracy in America*, ed. Phillips Bradley (New York: Alfred Knopf, 1945), vol. 2, p. 166.

9. On the various stages and aspects of the evolution of the corporation, see George L. Beer, *The Old Colonial System, 1660–1754*, 2 vols. (New York: The MacMillan Co., 1912); Oscar Handlin and Mary F. Handlin, "The Origins of the American Business Corporation," *Journal of Economic History* 5 (1966): 777; Morton J. Horowitz, *The Transformation of American Law*, 1780–1860 (Cambridge, Mass., 1977), esp. pp. 111ff.; Ronald E. Seavoy, *The Origins of the American Business Corporation, 1784–1855* (Westport, Conn.: Greenwood Press, 1982); Herbert Hovenkamp, *Enterprise and American Law, 1836–1937* (Cambridge, Mass.: Harvard University Press, 1991).

10. R. Kent Newmyer, *The Supreme Court Under Marshall and Taney* (Arlington Heights, Ill.: Harlan Davidson, Inc., 1969), p. 59.

11. *Testimony Before the Committee on Commerce of the United States House of Representatives, January 14, 15, and 16, 1880* (Washington, D.C., 1880), pp. 18–24.

12. A comprehensive discussion of the emergence of the Standard Oil Trust is Ralph W. Hidy and Muriel E. Hidy, *Pioneering in Big Business, 1882–1911* (New York: Harper, 1955), pp. 40–46. See also Daniel Yergin's magisterial treatment of the history of the petroleum industry, *The Prize: The Epic Quest for Oil, Money, and Power* (New York: Simon and Schuster, 1991).

13. On the merger wave see Thomas Navin and Marion Sears, "The Rise of a Market for Industrial Securities, 1887–1902," *Business History Review* 29 (1954): 105-38; Ralph Nelson, *Merger Movements in American Industry, 1895–1956* (Princeton, N.J.: Princeton University Press, 1959); Naomi Lamoreaux, *The Great Merger Movement in American Business, 1895–1904* (New York: Cambridge University Press, 1985).

14. In addition to the Chandlerian overview, some useful firm histories illustrating these strategic and administrative developments in detail are Thomas C. Cochran, *Railroad Leaders* (Cambridge, Mass.: Harvard University Press, 1953); Harold C. Livesay, *Andrew Carnegie and the Rise of Big Business* (Boston: Little Brown, 1975); Robert W. Garnet, *The Telephone Enterprise: The Evolution of the Bell System's Horizontal Structure, 1879–1909*, (Baltimore: Johns Hopkins University Press, 1985); George David Smith, *The Anatomy of a Business Strategy: Bell, Western Electric, and the Origins of the American Telephone Industry* (Baltimore: Johns Hopkins University Press, 1985).

15. On the U.S. Steel deal see George David Smith and Richard Sylla, *The Transformation of Financial Capitalism: An Essay on the History of Capital Markets*, in *Financial Markets, Institutions and Instruments* (New York: New York University Salomon Center, 1993), pp. 2–5.

16. See, note 14 above.

17. On scientific management see Daniel Nelson, *Frederick W. Taylor and the Rise of Scientific Management* (Madison, Wis.: University of Wisconsin Press, 1980). For a standard general history of automobiles, see John Rae, *American Automobile Manufacturers: The First Forty Years* (Philadelphia: Chilton, 1959). On Ford see Allan Nevins, *Ford: The Times, the Man, the Company* (New York: Scribners, 1954); and Robert Lacey, *Ford: The Men and the Machine* (Boston: Little Brown, 1985).

18. Leonard S. Reich, *The Making of American Industrial Research: Science and Business at GE and Bell, 1876–1926* (New York: Cambridge University Press, 1985); David A. Hounshell and John Kenly Smith Jr., *Science and Corporate: DuPont R&D, 1912–1980* (New York: Cambridge University Press, 1988); Margaret B. W. Graham and Bettye H. Pruitt, *R&D for Industry: A Century of Technological Innovation at Alcoa* (New York: Cambridge University Press, 1990).

19. On diversification and the development of multidivisional corporations, see Chandler, *Strategy and Structure*; for cases on Du Pont, Standard Oil, General Motors, and Sears, Roebuck; Alfred P. Sloan Jr., *My Years with General Motors* (New York: Doubleday, 1963); Davis Dyer and David B. Sicilia, *Labors of a Modern Hercules* (Boston: Harvard Business School Press, 1990).

20. Postwar diversification is analyzed in Richard P. Rumelt, *Strategy, Structure and Economic Performance* (Boston: Harvard University Press, 1974) and Milton Leontiades, *Managing the Unmanageable: Strategies for Success Within the Conglomerate* (Reading, Mass.: Addison Wesley, 1986).

21. Adolf Berle and Gardiner Means, *The Modern Corporation and Private Property* (New York: MacMillan, 1933), p. 122. This was not the first, or last, commentary on the problems of the separation of ownership and management, but its breadth and timeliness, coming at the height of the Great Depression, focused attention on the issue, which is now most closely associated with these two authors.

22. Edward S. Mason, ed., *The Corporation in Modern Society* (Cambridge, Mass: Harvard University Press, 1959), introduction.

23. *Historical Statistics of the United States*, pt. 1, series A 6–8, 57–72; series F 1–5; series D 11–25.

24. The attacks on big business and the development of regulation are usefully analyzed from different perspectives by Richard Hofstadter, *The Age of Reform* (New York: Alfred Knopf, 1955); Gabriel Kolko, *The Triumph of Conservatism: A Social Reinterpretation of American History, 1990–1916* (New York: Free Press of Glencoe, 1963); Robert Wiebe, *The Search for Order, 1877–1920* (New York: Hill and Wang, 1967); Louis Galambos, *The Public Image of Big Business in America: 1880–1940* (Baltimore: Johns Hopkins University Press, 1975); and Jonathan R. T. Hughes, *The Governmental Habit Redux: Economic Controls from Colonial Times to the Present* (Princeton, N.J.: Princeton University Press, 1991).

25. Overviews of U.S. antitrust history and policy are William Letwin, *Law and Economic Policy in America* (New York: Random House, 1965); Robert H. Bork,

The Antitrust Paradox: A Policy at War with Itself (New York: Basic Books, 1978); and Marc Allen Eisner, *Antitrust and the Triumph of Economics: Institutions, Expertise and Policy Change* (Chapel Hill: University of North Carolina Press, 1991).

26. In addition to Smith and Sylla, *Transformation of Financial Capitalism*, see Vincent P. Carosso, *Investment Banking in America: A History* (Cambridge, Mass.: Harvard University Press, 1970); and Richard Sylla, *The American Capital Market, 1846–1914* (New York: Arno Press, 1975). Good institutional studies are Harold van B. Cleveland and Thomas Huertas, *Citibank: 1812–1970* (Cambridge, Mass.: Harvard University Press, 1985); Robert Sobel, *The Life and Times of Dillon, Read* (New York: Truman Talley Books, 1989); and Ron Chernow, *The House of Morgan: An American Banking Dynasty and the Rise of Modern Finance* (New York: Atlantic Monthly Press, 1990).

27. See Thomas C. McCraw, *Prophets of Regulation: Charles Francis Adams, Louis D. Brandeis, James M. Landis, Alfred E. Kahn* (Cambridge, Mass.: Harvard University Press, 1984) for an intellectual biography of Brandeis and the currents of contemporary thought on the trust question. See also Walter Lippmann's *Drift and Mastery: An Attempt to Diagnose the Current Unrest* (Englewood Cliffs, N.J.: Prentice Hall, 1961), pp. 42–43; Arthur S. Link, ed., *The Papers of Woodrow Wilson*, vol. 25 (Princeton, N.J.: Princeton University Press, 1978), p. 153.

28. In addition to works cited in note 26, above, see John Brooks, *Once in Golconda: A True Drama of Wall Street, 1920–1938* (New York: Harper and Row, 1969) for a vivid chronicle of the disillusionment with the American financial system. Also useful is Joel Seligman, *The Transformation of Wall Street: The History of the Securities and Exchange Commission and Modern Corporate Finance* (Boston: Houghton Mifflin, 1982).

29. On labor history see David Brody, *Workers in Industrial America: Essays on the 20th Century Struggle* (New York: Oxford University Press, 1980); Sanford M. Jacoby, *Employing Bureaucracy: Managers, Unions and the Transformation of Work in American Industry, 1900–1945* (New York: Columbia University Press, 1985); Richard C. Edwards, *Contested Terrain: The Transformation of the Workplace in the Twentieth Century* (New York: Basic Books, 1985).

30. Useful general works are Robert Averitt, *The Dual Economy: The Dynamics of American Industry Structure* (New York: W. W. Norton, 1968); and Harold G. Vatter, *The United States Economy in the 1950's* (Chicago: University of Chicago Press, 1993).

31. George David Smith, *From Monopoly to Competition: The Transformations of Alcoa 1888–1986,* (New York: Cambridge University Press, 1988), chaps. 5–6.

32. On the rise and spread of multinational corporations, see Raymond Vernon, *Sovereignty at Bay: The Multinational Spread of U.S. Enterprises* (New York: Basic Books, 1971); and Mira Wilkins, *The Maturing of Multinational Enterprise: American Business Abroad from 1914 to 1970* (Cambridge, Mass.: Harvard University Press, 1974).

33. The emblematic steel story is chronicled in Thomas K. McCraw and Patricia A. O'Brien, "Production and Distribution: Competition Policy and Industry Structure" in *America Versus Japan*, ed. Thomas K. McCraw (Boston: Harvard Business School Press, 1986); Paul R. Lawrence and Davis Dyer, *Renewing American Industry: Organizing for Efficiency and Innovation* (New York: Basic Books, 1983), chap. 10; and Paul Tiffany, *The Decline of American Steel: How Management, Labor and Government Went Wrong* (New York: Oxford University Press, 1988).

34. The relative postwar decline of another major American industry, automobiles, is well documented in David Halberstam, *The Reckoning* (New York: Morrow, 1986); and Maryann Keller, *Rude Awakening: The Rise, Fall and Struggle for Recovery of General Motors* (New York: Morrow, 1989).

35. See the extended historical and legal discussion in Mark J. Roe, *Strong Managers, Weak Owners: The Political Roots of American Corporate Finance* (Princeton, N.J.: Princeton University Press, 1994).

36. Alan Auerbach, ed., *Mergers and Acquisitions* (Chicago: University of Chicago Press, 1988).

37. See, e.g., two of the typically adversarial, journalistic histories of the leveraged buyout wave: Connie Bruck, *The Predator's Ball: The Junk-Bond Raiders and the Man Who Staked Them* (New York: Simon and Schuster, 1988); and George Anders, *The Merchants of Debt: KKR and the Mortgaging of American Business* (New York: Basic Books, 1992).

38. See Andrei Shleifer and Robert Vishny, "The Takeover Wave of the 1980s," *Science*, 249 (August 1990): 745–49; Mark Mitchell and Kenneth Lehn, "Do Bad Bidders Become Good Targets?" *Journal of Political Economy* 2 (1990): 372–98; Dennis Mueller, "Mergers," in *New Palgrave Dictionary of Finance*, ed. Peter Newman, et al. (New York: Stockton Press, 1992); and Bronwyn H. Hall, "Corporate Restructuring and Investment Horizons in the United States, 1976–1987," *Business History Review*, 68 (spring 1994): 110–43. A somewhat less sympathetic view of leveraged buyouts, especially for mature "stable technology industries," is Alfred D. Chandler Jr., "The Competitive Performance of U.S. Industrial Enterprises Since the Second World War," in ibid, 1–72.

39. See note 20 above. For an entertaining history of some of the shortcomings of the conglomerate wave, see Robert Sobel, *The Rise and Fall of the Conglomerate Kings* (New York: Stein and Day, 1984). Scholarly treatments of conglomerate corporations, one successful, one not, are Bettye H. Pruitt, *The Making of Harcourt General: A History of Growth Through Diversification* (Cambridge, Mass.: Harvard Business School Press, 1994); and George P. Baker, "Beatrice: A Study in the Creation and Destruction of Value," *Journal of Finance* 47 (1992): 1081–119.

40. A representative argument to this point, building on years of scholarship into principal-agent problems, is Michael C. Jensen, "Corporate Control and the Politics of Finance," *Journal of Applied Corporate Finance* 4 (1991): 13–33.

41. See John Desmond Glover and Gerald A. Simon, *Chief Executives' Handbook* (Homewood, Ill.: Dow Jones-Irwin, 1976) for a discussion of the early stages of this trend.

42. Jacoby, *Employing Bureaucracy*; Thomas A. Kochan, Harry C. Katz, and Robert B. McKersie, *The Transformation of American Industrial Relations*, 2d ed. (Ithaca, N.Y.: Cornell University Press, 1994).

43. On job creation see Steve J. Davis and John Haltimeyer, "Gross Job Creation, Gross Job Destruction and Employment Reallocation," Federal Reserve Bank of Chicago, Working Paper series, WP-91-5, 1991.

44. Richard S. Tedlow, *Keeping the Corporate Image: Public Relations and Big Business, 1900–1950* (Greenwich, Conn.: JAI Press, 1979); and Marion G. Sobol, Gail E. Farrelly, and Jessica S. Taper, *Shaping the Corporate Image: An Analytical Guide for Executive Decision Makers* (New York: Quorum Press, 1992).

45. There is no authoritative history of planning, but for a recent statement by a leading authority on the subject, see Henry Mintzberg, *The Rise and Fall of Strategic Planning: Reconceiving Roles for Planning, Plans, Planners* (New York: Free Press, 1994).

46. The literature on the evolution and cultivation of the American market is vast, although, curiously, there is no history of the marketing function as big corporations carry it out. See Richard S. Tedlow, *New and Improved: The Story of Mass Marketing in America* (New York: Basic Books, 1985); Stephen Fox, *The Mirror Makers: A History of American Advertising and Its Creators* (New York: Morrow, 1984); and Philip Kotler and Gary Armstrong, *Marketing: An Introduction* (Englewood Cliffs, N.J.: Prentice Hall, 1993).

47. Peter G. W. Keen, *Every Manager's Guide to Information Technology: A Glossary of Key Terms and Concepts for Today's Business Leader* (Boston: Harvard Business School Press, 1991), contains a brief history of the evolution and spread of information technology in big business.

48. Modern diversification strategies flourished increasingly in the nonmanufacturing sector, as financial and other service firms looked for ways to expand beyond their core businesses into more profitable venues. The particular histories of such efforts wait to be written, but one good example of this trend had been carefully documented for a leading firm in the accounting industry: David Grayson Allen and Kathleen McDermott, *Accounting for Success: A History of Price Waterhouse in America, 1890–1990* (Boston: Harvard Business School Press, 1993), esp. chaps. 6–8.

49. In some ways the uniformity in language served to parody the process of corporate reporting. In preparing the text of an annual report or in speaking to a group of financial analysts, for example, the CEOs of very different companies came to say pretty much the same things: that they would only compete in markets in which they have the first or second leading position; that their goal was to "enhance shareholder value"; that they have become (or are working to become) "customer-driven"; that they have found new ways to capture and institutionalize learning; that

they have achieved enormous savings due to restructuring and downsizing; that a heightened concern for quality has forced reconceptualization of traditional processes and led to impressive gains in efficiency or cost position, as well as in quality; that the extent of teamwork and cross-functional integration inside companies is unprecedented and increasing; and on and on.

50. Excellent comparative histories of U.S. business ideology and that of other capitalist societies can be found in George C. Lodge and Ezra F. Vogel, *Ideology and National Competitiveness: An Analysis of Nine Countries* (Cambridge, Mass.: Harvard Business School Press, 1987); and Jeffrey E. Garten, *A Cold Peace: America, Japan, Germany, and the Struggle for Supremacy* (New York: Times Books, 1993).

51. The adoption of lean manufacturing techniques is particularly significant in that it represents the most fundamental development in managing the production process since the assembly line. This new trend is nicely captured and placed in historical context in a report of a five-year worldwide manufacturing study sponsored by the Massachusetts Institute of Technology. See James P. Womack, Daniel T. Jones, and Daniel Roos, *The Machine That Changed the World* (New York: Harper Collins, 1990).

3

How American Is the American Corporation?

✦

RAYMOND VERNON

Robert Reich's 1990 article—provocatively entitled "Who Is Us?"—has helped to revive a question almost as old as the corporation itself: To whom does the corporation owe its fealty? The question is particularly provocative in the United States in the final decade of the twentieth century because almost every major corporation headquartered in the country presides over a network of related enterprises that reaches over many countries. How are we to take into account the existence of these international networks as we address the question "Who Is Us?"

My conclusion is that the mushrooming of these international networks has not greatly dimmed the concept that American corporations exist, to be distinguished from corporations based in Europe or Japan or Brazil; the distinction continues to exercise power not only in the perceptions of the public but also in the policies of national governments. Nevertheless, the corporations themselves are far more constrained in recognizing their national identity as American. Their position as stewards presiding over a network of companies located in many countries introduces an element of ambiguity in their interests and in their loyalties that no amount of goodwill and open-mindedness can totally resolve. Mitigating these tensions will require a wide range of measures, many of which can be undertaken only by joint agreement among affected governments; but few of these measures have yet even appeared on the international agenda.

The Issue

The foreign activities of U.S.enterprises have grown to such an extent over the past four decades that they cannot fail to exercise a strong influence on the policies and practices of these firms in the United States. As Figure 3.1 indicates, the after-tax foreign earnings of U.S. corporations have increased dramatically over the past four decades relative to their after-tax earnings in the United States, reaching a level close to 50 percent by the latter 1980s.[1] In manufacturing, the foreign affiliates of U.S. parents report total employment equal to over 40 percent of the employment in the U.S. establishments of the parents; and in services, the comparable figure comes to about 24 percent.[2] Data on the sales and assets of the foreign affiliates of U.S. parents paint very much the same picture.[3] So U.S. enterprises can no longer manage their affairs without a constant reckoning of the effects of their decisions on their interests abroad.

Although the U.S.-based multinational enterprise is indisputably important for the U.S. economy, it is highly concentrated in the big-business sector of that economy. In the occasional censuses of the U.S. Department of Commerce, one finds only about two thousand U.S. firms with subsidiaries in foreign countries, with the average firm reporting eight such subsidiaries.[4] Moreover, in 1990 the five hundred largest such firms ac-

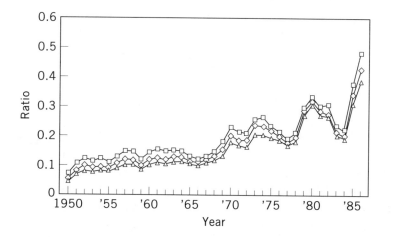

Figure 3.1. Ratio of after-tax foreign earnings to after-tax domestic earnings of U.S. corporations. The three lines reflect three different definitions of foreign earnings. *Source*: James R. Hines Jr., "The Flight Paths of Migratory Corporations," *Journal of Accounting, Auditing and Finance* 6, no. 4 (Fall 1991): 468.

Table 3.1. Shares Contributed to U.S. Gross Product in Manufacturing

	Percent U.S.-based parent firms	Percent foreign-owned subsidiaries in U.S.	Percent total
1977	68.8	3.4	72.4
1982	65.7	7.4	73.1
1989	61.1	11.3	72.4

counted for about 95 percent of the assets of all the foreign subsidiaries of U.S. parents. Nevertheless, smaller firms are developing multinational networks in increasing numbers; in fact, U.S.-based firms with fewer than five hundred employees made up about one-quarter of the two thousand U.S.-based multinationals.[5]

Viewed in the aggregate, U.S.-based enterprises that preside over international networks play a major role in the U.S. economy. According to an estimate of the United Nations, the manufacturing product of these enterprises generated in the United States in 1989 accounted for about 61 percent of the gross manufacturing product of the country in that year, with substantial (though lower) proportions for services and primary activities.[6] Neverthless, viewed from one perspective, one could say that the relative importance of the U.S.-based parent to the U.S. economy has been declining. Table 3.1, based on UN estimates, offers one measure of the position of these firms over time, with arresting implications. Evidently, U.S.-based firms with multinational networks in manufacturing have come to occupy a somewhat reduced position in U.S. manufacturing output. And, as their relative position in the United States has declined, the position of foreign-owned manufacturers in the United States has increased.

With the growing importance of foreign-owned subsidiaries in the United States, it is apparent that the country needs to respond not only to the question that makes up the title of this essay but to a companion question as well: How American is the foreign-owned subsidiary in America? For the present, I leave that critical question to be addressed by others. But it seems obvious that the growth of these foreign-owned firms lends added support to the proposition that any efforts to mitigate the tensions explored in this paper will require joint action on the part of the affected governments.

Although the United States was once seen as the principal country breeding multinational enterprises, the home bases of multinational enterprises today are to be found in many different countries. According to the UN's listing for 1990, the world's one hundred largest multinationals came from thirteen different countries. And the subsidiaries of these enterprises are to be found in every market economy on the globe.[7] The reasons for the spread of such enterprises from their home bases are well understood. For some products and services, these networks represent the most efficient way for the parent to penetrate markets or acquire raw materials, technology, and components, being superior to arm's-length trading in the open international market.[8] Moreover, in many situations, the parent sees the creation of a foreign subsidiary as the most effective way of reducing risks, including the risk of import restrictions, of exchange rate changes, and of preemptive threats by rivals.[9]

Yet despite the seeming ubiquity of the multinational enterprise phenomenon and the likelihood that it will continue to occupy a prominent place in international markets, governments in the countries in which most of these enterprises are based hestitate to discuss the basic anomalies associated with their existence. One detects the echoes of reactions sixty years ago when Adolf Berle and Gardiner Means took note of another basic anomaly associated with large U.S. corporations, namely, the separation of ownership from the control of their assets.[10] Then, as now, most business managers and politicians saw nothing to be gained by focusing on unresolved problems that offered no obvious solution.[11]

To be sure, in times past, scholars, politicians, and poets have sometimes raised fundamental questions about the nature of the multinational enterprise.[12] But their interest was at its peak at a time when the phenomenon was thought to be largely a manifestation of the Pax Americana, rather than a global trend in which parent firms from dozens of countries were creating their own multinational networks.

Today there is a widespread acknowledgment of the possibility that multinational enterprises may be benefiting all nations by contributing to global efficiency. The question, then, is how the cost and benefits generated by multinational enterprises are being shared among different national jurisdictions. That question is usually raised, however, in narrowly functional terms. How are such enterprises affecting economic development and job creation as they move their production activities across borders in pursuit of higher profits or greater security? How do they affect tax collections, as they account for the cross-border operations of their affiliated units? How do they affect competitive conditions in national markets as they engage in mergers and divestitures abroad? How do they affect national security, as they interact with foreign enterprises in world markets? What is their impact on environmental objectives as they search for a site for pollution-generating activities? And how do they relate to national democratic processes as they exercise their political rights in foreign countries? What is lacking, then, is not an interest in the issues generated by the multinational enterprise but an interest in searching for the underlying causes that generate the unease.

The Basic Dilemma

Although neither governments nor enterprises are eager to acknowledge a basic dilemma that the multinational enterprise embodies, the nature of that dilemma is painfully apparent. The multinational enterprise operates under the constraints imposed by two sets of obligations, and the two sets define goals that are bound at times to conflict.

The first set of obligations is to the governments that authorize the creation of the various corporations that constitute any multinational network. As numerous scholars have observed, governments have endowed the corporation with some extraordinary attributes: its claim to immortality; its right in most circumstances to make commitments in its own name, without direct participation in such decisions by its owners; and its capacity in most situations to shield its owners from financial liability.[13] In return, governments usually expect that the corporation's operations will be compatible with the national interests of the country that provides for its creation.

That expectation, I need hardly observe, is not always realized. The managers of large corporations are frequently accused of serving their own interests or those of their stockholders at the cost of the rest of the national economy that authorized their existence. But large enterprises that preside over a multinational network are recognized as being exposed to a very distinctive set of added pressures, namely, the pressures applied by foreign governments and other interests operating in the countries in which the foreign subsidiaries of the multinationals are located.

All governments are in competition for investment funds, technology, jobs, and exports. Each tries to persuade or compel the managers of the multinational network, as they execute their network strategies, to make the largest possible contribution to its national economy. In the pursuit of that objective, governments do not hesitate to apply their pressures even when it seems apparent that their gains would be at the cost of some other country. When the efforts of different governments blatantly conflict, as they often do, the managers of the multinational enterprise usually find themselves in the acutely uncomfortable position of parceling out their resources to different national economies. As a rule, they perform that uncomfortable task as quietly and unobtrusively as possible, but usually with a sense of the risks inherent in their position.

To be sure, a corporation that has no foreign subsidiaries to worry about can nevertheless affect its home country in ways that are hard to distinguish from those associated with multinational enterprises. A corporation without foreign subsidiaries that switches from a domestic supplier of components to an independent foreign supplier, for instance, can generate economic consequences indistinguishable from those that a parent company creates when it switches its purchases from a domestic source to one of its subsidiaries in a foreign country. But there is an implicit awareness among politicians and the public at large that the position of the corporation with foreign subsidiaries is especially exposed, as it seeks to juggle the foreign government's expectations regarding the subsidiary's contributions with the home government's expectations of the contributions of the parent.

At the same time, there is widespread acceptance of the idea that the multinational structure of enterprises can add to global efficiency, thus opening up the possibility that such enterprises may make a positive contribution to the welfare of all countries. Indeed, state-owned enterprises appear in relative decline; according to one compilation, governments between 1985 and 1993 sold off $328 billion of their state-owned enterprises to the private sector, in hundreds of transactions involving several scores of countries.[14] In some industries, notably telecommunications and mining, multinational enterprises based in the United States and other industrialized countries have been among the largest buyers of the state-owned properties under the hammer. Reflecting the importance of that trend, one source reports that in the years from 1985 to 1990 there were nearly 150 cross-border acquisitions of telecommunications companies, with value of about $20 billion;[15] all but a few of these involved shifts from state ownership to private ownership

As I shall point out in the following, however, the shift in global sentiment does not mean that governments are prepared to abandon their concerns over the issues that are inherent in the operations of multinational enterprises. Neither tax, antitrust, security, pollution, development, nor political participation issues in which multinationals are involved show signs of a systemic solution. Besides, multinationals from time to time are tempting targets for protesting the pain brought on by even larger issues, such as the grave risks that industrial change repeatedly brings to exposed workers and affected localities. The protests of U.S. labor against the North American Free Trade Agreement (NAFTA), of the "green" organizations against industrial pollution, and of the farmers of India against the green revolution, for instance, often take the form of an attack on multinationals as a class.

The quality of such protests, it is true, is vastly different from that of a few decades ago, as many foreign governments have come to recognize the counterproductive results of some of their interventions in the market, particularly those conducted through state monopolies and state-owned enterprises. But the current disposition of governments to rely more heavily on the performance of the market than at any time in the last half century does not mean that many of them are prepared to accept any outcome the market will generate. The member countries of OPEC still attempt to steer the course of world oil prices; the producers of coffee in Africa and Latin America make sporadic efforts to gain control of coffee prices; Europe, Japan, and the United States, among others, continue to ride herd on their markets for agricultural products; and the support for "industrial policies" in the advanced industrialized countries is still in evidence. Even as governments persist in their efforts to attract multinational enterprises, therefore, few of them will abandon their efforts to increase their share of the benefits generated by such enterprises.

Under present conditions, despite the history of Bhopal and United Fruit, multinational enterprises still can make as good a case for their performance as Winston Churchill once made for democracy. As compared with the available alternatives, such as state-owned enterprises and private national enterprises, the multinational enterprise must be rated a responsible and responsive form of business. But that is not enough to ensure an untroubled future. A global economy that is populated by multinational enterprises has yet to come to terms with a world that is organized by nation-states. In a global system organized by nation-states, a network made up of units of different nationalities that respond to a common strategy bristles with latent contradictions. Until some measures are taken to blunt the contradictions, the multinational enterprise faces an international environment of latent or active threat, which will constantly be placing impediments in the way of its efficient functioning and exacerbating relations between governments.

Business-Government Relations

For the United States, however, there is a more pointed reason to take an interest in the rules of the game relating to the operations of multinational enterprises. This is the prospect that, in the tug-of-war among different governments over the resources of the multinational enterprise, the U.S. government will perform relatively poorly, allowing other governments to capture more than their share.

The reasons for expecting this outcome arise in part from the marked distinctiveness of business-government relations in the United States. To be sure, large corporations everywhere share certain common characteristics. In the United States as elsewhere, the modern corporation emerged as a response to the needs and opportunities generated by technological advances in transportation and production. As long as the family-based business was the dominant form of enterprise, there were severe limits on the capacity of firms to assume the long-term obligations and to build the professional bureaucracies that are indispensable for exploiting significant economies of scale and scope. But, as various scholars have observed, the statutory basis for the creation of the modern corporation in the United States sprang from very different roots than in the United Kingdom or continental Europe, not to mention most countries in Asia or Latin America.

In other industrialized countries, the modern corporation grew out of the divine attributes of royal houses and the church. Whereas ordinary mortals could make only a temporary claim to life on earth, institutions of divine origin were blessed with the attribute of immortality. So corporations like the British East India Company and the Hudson's Bay Company were seen as extensions or agents of these divine institutions. The United States, on the other hand, owed its early political development to movements that were in flight from the centrist governments and state religions of Europe.[16] It is hardly surprising, therefore, that some Americans saw the corporation as an insidious menace, paving the way to large aggregations of capital and excessive concentrations of economic power.[17]

These diverse starting points produced very different paths in the development of the corporate persona. The statutory processes that authorized and empowered corporations outside of the United States consisted of a cautious step-by-step relaxation of a tightly guarded royal prerogative. In the United States, on the other hand, the idea that the federal government should authorize the creation of corporations initially met with considerable resistance. Eventually, it was the various sovereign states of the

United States that took over the process of authorizing the creation of corporations. There ensued a competitive race among the states, conducted vigorously over many decades, a process that in the end endowed all U.S. citizens with the precious rights of kings, including the right to immortality and the right to protection from creditors and other claimants.

Developments in the nineteenth and twentieth centuries served to preserve and extend these early differences. While the relations between big business and government outside the United States varied in detail from one country to the next, big businesses in Europe and Japan managed to maintain intimate links with their respective governments until the end of World War II. The highly concentrated banking structures and well-delineated national elites of these countries helped to maintain such links, making for a national strategy in which business and government were usually found performing complementary roles.

That pattern stood in sharp contrast with the chaotic relations between the public sector and business interests in the United States.[18] No other country could match the size of the vast giveaways of public resources to the private sector, exemplified in the building of the transcontinental railroads, in the subsidized leasing of public lands for mining and agriculture, and in the subsidized provision of water. But neither could other countries match the unprecedented efforts on the part of government agencies to rein in the power of big business, using antitrust laws, regulatory agencies, and the courts. The decree dissolving the Standard Oil Company in 1911 and the law directing the dissolution of the public utility holding companies in 1935, for instance, had no counterparts in other countries.

After World War II the exceptionalism of the United States continued to surface.[19] Before the war the United States had lagged decades behind Europe in the introduction of the social programs associated with the New Deal; an abortive effort to bring business in much closer contact with government through a National Recovery Administration was struck down by the Supreme Court before it was two years old. In the postwar period, U.S. business-government relations continued to follow a highly distinctive course, creating norms for U.S.-based enterprises that were markedly different from those they were to encounter in other parts of the world.

Following the war, countries all over the world experimented with various forms of state intervention aimed at speeding their growth, from the import-substitution policies of Latin America and Asia to the national planning efforts of France and Britain and the administrative guidance of Japan. In these experiments the close ties between big business and governments typically played a major role.[20] But the United States, almost alone, remained aloof from these experiments. After World War II, unlike other countries, the U.S. government dissolved the government-owned companies that it had created for its wartime needs. Thereafter, cooperation between the federal government and the private sector in the United States on foreign issues was episodic and opportunistic. From time to time the U.S. government used the CIA in an effort to destabilize foreign regimes that had been hostile to U.S.-based multinational enterprises, such as the Jacobo Arbenz regime in Guatemala in 1954 and the Salvador Allende regime in Chile in 1972. But the principal motive of the U.S. government behind those extraordinary episodes was to turn back the Soviet Union in the cold war rather than provide direct support to the affected enterprises.[21]

If there was any industry in which cooperation between government and industry had some measure of continuity and structure it was oil. That oil was an exceptional industry in this respect was apparent in numerous ways. Only oil, for instance, had its own official adviser inside the State Department; and only oil managed to get its own representatives on the staff of General Douglas MacArthur during the postwar occupation of Japan. Even in the case of oil, however, the relationships between business and government proved sporadic and contentious. There were periods of collaboration, such as the 1920s, when Washington supported the entry of U.S. oil companies into the Middle East, and the 1950s, when it unseated Prime Minister Mohammed Mossadegh and helped the U.S. oil companies gain a foothold in Iran. But there were other periods in which the major oil companies were under attack from Washington, as illustrated by the Supreme Court decision of 1911 liquidating the Standard Oil trust, by various federal lawsuits against the oil companies initiated in the 1940s, and by the oil import restrictions imposed by the U.S. government in the 1950s. Even in crises such as the closing of the Suez Canal and the oil embargo attending the Israeli-Egyptian war of 1973, the collaboration between the oil industry and the U.S. government was characterized by reserve and punctuated by acrimony.[22]

The experiences of the oil industry serve to identify some of the factors that distinguish the U.S. case from other countries. One such factor is the dispersion of power inside the U.S. government structure. At various times the power of the courts, the Congress, and the various states to challenge the executive branch in Washington has been clearly in evidence. Even inside the executive branch, various agencies have been able at times to strike out on their own initiatives. Another factor has been the diversity of interests within the oil industry itself, notably the deep split between the independent producers of oil in the United States and the majors producing oil all over the world.

Apart from oil, there have been very few industries with which the federal government has maintained some measure of sustained cooperation on foreign issues after World War II. But the aircraft and computer chip industries have occupied favored positions in this respect. It is no accident that, in both cases, the defense agencies have been deeply involved, providing research support and purchasing on preferential terms.[23]

Yet in both instances, U.S.-based enterprises that benefited from the U.S. government's support have not hesitated in striking off on their own, forging alliances and exchanging technology with firms based in Europe and Japan wherever they saw an advantage in doing so. That propensity has been especially in evidence in the semiconductor industry, in which, the U.S. government has established an ambitious program of financial support through SEMATECH, a consortium of fourteen chip-making firms which over the years have received over one billion dollars in U.S. funds. The individual members of SEMATECH, including Texas Instruments, Motorola, and AT&T, have still been free to enter into close alliances with Japanese and German firms in the same industry. And SEMATECH itself has funneled funds into various contractor firms, such as Semi-Gas Systems and Silicon Valley Group Lithograph, which in turn have established ties to Japanese competitors through the sale of equity and of technical information.[24]

In maintaining their independence to strike deals overseas, U.S. firms are behaving well within the norms that govern relationships between U.S. business and the federal government. One sees a pronounced reluctance among Americans in general and American business interests in particular to place power in the hands of a national bureaucracy, a reluctance that manifests itself in elaborate statutory guidelines and rights of appeal from the decisions of the bureaucracy.[25] True, most managers of big business in the United States see themselves as hemmed in by high corporate income taxes and suffocated by regulations covering labor relations, stockholder relations, the environment, and competitive behavior. Moreover, they see themselves treading warily among sovereign national governments, each such government with the arbitrary power to penalize and confiscate. At the same time, however, those with foreign experience usually recognize that their relationships to the U.S. government differ profoundly from business-government relationships prevailing in most of the countries where their foreign subsidiaries are located.[26]

So far, the exceptionalism of the United States continues to be tangible, distinguishing the behavior of U.S.-based enterprises toward their home government from the behavior of enterprises headquartered outside the United States. These latter enterprises, true to their origins, will tend to behave a little more like the agents (or, it may be, the partners) of their respective home governments than U.S.-based enterprises would be prepared to do.[27] That is to say, they will tend to call on their governments more readily for help, and they will tend to get that support with fewer questions asked. Moreover, like any valued agent or partner, they will at times have a larger hand in drafting the government's official line than any U.S. firm would normally expect to have; and, like any valued agent or partner, they will at times accept the informal guidance of the government to a degree that U.S. firms would usually find difficult to tolerate.

Sweeping generalizations such as these, of course, always require qualifications and nuances. Business-government relationships vary in detail, being affected, among other things, by the nature of the immediate issue, the industry involved, and the larger political and economic context in which the issue arises.[28] Moreover, developments in both Europe and Japan suggest the possibility that the close ties between governments and their largest enterprises that were so typical in the past may be diminishing a little, reducing the distinctions between business-government relations in those areas and in the United States;[29] but the differences remain palpable.

Indeed, for managers of the U.S.-based multinational enterprise, the implications of the subtle differences in business-government relations in foreign countries can sometimes be profound. Suppose that a foreign sovereign authorizes a U.S. parent corporation to create a subsidiary in its jurisdiction. What are the rights and responsibilities of the subsidiary? Is it to be regarded as an auslander, incapable of accepting the subtle remnants of agency that are inherent in the relationship between the authorizing state and locally owned corporations?[30] Or should it expect to receive all the rights and carry all the burdens of such corporations? And if the subsidiary is to be responsive to the government that authorized its existence, what of the responsibilities of the parent's managers in the United States as they direct the affairs of these subsidiaries in foreign countries, having in mind not only the expectations of the foreign countries but also those of the U.S. government and the stockholders of the parent enterprise?

Before closing in on that critical question, one has to address another aspect of the political environment in which the U.S.-based enterprises operate, namely, the foreign policies of the United States that affect their behavior overseas.

U.S. Policies

International discussions over the problems associated with the multinational enterprise have rarely raised fundamental issues regarding the nature of the institution and the dilemmas it faces. Such questions, as I have already suggested, tend to leave both governments and enterprises uncomfortable, posing large issues without obvious solutions.

In the case of the United States, the propensity to deal with such problems as if they were a series of unrelated functional issues is especially strong. The reasons for that tendency run very deep, being due in part to the diffusion of power in the U.S. government itself. Taxation lies in the province of the Bureau of Internal Revenue, with the Ways and Means Committee of the House and the Finance Committee of the Senate performing the oversight function; antitrust is the province of Justice and the Federal Trade Commission, with distinctly different ties to the congressional structure; "dirty tricks" are in the province of the CIA, with oversight from other committees of the two houses. And so it goes. Not surprisingly, then, in forums such as the UN, the Organization for Economic Cooperation and Development, and the General Agreement on Tariffs and Trade, the oversized delegations of the U.S. government have preferred to address the problems of the multinational enterprise functionally, passing the lead position to one agency or another according to the subject matter.

There has been a tendency, therefore, for the United States to generate policies that affect multinational enterprises function by function, risking inconsistencies and contradictions. The tendency has been enlarged a little by the independent role of the courts in interpreting U.S. law. Although cooperation between the public sector and the private sector has been difficult, U.S. courts and administrative agencies have had no hesitation, when it suited their needs, to assert their jurisdiction over U.S.-owned subsidiaries in foreign countries, even though those subsidiaries are created under foreign laws and do their business outside the United States.[31] The tendency is most in evidence in matters purportedly related to defense, such as security export controls. It also appears in other areas, however, such as the enforcement of the antitrust laws and the laws relating to securities markets. But because the laws involved are administered by different agencies and interpreted by different courts in the United States, the underlying criteria by which the United States claims an extraterritorial reach are quite obscure.

Despite these functional differences, the United States has typically demanded of foreign governments that they provide "national treatment" for the foreign subsidiaries of U.S.-based enterprises, that is, treatment indistinguishable from that provided to a national in similar circumstances. That position, however, has been undermined by various factors. In promoting this position, the U.S. government has usually preferred to disregard its own not-infrequent violations of the principle.[32] The occasional decisions of the U.S. government to exclude foreign-owned subsidiaries from official research grants in high-tech industries have contributed substantially to the undermining process.[33]

Moreover, when urging the principle of "national treatment" on other countries, U.S. policy makers appear to overlook the fact that government ministries abroad are frequently authorized and directed to shape their actions toward individual enterprises, whether domestic or foreign, without regard for the principle of nondiscrimination, using criteria that may violate that principle. In such cases, the application of "national treatment"still leaves governments free to discriminate. Added to that point is the fact that foreign-owned enterprises tend to cluster in distinctive sectors of the economy, such as those that require relatively large scale and relatively advanced technology, so that the "national treatment" standard does not exist.

Despite the precarious state and doubtful utility of the "national treatment" principle, remants of the principle are embodied in over four hundred bilateral agreements.[34] To be sure, the guarantee ordinarily does not cover all industries; activities such as radio and television broadcasting, coastwise shipping, and defense production, among others, are usually explicitly excluded. Indeed, the "national treatment" guarantee in many agreements does not extend to the foreigner's initial right to establish a subsidiary but is limited to the relations between the subsidiary and the host government after establishment.

Moreover, the principle has been weakened even further by the fact that governments have typically sought to supplement the "national treatment" rights for their subsidiaries in foreign countries with added rights that distinguish them from local enterprises. The U.S. government and other governments have demanded of other countries, for instance, that the subsidiaries of their nationals, in addition to receiving national treatment, should also receive most-favored-nation treatment, should be protected from the breach of any contractual commitments the government may have undertaken with respect to the subsidiary, and should be favored with any added rights that may exist in international law. In the end, therefore, foreign-owned enterprises often acquire rights that on paper seem to exceed those of the local enterprise.

Not surprisingly, these various provisions offer little in the way of guidance toward a general concept of the multinational enterprise. No doubt, their existence has some defensive value for the foreign investor when a dispute arises, especially if the issue does not touch a raw political nerve in the host country. Arbitration facilities offered by the World Bank and other organizations add a little more protection for the exposed investor.[35] But they do little to resolve the basic ambiguities regarding the nature of the multinational enterprise.

All told, then, U.S. policies toward the multinational enterprise do not offer any hint of an underlying concept regarding the nature of the institution. In practice, the American public has no trouble identifying "our" multinational enterprises from "theirs;" the Big Three automobile producers are "ours,"while Honda is "theirs." Presumably, the distinction turns in part on the national identity of stockholders; and foreigners' holdings of equity in U.S. parents are still comparatively small.[36] The distinction also may turn on the nationality of the managers at the apex of the organization. But this criterion is beginning to provide slightly more ambiguous signals; according to one survey, about one in six large companies in the United States now includes at least one director who is not a U.S. citizen.[37]

Eventually, identifying criteria of this kind will grow even softer. Takeovers by foreigners of long-established U.S. firms have already created a class of cases in which these criteria do not seem quite appropriate. As these criteria soften, the expectations of the U.S. government with regard to the behavior of multinationals will become even more ambiguous.

Behavioral Patterns of Enterprises

In the past, the driving force behind the multinationalization of large enterprises has been largely technological, a response to the fact that the cost of transportation and communication has fallen dramatically in real terms, and the added fact that the facilities for transborder movements of tangibles and intangibles have improved in quality to a degree never previously imagined. Whether the trend could have been aborted by a hostile set of public policies is unclear. But the cat, it appears, is forever out of the bag. And it seems plausible to assume, as I do, that space and distance will continue to shrink in importance in the locational decisions of business managers.

In such a world, will it matter if the United States continues to deal with the issues relating to multinational enterprises in its accustomed pattern, grappling with each issue as it arises until some inflammatory case seems to require a broader response? At the present state of our knowledge, one can only provide some highly conditional answers. To gain a sense of those complex answers, consider the state of U.S. policy in three fields that provide some of the raw stimuli in the creation of international economic frictions: the creation of jobs, the payment of taxes, and national security.

Creating Jobs

General Electronics closes a plant in Council Bluffs, Iowa, that produces the filaments for electric lamps and simultaneously opens up a plant in Hermosillo, Mexico, that produces the same product at lower labor cost. (The names have been altered to protect the innocent.) Is this an irrefutable case for the proposition that multinationalness can destroy jobs in the United States? The answer to that question is an unequivocal no. We cannot say what the job effect of General Electronic's decision will be unless we can picture what would have happened if the company had failed to make the transfer from Council Bluffs to Hermosillio. If General Electronics failed to make the move, would its bulbs have been priced out of the U.S. market and out of its markets abroad, such as Canada and Mexico? Or, alternatively, would General Electronics have risen to the competitive challenge by introducing some laborsaving means of production in its U.S. plants? And if it followed the latter course, by how much would it concurrently reduce its Council Bluffs staff?

It has not been for lack of research effort that such uncertainties have persisted regarding the job effects generated by the multinational structure of U.S. enterprises. Scholars have repeatedly tried to come to some overall judgments on that score, using both individual case studies and models of the U.S. economy.[38] As usual, both approaches provide wobbly conclusions. The case studies are too few in number to be reliably representative. And the models—notwithstanding the impressive ingenuity of some of the model builders—are still simplified caricatures of a more complex reality.[39]

Nevertheless, for what it is worth, a dominant judgment does appear to exist among academic economists who have addressed the question of the effects on the U.S. economy of the multinationalness of U.S.-based corporations: they appear to share a strong presumption, based largely on faith or on clinical experience, that the decisions of multinational enterprises under present world conditions have very little effect on jobs in the United States. Some worry about the effects on U.S. income distribution of the increasing international exchanges of goods and services, including those stimulated by the increase in the role of multinationals.[40] Some would not be averse to attempting consciously to increase the attractiveness of the United States as a locus for the future operations of such enterprises, through measures such as governmental support for job training and research, or a reduction in corporate income taxes, or even cautious doses of "industrial policy" aimed at a few selected industries.[41] But the dominant view among economists in the United States continues to be that trends in job creation in the country are not materially influenced by the multinationalness of enterprise

That conclusion, however, does not mean that the strenuous and costly efforts of the various states of the United States to retain and attract the units of multinational enterprises are without economic effect; at a minimum, they affect the distribution of the tax burden between individuals and business in the country. Nor does it mean that the countermeasures of other governments to retain and enlarge the activities of U.S.-owned subsidiaries in their jurisdictions are without effect; these could well be altering the content of jobs in the United States, even if they do not greatly affect the overall level of employment.

In the absence of some effective international restraints, it is doubtful that governments will suspend their efforts to bring jobs and investments into their jurisdictions. Indeed, the international economic battles of the future, once fought through competing tariffs and exchange rates, are likely to concentrate much more on capturing the resources of the multinational networks. In such a battle, governments will continue to use both blandishments and threats in their dealings with multinational enterprises—blandishments when the aim of government is to attract them into its jurisdiction, threats when they seem useful as a means of increasing the contributions of the enterprises to the economy. And the enterprises, especially the U.S.-based enterprises, can be expected to respond according to their business interests, rather than to the label that governments put upon them.

In a game of this sort, the United States is unlikely to fare well. The competition among the states will elevate the price that the country as a whole pays for retaining or attracting investment on U.S. soil. And if the negotiating function were passed up from the states to the federal level, some of the inherent characteristics of the federal system would hamper its negotiations so severely as to imperil the outcome. The propensity of the federal system to hold the executive branch to transparent standards entailing the least possible use of bureaucratic discretion would create one major handicap in the competitive struggle. The strong tendency of the federal system to require a wide sharing of benefits among the various states would create another. In uninhibited warfare, therefore, it would not be surprising to find some of the activities and investments of U.S.-based enterprises drawn to other countries. It would be a source of comfort—though cold comfort on the whole—to note that the blandishments of the individual states of the United States might attract some foreign direct investment in return.

In the tug-of-war between countries for the resources of multinational enterprises, general measures that made the United States attractive as an economic environment, such as the improvement of workforce skills, infrastructure, and tax structures, could play their usual important role. And, given the firmly embedded characteristics of the U.S. system of governance, the U.S. government would be wise to push for international agreements that restrained the use of blandishments and threats in the struggle for the resources of the multinational enterprises. U.S. efforts in this direction are already prominent in GATT and NAFTA. But these are policies that require patience and fortitude; and they are constantly threatened in the United States by the temptation to ape the aggressive unilateral policies of other countries.

Paying Taxes

There was a time, not very long ago, when the sovereign right to tax was a right to be defended by armed force. Today, less bellicose means would be employed in most cases to defend that right, but the right to tax remains a major concern of every sovereign state.

Fortunately, multinational enterprises themselves have a powerful interest in ensuring that the sovereigns find a way of settling their quarrels over the right to tax. Where taxes are concerned, the increasing sophistication of national tax collectors has posed a growing threat for multinational enterprises; as a consequence, these enterprises have gradually come around to the realization that their interests lie in helping governments resolve their conflicts, lest they end up the victims in the clash.

U.S. policies toward the taxation of multinational enterprises are shaped around two basic principles: that enterprises in the United States ought not to be required to pay taxes on income earned in other countries if foreign governments have already taxed that income at U.S. levels; and that the taxable income of the U.S. taxpayer can be separated from the income of its foreign subsidiaries and affiliates by objectively verifiable criteria.

To those who have seen the operations of multinational enterprises from close up, the second principle reflects a view of the multinational enterprise that bears little relation to reality. How substantial that distortion may be in the case of any multinational enterprise depends on the nature of the relations among the various units around the globe that make up the enterprise. But the distortion is severe in many cases, leading to demands by the U.S. authorities upon the taxpaying entity that are procrustean in nature.

In the tax issue, one sees in an explicit context the clash between the requirements of a nation-state system and the realities of the multinational enterprise. The various units of any multinational enterprise are commonly engaged in a stream of transfers of goods and services, transfers that would command a payment if undertaken with outside parties. Sometimes the transfers consist of tangible materials or components, sometimes of intangible managerial or industrial technology, sometimes of the right to use a trade name or manufacture a product protected by patents.[42] In response to the political need for autonomous decisions, most countries have adopted the principle that they will apportion costs among the units of a multinational enterprise by valuing these internal transfers on the basis of the prices they would fetch in an arm's-length transaction. Unfortunately, however, comparable arm's-length prices are usually not to be found.[43] Rare enough where tangible products are concerned, arm's-length prices are even rarer in the case of intangibles. So governments are reduced to imposing their own prices, or accepting the uninhibited declarations of the taxpayer, in order to determine the taxable profits of the units in their jurisdiction.

In response to deep-seated values rooted in history, the U.S. public assigns great value to the proposition that the federal bureaucracy should operate pursuant to objective standards, with the least possible scope for arbitrary bureaucratic determinations. So elaborate guidelines are provided, laid down by law and regulation. Several hundred economists in the Internal Revenue Service and thousands of lawyers and consultants representing the taxpaying multinationals struggle endlessly over the creation of these synthetic numbers.[44] And as the international transfers among the units of multinational enterprises have swelled, the processing times for tax returns have increased and the backlog of unresolved cases has piled up.[45] Nevertheless, the fact that the outcomes are hopelessly arbitrary remains starkly evident.[46]

U.S. authorities, conscious of the risks and costs of creating a hopelessly complex structure, have fallen back on various devices for trying to make the system work. With the support of the U.S. business community, they have entered into bilateral tax treaties with some forty-two countries, providing for formulas and processes that would avoid double taxation between them. In a few cases, U.S. authorities have gone a step further by agreeing on binding arbitration with another country in the event that differences arise between them; and they have agreed with a few large taxpayers in advance on acceptable cost-allocating formulas.[47] But the cost and complexities of developing such agreements suggest that they do not offer a solution for most taxpayers.

So far, however, there has been no groundswell among the leading countries to move to a system that would reestablish contact with reality, that is, a system which would recognize that in many cases the aggregate profits of the multinational enterprise resulting from operations in a number of different countries provide the only hard starting point for undertaking a national allocation of taxable profits. Part of the resistance to any such approach stems from those who have a stake in the present system, including the public and private bureaucracies that thrive on its existence. But there is another major problem as well: the fact that unless all major taxing jurisdictions adopt the same unitary approach, the risks of double taxation will be very high. It is not surprising, therefore, that when a few states in the United States took it upon themselves to introduce such a system, they were assailed from all directions.[48]

The odds are, therefore, that for some time to come U.S.-based multinationals will have to live with the present U.S. approach to the taxation of their global activities. And the probability is high, as well, that the procedures designed to justify the inescapably arbitrary outcomes of that approach will grow in complexity. That expectation stems in part from the fact that the transfers among the units of U.S.-based enterprises promise increasingly to consist of intangibles such as information and franchises; and the difficulties of creating a defensible transfer price for such resources prove, in practice, to be many times greater than those relating to tangibles.[49] With few signs of an international response to these growing problems, the reactions of U.S.-based multinationals to such trends is easy to predict: where legally possible and economically sensible, managers are likely to keep their international transfers outside the jurisdiction of U.S. tax authorities. In time, such responses will weaken the attachment of any enterprise to its U.S. identity.

National Security

Although official Washington as a rule has been slow to display much interest in the anomalous characteristics of U.S.-based multinational enterprises, that interest has been readily aroused when issues of national security appeared to be involved. With the Gulf War well in mind, U.S. planners remain eager to resist the proliferation of weapons of mass destruction and to maintain the technical lead that proved so critical for U.S. forces. The prospect that the U.S. military establishment will have to rely in the future on enterprises that maintain substantial operations in foreign countries can hardly be expected to sit comfortably with such planners. But, despite numerous official studies and analyses, no signs of a way out of that increasing difficulty are in evidence.

It is apparent even to the outsider, however, that the concerns of military planners are of a number of different kinds. One source of worry, reflecting the experiences of World War II and the ensuing half century of the cold war, is whether the U.S. economy could function adequately as the workhorse of a NATO alliance in providing the needed ingredients for a prolonged conventional war. As U.S. military leaders are thoroughly aware, the justification for planning for a prolonged conventional war has shrunk considerably with the dissolution of the Soviet Union and the increasing destructive capabilities of conventional arms; but the power of old assumptions usually continues in bureaucratic organizations such as the military long after their leadership has recognized them as obsolete. From time to time, therefore, Pentagon planners worry whether the capacity of an industry in the United States is sufficient to sustain the wartime needs of a fighting alliance. And as U.S.-based enterprises inexorably expand the multinational networks on which they rely for their materials and components, the worries of the planners grow apace.

A second worry for military planners is epitomized by the ancient tale of the missing horseshoe nail, on which a critical battle turned. This is a concern not so much for the conduct of prolonged wars as for the execution of rapid maneuvers, whether before the outbreak of hostilities or in actual war. The concern carries particular weight with U.S. military planners today for a number of reasons. For one thing, the U.S. government itself has repeatedly tried to withhold critical items from other countries, including countries that were friends and allies, if the United States did not approve of the use to which the item would be put. Accordingly, it is easy for U.S. planners to picture the United States at the receiving end of such a policy.[50] The fact that a U.S.-based multinational enterprise was relying on its Spanish or Indian subsidiary to provide some critical component for the U.S. armed forces, therefore, would be an obvious source of tension for the military planner.

Some trends in industrial production tend to reduce the risks to military preparedness arising out of the possibility that a horseshoe nail might be lacking in the heat of a crisis. In many areas, helped by computerized controls, the country's processing and production facilities are becoming less specialized and more versatile, capable on short notice of producing the output required to replace the missing nail.[51] On the other hand, the possibility that U.S. planners may overlook a critically needed nail has been increased exponentially in recent decades as a result of other factors. Large enterprises throughout the world have been rediscovering the virtues of contracting out many of the activities that heretofore they felt obliged to produce in tightly controlled subsidiary organizations, often turning to foreign sources for their intermediate needs.[52] At the same time, there have been giant increases in the complexity of military end products such as tanks and aircraft. This increased complexity means that the manufacture of such products has depended increasingly on successive layers of components, each fabricated and assembled in facilities devoted especially to the component. By the time the end product is assembled for delivery to the military, it is difficult for planners to pinpoint the sources of the critical components that have gone into the successive layers. The magnitude of the problem is suggested by an informed estimate that one-fifth of the value of equipment purchased by the U.S. military is of foreign origin.[53]

A more fundamental threat to U.S. military planning, however, may lie in the declining ability of the defense establishment to influence the long-term direction of the research and development activities of the enterprises on which it depends. To be sure, the multinationalization of U.S.-based firms is not the only factor that contributes to that declining trend. Probably more important is the fact that the expenditures of the defense establishment on hardware and software are shrinking, so that the requirements of the defense market will play a less substantial role in determining the general direction of future industrial developments.

But the declining influence of the military on the direction of industrial research and development may render the military even more resistant to the dilution of its control where such control still exists. It would not be surprising, therefore, to find the military increasingly active in attempting to block foreigners' takeovers of U.S.-based firms that they regard as useful for the long-term retention of U.S. military superiority.

It is overwhelmingly likely, however, that the U.S. objectives of maintaining technical superiority while preventing the proliferation of weapons of mass destruction will prove increasingly difficult to implement. The U.S. government will no doubt continue to apply some measures of export controls and denial; witness its efforts in 1993 to prevent China from helping Pakistan manufacture ballistic missiles.[54] But the liquidation of the Coordinating Committee (better known as COCOM) in 1994 and the drastic

curtailment of the range of U.S. export controls are signs that the present
U.S. administration is prepared reluctantly to acknowledge the futility of
most of its controls. Perhaps these measures presage an effort on the part
of the U.S. government to think more systematically about the place of
multinationals in defense policy. But for the present there are few signs of
such a development.

Conclusions

The multinational spread of U.S.-based enterprise is here to stay. Large enterprises are now obliged as a matter of survival to scan the global environment continuously for threats and opportunities. They may not always respond to those threats or opportunities by establishing a new subsidiary
abroad, but the need to establish or strengthen foreign ties of some sort will
prove irresistible. With changes of such power and magnitude, it is not surprising that the nature of the corporation is being transformed. Having
modified the concept of property over half a century ago, the adaptations of
large enterprises have begun to modify the concept of nationality.

Yet the idea of a global corporation, altogether lacking in national identification, remains remote; it is not even apparent that the world is moving
in that direction. What is clear is that the business entities created by the
acts of sovereign states cannot be expected to confine their activities to the
jurisdiction of the state that created them. And, while roaming the world,
they cannot avoid operating under uncertain rights and conflicting responsibilities, defined by standards that relate to an earlier era.

The solution to the resulting tensions does not lie in the hands of any
one state alone. Any substantial reduction in such tensions will require
agreements among governments. If history is any guide, agreements on a
few of these issues may be achieved, whether regionally or globally, whether
by mutual education or by the coercion of large countries. But history also
suggests that the speed and extent of such agreements will depend on when
and whether the multinational enterprises themselves accept the need for
them. And that recognition is proceeding very slowly.

Meanwhile, American corporations are taking their own measures to
deal with the ambiguities and tensions they confront in their roles as the
leaders of multinational networks. Responding to the persistent pressures
of governments and other interests abroad, they are being obliged to acknowledge the conflicting goals of these interests, and in accommodating to
those interests are bound to lose a little of their identity as American cor-

porations. Countervailing pressures from the United States are unlikely to offset the trend; and, in any case, they would only increase the tensions to which the enterprises were exposed. Only mediation through international agreement can provide a long-term response. But for the present, neither the U.S. government nor the U.S.-based multinational enterprises exhibit much desire to move in that direction.

Notes

My thanks to Kelly Corbet, Roberto Martinez, and Jeremy Tachau for their research support. I am also grateful to my coauthors and collaborators in the preparation of this volume, whose cogent comments helped sharpen various points in the presentation.

1. James R. Hines Jr., "The Flight Paths of Migratory Corporations," *Journal of Accounting, Auditing, and Finance* 6, no.4 (fall 1991): 468.

2. *World Investment Directory: Developed Countries*, vol. 3, (New York: United Nations, 1993), p. 499.

3. *World Investment Report, 1993* (New York: United Nations, 1993), pp. 26–27 provides such data for the twenty-seven largest U.S.-based enterprises.

4. The data reported here are drawn from various issues of *U.S. Parent Companies and their Foreign Affiliates* (Washington, D.C.: U.S. Department of Commerce, Bureau of Economic Analysis).

5. *World Investment Report, 1993*, p. 25, based on unpublished data received from the U.S. Department of Commerce.

6. *World Investment Report 1993*, p. 159.

7. *World Investment Report, 1993*, p. 26 and passim.

8. See, e.g., John H. Dunning, ed., *The Theory of Transnational Corporations* (New York: Routledge, 1993).

9. Raymond Vernon, "Organizational and Institutional Responses to International Risk," in *Managing International Risk*, ed. Richard J. Herring (New York: Cambridge University Press, 1983), pp. 191–216.

10. Adolf A. Berle Jr., and Gardiner C. Means, *The Modern Corporation and Private Property* (New York: Macmillan, 1935).

11. The legal profession, however, is beginning to recognize the need for new legal doctrines that reflect the existence of the multinational enterprise. See, e.g., Phillip I. Blumberg, *The Multinational Challenge to Corporate Law: The Search for a New Corporate Personality* (New York: Oxford University Press, 1993).

12. The literature is voluminous. For a sampling, see R. J. Barnet and R. E. Müller, *Global Reach* (New York: Simon and Schuster, 1974); Kari Levitt, *Silent Surrender: The Multinational Corporation in Canada* (New York: St. Martin's Press, 1970); L. G. Countinbo, *The Internationalization of Oligopoly Capital* (Ann Arbor,

Mich.: Xerox University Microfilms, 1975); and Osvaldo Sunkel, "Big Business and 'Dependencia': A Latin American View," *Foreign Affairs* 50, no. 3 (April 1972): 527.

13. These generalizations need to be qualified in various ways, notably, in the occasional decisions of governments to "pierce the corporate veil" and to determine the "nationality" of a corporation by factors other than the country of its incorporation. For these exceptions as they apply to multinational enterprises, see *World Investment Report, 1993*, pp. 183–200.

14 "Selling the State," *The Economist,* August 21, 1993, p. 18.

15. *World Investment Report, 1993*, Table III.7, p. 83.

16. See, e.g., Samuel P. Huntington, "Political Modernization: America vs. Europe," *World Politics* 18, no. 3 (April 1966): 378–414.

17. For a historical account see, e.g., the dissenting opinion of Supreme Court Justice Louis Brandeis in *Liggett v. Lee*, 53 Sup. Ct. 490 (1932); also Thomas K. McCraw, "The Evolution of the Corporation in the United States," in *The U.S. Business Corporation*, ed. John R. Meyer and James M. Gustafson (Cambridge Mass.: Ballinger, 1988), pp. 1–19.

18. A superb summary appears in Thomas K. McCraw, "The Historical Background," in *American Society: Public and Private Responsibilities*, ed. Winthrop Knowlton and Richard Zeckhauser (Cambridge Mass.: Ballinger, 1986), pp. 15–42.

19. The classic work on this subject is Louis Hartz, *The Liberal Tradition in America* (New York: Harcourt Brace, 1955).

20. See, e.g., Andrew Shonfield, *Modern Capitalism* (New York: Oxford University Press, 1965); Raymond Vernon, ed., *Big Business and the State* (Cambridge, Mass.: Harvard University Press, 1974); Chalmers Johnson, *MITI and the Japanese Miracle* (Stanford, Calif.: Stanford University Press, 1982), pp. 199–274.

21. For an early account see Stephen D. Krasner, *Defending the National Interest* (Princeton, N.J.: Princeton University Press, 1978), pp. 279–312. Krasner's interpretation regarding U.S. motivations is consistent with other interpretations of these incidents.

22. For accounts of these relationships see, e.g., Daniel Yergin, *The Prize* (New York: Simon and Schuster, 1991), esp. pp. 398, 483, 619; Krasner, *Defending the National Interest*, pp. 156–212, 245–270; Robert B. Stobaugh, "The Oil Companies in the Crisis," *The Oil Crisis*, ed. Raymond Vernon (Cambridge, Mass.: Harvard University Press, 1976), pp. 184–185; and Raymond Vernon, *Two Hungry Giants: The United States and Japan in the Quest for Oil and Ores* (Cambridge, Mass.: Harvard University Press, 1983), pp. 58–81.

23. For a comparison of U.S. efforts with those of other countries, see, e.g., U.S. Congress, Office of Technology Assessment, *Competing Economies* (Washington, D.C.: U.S. Government Printing Office, October 1991).

24. For a summary of SEMATECH's operations, see "Uncle Sam's Helping Hand," *The Economist*, April 2, 1994, pp. 77–79.

25. See, e.g., Sheila Jasonoff, "American Exceptionalism and the Political

Acknowledgment of Risk," in *Risk*, ed., Edward J. Burger Jr. (Ann Arbor: University of Michigan Press, 1990), pp. 61–81. A succession of studies in the health and environment fields comparing U.S. practices with those of other (mainly European) countries repeatedly reaffirms these differences.

26. A diffuse literature exists on business-government relations in countries outside the United States. See, e.g., Peter Katzenstein, ed., *Between Power and Plenty: Foreign Economic Policies of Advanced Industrial States* (Madison: University of Wisconsin Press, 1978); Ralf Dahrendorf, *Society and Democracy in Germany* (New York: Norton, 1979); Heidron Abromeit, "Government-Industry Relations in West Germany," in *Governments, Industries and Markets: Aspects of Government-Industry Relations in the UK, Japan, West Germany and the USA Since 1945*, ed. Martin Chick (Brookfield, Vt: Edward Elgar, 1990), pp. 61–83; Antonio Chiesi and Alberto Martinelli, "The Representation of Business Interests as a Mechanism of Social Regulation," in *State, Market, and Social Regulation: New Perspectives on Italy*, ed. Peter Lange and Marino Regini (New York: Cambridge University Press, 1989), pp. 187–213.

27. Scholars have sometimes debated whether big business was principal, agent, or partner in relation to the government. See, e.g., Richard J. Samuels, *The Business of the Japanese State* (Ithaca N.Y.: Cornell University Press, 1987), esp. pp. 257–290, in which he develops the concept of politics by mutual consent.

28. For a systematic effort to identify the relevant factors affecting the relationship, see Samuels, *The Business of the Japanese State*, esp. pp. 257–290.

29. In the case of member countries of the European Union, the business-government relations of large corporations are being divided between their home governments and Brussels, a consequence of the growing economic powers of the Union. See Loukas Tsoukalis, *The New European Community*, 2d ed. (New York: Oxford University Press, 1993), pp. 102–117; Matthew Bishop and John Kay, eds., *European Mergers and Merger Policy* (New York: Oxford University Press, 1993), pp. 294–317; and Maria Green Cowles, "The Rise of the European Multinational," *International Economic Insights*, July/August 1993, pp. 15–18. Samuels (*The Business of the Japanese State*, pp. 257–290) provides an account of business-government relations in Japan.

30. As with all such generalizations, one must recognize the existence of considerable variations among countries in how they identify "their" enterprises. In many counties of Europe, for instance, the concept of the *siège* of a corporation, corresponding to its principal place of business, figures centrally in a determination of its nationality. And in many countries the corporate veil is often pierced in making that determination. See *Restatement of the Law, Third, The Foreign Relations of the United States, Vol. 1* (St. Paul, Minn.: American Law Institute, 1987), p. 130.

31. See, e.g., Gary B. Born, "A Reappraisal of the Extraterritorial Reach of U.S. Law," *Law and Policy in International Business* 24, no. 1 (1993) 1–100; Phillip M. Blumberg, *The Multinational Challenge to Corporation Law* (Oxford: Oxford University Press, 1993), esp. pp. 168–215.

32. See, e.g., Jose E. Alvarez, "Political Protectionism and United States Investment Obligations in Conflict: The Hazards of Exon-Florio," *Virginia Journal of International Law* 30, no. 1 (1989): pp. 2–187.

33. Illustrations include U.S. government grants in support of semiconductors and battery-run automobiles. For an account of U.S. policies that condition the national treatment principle, see U.S. Congress, Office of Technology Assessment. *Multinationals and the U.S. Technology Base* (Washington, D.C.: U.S. Government Printing Office, September 1994), pp. 27–30.

34. *Bilateral Investment Treaties 1959–1991,* (New York: United Nations, 1992), esp. pp. 7–10.

35. See, e.g.,"ICSID Review," *Foreign Investment Law Journal* 7, no. 2 (1992): 336–38, which notes that reference to ICSID arbitration appears in "hundreds of large investment contracts." For an analysis of the reasons for ICSID's small caseload, see Wolfgang Peter, *Arbitration and Renegotiation of International Investment Agreements* (Dordrecht: Martinus Nijhoff, 1986), pp. 200–203.

36. Estimates by the New York Stock Exchange staff, based on the Federal Reserve Board's "Flow of Funds" data, place foreigners' holdings of U.S. corporate equity at less than 6 percent of the total outstanding at 1993 year end. Private communication.

37. Based on a survey of 589 companies in 1989, all members of the American Society of Corporate Secretaries, about half of them with annual sales in excess of one billion dollars. From Jeremy Bacon, *Membership and Organization of Corporate Boards* (New York: The Conference Board, 1990), p. 12.

38. R. G. Hawkins, "Jobs, Skills, and US Multinationals," in *Transnational Corporations and International Trade and Payments,* ed. H. Peter Gray (London: Routledge, 1993), pp. 252–264.

39. For a review of some of the models in a specific case, that of the effects of NAFTA on U.S. labor markets, see Nora Lustig, Barry P. Bosworth, and Robert Z. Lawrence, *North American Free Trade: Assessing the Impact* (Washington, D.C.: Brookings Books, 1992), pp. 78–94.

40. The debate over the merits of the NAFTA have brought that issue strongly to the fore. See, e.g., Jeff Faux, "The Failed Case for NAFTA," Report of the Economic Policy Institute, Washington, D.C.. June 29, 1993.

41. For a timely set of proposals for tax reform, see Gary C. Hufbauer, *U.S. Taxation of International Income: Blueprint for Reform* (Washington, D.C.: Institute for International Economics, 1992).

42. For a taste of the complexity of these relationships and the difficulties of assessing the value of the transfers entailed see Jill C. Pagan and J. Scott Wilkie, *Transfer Pricing Strategy in a Global Economy* (Amsterdam: IBFD Publications, 1993), esp. chap. 3, entitled "Anatomy of a Transfer Pricing Case."

43. How often genuine arm's-length prices can be found is a matter for some debate. One report of the U.S. Internal Revenue Service, reporting on 823 contested cases in 1980 and 1981, claims that about 60 percent of the income adjustments demanded by the IRS were based on "price" adjustments; but a report of the General

Accounting Office contends that only 3 percent of these "pricing" cases were based on true arm's-length prices, the rest being synthetic figures derived from the available cost data. For an account of these reports, see Roger Y. W. Tang, *Transfer Pricing in the 1990s* (Westport, Conn.: Quorum Books, 1993), p. 20.

44. For a glimpse of the actual process, see Pagan and Wilkie, *Transfer Pricing Strategy in a Global Economy*, chap. 3, "Anatomy of a Transfer Pricing Case."

45. See, e.g. John Turro, "U.S. Congressional Committee Blasts Foreign Firms for Tax Dodging," *Tax Notes International* 2, no. 8 (August 1990): 799; John E. O'Grady, "Apple and IRS Enter into First Arbitration Under U.S. Tax Court Rule," *Tax Notes International* 4, no. 11, (March 16, 1992): p. 519; Gary C. Hufbauer and Joanna van Rooij, "The Coming Global Tax War," *The International Economy*, January/February 1993, p. 20.

46. The gravity of the issue is gradually being recognized. See, e.g., Dale W. Wickman and Charles J. Kerster, "New Directions Needed for Solution of the International Pricing Tax Puzzle," *Tax Notes* 56, no. 3 (July 20, 1992): 349 and passim.

47. The measures are summarized in *World Investment Report 1993*, pp. 207–209. See also Pagan and Wilkie, *Transfer Pricing Strategy in a Global Economy*, pp. 185–206.

48. Various issues of the *Financial Times* report the most recent phase of the United Kingdom's protest regarding the California tax. See the following: "California Rethinks Unitary Tax System," August 18, 1993, p. 6; and "California Retreats on Taxation," August 20, 1993, p. 4.

49. That fact explains why the U.S. Treasury representative took the extraordinary step in the course of the 1993 GATT negotiations of proposing to withhold the national treatment guarantee in tax matters from foreign-owned subsidiaries engaged in services. See "US Fights Its Corner over Tax Demands," *Financial Times*, November 23, 1993, p. 6; and "Warning to U.S. over Tax Demands," *Financial Times*, November 24, 1993, p. 7.

50. See, e.g., Michael Mastanduno, "The United States Defiant: Export Controls in the Postwar Era" in *Defense and Dependence in a Global Economy*, ed. Raymond Vernon and Ethan B. Kapstein (Washington, D.C.: Congressional Quarterly, 1992), pp. 91–112.

51. For a summary of the relevant trends, written for lay consumption, see "Manufacturing Technology," *The Economist*, March 31, 1994, pp. S-3 to S-18.

52. See, e.g., Masaaki Kotabe, *Global Sourcing Strategy: R&D, Manufacturing, and Marketing Interfaces* (New York: Quorum Books, 1992).

53. Raymond Vernon and Ethan B. Kapstein, "National Needs, Global Resources," in *Defense and Dependence in a Global Economy*, ed. Raymond Vernon and Ethan B. Kapstein (Washington, D.C.: Congressional Quarterly Press, 1992), p. 5.

54. Indicative is the op-ed piece of Senator John Glenn, "China's Dangerous Arms Exports," *Washington Post*, December 3, 1993, p. A29.

4

From Antitrust to Corporation Governance? The Corporation and the Law: 1959–1994

✦

MARK J. ROE

About one-third of a century ago, the editor of *The Corporation in Modern Society* collected a set of essays on the state of the large public corporation in the United States, and to a modern reader the collection displays a consensus view of the American corporation, a view that must have reflected the unstated assumptions of many thoughtful Americans: the large corporation was a powerful creature that needed to be tamed. And that taming was the central task for public policy. Although the corporation was highly successful in producing wealth for Americans, public constraints had to stop it from running roughshod over employees and communities. It was a powerful actor that the public and the polity had to watch warily.

Edward Mason, the editor of *The Corporation in Modern Society*, said, "This powerful corporate machine, which so successfully grinds out the goods we want, seems to be running without any discernible controls."[1] One contributor said that the corporation had "produced a tension of power . . . [as] giant enterprises . . . come to rival the sovereignty of the state itself."[2] Carl Kaysen, a contributor then and the editor of this volume, concluded: "The proposition that a group of giant business corporations . . . embodies a significant and troublesome concentration of power is the cliché which serves this volume as a foundation stone."[3]

The earlier volume linked up to corporate law's biblical text, Berle and Means's *The Modern Corporation and Private Property*, a book that in 1932 announced that with the growth in size of the large firms a new organizational form had emerged: the public firm with managers controlling the big organizations that owned much property, with the managers themselves not owning the company. Adolph Berle, who was a corporate law professor at Columbia Law School when he had made his "discovery" in the 1930s, introduced the 1959 volume, writing that the motivation for the volume arose from the fact that corporate power has "become visible, and . . . this power [falls] outside the problems of power foreseen when American democracy was founded." Berle said there had often been a fear, expressed best by Brandeis, "that big business could never be good—and that its power, if allowed unrestrained expansion, could not be prevented from [upsetting] the principles of free democracy. [This view of Brandeis] may have been right; time only will tell." The curse of bigness, however, was not really as bad as Brandeis made out, Berle said. It could be coped with by government regulation.

The corporation as an economic success was not in doubt. But were workers, suppliers and customers getting their fair share? Mason asked.[4] There was no doubt that the "modern corporation wields economic and social power of the highest consequence for the condition of our polity . . . Let us accept [this, as all agree] as our first premise," said the first essayist, Abram Chayes.[5] Law's role is to "regulariz[e] and rationalize[e] the use of [corporate] power,"[6] power both to do evil and to accomplish social ends. In this mix of control and power back in the 1950s, shareholders seemed to be powerless.[7] "Management is typically . . . an autonomous center of decision . . . [S]tockholders . . . exercise little or no power of choice themselves." Maybe that was for the best, some commentators thought: shareholders ought not to have a voice in corporate governance; they "are not the governed of the corporation whose consent must be sought"; they should get financial information, not voice. "Antitrust and public regulation have, broadly speaking, been the characteristic response of American politics, government, and law to the problems posed by the modern corporation."[8]

More popular books, such as John Kenneth Galbraith's *New Industrial State*, echoed that volume's theme a few year's afterward. A decade before, Peter Drucker's homage to GM celebrated its managerial prowess.[9] Popular speculation abroad was that the American corporation was not just efficient, but was so perfect for the task of organizing economic activity that in short order it would dominate global production.[10]

The Mason volume's consensus view was that American corporate success could be taken for granted. The issue was how to tame it, how to make sure its power didn't displace that of government, and how to let employees and communities share in the bounty.[11]

No such consensus would be found today. Several successful colossuses of the 1950s have become struggling dinosaurs in the 1990s—GM, IBM, Sears, Westinghouse, and American Express. They are struggling to adapt, change, and renew themselves, and while their recent responses give rise to optimism, their success is not yet assured. In the 1950s, power was in the forefront; today power is less important than the responsibility to survive and be a vehicle of economic prosperity. Competitiveness and productivity, not power, are in the forefront.

Today's version of the Mason quote would not be: "This powerful corporate machine, which so successfully grinds out the goods we want, seems to be running without any discernible controls." It would be closer to: "This once powerful corporate machine is now successful in some places, unsuccessful in others, and, according to some, needs help to better be able to grind out the goods we want." Perhaps a modern-day Mason might add that "managers at less successful firms ought to be made more accountable than they have been."

This is not to say that the notion of power and privilege has disappeared. It has not, but it has changed. The public's dislike of corporate power seems to have been transferred to a public dislike of high corporate salaries, to an unease over corporate downsizing and layoffs, and, in the 1980s, to revulsion at the financial maneuvering in takeovers. Insiders were making too much money and not perceived to be providing enough (or any?) value in making firms run better. A few of these public likes and dislikes got reflected, albeit palely, in law: in Securities and Exchange Commission disclosure requirements on executive compensation, in tax rules on deductibility of salaries exceeding one million dollars, and in state antitakeover laws. The public was not in awe of the corporation's power and success, but annoyed that for the remuneration involved, managers ought to deliver more.

The view of shareholder power also differs today. Shareholders in the 1950s were seen as powerless (perhaps justifiably so).[12] Power shifted in the 1980s during the massive takeover wave. Shareholders could do something; managers were under siege. Although by the 1990s managers had recovered their balance and no longer had day-to-day worries about hostile takeovers, institutional investors by 1990 were no longer uniformly passive, and some were prodding boards to be more active. No one would say that institutional shareholders of the 1990s have been powerless.

· · · · ·

Thus the corporation as perceived today and as perceived four decades ago can be contrasted both in power and in competitive success. What were the sources of these perceptions of unrestrained power from 1959? And how and why did those perceptions change in the ensuing decades? Can a change in these perceptions (and in the underlying reality) help to explain changes in how law acts on the corporation?

In the 1950s the American economy was performing very well; derivatively, corporations seemed to be doing their jobs well. A sustained rise in productivity began after World War II and would continue until the early 1970s. And academics believed oligopolistic competition characterized many big manufacturing industries in the 1950s. The Big Three automakers, Big Steel, and the electrical equipment manufacturers all seemed immune to failure. They were powerful firms with powerful managers, often with above-normal profits.[13]

Over these supranormal profits managers had discretion. And this discretion over profits made the power of managers salient in 1959. Success, especially the perception of oligopolistic success, made firms and their managers appear to possess power. How would they distribute those supranormal profits? Would they distribute those profits to themselves—via high salaries, nice offices, and a quiet life—to shareholders, to employees, to charity, or to their customers via a better product? Had the biggest firms been barely able to meet expenses, were they struggling to survive, then they would not have appeared either to have been powerful or to have had enormous discretion over an excess of funds.

What happened to those oligopolistic profits? Why do those firms no longer seem to be the powerful giants they once seemed to be? Part of the answer is obvious: in the ensuing decades, international competition turned the three U.S. oligopolists in, say, the American automotive market in 1959 into three of ten competitive players in a globalized market in the 1990s.[14] A speedup in technological change upset several leaders in other industries. Their supranormal profits of the 1950s are gone. Indeed, the Big Three automakers in the 1980s would, without informal import quotas, have had no profits at all; and one of the Big Three, Chrysler, needed a billion-dollar government bailout in 1979 to survive. They are no longer the powerful colossuses that needed to be tamed, but, like GM in recent years, are faltering giants that need to revitalize themselves.[15]

Survival and prosperity—issues taken for granted in 1959—are central

issues of the 1990s. The transformation from an oligopolistic domestic
market to a competitive global market made the discretionary profits disappear; the image of the industrial corporation as powerful actor faded when
the biggest and most publicized are struggling to survive. The image of the
corporation as a sweating and not-always-successful competitor has become more vivid.

Moreover, the public goal of "taming" the large public firm expressed
itself in the "political" marketplace and became regularized. The rise of consumer and environmental groups, and their concomitant regulatory controls, reduced the range of corporate and managerial discretion.

I have not yet spoken much of law for a reason. I have thus far only
sketched the claim that a public perception that large corporations were
powerful creatures in need of taming faded as the economic source of that
perception—oligopoly and uniformly good performance—faded. I want
next to assert that business law is in important part derivative of a society's
view of the corporation. If a society views its corporations as powerful creatures whose strength rivals that of government, that society will tend to constrain the corporations' actions and focus on antitrust and other rules that
tranquilize the most powerful firms. If a society views its corporations as
weak from internal decay and under siege from international competitors
and takeover entrepreneurs, that society will tend to help those firms experiment with alternative organizational forms, relax its antitrust laws, and
protect firms and their managers from takeovers. In very broad outline this
is what happened in the thirty-five years between 1959 and today.

This transformation from undisputed success to striving can be told without referring to oligopoly, by looking at changes in productivity during the
postwar years. From 1945 to 1973 productivity in the United States
spurted; productivity growth in the years since has been mixed.[16] With the
whole economy performing well in the 1950s, academics had the luxury of
thinking that corporate power, not just corporate performance, was central.
Imports and foreign competition weren't important to the American economy. The 1959 cliché—corporate power, with success assumed—may have
depended on the fact that overall the American economy was doing quite
well in the 1950s. Since then, its success has been more uneven.

The supranormal profits of industry leaders in the 1950s could alternatively have been due to superior efficiency; and it could have been that efficiency—not oligopoly—gave GM and the other leaders their power. The
image shift from power to struggling giant by the 1980s could be seen as a
shift in identity of the most efficient automaker; profits and power might

still have accrued to the best performer in the 1980s; in the 1980s, though, those profits were going to Toyota.

Whatever way the decline is explained—the decay of an oligopoly, the slowing down of domestic productivity, a shift in some industries to foreign firms as the most efficient—it is partly this decline of the industry leaders, and in some instances of entire industries, that explains the image shift from power to struggle.

Let me here trace how two bodies of law interacted with these developments over four decades—first, antitrust law and, second, the laws governing the relationships between financial institutions and large firms.

Antitrust's concern, particularly in the 1950s, was with concentrations of economic power. The *Alcoa* decision crystallized the rhetoric against size and power: "It is possible, because of its indirect social or moral effect, to prefer a system of small producers . . . to one in which the great mass of those engaged must accept the direction of a few. . . . [G]reat industrial consolidations are inherently undesirable, regardless of their economic results."[17] Success and wealth, easily taken for granted when the United States accounted for half of the world's gross economic product just after World War II, led antitrust toward other aspirations, such as keeping business on a human, local scale, even if at economic cost. Although the 1945 *Alcoa* analysis required more than mere size to run afoul of the antitrust laws—the firm in question still had to commit some act of monopolization—nevertheless commentators, lawyers, and business-people often had trouble distinguishing aggressive business behavior (exercising skill, foresight, and ingenuity) from a prohibited act of monopolization.[18]

The effect of case law, particularly the effect of Learned Hand's articulate opinion in *Alcoa*, was to tell business leaders that the only sure defense against a suit for monopolization was to avoid being a monopoly, to avoid having a large share of the relevant market. Market leaders were said to refuse to seek that extra percentage of market share that might make them a monopoly in antitrust terms. GM, for example, was said to have been unwilling to compete fiercely in Studebaker's primary submarket[19] because it feared that if and when Studebaker went out of business, it was more likely to face a government antitrust suit. GM was rumored to have helped facilitate a merger among Studebaker and other smaller automakers to make a competitor that could take enough market share to forestall an antitrust suit against GM.[20]

The 1950's major antitrust action was the Justice Department's lawsuit against GM and Du Pont. (Du Pont owned about a quarter of GM's stock, and the Justice Department sought to have the company divest that stock. It succeeded.) During that time it was no secret that the government was contemplating a lawsuit to dissolve GM.[21] While the government never sought to dissolve GM, it did eventually launch an antitrust attack on two of the other colossuses, IBM in 1969 and AT&T in 1974.

At the same time, the government was developing a strict antimerger policy. The Cellar-Kefauver enhancements to the Clayton Act in 1950 were seen, particularly as interpreted in the Supreme Court's *Brown Shoe* opinion in 1962,[22] as making mergers between any substantial companies in the same industry difficult or impossible. The antitrust combination was powerful: merger law was tight, and the market leaders were at risk of a structural antitrust attack.

While antitrust rhetoric and case choice at the Justice Department militated toward seeking dissolution of the largest American firms—those with the most concentrated appearance of power—academic work focused on the problems of oligopoly. These were the firms that had "power," power to set prices, to raise them, to lower them; power to increase quantity of production; power to innovate or not.[23] Oligopoly was the problem; the Sherman Act, designed for simpler economies where price-fixing and naked predatory tactics were the principal problems, was not up to the task of dealing well with oligopolies.

If law had an effect here, it was to discourage the market leader from acquiring market share above, say, 60 percent (the gray zone for defining whether a firm had a monopoly in antitrust case law). Yet the firm with oligopoly profits had to decide what to do with its bounty. Senior managers did not want to part with that cash and the "power" it gave them. Tax laws discouraged them from parting with it, because the convenient ways of moving the money into shareholders' hands were taxed. Shareholders who were small, distant, and "powerless" had little effect on managers; they could not easily force the cash out and, with heavy taxation attaching to the most obvious way for cash to move out of firms—dividends—it was not always in shareholders' private interests for that cash to move out at the tax rates then in effect, which reached up to 90 percent of a dividend received.[24]

What were the firm and its managers to do? Managers wanted to retain their "power" and the cash that supported "power," but antitrust law discouraged expansion in the same industry. They could use their retained earnings to buy other companies in unrelated industries via conglomerate mergers, which attracted less antitrust attention than did horizontal mergers. Conglomerate mergers had other advantages as well: they kept the

IRS's hands off the base firms' earnings, and allowed managers to keep control over their firm's earnings and assets, without sending them up to shareholders.[25]

Did the harsh anti–horizontal merger policy help induce conglomerate acquisitions? Although some may think so,[26] this question deserves more analysis. A firm with profits that it wishes to retain and deploy faces three major nonconglomerate options: it can expand by horizontal acquisition, it can expand by new investment, or it can expand by vertical acquisition.

For horizontal acquisitions by a successful market leader, antitrust law stopped this outlet for expansion, but, and this point is often neglected, when the antitrust authorities get the market share numbers right in setting horizontal merger limits, the market leader's expansion via horizontal merger should be stopped. (Obviously, there is the question of degree and line drawing: not all horizontal mergers needed to have been stopped; the line could have been drawn farther out than, say, the limits set in the leading *Brown Shoe* opinion of 1962.) For the second type of expansion via new investment, the strict antimerger policy was irrelevant, but the fear of an Alcoa-type attack hindered firms from expanding in their core market. Antitrust as raising the critical barrier to this type of expansion, however, could have been overrated, because oligopolists rationally resist expansion. The third outlet via vertical acquisition could well have been foreclosed by aggressive antitrust attacks on vertical acquisition.[27]

Thus, to argue that antitrust authorities' general horizontal merger policy *improperly* encouraged conglomerate expansion may be incorrect. The antitrust culprit, if there is one, is more likely to lie in the policy-restricting vertical mergers, in the general fear of high market share, or in setting the horizontal limits too tightly. Law's role in conglomerate formation may well have been more in tax law and in facilitating governance structures that gave managers freer rein over corporate activities than they otherwise might have had.

Moreover, law might not have been central, because the conglomerate merger during its heyday was seen as a superior organizational structure. It had high theory behind it.[28] Shareholders in the large American firm were too distant, too small, and too powerless to monitor managers; the conglomerate added a dollop or more of monitoring, as central headquarters managers monitored the divisions managers. (True, as time would show, the headquarters' senior staff as much as anyone else needed monitoring. The headquarters staff expanded its sphere of control beyond its ability to effectively manage.) In the age of the mainframe computer, the conglomerate fit well with then-current technologies. Information was most cheaply processed centrally, and the conglomerate headquarters could do it well, or so it appeared.

The conglomerate did not last long as the quintessential business form. By the late 1970s it was under attack. The legal attacks fizzled; courts accepted no antitrust theory as a basis to attack a pure conglomerate merger. But business transactions began to destroy the conglomerate because it had become an unwieldy business form: many takeovers of the late 1970s and 1980s were directed at breaking up the conglomerates. (Some were breaking up even before the takeover wave inundated them.)[29]

The upside of conglomerates was that they allowed a central staff of strategic planners to monitor the divisions, to pull cash out from the cash cows and use it to finance the rising stars without the IRS taking a percentage as the money moved from one subsidiary to finance another. Their downside was that many ended up having managements controlling businesses about which they knew little. The structure might have been a good one if not overused, but by the 1980s it was overused. The *Economist* called the conglomerate "the biggest collective error ever made by American business."[30]

Bust-up takeovers of the 1980s tended to put the divisions and subsidiaries in the hands of managers who knew the firm's market better than the senior conglomerate managers.[31] Technology, in the meantime, had also changed; cheaper, smaller, local computing was replacing the large mainframe. Antitrust law was relaxed in the 1980s, allowing for many more mergers among the vertically related parts of an industry, and allowing for more mergers among the horizontal competitors. The large American corporation by the late 1970s and early 1980s was exemplified not so much by the powerhouse GM celebrated by Peter Drucker, circa 1950,[32] as by large firms campaigning for import protection and Chrysler's begging for and getting a billion-dollar loan. In that context—of a perception that these were no longer colossuses but were weakening firms in need of help—a conservative administration in Washington in the 1980s found it easy to relax many antitrust rules.

High theory came around too, in two dimensions. In the antitrust dimension, scholarship showed how many of the vertical practices once thought to be clearly predatory were either benign or efficient.[33] In the corporate dimension, theory could explain many of the bust-ups as ways to liberate the free cash flow from firms whose managers wanted to retain that cash and unprofitably reinvest it beyond what was needed to sustain profitable operations.[34]

These changes could not have arisen easily, or perhaps at all, if the underlying antitrust law had not changed. True, conglomerate mergers did not become any harder under antitrust law in the 1980s, but by the early 1980s the attitude toward vertical restraints and mergers eased up. While doctrine never made these "per se legal," enforcement policy starting in the Reagan years made them practically so. If the Justice Department and the Federal Trade Commission would not bring suit, there were few antitrust worries, even if judicial doctrine changed more slowly. And for horizontal mergers, the rollback, while not as far and broad as for vertical restraints and mergers, was still substantial. Large horizontal mergers in the 1950s and 1960s had been likely to be challenged; new Justice Department guidelines in the 1980s gave more leeway and signaled an even more deferential enforcement policy. Moreover, as industry internationalized, antitrust enforcement should have "naturally" receded: market power eroded due to the entry of new international competitors. At the same time, the old antitrust monopolization suits against the giants—IBM and AT&T—were settled or dismissed. The pressure that large American firms felt to avoid large market share among the American producers lifted, in part because international competition was redefining the competitive market. At the same time, the antitrust roadblock to many horizontal mergers was removed. These two changes enabled many of the 1980s bust-ups and resales to firms in the same or vertically related businesses.[35]

The oligopolies that seemed to prevail in the 1950s were not good candidates for the kind of takeovers that became widespread in the 1980s. Let me suggest why that was so: oligopolists try, and sometimes are able, to keep their prices well above cost. They may never formally agree to keep their prices up, but, because there are only a few players in the industry, each one knows that breaking an implicit pricing arrangement will likely lead to a price war that would lower its own profits. This much is familiar. But the interplay between this kind of oligopolistic pricing and a takeover market has not, as far as I know, been analyzed. For oligopolistic pricing to work, a firm's senior managers have to believe that the other one or two firms and their managers are playing ball, not secretly offering large rebates from "list" prices. With extra profits from oligopoly pricing, they might run their firm a bit inefficiently, giving middle-level managers and employees a piece of the oligopoly profits. Thus the wages of autoworkers and steelworkers have exceeded those of workers in similar but more competitive industries.

   To use the modern vocabulary, agency costs[36] should, I believe, be seen as partly produced by oligopoly. If product competition is quick and fierce, a firm's managers cannot slack off or distribute some of the excess profits to employees (in wages or in a quieter workplace), because competitors will get the slacker's business.[37] In perfect competition, high wages and a quiet workplace for managers can succeed only if the extra wages and quiet life enhance productivity enough to cover their cost.

Here's why that kind of an industry was not likely to produce good candidates for hostile takeovers. Imagine an oligopolistically organized industry of three or four firms operating in the 1950s and 1960s. Although oligopoly contributes to corporate profitability, industry structure alone does not determine profitable pricing. The key players—senior managers—have to "trust" one another. American antitrust law attacked explicit price-fixing schemes viciously, but courts did not control pure conscious parallelism, in which the key players in an industry reached an "understanding" on pricing without explicitly agreeing on high prices.[38] The oligopolist could arrange for industry trends to be analyzed at industry meetings. U.S. Steel could announce its price to a *Wall Street Journal* reporter on Monday; Bethlehem Steel could respond through the *Journal* on Tuesday.

This background sets us up for several insights about the law and the takeover wave of the 1980s. Imagine the dilemma a budding takeover entrepreneur, say a young T. Boone Pickens or Carl Icahn, would face in the 1950s or 1960s. True, he might run the firm more efficiently (to accept here an issue that was in dispute in the 1980s), or, more realistically, the threat of takeover might have made incumbent managers run it more efficiently. But could either young takeover entrepreneur have credibly threatened a takeover of a 1950s oligopolist that would have enhanced shareholder value?

I think not. They would likely have destroyed the "trust" developed among the handful of usually homogeneous senior managers in the industry. Destroying the oligopolistic understandings would destroy shareholder value, making a takeover unprofitable to the offeror: it might tighten up operations a bit but would then lose profits if the delicacies of oligopolistic pricing were ripped apart.[39]

To be sure, not everyone now believes that the Big Threes and the Big Fours extracted large oligopoly profits. George Stigler, for example, argued that behind uniform list prices were secret discounts, rebates, and competition. Even competitors who kept prices uniform might have competed away their excess profits in other dimensions, such as by providing additional service (with highly paid employees).[40] But even if we were to accept this side of the divided opinion, the argument I'm making here—that the 1950s oligopolists were not good candidates for hostile takeovers—would still apply. First, even if the players were wrong in believing there were oligopoly profits, the idea of oligopoly was widely believed. Belief would then deter the emergence of a hostile offeror. Second, even if the oligopoly profits were frittered away in other dimensions, there might in the end have been no profits for the hostile offeror. If the offeror succeeded, it would trigger increased competition from the other oligopolists, wiping out the offeror's profits, in a manner similar to how an errant oligopolist facing a "kinked" demand curve would see that if it decided to compete, it would find its hoped-for profits eliminated when the other oligopolists reacted and lowered their price.[41]

What changed by the 1980s? The oligopoly broke down not because of changing antitrust rules but (for most manufacturing firms) because Japan and Europe could get manufactured goods into the United States at competitive prices and quality. Many foreign manufacturers learned how to make competitive products; for other industries American macroeconomic policies (low taxes, a large budget deficit, and high interest rates) drove the dollar to high levels, making imports more competitive with domestic industry. In some other industries unaffected by import competition, technological change upset the soft oligopoly arrangements. Either way, the old cushion subsided.

And new economic understandings arose about what was needed to make for an oligopoly.[42] Academics often attributed supranormal profits in the 1950s to oligopoly; by the 1980s, more academics attributed above-normal profits to superior efficiency.

With the cushion gone—whether it was an oligopolistic cushion or an efficiency cushion—disruptive takeover entrepreneurs would no longer upset either the delicacies of oligoplistic pricing or the hum of a highly efficient organization, because international competition (or technological change) had already done that. The private profits of oligopoly and superior efficiency were gone, but the private (and public) costs of poorly organized firms were there to exploit.

There is a related reason why the takeovers that dominated the corporate stage in the 1980s were unfamiliar in the 1950s: the idea was strange. It needed time for business practice to come closer and perhaps for theory to provide a rationale.[43] The idea of severing the head of a firm—its senior management—at first must have seemed to be a crazy way to make money. Firms were living organizations. Severing the head of a firm, like severing the head of a living being, meant death.

The conglomerate changed the metaphor. With its rise—partly due to managers' desire to expand, tax law's preference for earnings retention, and firms' desire to retain the cash from their high earnings—managers learned that they could move subsidiaries and divisions around like pieces on a chessboard.

Conglomerates were assembled from separate firms, with a central headquarters directing the firm. Their widespread use in the 1960s taught managers that it was possible to mix and match corporate divisions. It was only a small leap of an organizational idea for a conglomerate to bring in an outside firm via a hostile acquisition in the 1970s, by buying up the target's stock and tucking the formerly independent firm in as one now managed from the conglomerate headquarters. From there it was only another small mental jump in the 1980s to understand that once the pieces of a conglomerate had been assembled, they could be disassembled as well.

As already noted, firms in oligopolies tend to share their excess profits with midlevel employees and workers. When by the 1980s international competition and technological change deflated the oligopolistic cushion (or changed the national identity of a few of the most efficient manufacturers from American to Japanese), takeover entrepreneurs could profit by tightening up the workplace, which could then be seen as a reneging on implicit contracts between the firm and its employees.[44] Even if there were no implicit contract to renege on, the workplace in those industries would be tighter than it had been.

Managers and employees did not just take it; they reacted, and reacted in a way that implicates how some corporate law gets made: the corporation and its constituents, mainly managers and employees, can actively seek the corporate law that they want. The managers and employees of firms in decaying industries in "Rust Belt" states—the firms that were often takeover targets in the 1980s—sought the antitakeover laws that state legislatures passed at the end of the 1980s. These laws (and the supporting judicial decisions)[45] did not outright ban takeovers, but they raised their costs.

Public opinion was on managers' and employees' sides. While the data suggest that takeovers affected blue-collar employment less than the public perceived,[46] public perceptions, even exaggerated perceptions, can drive lawmaking as much as reality can. Takeovers are done with *dollar* votes to buy stock, but *ballot box* votes elect the politicians who make takeover laws.[47] Some state antitakeover laws responded to distortive takeover tactics that favored raiders; distortions favoring incumbents went uncorrected, or the laws passed increased them. Although politicians' views of the "merits"—are takeovers functional or not?—affected how they would vote, factors other than the "merits" affect political outcomes, factors such as public opinion and political strength.

Voters were unsympathetic to hostile takeovers. One poll showed 58 percent of those polled as thinking hostile takeovers did more harm than good; only 8 percent thought hostile takeovers were beneficial.[48] They disrupted employees' lives, and the average person mistrusted takeovers and financial maneuverings. In popular novels, movies, and the press, takeovers were engineered by greedy, dysfunctional raiders and investment bankers.

Takeovers disrupted the status quo; bust-up takeovers were seen as throwing managers and employees out of work. Managers and employees at firms that were not yet targets were anxious and fearful (would they be next?) and sympathized with employees at targets. Managers who sought political protection did not climb uphill in the political arena; legislators who did managers' bidding did not have to fear reprisal from voters. It was the opposite. Politicians who bashed Wall Street and thwarted takeovers were rewarded by the average voter, not punished.

The politics behind these laws can be illustrated by the passage in 1990 of the Pennsylvania antitakeover law, one of the more stringent: "Behind the debate [on the merits] in Pennsylvania is a power struggle between the shareholders . . . and the directors and managers . . . Pennsylvania business groups supporting the bill are aligned with unions seeking to protect the jobs of their members . . . The bill's supporters point to a wave of populist revulsion with the takeover boom of the 1980s."[49] Labor and Pennsylvania's Chamber of Business and Industry lobbied hard:

> [The] lobbying effort is the product of teamwork between . . . Pennsylvania labor unions and a coalition of over two dozen corporations working for the passage of the bill under the well-organized direction of the Pennsylvania Chamber of Business and Industry. A hard-core group of a dozen manufacturing concerns, including Armstrong, Scott Paper Company, PPG Industries Inc., The Rorer Group Inc., Aluminum Co. of America, and Consolidated Rail Corporation—along with several banks and utilities—have been the most active supporters.[50]

International competition and other technological forces that affected even firms not sensitive to international competition took away that 1950s oligopolistic cushion, which had until then helped to make employees' and senior managers' working lives a bit softer than they otherwise might have been. Takeovers often became the change mechanism, and those who thought they'd be adversely affected—corporate managers and corporate employees—reacted and helped to make corporate law in the 1980s.

The takeover coalesced shareholders—the powerless corporate players in the 1950s—and made managers squawk. When hostile takeovers declined—whether because the best opportunities were gone by the late 1980s or because antitakeover laws raised their costs just enough to deter them, or both—there were fewer tools to make managers accountable. (The increase of international competition in manufacturing industries—the most basic tool of accountability—also made this lack of accountability less critical but more visible.) It was less critical because competitors could pick up the slack, but more visible because fierce competition quickly highlighted failures of accountability: profits dropped quickly.

Meanwhile, there were important changes in the structure of shareholding. In the 1950s the prototypical shareholder was the wealthy or upper-middle-class individual or family. By the 1990s the prototypical shareholder was the institutional investor, with the biggest change coming from the rise of the pension fund. Social trends account for much of this rise: longer life spans, earlier retirement, the breakup of the adult family. But law accounts for some of the trend, because pensions could be financed in a number of ways: unfunded promises from the company, insurance, private savings, tax-subsidized private savings (like IRAs or Keoghs).

Tax law and ERISA (The Employee Retirement Income Security Act of 1974) encouraged companies to fund their pension plans, putting aside money for their expected pension payments. Funding, which is not always required abroad, created a huge pool here of invested capital, a pool that changed the nature of shareholding in the United States. In 1994, pension funds owned more than 30 percent of the shares in the stock market, and these pension funds have the potential to play a more active role in the corporation. Their existence made the 1980s takeovers easier, because the pension funds were often willing to sell their stock quickly when offered a high price for a portfolio company's stock. The pension funds set up the potential today for change in relationships among shareholders, senior managers, and boards of directors.

This rise of institutional investors should be seen in some historical perspective. In the introduction to *The Corporation in Modern Society*, Edward Mason said that "the equity owner is joining the bond holder as a functionless rentier." As a statement of fact in the 1950s this was true; as a prediction of what would happen over the subsequent four decades it was wrong. The shareholder in the 1970s and 1980s was not a passive rentier but an active assistant to the takeover entrepreneurs, and in the 1990s that shareholder shows enough stirrings of activity that rentier is not the right name.[51]

Why was Mason's statement true in the 1950s? The standard thinking then was that technology and economies of scale demanded large-scale organizations. Large-scale organizations demanded that capital be held by many scattered shareholders. Distance and small size made the shareholder passive—a "rentier" in Mason's vocabulary. Financial intermediaries had the *potential* to be a counterweight to management, Rostow implied in his essay in the 1959 volume, but with their small holdings they preferred to sell rather than to fight when they detected problems with managers.[52] Rostow denigrated the reformers of the day who sought to improve shareholder democracy, because he thought the analogy to democracy was inapt. Those with small holdings would never invest the time, energy, and money needed to make corporate democracy work. Only raiders—exemplified later in the takeover boom of the 1980s—could do so, because their return would be commensurate with their effort.

But what neither Mason nor Rostow mentioned then—what wasn't in the consciousness of the contributors to the 1959 volume—was that rentier status was contingent on the organization of financial intermediaries. While individual shareholdings must usually be held rentier-style, institutional stockholdings could be held in large blocks and those institutions could, in theory, play an active role in the firm. It has rarely occurred in the United States and has never been widespread.

The probable reason for this is that concentrated ownership as an organizational form is roughly matched by the alternatives for most firms, making it unlikely that it would dominate the alternative forms. Because its efficiency benefits were small or nonexistent, and available only to some firms, law could play an important role in shaping the shareholders' relations with the firm, helping to make them Masonesque rentiers.

Law regulates the relationships at the very top of the large public firm—those among shareholders, the board of directors, and senior managers—and regulates what financial institutions can and cannot do. The rise of large stockholding pension funds needs to be contrasted with the historical suppression in the United States of the other potentially powerful financial intermediaries. From the destruction of the Second Bank of the United States, to the confinement of national banks to a single location until 1927 (and to not much more than that until recently), to Glass-Steagall's separation of commercial and investment banking, to various securities laws, the United States has had rules to keep financial institutions small and passive. The basic reason was the American public's dislike of concentrations of economic power. The subsidiary reasons were the weakness of American government for much of American history (making private power seem even more threatening) and the ability of interest groups (country banks in the past, and managers in modern times) to influence lawmaking when their goals matched the public goals of fragmentation of private economic power. Political actors wanted the shareholder to be a mere rentier.[53]

In financial and corporate law circles these relationships among share-holders, managers, and boards of directors are seen to be important. Some even suggest that the United States has some maladapted large firms because one choice on the evolutionary menu was closed off, namely, the possibility of more powerful shareholders with seats in the boardrooms of the largest firms. (It is not unusual, however, for specialists to exaggerate the importance of their specialty.)

Law is often thought to be unimportant in this triangular relationship. Or, more precisely, law is thought to be important, but its structure is thought to be enabling, permitting shareholders, boards, and senior managers to structure their relations in any way they want. Whatever restrictions there are on these relationships have usually been thought trivial.[54] I have challenged that view elsewhere.[55] While state corporate law roughly corresponds to this format, and Delaware—the state where a majority of large public firms are incorporated—comes closest, there are other quite powerful laws that affect that triangular corporate governance relationship, namely, the laws that historically regulated financial institutions' size, authority to own stock, and ability to enter boardrooms and wield influence.

The recent increase in institutional investor activism in the 1990s, small though it may thus far be, is the incipient rise of a new organizational form. Germany and Japan have had enhanced institutional presence at the top of the large firm (that form is under pressure there now, especially after the institutions have fumbled their responsibilities several times, but clearly it has been important, and may yet endure); the United States has not yet had that form.

With American firms under increasing competitive pressure, it is not surprising that they experiment with new organizational forms at the top, forms that might make management relatively weaker than it has been (although still the strongest of the three primary actors). Thus General Motors in crisis temporarily split the position of CEO and chairman of the board, and later used a lead outside director as a counterweight to the CEO-chairman. These changes shifted power from the CEO to the board. Other firms have been paying more attention to institutional investors. Institutional investors lobbied the SEC to roll back rules that inhibited the institutions from coordinating their activities.

This development was foreshadowed in the 1959 volume on the corporation in modern society, by John Lintner. If managers are powerful, said Lintner, there will be pressure to create a countervailing power, including a countervailing power from the institutions that own or finance the firm.[56] This is now happening, although so slowly that one hesitates to announce a trend, and it's happening for different reasons from those Lintner guessed at: the countervailing power is arising not so much because managers are powerful, but because some are seen not to be performing well. When an economy faces problems, there's a tendency to treat the problem similarly to how the owner of a baseball team deals with a losing team, by "firing the manager," that is, blaming the governance system and the surrounding legal framework for competitive slippage; in some circles in the United States, problems have been blamed partly on fragmented ownership. Similarly, as the German and Japanese economies have faltered, in some German and Japanese circles their problems are blamed on concentrated ownership.[57] (Whether organizational formats are maladaptations depends more on business practices that are unconnected to that triangle of relationships at the top. And competitiveness and productivity—the ultimate goals—depend more on macroeconomic policies, the education and motivation of employees, and technology, than on this triangle of corporate relations.)

The history of financial fragmentation has to be placed next to the assumptions of the 1959 volume, which grew out of the cliché "that a group of giant business corporations . . . embodies a significant and troublesome concentration of power."[58] If politics fragmented private concentrations of financial power, and the American public distrusted concentrations of corporate power as well, why didn't politics, politicians, and law go after corporate power as well?

If politics didn't fragment industrial firms as well as it fragmented financial intermediaries, it wasn't for lack of trying; much antitrust rhetoric and action were directed toward that end. Law used different means when fragmenting industrial firms, means that turned out to be less effective than those used to fragment finance, and antitrust wasn't as successful as the financial regulation. Antitrust fragmentation depended on a legal finding that, say, a merger would tend to create a monopoly or to lessen competition. In contrast, banks were confined for quite some time to their locality, with no "exception" for banking networks that would not tend toward monopoly or lessen competition. And perhaps financial fragmentation had only modest efficiency costs, but industrial fragmentation would have had more, so efforts to find organizational substitutes prevailed. Tax policy offset antitrust policy; by favoring retained earnings, tax law encouraged corporate growth; antitrust just affected where the growth would occur.

In other work I've argued that the American predisposition to thwart concentrations of economic power had its most severe effect on fragmenting financial institutions, and that this financial fragmentation greatly affected the structure at the top of the large public corporation.[59] The 1959 volume on the corporation in modern society focused on corporate concentration, because American politics had successfully deterred financial concentration.

In this essay I have sought to analyze what seem to have been the plausible changes in academic attitudes toward the corporation during the past thirty-five years, what the underlying bases for these changes might have been, and how these changes affected corporate law. One could not possibly write a short essay on all major laws affecting the large corporation. Surely that list would include not just antitrust but also ERISA's (and related tax law's) effects on the corporation's financing and its obligations to employees, employment and labor law, antidiscrimination law, securities law, corporate law, patent law, and environmental law. Moreover, firms in specific businesses are often highly regulated: banking law obviously affects banks, franchise and fuel efficiency laws regulate auto companies, licensing rules regulate electric utilities, patent and copyright law affects computer software.

When the first *The Corporation in Modern Society* symposium was held, today's corporate issues—competitiveness and survival—were hardly visible. America's large firms were colossuses bestriding the U.S. and the world economy. There was barely any question that they were fit for economic competition. They had vanquished every other economic form. Natural selection had made them the winners. The issues concerning the rule of law and the modern corporation were whether they were too successful, too powerful economically. The questions were whether law should cut them down to size, restrain their economic behavior, make them more responsive to communities and ordinary people.

These considerations could again become central. Worldwide changes could make the returns to capital high and returns to labor low (because the world has a lot of people and not enough capital, and open international markets push American returns on capital and labor to worldwide rates).[60] This and a widespread unsettled feeling about job security could, if the American economy weakens, create a free-floating hostility to the corporation, particularly if some inside the corporation do well and seem to take what seems to be more than their "fair" share, while others do not.

The shift from power to competitiveness is what I analyze here, but the point to which we have shifted need not be a resting place, the final arena for corporate issues, for all time. Indeed, I doubt that it is the stable finale.

The broad legal shifts in the decades since 1959 should be seen as resulting from the fading of that heroic but dangerous image of corporate colossuses bestriding the world economy. Antitrust attacks to break up the giants seemed so sensible when three oligopolists split the U.S., and sometimes the world, market. Such attacks made no sense when the three came to be embedded in a worldwide market of ten firms. Antitrust rules relaxed. Consumer laws and environmental laws sanded down a few of the rough corporate edges. ERISA's treatment of pensions, antidiscrimination laws, and health and safety laws all made the corporation seem fairer for its employees than it had been. The following help characterize the corporate changes in the past three and a half decades:

1. Corporate power was the central consideration in 1959; today, it would be competitiveness.

2. Underlying the 1959 urge to tame the large corporation was the widespread existence (or at least perception) of industrial oligopoly. It was oligopoly (or the superior efficiency of a few American manufacturing leaders) that gave the large firm slack and the perception of power.

3. That appearance of industrial oligopoly (or superior efficiency) subsequently disappeared, at least in heavy manufacturing, largely due to international competition and technological change. Oligopoly's disappearance changed that old image of powerful colossuses and replaced it with a new one, of faltering large corporations. The new image assisted change in antitrust laws, which relaxed the rules against horizontal mergers and lifted many against vertical mergers.

4. That relaxation in antitrust facilitated the merger boom of the 1980s, as has been noted by others. Antitrust's previous strong barriers to high market share and to horizontal (and many vertical) mergers had channeled corporate managers into conglomerate mergers. These conglomerates were not successfully challenged by antitrust, but they became one of the prime targets of the 1980s takeovers, which broke up many of them.

5. The 1950s perception of oligopoly was one reason why hostile takeovers appeared later and not then. A takeover entrepreneur would too easily upset the oligopolists' implicit understandings among themselves. If there were oligopoly profits, the takeover entrepreneur might lose them if he damaged those oligopolistic understandings. And a takeover entrepreneur who tried to tighten the workplace might fail (as Carl Icahn found out when taking over

TWA and Frank Lorenzo found out at Continental and Eastern). One who hoped to succeed would fear that other rivals would react to success by moving along the oligopolist's "kinked" demand curve to lower its price and tighten its own workplace, leaving the takeover entrepreneur with no profits, many expenses, and a chance of failure. When international competition, a strong dollar in the 1980s, and technological change took away the oligopoly and made it clear that firms had to react or would fail, then takeovers became more plausible.[61] Moreover, until conglomerates were widespread, managers didn't believe that corporate divisions could be moved around like pieces on a game board. This is not to say that perceptions of oligopoly were the only explanation for the lack of 1950s takeovers, but it is an underrecognized explanation.

Thirty-five years after the first volume on the corporation in modern society, some of those colossuses look now and again like dinosaurs: big, ferocious, and maybe on the verge of being naturally selected out. What happened is obvious: the reconstruction of Europe and Japan forced the colossuses to compete in the international arena; an accelerating pace of technological change made old structures obsolete and brought forth new domestic competitors. While many of the old industrial firms were, or became, fit to compete in the new international arena and to ride the waves of new technological change, some weren't. Even the fit ones have to sweat to survive and cannot relax as they did four decades ago. The notion of the rule of law to control corporate power faded, and the legal questions began to focus on whether law plays some role in hindering, or enhancing, corporate competitiveness.

Notes

Thanks go to Victor Goldberg, Harvey Goldschmid, Jeffrey Gordon, William Kenneth Jones, John Kasdan, and Milton Handler for comments on a prior draft.

1. Edward S. Mason "Introduction," in *The Corporation in Modern Society*, ed. Edward S. Mason [hereafter *Modern Society*] (New York: Atheneum, 1959), pp. 1, 4.

2. Earl Latham, "The Body Politic of the Corporation," in *Modern Society*, p. 218.

3. Carl Kaysen, "The Corporation: How Much Power? What Scope?" in *Modern Society*, p. 85.

4. Mason," Introduction," p. 11.

5. Abram Chayes, "The Modern Corporation and the Rule of Law," in *Modern Society*, pp. 25, 28.

6. Ibid., p. 32.

7. Chayes,"The Modern Corporation," p. 40; Kaysen, "The Corporation,"p. 91.

8. Chayes,"The Modern Corporation," p. 36.

9. Peter Drucker, *The Concept of the Corporation* (New York: The John Day Company, 1946).

10. Jean-Jacques Servan-Schreiber, *The American Challenge* (New York: Atheneum, 1967); Galbraith's *New Industrial State* was published in 1967 (Boston: Houghton Mifflin).

11. The only exception was Eugene Rostow's essay. Rostow prescribed shareholder profit maximization as the only sensible guideline. See Eugene V. Rostow, "To Whom and What Ends Is Corporate Management Responsible?" in *Modern Society*, p. 46. But note, as we shall inquire into later, that in an oligopolistic market, profit maximization (Rostow's prescription) does not equal social interest.

12. See Chayes, "The Modern Corporation."

13. Kaysen, in particular, made this point for the 1959 volume; See Mason, "Introduction, " p. 20.

Whether the profits from concentration were unusual has been disputed; see Harold Demsetz, "Economics as a Guide to Antitrust Regulation," *Journal of Law and Economics* 19 (1976): 371, 380, analyzing 1958–1967 profit data and concluding that profits rose when firm size rose, and not so much when industry concentration rose. Others argued that some of these profits were dissipated in rents paid to acquire monopoly power; see Richard A. Posner, "The Social Costs of Monopoly and Regulation, " *Journal of Political Economy* 83 (1975): 807. Other studies at the time correlated concentration, market share, and firm size with profit; see Marshall Hall and Leonard Weiss, "Firm Size and Profitability," *Review of Economics and Statistics* 49 (1967): 319; William G. Shepherd, "The Elements of Market Structure," *Review of Economic Studies* 54 (1972): 25.

14. The Herfindahl index, a standard measure of industry concentration, was cut in one-half, in some cases in one-third, for eight worldwide industries from the 1950s to the 1970s; see Raymond Vernon, *Storm over the Multinationals* (Cambridge, Mass.: Harvard University Press, 1977), p. 81.

15. Perceptions of power and concentration shifted to technological industries—Microsoft and Intel, for example—where the pace of change has thus far been so rapid so as not to create the same 1950s image of power.

16. Paul Krugman, *Peddling Prosperity* (New York: W. W. Norton), p. 57.

17. *United States v. Aluminum Co. of America*, 148 F. 2d 416, 427–28 (2d Cir. 1945).

18. For an aggressive statement of this view, see Robert H. Bork, *The Antitrust Paradox* (New York: Basic Books, 1978), pp. 58–61. Attributing to antitrust an as-

piration to bring business down to a human scale is hard to prove, and may in fact be unprovable, because few decisions make the aspiration explicit. Only a very rich nation—or a nation that perceived itself as rich—could let such sentiments seep into business policy. By the late 1970s and 1980s courts needed more than the Alcoa court had needed to find a violation of the Sherman Act's ban on monopolization; see *Aspen Skiing Co. v. Aspen Highlands Skiing Corp.*, 472 U.S. 585 (1985); *Olympia Equipment Leasing Co. v. Western Union Telegraph*, 797 F. 2d 370, 375–76 (7th Cir. 1986), cert. denied, 480 U.S. 934 (1987); *Berkey Photo, Inc. v. Eastman Kodak Co.*, 603 F. 2d 263 (2d Cir. 1979), cert. denied, 444 U.S. 1093.

19. Ed Cray, *Chrome Colossus* (New York: McGraw-Hill, 1980), p. 402.

20. "Larger Companies Encourage Merger to Take Pressure Off 'Big Three,'" *New York Times*, July 12, 1954, p. 27.

21. E.g., Anthony Lewis, "U.S. Aide Suggests G.M. Give Up Unit," *New York Times*, March 9, 1956, p. 1. Cf. Donald Dewey, *The Antitrust Experiment in America* (New York: Columbia University Press, 1990), p. 40: The "break-up [of] General Motors . . . was[] seriously debated at professional [economics] meetings in the 1950s . . . ".

22. *Brown Shoe Co. v. United States*, 370 U.S. 294 (1962).

23. Phillip E. Areeda and Donald Turner, *Antitrust Law*, vol. 3 (Boston: Little Brown, 1994), pp. 359-90; Carl Kaysen and Donald F. Turner, *Antitrust Policy: An Economic and Legal Analysis* (Cambridge, Mass.: Harvard University Press, 1959); Donald Turner, "The Definition of Agreement Under the Sherman Act," *Harvard Law Review* 75 (1962): 655.

24. For reasons that should be explored carefully by a tax historian, slightly more complex mechanisms of getting the cash out to shareholders at low tax rates, such as a company repurchasing its own shares, were apparently unpopular in the 1950s and 1960s but became common in the 1980s.

25. When the conglomerate bought a target for cash, the buy-up could be seen as a tax-favored way of getting cash out from corporate coffers into shareholders' hands, although the recipients were the target firm's shareholders, not the base firm's shareholders.

26. Lawrence Sullivan, *Handbook of the Law of Antitrust* (St. Paul, Minn.: West, 1977), p. 598; F. M. Scherer, *Industrial Market Structure and Economic Performance*, 3d ed. (Chicago: Rand McNally, 1980), p. 156.

27. See *Brown Shoe Co. v. United States*, 370 U.S. 294, 323–34 (Chicago: Rand McNally, 1962).

28. Oliver Williamson, *Markets and Hierarchies: Analysis and Antitrust Implications* (New York: Free Press, 1975).

29. David J. Ravenscraft and F. M. Scherer, *Mergers, Sell-Offs, and Economic Efficiency* (Washington, D.C.: Brookings Institution, 1987).

30. *The Economist*, April 27, 1991; Gerald F. Davis, Kristina A. Diekmann, and Catherine H. Tinsley, "The Decline and Fall of the Conglomerate Firm in the 1980s: The Institutionalization of an Organizational Form," *American Sociological Review* 59 (1994): 547–48.

31. Sanjay Bhagat, Andrei Shleifer, and Robert Vishny, *Hostile Takeovers in the 1980s: The Return to Specialization*, 1990 Brookings Papers on Economic Activity: Microeconomics, p. 1.

32. Drucker, *The Concept of the Corporation* .

33. Again, see Williamson, *Markets and Hierarchies*; see also Milton Handler, Harlan M. Blake, Robert Pitofsky and Harvey J. Goldschmid, *Cases and Materials on Trade Regulation*, 3d ed. (Westbury, N.Y.: Foundation, 1990), pp. 670–71, citing prominent academic works on vertical restraints.

34. Michael C. Jensen, "Agency Costs of Free Cash Flow," *American Economic Review* 76 (1986): 323.

35. There is some irony here: "Big is bad" led to the two big antitrust suits of the past four decades, those against IBM and AT&T. AT&T accepted a breakup settlement; IBM won dismissal. Thus far, the broken up, competitive parts of AT&T are doing better than the still big IBM, which is only slowly reacting to the changing technologies and markets of the 1980s.

There is a conceptual irony here as well: some managers slack off. Firms in concentrated industries might not compete as fiercely as they should. The best firms to take over those with managerial laggards were other firms in the same industry. This makes for a trade-off in what causes slack and underperformance: in the 1980s, relaxation of the antitrust rules made for enhanced monitoring of management, at the potential price of decreased domestic product market competition. (In industries where international competition was sufficient, there was no trade-off.)

36. Michael C. Jensen and William H. Meckling, "Theory of the Firm: Managerial Behavior, Agency Costs and Ownership Structure," *Journal of Financial Economics* 3 (1976): 305.

37. Thus airline employees took some of the industry gains when the airline industry avoided price competition. When the auto industry was oligopolistically organized, employees got some of the oligopoly profits. When deregulation introduced price competition in the airline industry and the rise of Japanese automakers introduced competition in the auto industry, the firms had to bargain internally on where to adjust: on the wage rate, the stock value, or managers' incomes.

38. Areeda and Turner, *Antitrust Law*, vol. 5, pp. 177ff.

39. It is possible that the takeover entrepreneur could take over the company, refuse to lower prices (a move that would upset the oligopoly), but then tighten the workplace and keep the resulting profits. Whether this could have been a viable strategy is open to question. Few 1980s takeovers had this as their central strategy. In a few where it was central, the takeover entrepreneur failed. In the 1950s setting, perhaps the tough individuals who would seek to tighten the workplace would also be seen as untrustworthy by the other oligopolists. The profits gained from tightening the workplace would be offset by the probability of profits lost when competition broke out.

40. George J. Stigler, *The Organization of Industry* (Homewood, Ill.: Irwin, 1968), pp. 45, 56–60.

41. Moreover, I'm not here arguing that we should ignore other changes by the

1980s: changes in corporate culture—nice people at one time didn't make unsolicited takeover bids but by the 1980s they could; the rise of new financing techniques; antitrust changes that allowed corporate divisions to be marketed easily; and an institutionalization of stockholding, which made for a big supply of "hot" stock, ready to tender to the highest bidder.

Proxy fights in the early 1950s contradict my argument here. Raiders who engaged in proxy fights in the early 1950s were as disruptive as takeover raiders would have been. One response might be that the proxy raiders disappeared, perhaps because they couldn't make money due in part to the reasons analyzed here. Alternatively, they disappeared because new proxy rules in the mid-1950s raised their costs. Given the unprofitability of raiding in an oligopolistic market, the incentive for innovation by finding a new tactic—the takeover—was insufficient.

42. The thinking in 1959 classified 60 percent of large manufacturing industries as structurally oligopolistic, industries that, although they could be competitive, could with additional ingredients beyond structure be less than fully competitive; see Kaysen and Turner, *Antitrust Policy*, pp. 30–31. The 1959 notion of a potentially oligopolistic structure—an industry with the first eight firms making 33 percent of the goods—was one that economists a few decades later would tend to think of as a competitive industry.

43. Theoretic change could be seen as starting with Henry G. Manne, "Mergers and the Market for Corporate Control," *Journal of Political Economy* 73 (1964): 110.

44. Andrei Shleifer and Lawrence Summers, "Breach of Trust in Hostile Takeovers," in *Corporate Takeovers: Causes and Consequences*, ed. Alan Auerbach (Chicago: University of Chicago Press, 1988), p. 33. Although this kind of tightening does not seem to be central to the broad run of 1980s mergers, it is central to the popular image of those takeovers.

45. True, state statutes were not absolute showstoppers; some just raised the costs of takeovers but did not absolutely bar them. Court decisions that validated the poison pill were more important because the pill could stop a takeover cold. The "pill," when adopted by a target company, would force any successful offering company to buy out remaining shareholders at an inflated price, thereby thwarting many takeovers because the offeror did not want to swallow the financial "pill." State legislatures could have banned the pill but did not.

46. Frank R. Lichtenberg and Donald Siegel, "The Effects of Leveraged Buyouts on Productivity and Related Aspects of Firm Behavior," *Journal of Financial Economics* 27 (1991): 165.

47. The next four paragraphs draw on my "Takeover Politics," in *The Deal Decade*, ed. Margaret Blair (Washington, D.C.: Brookings Institution, 1993), 321.

48. "Who Likes Takeovers?" Forbes, May 18, 1987, p. 12; Roberta Romano, "The Future of Hostile Takeovers: Legislation and Public Opinion," *University of Cincinnati Law Review* 57 (1988): 457.

49. Leslie Wayne, "Pennsylvania Lends Force to Antitakeover Trend," *New York Times*, April 19, 1990, p. A1.

50. "Management and Labor Join Forces to Stiff-arm Raiders in Pennsylvania," *Corporate Control Alert* 7 (January 1990): 1, 8.

51. Mason, "Introduction," p. 2. The ultimate beneficiaries of the new institutions—the pensioner or the mutual fund owner—are rentiers, but the pension and mutual funds need not be, and often are not.

52. Rostow, "To Whom and What Ends Is Corporate Management Responsible?" p. 54.

53. I first developed this theme in some detail in "Political and Legal Restraints on Corporate Control," *Journal of Financial Economics* 27 (1990): 7; and "A Political Theory of American Corporate Finance," *Columbia Law Review* 91 (1991); 10. I developed it in yet more detail in *Strong Managers, Weak Owners: The Political Roots of American Corporate Finance* (Princeton: Princeton University Press, 1994).

54. Frank H. Easterbrook and Daniel R. Fischel, The Economic Structure of Corporate Law (Cambridge, Mass.: Harvard Universty Press, 1991); Bernard S. Black, "Is Corporate Law Trivial?: A Political and Economic Analysis," *Northwestern Law Review* 84 (1990): 542.

55. Roe, *Strong Managers, Weak Owners*.

56. John Lintner, "The Financing of Corporations," in *Modern Society*, pp. 166, 193–94.

57. An economy that had concentrated shareholder voice in large firms could be inferior to one that had weak shareholder voice. But since concentration seems to have some organizational benefits for some firms (theoretically and by comparison), a plausible policy prescription would be to permit competition among organizational forms, not to suppress (or encourage) one or the other.

58. Kaysen, "The Corporation," p. 85.

59. See n. 53.

60. See Lester Thurow's essay, Ch. 12.

61. While this helps to explain Rust Belt and conglomerate takeovers, it doesn't help to explain the other big category in the 1980s takeovers, that of the oil company takeovers, whose explanation lies elsewhere. In the 1980s, oil prices soared, but Wall Street believed the rise was unsustainable. Oil companies nevertheless spent massive sums on exploration, with costs that Wall Street believed exceeded the long-run sales price of oil. Hence, there was an opportunity for takeover entrepreneurs to profit by inducing the heaviest explorers to shut down their exploration departments.

5

Financing the American Corporation: The Changing Menu of Financial Relationships

◆

CHARLES W. CALOMIRIS

CARLOS D. RAMIREZ

The history of the financing of the American corporation can be described along many dimensions—variation in the relative importance of particular contracting forms (e.g., debt vs. equity) as marginal sources of funds, changes in the use of retained earnings vs. external finance, shifts in the relative importance of lending from commercial banks or similar intermediaries (sometimes referred to as "insider" lending) vs. financing from public markets. Each of these potential measures of the historical evolution of corporate finance has been used by financial historians to address particular questions. For example, variation in the relative importance of debt, preferred stock, and common stock as sources of external finance can help gauge the effects of innovations in bankruptcy laws on corporate finance costs. Reductions in the role of banks in financing corporations, often induced by regulatory change, can help measure the importance of regulatory restrictions on banks for corporate finance costs. Changes in the relative cost of external finance through public markets can be related to institutional factors that reduce the costs of public securities offerings.

Our central point in this paper is that there is a single general historical pattern that lies behind each of these three measures of historical change in corporate finance (contracting form, reliance on funds from intermediaries, and costs of external finance). In essence, the history of American corporate finance along all three dimensions is the history of altering the range of feasible relationships between corporations and particular intermediaries, which in turn redefines the cost-minimizing means of financing the corporation.

Virtually every financial transaction involves at least one intermediary. Indeed, the distinction between using intermediaries and using "the market" is a false dichotomy. Public securities issuance requires the reliance on intermediaries (investment bankers, commercial paper dealers) to perform services similar to those provided by banks making loans, life insurance companies holding private placements of corporate debt, or venture capitalists investing in corporate equity. Each of these intermediaries can be seen as one of many mechanisms for solving a combination of problems or reducing "frictions"—communicating information, controlling the use of funds, and physically transacting with corporations—all of which arise from a corporation's financing needs.

The fundamental problem of the corporation is to secure funding from people who are not directly in control of the use of those funds. Ultimate suppliers of funds typically lack knowledge about the corporation's ex ante creditworthiness, lack the means of observing or controlling the actions of the firm once it obtains their funds, and lack a convenient means of transferring the funds physically. In the face of these information and transaction costs, suppliers of funds may not find it worthwhile to transfer their savings to corporations, even though corporations have access to worthwhile (positive net present value) investment projects. Intermediaries of all kinds exist to help overcome these obstacles. Of course the services of intermediaries are not supplied gratis. The fees (and other costs) of using any of these intermediaries can be significant, and reflect the costs of investing resources in information processing, information signaling (marketing), physical transacting, and controlling corporate management.

Presumably, the variation across corporations and over time in the reliance on different intermediation relationships reflects variation across firms and over time in the costs and benefits of those relationships. Firms should choose the profit-maximizing relationship, after taking into account all the benefits and costs associated with the various choices.

The menu of financial relationship choices available to firms varies over time. That changing menu, we argue, has been the driving force behind the history of American corporate finance. A survey of the history of changes in the feasible ranges of relationships between nonfinancial corporations and intermediaries reveals how transformations have occurred, and what the consequences of those developments have been for corporate financing costs. Changing ranges of relationships have sometimes been dictated by conscious regulatory policy, and sometimes by "induced" private financial innovations. In the latter case, innovations have often been the unintended consequence of other government actions (notably, regulations of intermediaries or financial markets, wars, tax policies, and bankruptcy rules). The changes in the range of feasible relationships have evolved as a historical, and therefore "path-dependent," process. New relationships grow out of the combination of preexisting relationships and new circumstances.

This survey shows how the relative importance of certain intermediaries, the relative reliance on outsiders, and the forms of financial claims often reflect restrictions placed on the range of relationships. The peculiarities of U.S. corporate finance along several dimensions are, we argue, traceable to the same underlying regulatory distortions that limited the range of bank-firm relationships. In large part, the history of institutional change and financial innovation in the United States has been the history of attempts to work around costly restrictions on relationships not faced by corporations in most other countries.

We begin with a theoretical survey of the financial frictions that make financial relationships necessary, and we argue that breadth and continuity in financial relationships ("universal banking") has many desirable features. We trace the way financing frictions have been addressed over the course of American history with a changing set of financial relationships, and consider the merits and limitations of each. We conclude by considering the potential benefits and likelihood of current reforms of the banking system in the light of theoretical and historical lessons.

Finance Theory: The Menu of Intermediary Relationships

Financial Frictions and the Role of Intermediaries

What would prevent a corporation with a worthwhile project from being able to secure financing? Five broad categories of frictions can prevent efficient capital allocation from taking place. First, suppliers of funds may not be able to identify "good" firms. If so, "bad" firms may have an incentive to pretend to be good firms. The difficulty of distinguishing good from bad firms raises the cost of borrowing for good firms and may even lead to a collapse of the market for funds to the pooled class of firms.[1]

Second, even if firms seeking to raise funds are ex ante identical, and even if firms have access to profitable projects, managers may not have the necessary incentives to invest in those projects once they have received funding. For one thing, successful investment may require costly managerial effort, which the manager may wish to withhold. Furthermore, after contracting with fund suppliers, managers may find it in their interest to choose an inferior project as a result of the incentives created by the contract between fund suppliers and the firm. For example, managers who are also residual claimants to firm profits (either directly as stockholders, or indirectly through bonuses) may prefer to allocate funds suboptimally (investing in projects of lower or even negative net present value) because doing so substantially increases their share of the (smaller) pie. Financing choices often involve a trade-off between these two incentive problems. Debt contracts tend to provide greater incentives for managerial effort (by making managers residual claimants), but they also provide incentives to managers to prefer projects that deliver large "upper tails" (low-probability large payoffs) to superior projects with smaller upper tails.[2]

Third, even if firms' types are known and the investment choices of managers can be controlled easily by suppliers of funds, managers may be able to exploit the fact that it is costly to verify the outcome of the investment on which the financial claims of suppliers are based.[3] That is, managers may try to "hide" profits to reduce the profit-contingent payments they have promised suppliers of funds. Knowing this, suppliers of funds cannot trust the reports of managers, and will have to invest in "costly state verification" (which can be thought of as requiring a court audit or bankruptcy proceeding to verify outcomes). Debt contracts can minimize these costs by reducing the number of states of the world in which verification must occur (i.e., no verification occurs so long as the promised payment is made).

Fourth, managers can do damage ex post by "absconding," which we will define as any wasteful action by the manager after the outcome has occurred that has the effect of increasing the manager's wealth. Models of such behavior sometimes assume that managerial waste from absconding is proportional to the wealth of the firm, and that the manager is a residual claimant of the firm (through stock ownership or bonus schemes). This in turn implies that the manager's incentive to abscond is greater when outcomes are poor. Preventing such behavior requires the observability of the state (on which the manager's absconding decision is based), and an effective enforcement technology for preventing absconding.[4]

Finally, market segmentation (due, e.g., to natural boundaries that impose physical barriers between savers and investors) can prevent efficient transfers of funds from occurring, even in the absence of the problems of information and control discussed earlier. Moreover, such physical costs also imply related problems of information and control. To the extent that ultimate suppliers of funds are scattered and distant from ultimate users, information and control costs will be exacerbated. Problems of market segmentation have been particularly severe in the United States, because of its highly fragmented commercial banking system. Such segmentation is reflected in substantial variation across locations in the cost of funds and the profits of corporations historically.[5]

Of course, if funds suppliers could costlessly transfer funds, screen applicants accurately, monitor the actions of managers and the outcomes of investments, and write contracts to enforce penalties against improper investment or absconding behavior by managers, then there would be no need to invest resources in the financial system. In such a world all positive net present value investments would be realized, and intermediaries would have no active role in corporate finance. Such is not the world in which we live.

The role for intermediaries comes from advantages of appointing a specialist to transfer funds, screen applicants, monitor managerial performance and firm profits, and design and enforce specific contractual covenants that discipline managers. Virtually every model of a "bank" has as its fundamental features some advantage from delegating decision making to a specialist, and the need to ensure that the "delegated monitor" faces incentives to behave appropriately. A useful definition of a viable financial intermediary is a financial agent that reduces net incentive and control problems—the sum of those that result from the frictions outlined earlier and those that are *added* as the result of the actions of the intermediary.

Why is it beneficial to use an intermediary? First and foremost, given the multiple suppliers of funds to any use, intermediaries avoid redundancy of screening, monitoring, and enforcement costs, and enjoy physical law-of-large-numbers economies in cash management (netting of transfers). Given transaction costs in securities markets, intermediaries also offer low-cost portfolio diversification. The concentration of claims in the hands of an intermediary also avoids coordination costs in the relationship between firms and their funds suppliers. For example, debt renegotiation costs are much lower when the number of parties to the renegotiation is small.[6] Information costs and coordination costs are often related. If a banker has all or most of the outstanding debt of the firm, then it pays for the banker to invest more in monitoring the firm because the banker's ability to make use of information is greater when he can act with greater authority in a renegotiation/bankruptcy. Firms with large numbers of claimants can play one off against the other, and can reduce the benefit to any claimant of investing effort in monitoring the firm.

From the standpoint of a firm in need of funds, the menu of intermediaries and contracting forms offers alternative "mechanisms"—each is an answer to the question of how one might raise funds, and presumably the least costly mechanism is chosen by the firm, after taking account of and weighing the advantages and disadvantages of each potential relationship along a variety of dimensions. Some forms of intermediation cost more "up front" than others. For example, some intermediaries charge higher fees, or restrict the behavior of the firm more with strict debt covenants, or create a powerful new outside stockholder with direct control over management— and these restrictions may inhibit some potentially profitable behavior.[7] But those higher up-front costs may be warranted if those restrictions imply significant *contingent benefits* to the firm (like low costs of finance contingent on a decline in earnings in the future), or if other forms of finance are more costly to the firm because they do not resolve incentive and control problems facing the firm.

For firms that have a wide range of choices about which intermediation relationship or financing mechanism to use (say, large, well-established firms with access to many financing vehicles), choosing the optimal mechanism requires estimating the probabilities of many potential states of the world, and estimating the benefits of each possible mechanism in each potential state. For example, hiring an underwriter to place a widely held bond issue may offer the advantage of a higher price of debt (or larger amount of debt) than could be secured from a bank. On the other hand, in states of the world where the firm enters financial distress (where it is unable to cover its interest expenses with current income), the costs of that distress (reduced investment and other disruptions) will likely be greater if its debt is in the form of a widely held bond issue. The costs of financial distress may differ according to firm characteristics (e.g., firms with clearly observable profitable investment opportunities would suffer less costs than others). Thus one possible interpretation of a firm's decision to use public debt as opposed to bank loans is that it perceives the likelihood and anticipated costs of financial distress to be low.

There are many other contingencies to consider, and there are many more dimensions to corporate finance choice than the decision over whether to use public debt or bank loans. Financial distress is an extreme case. More generally, firms will be concerned about the implications of their financing relationships for the costs of finance when they experience a sudden decline in internally generated earnings. Firms are aware, for example, that short of financial distress they may face constraints on access to funds because of the costs of external finance. Several studies have measured the importance of internally generated funds in firms' investment decisions, and have traced that importance to the high costs of financing activity from external sources.[8] The higher the shadow cost of external finance (which reflects the extent to which firms are vulnerable to the various frictions mentioned earlier), the greater the excessive sensitivity of investment to cash flow.[9]

For our purposes, what is most important about the potential costs of external finance is their connection to choices about financial relationships. From this perspective, two important points have been stressed in the literature. First, firms facing the greatest frictions in capital markets tend to rely more on close relationships with intermediaries. Some markets—notably the public bond and commercial paper markets—are not accessible to all firms because of the prohibitive costs of financial frictions. Firms tend to progress through a financial "life cycle." They begin with access only to the endowments of a close-knit group of entrepreneurs. Over time they rely on lending from banks or venture capitalists, which retain close control over the firm. Later, as firms' prospects become a matter of common knowledge, and as their internal resources become larger relative to their funding needs, firms can rely on "outside" sources of funds in public markets, and intermediaries take on the role of underwriters rather than suppliers of funds through loans or equity investments.

Second, a firm's ability to raise funds during times when cash flow is small relative to investment opportunities depends importantly on whether it has a preexisting financing relationship, and on the strength of that relationship. The uniqueness of bank lending relationships has been the subject of many recent studies of banking. Other banklike intermediaries (finance companies and life insurance companies) engage in lending agreements similar to bank loans, and monitor and control firm behavior through the verification and enforcement of covenants. Studies of these intermediaries have found that they, like banks, have access to special information and control devices, and are therefore properly viewed as "insider" lenders.[10]

Lest one be carried away by the wonders of "discipline," it is worth bearing in mind that discipline has its costs, which explains why it is not the preferred means of financing relationship for all firms. In Japan, for example, firms sometimes opt out of close firm-bank relationships, and in doing so increase their reliance on internal funds to finance investment.[11] Given that many of those firms were closely controlled by banks prior to the decision to break off the close relationship, it is hard to argue that Japanese firms cut their ties to banks because the firms' managers wish to avoid efficient discipline in order to abuse "free cash flow." Why would value-maximizing firms voluntarily increase their costs of raising external funds in the future? One simple explanation is that there are fixed costs to establishing and maintaining financing relationships—for example, the costs of designing and enforcing appropriate standards of behavior. Another cost to buying discipline may be the inflexibility of the disciplinarian. For example, financial covenants are a form of regulation that could be viewed as a substitute for constant scrutiny of the firm. By establishing a set of easily verified covenants, the firm is able to reduce the costs charged by the intermediary for monitoring. Other covenants typically restrict the use of funds, as well as changes in the operations of the firm. Despite the obvious benefits of such covenants in reducing costs of control, they may be costly by limiting the flexibility of the firm to respond to changing circumstances. Thus, as firms reach the advanced stage of the financial life cycle and become seasoned credit risks with smaller relative reliance on external finance, the costs of strong relationships may be greater than the attendant benefits and they may choose to switch to financing relationships that entail weaker ties to intermediaries. There is empirical support for the notion that stronger banking relationships entail higher costs.[12]

Intermediaries in Securities Markets

Intermediaries specializing in the creation of insider debts of corporations—commercial banks, finance companies, and life insurance companies—are not the only intermediaries that develop beneficial relationships with firms. Investment bankers in the pre–World War I era (and J. P. Morgan, in particular) developed close relationships with their clients—involving underwriting, assistance in corporate reorganization, and involvement in corporate boards of directors. De Long (1991) and Ramirez (1995) have argued that the "Morgan collar" was a source of discipline that removed financial constraints on firms that were willing to "wear" it with pride.

Calomiris and Raff (1995) argue that the rise of institutional investors (pensions and mutuals) since the 1950s—which own large shares of corporate equity and participate actively in initial public offerings—was among the most important "intermediary innovations" of the post–World War II era. The rise of pensions and mutual funds as large block purchasers of equity in primary and secondary markets dramatically reduced the costs of placing equity and produced a permanent shift toward common stock issues by industrial firms.

The role of investment bankers and institutional buyers of securities in facilitating the marketing of securities has received less attention from finance economists than the role of intermediaries as lenders. Theoretical models of investment banking tend to stress the importance of the investment bankers' information and sales networks and the development of long-term relationships and reputation. Empirical analyses of the variation across firms and over time in the costs of securities flotations emphasize the importance of information cost and marketing in explaining flotation cost differences. This literature emphasizes that continuing relationships among buyers and investment bankers, and concentrations of shares (and voting power) in small numbers of investors (pensions, mutuals, and trusts) help to reduce issuing costs by reducing information problems ex ante and corporate control costs ex post.[13]

Relationships and the Forms of Claims

In emphasizing firm-intermediary relationships as the defining aspect of the corporate finance decision, we are not arguing that the form of financial claims is irrelevant to financing cost. But the benefits of choosing a particular form of claim depend on the relationship that gives rise to the financial contract. Mackie-Mason (1990) finds that the firm's choice of financing relationship (whether to rely on private or public sources of funds) is more closely related to inherent characteristics of the firm than the choice of financing with debt or equity.

Other studies have found that the importance of the form of the claim issued depends on the relationship chosen. The effectiveness of debt or equity as a disciplinary device depends on the concentration of debt or equity holdings, and the concentration of claims depends on the financing relationship. Bank lending permits concentration of debt holdings, which provides incentive for the monitoring and enforcement of lending covenants, and avoids free-rider problems in the event a "workout" is necessary. Concentrated equity holdings—a central feature of German and Japanese banking, and an important consequence of the rise of institutional investors in the United States after the 1950s—allow stockholders (or their agents) to exert more control over managerial decision-making. While the form of the optimal claim on the firm likely depends on which of the "five frictions" outlined previously is most important, the concentration of claims has an important influence on the costs of achieving the desired disciplinary advantages from any financing arrangement.

Also, requiring an insider lender to own junior claims on the firm can strengthen the lender's incentives to monitor the firm or to honestly reveal the firm's characteristics when underwriting a public offering of stock.[14]

American Financial Fragmentation and Relationship Constraints

One of the most remarkable features of American finance—perhaps the single feature that has set American financial history apart from that of other countries—is the number and variety of intermediaries available and their independence from one another. Unlike in other countries, the American corporate financing system is not organized around a set of "universal banks" performing a variety of functions for their clients.

We will argue that limits on the size and scope of banks in the United States have placed important constraints on the feasible menu of financing relationships of corporations. In the United States, it has been harder to concentrate financial claims on firms. The concentration of debt claims has been limited by the size of banks (due to restrictions on branching and consolidation). Furthermore, intermediaries have been prohibited from involvement in selling, managing, and holding large interests in firms, sometimes by limitations on the size and geographic range of intermediaries, and sometimes by limits on the equity-holding powers of intermediaries. Finally, government restrictions that forced intermediaries to specialize in particular functions have limited the beneficial combining of activities within the same intermediary.

In discussing the costs of prohibiting "universal banking" in the United States, it is useful to consider the advantages that other countries have enjoyed from such a system. "Universal banking" takes different forms in different countries, and there is no clear agreement regarding the essential, defining characteristics of universal banks. For our purposes we define universal banks to be intermediaries with three sets of characteristics: (1) they operate large networks over a wide geographic range (they are large and locationally "universal"); (2) they provide customers with access to a wide scope of activities, including lending, underwriting, portfolio management, and deposit taking; and (3) they are permitted to hold a variety of types of claims (e.g., debt and equity) on their corporate customers. In our historical discussion of the United States, this definition will prove useful for distinguishing between the U.S. and German banking systems, and for distinguishing between "full-fledged" universal banking in Germany and partial and intermittent attempts to concentrate and combine financial services historically in the United States.

The benefits of universal banking divide usefully into four categories. First, there are the simple benefits of concentration that come from allowing banks to be large—reducing costs of coordination among claimants and thus strengthening the intermediary's incentives to screen, monitor, control, and negotiate with the firm efficiently.[15]

Second, there are information and network economies from combining various functions within the same intermediary. Intermediaries that can combine different functions can save on information and enforcement costs and "brick and mortar" costs by spreading fixed costs over more transactions.[16]

Third, there are incentive and signaling benefits from combining activities. Providing a variety of services and holding various claims on a firm can strengthen the incentives of intermediaries to monitor and enforce properly, and can improve their ability to signal information to outsiders when marketing securities. A bank may find it easier and more desirable to monitor a borrower in which it maintains a junior stake.[17] Also, it may be easier for a bank to underwrite equity of a firm in which it also has a stake. For example, if a bank holds (or controls for its trust customers) stock in a corporation, the bank stands to lose from managerial errors or misbehavior of that corporation (i.e., lost profits on stock or disgruntled trust customers). Potential buyers of equity are more likely to trust the opinion of a universal bank underwriter that is taking a junior stake in the firm whose shares are being sold, especially if the underwriter retains significant control of the firm after the issue.[18]

Fourth, universal banking can promote low-cost diversification of the intermediary, and thereby reduce its cost of funds. Eugene White (1986) and Elijah Brewer (1989) have argued from the evidence of limited universal banking in the United States (historically and currently) that universal banks are better able to diversify because the incomes from the various services they offer are not highly correlated.[19]

From the perspective of these theoretical arguments, regulatory restrictions on the geographic range and scope of activities of intermediaries may be very costly. Indeed, we will argue that such costly restrictions explain the peculiar history of the development of American financial intermediaries, and the high costs of industrial finance in the United States.

Summary

Corporate finance theory seeks to explain financing decisions as choices among the menu of available intermediation mechanisms in the presence of financing frictions. Cross-sectional differences in those choices reflect the differing importance of particular frictions for particular firms, which in turn is closely related to the firm's financial maturity. Possible intermediation arrangements include insider lending from banks, finance companies, and life insurance companies, venture capital finance, or public debt or stock issuance through an investment bank (and its network of institutional dealers and purchasers).

Regardless of the form of financial claim chosen, the concentration of claims and transactions in large-scale, "universal banks" tends to facilitate several functions of intermediaries—especially monitoring, corporate control, and signaling. Limitations on concentration have been a hallmark of the American financial system, and an important constraint on the development of firm-bank relationships. The U.S. financial system has been unusually restrictive, both in allowing the concentration of claims, and in allowing particular intermediaries to be involved in a variety of types of financial transactions.

In the next section, we analyze the historical circumstances that gave rise to the peculiar constraints of American corporate finance, discuss their costs, and describe the forces that changed those constraints over time. We argue that during its early history (prior to the Civil War), the United States was able to develop a very efficient intermediation system, particularly in New England. In many respects, that system enjoyed the advantages of a universal banking system by virtue of the close ties among industrial borrowers, commercial banks, underwriters, and securities portfolio managers. But that system of "insider finance" broke down by the 1890s in the face of restrictions on bank branching and consolidation and the expansion in the scale of industrial firms. Further limitations on bank involvement in boards of directors (the Clayton Act of 1914) and the forced separation of commercial and investment banking (the Glass-Steagall Act of 1933) further limited intermediaries' abilities to reap the gains outlined earlier.

The subsequent history of American financial intermediation—or the history of the menu of financial relationships available to corporations—can be described as the history of finding "second-best" solutions in the face of these restrictions, which entailed the creation of new intermediaries and new financial claims (commercial paper houses and commercial paper, insurance companies and private placements, pensions, mutuals and venture capitalists participating in venture capital funds and investment banking syndicates).

These financial developments involved new methods of cooperation among intermediaries (especially among venture capitalists, trusts, pensions, and investment bankers) that had some elements in common with early arrangements in New England and universal banking systems. Today commercial banks themselves have become involved in these new coalitions of intermediaries, and may become the platform on which true American universal banks will be built. Some of these changes after the Great Depression were direct reactions to regulatory restrictions, while others were largely the unintended benefits of developments that had other sources.

American Corporate Finance: A Changing Menu of Relationships

Corporate Chartering, Bank Chartering, and Limited Entry: The "Mercantilist" System

The defining characteristic of a corporation, as opposed to a proprietorship or partnership, is the structure of its financial claims and the limited liability of corporate shareholders. Limited liability is a useful device for financing large-scale corporations for two reasons. First, "outside" shareholders in a world of asymmetrical information and imperfect corporate control will be reluctant to purchase shares in a risky venture if there is no limit to downside risk. Second, risk-averse outside and inside shareholders alike benefit from limiting the risk of ownership.

Governments understood that corporate chartering was an effective means of attracting funds to new, risky ventures. The mercantilist strategy had corporations at its center. By restricting the number of corporations, monarchs were able to give "charter value" to the corporations they permitted to form. These corporations were typically given monopoly rights too, which added to their charter values. Charter values served as a "bootstrapping" device for financing the development of the empire. Newly formed corporations could lever their charter capital values by borrowing or floating shares publicly. Restricting chartering of enterprises was an effective means to channel private funds to the government's top priorities—which included banks and various trading companies designated to capture foreign markets.

Thus the financial relationships of the mercantilist corporation were largely a matter of government policy—selecting a set of activities to receive special access to the privilege of incorporation, which implied special access to sources of funds. This mercantilist tradition was well understood in the American colonies, and underlay part of the conflict between the British empire and the colonies. The chartering of banks was viewed by colonists like Benjamin Franklin (in his classic 1738 pamphlet on the topic) as an important means for promoting the development of the economy and expansion westward. Franklin advocated land banks as a means to convert illiquid claims on the future (future returns from land) into current liquid funds that could be used to import needed capital from abroad, and to encourage immigration. Such plans were thwarted by the crown, which saw the chartering of banks, and the orientation of commerce toward interior development, as contrary to British interests. The crown wanted the credit supply to remain in the hands of British merchants (providing trade credit for exports), and wanted to restrict autonomous economic development on the frontier. After all, the purpose of the colonies from the perspective of the crown was to serve as a source of exports for the empire, not to become an economically self-reliant group of settlements demanding ever more expensive protection from the French and Indians on the western frontier. The conflict over corporate chartering, and bank chartering in particular, reflected the central conflict between the interests and aspirations of the colonists and those of the empire.[20]

The mercantilist view of corporations as a privilege to be conferred by the government to achieve government priorities extended into the early history of the new nation. The Constitution did not centralize authority over the chartering of corporations or banks. The federal government experimented with the chartering of two banks (the Bank of the United States and the Second Bank of the United States) from 1791 to 1811 and 1816 to 1836 respectively. These banks were founded to serve the financial needs of the federal government—as a source of revenue, as a means of collecting taxes, and as a network for placing government securities. The main chartering authorities for banks prior to the Civil War were the individual states. During the early antebellum period (prior to the late 1830s), most bank charters were granted to finance particular needs, and were acts of the state legislatures. Sometimes banking powers were attached to other corporate authorities—for example, to build canals, roads, or water systems.[21]

The restriction of bank charters was an important source of charter value that helped banks raise additional funds, and thereby helped the corporations that were connected to those banks gain access to funds. Models of the "delegated monitoring" problem of a bank have the common feature that an insufficient amount of insider capital can limit the amount of funds banks can raise from outside shareholders or depositors, and those models consider alternative means to solve the delegation problem.[22] From this perspective, because charter value helped to create an instant concentration of wealth in the hands of bank insiders (a fact that led to much political controversy over who would obtain a charter), it had a positive allocative role in capital markets.

By the 1820s, the need for creating concentrations of wealth through limited chartering to "bootstrap" banks was no longer as necessary. The transformation of merchant capital into industrial uses and banking during the period of national isolation produced by the Napoleonic Wars saw the creation of a new class of banker-industrialists—a large number of wealthy industrial-financial entrepreneurs. It is understandable, therefore, that free entry into banking (and into corporate chartering more generally) would be considered increasingly desirable, and that the 1830s would see major changes in the form of the "free banking" era (the unlimited chartering of banks under a common set of regulations).

The Mature Antebellum System: Pseudo-Universal Banking in New England

New England banking and financial markets were the best developed during the antebellum period, and recent empirical work has emphasized the relative efficiency of New England banks. Perhaps surprisingly, New England enjoyed a universal banking system of a sort long before "true" universal banking was established in Germany in the last three decades of the nineteenth century. The relationship between the nonbank corporation and the bank remained the focus of the corporation's financial relationship, but that relationship became increasingly complex, and involved securities flotations and investments by related intermediaries (savings banks), as well as funding by commercial banks.[23]

New England's antebellum banks were a primary source of funding for New England industrialists. The links between industry and banking in New England were very close, and the banks were closely affiliated with other financial institutions that underwrote securities issues and managed securities portfolios. The banks were chartered to provide credit to their industrialist founders. In many cases the officers and directors of the banks were their principal borrowers. Like German universal banks, and unlike U.S.

banks later in the nineteenth century, the stock of antebellum New England banks was widely issued.

New England banks were able to attract large numbers of outside stockholders and pay lower returns on equity than other banks because their institutional arrangements mitigated information problems. Each bank's borrower-insiders had strong incentives to monitor one another to ensure the continuation of the flow of credit to their own enterprises in the future. Moreover, interbank relationships ensured monitoring among members of the Suffolk system and among commercial banks and savings banks (which financed much of commercial banks' activities).[24]

Postbellum Industrial Finance and the Shrinking Role of Commercial Banks

Postbellum industrialization posed new challenges for the financial system, and these challenges seem not to have been met as effectively as before by banks. As Alfred Chandler (1977) and others have stressed, the "second industrial revolution" of the postbellum era saw the creation of whole new industries (electricity, steel, and chemicals), the development of a transcontinental network of railroads, and the creation of the large modern corporation, vertically and horizontally integrated, and controlled by a large bureaucratic managerial hierarchy.

Two of the most important roles of a financial intermediary are to reduce the degree of asymmetrical information between lenders and borrowers, and to provide a credible means for controlling management's use of the funds allocated to it. In a rapidly growing industrial economy, with many new products, new forms of producing, organizing, and distributing products, and an enormous increase in the scale of production, the challenges faced by the financial system to resolve information and control problems were enormous.

Financial and economic historians generally have argued that the U.S. financial system faced problems in adapting to these new challenges. U.S. regional financial markets remained largely isolated from one another during the late nineteenth century, and financial markets were slow to channel funds from low-growth sectors to high-growth sectors. Large, persisting regional differences in interest rates—an indication of a fragmented financial system—were a unique feature of American financial markets. Although these differences declined over time, they remained large relative to those of other countries before and after World War I. As late as the

1920s, bank loan interest rate differentials across regions on similar types of loans were as large as 3 percent. Interestingly, antebellum interest rate data do not show similar regional differences. Apparently, postbellum economic growth—with its new geographic frontiers and new industrial sectors—brought increasing capital market segmentation.[25]

Evidence from the profitability of manufacturing firms confirms the impression that there were significant impediments to moving capital across regions and across sectors from low-profit to high-profit uses. In a unique study of census data on manufacturing establishments during the postbellum period, Atack and Bateman (1994) examine profit differences across regions and sectors and find large persistent differences in profitability.

Evidence on the role of commercial banks in the industrialization process is consistent with the view that sources of funding for industrial firms were inadequate. Links between industrial firms and banks were much weaker in the United States than in other countries (notably, much weaker than in Germany's universal banking system). This reflected primarily the small size of incorporated banks relative to the large needs of industrial borrowers. There were more than twenty-six thousand banks operating in 1914, and the overwhelming majority of these were not permitted to operate branches, even within their home state. Small banks operating in a restricted location simply were incapable of financing, monitoring, and disciplining large industrial borrowers operating throughout the nation.

To the extent banks were involved with industrial finance, much of bank financing of firms occurred without any direct (much less ongoing) relationship between the bank and the firms it financed. Intermediaries' claims on firms primarily took the form of corporate bond holdings placed through syndicates. According to Raymond Goldsmith, for the period 1901–1912, bonds held by all intermediaries accounted for 18 percent of funds supplied by external sources (that is, excluding retained earnings) to nonfinancial firms. Commercial banks accounted for two-thirds of corporate bond holdings by intermediaries in 1912. Based on flow-of-funds accounting, bank loans (for all purposes) accounted for 12 percent of externally supplied funds for 1901–1912. For this period, bank loans amounted to roughly 10 percent of firms' debts, and less than 5 percent of firms' assets. Bonds and notes accounted for roughly half of firms' debts, and trade debt constituted 15 percent.[26]

Reliance on bank loans was relatively high for small firms. Large, established manufacturing firms relied more on bond issues as a means of indirect bank finance and less on loans from banks as a source of financing, especially prior to the 1940s.[27] Of course, under a unit banking system, large-scale firms operating throughout the country would have had to borrow from many small unit banks simultaneously. Bond market syndications facilitated this transaction by providing a means for banks to share risk and coordinate capital allocations.

A study of funding sources for a sample of fourteen large manufacturing firms from 1900 to 1910, based on accounting records of sources of net inflows of funds, indicates little reliance on bank lending. For the period 1900 to 1910 these firms reported a total financial inflow of $1.2 billion, of which $357 million came from external finance. Of this only $29 million was in the form of short-term debt. Some bank loans during this period also took the form of long-term debt, but long-term loans from commercial banks were relatively uncommon around the turn of the century.[28]

While small firms relied more on banks, it does not follow that banks contributed to the financing of industrial capital expansion by small firms any more than they did to that of large firms. Two detailed studies of the sources of capital in manufacturing provide a glimpse of the contribution of banks to industrial expansion in Illinois and California in the middle to late nineteenth century.[29] In the case of California, thirty-three of seventy-one manufacturing firms studied over the period 1859 to 1880 financed their investment entirely from internal sources. The others incorporated, took in partners, and supplemented these sources with earnings of existing partners from other sources, sale of stock or real estate, "eastern capital" (in three cases), and loans from a private banker (the same banker in both instances). Clearly, commercial banks had no role in the expansion of manufacturing capital in California prior to 1880.

Illinois' experience was similar, but the role of banks in financing industrial expansion may have been greater. The rapid expansion of manufacturing in Illinois began in the 1860s. From 1860 to 1870, manufacturing production and capital each increased sevenfold, and employment increased sixfold. From 1870 to 1880, manufacturing production doubled. The personal and business histories of fifty entrepreneurs show that these firms were financed initially from accumulated savings of would-be manufacturing entrepreneurs, or by entrepreneurs taking on a partner with savings. Subsequent funding typically was provided by retained earnings. Occasionally, this was supplemented by the sale of entrepreneurial assets, the expansion of the partnership, or incorporation. In twenty-six out of fifty cases, manufacturing entrepreneurs of relatively mature firms used profits to invest in an interest in a bank, which "marked the beginning of more rapid success for them. They owned in part or had access to, funds, either

large or small, which would enable them to grow and to progress." This was
especially important in the 1860s because manufacturing was moving
rapidly toward mechanization and opportunities for expansion outpaced accumulated profits.[30]

To summarize, firms progressed up the financial "pecking order" as
they matured. Entrepreneurs sometimes secured access to external funds
by investing in banks, on which they could rely for limited funding. While
the experience of Illinois' entrepreneurs does indicate a role for banks in industrial finance, it says as much about the limits of that role as it does about
banks' potential importance. Access to bank funds was extremely limited,
and bank stockholders were given preference as bank borrowers. While
banks may have played some role in financing industrial expansion in
Illinois and elsewhere, the importance of this role was greatest during the
"adolescent" stage of the firm's life cycle—after the firm had become mature enough to invest in becoming a bank insider but before it had become
too large to rely on a bank for its funding needs. Even this role of bank lending in industrial finance is apparent only in the histories of roughly half of
the case studies examined.

Why were commercial banks unable to expand to meet the challenges
of financing the new large-scale industrial producers? Naomi Lamoreaux's
(1991a, 1991b, 1994) studies of New England banking provide an interesting perspective on that question. She shows that large-scale banking would
have been profitable in New England, but that profitable consolidation was
not permitted by bank regulators. Many New England banks wanted to
merge in response to the growing scale of firms, and the consequent
economies of scope and scale in providing industrial finance. When banks
were able to merge, their profits increased substantially. Ultimately, however, national and state banking laws stood in the way of bank mergers or
branching, as unit bankers blocked attempts to liberalize branching laws
and prevented attempted mergers. The economic costs of the political
power of small unit bankers is an important theme throughout the history
of American financial regulation.[31]

Regulatory barriers on the scale of banking changed the functions of
New England banks. As already discussed, New England banks had been
important sources of finance, monitoring, and control for antebellum industrial enterprises, and the manager/owners of those enterprises were
bank "insiders." Those arrangements changed by the late nineteenth century. By 1900, New England's banks had moved toward financing the commercial (rather than industrial) undertakings of bank outsiders. These
changes reflected the growing mismatch between large-scale firms, and in-

herently small unit banks. As firms became larger, small banks found it increasingly difficult to satisfy the investment-financing needs of large customers, given the desirability of maintaining a diversified loan portfolio.

Filling the Gap: The Dawn of "Financial Capitalism"

The fragmented banking system's inability to finance industrial growth induced innovative new financing methods for corporate borrowers. These included the development of a market for commercial paper (a short-term, highly liquid debt instrument, mainly held by banks), and the rise of investment banking syndicates. Both of these financing mechanisms were available only to the largest, most established firms. Syndicates were used to finance corporate consolidations and reorganizations, as well as to market new issues of bonds and preferred stocks.

The commercial paper market (a unique innovation of the American financial system) met the short-term borrowing needs of large, high-quality borrowers. From humble beginnings in the 1870s, it reached its pre–World War II peak in 1920 at $1.3 billion, consisting of the debts of over four thousand borrowers.[32] Commercial paper houses provided a means for the highest-quality borrowers to locate cheaper sources of funds outside their local markets. Commercial paper brokers received short-term bridge financing from local banks, which was repaid once they had sold their paper (generally to banks in relatively low-credit-demand locations).

The commercial paper market was not open to all firms and was not useful for all purposes. Because commercial paper was used as a money substitute (essentially, a form of interest-bearing bank reserves), only the lowest-risk borrowers were permitted to enter the market, and the maturity of paper was kept short. These restrictions ensured that credit risk was very small in the market, and made it easier to sell paper in the secondary market.[33] Even for high-quality borrowers, the high costs and high frequency of rollover in the commercial paper market meant that long-term financing needs could not be addressed adequately through commercial paper finance.

The vehicle for long-term finance was the investment banking syndicate. Investment banking syndicates operated as multitiered financing mechanisms. At the top were Wall Street investment bankers who planned, priced, and underwrote the issue. Sales occurred through a network of local dealers, many of whom maintained close ties with local commercial banks, who bought securities for themselves and for their customers. As Vincent Carosso (1970) points out in his classic study of investment banking, this selling network developed during the Civil War as a means of placing large issues of government bonds. The network of relationships remained after the Civil War, and provided a basis for continuing distributions of private securities.

The central challenge facing an investment banking syndicate is convincing buyers to purchase the securities of firms about which they know little or nothing. How could a Wall Street financier assure potential American (and foreign) investors that American railroad and industrial securities were sound investments? Why should buyers believe that investment bankers or their dealers will truthfully identify which are the good companies and which are the bad ones?

Clearly, reputation building, effective signaling, and information sharing are the key ingredients to resolving the problems of marketing securities to outsiders.[34] The marketing of securities also can be enhanced by the continuing involvement of the investment banker with the issuing firm. As noted in our theoretical discussion, some of the frictions that discourage outside investors from financing firms come from the inability of outside investors to prevent firms from misusing funds (e.g., taking on excessive risk after placing a large debt issue). For investment bankers to be successful in marketing securities, they must be able to convince outside investors that they possess and accurately communicate information about firms ex ante, and the value of the securities sold will be enhanced if bankers can limit opportunistic behavior by firms ex post.

An important tradition in American corporate finance emerged as a response to these concerns—the presence of a powerful financier on the board of directors of a corporation seeking funding through an investment banking syndicate. This became a prevalent practice during the last two decades of the nineteenth century. Indeed, the rise of "financial capitalism"—as this practice came to be known—has its American origins with the railroad financings of the 1870s and '80s.

Investment Banking and Corporate Finance
Prior to World War I

The rise of the modern industrial corporation during the last quarter of the nineteenth century encouraged this type of affiliation between bankers and companies to make the rapid industrial growth of that period feasible. Spectacular growth of "mass production" with "mass distribution" took place during the 1890s and the first decade of the twentieth century. This process required huge outlays of capital—more than any single lender could command or risk. The challenge to financing such growth on such a large scale was to find a means to intermediate between creditworthy firms and a large number of uninformed suppliers of funds—to design an effective mechanism to screen, monitor, and control large-scale users of funds raised in centralized capital markets.

The growth of financial capitalism reflected other changes in the economy in addition to the growth of new large-scale industries. Three other influences were particularly important, and operated largely through the incentives that they created for developing means of restructuring existing financial claims on existing real assets, rather than creating new claims to finance new assets. These include changes in law—especially bankruptcy law—that promoted innovations in financial instruments (preferred stock issues) and encouraged the restructuring of corporate balance sheets; episodes of macroeconomic financial distress that encouraged corporate restructurings and consolidations; and the incentives for consolidation created by the Sherman Antitrust Act of 1890.[35] These three influences not only created increased demand for securities marketing by investment banks; they increased the need for involvement of investment bankers in corporate decision making.

For most of the nineteenth century the United States lacked a comprehensive law on bankruptcy. The frequent episodes of financial distress that resulted in a large number of railroad failures had not influenced policy makers enough to motivate the formation of a bankruptcy law until 1898. The process of equity receivership underwent constant change in response to ongoing legal innovations in the bankruptcy process. Revisions in the nineteenth-century legal process included (1) the right of receivers to issue claims with a seniority level higher than the prior senior claimants; (2) the right of courts to secure the claims of unsecured debtholders; and (3) the imposition of "fees" on stakeholders as a method of raising funds to complete the reorganization.

Along with these legal innovations in the bankruptcy process, new methods of financial reorganization were being introduced during this period. These methods included the more frequent use of preferred stock, the collection of assessments to raise cash during reorganizations, and the use of voting trusts. These developments occurred partly as a response to the recurring financial problems from which most corporations were suffering. Preferred stock, for example, was more frequently used during the reorganizations of the 1890s, as bond financing and floating debt used during previous organizations only resulted in an increased chance of default. After the unsuccessful reorganizations of the 1870s, railroad financiers and investors experimented with different, innovative methods of reorganization designed to reestablish the financial health of their troubled companies. The Wabash experience of the 1880s served as a successful model of reorganization for other firms.[36]

Extensive use of the voting trust along with the more widespread use of preferred stock as a tool for raising capital in external markets increased the demand for banker representation on the boards of directors of client corporations. The complexity of these financial innovations, and the use of (riskier) preferred stock rather than simple debt magnified the importance of investment bankers as advisers and controllers of corporate decision making.

Clearly, episodes of financial distress furthered the movement toward investment banker involvement in corporate management by encouraging the legal innovations of the late nineteenth century and the financial innovations that responded to them. Experiences with distress also taught firms the potential advantages of maintaining an ongoing relationship with an investment banking firm as a form of insurance against the costs of future financial distress. The investment banker's role in this respect depended on his ability to buy and sell large amounts of securities in a short period of time. In times of precarious financial conditions such as the panics of 1861, 1873, and 1893, prestigious investment banking firms were very much in demand for representation and financial advice. During economic downturns, when the rate of railroad and commercial failures increased, reorganizations and necessary mergers were more easily performed by a financial expert who was "inside" the corporation.

The Sherman Antitrust Act of 1890 also added to the demand for investment bank involvement in corporate management. The Sherman Act did not explicitly prohibit the formation of holding companies. Banker representation facilitated the circumventing of new regulations by creating legal holding companies to replace the now illegal trusts. Thus the Sherman Antitrust Act encouraged the biggest merger movement in U.S. history. Perhaps as much as one-half of U.S. manufacturing capacity took part in the merger during the years 1898–1902.[37] The U.S. Steel merger, orchestrated by J. P. Morgan and Company was by far the largest of these in capitalization.

More formal empirical analysis of financial capitalism confirms its importance in facilitating the financing of industry. Recent studies have shown that maintaining a close relationship with a major investment banking house was associated with improved corporate performance and greater access to external finance. DeLong (1991) finds that the performance of firms affiliated with Morgan was higher than that of nonaffiliated firms, and Ramirez (1995) finds that Morgan firms did not display the excessive cash-flow sensitivity of investment found in other firms.

Although financial capitalism was evolving during the last two decades of the nineteenth century and the first decade of the twentieth, it never developed into universal banking in the German sense, nor the zaibatsu system that existed in Japan prior to World War II. Despite its successes, in comparison to the German universal banking system the American system entailed high costs of external finance for all corporate borrowers, and especially high costs for immature firms, which lacked access to the high-flying financial capitalism of Morgan and his counterparts.

Calomiris (1995) argues that the relatively high costs of American corporate finance are visible in a number of comparisons between German and American corporations. In particular, the high fees for issuing common stock in the United States and the paucity of stock issues (especially of common stock) by American firms indicate that information and control problems were better solved by German capital markets. German firms issued far more public equity than debt, most of which was in the form of new common stock issues. American firms issued very little common stock on the public market prior to World War I. The commissions on common stock flotations charged by German universal banks were roughly 4 percent and did not significantly vary by the size of the firm or the size of the issue. In the United States, commissions averaged above 20 percent, and the costs were prohibitive for any but the largest firms.

The paucity of equity issues and the high commissions charged on junior instruments (common stock issues) in the United States reflected the difficulty of credibly communicating information about firms and controlling corporate behavior. J. P. Morgan was willing to make a large investment in information about and control over its established industrial clients. But U.S. industry in large measure was left behind by the capital markets. In Germany the situation was different. Even small firms and firms in growing industries could gain access to capital markets, typically through stock issues. The key difference between the German and American financial systems was that German universal banks could take deposits, lend, underwrite securities, place issues, and manage portfolios all within the same financial institution, and that institution could operate throughout Germany. Because German banks could branch freely, they were able to use the same network of offices for all these functions. This allowed them to "internalize" the costs and benefits of monitoring and controlling their industrial clients. Before underwriting a security, they had lent to, and developed a relationship with, the issuing firm for some time. After underwriting the issue, they placed it internally with their own trust customers. After placing an equity issue, the bank retained control over the votes of the shareholders, which concentrated control in the bank.[38]

German banks thus had preexisting knowledge at the time of the underwriting that helped to reduce information costs. More important, the bank's function as a portfolio manager gave it a way to control the subsequent behavior of the firm, and a continuing incentive to monitor and signal the quality of its industrial clients honestly (since it competed with other banks for the privilege of managing customers' portfolios).

Another indicator of the high relative cost of finance in the United States is the choice of factors of production. The U.S. tendency to avoid fixed capital in the production process has been widely discussed by economic historians, and linked to the high cost of external finance. Firms facing high external finance costs may rely more on liquid assets in the production process (materials) because liquid assets are easy to sell during a cash crunch, and they command better terms as collateral for bank loans. Historical analysis of the U.S. production process has stressed the reliance placed by the United States on substitutes for capital in the production process, especially natural resources. The reliance on substitutes for fixed capital increased during the late nineteenth and early twentieth centuries. By 1928, resource intensity of exports was 50 percent higher than its 1879 level.[39]

The historical literature on U.S. factor choice shows that the reliance on resources was not exogenously determined. America's natural resource base is not among the richest in the world. Rather, the American reliance on natural resources, the development of production techniques that were resource-intensive, and the emergence of high-throughput production and distribution processes were induced in part by the high cost of raising capital.

Studies of variation in asset structures across firms using post–World War II data are also consistent with this argument. These studies find that high fixed capital intensivity is associated with lower-cost access to external finance (as measured either by cross-sectional differences in underwriting costs or by differences in access to bond and commercial paper markets).[40]

Changes in Financial Capitalism
During the Interwar Era

The initial failure of universal banking in the United States, we have argued, was attributable to constraints on the ability of commercial banks to branch, since this limited any intermediary's ability to lend to (much less underwrite for) large-scale firms on a national scale. But those initial barriers were not the only limitations that would be imposed on the relationships of financial capitalism. In the wake of populist congressional "investigations," first in 1912, later in 1932, Congress acted to circumscribe banking powers and limit financial capitalism. The second intervention, in 1933, was the more important. The early legislation had little effect, and other trends began to favor the development of "incipient" universal banking in the 1920s—notably, the wave of deregulation of bank consolidation and branching during the 1920s. The restrictions imposed by the Banking Act of 1933 and the revival of protection for unit banks brought an end to these experiments.

During the first decade of the twentieth century there was a growing public perception that financial capitalism was growing too concentrated and that a "Money Trust" had been formed among the few and powerful investment banking houses during the period. This negative view of financial capitalism was magnified by the panics of 1902 and 1907. This concern became the source of a bitter political debate that culminated in a congressional investigation of the so-called Money Trust. Progressives such as Arsene Pujo, a Louisiana representative who chaired the Money Trust investigation, together with Samuel Untermyer (chief counsel of the committee), and Louis D. Brandeis, a very influential and ambitious Boston lawyer (who would later become a Supreme Court justice) questioned the influence and power that these few investment banking houses had over a large sector of the economy. The committee cross-examined members of the largest investment banking houses and their client firms during the hearings. Although they never accomplished it, their intention was to show the existence of trusts that controlled a substantial share of capital and abused their strategic position.

Mark Roe (see chapter 4 in this volume) points out that U.S. regulation evolved largely in response to public perceptions of who or what was wrong in the existing system. The Pujo investigation of 1912 and the enactment of the Clayton Act of 1914 were clearly products of this public outcry. Public sentiments had been stirred up after the Panic of 1907 and were further highlighted when Brandeis held J. P. Morgan and Charles Mellen (CEO of the New York, New Haven, and Hartford Railroad) responsible for the deteriorated financial condition of the railroad. "The evils of monopoly" caused the New Haven to go into receivership in 1914, according to Brandeis's *Other Peoples' Money*.

But the momentum of legislation from the Progressive Era waned substantially after 1914 due to the involvement of investment banks in the war effort. The perception changed in favor of Wall Street once again, as it came to be viewed as a major contributor to the financing of the Allies' war expenditures. During this period the role of the investment and commercial bankers shifted from financing domestic corporations to financing domestic and foreign governments. In the wake of these changes, there was little effort to enforce and strengthen the Clayton Act's weak limitations on bank involvement in boards of directors.

Two mutually reinforcing developments during the 1920s changed the menu of feasible relationships between financiers and corporations, and led to "incipient" universal banking. First, partly as a consequence of how the war was financed, the American public had increased its appetite for financial securities. Even small, unsophisticated investors wanted to partake in the securities boom of the 1920s. Second, largely in response to a wave of bank failures (produced by agricultural income declines after World War I), many states liberalized their regulations on bank branching and consolidation. From 1920 to 1929, nearly four thousand banks were absorbed by merger. The number of bank offices operated by branching banks rose from 1,811 to 4,117.[41]

This meant a substantial increase in the scale and geographic range of many U.S. banks. It also meant that many commercial banks were becoming large enough to reap the advantages of scope from becoming universal banks. Commercial banks were not permitted to sell or own stock directly but could do so through wholly owned affiliates that effectively operated as organs of the bank. The first three investment affiliates of national banks were organized between 1908 and 1917, and served as models for the growth of affiliates in the 1920s. By 1929, 591 banks operated affiliates.[42]

In 1929, securities market optimism was suddenly shattered. The stock market crash and the subsequent Great Depression left a bitter taste with the public, and once again, the negative sentiments against the financial community had been awakened. The investment and commercial banking industry had few political defenders in Washington. Soon another congressional investigation was initiated, this time under the chairmanship of Ferdinand Pecora. This investigation intended to show that rampant abuses, fraud, and conflict of interest had resulted in the systematic fooling of securities investors.

These critics argued for the end of bank affiliates because they believed that preexisting (senior) debt obligations of issuing firms, if held by the bank managing a new issue, created a conflict of interest. It was argued that banks had an incentive to mislead investors when selling junior securities of the firm because doing so would increase the value of existing bank-held debts of issuing firms. Other opponents to affiliates based their opposition on the supposed connection between the stock market collapse and subsequent bank failures. The investigation was a biased search for embarrassing examples, not a scientific analysis of the operation of bankers and investment bankers.[43]

These hearings, unlike their Progressive Era predecessor, did culminate in far-reaching regulations in the financial community. These included the Securities Acts of 1933 and 1934 (which required complete disclosure of financial information) and the (Glass-Steagall) Banking Act of 1933 (which separated commercial banking activities from investment banking, created federal deposit insurance, and imposed Regulation Q ceilings on bank deposits).[44]

From the standpoint of incipient universal banking, these changes meant the end of a brief experiment. That was clearly the intent of Congress. The Banking Act of 1933 was a compromise among various positions, and there were great differences between Glass's and Steagall's regulatory goals. The compromise they reached was intended to reverse the demise of small banks and to remove commercial banks from their connections to securities markets. Deposit insurance (Representative Steagall's hobbyhorse) was understood to be a mandated subsidy from large banks to small banks, and was viewed as an alternative to expanding branching and consolidation as a means to stabilize the banking system. The separation of commercial and investment banking followed from Glass's view that the stock market had been the ruin of the banking system. Glass pushed for Regulation Q as a further means to insulate banks from securities markets. He argued that removing interest on deposits would discourage banks from reserve pyramiding in New York, and thereby break the link between the banking system and the call loan market for brokers and dealers on Wall Street.

It is ironic how this "new" negative perception in Washington contrasts with the one prevalent during the Progressive Era. During the Pujo investigations, Brandeis focused on the oligopolistic behavior of the financial community as the main source of evil that plagued the industry. Indeed, the concept of a "Money Trust" was specifically derived from the public perception that the financial industry was too concentrated, and thus easily controllable by a few influential financiers. The Pecora investigation of the 1930s, by contrast, indirectly highlighted more the competitive scenario of the securities industry as a direct or indirect cause of the "evils" that beset the market during the late 1920s. Typical accusations alleged that bank affiliates were unloading securities of poor quality onto the innocent public largely through "misleading" advertisements. But these advertisements were a symbol of the increased competition and entry that had taken place in the 1920s.

The principal accusations of the Pecora hearings have been discredited by recent research. Benston (1989) criticizes the methods of the hearings and finds no evidence to support their "findings." White (1986) finds that banks that operated affiliates had lower failure propensities than other banks, and traces this fact to the income diversification that nonbank activities offered. Kroszner and Rajan (1994) argue that the alleged conflicts of interest that supposedly led bank-affiliated investment bankers to cheat their clients did not exist. They show that the securities promoted by commercial bank affiliates were of comparable quality to those underwritten and sponsored by investment banking houses. Bank affiliates likely avoided conflicts of interest, in part, by themselves purchasing sufficient quantities of junior issues for sufficient lengths of time to quell any suspicions of an incentive to overprice issues. For example, Harris Bank and Trust in Chicago prided itself on its willingness to purchase shares that it underwrote, and incorporated that fact into its motto ("we sell and hold"). Furthermore, reputational considerations discourage underwriters from overpricing securities. Such behavior would be punished by less demand for purchases in the future, and by the loss of trust accounts of securities purchasers who suffered loss on the transaction.

Ramirez and DeLong (1994) argue that New Deal reforms undermined beneficial relationships between firms and their bankers. Benefits to corporations from being affiliated to a bank prior to the banking reforms of the New Deal were reflected in a higher market value of affiliated firms. After the New Deal reforms, bank-firm relationships did not have any significant effect on firms' market values. From this standpoint, the enactment of the New Deal reforms imposed significant financing costs on corporations.

What is the mechanism behind Ramirez and DeLong's findings? New Deal reforms limited the relationship between financial intermediaries and corporations. By separating investment banking from commercial banking, the Glass-Steagall Act reduced the influence that both commercial and investment banks had over client corporations. For commercial banks this was clearly the case since now they were not allowed to own corporate stocks as assets. It also reduced the influence of investment banks since the contacts and financial resources that connected them to the commercial banks had been eliminated. Investment bankers had to rely solely on their ability to search for individual clients to purchase securities, and not on the financial backing of commercial banks that stood ready to purchase blocks of securities. For the client corporation, it indirectly increased the cost of raising funds in external markets. To the extent that financiers were representing shareholders, the separation of ownership and control over the resources of the corporation had become more acute (see Berle and Means, 1932).

There is also indirect evidence supporting the claim that the cost of raising funds in public financial markets increased in the aftermath of New Deal financial reforms. Private placements (private debt issues held by life insurance companies) increased dramatically after the 1930s. Other factors may have contributed to the long-term growth of private placements during the late 1940s and '50s, but the timing of the early growth spurt in the late 1930s and early 1940s supports the notion that private placements were favored by the rising cost of issuing public securities.[45]

The financial devastation of the Great Depression (and the restrictive financial regulations that followed) increased the cost of corporate finance and reduced the relative importance of finance from sources other than retained earnings.[46] Flow-of-funds data indicate that the corporate sector as a whole obtained more than 100 percent of its financing from retained earnings. There was a net repayment of debt claims and virtually no stock issues during this period. Over the period 1940–1945, retained earnings still accounted for 80 percent of corporate finance sources. For periods of similar length prior to and after the Great Depression, internal funds typically provided between one-half and two-thirds of funding.[47]

To the extent that sources other than earnings were forthcoming in the late 1930s and '40s, they increasingly took the form of private placements. From 1934 to 1937, private placements accounted for 12 percent of a small total of corporate offerings. By 1951, private placements accounted for 44 percent of all corporate offerings, 58 percent of all debt issues, and 82 percent of all debt issues of manufacturing firms. From the beginning, life insurance companies accounted for the overwhelming majority of these purchases (93 percent in 1947, 83 percent in 1950) with the remainder held largely by banks (2.7 percent in 1947, 12.1 percent in 1950). For the period 1990–1992, life insurance companies and banks (broadly defined) maintained respective shares of 83 and 11 percent of the private placement market.[48]

Bank loans also increased in importance in the 1940s and '50s. Indeed, the growth in private placements during the 1940s was matched by growth in commercial bank lending to corporations. From 1939 to 1952, life insurance company outstanding holdings of corporate debt rose from $10.4 billion to $34.7 billion. From 1939 to 1952, total outstanding loans from operating commercial banks to nonfinancial corporations increased from

$6.2 billion to $21.9 billion. Over that same period, bank holdings of bonds and notes rose little by comparison—from $3.0 billion to $3.4 billion. Over this period, during which bank and insurance company holdings of corporate debt tripled, producer prices roughly doubled; thus real growth in inside debt was significant.[49]

Regressive Changes in Financing Relationships
After the 1930s

Although inside debt was the most active margin of external finance during the 1940s, the growth of inside debt from the 1930s to the 1950s did not provide an adequate substitute for predepression financial relationships under "incipient" universal banking, as indicated by Ramirez and DeLong's (1994) evidence on the weakening of banking relationships after 1933. Why were private placements and bank debt inadequate substitutes for earlier financial arrangements? There are two (closely related) potential explanations—inside debt was in the form of the most senior obligations of corporations, and inside debt remained small relative to assets. These explanations are related because debt seniority is enhanced when senior debt remains small relative to total assets. The information and control requirements of relationships that entail the supply of small quantities of senior debt are very limited. Banks and insurance companies are able to protect themselves by restricting debt ratios, holding secured (collateralized) debt, and designing and enforcing financial and behavioral covenants defined in ways that are relatively easy to observe.

Those financial relationships, however, will not necessarily guarantee that management will be effectively disciplined to avoid conflicts of interest between managers and stockholders. As Michael Jensen (1986) has stressed, absent large quantities of debt (which force managers to maximize operating profits to avoid financial distress), managers will be able to use the "free cash flow" of firms at the expense of stockholders. Banks and insurance companies holding small amounts of corporate debt (relative to assets) are, therefore, no substitute for universal banks, which are both junior and senior stakeholders in the firm, and which control a significant share of the voting power of the stockholders.

Thus a lack of discipline over managers was especially likely in the 1940s and '50s—after the collapse of "incipient" universal banking and during an era of high cash flow and low debt. The 1940s and '50s were a time of unusually low debt ratios when compared with earlier or later periods. For example, data on the ratio of the market value of corporate debt to the market value of corporate assets indicate debt-to-asset ratios during the 1940s and '50s of roughly 15 percent. Another measure, based on different estimates, shows an average ratio of 18 percent for the 1950s. Estimates for the same measure average 32 percent for four selected years between 1900 and 1929. Leverage rose significantly beginning in the 1960s and reached ratios in the 25 to 40 percent range for most of the 1970s and '80s.[50] The 1940s and '50s were a time of unusually low debt ratios historically, and senior, inside debt relationships were an imperfect substitute for the richer corporate finance relationships of the predepression era.[51]

To summarize, in the immediate postwar period, the continuing growth of the size of corporations and the lack of any external concentration of power to control corporate decision-making weakened the efficiency of capital market allocations and increased the costs of corporate finance. The concentration of power over the resources of the corporation had shifted somewhat from the hands of owners (and their financier agents) to those of management.

Institutional Investors and the
New Financial Capitalism

The relative importance of retained earnings and senior inside debt finance during the 1940s and '50s was a short-lived phenomenon.[52] Private placements as a percentage of securities offerings peaked in the mid-1960s. The resurgence in public offerings of bonds and stocks, beginning in the 1950s, reduced the share of private placements to only 14 percent of total securities issues by 1970.[53] That trend accelerated in the early 1970s, and continues into the present, with dramatic growth over the 1980s and '90s in public issues of debt and equity, and a relative decline in the share of inside debt relative to total financing sources. What caused this resurgence of public debt and equity issuance?

The boom in equity issues, beginning in the 1960s, was so dramatic that in 1971 the Securities and Exchange Commission published an enormous multivolume study and Congress held hearings examining these changes. That study concluded that, in the market for new common stock issues, institutional investors (pensions, mutuals, and trusts) had changed the way equity issues were sold.[54] By acting as purchasers of large amounts of stock, particularly in unseasoned companies, they reduced the marketing costs normally associated with placing such stock. The Securities and Exchange Commission found that institutional investors accounted for 24 percent of all purchases of 1,684 initial public offerings (IPOs) of common stock from January 1967 to March 1970. Despite enormous short-term profits that some investors realized from rapid sales of initially underpriced IPOs, most institutional investors bought stocks in the primary market to hold as long-term investments.[55] Seventy percent of institutional IPO purchases remained unsold after twelve weeks. Institutional investors did not discriminate in their purchasing according to the size of the issuer, but did tend to deal only with the largest underwriters.[56]

Involvement by institutional investors has been an important contributor to the decline in the cost of public issues of equity after the 1950s. As one study argued, "These institutions, which first sparked the cult of common stocks, later attracted public attention to 'growth' stocks and created the fashion for instant performance. Innovative and inventive, institutional money managers have ventured into areas where older and more prudent investment men feared to tread, *taking positions in the stocks of unseasoned companies*, setting up hedge funds, devising new types of securities" (emphasis added).[57] Part of the Securities and Exchange Commission's (1971) study focuses on the impact of institutional investors on corporate issuers. It emphasizes that, by selling in block to institutional buyers of primary public common stock offerings, investment bankers could economize on the costs of marketing securities. It was easier for underwriters to credibly communicate the characteristics of issuers to a few block buyers, especially if those block buyers were institutional investors with large trust accounts managed by New York banks. Additionally, the concentration of stockholdings of unseasoned firms may have facilitated control over management, and thus reduced the potential risk of stock purchases and the need for information about the firm at the time of the offering.

The Securities and Exchange Commission argued that the benefits of institutional purchasing for reducing issue costs on public equity exceeded the direct consequences of placing shares in the hands of institutional investors. The participation of institutional buyers in an offering also made it easier to sell the remainder of the offering to individual investors:

> Retail members of the syndicate have been known to advise their customers in advance of the offering that institutions have indicated their intent to buy the issue. . . . While this knowledge of institutional interest may increase the public's appetite for any stock, the effect is greater for small, less established issuers than for large established issuers and still more so for first offerings of such small companies . . . The possible public impression that institutions, with their purported research capabilities and sophistication, would not allow themselves to be bilked helps explain individual investors' attitudes toward institutional interest. The result, then, of supposed or revealed institutional interest in an offering is to enhance retail interest as well.[58]

More formal empirical studies of issuing costs have confirmed the importance of institutional investors in reducing costs, and have shown that small, unseasoned issuers were among the largest beneficiaries. Mendelson (1967) and Calomiris and Raff (1994) argue that the costs of public common stock issues (measured by underwriting commissions, or commissions plus expenses) fell dramatically from 1950 to 1970, and that this decline was especially pronounced for small, relatively unseasoned firms (those for which information problems and marketing costs were greatest). These authors relate the decline in the costs of public issues to the role of institutional investors making block purchases of stock, which reduced costs of information and control in the market for public securities.[59]

The growth of pension funds' and mutual funds' holdings of equity in the late 1950s and '60s was dramatic. In 1946, investment companies (mutual funds) and private pension funds held 2.0 percent and 0.8 percent respective shares of corporate equities. By 1970, those shares had risen to 5.3 and 7.8 percent, respectively. By 1980, private pensions held 10.4 percent of corporate equity, while investment companies held 4.6 percent. The growth of equity holdings by pension funds reflected more than the 17-fold growth in total assets of these intermediaries from 1950 to 1971. Private pension funds' holdings of common stock grew from 12 percent of their total assets in 1951 to 68 percent in 1971.[60]

Did these intermediaries arise in response to high corporate finance cost, or for other reasons? The answer seems to be the latter, but their continuing growth, in part, reflected their unique abilities and incentives to invest in information and control corporate performance. The principal sources of early growth in pension funds were the wage controls of World War II (which favored the use of nonwage compensation for employees) and the tax exemptions enjoyed by pensions, which became increasingly valuable during the 1960s.

Institutional investors were very active in the venture capital market as well. In addition to their $1.4 billion in public IPO purchases during the period 1967–1970, institutional investors purchased $3.5 billion of nonpublicly traded "restricted" securities (venture capital investments in equity or debt with equity features), which mainly benefited small, young firms.[61]

Venture capitalists provide a combination of discipline and funding for a class of firms very different from those affiliated with Morgan in the pre–World War I era (which were among the largest and best-seasoned credit risks in the economy). Venture capitalists finance unseasoned firms that lack access to public markets and play an important role in managing the financial arrangements of these firms.

Venture capital funds, which became especially popular in the 1970s, operate as two-tiered sets of relationships with spillover effects over the firm life cycle. Large institutional investors hold shares of the fund, which invests in many firms. The venture capitalist also retains a stake in the fund. Large institutional investors (especially private pension funds) learn about the firms being financed by the venture capital fund through their participation in the fund. Those same institutional investors often participate in the initial public offerings of the firms that they helped finance earlier.

Government policy has had important influences on the venture capital market, and on the involvement of institutional investors and commercial banks in venture capital funds. The history of modern American venture capitalism begins with the formation in 1946 of the American Research and Development Corporation. The investment of this firm in Digital Equipment Company during the late 1950s remains one of the great success stories of venture capitalism. Regulatory changes that favored limited commercial bank entry into equity funds to finance small businesses (under the Small Business Investment Company Act of 1958) provided an early impetus for expansion. In 1971 the Bank Holding Company Act further relaxed restrictions on bank entry into venture capital, and there was a significant influx of bank capital into venture capital affiliates. Pension companies had initially been slow to involve themselves in venture capital funds. Trustees faced the threat of personal liability for "imprudent" activities (which seemed to include venture capital investments). Reforms to the Employee Retirement Income Security Act (ERISA) in the late 1970s, however, redefined the "prudent man rule" to emphasize overall portfolio diversification rather than individual investments, and this encouraged substantial entry during the 1970s (with pensions typically holding 5 percent of their assets in venture funds).[62]

The growth of new institutional investors after the 1960s brought with it a new scope to financial relationships—one very reminiscent of predepression financial capitalism. A multitiered intermediation arrangement involving institutional investors, trust bankers, venture capitalists, large commercial banks, and investment bank underwriters became involved in long-term relationships among themselves, and with corporations in need of funds. While these arrangements are still a far cry from universal banking, they share some important advantages. The scale of funding sources is large relative to the needs of firms (which economizes on the costs of placement), there is often continuity in the relationships between firms and intermediaries over time, and intermediaries are junior as well as senior claimants of the firm (which provides incentives and means for intermediaries to monitor and control corporations).

Other Developments in Corporate Finance
and Control Since the 1960s

The growth of institutional investors and of venture capitalists are two important institutional developments that have helped reduce financing costs associated with asymmetrical information problems and potential conflicts between managers and shareholders. Other market-driven mechanisms that have become increasingly important since the 1960s include increased product market competition; the use of takeovers as a mechanism for corporate control; increased reliance on debt finance; and incentive-based management compensation packages.

The first of these mechanisms, product market competition, helps to impose discipline on managerial behavior by exposing managerial errors more quickly and making financial distress a more likely outcome of managerial errors. A seemingly unimportant managerial mistake can have catastrophic consequences for a firm in a highly competitive industry. For example, even a company with an efficient production process may lose substantial market share to its competitors due to a marketing error.[63] Naturally, companies under poor management are much more likely to lose out to their competitors.

Product market competition has become increasingly important during the last twenty years, partly as a result of the heightened foreign competition facing American enterprises. During the last three decades many nations, notably Japan and other Asian countries, have improved their production processes and increased their productivity levels dramatically. Accompanying this trend was the steady reduction of tariff barriers in the United States and in other industrialized countries.

It is hard to measure the extent to which foreign competition has improved managerial discipline. Nevertheless, casual empiricism suggests that it has been substantial, especially when one considers the structural changes that have taken place in American corporations in recent years. "Reengineering," "downsizing," and "restructuring" are all part of the transformation companies have experienced recently as a response to the challenge to become more competitive in the world market. The internal organization that seemed to have served the American company well forty or fifty years ago is now seen as an inefficient system that creates layers of unnecessary managerial staff.

While competition helps to expose managerial waste and increases the chance that inefficiency will translate into financial failure, takeovers improve stockholders' abilities to discipline wasteful managers without depending on competition-induced financial distress.[64] If the market perceives that a company is undervalued because of poor managerial talent, a successful takeover can replace management and increase the market value of the targeted firm. Even the management of a company that is not taken over is affected by the new takeover technology; the threat of a takeover itself reduces managerial incentives to invest company resources in value-reducing ways.[65]

Have takeovers been beneficial to society as a whole (including shareholders and employees of the targeted firm and those of bidding firms), or have they only benefited shareholders of targeted firms at the expense of other groups? Evidence indicates that takeovers have brought net economic gains. Michael Jensen estimates that the net gain to society from the takeover activity during the 1977–1986 period has been in the neighborhood of four hundred billion dollars (1986 dollars).[66] The gains are highest when a well-managed firm makes a bid for a poorly managed one. By contrast, they are lowest (even negative) when a poorly managed firm intends to take over a well-managed one.[67]

Although takeovers in general are motivated by one of the world's great constants—the search for profit—the wave that came in the 1980s seems to have been facilitated by the relaxation of restrictions on mergers that antitrust regulators would have opposed in earlier periods. In fact, industries that experienced a great deal of deregulation, such as transportation, gas and oil, and financial services, also experienced an increase in the level of merger activity during the 1980s.[68]

Jensen (1986) argues that actual or potential takeovers can reduce managerial incentive problems. For example, if managers were motivated by the objective of maximizing the value of their firms, then any cash flow left over after all positive net present value projects have been financed should be distributed in the form of dividends or stock buybacks to shareholders. The "free cash flow problem" arises because managers who have discretion over these funds may instead have an incentive to use "excess funds" to finance the acquisitions of other businesses, including those producing different products or operating in different industries.[69] Even if doing so reduces the value of the firm, increasing firm size and reducing firm risk may increase managers' perquisites and reduce the risk of firm failure (i.e., unemployment of the manager). In a recent study Lang and Stulz (1994) report evidence for the 1970s and '80s indicating that the market places a higher value on single-industry firms than on conglomerates with diversified portfolios of businesses. In other words, a firm that pursues a diversification strategy tends to be penalized in financial markets with a reduced market value. This evidence suggests that conglomerate acquisitions may serve the interests of managers at the expense of stockholders.

It follows that a takeover can add economic value by taking control of an inefficient, diversified firm away from its management, and selling its divisions as independent businesses. Because creating a conglomerate is a reversible corporate strategy, takeovers provide a means to improve efficiency, which may make takeover threats sufficient to discourage some managers from pursuing wasteful strategies in the first place.[70]

As mentioned earlier, one well-documented trend of the past thirty years has been the rise of corporate debt relative to equity.[71] There are many reasons why companies might find debt issuance appealing. Among them, debt financing carries attractive tax advantages over equity financing.[72] Others have emphasized the advantages of debt as a disciplinary device. By taking on debt, managers increase their debt service relative to operating profits, and thereby constrain themselves to maximize profits and avoid abusing "free cash flow" (using cash flows to finance endeavors that give the manager a personal benefit but do not increase the value of the firm). From this perspective the rise in corporate leverage may have been induced, in part, to reverse the post-1930s trend toward managerial autonomy and away from supervision and control by shareholders.

Gertler and Hubbard (1990) argue that tax advantages have been the more important motivation behind the run-up in corporate debt. They point to offsetting costs of debt that may outweigh the disciplinary advantages stressed by Jensen. Debt increases the potential for financial distress because the firm's promised payments are not indexed to the state of the economy. Furthermore, Gertler and Hubbard argue that the disciplinary advantages of debt could be achieved, and much of its financial distress costs eliminated, by choosing an alternative contracting structure that shares features of both debt and equity and indexes firms' payments to observable macroeconomic state variables.

Gertler and Hubbard (1990) may be right to attribute most of the run-up of debt to tax considerations, and to emphasize the costs of financial distress wrought by debt financing.[73] Nevertheless, whether or not the debt run-up was designed as a disciplinary device, greater corporate discipline has been a by-product of higher leverage. It is an open question whether those benefits outweigh the other corporate finance costs of higher leverage, which include physical costs of financial distress, forgone investments that result from financial distress, and negative spillovers in financial markets as intermediaries become more concerned about the fragility of the financial system, and thereby apprehensive about the issuance of new debt.

The design of the management compensation contract is another device the market uses to alleviate the conflict of interest between managers and shareholders. To the extent that these contracts include incentives to induce managers to undertake actions in the interest of shareholders, they can reduce the need for monitoring and control of managers by stockholders. By tying the financial remuneration of senior management (the CEO, for example) to a measure of company performance (such as accounting earnings or the market value of the firm), the CEO's stake in the corporation is more directly related to that of shareholders.

Pay-for-performance contracts can take many different forms and may differ in the types of incentives they offer. These incentives include performance-based bonuses and salary increases, and stock options. Often implicit in such contracts is the possibility of removal from a senior position due to poor performance. In a recent study Jensen and Murphy (1990) estimate the sensitivity of managerial incentives to shareholder wealth (a variable directly proportional to the market value of the firm) and conclude that the total CEO compensation package changes by $3.25 for every $1,000 change in shareholder wealth. This sensitivity measure is significantly lower for larger firms ($1.85 per $1,000 for the top half of their sample versus $8.05 per $1,000 for the bottom half).

The lower estimated sensitivity for larger firms could be justified in theory as the result of managerial risk aversion—especially if executive compensation (and wealth) is not strictly proportional to firm size. As the size of the firm becomes larger, maintaining the same sensitivity of managerial earnings to firm earnings requires greater variation in managerial earnings. Another explanation for Jensen and Murphy's finding might be that monitoring costs are not important enough to render pay-for-performance contracts necessary. A third possibility is that managers of large firms are more insulated from stockholder discipline, and thus are able to avoid making their salaries as sensitive to firm performance. Finally, Jensen and Murphy argue that some of the low sensitivity of managerial compensation to performance reflects other external factors. Political and regulatory issues inside and outside the corporation seem to play an important role in the construction of CEO compensations.

In summary, market-driven mechanisms that grew in importance after the 1960s have mitigated asymmetrical information problems and shareholder-management conflicts to some extent. In our view, however, such devices are imperfect substitutes for properly structured universal banking relationships. First, although product market competition can expose managerial incompetence or waste, and may punish inefficiency by making financial distress a more likely outcome, this is an indirect and costly means of discipline. This mechanism imposes costs not only on the management but also on other constituents of the corporation, including its stockholders, employees, and creditors. Frequent restructuring and reorganization in response to product market conditions is socially costly.

As for takeovers, it is important to understand that they are effective only to the extent that management behavior is observable. The trouble is that management actions and decision making may be observable to outsiders only dimly and only after the fact. If value-reducing actions are reversible, such as in the case of diversification mergers, a takeover might undo them successfully. However, if they are not, all that a takeover can do is prevent continuing losses from those actions. In addition, it is important to consider the social readjustment costs of a takeover, since they might also be expensive for the employees and the community, and can impose large transaction costs on shareholders. Being able to undo investments that should never have been undertaken is not as beneficial as being able to prevent value-reducing investments from being undertaken in the first place—one of the potential advantages of a universal banking relationship.

Neither is debt an effective substitute for the benefits provided by universal banking. As discussed earlier, debt might alleviate the free cash flow problem, but it creates other problems. In particular, it increases the probability and the costs of bankruptcy.

Pay-for-performance as a device to influence managerial incentives would seem to be less wasteful than product market competition, takeovers, or high leverage to improve managerial behavior. The trouble is that the available evidence indicates that there are practical limits to the extent to which pay-for-performance schemes can reduce the conflict between managers and shareholders. Managers are risk-averse, and this places limits on feasible incentive schemes in their compensation packages.

Most importantly, managerial compensation—like the other three market-driven mechanisms—can solve problems of managerial misbehavior but does nothing to mitigate financing costs that result from asymmetrical information between insiders and outsiders. Even if firms are perfectly controlled by stockholders, they will face financing costs associated with lack of information about the value of their opportunities and the potential for stockholders to act in their own self interest and contrary to the interest of their creditors. Universal banking, however, can address conflicts of interest both between managers and shareholders, and between informed shareholders and uninformed creditors or potential shareholders, and can do so without the large transaction costs, information costs, and disruption inherent in other potential mechanisms for solving those problems.

Financial Innovations and Relationships

It has become a commonplace to argue that the rapid growth in securities transactions during the 1980s, domestically and internationally, is evidence that financial relationships matter less than they used to. Such arguments usually point vaguely toward computers as the source of the new technological breakthroughs (reflected in common stock market growth in developing countries; in the surge in bank loan sales, syndications, and asset-backed securitizations in the United States; and in the growth of derivative transactions worldwide). Some would argue that innovation has made it possible to resolve information and control problems without resort to traditional relationships. We believe this view that "transactional" intermediation is replacing "relationship" intermediation in American corporate finance is flawed for several reasons.

First, one of the main indicators of the demise of relationships—the decline in domestic commercial bank holdings of corporate debt—has been misinterpreted. While it is true that foreign bank entrants and asset-backed securities significantly increased their asset market shares of corporate debt during the 1980s, for many borrowers those changes in the identities of ultimate holders of debt did not imply changes in their banking relationships. Domestic banks often originated and sold loans to foreign banks, or managed syndicated loans in which foreign banks participated. Similarly, asset-backed securitizations require origination, and often "credit enhancement." Bankers change the packaging of the credit service, but fulfill essentially familiar roles as screeners, monitors, and marketers for their client firms. Foreign bank entry into loan origination during the 1980s was largely confined to large, creditworthy firms with access to public debt markets, not to the vast majority of firms, which lack such access and which depend on continuing relationships with intermediaries to meet their financing needs economically.[74]

Computers have not single-handedly repealed the laws of economics. They have not provided any new, magical solutions to creditors' problems of monitoring and controlling the behavior of owners, or to stockholders' problems of controlling managers. Computers have facilitated the dissemination of statistical credit analysis, and thus encouraged financial innovations that allow the sharing of risk among institutions, nationally and internationally.

But they have not fundamentally changed the fact that corporate finance (for the vast majority of firms) is relationship-based.

Indeed, one could argue that new financial innovations are more rapidly propelling financial intermediaries toward universal banking. Once the fixed costs of providing multiple products are reduced, there is more room for "relationship economies of scope" to influence the structure of the financial services industry. By expanding the feasible menu of services that any intermediary can deliver, technological progress may enhance the strength of long-term relationships between clients and their intermediaries.

Universal Banking in the 1990s?

The most recent important change in corporate finance technology has come from relaxation of restrictions on bank scale and scope. Limits on branching—the single most important impediment to an efficient system of corporate finance throughout American history—have been eliminated. Banks have gained entry to nontraditional banking activities—including securities underwriting, derivatives sales, mutual fund management, and venture capital finance. As Kaufman and Mote (1990) show, most of the expansion in banking powers has followed discretionary relaxation of regulatory policy rather than legislative action, and there are still some important barriers to true universal banking. Although important political obstacles remain, the tide clearly has turned, and many academics and regulators have come out in support of removing existing barriers.[75]

Why the sudden change? As in the 1920s (the earlier period that witnessed widespread relaxation of branching and consolidation restrictions and expanded bank powers), regulators and politicians responded to a crisis. The collapse of small, rural banks brought on by the agricultural bust of the 1920s prompted a bank consolidation movement (which, in turn, encouraged the expansion of powers). Most states relaxed branching laws between 1920 and 1939 to encourage entry by banks amid widespread economic distress. In the 1980s, once again it was the collapse of many small banks and thrifts that prompted action. Between 1979 and 1990 most states significantly relaxed their internal branching laws prior to any federal action.[76]

Federal regulators—notably Allan Greenspan—were also concerned about declining profits of banks in the late 1980s and the increased competition banks faced from abroad, which was the single most important source of lost commercial and industrial lending business for domestic banks. Regulators argued that expanded powers were necessary to level the playing field between universal banks in other countries and American commercial banks. The United States followed a pattern similar to many other countries of deregulation in response to global competition in financial services.[77]

An emphasis on the relationship benefits of universal banking raises interesting issues for current regulatory reform. For example, it may be that a repeal of restrictions on equity holdings by banks (which might reduce costs of corporate governance and financial distress for bank clients) would have greater benefits for corporate finance than allowing banks to sell insurance (which receives comparatively greater attention in most of the current discussions of universal banking). Furthermore, repealing underwriting restrictions may imply greater relationship-cost savings if banks are also allowed to sell the issues they underwrite to their own customers (contrary to current regulations) and thus retain control over stock voting rights of client firms (as German banks do).

Conclusion

The history of the American financial system, and of corporate financial relationships within that system, reflects the interplay among financial frictions (information and control costs of corporate finance), government policies (bank and financial market regulations, tax policies, pension laws, bankruptcy laws), financial crises, and financial innovations. These influences together determine the "menu" of financial relationships available to corporations over time. With respect to the ability of the financial system to mitigate frictions due to problems of asymmetrical information and corporate control, the history of American institutional and regulatory change has seen moments of progress, as well as reversals. Three relatively successful cases—the antebellum New England system, incipient universal banking in the 1920s, and the "new" financial capitalism—are separated by periods that offered poorer menus of financial relationships. While over the very long run there may be a tendency for efficient financial relationships (like universal banking) to be allowed by government, over significant intervals (many decades) government interventions have stood in the way of these beneficial relationships. Thus, history has not been a process of steady or rapid convergence toward the most efficient set of relationships.

Whether recent trends toward the expansion of the scale and scope of commercial bank operations will usher in a new, lasting era of true universal banking in the United States, and its accompanying benefits for the costs of corporate finance, remains an open question. We suspect that the road ahead will be as bumpy as that which has already been traversed. The future menu of relationships is hard to predict; institutional change is path-dependent and subject to the unforecastable influences of financial crises and government policy. Despite the potential for improvement in banking regulation brought by global competition, for example, the next financial crisis—possibly a costly insolvency of a financial intermediary involved in complicated derivative transactions—could reverse much of the progress that has been made in broadening banks' involvement in nontraditional corporate finance. Just as important, government policies not directed toward financial markets or intermediaries (like tax or health care policies) may have important unforeseen consequences for corporate financing arrangements.

Notes

The authors thank Carl Kaysen and other contributors to this volume for helpful suggestions in revising this chapter.

   1. See Akerlof (1970); Stiglitz and Weiss (1981); Myers and Majluf (1984); and Calomiris and Hubbard (1990).

   2. The classic statements of these problems can be found in Jensen and Meckling (1976) and in Myers (1977).

   3. The connection between costly verification and debt is studied in Townsend (1979); Diamond (1984); and Gale and Hellwig (1985).

   4. Our definition of absconding subsumes managerial waste of "free cash flow," as discussed in the classic work by Berle and Means (1932), and emphasized recently by Jensen (1986). For a discussion of how absconding incentives may increase during times of poor performance, and the role of debt in mitigating such problems, see Calomiris and Kahn (1991).

   5. See Atack and Bateman (1994) for a discussion of regional differences in manufacturing profits historically, and Calomiris (1993a) for a review of similar regional differences in interest rates.

   6. Gilson, John, and Lang (1990) examine the factors determining successful restructurings of distressed firms, and find that bank involvement and the concentration of debt make success more likely.

   7. As we argue later, intermediaries may choose to "regulate" as an alternative to investing in information, or may lack the special skills of the entrepreneur and may impose excessively conservative rules on entrepreneurial behavior. Thus, there may be deadweight losses associated with discipline, as well as advantages.

   8. Excess sensitivity of fixed capital investment and working capital investment is measured after controlling for fundamental firm investment opportunities

using either a sales-accelerator model or a Tobin's Q model of investment. Recent contributions to this literature include Fazzari, Hubbard, and Petersen (1988); Himmelberg (1990); Whited (1992); Gilchrist and Himmelberg (1993); Himmelberg and Petersen (1994); Calomiris and Hubbard (1995); Calomiris and Himmelberg (1995); and Calomiris, Himmelberg, and Wachtel (1995).

9. In addition to a dependence on inside lenders, unseasoned credit risks tend to exhibit other related behavioral characteristics. Because of their financing constraints they tend to substitute liquid capital for fixed capital and maintain higher ratios of inventories and liquid assets to sales. This behavior allows the firms to self-insure against shortfalls of cash flow, and provides them with highly liquid collateral that can help reduce the costs of borrowing from inside lenders (Fazzari and Petersen, 1993; Calomiris and Hubbard, 1995; Calomiris, Himmelberg, and Wachtel, 1995; Calomiris and Himmelberg, 1995).

10. For empirical evidence that banks maintain close relationships with relatively "unseasoned" credit risks, and produce unique information about their creditworthiness, see James (1987); Mackie-Mason (1990); Best and Zhang (1993); Billett, Flannery, and Garfinkel (1995); and Petersen and Rajan (1994). For evidence on the characteristics of firms with access to public debt markets, see Calomiris, Himmelberg, and Wachtel (1995). For qualitative discussions of the financial "life cycle" of firms, see Butters and Lintner (1945).

A subset of the new literature on bank lending relationships has shown that not all bank relationships have the same consequences for firm financing costs. Morgan (1993) finds that the cash flow sensitivity of investment for bank borrowers is significantly reduced if borrowers are willing to accept the discipline of financial covenants (restrictions on leverage, dividend payments, and ratios of liquid to illiquid assets). Slovin, Sushka, and Polonchek (1992) find that when Continental Bank faced the threat of liquidation in 1983, the stock values of borrowers that relied on their relationship with Continental fell significantly, while those of other Continental borrowers (those with many other bank relationships, and those with access to public markets) did not react to the threat to Continental. Hoshi, Kashyap, and Scharfstein (1990a, 1990b, 1991) find that when Japanese firms are willing to become part of a *keiretsu*—which entails a very close relationship with the *keiretsu*'s main bank, including lending, stock ownership, and involvement by the bank in the board of directors of the firm—their cash-flow sensitivity of investment (controlling for opportunities) is reduced, as is the cost of financial distress (measured by investment contractions during distress episodes).

11. See Hoshi, Kashyap, and Scharfstein (1990b).

12. For a complementary perspective on the change from a bank to a nonbank financing choice, see Diamond (1991). This model emphasizes the role of banks in helping firms generate information about themselves that can be of use in moving to securities markets later. For evidence on the transfer of information from prior bank lending to securities markets, see James and Wier (1990) and Booth (1991).

Weinstein and Yafeh (1994) present evidence consistent with the notion that bank lending in close firm-bank relationships is relatively costly. They find that

Japanese "main bank" relationships entail higher interest costs than other Japanese bank loans. They use this evidence to challenge the benefits of main bank lending, but in fact their evidence is quite consistent with beneficial main bank relationships. Higher interest likely reflects greater costs of lending (more intensive monitoring and control) rather than rent extraction by banks. As Rajan (1992) shows, even if close bank relationships do give banks the power to extract quasi rents (which would show up as higher interest costs on loans), those quasi rents will be bid away at the time the bank relationship is established, if the market for relationships is competitive ex ante.

13. Theoretical models include Benveniste and Spindt (1989), Benveniste and Wilhelm (1990), and Chemmanur and Fulghieri (1994). Studies of post–World War II flotation costs include Mendelson (1967), Hansen and Torregrossa (1992), and Calomiris and Himmelberg (1995). Analyses of cross-country differences and changes in costs over time in the United States are provided in Calomiris (1995) and Calomiris and Raff (1995).

14. Rajan (1994) shows that a banker with a debt claim on a firm may have an incentive to misrepresent the firm's financial position to potential purchasers of new shares in order to raise the value of the firm's debt. So long as the banker also subscribes to a sufficient amount of the stock, however, that potential conflict of interest will not arise.

15. E.g., Gorton and Schmidt (1994) relate the size of the equity stakes of German universal banks to the performance of their corporations.

16. Network economies can be particularly important when securities must be sold to many ultimate holders. Restrictions on commercial bank branching, for example, may make universal banking infeasible. If banks are not allowed to develop nationwide networks for taking deposits, as was the case in the United States, they may find the costs of setting up a network of branches throughout the country to sell securities, manage portfolios, and make loans prohibitively high. Calomiris (1995) emphasizes the importance of network economies for explaining some of the advantages of universal banking in Germany. He finds that underwriting fees charged by German banks were much smaller than those charged in the United States. That cost difference may reflect a variety of economies of universal banking. Calomiris also finds no significant cost difference in placing large and small issues in Germany. In the United States, in contrast, the size of issues is the single most important predictor of the underwriting commission rate. Calomiris argues that the ability of universal banks to place securities internally within their network of securities purchasers explains this fact.

17. See Sheard (1989) and Hoshi, Kashyap, and Scharfstein (1990a, 1990b) for evidence of the importance of bank equity ownership in its clients (a key ingredient in the Japanese "main banking" relationship) in reducing the costs of raising funds from the bank.

18. Calomiris (1995) argues that network, information, and signaling economies can explain the low costs of equity flotation in Germany historically under universal banking.

19. Some commentators on universal banking have argued that there are disadvantages to concentrating so much power within one intermediary or a small set of intermediaries. It is argued that financial intermediaries may become oligopolistic if there are too few of them, or that a few powerful intermediaries may help to enforce cartels among industrial firms (as a device for coordinating penalties to be imposed on firms that deviate from the cartel's agreement). But pointing to such costs of universal banking does not amount to an indictment of universal banking per se. First, fragmentation of financial services may create more monopoly power by banks than universal banking. Recent research on the United States and Canada, for example, indicates that the concentrated Canadian banking system prices more competitively than its American counterparts (Calomiris 1993a; Shaffer 1993). Unit banking protects banks from competition, while branch banking promotes competition among several banks. Second, with respect to banks' abilities to enforce industrial cartels, bank enforcement is neither a necessary nor a sufficient condition for successful cartelization. In the United States, cartels developed in the absence of universal banking. Moreover, aggressive antitrust enforcement can overcome industrial cartelization effectively, whether or not universal banks exist.

20. For a review of banking and finance during the colonial and early national period, see Perkins (1994).

21. For discussion of the connection between banks and other special-purpose corporations, see Knox (1900); Legler, Sylla, and Wallis (1990); and Schweikart (1988).

22. See Campbell and Kracaw (1980); Diamond (1984); and Calomiris and Kahn (1991).

23. Calomiris and Kahn (1996) argue for the relative efficiency of New England banks. Davis (1957, 1960) and Lamoreaux (1991a, 1994) provide detailed analyses of the links between New England banks and industrial enterprises.

24. It is interesting to note the many similarities to the German system, including the close relationships between banks and firms, and the use of savings institutions as investors in industrial banks. Savings institutions (Kreditgenossenschaften) were large depositors in the German credit banks (Riesser, 1911, pp. 198–202).

25. Baskin (1988), Davis (1966), and Calomiris (1993a, 1995) describe the development of American capital markets and their limitations. Davis (1963, 1965), Sylla (1969), James (1978), and Calomiris (1993a) examine data on postwar interest rate differences relevant for commercial and industrial lending. Riefler (1930) provides data on actual bank lending rates during the 1920s. Bodenhorn (1990) examines regional interest rate differences during the antebellum period.

26. Goldsmith (1958, pp. 222, 335) gives intermediaries holdings of bonds. On pages 339–40 he provides data on commercial banks' bond holdings, decomposed according to type of issuer. Goldsmith, Lipsey, and Mendelsohn (1963, p.146) provide data on composition of debts for nonfinancial corporations.

27. Goldsmith (1958, pp. 217–18).

28. Goldsmith (1958, pp. 335, 339) is the source for data on short- and long-

term lending by commercial banks. The study of large manufacturing firms is described in Dobrovolsky and Bernstein (1960, pp. 141–42).

29. Marquardt (1960) studies enterprises in Illinois, while Trusk (1960) studies firms in California.

30. Marquardt (1960, p. 507).

31. See Calomiris (1993a) and Calomiris and White (1994).

32. For reviews of the history of the commercial paper market, see Greef (1938); Foulke (1931); and Selden (1963).

33. For a discussion of the theoretical connection between low risk and liquidity, see Gorton and Pennacchi (1990). For an empirical study of the characteristics of issuers, see Calomiris, Himmelberg, and Wachtel (1995).

34. Theoretical models of investment banking include Benveniste and Spindt (1989); Benveniste and Wilhelm (1990); and Chemmanur and Fulghieri (1994).

35. For a discussion of the origins of preferred stock, see Tufano (1992). Campbell (1938) and Carosso (1970) discuss the importance of restructurings, and Smith and Sylla (1993) provide a lively analysis of the biggest of these cases—the formation of U.S. Steel. Bittilingmayer (1985) and Cleveland and Huertas (1986) discuss bankruptcy law changes and the Sherman Act.

36. See Martin (1972).

37. Bittilingmayer (1985, p. 77).

38. The failure of the U.S. banking system to develop German-style universal banking cannot be attributed to ignorance. The successes of German banking were widely appreciated by contemporaries from an early date (e.g., Jeidels, 1905). Jacob Riesser's (1911) classic study of German banking—which focused on advantages from corporate control by universal bankers—was commissioned by the U.S. National Monetary Commission as part of its study of alternative financial arrangements. But in drafting its proposals for what would become the Federal Reserve System, the National Monetary Commission took as given the fragmented structure of the American banking system and the lack of universal banking.

39. Wright (1990, p. 658) notes that U.S. exports had far higher resource content than imports and that the resource intensity of exports increased substantially during late nineteenth-century industrialization. Wright follows Piore and Sabel (1984) and Williamson (1980) in linking the American utilization of resources with the "high throughput" system of manufacture emphasized by Chandler (1977), which Field (1983, 1987) points out is a means to economize on capital costs.

40. Calomiris, Himmelberg, and Wachtel (1995); and Calomiris and Himmelberg (1995).

41. Calomiris (1995).

42. Peach (1941, pp. 18–20, 61–64).

43. Benston (1989) provides a detailed critique of the hearings.

44. See Carosso (1970); Smith and Sylla (1993); Calomiris and Raff (1995); and Calomiris and White (1994) for descriptions of the New Deal financial market and banking reforms and their effects.

45. For detailed discussions of the rise of private placements, see Carosso (1970); Jarrell (1981); and Calomiris and Raff (1995). The growth of life insurance companies (the primary holders of private placements), and the advantages of concentrated control in private placements of debt, were also important in explaining their growth. Private placements permitted the writing and enforcing of covenants that were not feasible for public bonds. The concentration of control in private placements implied far greater incentives for holders of debt to collect and use information to control corporate behavior and limit risk.

46. See Bernanke (1983); Calomiris (1993b); and Calomiris and Raff (1995).

47. Data on the shares of external and internal funding are from Taggart (1985, p. 26). Part of this reliance on retained earnings during the early 1940s may reflect the crowding out of corporate fund-raising by government bond issues. Much of the growth in insurance company holdings of private debt in the late 1940s and '50s, for example, coincided with a decline in holdings of government debt.

48. Data on private placements are from Securities and Exchange Commission (1952, pp. 3–6); and Carey et al. (1993).

49. Data on bank holdings of bonds and notes are from Goldsmith (1958, 339, 364). Producer price data are from Council of Economic Advisers (1974, p. 252).

50. Data on debt ratios are from Taggart (1985, pp. 24–28).

51. Myers (1976) points to unprofitable mergers as an example of lack of discipline over corporate management during the 1960s.

52. The discussion in this section borrows heavily from Calomiris and Raff (1995).

53. Jarrell (1981).

54. In the secondary market, institutional holders gave rise to the "two-tier" market for equity trading. In addition to the traditional small transactions for individual holders, a new market arose in block trades among large money managers, which included pension fund managers or their investment managers (particularly, Morgan Guaranty, Bankers Trust, and Citibank, which collectively managed 80 percent of the trust accounts of employee benefit plans—Munnell, 1982, p. 121). The main advantages of this development were improvements in market liquidity, as it became much easier to move large amounts of shares over small periods of time. See also Blume, Crockett, and Friend (1974).

55. Those that sold immediately after buying primary issues reaped similar profits to other IPO purchasers (a capital gain averaging 18 percent for the first week after the issue).

56. Securities and Exchange Commission (1971, pp. 2348–56).

57. Friend, Blume, and Crockett (1970, p. vii).

58. Securities and Exchange Commission (1971, p. 2393).

59. In a study of the determinants of underwriting fees for recent common stock issues, Hansen and Torregrossa (1992) show that institutional investor purchases of common stock issues are associated with lower issuing fees.

60. Useful studies of the development of institutional investors include Andrews (1964); Greenough and King (1976); Ture (1976); and Munnell (1982).

61. Securities and Exchange Commission (1971).

62. Bank-holding-company-owned venture capital affiliates have been playing an increasingly important role in the growth of private equity finance.

63. Kremer (1993) refers to O-ring defects in the *Challenger* disaster as an example of the low tolerance for managerial error in modern production processes.

64. A takeover of a targeted company is initiated when a potential acquirer makes a tender offer to its shareholders. If the shareholders accept the offer, the company changes ownership and the takeover is completed.

65. To be sure, takeovers are not exclusively done to enforce managerial discipline. There are other important considerations. For more on this see Brealey and Myers (1991).

66. See Jensen (1988, pp. 21–22).

67. This and other evidence is found in the studies of Lang, Stulz, and Walkling (1989), Shleifer and Vishny (1990, 1992), Servaes (1991), and Healy, Palepu, and Ruback (1992). These figures, however, do not say anything about the substantial amount of redistribution that takes place after a takeover is completed. There are many aspects which we do not address, as they would take us beyond the scope of our discussion. For a comprehensive evaluation of the consequences of takeovers, see Auerbach (1988).

68. See Jensen (1988) and Jarrell, Brickley, and Netter (1988) for a more detailed discussion of these issues.

69. Managers typically justify such acquisitions with two arguments. First, by acquiring other lines of businesses, firms can exploit economies of scale and scope. Second, by organizing an internal capital market, the firm will presumably be more efficient at allocating capital resources than an external market. For a comprehensive discussion, see Brealey and Myers (1991) and Morck, Schleifer, and Vishny (1990).

70. Indirect evidence of this can be found in Bhagat, Shleifer, and Vishny (1990); Kaplan and Weisbach (1992); and Mitchell and Lehn (1990); all of whom report that it is common to observe substantial sales of assets after a takeover. More direct evidence is presented by Berger and Ofek (1995), who find that the probability of a takeover increases with the amount of value destroyed by a diversification strategy.

71. This trend is emphasized by Taggart (1985) with respect to the 1960s and '70s, and by Friedman (1986) and Bernanke and Campbell (1988, 1990) for the 1970s and '80s. See also Jefferis (1990) and Gertler and Hubbard (1990).

72. See Miller (1977) and Auerbach (1981).

73. Indeed, Warner (1977) and Calomiris, Orphanides, and Sharpe (1994) find that these costs are substantial.

74. For a bold prediction that relationships are in decline, see Crook (1992).

For the opposite point of view, see Calomiris and Carey (1994); Boyd and Gertler (1994); and Calomiris (1996).

75. The most important obstacle to deregulation of bank powers is finding a way to limit the risks faced by the deposit insurance system from allowing banks to engage in nontraditional activities.

76. See Mengle (1990).

77. See Calomiris and Carey (1994) for a discussion of foreign bank entry into commercial and industrial lending. Crook (1992) discusses the forces behind global deregulation of financial markets.

References

Akerlof, G. A. (1970). "The Market for 'Lemons': Quality Uncertainty and the Market Mechanism." *Quarterly Journal of Economics* 84 (August): 488–500.

Andrews, V. L. (1964). "Noninsured Corporate and State and Local Government Retirement Funds in the Financial Structure," In *Private Capital Markets*, I. Friend, H. P. Minsky, and V. L. Andrews, eds., Englewood Cliffs, N.J.: Prentice-Hall, Inc., 381–531.

Atack, J., and F. Bateman. (1994). "Did the United States Industrialize Too Slowly?" Working paper, Vanderbilt University.

Auerbach, A. (1981). "Inflation and the Tax Treatment of Firm Behavior." *American Economic Review* 71 (May): 419–423.

———. (1988). *Corporate Takeovers: Causes and Consequences.* Chicago: University of Chicago Press.

Baskin, J. (1988). "The Development of Corporate Financial Markets in Britain and the United States, 1600–1914: Overcoming Asymmetric Information." *Business History Review* 62: 199–237.

Benston, G. J. (1989). *The Separation of Commercial and Investment Banking: The Glass-Steagall Act Revisited and Reconsidered.* Norwell: Kluwer Academic.

Benveniste, L. M., and P. A. Spindt. (1989). "How Investment Bankers Determine the Offer Price and Allocation of New Issues." *Journal of Financial Economics* 24 (October): 343–61.

Benveniste, L. M., and W. J. Wilhelm. (1990). "A Comparative Analysis of IPO Proceeds Under Alternative Regulatory Environments." *Journal of Financial Economics* 28 (November–December): 173–207.

Berger, P. G., and E. Ofek. (1995). "Bustup Takeovers of Value-Destroying Diversified Firms." Working paper, New York University.

Berle, A., and G. Means. (1932). *The Modern Corporation and Private Property.* New York: Macmillan.

Bernanke, B. S. (1983). "Nonmonetary Effects of the Financial Crisis in the Propagation of the Great Depression." *American Economic Review* 73 (June): 257–76.

Bernanke, B. S., and J. Y. Campbell. (1988). "Is There a Corporate Debt Crisis?" *Brookings Papers on Economic Activity* (1): 83–125.

———. (1990). "U.S. Corporate Leverage: Developments in 1987 and 1988," *Brookings Papers on Economic Activity* (1): 255–78

Best, R., and H. Zhang. (1993). "Alternative Information Sources and the Information Content of Bank Loans." *Journal of Finance* 48 (September): 1507-22.

Bhagat, S., A. Shleifer, and R. W. Vishny. (1990). "Hostile Takeovers in the 1980s: The Return to Corporate Specialization." *Brookings Papers on Economic Activity* (Microeconomics): 1–72.

Billett, M. T., M. J. Flannery, and J. A. Garfinkel. (1995). "The Effect of Lender Identity on a Borrowing Firm's Equity Return." *Journal of Finance* 50 (June): 699-719.

Bittilingmayer, G. (1985). "Did Antitrust Policy Cause the Great Merger Wave?" *Journal of Law and Economics* 28 (April): 77–118.

Blume, M. E., J. Crockett, and I. Friend. (1974). "Stockownership in the United States: Characteristics and Trends." *Survey of Current Business* 54 (November): 16–40.

Bodenhorn, H. (1990). "Capital Mobility and Financial Integration in Antebellum America." *Journal of Economic History* 52 (September): 585–610.

Booth, J. R. (1991). "Contract Costs, Bank Loans, and the Cross-Monitoring Hypothesis." *Journal of Financial Economics* 31 (February): 25–41.

Boyd, J. H., and M. Gertler. (1994). "Are Banks Dead? Or Are the Reports Greatly Exaggerated?" *Quarterly Review*, Federal Reserve Bank of Minneapolis, Summer, 2–23.

Brealey, R., and S. Myers. (1991). *Principles of Corporate Finance*. New York: McGraw-Hill.

Brewer, E. (1989). "Relationship between Bank Holding Company Risk and Nonbank Activity." *Journal of Economics and Business* 41 (November): 337–53.

Butters, J. K., and J. Lintner (1945). *Effects of Federal Taxes on Growing Enterprises*. Boston: Harvard University Press.

Calomiris, C. W. (1993a). "Regulation, Industrial Structure, and Instability in U.S. Banking: An Historical Perspective."In *Structural Change in Banking*, M. Klausner and L. J. White, eds. Homewood, Ill.: Business One-Irwin, 19–115.

———. (1993b). "Financial Factors in the Great Depression." *Journal of Economic Perspectives* 7 (Spring): 61–85.

———. (1995). "The Costs of Rejecting Universal Banking: American Finance in the German Mirror, 1870–1914." In *The Coordination of Activity Within and Between Firms*, N. Lamoreaux and D. M. G. Raff, eds. Chicago: University of Chicago Press, 257–315.

———. (1996). "Is Universal Banking Right for the United States," Working paper, American Enterprise Institute.

Calomiris, C. W., and M. Carey. (1994). "Loan Market Competition Between

Foreign and U.S. Banks: Some Facts About Loans and Borrowers." In *Proceedings of the 30th Annual Conference on Bank Structure and Competition*. Chicago: Federal Reserve Bank of Chicago.

Calomiris, C. W., and C. P. Himmelberg. (1995). "Investment Banking Spreads as a Measure of the Cost of Access to External Finance." Working paper, University of Illinois.

Calomiris, C. W., C. P. Himmelberg, and P. Wachtel (forthcoming). "Commercial Paper, Corporate Finance, and the Business Cycle: A Microeconomic Perspective." *Carnegie-Rochester Series on Public Policy*.

Calomiris, C. W., and R. G. Hubbard. (1990). "Firm Heterogeneity, Internal Finance and 'Credit Rationing,'" *Economic Journal* 100 (March): 90–104.

———. (1995). "Internal Finance and Investment: Evidence frome the Undistributed Profits Tax of 1936–1937." *Journal of Business* 68 (October): 443–82.

Calomiris, C. W., and C. M. Kahn (1991). "The Role of Demandable Debt in Structuring Optimal Bank Arrangements." *American Economic Review* 81 (June): 497–513.

———. (forthcoming). "The Efficiency of Self-Regulated Payments Systems: Learning from the Suffolk System." *Journal of Money, Credit, and Banking*.

Calomiris, C. W., A. Orphanides, and S. Sharpe. (1994). "Leverage as a State Variable for Employment, Inventory Accumulation, and Fixed Investment." National Bureau of Economic Research Working Paper No. 4800, July.

Calomiris, C. W., and D. M. G. Raff (forthcoming). "The Evolution of Market Structure, Information, and Spreads in American Investment Banking." In *Anglo-American Finance: Financial Markets and Institutions in 20th-Century North America and the U.K.*, R Sylla and M. Bordo, eds. Homewood, Ill.: Business One-Irwin.

Calomiris, C. W., and E. N. White (1994). "The Origins of Federal Deposit Insurance." In *The Regulated Economy: A Historical Approach to Political Economy*, C. Goldin and G. Libecap, eds. Chicago: University of Chicago Press, 145–188.

Campbell, E. G. (1938). *The Reorganization of the American Railroad System, 1893–1900*. New York: Columbia University Press.

Campbell, T., and W. Kracaw. (1980). "Information Production, Market Signalling and the Theory of Financial Intermediation." *Journal of Finance* 35 (September): 863–81.

Carey, M., S. Prowse, J. Rea, and G. Udell. (1993). "The Economics of Private Placements: A New Look." *Financial Markets, Institutions, and Instruments* 2(3): 1–67.

Carosso, V. P. (1970). *Investment Banking in America*. Cambridge: Harvard University Press.

Chandler, A. D. (1977). *The Visible Hand: The Managerial Revolution in American Business*. Cambridge: Harvard University Press.

Chemmanur, T.J., and P. Fulghieri. (1994). "Investment Bank Repudiation,

Information Production, and Financial Intermendiation." *Journal of Finance* 49 (March): 57–79.

Cleveland, H., and T. Huertas. (1986). *Citibank*, 1812–1970. Cambridge: Harvard University Press.

Council of Economic Advisers. (1974). *Economic Report of the President*. Washington, D.C.: U.S. Government Printing Office.

Crook, C. (1992). "Fear of Finance." *The Economist*, September 19, 1992, 5–18.

Davis, L. (1957). "Sources of Industrial Finance: The American Textile Industry, A Case Study." *Explorations in Entrepreneurial History* 9: 190–203.

———. (1960). "The New England Textile Mills and the Capital Markets: A Study of Industrial Borrowing, 1840–1860." *Journal of Economic History* 20: 1–30.

———. (1963). "Capital Immobilities and Finance Capitalism: A Study of Economic Evolution in the United States, 1820–1920." *Explorations in Entrepreneurial History* (Fall): 88–105.

———. (1965). "The Investment Market, 1870–1914: The Evolution of a National Market." *Journal of Economic History* 25 (September): 355–99.

———. (1966). "The Capital Markets and Industrial Concerns: The U.S. and the U.K., A Comparative Study." *Economic History Review* 19: 255–72.

De Long, J. B. (1991). "Did J. P. Morgan's Men Add Value? An Economist's Perspective on Financial Capitalism." In *Inside the Business Enterprise: Historical Perspectives on the Use of Information*, P. Temin, ed. Chicago: University of Chicago Press, 205–36.

Diamond, D. (1984). "Financial Intermediation and Delegated Monitoring." *Review of Economic Studies* 51 (July): 393–414.

———. (1991). "Monitoring and Reputation: The Choice between Bank Loans and Directly Placed Debt." *Journal of Political Economy* 99 (August): 689–721.

Dobrovolsky, S. P., and M. Bernstein. (1960). "Long Term Trends in Capital Financing." In *Capital in Manufacturing and Mining: Its Formation and Financing*, D. Creamer, S. P. Dobrovolsky, I. Borenstein, eds. Princeton: Princeton University Press, 109–93.

Fazzari, S. M., and B. C. Petersen. (1993). "Working Capital and Fixed Investment: New Evidence on Financing Constraints." *Rand Journal of Economics* 24 (Autum): 328–42.

Fazzari, S. M., R. G. Hubbard, and B. C. Petersen. (1988). "Financing Constraints and Corporate Investment." *Brookings Papers on Economic Activity* (1): 141–95.

Field, A. (1983). "Land Abundance, Interest/Profit Rates and Nineteenth-Century American and British Technology." *Journal of Economic History* 42 (June): 405–31.

———. (1987). "Modern Business Enterprise as a Capital-Saving Innovation." *Journal of Economic History* 46 (June); 473–85.

Foulke, R. A. (1931). *The Commercial Paper Market*. New York: Bankers' Publishing Co.

Friedman, B. M. (1986). "Increasing Indebtness and Financial Instability in the

United States." In *Debt, Financial Stability, and Public Policy*. Kansas City: Federal Reserve Bank of Kansas City, 27–53.

Friend, I., M. Blume, and J. Crockett. (1970). *Mutual Funds and Other Institutional Investors*. New York: McGraw-Hill.

Gale, D., and M. Hellwig. (1985). "Incentive-Compatible Debt Contracts: The One Period Problem." *Review of Economic Studies* (October): 647–63.

Gertler, M., and R. G. Hubbard. (1990). "Taxation, Corporate Capital Structure, and Financial Distress." *Tax Policy and the Economy* 4: 43–71.

Gilchrist, S., and C. P. Himmelberg. (1993). "Evidence on the Role of Cash Flow for Investment." Board of Governors of the Federal Reserve System, Finance and Economics Discussion Series. Working paper, 93–7.

Gilson, S. C., K. John, and L. H. P. Lang. (1990). "Troubled Debt Restructurings." *Journal of Financial Economics* 27: 315–53.

Goldsmith, R. W. (1958). *Financial Intermediaries in the American Economy Since 1900*. Princeton: Princeton University Press.

Goldsmith, R. W., R. E. Lipsey, and M. Mendelsohn. (1963). *Studies in the National Balance Sheet of the United States*. Princeton: Princeton University Press.

Gorton, G., and G. Pennacchi. (1990). "Financial Intermediaries and Liquidity Creation." *Journal of Finance* 45 (March): 49–71.

Gorton, G., and F. A. Schmidt. (1994). "Universal Banking and the Performance of German Firms." Working paper, University of Pennsylvania.

Greef, A. O. (1938). *The Commercial Paper House in the United States*. Cambridge: Harvard University Press.

Greenough, W. C., and F. P. King. (1976). *Pension Plans and Public Policy*. New York: Columbia University Press.

Hansen, R. S., and P. Torregrossa. (1992). "Underwriter Compensation and Corporate Monitoring." *Journal of Finance* 47 (September): 1537–55.

Healy, P. M., K. G. Palepu, and R. S. Ruback. (1992). "Does Corporate Performance Improve After Mergers? *Journal of Financial Economics* 31: 135–175.

Himmelberg, C. P. (1990). "Essays on the Relationship between Investment and Internal Finance." Ph. D. dissertation, Northwestern University.

Himmelberg, C. P., and B. C. Petersen (1994). "R&D and Internal Finance: A Panel Study of Small Firms in High-Tech Industries." *Review of Economics and Statistics*: 38–51.

Hoshi, T., A. Kashyap, and D. Scharfstein. (1990a). "The Role of Banks in Reducing the Costs of Financial Distress." *Journal of Financial Economics* 27 (September): 67–88.

———. (1990b). "Bank Monitoring and Investment: Evidence from the Changing Structure of Japanese Corporate Banking Relationships." In *Asymmetric Information, Corporate Finance, and Investment*, R. G. Hubbard, ed. Chicago: University of Chicago Press, 105–26.

———. (1991). "Corporate Structure, Liquidity, and Investment: Evidence from Japanese Industrial Groups." *Quarterly Journal of Economics* 106: 33–60.

James, C. (1987). "Some Evidence on the Uniqueness of Bank Loans." *Journal of Financial Economics* 19: 217–235.

James, C., and P. Wier. (1990). "Are Bank Loans Different? Some Evidence from the Stock Market." *Journal of Applied Corporate Finance*: 46–54.

James, J. (1978). *Money and Capital Markets in Postbellum America*. Princeton: Princeton University Press.

Jarrell, G.A. (1981). "The Economic Effects of Federal Regulation of the Market for New Security Issues." *Journal of Law and Economics* 24 (December): 613–75.

Jarrell, G. A., J. A. Brickley, and J. M. Netter. (1988). "The Market for Corporate Control: The Empirical Evidence Since 1980." *Journal of Economic Perspectives* 2 (Winter): 49–68

Jefferis, R. (1990). "The High-Yield Debt Market, 1980–1990," *Economic Commentary* (April): 113–18.

Jeidels, O. (1905). *Das Verhaltnis der deutschen Grossbanken zur Industrie, mit besonderer Berucksichtung der Eisenindustrie*. Berlin: Schmollers Forschungen.

Jensen, M. C. (1986). "Agency Costs of Free Cash Flow, Corporate Finance and Takeovers." *American Economic Association Papers and Proceedings* 76 (May): 323–29.

———. (1988). "Takeovers: Their Causes and Consequences." *Journal of Economic Perspectives* 2 (Winter): 21–48.

Jensen, M. C., and W. H. Meckling. (1976). "Theory of the Firm: Managerial Behavior, Agency Costs and Ownership Structure." *Journal of Financial Economics* 3: 305–60.

Jensen, M. C., and K. J. Murphy. (1990). "Performance Pay and Top-Management Incentives." *Journal of Political Economy* 98: 225–64.

Kaplan, S. N., and M. S. Weisbach. (1992). "The Success of Acquisitions: Evidence from Divestures. *Journal of Finance* 47 (March): 107–38.

Kaufman, G., and L. Mote. (1990). "Glass-Steagall: Repeal By Regulatory and Judicial Reinterpretation." *Banking Law Journal* (September–October): 388–421.

Knox, J. J. (1900). *A History of Banking in the United States*. New York: Bradford Rhodes & Co.

Kremer, M. (1993). "The O-Ring Theory of Economic Development." *Quarterly Journal of Economics* 108 (August): 551–75.

Kroszner, R. S., and R. G. Rajan. (1994). "Is the Glass-Steagall Act Justified? A Study of the U.S. Experience with Universal Banking before 1933." *American Economic Review* 84 (September): 810–32.

Lamoreaux, N. (1991a). "Information Problems and Banks: Specialization in Short-Term Commercial Lending, New England in the Nineteenth Century." In *Inside the Business Enterprise: Historical Perspectives on the Use of Information*, P. Temin, ed. Chicago: University of Chicago Press, 154–95.

———. (1991b). "Bank Mergers in Late Nineteenth-Century New England: The Contingent Nature of Structural Change." *Journal of Economic History* 51 (September): 537–58.

————. (1994). *Insider Lending: Banks, Personal Connections, and Economic Development in Industrial New England, 1784–1912.* Cambridge: Cambridge University Press.

Lang, L. H. P., and R. Stulz (1994). "Tobin's q, Corporate Diversification, and Firm Performance," *Journal of Political Economy* 102: 1248–80.

Lang, L. H. P., R. Stulz, and R. A. Walkling. (1989). "Managerial Performance, Tobin's q, and the Gains From Successful Tender Offers." *Journal of Financial Economics* 24: 137–54.

Legler, J. B., R. Sylla, and J. J. Wallis (1990). "U.S. City Finances and the Growth of Government, 1859–1902." *Journal of Economic History* 48 (June): 347–56.

Mackie-Mason, J. K. (1990). "Do Firms Care Who Provides Their Financing?" In *Asymmetric Information, Corporate Finance, and Investment*, R.G. Hubbard, ed. Chicago: University of Chicago Press, 63–104.

Marquardt, M. O. (1960). "Sources of Capital of Early Illinois Manufacturers, 1840–1880." Ph.D. dissertation, University of Illinois.

Martin, A. (1972). "Railroads and the Equity Receivership: An Essay on Institutional Change." *Journal of Economic History* 34 (September): 685–709.

Mendelson, M. (1967). "Underwriting Compensation." In *Investment Banking and the New Issues Market*, I. Friend et al., eds. New York: The World Publishing Company, 394–479.

Mengle, D. L. (1990). "The Case for Interstate Branch Banking." *Federal Reserve Bank of Richmond Economic Review* 76 (November/December), 3–17.

Miller, M. (1977). "Debt and Taxes." *Journal of Finance* 32 (May): 261–75.

Mitchell, M. L., and K. Lehn. (1990). "Do Bad Bidders Become Good Targets?" *Journal of Political Economy* 98: 372–98.

Morck, R., A. Shleifer, and R. W. Vishny. (1990). "Do Managerial Objectives Drive Bad Acquisitions?" *Journal of Finance* 45 (March): 31–48.

Morgan, D. (1993). "Bank Monitoring Mitigates Agency Problems: New Evidence Using the Financial Covenants in Bank Loan Commitments." Federal Reserve Bank of Kansas City, Working paper 93–116.

Munnell, A. H. (1982). *The Economics of Private Pensions*. Washington D.C.: Brookings Institution.

Myers, S. C. (1976). "A Framework for Evaluating Mergers." In *Modern Developments in Financial Management*, S. C. Myers, ed. New York: Frederick A. Praeger.

————. (1977). "Determinants of Corporate Borrowing." *Journal of Financial Economics* 5: 147–75.

Myers, S. C. and N. Majluf. (1984). "Corporate Financing and Investment Decisions When Firms Have Information That Investors Do Not Have." *Journal of Financial Economics* 13: 187–221.

Peach, W. P. (1941). *The Security Affiliates of National Banks*. Baltimore: John Hopkins University Press.

Perkins, E. (1994). *American Public Finance and Financial Services, 1700–1815.* Columbus: Ohio State University Press.

Petersen, M., and R. Rajan. (1994). "The Benefits of Lending Relationships: Evidence from Small Business Data." *Journal of Finance* 49 (March): 3–37.

Piore, M. and C. F. Sabel. (1984). *The Second Industrial Divide*. New York: Basic Books.

Rajan, R. (1992). "Insiders and Outsiders: The Choice between Relationships and Arms-Length Debt," *Journal of Finance* 47 (September): 1367–1400.

———. (1994). "A Theory of the Costs and Benefits of Universal Banking." Working paper, University of Chicago.

Ramirez, C. D. (1995). "Did J. P. Morgan's Men Add Liquidity? Cash Flow, Corporate Finance and Investment at the Turn of the Twentieth Century." *Journal of Finance* 50, (June): 661–78.

Ramirez, C. D., and J. B. De Long. (1993). "Banker Influence and Business Economic Performance: Assessing the Impact of Depression-Era Financial Market Reforms." Working paper, George Mason University.

Riefler, W. W. (1930). *Money Rates and Money Markets in the United States*. New York: Harper and Brothers.

Riesser, J. (1911). *The Great German Banks and Their Concentration in Connection with the Economic Development of Germany*. 3d ed., trans. Washington, D.C.: U.S. Government Printing Office.

Schweikart, L. (1988). *Banking in the American South from the Age of Jackson to Reconstruction*. Baton Rouge: Louisiana State University Press.

Securities and Exchange Commission (1952). *Privately-Placed Securities: Cost of Flotation*. Washington D.C.

———. (1971). *Cost of Flotation of Registered Equity Issues, 1963–1965*. Washington, D.C.

Selden, R. T. (1963). "Trends and Cycles in the Commercial Paper Market." NBER Occasional Paper No. 85. New York: National Bureau of Economic Research.

Servaes, H. (1991). "Tobin's q and the Gains From Takeover." *Journal of Finance* 46 (March): 409–19.

Shaffer S. (1993). "A Test of Competition in Canadian Banking." *Journal of Money, Credit, and Banking* 25 (February): 49–61.

Sheard, P. (1989). "The Main Bank System and Corporate Monitoring and Control in Japan." *Journal of Economic Behavior and Organization* 11: 399–422.

Shleifer, A. and R. W. Vishny. (1990). "The Takeover Wave of the 1980s." *Science* 249 (August): 745–49.

———. (1992). "Liquidation Values and Debt Capacity: A Market Equilibrium Approach." *Journal of Finance* 47 (September): 1343–65.

Slovin, M. B., M. E. Sushka, and J. A. Polonchek. (1992). "The Value of Bank Durability: Borrowers as Bank Stakeholders." *Journal of Finance* 48 (March): 247–66.

Smith, G. D. and R. Sylla. (1993). "The Transformation of Financial Capitalism: An Essay on the History of American Capital Markets." *Financial Markets, Institutions, and Instruments* 2 (May): 1–62.

Stiglitz, J. and A. Weiss. (1981). "Credit Rationing in Markets With Imperfect Information." *American Economic Review* 71: 393–410.

Sylla, R. (1969). "Federal Policy, Banking Market Structure, and Capital Mobilization in the United States, 1863–1913." *Journal of Economic History* 29 (December): 657–86.

Taggart, R. A. (1985). "Secular Patterns in the Financing of U.S. Corporations." In *Corporate Capital Structures in the United States*, B. M. Friedman, ed. Chicago: University of Chicago Press, 13–80.

Townsend, R. (1979). "Optimal Contracts and Competitive Markets with Costly State Verification." *Journal of Economic Theory* (October): 265–93.

Trusk, R. J. (1960). "Sources of Capital of Early California Manufacturers, 1850 to 1880." Ph.D. dissertation, University of Illinois.

Tufano, P. (1992). "Business Failure, Legal Innovation, and Financial Innovation in Historical Perspective." Working paper, Harvard University.

Ture, Norman B. (1976). *The Future of Private Pension Plans*. Washington D.C.: American Enterprise Institute.

Warner, J. B. (1977). "Bankruptcy Costs: Some Evidence." *Journal of Finance* 32 (May): 337–47.

Weinstein, D. E., and Y. Yafeh. (1994). "On the Costs of Universal Banking: Evidence from the Changing Main Bank Relations in Japan." Working paper, Harvard University.

White, E. N. (1986). "Before the Glass-Steagall Act: An Analysis of the Investment Banking Activities of National Banks." *Explorations in Economic History* 23 (January); 33–55.

Whited, T. M. (1992). "Debt, Liquidity Constraints, and Corporate Investment: Evidence From Panel Data." *Journal of Finance* 47 (September): 1425–60.

Williamson, O. (1980). "Emergence of the Visible Hand." in *Managerial Hierarchies*, A. D. Chandler and J. Daems, eds. Cambridge: Harvard University Press.

Williamson, O. (1988). "Corporate Finance and Corporate Governance." *Journal of Finance* 18: 567–91.

Wright, G. (1990). "The Origins of American Industrial Success, 1879–1940." *American Economic Review* 80 (September): 651–68.

6

The U.S. Corporation and Technical Progress

✦

DAVID C. MOWERY

RICHARD R. NELSON

In his magisterial *Capitalism, Socialism, and Democracy* (Schumpeter 1950), first published over fifty years ago, Joseph Schumpeter argued that contemporary neoclassical economic models of capitalism and competition overlooked the key characteristics of these phenomena. Capitalism and competition essentially were about technical innovation and economic growth, rather than the achievement of static "economic efficiency." Large firms with considerable market power were, in Schumpeter's view, the major sources of technical innovation. One of the concomitants of the dynamic power of modern capitalism was that the system always seemed to be operating somewhat inefficiently in the static sense, at least in comparison with the economists' theoretical norm of perfect competition. But according to Schumpeter, the dynamic gains to society from the economic growth generated by this system vastly outweighed such theoretical and imaginary static inefficiencies.

In so arguing, Schumpeter rekindled an old debate about how to view the large corporations that had grown up in the United States since the turn of the century. Should they be understood largely as causes of static economic inefficiency associated with monopoly pricing and sources of politically dangerous concentrations of political power? Or should they instead be welcomed as the principal and indispensable vehicle through which the United States and other advanced industrial nations lifted their standards of living and achieved the kind of democracy that is possible only in high-income societies? When *The Corporation in Modern Society* (Mason 1959) was published, this question, or rather its narrower version—"Is large firm size and concentrated markets a necessary basis for or consequence of rapid technical progress?"—had just begun to be probed by economists empirically. Jacob Schmookler's essay in that volume, "Technological Progress and the Modern American Corporation" (Schmookler 1959), discussed the issues posed above, and reported on some of the early empirical evidence bearing on them.

Despite the evidence that has accumulated over the past thirty years, or perhaps because of it, the debate refuses to go away. Recently, however, the form of the debate has changed and international competition has given it a new dimension. In particular, the rise of Japan as an economic and technological power, and the ability of Japanese companies in such industries as automobiles and electronics to take markets away from the American firms that formerly dominated them, have led to much critical scrutiny of the management and governance of large American firms. The recent study of U.S. competitiveness, *Made in America* (Dertouzos, Lester, and Solow 1989), illustrates this new strand of analysis.

Other elements of this new discussion take on an explicitly historical form. To oversimplify somewhat, one side of the debate is occupied by Alfred Chandler (1977, 1990) and his colleagues, who have described the central role played by large corporations in the development of the industries like steel, chemical products, automobiles, consumer durables, food processing, electrical equipment, and electronics that defined mid-twentieth-century capitalism. The description contains a strong note of approbation, an ode to the modern horizontally and vertically integrated capitalist firm that approves of managerial discretion.

A different view comes from scholars who argue that modern capitalism need not have developed along this path. Piore and Sabel (1984) point to industries and areas where modern technology was implemented through a structure of small and medium-sized firms that were linked horizontally and vertically through a variety of networking arrangements. Some apparent support for this view comes from the difficulties of such giant firms as Bethlehem Steel and IBM during the past dozen years, as these giant firms face increasing competition from firms that are smaller and less integrated. The 1980s also witnessed an unprecedented wave of horizontal and vertical dis-integration within many formerly large and diversified companies.

Was the heyday of the Schumpeterian or Chandlerian firm but a transient episode in U.S. economic history? Does the future belonging to smaller, less diversified firms that are linked to other firms through a variety of cooperative arrangements?

Although elements of the older debates are present in the new ones, the style and substance have changed. We treat some of these issues later in this essay, but adopt a broader focus. In particular, we wish to consider the role of corporations within the broader set of national institutions that support the advance of technology, as well as discussing changes in this role over time. More generally, this essay focuses on the changing role of corporations in national innovation systems.

Schumpeter's analysis of fifty years ago devoted remarkably little attention to the broader system of public and private institutions that support technological advance in industry. One important part of that broader system is universities, which train the scientists and engineers who go into corporate R&D and do much of the basic research that underpins the applied R&D efforts of firms. Schumpeter paid little attention to universities, and neither did Schmookler. Nor has Chandler or Piore and Sabel had much to say about universities.

These writers also rarely consider the role of government in much detail. Yet even at the time of Schumpeter's prophetic work, that role was substantial. Twenty years later, when Schmookler's work appeared, the role of government in the national innovation systems of the United States and the other major industrial powers had grown substantially in size and complexity. Nevertheless, Schmookler devoted little space to this role, although he did recognize that the U.S. system has been shaped to a considerable degree by public policies.

In order to understand how technical innovation proceeds in modern capitalist economies, one must pay considerable attention to universities, government, and a number of other institutional actors, in addition to considering the behavior of corporations or business firms. Corporations are one part of a complex institutional system, and their role cannot be understood in isolation. In our view, one of the most interesting recent developments in corporate R&D is the changing relationship between corporations and universities. U.S. corporate R&D also has been heavily affected by the expanded role of government in this nation's R&D system, especially changes in the range of government programs supporting corporate R&D.

The following section is historical, and examines the role of corporate R&D, and other parts of the modern innovation system as they evolved from the late nineteenth century through 1940. We focus mainly on the United States but discuss similarities and differences between the United States and other major industrial nations during this period, suggesting some possible explanations for these differences.

World War II was a watershed, and in the third section we consider the evolving role of corporations, and the other institutional actors, principally government, in the postwar period. In the two decades after World War II, U.S. companies had enormous productivity and technological advantages over corporations in other countries; since 1970, however, other countries have caught up, or have come close to doing so. Competition has become global in scope, and the structure of most major U.S. companies now is transnational. We will consider these developments in the fourth section. The final section considers the current situation and associated debates.

The Evolution of the U.S. R&D "System," 1900–1945

The science-based industries that figure so large in the U.S. and other industrial economies are of relatively recent origin, and are characterized by several key components. The first, which is extensively discussed here is the industrial research laboratory, a research facility (or facilities) owned by a business firm, staffed by university-trained scientists and engineers, and dedicated to improving the parent firm's products and processes. A second characteristic of most science-based industries is their close links to particular fields of university training and research. Fields such as chemical engineering, electrical engineering, and metallurgy established places within U.S. universities in the late nineteenth and early twentieth centuries, and strengthened the American industries that drew on them.

The Origins of U.S. Industrial Research

As David (1975), Rosenberg (1972), and others have noted, growth in manufacturing productivity and output in the nineteenth-century U.S. economy was closely associated with the development of the "American system of manufactures" for the production of light machines and other mechanical devices. The inventions behind this development were drawn forth by the very large American market for machinery for agriculture and transportation, and the fact that American manufacturing was largely protected from foreign competition.[1] Americans were able to exploit foreign sources of knowledge, including importation of both blueprints and skilled mechanics from Europe and elsewhere; but these inventions seldom required much scientific research.[2] The large-scale mass-production firms that arose out of these inventions were associated with a system of work organization involving a hierarchical and complex internal division of labor that was more fully developed in the United States than in contemporary industrial economies.

By and large the establishment of large-scale hierarchical firms preceded the development of industrial R&D, and set the stage and context for it.

The materials analysis and quality control laboratories that were established within many of these large factories were among the first U.S. industrial employers of scientists and research personnel. These plant-level laboratories gradually expanded and were supplemented by the foundation of central laboratories devoted to longer-term research. Although the development of much of the original testing and materials analysis research was a response to changes in the structure of production, the expansion and elaboration of these activities reflected changes in the organizational structure of the firm. The development of these research facilities was associated with expansion and diversification of the firm's activities and products and substitution of intrafirm control of these activities for market control.

The growth of industrial R&D was influenced by the dramatic advances in physics and chemistry during the last third of the nineteenth century, which created considerable potential for the profitable application of scientific and technical knowledge. Indeed, many of the earliest corporate investors in industrial R&D, such as General Electric and Alcoa, were founded on product or process innovations that drew on recent advances in physics and chemistry, and would not have been possible without them. But change in the scientific and technological knowledge base does not suffice to explain the growth of industrial R&D within the U.S. corporation. Although changing technical opportunities influenced the decision to invest in industrial R&D, they do not account for the growing share of R&D activity within the boundaries of the firm. A substantial network of independent R&D laboratories provided research services on a contractual basis throughout the formative years of industrial R&D in the United States. These contract research organizations' share of total R&D employment, however, declined during the first half of the century, and many of their clients were among the first to establish in-house R&D facilities.

The corporate R&D laboratory brought more of the process of developing and improving industrial technology into U.S. manufacturing firms, reducing the importance of the independent inventor as a source of patents (Schmookler 1957). But the in-house research facilities of large U.S. firms were concerned with more than just the creation of new technology. They also monitored technological developments outside of the firm and advised corporate managers on the acquisition of externally developed technologies.

The advantages of placing R&D within the firm reflected the fact that the sources of many commercially valuable innovations did not lie exclusively or even largely in scientific laboratory research. Much of the knowledge employed in industrial innovation flowed from the firm's production and marketing activities, and the knowledge produced by the interaction of R&D and other functions often was and is highly specific to a given firm. Moreover, transferring this information within or between organizations requires considerable shared expertise and knowledge, as well as sufficient expertise to absorb and apply the knowledge within the recipient division or firm.

Because interaction among the different functions within the firm contributes to a stock of firm-specific knowledge that is not easily transferred across organizational boundaries, organizations that do not conduct "downstream" activities such as manufacturing or marketing may be unable to develop specific bodies of know-how. Contracting problems also limit a firm's reliance on market-based forms of organization in R&D, especially for specialized projects. These types of projects are likely to involve investments in specialized physical or human capital, they typically involve small numbers of buyers and sellers, and they are often subject to considerable uncertainty concerning outcomes. Transaction-specific investments in an R&D project that cannot be easily redeployed to other uses or sold make it easier for one party to a contract to "hold up" the other, threatening to break the contract and negate the value of the other party's investment. The thin market, that is, the small number of buyers and sellers, for specialized research services makes opportunistic behavior more likely and discourages reliance on contracts for these forms of R&D (see Teece [1988] and Williamson [1985] for a more detailed discussion of contracting problems).

The very uncertainties that discouraged firms from contracting for some R&D services also prevented them from relying exclusively on in-house R&D for new technologies; no firm could ensure that all technological threats and opportunities would be pursued successfully in-house. Precisely because the outcomes of many research projects cannot be known ex ante, the portfolio of in-house projects may not adequately cover all technological alternatives, and important developments are likely to emerge from sources other than intrafirm R&D. Many firms therefore used their in-house R&D for two "outward-oriented" activities: monitoring their technological environment, often through research links with universities, and acquiring innovations from external sources. Contractual governance was infeasible for the provision of some classes of R&D services, but market mechanisms could be and were used, with the aid of internal R&D, to acquire the products of independent inventors and other manufacturing firms. Internal R&D facilities also monitored and interpreted the progress of research in other laboratories.

The structural change in many large U.S. manufacturing firms that underpinned investment in industrial research was strongly influenced by U.S. antitrust policy. By the late nineteenth century, judicial interpretations of the Sherman Antitrust Act had made agreements among firms for the control of prices and output targets of civil prosecution, and contributed to the 1895–1904 merger wave, particularly the surge in mergers after 1898.[3]

In 1904 the *Northern Securities* decision, which attacked market control through horizontal merger, caused an end of the merger wave, caused large U.S. firms to seek alternative means for corporate growth. For some of these firms, the threat of antitrust action sparked efforts to diversify into other areas, and these efforts often relied on the commercialization of new technologies that were developed internally or purchased from external sources.[4]

Although it discouraged horizontal mergers among large firms, U.S. antitrust policy through much of the pre-1940 period did not discourage efforts by these firms' research laboratories to acquire new technologies from external sources. Many of the sources of Du Pont's major product and process innovations during this period were obtained from outside the firm, which proceeded to further develop and commercialize them within the U.S. market (Mueller 1962; Hounshell and Smith 1988). The research facilities of AT&T were instrumental in the procurement and further development of the "triode" from independent inventor Lee de Forest, and also were involved in the corporation's decision to obtain loading-coil technology from Pupin (Reich 1985). General Electric's research operations monitored foreign technological advances in lamp filaments and the inventive activities of outside firms or individuals, and pursued patent rights to innovations developed all over the world (Reich 1985, p. 61).[5] To the extent that federal antitrust policy motivated industrial research investment by large U.S. firms before and during the interwar period, the policy paradoxically may have aided the survival of these firms and the growth of a relatively stable, oligopolistic market structure in some U.S. manufacturing industries.[6]

The effects of U.S. antitrust policy on the growth of industrial research were reinforced by judicial and legislative actions in the late nineteenth and early twentieth centuries that strengthened intellectual property rights. The congressional revision of patent laws that took effect in 1898 extended the duration of protection provided by U.S. patents covering inventions first patented in other countries (Bright 1949, p. 91).[7] The Supreme Court's 1908 decision (*Continental Paper Bag Company v. Eastern Paper Bag Company*) that patents covering goods not in production were valid (Neal and Goyder 1980, p. 324) expanded the utility of large patent portfolios for defensive purposes. Other congressional actions in the first three decades of this century increased the number of Patent Office examiners, stream-lined internal review procedures, and transferred the Office from the Interior to the Commerce Department (Noble 1977, pp. 107–8). Stronger and clearer intellectual property rights facilitated the development of a market for the acquisition and sale of industrial technologies. Judicial tolerance for restrictive patent licensing policies (see later text) further increased the value of patents in corporate research strategies.

Although the search for new patents provided one incentive to pursue industrial research, their imminent demise was another important impetus for the establishment of industrial research laboratories. The impending expiration of patents protecting core technologies, as well as the growth of competing technologies, led to the establishment or expansion of in-house research laboratories. Both AT&T and General Electric, for example, established or expanded their in-house laboratories in response to the intensified competitive pressure that resulted from the expiration of key patents (Reich 1985; Millard 1990, p. 156). In both of these firms, efforts to improve and protect corporate technological assets were combined with the acquisition of patents in related technologies from other firms and independent inventors.

Patents also provided a mechanism for some firms to retain market power without running afoul of antitrust law. The 1911 consent decree settling the federal government's antitrust suit against General Electric left GE's patent licensing scheme largely untouched, allowing the firm considerable latitude to set the terms and conditions of sales of lamps produced by its licensees, maintaining an effective cartel within the U.S. electric lamp market (Bright 1949, p. 158). Patent licensing provided the basis for the participation by General Electric and Du Pont in the international cartels of the interwar chemical and electrical equipment industries. U.S. participants in these international agreements took pains to characterize them as patent licensing schemes, arguing that exclusive license arrangements and restrictions on the commercial exploitation of patents would not run afoul of U.S. antitrust enforcement (Taylor and Sudnik 1984, p. 126).

The Growth of U.S. Industrial Research, 1921–1946

The limited data on the growth of industrial research activity during the early twentieth century suggest that the bulk of the laboratories and of research employment was located in the chemical products and related industries. The chemicals, glass, rubber, and petroleum industries accounted for nearly 40 percent of the number of laboratories founded during 1899–1946, and the chemicals sector dominated research employment during 1921–1946.[8] While much recent historiography of U.S. industrial research has focused on the electrical products industries, growth of industrial R&D in this industry lagged behind that in chemicals. Electrical machinery and instruments accounted for less than 10 percent of total research employment in 1921. By 1946, however, these latter two industries contained more than 20 percent of all scientists and engineers employed in industrial research in U.S. manufacturing.

Table 6.1 provides data on research laboratory employment for 1921, 1927, 1933, 1944, and 1946 in nineteen two-digit manufacturing industries and in manufacturing overall (excluding miscellaneous manufacturing industries). Employment of scientists and engineers in industrial research within manufacturing grew from roughly three thousand in 1921 to nearly forty-six thousand by 1946.[9] Chemicals, rubber, petroleum, and electrical machinery are among the most research-intensive industries, accounting for 48 to 58 percent of total employment of scientists and engineers in industrial research within manufacturing, throughout this period. The major prewar research employers remained among the most research-intensive industries well into the postwar period despite the growth in federal funding for research in industry. Chemicals, rubber, petroleum, and electrical machinery accounted for more than 53 percent of industrial research employment in 1940 and represented 40.3 percent of research employment in industry in 1984 (National Science Foundation 1987).

Schumpeter argued (1950)[10] that in-house industrial research had supplanted the inventor-entrepreneur (a hypothesis supported by Schmookler 1957) and would reinforce, rather than erode, the position of dominant firms. The data on research employment and firm turnover among the two hundred largest firms suggest that during 1921–1946 at least, the effects of industrial research were consistent with his predictions. Industrial research significantly improved firms' prospects for remaining in the ranks of the two hundred largest firms during this period (Mowery 1983).

The Universities

The pursuit of research was recognized as an important professional activity within both U.S. industry and higher education only in the late nineteenth century, and research in both venues was influenced by the example (and in the case of U.S. industry, by the competitive pressure) of German industry and academia. The reliance of many U.S. universities on state gov-

Table 6.1. Employment of Scientists and Engineers in Industrial Research Laboratories in U.S. Manufacturing Firms, 1921–1946

	1921	1927	1933	1940	1946
Food/beverages	116	353	651	1712	2510
	(.19)	(.53)	(.973)	(2.13)	(2.26)
Tobacco	—	4	17	54	67
		(.031)	(.19)	(.61)	(.65)
Textiles	15	79	149	254	434
	(.015)	(.07)	(.15)	(.23)	(.38)
Apparel	—	—	—	4	25
				(.005)	(.03)
Lumber products	30	50	65	128	187
	(.043)	(.16)	(.22)	(.30)	(.31)
Furniture	—	—	5	19	19
			(.041)	(.10)	(.07)
Paper	89	189	302	752	770
	(.49)	(.87)	(1.54)	(2.79)	(1.96)
Publishing	—	—	4	9	28
			(.015)	(.03)	(.06)
Chemicals	1102	1812	3255	7675	14066
	(5.2)	(6.52)	(12.81)	(27.81)	(30.31)
Petroleum	159	465	994	2849	4750
	(1.83)	(4.65)	(11.04)	(26.38)	(28.79)
Rubber products	297	361	564	1000	1069
	(2.04)	(2.56)	(5.65)	(8.35)	(5.2)
Leather	25	35	67	68	86
	(.09)	(.11)	(.24)	(.21)	(.25)
Stone/clay/glass	96	410	569	1334	1508
	(.38)	(1.18)	(3.25)	(5.0)	(3.72)
Primary metals	297	538	850	2113	2460
	(.78)	(.93)	(2.0)	(3.13)	(2.39)
Fabricated metal products	103	334	500	1332	1489
	(.27)	(.63)	(1.53)	(2.95)	(1.81)
Nonelectrical machinery	127	421	629	2122	2743
	(.25)	(.65)	(1.68)	(3.96)	(2.2)
Electrical machinery	199	732	1322	3269	6993
	(1.11)	(2.86)	(8.06)	(13.18)	(11.01)
Transportation equipment	83	256	394	1765	4491
	(.204)	(.52)	(1.28)	(3.24)	(4.58)
Instruments	127	234	581	1318	2246
	(.396)	(.63)	(2.69)	(4.04)	(3.81)
Total	2,775	6,320	10,927	27,777	45,941

Note: Figures in parentheses represent research intensity, defined as employment of scientists and engineers per 1,000 production workers.

Source: Mowery (1981).

ernment funding, the modest scope of this funding, and the rapid expansion of their training activities all supported the growth of formal and informal linkages between industry and university research.

U.S. universities were a focal point for the external monitoring activities of many U.S. industrial research laboratories before 1940. In some cases these linkages themselves included industrial development and commercialization of new technologies or products. But more often than not, these relationships supported industrial firms' observation of emerging developments in scientific and technological research.

Linkages between academic and industrial research were powerfully influenced by the decentralized structure and funding of U.S. higher education, especially the public institutions within the system. Public funding created a U.S. higher education system that was substantially larger than that of such European nations as Great Britain.[11] The source of this public funding, however, was equally important. The prominent role of state governments in financing the prewar U.S. higher education system led public universities to seek to provide economic benefits to their regions through formal and informal links to industry (Rosenberg and Nelson 1994).

Both the curriculum and research within U.S. higher education were more closely geared to commercial opportunities than was true in many European systems of higher education (with the possible exception of Germany in chemical products; see Beer 1959). Swann (1988) describes the extensive relationships between U.S. academic researchers, in both public and private educational institutions and in U.S. ethical drug firms that developed after World War I.[12] Hounshell and Smith (1988, pp. 290–92) document a similar trend for the Du Pont Company, which funded graduate fellowships at twenty-five universities during the 1920s and expanded its program during the 1930s to include support for postdoctoral researchers.[13]

Many state university systems introduced new programs in engineering, mining, and metallurgy in response to the requirements of local industry. Although they never received federal financial support, the first engineering experiment stations were established early in the twentieth century, and by 1938 there were thirty-eight. These installations focused mainly on applied, rather than basic, research.[14] The University of Minnesota's Mines Experiment Station, equipped with a blast furnace and foundry, conducted research that led to techniques for the commercial exploitation of the state's vast taconite deposits (Mowery and Rosenberg 1989b, p. 95). In 1906, MIT's electrical engineering department established an advisory committee that included senior managers from General Electric, the

Edison Electric Illuminating Company of Boston, AT&T, the Chicago Edison Company, and Westinghouse (Wildes and Lindgren 1985, pp. 42–43).[15] The department's Division of Electrical Engineering Research, established in 1913, received regular contributions from General Electric, AT&T, and Stone and Webster, among other firms.

But perhaps the most important linkage between higher education and industrial research operated through the training by public universities of scientists and engineers for employment in industrial research. The Ph.D.'s trained in public universities were essential participants in the expansion of industrial research employment during this period (Thackray 1982, p. 211).[16] The sheer scale of the U.S. higher educational system meant that it served as a device for the diffusion and utilization of advanced scientific and engineering knowledge.

Although the situation was improving in the decade before 1940, Cohen (1976) noted that virtually all "serious" U.S. scientists completed their studies at European universities, and Thackray et al. (1985) argue that American chemistry research during this period attracted attention (in the form of citations in other scientific papers) as much because of its quantity as its quality.[17]

Regardless of the quality of the scientific research performed within the U.S. research system before World War II, it was the larger body of scientific knowledge, and not merely frontier science, that usually was relevant to the needs of an expanding industrial establishment.[18] Thus, engineers and other technically trained personnel served as valuable carriers of scientific knowledge. As a result, the number of people bringing the knowledge and methods of science to bear upon industrial problems was vastly greater than the limited number of individuals that society chose to label "scientists" at any particular time. Even where it did not advance the knowledge frontier, higher education appears to have been an important instrument for scientific and engineering "catch-up" in the United States during the early twentieth century.

The Federal Role in U.S. R&D Before 1940

In spite of the permissive implications of the "general welfare" clause of the U.S. Constitution, federal support for science prior to World War II was limited by a strict interpretation of the role of the federal government. During World War I the military operated the R&D and production facilities for the war effort, with the exception of the munitions industry, where the federal government relied on Du Pont. When one of the armed services identified a scientific need that could not be met by in-service personnel, a person with the appropriate qualifications was drafted into that branch; very little use was otherwise made of the civilian scientific establishment (Sapolsky 1990).

One important exception was the National Advisory Committee on Aeronautics (NACA), founded in 1915 to "investigate the scientific problems involved in flight and to give advice to the military air services and other aviation services of the government" (Ames 1925). NACA, which was absorbed by the National Aeronautics and Space Administration (NASA) in 1958, made important contributions to the development of new aeronautics technologies for both civilian and military applications throughout its existence but was particularly important during the pre-1940 era.

For 1940, the last year that was not dominated by the vast expenditures associated with wartime mobilization, total federal expenditures for research, development, and R&D plant amounted to $74.1 million. Of that, Department of Agriculture expenditures amounted to $29.1 million, or 39 percent. In 1940 the Department of Agriculture's research budget exceeded that of the agencies that would eventually be combined in the Department of Defense, whose total research budget amounted to $26.4 million. Between them, these categories accounted for 75 percent of all federal R&D expenditures. The claimants on the remaining 25 percent, in descending order of importance, were the Department of the Interior ($7.9 million), the Department of Commerce ($3.3 million), the Public Health Service ($2.8 million), and the National Advisory Committee on Aeronautics ($2.2 million).

Conclusion

Much of the structure of the private sector components of the U.S. R&D system took shape during the 1900–1940 period. Closely linked with the rise of the giant multiproduct corporation that began at the turn of the century, industrial research contributed to the stability and survival of these firms. Industrial research laboratories were a key part of a prewar U.S. R&D system in which federal funds played a modest role. Industry accounted for roughly two-thirds of total national expenditures on R&D (see Mowery and Rosenberg 1989b, p. 93, and National Resources Planning Board 1942, p. 178). The industrially funded R&D that loomed so large in the prewar period's R&D spending was conducted mainly within the boundaries of U.S. firms. By 1940 there were nearly two thousand industrial research laboratories within U.S. manufacturing firms, a dramatic increase from the number (slightly more than one hundred)[19] that appear to have been active in 1900 (Mowery and Rosenberg 1989b, Table 4.1). Although they were located within the firm, these novel entities also looked outside the firm, monitoring the external environment of research in universities and industry, and supporting the technology acquisition strategies that played an important part in the development of large U.S. manufacturing firms during this period.

World War II and Postwar Technological and Economic Dominance, 1940–1975

The U.S. entry into World War II, which began a process of industrial mobilization for wartime and the subsequent cold war, was a watershed in the history of the U.S. R&D "system." Both the sharply increased level of federal resources devoted to defense-related R&D and the ways in which this investment was organized established the basis for the U.S. technological dominance that lasted into the 1970s.

The size of the increase in federal resources allocated to military R&D during the war is staggering. Total federal R&D expenditures (in 1930 dollars) rose from $83.2 million in 1940 to a peak of $1,313.6 million in 1945. Much of this increase was financed by Department of Defense R&D spending, which rose from $29.6 million to $423.6 million (in 1930 dollars). The remaining growth in R&D spending was associated with activities such as the Manhattan Project's development of the atomic bomb, expenditures for which were separate from Defense Department R&D expenditures.

In contrast to the structure of wartime R&D during World War I, when the military services assumed direct responsibility for both the oversight and the performance of much of this activity, the civilian-controlled Office of Scientific Research and Development (OSRD) managed a more decentralized effort during World War II, in which universities and industry played prominent roles. This contrast reflects the far more advanced university and private sector research capabilities during the second global conflict. The contractual arrangements developed during the war allowed the OSRD to tap the broad array of private sector scientific capabilities that had developed during the interwar period.[20] Members of the scientific community were called upon to recommend and to guide as well as to participate in scientific research with military payoffs. The OSRD was not subordinated to the military and had direct access to the president and to the pertinent congressional appropriations committees.

The success of these wartime contractual arrangements, as well as the demonstration of the power of large-scale technology development programs for national defense, contributed to the postwar transformation of the U.S. R&D system. The blueprint for this postwar system was drafted by Vannevar Bush, wartime head of the OSRD, whose *Science: The Endless Frontier* (1945) provided a justification and proposed an administrative structure for federal support of science and technology in the postwar era. Congressional and federal policy makers moved quickly to act on the justification provided by the Bush report.

But Bush's proposal for a coordinated research structure under the control of scientists never materialized. The Defense Department and its uniformed services quickly filled the vacuum created by the political stalemate over the adoption of the Bush report's administrative recommendations, and agencies such as the Office of Naval Research were among the leading supporters of basic research in the late 1940s. A greatly expanded National Institutes of Health took control of research support in the biomedical sciences. The National Science Foundation, the centerpiece of the Bush report's proposed structure, was established only in 1950, and controlled a research budget that was dwarfed by those of the Defense Department, the Atomic Energy Commission, and the National Institutes of Health.

The wartime and postwar debates created a U.S. R&D structure that was clearly distinguished both from the prewar period and from other countries, and had three key features. First, the bulk of federal R&D support was allocated to private firms undertaking work for the Defense Department, the Atomic Energy Commission (the AEC, later absorbed by the Department of Energy), and later, NASA. The Department of Defense and the AEC also became major supporters of university research, and supported numerous large federal laboratories. But as a direct result of wartime management techniques, and consistent with the postwar approach of privatization and decentralization, many of these new laboratories were managed by private firms or universities for the federal government. The dominant role of nongovernmental organizations in performing federally financed R&D was a new element in the U.S. system, and one that distinguished and distinguishes it from the emergent R&D systems of most other industrial economies.

Second, as noted earlier, the National Institutes of Health (NIH) became the leading government research support agency in the fields germane to its mandate. Much of this NIH funding went to universities, and the Institutes grew to become the largest single federal supporter of university research, a status the NIH continues to enjoy. Finally, the National Science Foundation and the National Science Board, established only in 1950, assumed a role out of proportion to their budget as champions of the U.S. academic research enterprise.

Postwar R&D Spending

Through the programs and new initiatives summarized here, the federal government assumed a much larger role in the funding of overall U.S. R&D during the postwar era than was true of the prewar period. Indeed, until the mid-1970s, federal R&D spending accounted for at least 50 percent of to-

Table 6.2. U.S. R&D Spending, 1970–1993: Source of Funds (Percent)

	Federal government	Industry	Universities	Other nonprofits
1970	57	40	2	1
1971	56	41	2	1
1972	56	41	2	1
1973	53	43	2	1
1974	51	45	2	1
1975	51	45	2	2
1976	51	45	2	2
1977	50	46	2	2
1978	50	47	2	2
1979	49	47	2	2
1980	47	49	2	1
1981	46	50	2	1
1982	46	51	2	1
1983	46	51	2	1
1984	45	52	2	1
1985	46	51	2	1
1986	45	51	2	1
1987	46	50	3	1
1988	46	50	3	1
1989	44	51	3	1
1990	44	52	3	2
1991	41	54	3	2
1992	52	52	3	2
1993	42	52	4	2

Note: Totals may not add to 100% due to rounding.

Source: National Science Board (1993).

tal U.S. R&D spending (National Science Foundation 1991), and 48 percent of federally funded R&D for fiscal 1993 was performed in private industry (see Tables 6.2 and 6.3 for a tabulation of the sources of R&D finance and the institutional location of R&D performance in 1970–90).

Private R&D spending also grew significantly during this period. Federal funds were the primary source of R&D spending within aerospace throughout the postwar era. In electronics, federal and private sources accounted for similar proportions of industrial R&D performance. In the chemical and pharmaceuticals industries, however, virtually all of the R&D performed within industry was financed by industry. The total volume of resources devoted to R&D since the end of World War II is large not only

Table 6.3. U.S. R&D Spending, 1970–1993: R&D Performers (Percent)

	Federal government	Industry	Universities	University FFRDCs	Other nonprofits
1970	16	69	9	3	4
1971	16	69	9	3	3
1972	16	69	9	3	3
1973	16	69	9	3	3
1974	15	70	9	3	4
1975	15	69	10	3	4
1976	15	69	10	3	4
1977	14	70	10	3	3
1978	14	69	10	4	3
1979	13	70	10	4	4
1980	12	71	10	4	3
1981	12	72	10	3	3
1982	11	73	9	3	3
1983	12	73	9	3	3
1984	11	74	9	3	3
1985	11	74	9	3	3
1986	11	73	9	3	3
1987	11	74	10	3	3
1988	11	73	10	3	3
1989	11	72	11	3	3
1990	11	71	11	3	3
1991	10	70	12	3	4
1992	11	70	12	3	4
1993	10	70	13	3	4

Note: Totals may not add to 100% due to rounding.

Source: National Science Board (1993).

by comparison with our earlier history, but also by comparison with other Organization for Economic Cooperation and Development (OECD) member countries. Indeed, as late as 1969, when the combined R&D expenditures of the largest foreign industrial economies (West Germany, France, the United Kingdom, and Japan) were $11.3 billion, those for the United States were $25.6 billion. Not until the late 1970s did the combined total for these four countries exceed that of the United States (Danhof 1968, p. 192).

Changing Roles for University Research

The postwar era saw a vast expansion of research in U.S. institutions of higher learning. From an estimated level of nearly $420 million in 1935–1936, university research (excluding federally financed R&D centers [FFRDCs]) grew to more than $2 billion in 1960 and $13.9 billion in 1993 (all amounts in 1982 dollars), nearly doubling as a share of GNP during 1960–1993 (from 0.13 percent to 0.32 percent). The increase in federal support of university research transformed major U.S. universities into centers for the performance of scientific research, an unprecedented role.

One consequence of the upsurge in federal funding of university research appears to have been the weakening of some of the prewar links between corporate and university research (Leslie [1993] presents a similar view of the effects of defense-related research funding on the postwar research activities of MIT and Stanford University). Universities no longer sought industrial research sponsors as aggressively as they had before 1940, since abundant research funding was available from federal sources.[21] Some leading U.S. firms also reduced their university research links; Du Pont's research director argued in 1945 that the firm no longer could rely as heavily on university research as it had before World War II (Hounshell and Smith 1988, p. 355), in part because the firm's competitors, strengthened by World War II, were equally capable of exploiting such research. No longer able to use its superior ability to commercialize the results of basic research performed outside the firm, Du Pont found another reason to rely more heavily on internal sources of new scientific and technical knowledge. Swann (1988, pp. 170–71) also argues that research links between U.S. universities and the pharmaceuticals industry were weakened in the immediate aftermath of World War II by increased federal research funding for academic research in the health sciences.

Nevertheless, the great increases in industrial R&D during the postwar period would have been impossible without the expanded flow of university-trained scientists and engineers who were entering the workforce. In national security–related fields such as computer technology, Defense Department projects often brought university and industry scientists and engineers into close contact. The university research supported by the NIH provided important knowledge and techniques to help pharmaceutical research, and NIH fellowships led to a vast increase in the number of Americans trained in the biomedical sciences. Pharmaceutical companies relied extensively on medical school hospitals for drug testing. And U.S. university research provided a fertile spawning ground for new technologies and new firms.

Research in Industry

During this period, employment within industrial research grew from less than 50,000 in 1946 (Table 6.1) to roughly 300,000 scientists and engineers in 1962, 376,000 in 1970, and almost 600,000 in 1985 (Birr 1966; U.S. Bureau of the Census 1987, p. 570). A good part of the growth during the early part of this period was the result of large-scale funding by the Defense Department and NASA of systems development projects, primarily in the aerospace industry, but also in electrical equipment and electronics. Indeed, from the early postwar years to the late 1960s, the federal government accounted for half or more of total industrial R&D spending (National Science Board 1993, p. 330).

Corporate R&D funding also grew rapidly in chemical products and pharmaceuticals, where, however, government funding of industrial R&D was minimal, and in civilian electronics and civil aircraft. By the late 1960s company-funded R&D in industry exceeded government-funded R&D in industry; by the late 1980s it accounted for more than two-thirds of total R&D performed in industry, including virtually all of it outside aerospace and military electronics.

U.S. antitrust policy continued to influence U.S. industrial research and innovation during the postwar period, but both the policy and the nature of its influence changed. The appointment of Thurman Arnold in 1938 to head the Antitrust Division of the Justice Department, combined with growing criticism of large firms and economic concentration (e.g., the investigations of the federal Temporary National Economic Committee), produced a much tougher antitrust policy that extended well into the 1970s.

This revised antitrust policy made it more difficult for large U.S. firms to acquire firms in "related" technologies or industries,[22] and led them to rely more heavily on intrafirm sources for new technologies. In the case of Du Pont, the use of the central laboratory and development department to seek technologies developed initially by other firms for acquisition was ruled out by senior management as a result of the perceived antitrust restrictions. As a result, internal discovery (rather than development) of new products became paramount (Hounshell and Smith [1988] emphasize the firm's postwar expansion in R&D and its search for "new nylons"),[23] in contrast to the firm's R&D strategy before World War II.

In hindsight, it appears that the strategy of seeking "new nylons" from central corporate research tended to separate these fundamental research activities from the rest of the corporation, and central research laboratories could no longer benefit from close links with the markets and capabilities of the parent firm. Worse yet, in a number of cases when the labs did create technologies of significant potential value, the parent corporation failed to recognize their commercial potential; we return to this issue later.

At the same time that established firms like Du Pont were shifting the R&D strategies that many had employed since the early twentieth century, new firms began to play an important role in the development of the technologies spawned by the postwar U.S. R&D system. The prominence of new firms in commercializing new electronics technologies in the postwar United States, for example, contrasts with their more modest role in this industry in the interwar period. In industries that effectively did not exist before 1940, such as computers, semiconductors, and biotechnology, major innovations were commercialized largely through the efforts of new firms.[24] The postwar United States differs in this respect not only from the prewar United States but also from Japan and most Western European economies, where established firms dominated technology commercialization in electronics and pharmaceuticals.

In semiconductors, the activities of new firms in the commercialization of new technologies often built on the R&D investments and patents of larger firms (Tilton 1971, p. 69). In a near reversal of the prewar situation, the R&D facilities of large firms provided many of the basic technological advances that were commercialized by new firms. Small-firm entrants' contribution to semiconductor-industry patents grew steadily during 1952–1968, but their most significant role was in introducing new products, reflected in their often-dominant share of markets in new semiconductor devices.[25] In mainframe computers, established firms, such as IBM, Burroughs, and NCR, retained important roles. But in other emerging segments, such as minicomputers and supercomputers, new firms, including CDC, DEC, Data General, and Cray, achieved dominant positions, a point overlooked in Chandler's analysis (1990). Microcomputers also saw an influx of new firms, such as Compaq and Apple, along with established enterprises like IBM. In the U.S. biotechnology industry, new firms played an even more important role in developing and patenting new techniques and products than was true of semiconductors (Pisano, Shan, and Teece 1988, p. 189).

Several factors contributed to this prominent role of new, small firms in the postwar U.S. innovation system. The large basic research establishments in universities, government, and a number of private firms served as important "incubators" for the development of innovations that "walked out the door" with individuals who established firms to commercialize them. This pattern has been particularly significant in the biotechnology, microelectronics, and computer industries. Indeed, high levels of labor mobility within regional agglomerations of high-technology firms, including movement of people from universities to industry, have served both as an important channel for technology diffusion and as a magnet for other firms in similar or related industries.

The foundation and survival of vigorous new firms also depended on sophisticated private financial mechanisms that could support new firms during their infancy. The U.S. venture capital market played an especially important role in the establishment of many microelectronics firms during the 1950s and '60s, and contributed to the growth of the biotechnology and computer industries. According to the Office of Technology Assessment (1984, p. 274), the annual flow of venture capital into industrial investments ranged between $2.5 and $3.0 billion during 1969–1977. Venture capital–supported investments in new firms, however, were substantially smaller, averaging roughly $500 million annually during the 1980s (Florida and Smith 1990). Investment funds from venture capital were gradually supplemented by public equity offerings.[26]

Although even these totals likely are a small function of total investment financing in the United States (it is not simple to calculate a comparable total), most observers believe that the availability of venture capital in the United States vastly exceeded that elsewhere. Western European economies have yet to spawn similarly abundant sources of risk capital for new enterprises in high-technology industries. Okimoto (1986, p. 562) estimated that Japanese venture capital firms provided no more than $100 million in financing in 1986.

Commercialization of microelectronics and biotechnology innovations by new firms was aided by a relatively permissive intellectual property regime in these industries that aided technology diffusion and reduced the burden on young firms of litigation over innovations that may have originated in part within established firms or other research installations. In microelectronics, liberal licensing and cross-licensing policies were one byproduct of the 1956 consent decree that settled the federal antitrust suit against AT&T. In biotechnology, continuing uncertainty over the strength and breadth of intellectual property protection may have discouraged litigation.

Postwar U.S. antitrust policy also contributed to the importance of start-up firms. The 1956 settlement of the AT&T case significantly improved the environment for start-up firms in microelectronics, because of the liberal patent licensing terms of the consent decree and because the decree led AT&T to withdraw from commercial activities outside of telecommunications. As a result, the firm with the greatest technological capabilities in microelectronics was effectively forestalled from entry into commercial production of microelectronic devices, creating substantial opportunities for entry by start-up firms. A 1956 consent decree settling another antitrust suit against IBM also mandated liberal licensing by this pioneer computer firm of its punch card and computer patents at reasonable rates (Flamm 1988).

In addition to antitrust policy, U.S. military procurement aided the growth of new firms. As noted earlier, the U.S. military market in the 1950s and '60s provided an important springboard for start-up firms in microelectronics and computers, who faced relatively low marketing and distribution barriers to entry into this market.[27] The benefits of the military market were enhanced further by the substantial possibilities for technological spillovers from military to civilian applications. Some of the effects of military procurement on start-up firms' success, and on the spillovers from military to commercial applications, were a result of policy. In contrast to European military procurement, the U.S. armed services were willing to award major procurement contracts to firms with little track record in serving the military (or, in many cases, any) market.[28]

The System Under Pressure: Developments Since 1970

The Erosion of U.S. Dominance

For the quarter century after World War II, the United States was the world's dominant economic and technological power. This dominance rested in part on the sheer size of the American economy. In 1960 the population of the United States alone roughly equaled the combined population of the four largest Western European countries, and was twice as large as that of Japan. The real GNP of the United States was more than double that of Western Europe and roughly six times that of Japan. As these latter numbers imply, U.S. dominance was as much a matter of productivity as of size. U.S. GNP per worker in 1960 was double that in Western Europe, and fourfold that in Japan. U.S. productivity exceeded that of Japan and Western European nations in almost all manufacturing industries, and in manufacturing industries characterized by rapid product innovation, American firms were among the leaders.

The earlier sections of this essay have identified two sources of American dominance in manufacturing and two eras during which that dominance was attained. In the early part of the twentieth century, American firms gained preeminence in mass-production technology, acquiring significant productivity advantages over European firms in such industries as steel, concrete, automobiles, and a wide range of consumer durables. The rise of U.S. dominance in these sectors during this period reflected the nation's status as the world's largest single industrial market, in an international environment characterized by significant barriers to international trade in manufactured goods. The American lead in "high-technology" products largely came into being after World War II, as the result of massive public investments in training of scientists and engineers and large public and private investments in industrial R&D. In aircraft, electronics, and computer technologies, U.S. firms also benefited from Department of Defense expenditures on procurement and R&D.

By the 1960s, however, firms in the major European nations and Japan were rapidly catching up to their American counterparts in productivity. This both caused, and is reflected in, the convergence of GNP per worker shown in Figure 6.1. The product design capabilities of European and

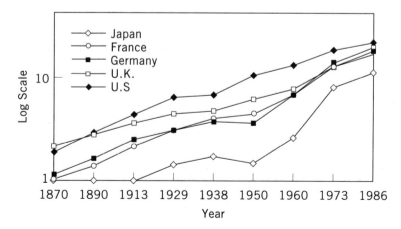

Figure 6.1. Gross domestic product per hour, 1870–1986. *Source:* Maddison (1987, 1989).

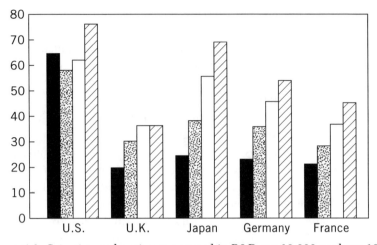

Figure 6.2. Scientists and engineers engaged in R&D per 10,000 workers: 1965, 1972, 1981, 1987. *Source:* U.S. National Science Board (1989, 1991), Appendix Table 3-19.

Japanese firms also were catching up to those of U.S. firms in a number of industries that they formerly had dominated. This convergence was one result of large-scale investments in the training of scientists and engineers, as well as in R&D, that were made in Japan and Western Europe (see Figure 6.2).

Foreign firms began to compete effectively with American firms in the American market during the 1960s. First in textiles, somewhat later in steel, then in consumer electronics, automobiles, semiconductors, and other areas of sophisticated manufacturing, foreign firms took a significant and growing share of the American market. By the mid-1970s, many Americans were expressing concern, and by the 1980s the concern had turned to alarm. Less than twenty-five years elapsed between the publication by Jean-Jacques Servan-Schreiber of his book *The American Challenge* (1968), which raised the specter to Europeans of growing subservience to an all-competent United States, and the publication of the MIT Commission on Industrial Productivity's *Made in America,* (Dertouzos, Lester, and Solow 1989), which argued that the United States had lost important manufacturing strengths.

Correlates and Causes

What factors lay behind this postwar decline in U.S. dominance? The most important was the reconstruction of the European and Japanese economies, within a global economy characterized by regional and global liberalization in trade and investment flows. Lower trade barriers made it possible for European and Japanese firms to exploit the economies of large-scale production that had been monopolized for so long by American firms manufacturing largely for their domestic market. Heavy investment in new plant and equipment, rapid productivity growth associated with the adoption of American-pioneered technology and management styles, and a surge of exports from European and Japanese firms were the result. Similarly, European and Japanese governments revamped their education systems to expand production of scientists and engineers, and European and Japanese firms increased their R&D expenditures, absorbing the newly enhanced supply of scientific and technical manpower.

To be sure, the opening of the postwar U.S. economy to international flows of goods and capital benefited much of American industry. U.S. trade with other nations (imports plus exports) grew from 9 percent of GDP in 1960 to 22 percent in 1993. Major American industries like aircraft, computers, and semiconductors now sell a significant fraction of their output on foreign markets, have significant foreign investments, or work closely with foreign partners. Nonetheless, the opening of the postwar economy probably was more beneficial to European and Japanese firms than to U.S. enterprises (see Abramovitz 1986; Nelson and Wright 1992).

The post-1970 period has been marked not only by the rise of formidable foreign competitors to American firms but also by slower growth in U.S. productivity and incomes. Foreign competition had little to do with the slowdown in U.S. productivity growth, which also afflicted the other OECD economies, but this slowdown enabled foreign firms (especially those from newly industrializing economies) to narrow performance gaps with U.S. firms more rapidly than they otherwise would have. Slower growth in real household incomes after 1970 was associated with declines in U.S. private and public savings. Schultze (1990) estimated that net national saving amounted to 8 percent of national income during 1951–1980, but dropped to 3.1 percent during 1984–1985 and 3.2 percent in 1989, as a result of declining rates of private saving and sharp increases in government dissaving. Partly in response to these developments in national savings behavior, business-sector gross fixed capital investment in the U.S. economy averaged 12 to 14 percent of net output during 1965–1985, well above U.S. savings but well below the levels observed in Japan and Germany during this period (Dertouzos, Lester, and Solow 1989). The gap between U.S. investments and U.S. savings was covered by a trade deficit.

The post-1970 era also was marked by two other developments with mixed consequences for industrial R&D and U.S. innovative performance.

One was the growing popularity of the idea that a corporation should be re-garded as the holder of a "portfolio" of business units that need have very little in common by way of markets, technology, or products. To some ex-tent, the popularity of unrelated diversification was a response by senior U.S. managers to severe antitrust restrictions on corporate acquisitions in related industries. The principal role of central management, according to this view of the corporation, was to allocate funds across its business units, rewarding or replacing management of those units according to their profit and loss statement.[29] Conglomerate mergers were the result.

By the 1980s, however, the disappointing operating results of these conglomerate mergers provided an important impetus to another great wave of corporate restructuring that reversed the results of many of the conglomerate mergers of the previous decade. In sharp contrast to the early merger movements, however, a large share of the transactions effected dur-ing the 1980s involved hostile takeovers (Shleifer and Vishny 1991).

Both the conglomerate mergers of the 1970s and their reversal during the 1980s were made possible by developments in the U.S. capital market that gave new life to the U.S. market for corporate control. Beginning in the 1960s, growth in pension funds and other institutional portfolios signifi-cantly expanded the portion of shares administered on behalf of their ulti-mate beneficiaries by institutional managers.[30] In 1955 pension funds owned 2 percent of the value of all U.S. equities outstanding, and house-holds owned 91 percent. By 1985 these shares had shifted to 22 percent and 60 percent, respectively. During the 1980s "junk bonds" and other new instruments enabled vast quantities of funds, often managed by institutions on behalf of mutual fund shareholders or pension beneficiaries, to be col-lected quickly for purchases of the stock of targeted corporations and to make offers to the remaining stockholders of intended takeovers.

Although these changes most significantly affected divestiture and ac-quisition behavior in less R&D-intensive industries, they almost certainly affected R&D investment decisions in R&D-intensive sectors as well. In many of the large U.S. firms that had pioneered industrial research, the rise of conglomerate strategies weakened senior management understanding of and commitment to the development of the technologies that historically had been essential to the competitive success of the firm, eroding the qual-ity and consistency of decision making on technology-related issues. RCA, for example, pursued a conglomerate diversification strategy while main-taining its large fundamental research "campus" near Princeton, New Jersey, that made important research contributions to military and con-sumer electronics technologies. The firm encountered growing difficulties, however, in reaping the commercial returns to its considerable research capabilities, often because of poor strategic judgments that were the result of a management that no longer had special expertise in the traditional core business. RCA's decision to pursue development of the expensive and unsuccessful videodisc home-entertainment technology (Graham 1986b) and its neglect of its dominant position in color television receivers jointly led to the company's demise.

More generally, the sharp separation of R&D from the other parts of the corporation, which, as noted earlier, was part of the strategy adopted by many firms during the 1960s, began to cause serious problems in the late 1970s and 1980s. The Palo Alto Research Center of Xerox and the Watson Research Laboratories of IBM in Yorktown were extremely productive scientific research laboratories, but other firms often beat IBM and Xerox to market with products based on this research. The separation of product design and development from production and marketing that marked many American corporations also became a significant liability when the Americans were forced to compete with Japanese firms that maintained closer integration of design and development with production and marketing.

The role of another pillar of the postwar U.S. R&D system, defense R&D, shifted, and its contribution to advances in civilian technologies arguably declined, after the 1960s. Defense-related spending on procurement and R&D during the 1950s and '60s spawned a number of important commercial innovations and innovative firms. By the 1970s, however, military needs in many advanced technologies had diverged from those of civilian users sufficiently to reduce the importance of defense-related spending as a source of support for the development of new commercial technologies within the United States. By the 1980s, civilian R&D and product design determined the pace of advances in military technologies to a growing extent in such industries as semiconductors and computers, even as the share of total demand within these industries accounted for by the U.S. military shrank. In addition, the share of U.S. military spending allocated to research, as opposed to development, declined during the 1970s and 1980s, further weakening the potential "spillovers" from these expenditures.

The returns to R&D investment in the U.S. economy during the mid-1970s appear to have declined,[31] and the rate of growth in real industry expenditures on R&D declined. Industry funding of basic research shrank, and many of the central research facilities of the giant corporations entered a period of budgetary austerity or cutbacks. After a resurgence in the early 1980s, the rate of growth in industry-funded R&D fell off again, and the

National Science Foundation in early 1990 reported that real industry-financed R&D had actually declined during 1988–1989.[32]

Corporate and System Responses

The 1980s and early 1990s witnessed what we believe are the early stages of a significant restructuring in U.S. corporate R&D. This restructuring has manifested itself in the growth of external R&D "alliances" between U.S. firms and U.S. universities, U.S. and foreign firms, and in significant reductions in corporate support for the corporate research laboratories that were prominent in corporate R&D strategies of the 1950s and '60s. There is a clear central theme in these changes—the end of the separation of R&D from other activities within the firm and the end of the "inward-oriented" R&D strategies that many large U.S. firms pursued during the early postwar period, and a revival of some elements of the prewar system.

One striking development has been the reorganization of applied R&D to bring that activity closer to production and marketing. In many large firms, product divisions now have more control over R&D, and efforts continue to reduce barriers to communication and cooperation between R&D and other corporate functions. One consequence is a significant reduction in the time from product conception to full-scale production that a number of American companies have achieved. Both Ford and Chrysler, for example, have reduced the length of time required to develop new models by at least 30 percent (White and Suris 1993; *Business Week* 1993), and examples of similar or greater reductions can be found at Motorola, Eastman Kodak, and Hewlett Packard (see Wheelwright and Clark 1992; Bowen et al. 1994).

Another effect of the reorientation of U.S. corporate R&D has been a reduction in the fraction of corporate R&D invested in long run-fundamental research. Companies now focus much of their R&D attention on this and at most one future generation of products, looking outside their boundaries for the basic advances that will establish the technologies of the future.

As Rosenberg and Nelson (1994), Cohen, Florida, and Goe (1994), and others have noted, U.S. firms have expanded their funding for and relationships with university-based research since 1980. The central role of the federal government in supporting academic research has been supplemented by increased funding from industry. Financial support from industry has established a number of research facilities on university campuses to conduct research with potential commercial value. The phenomenon of university-industry research collaboration is not new, having been well established before 1940. The share of university research expenditures financed by industry nevertheless appears to have declined through much of the postwar period. In 1953, industry financed 11 percent of university research, a share that declined to 5.5 percent in 1960 and 2.7 percent in 1978. By 1985–1986, estimates suggest that industrial funds accounted for no more than 5 percent of university research, a share that had increased by 1992 to as much as 7 percent. The recent development of closer research ties between universities and industry represents a restoration of a linkage that was weakened during the 1950s and '60s.[33]

The growing role of U.S. universities in the performance of basic research has been associated with a recognition by U.S. industry that more fields of research at the universities now hold out significant promise of generating findings that may be of great commercial significance. The connection between university research and commercial technology appears to be particularly close in biotechnology, a factor that influences the character of many university-industry research relationships in this field, and may distinguish them from university-industry research collaborations in other fields.[34] Increased pressure to reduce R&D costs, to monitor a wider range of emerging areas of scientific research, and to speed the commercialization of scientific research have driven many U.S. firms to attempt to develop relationships with an array of external institutions (see later text for additional discussion), including research universities in the United States and abroad, to complement and enhance the payoff from their in-house R&D activities.[35]

The expanded international R&D collaborations of U.S. firms, most of which focus on near-term product development, manufacturing, and marketing, reflect the influence of several factors beyond those that have contributed to increased domestic R&D collaboration with other firms and universities. The improved technological capabilities of many foreign firms that have resulted from the broad trends described earlier now make them far more attractive partners for such international collaborative ventures. Foreign firms' stronger technological capabilities also have intensified their interest in using these international alliances as opportunities for learning such complex, noncodified technological skills as systems integration in airframe design and development. The willingness of foreign governments in Japan and Western Europe to subsidize (through grants or low-interest loans) the risk capital employed by their firms in these ventures also means that U.S. firms can both spread risk and lower their cost of capital by teaming up with foreign firms. Finally, significant nontariff barriers to international trade in such industries as telecommunications equipment and commercial aircraft mean that international joint ventures can facilitate access to foreign markets that are growing rapidly and whose revenues are more important than ever in offsetting rising development costs.

Government policy has been an important influence on the evolving structure of U.S. industrial R&D through this century, and the 1980s were no exception. Despite the Reagan and Bush administrations' rejection of any intimation of intervention in the market, significant initiatives, such as the semiconductor research consortium Semiconductor Manufacturing Technology (SEMATECH), were in fact undertaken under Reagan, and both administrations (with the political support of Congress, controlled by the opposition party for much of this period) made significant changes in two key policy areas, antitrust and intellectual property rights. U.S. initiatives in technology policy during the Reagan and Bush administrations improved enforcement of intellectual property protection and reduced antitrust restrictions on collaboration in research. The 1982 legislation that established the court of appeals for the federal circuit strengthened the protection granted to patent holders.[36] The U.S. government also pursued stronger international protection for intellectual property rights in both bilateral and multilateral international trade negotiations.

The widespread faith in strong intellectual property rights as a critical policy tool in improving U.S. competitiveness was exemplified in two other important statutes of the early 1980s that sought to transform the large system of federal laboratories into sources of innovations for U.S. firms. The Bayh-Dole Patent and Trademark Amendments Act and the Stevenson-Wydler Act changed several aspects of federal policy toward the federal government laboratories. The Bayh-Dole Act strongly encouraged federal agencies to grant licenses to small businesses and nonprofit institutions, especially universities, for patents deriving from research funded by federal agencies at federal and contractor-operated laboratories. The Federal Technology Transfer Act of 1986 authorized the negotiation of cooperative R&D agreements (CRADAs) between government-operated laboratories and private firms. A CRADA specifies terms under which a private organization provides personnel, equipment, or financing for R&D activities that are consistent with a specific laboratory's broader mission.[37] Included in most CRADAs are provisions that cover the sharing of intellectual property rights to any technologies developed under their auspices.

In antitrust policy, the Reagan administration adopted a substantially more lenient enforcement posture than its predecessors, arguing that international competition had significantly reduced the dangers of market power being acquired through domestic merger and acquisition activity. Justice Department guidelines and review procedures for mergers were relaxed somewhat, and major federal antitrust suits against high-technology firms were dropped or settled in the early 1980s. The Reagan administration supported the 1984 National Cooperative Research Act (NCRA), which reduced the antitrust penalties for collaboration among firms in precommercial research. The NCRA has been credited with easing the founding of the Microelectronics and Computer Technology Corporation, an early research consortium involving U.S. computer and electronics firms.

Federal technology policy has undergone a substantial shift since the mid-1980s. Faced with far more intense foreign competition by firms that had greatly improved their abilities to exploit scientific advances made in U.S. and other foreign laboratories, federal policy makers began to experiment with "strategic" programs that seek to strengthen civilian technological capabilities. Programs such as the National Center for Manufacturing Sciences, SEMATECH, the Advanced Technology Program of the Department of Commerce, and even the National Science Foundation's Engineering Research Centers all represent significant departures from the established postwar structure of federal science and technology policy. The Commerce Department's share of total federal R&D spending more than doubled between fiscal 1993 and fiscal 1995, as a direct result of the new focus on support for "precommercial" technology programs. In addition, the Clinton administration announced its intention to increase civilian R&D spending to at least 50 percent of the total federal R&D budget by 1998.

In addition to foreign competition, of course, these experiments were motivated by the belief (often based on little evidence) that foreign government R&D programs had contributed to the competitive strength of non-U.S. firms. The changing relationship between defense-related and civilian technologies that we noted earlier also influenced this shift, not least by engaging the attention of the federal agency with the largest single R&D budget, the Defense Department. Both SEMATECH and the National Center for Manufacturing Sciences received federal funds from Defense Department programs. In both cases these funds were granted to programs seeking to enhance civilian technological strengths in the belief that the U.S. high-technology defense industrial base rested on the commercial technological and competitive capabilities of defense suppliers.

All of these initiatives in U.S. technology policy predate the Clinton administration. Indeed, programs such as SEMATECH and the Advanced Technology Program originated in Congress in the face of indifference or hostility from the White House. This point is an important one, in our view, because it suggests that the political foundations of this shift in technology are in fact more bipartisan and robust in nature than is sometimes assumed. The prominent congressional role in these initiatives also increases considerably the risks that the design and implementation of these programs will be dominated by redistributive politics. Although it was hardly immune to the force of distributive politics, the "national security" rationale for postwar R&D spending provided a clearer mission and restricted some of the creative redefinition of program goals and priorities that such amorphous objectives as "national competitiveness" invite.

American Corporations and Technical Advance in a Global Economy

This essay has focused on the American corporation and the role it has played in technical advance, but in many places we have compared the American scene with that in Europe, and more lately Japan, in order to highlight what was distinctive about American corporations and the American innovation system more generally. From the end of the nineteenth century through the 1960s, one of the key factors that distinguished American corporations from their foreign counterparts was the much larger size of their market, in both numbers of customers and their affluence. Through much of the post–World War II era, American corporations in many industries benefited from large American defense expenditures. Throughout the post–World War II era, the American university research system has been by far the world's strongest, and this has lent advantage to American corporations in several industries. Antitrust policies have been much stronger in the United States than abroad. On the other hand, active government civilian technology policy has been much more muted.

During the last thirty years, as our discussion in the preceding section suggested, nearly all of the features that made the postwar American corporation and the postwar American R&D system distinctive have faded in significance. Today the American corporation, and the American national innovation system in which it is embedded, looks much more like those in other major industrial nations. This trend reflects change in both the U.S. and foreign economies. We noted the dismantling in the post–World War II era of barriers to trade and investment, which enabled foreign corporations to face markets of comparable size to those faced by American companies. This was reflected both in improvement in foreign firms' access to the American market, and in growth in the European and Japanese markets. Much of the fall from dominance of American corporations in mass production industries is attributable to this equalization of the size of the playing fields.

Although even in the wake of the cold war, the American military budget remains far larger than those of other industrial nations, by the mid-1970s U.S. military procurement and R&D spending no longer provided commercial advantage to U.S. companies. As military procurement demand became more specialized, military contracts gave companies much less advantage in commercial markets. At the same time, civilian markets, especially in telecommunications and electronics, enjoyed more rapid innovation and exploited technologies that in many areas were more advanced than those available to the military.

The American university research system remains the world's largest, but many foreign companies have established branch operations in the United States, or have established their own direct connections with American universities. And the American university research system itself is under considerable pressure. Although for the foreseeable future the strength of the American university research system will continue to lend some special advantages to American companies in areas where close university ties are important, this element of American distinctiveness now appears to be less important than once was true.

There has been a certain amount of convergence of both antitrust and technology policies across the advanced industrial nations. The relaxation of U.S. antitrust policy described in the preceding sections may reduce the ability of new firms to enter industries and effectively challenge the prevailing dominant ones, a feature that in the postwar era has been much more common in the United States than in Europe and Japan. On the other hand, the "competition policy" of the European Union appears to be growing in stringency. Dramatic evidence of the "convergence" of the competition policies of the European Union and the United States may be found in the efforts by the U.S. Department of Justice to coordinate its actions on the Microsoft antitrust case with those of the European Union (see Novak 1994). Partly in response to pressure from the United States and the governments of other industrial nations, Japan is also beginning to adopt a tougher posture on competition policy. Thus, while the formation of new firms in high-technology fields may become more difficult in the United States, it may become somewhat easier in Europe and Japan.

National technology policies also seem to be converging. The United States has initiated significant new programs in public-private cooperation in civilian technologies, such as SEMATECH and the Advanced Technologies Program, during the 1980s, in some cases in the face of opposition from the Reagan and Bush administrations. The Clinton administration has embraced these policies much more warmly. Although the U. S. government (or at least, the trade policy components thereof) continues to argue that government support of civilian technologies should not go beyond the "precommercial" stage, a threshold may have been crossed in the recently announced Pentagon initiative for supporting U.S. development and production of flat panel displays, which combines federal grants for R&D with financial help for the establishment by U.S. firms of production facilities (Davis and Zachary 1994). Having for years criticized European governments for their production subsidies on such enterprises as Airbus Industrie, the U.S. government now seems to be wading in the same pond.

Future American corporations thus are likely to resemble their European and Japanese counterparts somewhat more closely, and they will be supported by and linked into the rest of their national innovation system in similar ways. What does such similarity imply for the behavior of the global innovation system? In a number of industries the range of technologies that a corporation needs to be able to tap into in order to be an effective competitor has widened significantly. This is reflected in the increasing number of fields in which large corporations are patenting (see Pavitt and Patel 1994). This is one among a variety of forces that are causing corporations to recognize expressly that they cannot be "an island unto themselves" so far as technology generation is concerned but must develop a network of relationships with other institutions.

The expanding network of intercorporate technology linkages includes numerous transnational linkages. In industries such as commercial aircraft, new product development and manufacture have been dominated by such "alliances" for most of the past two decades. These international linkages are one consequence of the evening out of technological capabilities across corporations in different nations, but they also provide important risk-sharing advantages to the participants. They also reflect the operation of national policies of "technonationalism" that seek to support domestic firms: paradoxically, these "national" or "regional" champions must form transnational links as a means of gaining access to foreign markets, foreign technology development programs, and the like.

How do these developments resolve the debate between those who have a Chandlerian vision of the importance of large firms that make significant long-term investments, and the proponents of the Sabel-Piore position that the future lies with smaller firms linked in networks? The evolving U.S. corporate innovation system has many elements of both visions. In aircraft, electronics, automobiles, and a number of other industries, one sees networks of large firms and growth in international alliances that is supported in some cases by government policies of "managed trade." This development has spawned concern that these global industries will become cartelized. In other areas of electronics, as well as biotechnology and software, networks link small and large firms, and provide opportunities for smaller firms to gain access to foreign sources of capital and foreign markets. Moreover, with the possible exception of commercial aircraft, the success of any efforts by firms and governments throughout the industrial world to "control" competition in such products as dynamic random-access memories (DRAMs) or computers has been undercut by the entry of new firms, in some cases from such nations as Taiwan and South Korea. In contrast to the interwar years, technological opportunities and capabilities appear to be sufficiently widely distributed within the global economy, and capital and labor mobility sufficiently high, that effective cartelization of high-technology products is now difficult if not impossible.

There is little agreement on the consequences of these tendencies toward convergence in the corporate and national R&D systems of the industrial economies. Robert Reich (1991) argues that the modern manufacturing corporation has become largely an organization that coordinates work done all over the world, in many cases by firms and individuals connected to the coordinating firm only through short-term contracts. His famous question—"Who is us?"—asserts that manufacturing firms are so transnational that the concept of an "American firm" has become quite ambiguous. On the other side, Michael Porter (1990) insists that the incidence and character of transnationalism has been exaggerated. Although a modern manufacturing company may sell a good portion of its products abroad, and have sizable production and R&D operations abroad, its heart and roots (to combine two metaphors) remain at home. In their empirical analysis of corporate patenting, Pavitt and Patel (1994) show that with the exception of companies headquartered in very small countries (like the Netherlands and Belgium), the bulk of the patents obtained by large manufacturing corporations are based on work done in the country of the corporate headquarters. On the other hand, however, 30 to 50 percent of the value added in Boeing's 767 transport as of 1991 was from its Japanese risk-sharing partners (Friedman and Samuels 1992, p. 23), and this firm predicts that North America will account for no more than 30 percent of its sales of wide-body commercial transports during the next twenty-five years (Kandebo 1994). By 1990, the U.S. Department of Commerce estimated that more than 20 percent of the cars assembled in the United States were produced by Japanese-owned companies; the average "U.S. content" of these automobiles was 50 percent as of 1989 (U.S. Department of Commerce 1991).

In our concluding remarks, we want to call attention to some implications of this controversy. One important consequence is a growing tension between the aim of national governments and the behaviors of international business. American corporations are increasingly transnational, and a larger share of manufacturing plants located in the United States now have foreign owners than at any time in the postwar era. In spite or because of this development, the notion that the American government ought to support and protect "American business" has, if anything, gained in political currency. The history of U.S. policy toward the semiconductor industry is a good case in point. During the late 1970s and early 1980s, a growing fraction of the output of American-owned semiconductor companies was produced abroad. The significant increases in American imports of semiconductors that occurred during the early and middle 1980s included a significant amount of semiconductors produced by American-owned companies abroad, as well as semiconductors produced by Japanese and other foreign companies. The political debate that led to the semiconductor trade agreement virtually ignored this fact. It was a political imperative that SEMATECH admit as members only U.S.-owned companies, despite the fact that during this period the same U.S. companies had developed a network of technology agreements with Japanese- and European-owned companies. It is ironic, but merits more notice than it has received thus far, that the U.S.-Japanese semiconductor agreement set a floor under the prices of Japanese semiconductors, and thereby supported an increase in Korean production of semiconductors for the U.S. market.

Another consequence is that, in their zeal to help national competitiveness, governments seem to be shifting their own R&D support portfolios toward projects that have short-term and predictable payoffs, and away from long-run fundamental research, just as at the same time companies have been doing the same thing. Projects like SEMATECH may help the competitiveness of the American semiconductor industry vis-à-vis the Japanese. But such projects will not compensate for the decline of the corporate central research in the major electronics companies. This is a problem that national innovation systems have yet to solve.

Notes

1. Abramovitz (1986) notes,

The path of technological change which in those years [1870–1945] offered the greatest opportunities for advance was at once heavily scale-dependent and biased in a labor-saving but capital- and resource-using direction. In both respects America enjoyed great advantages compared with Europe or Japan. Large-scale production was favored by a large, rapidly growing, and increasingly prosperous population. It was supported also by a striking homogeneity of tastes. This reflected the country's comparative youth, its rapid settlement by migration from a common base on the Atlantic, and the weakness and fluidity of its class divisions. Further, insofar as the population grew by immigration, the new Americans and their children quickly accepted the consumption patterns of their adopted country because the prevailing ethos favored assimilation to the dominant native white culture. At the same time, American industry was encouraged to explore the rich possibilities of a labor-saving but capital- and resource-using path of advance. The country's resources of land, forest, and minerals were particularly rich and abundant, and supplies of capital grew rapidly in response to high returns. (P. 397)

2. As described by Mowery and Rosenberg (1989b),

The coupling between science and technological innovation remained very loose during this period [the nineteenth century] because, in many industrial activities, innovations did not require scientific knowledge. This was true of the broad range of metal-using industries in the second half of the nineteenth century, in which the United States took a position of distinct technological leadership. Indeed, following the American display at the Crystal Palace Exhibition in 1851, the British came to speak routinely of "the American system of manufactures." . . . In the second half of the nineteenth century, America provided the leadership in developing a new production technology for manufacturing such products as reapers, threshers, cultivators, repeating rifles, hardware, watches, sewing machines, typewriters, and bicycles. (P. 27)

3. See Stigler (1968). The Supreme Court ruled in the *Trans Missouri Association* case in 1898 and the *Addyston Pipe* case in 1899 that the Sherman Act outlawed all agreements among firms on prices or market sharing. Data in Thorelli (1954) and Lamoreaux (1985) indicate an increase in merger activity between the 1895–1898 and 1899–1902 periods. Lamoreaux (1985) argues that other factors, including the increasing capital intensity of production technologies and the resulting rise in fixed costs, were more important influences on the U.S. merger wave, but her account (p. 109) also acknowledges the importance of the Sherman Act in the peak of the merger wave. Lamoreaux also emphasizes the incentives created by

tighter Sherman Act enforcement after 1904 for firms to pursue alternatives to merger or cartelization as strategies for attaining or preserving market power.

4. Threatened with antitrust suits from state as well as federal agencies, George Eastman saw industrial research as a means of supporting the diversification and growth of Eastman Kodak (Sturchio 1985, p. 8). Facing a hostile political environment during the first decade of this century, the Du Pont Company used industrial research to diversify out of the black and smokeless powder businesses even before the 1913 antitrust decision that forced the divestiture of a portion of the firm's black powder and dynamite businesses (Hounshell and Smith 1988, p. 57).

5. Other examples include the establishment by the Standard Oil Company of New Jersey of a development department to carry out development of technologies obtained from other sources, rather than for original research (Gibb and Knowlton 1956, p. 525); Alcoa's R&D operations also closely monitored and frequently purchased process innovations from external sources (Graham and Pruitt 1990, pp. 145–47).

6. During 1921–1946, the growth of intrafirm industrial research was associated with a decline in turnover among the largest U.S. manufacturing firms during this period (Mowery 1983; Edwards 1975; Kaplan 1964; Collins and Preston 1961). Interestingly, and in contrast to the usual formulation of one of the Schumpeterian "hypotheses," these results suggest that firm conduct (R&D employment) was an important influence on market structure (turnover). They are also broadly consistent with the results of studies of more recent data on the market structure–R&D investment relationship that suggest that structure and R&D investment are jointly determined (Levin, Cohen, and Mowery 1985).

7. The original provision of the U.S. patent law, and the timing of its change, indicate the growing role of the United States as a source of industrial technology, and the change in its historic status as a "borrower" of industrial technology from foreign sources. As Bright (1949) notes, "The U.S. patent laws at that time [the 1890s] contained a provision that an American patent was valid only as long as the shortest-lived patent in a foreign country, if the foreign patent had been issued first. The Canadian patent [for Edison's carbon filament] was declared invalid by the Canadian Deputy Commissioner of Patents, on February 26, 1889, for non-compliance with Canadian statutes regarding manufacture and importation. If that decision had been allowed to stand, the American patent would probably have become void also, since the Canadian patent had been granted before the American patent (p. 88)." Pressure from U.S. firms that had become patent holders led to revision in this statute: "The American patent laws were revised as of January 1, 1898, to include a provision that domestic applications for patents could be filed anytime within seven months of the earliest foreign application without prejudicing the full seventeen-year term of the American patent, regardless of its date of issue. The revision resulted in large part from agitation created during the early nineties when the Edison patent and a few fundamental patents in other industries were cut short

before their full terms. The modification had an important bearing on the length of patent protection in incandescent lighting after that date" (Bright 1949, p. 91).

8. In 1921 the chemicals, petroleum, and rubber industries accounted for slightly more than 40 percent of total research scientists and engineers in manufacturing.

9. The data in Table 6.1 were drawn originally from the National Research Council surveys of industrial research employment, as tabulated in Mowery (1981). The surveys' coverage of research laboratories in 1921 is somewhat suspect, and the data for that year should be treated with caution.

10. "Innovation is being reduced to routine. Technological progress is increasingly becoming the business of teams of trained specialists who turn out what is required and make it work in predictable ways. The romance of earlier commercial adventure is rapidly wearing away" (Schumpeter 1950, p. 132).

11. In the early 1920s, roughly 42,000 students were enrolled in British universities; the figure rose to 50,000–60,000 by the late 1930s. By contrast, American institutions of higher learning awarded over 48,000 *degrees* in 1913 and more than 216,000 in 1940. With a total population 35 percent that of the United States, Britain had only about 6 percent as many students in higher education in the late 1930s. See Briggs (1981); U.S. Bureau of the Census (1975).

12. According to Swann (1988, p. 50), Squibb's support of university research fellowships expanded (in current dollars) from $18,400 in 1925 to more than $48,000 in 1930, and accounted for one-seventh of the firm's total R&D budget for the period. By 1943, according to Swann (p. 50), university research fellowships amounting to more than $87,000 accounted for 11 percent of Eli Lilly and Company's R&D budget. Swann cites similarly ambitious university research programs sponsored by Merck and Upjohn.

13. During the 1920s, colleges and universities to which the firm provided funds for graduate research fellowships also asked Du Pont for suggestions for research, and in 1938 a leading Du Pont researcher left the firm to head the chemical engineering department at the University of Delaware (Hounshell and Smith 1988, p. 295).

14. The contribution of universities to U.S. technological performance is particularly interesting in view of the fact that for much of the pre-1940 period there were few areas of scientific research in which U.S. universities or scholars could be described as substantially stronger than their European counterparts. This portion of the historical record suggests that the linkage between excellence in scientific research and growth in U.S. national income or productivity is tenuous, a point consistent with postwar evidence and with the conclusions of Nelson and Wright (1992).

15. The MIT example also illustrates the effects of reductions in state funding on universities' eagerness to seek out industrial research sponsors. Wildes and Lindgren (1985, p. 63) note that the 1919 withdrawal by the Massachusetts state

legislature of financial support for MIT, along with the termination of the institute's agreement with Harvard University to teach Harvard engineering courses, led MIT President Richard C. Mclaurin to establish the Division of Industrial Cooperation and Research. This organization was financed by industrial firms that gained access to MIT libraries, laboratories, and staff for consultation on industrial problems. Still another institutional link between MIT and a research-intensive U.S. industry, the Institute's School of Chemical Engineering Practice, was established in 1916 (Mattill 1991).

16. Hounshell and Smith (1988, p. 298) report that 46 of the 176 Ph.D.'s overseen by Carl Marvel, longtime professor in the University of Illinois chemistry department, went to work for one firm, Du Pont. According to Thackray (1982, p. 221), 65 percent of the 184 Ph.D.'s overseen by Professor Roger Adams of the University of Illinois during 1918–58 went directly into industrial employment. In 1940, 30 of the 46 Ph.D.'s produced by the University of Illinois chemistry department were first employed in industry.

17. As Thackray et al. (1985) note,

From comparative obscurity before World War I, American chemistry rose steadily in esteem to a position of international dominance. Almost half the citations in the *Annual Reports* [*Annual Reports in Chemistry*, described on the page as "a central British review journal"] in 1975 were to American publications. Similarly, almost half the citations to non-German-language literature in *Chemische Berichte* [the "central German chemical journal"] in 1975 went to American work. It is striking that this hegemony is the culmination of a fifty-year trend of increasing presence, and not merely the result of post–World War II developments. Second, it is clear that the increasing attention received in the two decades before World War II reflected the growing *volume* of American chemistry, rather than a changed assessment of its worth. Since World War II, however, in both *Chemische Berichte* and the *Annual Reports*, American chemistry has been cited proportionately more than is warranted by increasing quantity alone. The prominence of American work within the international literature has been sustained by quality. (P. 157; emphasis in original)

18. Moreover, to a much greater extent in the United States than Great Britain, technically trained engineers moved into positions of industrial leadership. See Chandler (1962, p. 317).

19. As Hounshell (1993) has pointed out, the estimate of the number of industrial research laboratories in Mowery and Rosenberg (1989) may be high; he argues that the number of in-house research laboratories that did more than simple materials testing or quality control was in fact far smaller. The estimate in Mowery and Rosenberg is based on the reported foundation dates of laboratories listed in the 1940 edition of the National Research Council survey (1940), and therefore is subject to the vagaries of corporate memory, as well as differences among firms over the definition of an industrial research laboratory. The employment data reported in

Table 6.1 are less likely to suffer from this flaw, since they are gathered from contemporaneous surveys published by the National Research Council.

20. The differences in the arrangements during the two world wars between the federal government and the private sector for defense-related research and development had significant effects on the diffusion of technological know-how during and after each conflict. Limited involvement by private firms in military R&D during World War I meant that "spillovers" from military to commercial innovation were limited. World War II appears to have had a different effect. In the chemicals industry, for example, Hounshell and Smith (1988) argue that World War II created significant new competitive threats to the Du Pont Company, because of the large-scale involvement of private firms in the operation of complex chemical production processes: "Because the wartime emergency served as a great leveler—exposing other companies to truly large-scale projects and manufacturing operations while forcing Du Pont to yield much of its proprietary knowledge—Du Pont's executives foresaw that firms such as Allied, Union Carbide, Monsanto, and Dow would become far more competitive after the war. This competition would be manifested not only in the marketplace but also in the laboratory" (p. 332).

21. Lowen (1991) points out that in some cases (e.g., Stanford University), university administrators entered the postwar era with ambitious plans to expand industrial support of university research. In the case of Stanford University, the foundation in 1946 of the Stanford Research Institute was one component of such a strategy, which largely disappeared under the flood of federal research funds that soon materialized:

> The turn to government support in the years following the war coincided with a realization within the university that industry support would be inadequate to meet the goal of elevating Stanford's prestige. . . . Stanford's administration would continue in the next decades to seek collaboration with industry, but in the late 1940s, it had begun to recognize the usefulness of federal support, and to appreciate the relatively unrestricted terms for its acceptance. After the Korean War, the interest in using federal funds to support expensive and nationally prestigious fields of research would grow (Lowen 1991, pp. 386–87).

22. Hawley (1966) analyzes the shifting antitrust policies of the New Deal. Arnold took office in 1938, and during 1938–1942 filed 312 antitrust cases, considerably more than the 46 filed during 1932–1937 or the 70 filed during 1926–1931 (Fligstein 1990, p. 168).

23. Hounshell and Smith (1988) and Mueller (1962) both argue that the discovery and development of nylon, one of Du Pont's most commercially successful innovations, was in fact atypical of the firm's pre-1940 R&D strategy. Rather than being developed to the point of commercialization following its acquisition by Du Pont, nylon was based on the basic research of Carothers within Du Pont's central corporate research facilities. The successful development of nylon from basic research through to commercialization nevertheless exerted a strong influence on Du

Pont's postwar R&D strategy, not least because of the fact that many senior Du Pont executives had direct experience with the nylon project. Hounshell (1993) argues that Du Pont had far less success in employing the "lessons of nylon" to manage such costly postwar synthetic fiber innovations as Delrin.

24. This is not to deny the major role played by such large firms as IBM in computers and AT&T in microelectronics. In other instances, large firms have acquired smaller enterprises and applied their production or marketing expertise to expand markets for a new product technology. Nonetheless, it seems apparent that start-up firms have been far more active in commercializing new technologies in the United States than in other industrial economies. Malerba (1985) and Tilton (1971) stress the importance of new, small firms in the U.S. semiconductor industry; Flamm (1988) describes their significant role in computer technology; and Orsenigo (1989) and Pisano, Shan, and Teece (1988) discuss the importance of these firms in the U.S. biotechnology industry. Bollinger, Hope, and Utterback (1983) survey some of the literature on the "new technology-based firm."

25. The contribution of new firms to major innovations increased substantially after 1960, the era of integrated circuits that combined in a single chip the functions formerly performed by discrete semiconductor components. Levin (1982, p. 55) noted that only one of the firms (Motorola) identified as having produced major innovations or new product families during 1960–1977 had been active in the electronics industry before the invention of the transistor.

26. See Perry (1986) and Mowery and Steinmueller (1991). Sharp (1989) argues that

> the venture capital market in Europe is underdeveloped. The most active venture capital market is in the UK where some half dozen funds specialising in investment in biotechnology are active and an estimated total of over $1 billion invested since 1980. . . . The doyen of this market is the Rothschild Fund Biotechnology Investments Ltd (BIL)—now capitalised at $200 million and the largest specialist fund in Europe. By contrast, the largest German venture capital fund, Techno Venture Management, established in 1984, had an initial capitalisation of $10 million and in 1989 is worth only $50 million. The availability of venture capital, however, is only one part of the equation. BIL, for example, whose investments span biotechnology and medical technology, have not found in Europe the quality of investment they are seeking. 75 per cent of their investments are in the US, only 25 per cent in Europe, and these concentrated almost entirely in the UK. This pattern of investment is mirrored by nearly all the investment funds, all of which invest a large proportion of their investments in biotechnology in the small firm sector in the US, and only a very small proportion in small firms in Europe." (Pp. 9–10)

27. Discussing the early years of the semiconductor industry, Tilton (1971) noted, "The defense market has been particularly important for new firms . . . these

firms often have started by introducing new products and concentrating in new semiconductor fields where the military has usually provided the major or only market. Fortunately for them, the armed forces have not hesitated to buy from new and untried firms. In early 1953, for example, before Transitron had made any significant sales, the military authorized the use of its gold-bonded diode. This approval has been called the real turning point for the new firms. During 1959, new firms accounted for 63 percent of all semiconductor sales and 69 percent of military sales" (p. 91). Describing a similar situation in the early computer industry, Flamm (1988) argues that "the many start-up computer firms entering the U.S. industry in the early and middle 1950s were chasing after a reasonably large market, dominated by military demand. For almost all of these producers, the military was the first, and generally the best customer. About eighty different organizations, including numerous small start-ups that later merged with larger producers or disappeared, produced computers in the United States during the 1950s. The U.S. military, or defense contractors, paid for or purchased the first machines made by most of these groups" (pp. 78–79).

28. "European governments provided only limited funds to support the development of both electronic component and computer technology in the 1950s and were reluctant to purchase new and untried technology for use in their military and other systems. European governments also concentrated their limited support on defense-oriented engineering and electronics firms. The American practice was to support military technology projects undertaken by industrial and business equipment firms that were mainly interested in commercial markets. These firms viewed their military business as a development vehicle for technology that eventually would be adapted and sold in the open marketplace" (Flamm 1988, p. 134).

29. As Williamson argued in 1975,

The capital market in an environment of U-form firms was earlier regarded as a less than efficacious surveillance and correction mechanism for three reasons: its external relation to the firm places it at a serious information disadvantage; it is restricted to nonmarginal adjustments; it experiences nontrivial displacement costs. The general office of the M-form organization has superior properties in each of these respects. First, it is an internal rather than external control mechanism with the constitutional authority and expertise to make detailed evaluations of the performance of each of its operating parts. Second, it can make fine-tuning as well as discrete adjustments. This permits it both to intervene early in a selective, preventative way (a capability which the capital market lacks altogether), as well as to perform ex post corrective adjustments, in response to evidence of performance failure, with a surgical precision that the capital market lacks (the scalpel versus the ax is an appropriate analogy). Finally, the costs of intervention by the general office are relatively low. Altogether, therefore, a profit-oriented general office in an M-form enterprise might be expected to secure superior performance to that which the unassisted capital market can enforce. The M-form organization might thus be viewed as capitalism's creative response to the evident limits which the capital market experiences in its relations to the firm. (Pp. 158–59)

By the late 1980s, however, Rumelt (1988) expressed considerable skepticism concerning internal capital markets: "Given mobility, the [middle] manager must temper his view of how a project's future influences his reputation or income with the possibility that he will no longer be in the organization. The net effect is that mobile managers will discount future cash flows more heavily than would be indicated by their personal discount rates on wealth or their employer's cost of capital. Given the fact that top management must choose among the projects that are actually proposed, the corporation as a whole will appear more myopic than are its members" (1988, pp. 153–54).

   30. According to Chandler (1994), institutional managers held 8 percent of all publicly listed securities in 1950, a share that had grown to 55 to 60 percent by 1990. Individuals held 30 to 35 percent of all listed securities in 1990.

   31. See Baily and Chakrabarti (1988, esp. pp. 42–43), who argue that such a decline did occur but attribute it largely to exhaustion of technological opportunities. The empirical research on the returns to R&D investment, to say nothing of fluctuations in these returns over time, yields mixed results: Scherer (1983) and Griliches (1986) do not find a decline in the rate of return to R&D, although Griliches (1980) did find such a decline.

   32. Markoff (1989) reports that recent survey data from the National Science Foundation indicate that inflation-adjusted R&D spending by industry shrank by 0.9 percent between 1988 and 1989, the first reduction in real industry-funded R&D spending since 1974–1975. For a less gloomy assessment of this development, see the *Economist* (1990, pp. 65–72).

   33. Indeed one might argue that the weakening of university-industry research linkages during a significant portion of the postwar period was the real departure from historical trends. Hounshell and Smith (1988) cite a 1945 memo from Elmer Bolton, director of what was to become the Du Pont Company's central research laboratory, that made a case for greater self-reliance by the firm in its basic research:

   Three things were necessary: Du Pont had to strengthen its research organizations and house them in modern research facilities; the company's existing processes had to be improved and new processes and products developed; and "fundamental research, which will serve as a background for new advances in applied chemistry, should be expanded not only in the Chemical Department but should [also] be increased in our industrial research laboratories and the Engineering Department." Bolton stressed that it was no longer "possible to rely to the same extent as in the past upon university research to supply this background so that in the future years it will be necessary for the Company to provide this knowledge to a far greater extent through its own efforts." To "retain its leadership" Du Pont had "to undertake on a much broader scale fundamental research in order to provide more knowledge to serve as a basis for applied research." (P. 355)

Swann (1988, pp. 170–81) also argues that research links between U.S. universities and the pharmaceuticals industry weakened significantly in the immediate aftermath of World War II, in part as a result of vastly increased federal research funding for academic research in the health sciences.

34. This close relationship is due in part to the nature of biotechnology. Recombinant DNA and genetic engineering techniques in many ways represent radical scientific breakthroughs that are being transferred to industry and reduced to practice. In Gomory's terminology (1988), biotechnology is a "ladder" technology, that is, a case in which "the new idea is dominant and the product forms itself around the new idea or new technology. Those who understand that idea or technology are often scientists, and they therefore play leading roles in its introduction" (p. 11). Another example of a ladder technology cited by Gomory is the transistor. In contrast to biotechnology, of course, the transistor was first developed within industry. The different origin of these two major scientific discoveries may reflect the shifting role of industry and universities as basic research performers. An interesting empirical study of university-industry research collaboration that tends to support the characterization of biotechnology as a unique area of interaction is Blumenthal et al. (1986).

35. An OECD study (Organization for Economic Cooperation and Development 1984) quotes a Xerox Corporation research executive's description of the firm's investment in the Center for Integrated Systems at Stanford University: "Xerox's contribution to CIS is very small compared to what we are investing internally in the same kind of research. For little additional investment we enlarge our perspective by participating in a broad program of basic research. We envision opportunities for joint interaction with the university and with other companies, as well as the ability to recruit students. On a per-dollar basis it should be a good investment" (quoted in OECD 1984, p. 47).

36. See Perry (1986), among other accounts. According to Katz and Ordover (1990), at least fourteen congressional bills passed during the 1980s focused on strengthening domestic and international protection for intellectual property rights, and the court of appeals for the federal circuit created in 1982 has upheld patent rights in roughly 80 percent of the cases argued before it, a considerable increase from the pre-1982 rate of 30 percent for the federal bench.

37. The 1958 Space Act that created NASA provided authority to this agency's laboratories to enter into similar agreements with industry.

References

Abramovitz, M. 1986. "Catching Up, Forging Ahead, and Falling Behind." *Journal of Economic History* 46: 385–406.

————. 1990. "The Catch-Up Factor in Postwar Economic Growth." *Economic Inquiry* 28: 1–18.

Ames, J. 1925. *Statement of NACA Chairman to the President's Aircraft Board.* Washington, D.C.: U.S. Government Printing Office.

Baily, M. N., and A. K. Chakrabarti. 1988. *Innovation and the Productivity Crisis.* Washington, D.C.: Brookings Institution.

Barfield, C. E. 1982. *Science Policy from Ford to Reagan.* Washington, D.C.: American Enterprise Institute.

Beer, J. H. 1959. *The Emergence of the German Dye Industry.* Urbana: University of Illinois Press.

Birr, K. 1966. "Science in American Industry." In *Science and Society in the U.S.,* edited by D. Van Tassel and M. Hall. Homewood, Ill.: Dorsey.

Blumenthal, D., M. Gluck, K. S. Louis, and D. Wise. 1986. "Industrial Support of University Research in Biotechnology." *Science* 231: 242–46.

Bollinger, L., K. Hope, and J. M. Utterback. 1983. "A Review of Literature and Hypotheses on New Technology-Based Firms." *Research Policy* 12: 1–14.

Borrus, M. G. 1988. *Competing for Control.* Cambridge, Mass.: Ballinger.

Bowen, H. K., K. B. Clark, C. A. Holloway, and S. C. Wheelwright. 1994. *The Perpetual Enterprise Machine.* New York: Oxford University Press.

Briggs, A. 1981. "Social History 1900–1945." In *The Economic History of Britain since 1700,* vol. 2, edited by R. Floud and D. W. McCloskey. Cambridge: Cambridge University Press.

Bright, A. A. 1949. *The Electric-Lamp Industry.* New York: Macmillan.

Bush, V. 1945. *Science: The Endless Frontier.* Washington, D.C.: U.S. Government Printing Office.

Business Week. 1989a. "Advanced Bio Class? That's over in Hitachi Hall." August 7, pp. 73–74.

————. 1989b. "Is the U.S. Selling Its High-Tech Soul to Japan?" June 26, pp. 117–18.

————. 1993. "Chrysler's Neon: Is This the Small Car Detroit Couldn't Build?" May 3, pp. 116–26.

Chandler, A. D., Jr. 1962. *Strategy and Structure: Chapters in the History of Industrial Enterprise.* Cambridge, Mass.: MIT Press.

————. 1974. "Structure and Investment Decisions in the United States." In *The Rise of Managerial Capitalism,* edited by H. Daems and H. v.d. Wee. The Hague: Martinus Nijhoff.

————. 1976. "The Development of Modern Management Structure in the US and UK." In *Management Strategy and Business Development,* edited by L. Hannah. London: Macmillan.

————. 1977. *The Visible Hand.* Cambridge, Mass.: Harvard University Press.

————. 1978. "The United States: Evolution of Enterprise." In *The Cambridge Economic History of Europe.* Vol. 7, P. Mathias and M. Postan, eds., *The*

Industrial Economies: Capital, Labour, and Enterprise, pt. 2. Cambridge: Cambridge University Press.

———. 1980a. "The Growth of the Transnational Industrial Firm in the United States and the United Kingdom: A Comparative Analysis." *Economic History Review,* 2d ser., 33: 396–410.

———. 1980b. "The United States: Seedbed of Managerial Capitalism." In *Managerial Hierarchies,* edited by A. D. Chandler and H. Daems. Cambridge, Mass.: Harvard University Press.

———. 1990. *Scale and Scope.* Cambridge, Mass.: Harvard University Press.

———. 1994. "The Competitive Performance of U.S. Industrial Enterprises Since the Second World War." *Business History Review* 68: 1–72.

Chesnais, F. 1988. "Technical Co-Operation Agreements Between Firms." *STI Review* 4: 51–119.

Cohen, I. B. 1976. "Science and the Growth of the American Republic." *Review of Politics* 38: 359–98.

Cohen, W. M., and D. C. Mowery. 1989. "The Influence of the Correlates of Firm Size on Product-Line R&D Investment." Unpublished manuscript.

Cohen, W. M., R. Florida, and R. Goe. 1994. *University-Industry Research Centers.* Pittsburgh: Carnegie-Mellon University.

Collins, N. R., and L. E. Preston. 1961. "The Size Structure of the Largest Industrial Firms." *American Economic Review* 51: 986–1011.

Congressional Budget Office. 1984. *Federal Support for R&D and Innovation.* Washington, D.C.: Congressional Budget Office.

Danhof, C. 1968. *Government Contracting and Technological Change.* Washington, D.C.: Brookings Institution.

David, P. A. 1975. *Technical Choice, Innovation, and Economic Growth.* New York: Cambridge University Press.

———. 1986. "Technology Diffusion, Public Policy, and Industrial Competitiveness." In *The Positive Sum Strategy: Harnessing Technology for Economic Growth,* edited by R. Landau and N. Rosenberg. Washington, D.C.: National Academy Press.

Davis, B. 1989. "Pentagon Seeks to Spur U.S. Effort to Develop 'High-Definition' TV." *Wall Street Journal,* January 4, p. 29.

Davis, B., and G. P. Zachary. 1994. "Electronics Firms Get Push from Clinton to Join Industrial Policy Initiative in Flat-Panel Displays." *Wall Street Journal,* April 28, p. A16.

Davis, L. E., and D. C. North. 1971. *Institutional Change and American Economic Growth.* New York: Cambridge University Press.

Dertouzos, M., R. Lester, and R. Solow, eds. 1989. *Made in America.* Cambridge, Mass.: MIT Press.

Economist. 1989."Test-tube Trauma," February 10, p. 67.

————. 1989. "Venture-Capital Drought," June 24, pp. 73–74.

————. 1990. "Out of the Ivory Tower," February 3, pp. 65–72.

Edwards, R. C. 1975. "Stages in Corporate Stability and Risks of Corporate Failure." *Journal of Economic History* 35: 418–57.

Ergas, H. 1987. "Does Technology Policy Matter?" In *Technology and Global Industry,* edited by H. Brooks and B. Guile. Washington, D.C.: National Academy Press.

Evenson, R. E. 1982. "Agriculture." In *Government and Technical Progress,* edited by R. R. Nelson. New York: Pergamon.

————. 1983. "Intellectual Property Rights and Agribusiness Research and Development: Implications for the Public Agricultural Research System." *American Journal of Agricultural Economics* 65: 967–76.

Ferguson, C. H. 1983. "The Microelectronics Industry in Distress." *Technology Review* 86: 24–37.

————. 1988. "From the People Who Brought You Voodoo Economics." *Harvard Business Review* 66: 55–62.

Flamm, K. 1988. *Creating the Computer.* Washington, D.C.: Brookings Institution.

Flamm, K., and T. McNaugher. 1989. "Rationalizing Technology Investments." In *Restructuring American Foreign Policy,* edited by J. D. Steinbruner. Washington, D.C.: Brookings Institution.

Fligstein, N. 1990. *The Transformation of Corporate Control.* Cambridge, Mass.: Harvard University Press.

Florida, R. L., and M. Kenney. 1988. "Venture Capital-Financed Innovation and Technological Change in the USA." *Research Policy* 17: 119–37.

Florida, R. L., and D. F. Smith. 1990. "Venture Capital, Innovation, and Economic Development." *Economic Development Quarterly* 4: 345–60.

Friedman, D. B., and R. J. Samuels. 1992. "How to Succeed Without Really Flying: The Japanese Aircraft Industry and Japan's Technology Ideology." MIT Japan Program paper 92-01.

Galambos, L. 1966. *Competition and Cooperation.* Baltimore, Md.: Johns Hopkins University Press.

Gerschenkron, A. 1962. "Economic Backwardness in Historical Perspective." In *Economic Backwardness in Historical Perspective,* ed. A. Gerschenkron. Cambridge, Mass.: Harvard University Press.

Gibb, G. S., and E. H. Knowlton. *The Resurgent Years: History of Standard Oil Company (New Jersey), 1911–1927.* New York: Harper.

Gomory, R. E. 1988. "Reduction to Practice: The Development and Manufacturing Cycle." In *Industrial R&D and U.S. Technological Leadership.* Washington, D.C.: National Academy Press.

Gorte, J. F.. 1989. Testimony Before the Subcommittee on Science, Research, and Technology, Committee on Science, Space, and Technology, U.S. House of Representatives. July 13.

Graham, M. B. W. 1986a., "Corporate Research and Development: The Latest Transformation." *Technology in Society* 7: 179–95.

———. 1986b. *RCA and the Videodisc: The Business of Research.* Cambridge: Cambridge University Press.

———. 1988. "R&D and Competition in England and the United States: The Case of the Aluminum Dirigible." *Business History Review* 62: 261–85.

Graham, M. B. W., and B. H. Pruitt. 1990. *R&D for Industry: A Century of Technical Innovation at Alcoa.* New York: Cambridge University Press.

Griliches, Z. 1980. "R&D and the Productivity Slowdown." *American Economic Review* 70: 343–48.

———. 1986. "Productivity, R&D, and Basic Research at the Firm Level in the 1970s." *American Economic Review* 76: 141–54.

Gupta, U. 1982. "Biotech Start-Ups Are Increasingly Bred Just to Be Sold." *Wall Street Journal*, July 19, p. B2.

———. 1988. "Start-Ups Face Big-Time Legal Artillery." *Wall Street Journal*, November 20, p. B2.

Hall, B. H. 1988. "The Effect of Takeover Activity on Corporate Research and Development." In *Corporate Takeovers: Causes and Consequences*, edited by A. Auerbach. Chicago: University of Chicago Press.

Harris, R. G., and D. C. Mowery. 1990. "New Plans for Joint Ventures: The Results May Be an Unwelcome Surprise." *The American Enterprise,* September/October.

Hawley, E. 1966. *The New Deal and the Problem of Monopoly.* Princeton, N.J.: Princeton University Press.

Hodder, J. E. 1988. "Corporate Capital Structure in the United States and Japan: Financial Intermediation and Implications of Financial Deregulation." In *Government Policy Towards Industry in the United States and Japan*, edited by J. B. Shoven. New York: Cambridge University Press.

Hounshell, D. A. 1993, "Industrial R&D in the United States: An Exploratory History." Paper presented at the conference "The Future of Industrial Research," Harvard Business School, Boston, February 10–12.

Hounshell, D. A., and J. K. Smith. 1985. "Du Pont: Better Things for Better Living Through Research." Paper presented at "The R&D Pioneers," Hagley Museum and Library, Wilmington, Delaware, October 7.

———. 1988. *Science and Corporate Strategy: Du Pont R&D, 1902–1980.* New York: Cambridge University Press.

Jorde, T. M., and D. J. Teece. 1989. "Competition and Cooperation: Striking the Right Balance." *California Management Review* 31: 25–37.

Kandebo, S. W. 1994. "Market Forces Recast Propulsion Industry." *Aviation Week & Space Technology*, March 14, p. 71.

Kaplan, A. D. H. 1964. *Big Business in a Competitive System.* Washington, D.C.: Brookings Institution.

Katz, M. L., and J. A. Ordover. 1990. "R&D Competition and Cooperation." *Brookings Papers on Economic Activity: Microeconomics 1990*: 137–92.

Lamoreaux, N. 1985. *The Great Merger Movement in American Business, 1895–1904*. New York: Cambridge University Press.

Lazonick, W. 1992. "Controlling the Market for Corporate Control: The Historical Significance of Managerial Capitalism." *Industrial and Corporate Change* 1: 445–88.

Leslie, S. W. 1993. *The Cold War and American Science: The Military-Industrial-Academic Complex at M.I.T. and Stanford*. New York: Columbia University Press.

Levin, R. C. 1982. "The Semiconductor Industry." In *Government and Technical Progress: A Cross-Industry Comparison*, edited by R. R. Nelson. New York: Pergamon Press.

Levin, R. C., W. M. Cohen, and D. C. Mowery. 1985. "R&D, Appropriability, Opportunity, and Market Structure: New Evidence on Some Schumpeterian Hypotheses." *American Economic Review Papers and Proceedings* 75: 20–24.

Lichtenberg, F. R., and D. Siegel. 1989. "The Effects of Leveraged Buyouts on Productivity and Related Aspects of Firm Behavior." Unpublished manuscript.

Lorell, M. A. 1980. *Multinational Development of Large Aircraft: The European Experience*. Santa Monica, Calif.: RAND Corporation.

Lowen, R. S. 1991. "Transforming the University: Administrators, Physicists, and Industrial and Federal Patronage at Stanford, 1935–49." *History of Education Quarterly* 31: 365–88.

Maddison, A. 1987. "Growth and Slowdown in Advanced Capitalist Economies." *Journal of Economic Literature* 25: 649–69.

———. 1989. *The World Economy in the 20th Century*. Paris: OECD.

Malerba, F. 1985. *The Semiconductor Business*. Madison: University of Wisconsin Press.

Markoff, J. 1989. "A Corporate Lag in Research Funds Is Causing Worry." *New York Times*, January 23, p. A1.

Mattill, J. 1991. *The Flagship: The M.I.T. School of Chemical Engineering Practice, 1916–1991*. Cambridge, Mass.: Koch School of Chemical Engineering Practice, MIT.

Millard, A. 1990. *Edison and the Business of Innovation*. Baltimore, Md.: Johns Hopkins University Press.

Mowery, D. C. 1981. "The Emergence and Growth of Industrial Research in American Manufacturing, 1899–1946." Ph.D. diss., Stanford University.

———. 1983. "Industrial Research, Firm Size, Growth, and Survival, 1921–1946." *Journal of Economic History* 43: 953–80.

———. 1984. "Firm Structure, Government Policy, and the Organization of Industrial Research: Great Britain and the United States, 1900–1950." *Business History Review* 58: 504–31.

Mowery, D. C., and N. Rosenberg. 1989a. "New Developments in U.S. Technology Policy: Implications for Competitiveness and International Trade Policy." *California Management Review* 27: 107–24.

———. 1989b. *Technology and the Pursuit of Economic Growth.* New York: Cambridge University Press.

Mowery, D. C., and W. E. Steinmueller. 1991. "Government Policy and Industry Evolution in the U.S. Integrated Circuit Industry: What Lessons for Newly Industrializing Economies?" CCC Working Paper, Center for Research in Management, University of California, Berkeley.

Mueller, W. F. 1962. "The Origins of the Basic Inventions Underlying Du Pont's Major Product and Process Innovations, 1920 to 1950." In *The Rate and Direction of Inventive Activity*, edited by R. Nelson. Princeton, N.J.: Princeton University Press.

National Research Council. 1982. "Research in Europe and the United States." In *Outlook for Science and Technology: The Next Five Years.* San Francisco: W. H. Freeman.

National Resources Planning Board. 1942. *Research—A National Resource,* vol. 1. Washington, D.C.: U.S. Government Printing Office.

National Science Board. 1981. *Science Indicators, 1980.* Washington, D.C.: U.S. Government Printing Office.

———. 1983. *Science Indicators, 1982.* Washington, D.C.: U.S. Government Printing Office.

———. 1993. *Science Indicators, 1993.* Washington, D.C.: U.S. Government Printing Office.

National Science Foundation. 1985. *Science and Technology Data Book.* Washington, D.C.: National Science Foundation.

———. 1987. *Research and Development in Industry, 1986.* Washington, D.C.: National Science Foundation.

———. 1991. *International Science and Technology Data Update: 1991.* Washington, D.C.: National Science Foundation.

Navin, R., and M. V. Sears. 1955. "The Rise of a Market for Industrial Securities." *Business History Review* 29, no. 2: 105–38.

Neal, A. D., and D. G. Goyder. 1980. *The Antitrust Laws of the U.S.A.* 3d ed. Cambridge: Cambridge University Press.

Nelson, R. R. 1984. *High-Technology Policies: A Five-Nation Comparison.* Washington, D.C.: American Enterprise Institute.

Nelson, R. R., and G. Wright. 1992. "The Rise and Fall of American Technological Leadership: The Postwar Era in Historical Perspective." *Journal of Economic Literature* 30, no. 3: 1931–64.

———. 1994. "The Erosion of U.S. Technological Leadership as a Factor in Postwar Economic Convergence." In *Convergence of Productivity*, edited by W. J. Baumol, R. R. Nelson, and E. N. Wolff. New York: Oxford University Press.

Noble, D. 1977. *America by Design*. New York: Knopf.

Novak, V. 1994. "Antitrust's Bingaman Talks Tough on Microsoft Case." *Wall Street Journal*, July 19, p. B1.

Office of Technology Assessment, U.S. Congress. 1984. *Commercial Biotechnology: An International Analysis*. Washington, D.C.: U.S. Government Printing Office.

Okimoto, D. I. 1986. "Regime Characteristics of Japanese Industrial Policy." In *Japan's High Technology Industries: Lessons and Limitations of Industrial Policy*, edited by H. Patrick and K. Yamamura. Seattle: University of Washington Press.

Okimoto, D. I., and G. R. Saxonhouse. 1987. "Technology and the Future of the Economy." In *The Political Economy of Japan*. Vol. 1, *The Domestic Transformation*, edited by K. Yamamura and Y. Yasuba. Stanford, Calif.: Stanford University Press.

Organization for Economic Cooperation and Development (OECD). 1984. *Industry and University: New Forms of Co-operation and Communication*. Paris: OECD.

Orsenigo, L. 1989. *The Emergence of Biotechnology*. London: Pinter Publishing.

Ostry, S. 1990. *The Political Economy of Policy Making: Trade and Innovation Policies in the Triad*. New York: Council on Foreign Relations.

Parker, W. N. 1972. "Agriculture." In *An Economist's History of the United States*, edited by L. E. Davis, R. A. Easterlin, and W. N. Parker. New York: Harper and Row.

Patel, P., and K. Pavitt. 1986. "Measuring Europe's Technological Performance: Results and Prospects." In *A European Future in High Technology?* edited by H. Ergas. Brussels: Center for European Policy Studies.

Pavitt, K., and P. Patel. 1994. "Technological Competencies in the World's Largest Firms: Characteristics, Constraints, and Scope for Managerial Choice," SPRU-STEEP Discussion Paper no.13, University of Sussex.

Perry, N. J. 1986. "The Surprising Power of Patents." *Fortune*, June 25, pp. 57–63.

Perry, W. J. 1986. "Cultivating Technological Innovation." In *The Positive Sum Strategy*, edited by R. Landau and N. Rosenberg. Washington, D.C.: National Academy Press.

Piore, M. J., and C. F. Sabel. 1984. *The Second Industrial Divide*. New York: Basic Books.

Pisano, G. P., W. Shan, and D. J. Teece. 1988. "Joint Ventures and Collaboration in the Biotechnology Industry." In *International Collaborative Ventures in U.S. Manufacturing*, edited by D. C. Mowery. Cambridge, Mass.: Ballinger Publishing Company.

Pollack, A. 1990. "Technology Company Gets $4 Million U.S. Investment." *New York Times*, April 10, p. C17.

Porter, M. 1990. *The Competitive Advantage of Nations*. New York: Free Press.

Pursell, C. 1977. "Science Agencies in World War II: The OSRD and Its Challengers." In *The Sciences in the American Context*, edited by N. Reingold. Washington, D.C.: Smithsonian Institution.

Rauch, J. 1994. "The Visible Hand." *National Journal,* July 9, pp. 1612–17.

Reich, L. S. 1985. *The Making of American Industrial Research.* New York: Cambridge University Press, 1985.

Reich, R. B. 1991. *The Work of Nations.* New York: Knopf.

Reich, R. B., and E. Mankin. 1986. "Joint Ventures with Japan Give Away Our Future." *Harvard Business Review* 64: 78–86.

Reid, P. P. 1989. "Private and Public Regimes: International Cartelization of the Electrical Equipment Industry in an Era of Hegemonic Change, 1919–1939." Ph.D. diss., Johns Hopkins School of Advanced International Studies.

Rodgers, T. J. 1990. "Landmark Messages from the Microcosm." *Harvard Business Review* 68 (January–February): 24–30.

Rosenberg, N. 1972. *Technological and American Economic Growth.* New York: Harper and Row.

Rosenberg, N., and R. R. Nelson. 1994. "American Universities and Technical Advance." *Research Policy* 24: 323–48.

Rosenberg, N., and W. E. Steinmueller. 1988. "Why Are Americans Such Poor Imitators?" *American Economic Review* 78: 229–234.

Rosenbloom, R. S. 1985. "The R&D Pioneers, Then and Now." Paper presented at "The R&D Pioneers," Hagley Museum and Library, Wilmington, Delaware, October 7.

Rumelt, R. P. 1988. "Theory, Strategy, and Entrepreneurship." In *The Competitive Challenge,* edited by D. J. Teece. Cambridge, Mass.: Ballinger.

Salter, M. S., and W. A. Weinhold. 1980. *Merger Trends and Prospects.* Report for the Office of Policy, U.S. Department of Commerce. Washington, D.C.: U.S. Government Printing Office.

Sapolsky, H. 1990. *Science and the Navy.* Princeton, N.J.: Princeton University Press.

Scherer, F. M. 1983. "R&D and Declining Productivity Growth." *American Economic Review* 73: 215–18.

Schmookler, J. 1957. "Inventors Past and Present." *Review of Economics and Statistics* 39: 321–33.

———. 1959. "Technological Progress and the Modern American Corporation." In *The Corporation in Modern Society,* edited by E. Mason. Cambridge, Mass.: Harvard University Press.

Schultze, C. L. 1990. "The Federal Budget and the Nation's Economic Health." In *Setting National Priorities: Policy for the Nineties,* edited by H. J. Aaron. Washington, D.C.: Brookings Institution.

Schumpeter, J. A. 1950. *Capitalism, Socialism, and Democracy.* 3d ed. New York: Harper and Row.

Servan-Schreiber, J.-J. 1968. *The American Challenge.* New York: Atheneum Press.

Sharp, M. 1989. "European Countries in Science-Based Competition: The Case of Biotechnology." DRC Discussion Paper no. 72, SPRU, University of Sussex.

Shleifer, A., and R. W. Vishny. 1991. "Takeovers in the '60s and the '80s: Evidence and Implications." *Strategic Management Journal* 12: 51–59.

Stigler, G. J. 1968. "Monopoly and Oligopoly by Merger." In *The Organization of Industry*, edited by G. J. Stigler. Homewood, Ill.: Irwin.

Sturchio, J. L. 1985. "Experimenting with Research: Kenneth Mees, Eastman Kodak, and the Challenges of Diversification." Paper presented at "The R&D Pioneers," Hagley Museum and Library, Wilmington, Delaware, October 7.

Swann, J. P. 1988. *Academic Scientists and the Pharmaceutical Industry*. Baltimore, Md.: Johns Hopkins University Press.

Taylor, G. D., and P. E. Sudnik. 1984. *Du Pont and the International Chemical Industry*. Boston: Twayne.

Teece, D. J. 1988. "Technological Change and the Nature of the Firm." In *Technical Change and Economic Theory*, edited by G. Dosi, C. Freeman, R. Nelson, G. Silverberg, and L. Soete. London: Frances Pinter.

Thackray, A. 1982. "University-Industry Connections and Chemical Research: An Historical Perspective." In *University-Industry Research Relationships*. Washington, D.C.: National Science Board.

Thackray, A., J. L. Sturchio, P. T. Carroll, and R. Bud. 1985. *Chemistry in America, 1876–1976: Historical Indicators*. Dordrecht: Reidel.

Thorelli, H. B. 1954. *Federal Antitrust Policy*. Baltimore, Md.: Johns Hopkins University Press.

Tilton, J. E. 1971. *The International Diffusion of Technology: The Case of Transistors*. Washington, D.C.: Brookings Institution.

U.S. Bureau of the Census. 1975. *Historical Statistics of the United States: Colonial Times to 1970*. Vol. 1. Washington, D.C.: U.S. Government Printing Office.

———. 1987. *1987 Statistical Abstract of the United States*. Washington, D.C.: U.S. Government Printing Office.

U.S. Congressional Office of Technology Assessment. 1981. *An Assessment of the United States Food and Agricultural Research System*. Washington, D.C.: U.S. Government Printing Office.

———. 1986. *Technology, Public Policy, and the Changing Structure of American Agriculture*. Washington, D.C.: U.S. Government Printing Office.

U.S. Department of Commerce, Economics and Statistics Administration. 1991. *Foreign Direct Investment in the United States: Review and Analysis of Current Developments*. Washington, D.C.: U.S. Department of Commerce.

U.S. National Science Board. 1989. *Science Indicators, 1989*. Washington, D.C.: U.S. Government Printing Office and U.S. National Science Board.

———. 1991. *Science Indicators, 1991*. Washington, D.C.: U.S. Government Printing Office.

Utterback, J. M., and A. E. Murray. 1977. "The Influence of Defense Procurement and Sponsorship of Research and Development on the Development of the Civilian Electronics Industry." MIT Center for Policy Alternatives Working Paper no. 77–5.

Weart, S. 1979. "The Physics Business in America, 1919–1940." In *The Sciences in the American Perspective*, edited by N. Reingold. Washington, D.C.: Smithsonian Institution.

Wheelwright, S. C. and K. B. Clark. 1992. *Revolutionizing Product Development*. New York: Free Press.

White, J. B., and O. Suris. 1993. "How a 'Skunk Works' Kept Mustang Alive—On a Tight Budget." *Wall Street Journal*, September 21, p. A1.

White House Science Council. 1988. *High-Temperature Superconductivity: Perseverance and Cooperation on the Road to Commercialization*. Washington, D.C.: Office of Science and Technology Policy.

Wildes, K. L., and N. A. Lindgren. 1985. *A Century of Electrical Engineering and Computer Science at MIT, 1882–1982*. Cambridge, Mass.: MIT Press.

Williamson, O. E. 1975. *Markets and Hierarchies*. New York: Free Press.

———. 1985. *The Economic Institutions of Capitalism*. New York: Free Press.

Wise, G. 1985. "R&D at General Electric, 1878–1985." Paper presented at "The R&D Pioneers," Hagley Museum and Library, Wilmington, Delaware, October 7.

Wolf, J. 1989. "Europeans Fear Obstacles by U.S. on Advanced TV." *Wall Street Journal*, May 31, p. A16.

7

The American Corporation as an Employer: Past, Present, and Future Possibilities

◆

THOMAS A. KOCHAN

Much speculation has appeared in recent years on the nature of the corporation of the twenty-first century. Visions abound of networked firms, virtual organizations, flat and flexible structures, and global operations that transcend national boundaries. Missing from many of these analyses is a well-grounded understanding of the role of the corporation as an employer and manager of human resources. Yet how firms treat those who work for them will have important effects on the viability of the organizational forms envisioned for the corporation of the future.

Human resource issues are often overlooked in the mistaken view that an organization's employment practices are shaped by some deterministic trajectory of market or technological forces or that the most efficient or "best" practices of leading-edge firms naturally spread to other firms and employment relationships across the economy. Yet a deeper historical perspective suggests that employment practices are also influenced by labor market and labor force characteristics, unions and other institutions that speak for workers, and government policies that regulate employment relations. These factors therefore need to be more fully taken into account in predictions about the future of the American corporation.

This essay examines the modern American corporation as an employer and manager of human resources. It starts with an examination of the fundamental, enduring features of employment relationships. With this as a foundation, I then adopt a historical perspective by tracing what has changed in the labor force, in the environment of the firm, and in managerial structures and practices over the past decades that lead many to predict that we are in the midst of a fundamental transformation of organizational and employment relations. The role of human resources in American corporations is then put in an international context by describing several critical differences in the relationship of human resource practices and corporate governance arrangements in Japanese and German firms, where, either through law or through the nature of industrial organization, employees are more influential stakeholders than in the United States.

Throughout all this analysis comes a crucial point: the future of the American corporation as an employer is not preordained or uniquely determined by market or technological forces but rather is shaped by the interplay of external market, technical, and social pressures and the strategies and choices of managers, employees and those who represent them, and government policy makers who share responsibility for shaping the rules governing employment relationships. The final section of this chapter therefore focuses on some of the critical choices and options open to these parties in shaping the corporation of the future and its role as an employer.

Basic Principles of Employment Relationships

Since the emergence of free labor markets, the relationship between employers and employees has been mixed-motive in nature.[1] That is, the parties are bound together in an interdependent relationship that involves elements of both common and conflicting interests. Depending on how the relationship is governed and managed, the outcomes can vary from an inefficient bargain where both parties lose, to a highly distributive win-lose relationship whereby one party to the transaction gains at the expense of the other, to an integrative or win-win outcome where both parties' interests are well served by the relationship.

From the standpoint of the firm, employees are both potential assets which if mobilized and fully utilized can serve as a source of competitive advantage and, costs that, if not controlled properly, will serve as a competitive liability. From the employee's perspective the firm provides both a job and the source of one's economic livelihood as well a network of human and social relationships and a source of personal identity and psychological fulfillment. Alternatively, an employer can be a major source of economic insecurity, frustration, or stress in an employee's life.

Corporate Employment Practices:
1930s to 1950s

From the 1930s through the 1950s, employment practices of American corporations were managed through professional personnel and labor relations departments subject to what Galbraith described as the countervailing power of trade unions.[2] Unions grew to be large, powerful bargaining partners and adversaries that negotiated directly on behalf of employees with the majority of large firms and created strong incentives for those firms that were unorganized to match the economic benefits and social conditions achieved through collective bargaining. The New Deal legislation of the 1930s set a floor on employment standards on issues such as minimum wages, hours of work, and overtime requirements, and later on safety and health, equal employment opportunity, and a range of other employment conditions.

Through these two processes wages and working conditions were, in general, "taken out of competition" sufficiently to ward off incentives or opportunities for firms to seek competitive advantage by cutting wages and working conditions. As a result, real incomes of employees generally improved in tandem with the long-term rates of growth in productivity, thereby sharing the gains of economic progress with other stakeholders of the corporation and in society.

Managers and professional employees were generally treated by corporations as fixed assets who would enjoy long-term security and careers as long as they conformed to the expectations of the prevailing corporate culture that respected hierarchy and conformity and were prepared to move their families when a transfer or promotion was offered.[3] Managerial status and rewards were determined by one's level in the hierarchy.

The success and social stability achieved in American employment relations served as a model for the rest of the world. After World War II, American foreign policy makers encouraged Japan, Germany, and the newly industrializing countries to adopt our managerial and labor practices to both rebuild or develop their economies and strengthen their societies against the threat of communism or other forms of totalitarianism. Thus, the images that best characterize the American corporation as an employer in the 1950s are ones of stability and uniformity, shared gains among multiple stakeholders, and model for the rest of the world. By the 1990s, however, these images were replaced by ones of transformation and change, workforce diversity, efforts to deemphasize hierarchy in organizational designs, and a serious questioning of how to adapt the management and labor practices of competitors from abroad.

Effects of Increased Product
Market Competition

Increased competition in both international and domestic markets provided the initial stimulus for these developments. Competition from lower-wage countries made it impossible to "take wages out of competition." The same was true in domestic markets that were deregulated in the 1980s in critical industries such as telecommunications, transportation (air, trucking, railroads), and financial services. The combined effects of years of incremental improvements in wages and working conditions achieved through collective bargaining and in the comprehensive human resource policies and long-term employment relations in large (union and nonunion) corporations put these firms at a cost disadvantage when new competitors could enter their markets with lower labor cost structures and state-of-the-art products. This put tremendous pressure on existing firms to adopt new competitive strategies. Their options were to cut costs, exploit some other competitive advantage by developing new and higher-quality products and services, leave the market to the new competitors, or gradually lose market share. Each of these strategic responses required changes in employment practices that had been built up over the years. Emphasis on higher-value-added products required greater investments in training, flexibility in job assignments and work rules, and cooperation and participation from employees and unions. Lowering costs required wage moderation and often wage and benefit concessions. Restructuring and downsizing produced permanent job losses first for blue-collar and later for white-collar and managerial employees. (See chapter 9 in this volume for more detailed data and discussion of the magnitude and effects of restructuring.)

These product market developments interacted with equally profound developments in the labor markets and labor force characteristics and the institutional and public policy environments facing American firms, discussed in the following.

Labor Force Trends: 1950s to 1990s

The changes that have occurred in the labor force since the 1950s can be summed up in two words: increased diversity.[4] This diversity has multiple dimensions including differences in gender, race, age, educational attainment, occupational status, attachment to an employer, composition of the unemployed, and career patterns.

Population and Labor Force Growth

Between 1950 and 1993, the U.S. population increased by approximately 60 percent while the labor force doubled, rising from 62 million to 128 million workers. Thus a larger percentage of the country's population now is active in the labor force, growing from 59 percent in 1950 to 66 percent in 1993. Most of this growth has been due to the increased labor force participation rates of women. In 1950, 32 percent of women were in the labor force, compared with 58 percent in 1993. Changing patterns of labor force participation along with changes in family composition have produced the result that only 17 percent of the labor force now fits what was conceived of as the "typical" household earlier in the century, that is, one in which a husband worked full-time with a wife at home caring for their children on a full-time basis. (How American corporations responded to increased gender and racial diversity is discussed in the chapter 8 in this volume.)

Age Distribution

The labor force grew rapidly in the late 1960s and '70s as the postwar baby boom came of age and then slowed considerably in the 1980s. From 1965 to 1979 the labor force grew at an annual rate of 3.0 percent; the average growth rate fell to 1.5 percent from 1980 to 1993 and is projected by the Bureau of Labor Statistics (BLS) to grow at a still lower annual rate of 1.3 percent (using the BLS "moderate" assumptions about the future rate of economic growth). These changes in growth rates imply that the age composition of the labor force has also changed significantly over the past several decades. The dominant feature is the aging of the postwar baby boom. In 1960, just before this cohort began entering the labor force, the median age of workers was 40. By 1980 the median age had fallen to thirty-four and then began a slow steady rise to thirty-six in 1990 and will continue to rise to forty shortly after the turn of the century. The rise in age, combined with gradual increases in life expectancy, means that the United States will experience increased demand for services and benefits (health care, pensions, Social Security benefits, elder care, etc.) associated with an aging workforce and population.

Racial Composition

While white males continue to be the largest single demographic group in the labor force, all other categories of workers have grown and will continue to grow at a faster rate. For example, white males accounted for 60 percent of the labor force in 1960 and 47 percent in 1993. But between 1975 and 1993 the annual labor force growth rate of white males was only 1.2 percent, compared with 2.5 percent for blacks, 6.2 percent for Asians, and 5.9 for Hispanics. Because on average they are older than members of other groups, white males will be leaving the labor force through retirement or death at a higher rate than other groups. Over 85 percent of the net growth in the labor force between 1990 and 2000 will therefore come from women, minorities, and/or immigrants. Thus, the combination of an aging white male labor force, an increased participation rate of females, and a rising population of younger minorities and immigrants has created the diversity we now find in today's labor force, a diversity that will continue to increase in the years to come.

Education Levels

The American workforce is the most highly educated in the world, if measured by the number of years of education received by the average employee. In 1992, 52 percent of the American labor force had more than twelve years of schooling, 25 percent had attended some college, and 26 percent were college graduates. But there are reasons to be concerned about the quality of this education, its unequal distribution, and a serious weakness in the ability of one critical segment of the labor force to compete effectively in the labor market of the future, namely, those who enter the labor market with a high school education (or less) and do not go on to obtain a college degree or additional technical training. Nearly 25 percent of children today do not graduate from high school (over 40 percent of inner-city youth). International comparisons of educational achievement, even after controlling for compositional differences of those taking these tests in different countries, consistently show that American students score below students in countries as diverse as Japan, Germany, Korea, and Singapore. Fewer than 25 percent of those who do not go on to college graduate from a technical school or from a formal apprenticeship program.

These features of American education and school-to-work transition arrangements produce a large number of new labor force entrants who are poorly prepared to exercise the cognitive, analytic, and interpersonal skills demanded in organizations that are attempting to encourage decentralized decision making, employee participation and problem solving, and team-work. Thus, the burden on American corporations to continue the basic ed-ucation and training of the labor force is also considerably higher than that of corporations located in other countries.

Industry and Occupational Distribution

While the modal worker of the 1950s was a white male working in a blue-collar or white-collar job for a large industrial firm, this description now fits only a shrinking minority of employees. In 1950 goods-producing industries represented 41 percent of total employment, compared with 21 percent in 1993. Manufacturing now accounts for approximately 16 percent of the la-bor force. The fastest-growing service-sector industries have been whole-sale and retail trade, finance, insurance, real estate, and general services. Within the category of general services, business services have grown dra-matically, at a rate of over 10 percent per year in the 1980s, reflecting the growing use of temporary or contract employees in clerical, professional, and managerial jobs. State and local government employment also grew by approximately 3 percentage points over this time period.

The occupations that have grown the fastest over the past several decades lie at both tails of the wage distribution. The number of executives and managers increased by 83 percent between 1975 and 1990, compared with a growth rate of 37 percent for all workers. The slowest growth was ex-perienced in what in the past was called semiskilled production and service jobs—those of operators, assemblers, production workers, materials han-dlers, and laborers. At the same time the service sector created a large num-ber of relatively low-wage jobs such as janitors and service employees in the hotel, restaurant, and health care sectors. Thus many of the jobs that pro-duced relatively good middle-class incomes and living conditions for blue-collar workers with high school education (or less) in the postwar period have been shrinking. (The full dimensions of the wage and income inequal-ities produced by these changes are discussed in chapter 12 in this volume.)

More recently, the turbulence in the labor market has moved higher up in the occupational hierarchy to affect middle- and upper-level managers and professionals as firms restructure and downsize. In 1982, the first year for which reliable data of this kind are available, white-collar workers made up about 20 percent of the total unemployed; in 1992 they accounted for about 33 percent of the unemployed. Moreover, an increasing percentage of those who are laid off are permanently rather than temporarily displaced. For example, in the four recessions between 1960 and 1990, 44 percent of those laid off expected to be recalled by their employers, whereas only 14 percent of those laid off in the 1990–1992 recession expected to be recalled. In 1992 one national survey found that 42 percent of the labor force experienced downsizing at their workplaces, and 33 percent felt vulnerable to layoffs or permanent job loss. Thus, unemployment has changed in composition to affect a wider spectrum of the labor force, and is more likely to require the laid-off worker to find a new job with a new employer and often in a new industry rather than to await recall by a former employer.

As a result of this increased uncertainty, the average worker is likely to change employers approximately six to seven times over the course of his or her career. While the lack of good historical comparisons makes it difficult to determine whether this is an increase over the past, the general expectation is that, if anything, it is likely to increase in the future. This increased mobility (voluntary and involuntary) has important implications for the psychological contract between workers and American firms and the public policies and institutions that govern employment relationships.

Workers' Values and Expectations

Despite periodic concerns voiced to the contrary, American workers have not lost their work ethic or become less concerned with or motivated by the economic benefits associated with their jobs. These were popular arguments particularly throughout the 1960s and '70s during periods of social turbulence, questioning of authority, and relatively tight labor markets. But both objective measures of work effort, such as labor force participation rates and number of hours worked, as well as subjective indicators contained in attitude surveys show that work effort remains high among Americans. Americans continue to place a high value on the incomes and economic security associated with their jobs. What does appear to be true, however, is that the expectations workers bring to their jobs are more varied now than in the past, again reflecting the greater diversity in the characteristics and family roles of contemporary workers. For example, a 1993 survey showed that workers place a very high value on having access to information about their job and about the factors that will affect their career. Concerns for balancing work and family issues also rank high among a majority of American workers, an item that surveyors didn't even consider important enough to ask about in prior decades.

The effects of these changes in the labor force on corporate practices are discussed more fully in chapters 8, 9, and 12 in this volume. For the purposes of this chapter it is sufficient to note that increased labor force diversity put pressures on corporations, unions, and policy makers alike to update their practices and, therefore, served as another force driving change.

Institutional Trends

Declining Union Membership

The most significant institutional change since the 1950s in U.S. employment settings has been the decline in union membership and the coverage of collective bargaining. In 1955 approximately one-third of the American workforce and a majority of the hourly workers employed by large corporations were covered by collective bargaining agreements. By 1995 only 16 percent of the overall labor force and less than 11 percent of the private-sector labor force were organized. The biggest change in the composition of union membership between 1960 and 1990 reflected the growth of unions and collective bargaining in local, state, and federal government and the decline of private-sector union membership. Union membership among government employees rose from being a negligible force prior to 1960 to cover approximately 37 percent of government workers by 1975 and has remained at that level ever since. Union membership experienced a forty-year decline among private-sector workers, resulting in membership levels as low now as they were in the early 1930s just before the enactment of the National Labor Relations Act (NLRA) that granted workers protection for the right to organize and bargain with their employers through independent trade unions.

No single factor accounts for the decline of unions. Instead, research specialists on this topic emphasize the interactive effects of changes in the structure of the economy and labor force, improved personnel practices that reduce the incentive for workers to organize, increased managerial resistance to unions through legal and illegal means, and the slowness of unions to adapt to all of these changes. For our purposes, the changes in corporate practices are of greatest interest. Both the ability and the motiva-

tion to resist unions increased in the 1960s through the 1980s. The motivation increased because the union-nonunion wage and fringe benefit differentials increased. The ability to avoid unions increased because advanced human resource policies improved, thereby reducing the incentive
for workers to unionize, and the law regulating union representation elections failed to provide workers with access to unions without a long, protracted battle, thereby making it more difficulty and risky for workers who
want union representation to get it. I will return to this latter issue later in
the discussion of the role of public policy.

The decline of unions, juxtaposed against the data reviewed earlier on
worker expectations and interests, has led some to argue that there is a serious "representation gap" in American workplaces. Several surveys have
shown, for example, that approximately 30 percent of the nonunion labor
force would prefer to be represented by a union.[5] An even larger number, as
much as 80 percent of the labor force according to some surveys, would
prefer to have greater opportunity to participate in some fashion in decisions affecting their jobs and their careers.[6] However, for most of these
workers, collective bargaining is not a viable option. Employer resistance to
unions is too strong and American labor law is too weak to protect workers
who face an employer that is determined to resist unionization.[7] While, as
will be noted later, a growing number of firms have introduced various
forms of employee participation, these remain at the discretion of senior
management. Few employees believe they have the opportunity to initiate
group forms of participation in the absence of top management initiative or
encouragement.

Increased Government Regulation
of Employment

Part of the void left by the decline in union representation has been filled
by the growing number of laws regulating employment practices and relations. One estimate indicates that the number of such regulations increased from approximately 40 in the 1960s to over 150 by the 1990s.
Accompanying the growth in regulations covering issues such as equal employment opportunity, occupational safety and health, wage and hour regulations, pensions, and family and medical leave has been an increase in litigation before administrative agencies and state and federal courts. The
number of lawsuits filed in federal courts increased by over 400 percent between 1970 and 1990.[8] In response, some organizations have established
internal alternative dispute-resolution procedures involving use of ombuds-

men or other neutrals, mediation, peer review of discipline cases, and, in a small number of organizations, arbitration. Whether these internal private dispute-resolution procedures can be expanded in ways that both resolve problems more equitably and efficiently and reduce reliance on government regulations and litigation is an issue of considerable debate in public policy circles today.[9]

Organizational Trends

Changes in the labor force, unions, and government policies represent only one side of the equation shaping employment relationships. Equally fundamental changes in managerial values, structures, and practices are at work. Among these most prominent are the movement to decentralize decision making and flatten organizational structures, and to make greater use of teams to coordinate across traditional jobs, functions, and departments. Firms have also been introducing greater flexibility in defining their boundaries and in the types of employment contracts used to get work done. Finally, the very definition of what is an "American" corporation has been called into question.

Decentralization and Employee Involvement

The drive to move decision making down to front-line workers, to flatten organizational hierarchies, and to empower workers in various ways has clearly grown in both rhetoric and practice. This is most visible with respect to lower-level employees. By 1992 surveys showed that employee participation programs had been adopted by over 80 percent of American firms and diffused to perhaps as much as one-fifth to one-third of the nonmanagerial labor force.[10] While many of these programs experience limited half-lives, others have survived over time, and the level of interest and commitment among managers, workers, and union leaders has grown considerably over the past several decades. By no means, however, is this commitment universal, or even spread to a majority of managers or workers, thereby adding another element to the diversity found in contemporary workplaces.

Cross-functional Teams and Coordination

One of the clearest developments has been the effort to make greater use of teams, and to rely less on functional specialization in decision making. This trend is visible among both blue-collar and white-collar workers. For blue-collar workers variants of semiautonomous work groups are delegated authority to do work that in the past was done by supervisors (e.g., scheduling, work assignments, training, materials ordering) and the work of a unit is shared among workers who are cross-trained in the various tasks rather than divided into separate, narrowly defined jobs. Among white-collar workers, cross-functional teams bring together professionals from multiple disciplines or processes to improve the speed and quality of product development, introduction of new technologies, or to work on specific, time-limited projects. Such teamlike arrangements are reported to be found in nearly 40 percent of workplaces today.

The existence of team structures does not, however, guarantee that "high-performance" teams will result. The empirical evidence for blue-collar teams, product development teams, and teams that mix engineers, managers, and blue-collar workers together to introduce new technologies or improve existing processes and procedures shows great variation in performance.[11] Skill in managing diversity, communications, problem solving, decision making, and conflict resolution appear to be critical ingredients needed to transform work groups into high-performance teams. Moreover, teams do not exist in an organizational vacuum. Their ability to negotiate for support and resources with others in their organizations and the reinforcement of human resource practices such as training, career development, and reward systems are critical to either reinforcing or constraining teamwork in organizations. Few corporations have successfully adapted these policies and structures sufficiently to gain the full value from teams. Thus, the rate of attrition in the use of teams continues to be rather high.

Flexibility and Blurred Boundaries

The rise of the "networked" organization has profound effects on employee relations. It accounts for much of the growth in contingent, contract, and temporary employment as firms focus on their "core competencies" and contract out functions that were internalized in the more vertically integrated corporations of the past. The most profound employment relations effect of the move to networked organization design is that the lines of authority and responsibility become blurred regarding who is the employer responsible for supervising and setting the terms and conditions of employment for employees. Most U.S. employment policies and institutional arrangements are designed for employment settings where there is a single employer, a fixed work site, and an ongoing long-term employment relationship. Public policies governing pensions, training, supervision, safety and health, workers compensation, health insurance, union representation, and collective bargaining all were designed with this traditional model in mind.

Two examples illustrate the effects on employment relations that arise in the blurred boundaries of networked firms. One comes from an older industrial setting and one from the newer high-technology industry in Silicon Valley.

A study of the consequences of the growth in the use of contract workers to perform maintenance and specialty work in petrochemical plants was prompted by an explosion in a Texas chemical plant that killed twenty-three workers and injured another two hundred in 1989. Because contract workers were working on the unit that ignited the explosion, this accident highlighted the long-standing claim by the chemical workers' union that the increased use of low-wage, less experienced, poorly trained (and generally nonunion) contract workers was increasing the risk of accidents in this industry.

The results of a two-year study generally supported the union's claims.[12] This study found that contract workers were (1) growing in number and taking on more of the high-risk maintenance and repair work previously done by permanent employees; (2) lower-paid, less educated, received less training, less experienced in the industry, and had shorter tenures with their current employer; (3) less likely to be covered by a labor-management safety committee or a union contract; and (4) more likely to experience injuries and accidents. Moreover, managers of the petrochemical plants were instructed by their lawyers to be careful to keep an arm's-length relationship with contract workers.

Managers were advised to not take responsibility for either training or supervising these workers but instead to leave these issues to the contracting firm in order to avoid "coemployment" liabilities for these employees' workers' compensation premiums, other fringe benefits, or potential union activity or collective bargaining coverage. As a result, the highly sophisticated safety management systems and practices covering permanent employees of the petrochemical firms were not extended to contract workers on these sites, who were often doing some of the most high-risk work. Not surprisingly, this issue served as a source of considerable tension among unions, the Occupational Safety and Health Administration (OSHA), petrochemical firms, and contractors in this industry. This example illustrates the consequences of a situation in which neither public policies gov-

erning safety and health or labor relations nor labor-management institutions have been successful in adapting to a situation where the locus of
managerial responsibility is shifting from a single, large firm to a network of
firms where managerial authority is shared and the boundary between organizations is blurred.

The high-technology firms in Silicon Valley present yet another picture
of the dynamics of the networked corporation. This industry grew up as the
prototype of the networked corporation.[13] From 1970 to 1984 employment
in Silicon Valley grew at a rate of 7 percent, compared with less than 3 percent for the overall American economy. Turnover of technical professionals
was high, as they moved across the large number of new start-up companies. By 1990 the product and labor market situation changed dramatically
even as the rate of technological and product innovation continued to produce increases in productivity and output. From 1989 to 1992, for example,
output in the Silicon Valley semiconductor industry grew by over 40 percent, while employment remained stable as a result of the industry's significant growth in productivity. At the same time employment in other high-
technology industries in the region declined as defense and aerospace
budgets were reduced and international competition intensified in the computer industry. The composition of jobs also changed considerably as firms
contracted out more of their janitorial, cafeteria, software, clerical, and professional services. While full-time jobs in the large firms were declining, the
temporary help industry was expanding. In 1990 approximately thirty thousand people were employed by temporary help firms in the Silicon Valley
four-county region. The result is best captured by the theme of a 1994 government commission hearing on worker-management relations in Silicon
Valley. The commission was presented with a "Tale of Two Valleys." On the
one hand, representatives of the high-technology firms described the area
as the best place in the world to establish a high-technology, electronics-
based firm for its access to the network of highly educated professionals
needed to staff these operations. At the same time, workforce advocates focused on the bifurcation of society found in the area, with 30 percent of the
employed workforce earning less than fifteen thousand dollars per year,
while another strata of highly educated engineers, computer scientists, and
executives earn incomes that put them in the other tail of the income distribution. What is not being replicated are the middle-income blue-collar
and low-level professional jobs common to the large industrial firms of the
past.[14]

Globalization

In a global economy where technological, financial, and human resources travel quickly across national boundaries, it is increasingly difficult to discern the national identity and loyalty of a firm. This blurring of national identities is further complicated by the growth in strategic alliances, joint ventures, and other transnational partnerships among firms. Of the patents issued in the United States in 1978, 38 percent were issued to foreign firms; by 1991 this increased to 47 percent. In 1974, 1.2 percent of the U.S. labor force worked for U.S. affiliates of foreign-owned companies; in 1989 this increased to 4.4 million, or 3.8 percent of the labor force.

Globalization has a number of effects on employment practices of firms. First, it further increases the diversity of the workforce and the cultural environments in which work and managerial tasks are performed. Thus, all the U.S. labor force trends that lead to increased diversity and their implications for organizational practices are reinforced by the internationalization of corporate operations. Second, international operations offer increased opportunities for learning and comparison of managerial and labor practices since managers operating in their nonnative countries face decisions on which, if any, of their domestic practices to carry over into the new environment and which local practices to follow. What often evolves out of this amalgam are new innovations.[15] Third, it increases the range of choices over where to locate work and over the type of human resource values and strategies to embed in the operations. This therefore increases the need for those who speak for employee and human resource concerns to be part of these strategic decision-making processes and centers of power. These second and third features are discussed in more detail in the following.

Importing Employment Innovations

The auto industry provides the best contemporary example of the process by which internationalization can foster organizational learning and innovation in employment practices of American corporations. The rise in Japanese transplants in the 1980s served as perhaps the most visible laboratory for learning in the history of U.S. manufacturing. From 1982 to 1985, Honda, Nissan, Toyota, Mazda, Mitsubishi, and Suzuki all opened assembly facilities in the United States either on their own or in partnership with one of the Big Three American producers. Several of these, especially the Honda plant in Ohio and the Toyota-GM joint venture in California known as the New United Motors Manufacturing Inc. (NUMMI), quickly became among the highest-productivity and highest-quality plants in the industry.[16]

NUMMI, in particular, served as a visible example for the rest of American management since the plant and workforce in this facility had previously been managed by General Motors and had one of the worst labor relations, productivity, and quality records in the industry. Within two years after the start of the joint venture, this plant, with the same workforce, same union, but very different union-management relationship, was out-performing all other assembly plants in the country. It was even outper-forming a number of other GM plants that had been infused with consider-ably more high-technology equipment than was in place at NUMMI.

The lessons of NUMMI were not lost on the rest of the auto industry. By the early 1990s all three of the U.S. producers were adopting their own versions of the flexible production methods, teamwork systems of work or-ganization, and employee participation in problem solving found at NUMMI. While it is a mistake to attribute all of the diffusion of innovation in this industry to the role of the transplants, there is no doubt that it ac-celerated what had already begun and convinced others to move more ag-gressively in this direction.

Human Resources, Strategic Decision Making, and Corporate Governance

The increased options for locating work move the critical decisions that af-fect the long-term welfare of employees up to a higher level in the organi-zational hierarchy than was envisioned in the more stable employment sys-tems of the past. This changes the locus of power in corporations where employee voice or those responsible for championing human resource is-sues is needed most critically. No longer are the critical decisions made by human resource specialists or bilaterally between union and management negotiators in collective bargaining, but instead the critical decisions re-garding where new jobs will be created and others eliminated are made by strategic planners or executives who allocate investment resources to dif-ferent operations around the world. This, in turns, puts considerable pres-sure on human resource professionals and labor-management representa-tives to gain access to these higher levels of strategic decision making within corporations.[17]

This has proven to be especially difficult for both human resource and labor-management representatives in U.S. corporations. Despite much rhetoric to the contrary among personnel specialists, human resource managers continue to be among the weakest and most marginal of all functional groups in American corporations. This is true whether measured by the relative salaries of human resource executives compared with their counterparts in finance (the ratio is about 58 percent in the largest U.S. firms) or by surveys of experts or employees.[18]

Why is this the case? One way to understand the sources of weakness of both human resource executives and employees as stakeholders in corporate decision making is to compare their position in U.S., Japanese, and German corporations.

Japanese firms are sometimes described as a coalition of shareholders and employees with managers acting as mediating agents.[19] Individual shareholders receive a return on their investment through long-term capital gains more than through dividends or rapid turnover of stocks. Institutional investors (banks, other firms, insurance companies, and so forth), which own nearly 75 percent of the shares of large Japanese companies, also receive income from long-term capital gains, but they receive significant income from the interest paid on debt they hold and from income derived from goods and services sold to the firm. The dense networks of cross-shareholdings, customer relationships, and creditors are strongest in the sixteen or so keiretsu—large company networks tied together by a lead bank—such as Mitsubishi, Hitachi, or Matsushita.

Employees, in turn, receive their most significant rewards in the form of long tenure and meritorious service—lifetime employment in firms in which promotion to top-paying and high-status jobs depends on a combination of length of service and demonstrated individual performance. Other human resource practices are designed to make this coalitional model work by delivering long-tenure, loyal, and motivated employees who share a deep interest in the performance and growth of the firm. These practices include internal promotion, an informal training and development system that relies on job rotation and lateral transfers, steep age earnings profiles (the average retirement wage in Japan is 257 percent of the entry wage, compared with 107 percent in the United States), large retirement bonuses, enterprise unions, frequent and broad-based labor-management consultation, and annual bonuses. Thus it is easy to understand why human resource executives are influential in Japanese firms. The policies they develop and administer must reinforce this long-term orientation and commitment, or the mutual gains to employees and shareholders will not be realized.

The governance structure of Japanese corporations reflects these differences. The boards of directors of large corporations are composed of several outsiders, usually a representative of the company's main bank, and a group of internal senior managers—normally the heads of the key departments of personnel, finance, R&D, and the main factories or business units. The chairman of the board serves as the chief executive of the company. Retiring chairmen normally pick their successors. The board also appoints a "full-time board"—essentially a subgroup of the board composed mainly of the heads of the departments and the CEO. Thus, the board is not a pure representative of the shareholders but a coalition of insiders and outsiders, with the insiders holding the most important positions.

The company's main bank, which normally holds up to the legal limit of 5 percent of the shares of the company, is the key monitoring agent for other shareholders. Not only does it have equity and creditor stakes in the company, it has a reputational stake as well. This helps explain why, if a firm gets in financial trouble, the main bank often works closely with management to help solve the problem. In doing so it protects its reputation (as well as its investment). These financial and governance structures of the Japanese corporation make it difficult for a hostile takeover threat to surface or serve as a source of discipline on management. The intricate intercorporate shareholding simply makes it almost impossible for an outside investor to accumulate a large portion of the shares.

Japanese corporations are experiencing intense pressures to change toward more of an American model, in part in response to recent scandals involving business leaders and high government officials and in part because of the need to speed up the process of restructuring Japanese firms and capital markets in the face of increased competitive pressures. Yet the point of this comparison is clear: there is a close interdependence among the characteristics of capital markets, human resource practices, and corporate governance structures.

Germany presents yet another approach to corporate governance that produces a high level of influence for human resource issues and interests.[20] As in Japan, German banks hold equity stakes in the companies they loan money to; moreover, they normally hold the proxy rights to the shares of other stockholders who deposit their securities in the bank. Thus banks control appointments to the supervisory board. The supervisory board is the functional equivalent of a U.S. board of directors and is made up of a majority of outside directors plus one or more representatives of the firm's employees. Normally the lead bank has a representative on this board.

As in Japan, internal governance and human resource practices reinforce long-term time horizons and the importance of human resources in corporate decision making. As noted, by law, an employee representative sits on the supervisory board of all companies with more than two thousand employees. In the iron and steel industry a special law gives employees one less than a majority of seats on the supervisory boards. In addition, German companies have what is often referred to as a "dual-board structure." A management board consisting of employee- and management-nominated representatives serves as an internal board. One member of this board, the "Arbeitsdirecktor," is the equivalent of the head of the human resources department in a U.S. firm and can be removed by employees if they lose confidence in his or her behavior.

The key conclusion to be drawn from comparing employment systems and corporate governance arrangements is that American workers and the labor and management professionals who speak for them have less influence in U.S. corporations than in corporations in Germany or Japan where legal and institutional arrangements make employees important stakeholders in corporate governance. While this is not a new development, the impact of the weakness of human resources has more profound effects now than in the past given the increased range of options top executives have in choosing where to locate, how to compete, and what type of employment relations strategy to adopt.

Labor and Employment Policies

Public policies governing employment relations have not kept pace with changes in the structures and practices of American corporations or with the increased diversity of the American workforce. This is due in part to the political stalemate that has characterized labor policy making over the past two decades. Neither labor nor business groups have been able to pass major reforms they favor, yet each has been able to block proposals favored by the other. Moreover, government leaders have not be successful in forming a coalition capable of achieving significant change. In 1993 the newly elected Clinton administration took steps to break the stalemate by appointing a national Commission on the Future of Worker Management Relations and asking it to take a comprehensive look at the labor and employment laws that have been in place since the days of the New Deal. Then, following the 1994 congressional elections, Republican leaders in Congress began their own campaign to make fundamental but significantly different changes in employment law. Whatever results from this political contest could have profound effects on the future employment practices of American corporations.

The Clinton administration commission identified four aspects of the law that needed attention.[21] First, it concluded that the provisions in labor law limiting the forms of employee participation that are allowed in nonunion firms needed to be updated to support contemporary practice. The critical provisions in question were included in the 1935 NLRA to protect against the use of "company-dominated unions" to thwart employee free choice of independent union representation. Applying this provision of the law renders some contemporary forms of employee participation and self-managed work teams illegal in nonunion settings. The commission concluded that it is in the interests of firms, workers, and the national economy to promote continued expansion in employee participation. It recommended changing the law to not only allow for but encourage and support wider diffusion of employee participation in both union and nonunion settings. At the same time, the commission recommended maintaining the ban on company-dominated unions.

This recommendation was strongly criticized by the labor movement for two reasons. First, labor felt it would further undermine the ability of workers to organize into independent unions and would in fact lead to a return of company-dominated labor organizations. Second, labor feared that the Republican-dominated Congress would accept this part of the commission's recommendations, implement it, and ignore those outlined below regarding the need to strengthen worker protections in union organizing drives. Thus, the net result would be to further weaken worker rights and representation.

Second, the same 1935 law promised to provide workers with the right to choose whether or not to join a union, however, the evidence presented to the commission demonstrated that the law is failing to deliver on this promise. Instead the evidence showed: (1) that efforts of workers to unionize are met with high levels of conflict, legalistic delays, and resistance by employers, (2) that the likelihood that a worker will be illegally fired for supporting a union increased in the past two decades, and (3) that more than one-third of those work groups that vote to be represented by a union are not successful in getting a first contract and establishing an ongoing bargaining relationship because the conflicts from the organizing drive simply spill over to the negotiations process. Moreover, as noted earlier, surveys from the late 1970s through 1994 have consistently shown that about 30 percent of the nonunion labor force indicate an interest in being represented by a union. This suggests there is an unmet demand for union representation among workers today.

Given these facts, the commission recommended modifying the law to reduce delays and speed up the representation election process, ensure prompt reinstatement of workers who are illegally discharged, and provide for arbitration of first contracts that cannot be resolved through negotiations and mediation. Despite this evidence, business groups uniformly opposed any changes in the law or procedures governing union organizing that would make it easier for workers to exercise their rights to join a union and engage in collective bargaining.

Third, the commission concluded that the growth in employment regulation and litigation needed to be arrested by making greater use of private arbitration and other self-regulation procedures. The commission therefore urged employers, worker groups, and unions to develop effective workplace institutions to deal with issues such as safety and health, and to create private alternative dispute systems to deal with issues such as discrimination, sexual harassment, wage and hour regulations, and so on. Moving in this direction would decentralize part of the responsibility for enforcing workers' public rights to private institutions.

Whether or not fair private systems can be created in the face of the lack of strong institutions for worker representation in American corporations is a major unresolved question for those favoring expansion of private dispute resolution. Management spokespersons believe this is feasible; however, women's groups and other civil rights organizations argue that workers need independent representation to make private dispute resolution procedures fair and effective. This is likely to be a source of considerable debate and experimentation in the years ahead.

Fourth, the commission concluded that employment law needed to be updated to better cover workers in contingent employment relationships. The current law gives employers an incentive to reclassify regular employees as independent contractors and thereby escape payment of Social Security or unemployment insurance taxes. Moreover, as the study of contract workers in the petrochemical industry illustrated, contingent work creates new ambiguities over which employer is responsible for complying with the obligations of labor relations and safety and health laws. Thus, the growth of contingent employment relationships associated with networked organizations has proven to be one of the most difficult challenges to prevailing employment policies.

Yet there are no easy or simple solutions to the problem of how to regulate contingent employment relationships. The commission favored clarifying existing laws to ensure that a common definition and set of standards are used to determine employer and employee status under all laws governing the workplace, and it suggested several reforms that would make both

the host firm and the contractor jointly responsible for complying with labor and safety laws.

Taken together, the recommendations of the commission would encourage employee participation, strengthen worker protections if workers
want to joint a union, encourage voluntary dispute resolution, and internalize the enforcement of some government regulations. While they do not call
for a complete overhaul of current policies, they represent the most comprehensive set of proposals for modernizing these policies to come along in
many years.

Republican leaders in Congress favor a very different set of reforms, the
net effect of which would be to reduce the effects of government regulations
and increase employer discretion in employment practices without addressing the representation gap issue. Among the changes proposed would be the
elimination of all constraints on employee participation in nonunion firms,
elimination or weakening of prevailing wage and minimum wage laws, reductions in the penalties government agencies or the courts could impose
on firms for violating workplace safety or discrimination laws, and tightened
eligibility rules for unemployment compensation. The Republican agenda
also includes strong support for alternative dispute resolution procedures.[22]
Thus, while there is general agreement that the labor and employment policies are no longer well matched to the labor markets and corporate practices
of today, as yet there is no consensus on the direction, much less on the specific content, of the changes required. Unless this stalemate is broken, the
gap will continue to widen between the labor policies designed for the corporate and employment settings of the 1930s and the practices and characteristics of today's corporations and labor markets.

Summary and Conclusions

Changes in product and labor markets, the decline of unions, and the failure of employment regulations to keep pace with changes in the economy
have both created pressures on American corporations to change their employment practices and given them more discretion over how to do so. As a
result, there is more variation in the employment practices of American corporations today than was true in previous decades. Some of the increased
managerial discretion has been used to improve the quality of employment
opportunities and relationships available to the American workforce, that is,
to produce mutual gains for workers and shareholders. This is more true for
the more highly educated members of society than for those with less edu-

cation; for professional and high-level executives than for middle managers, supervisors, and hourly employees; and for younger, highly mobile workers than for middle- or advanced-aged employees with family, financial, or social obligations that limit their geographic or occupational mobility.

The net result of these changes is a highly dynamic labor market where loyalty to a single employer is reduced, incomes are more unequally distributed, responsibility and authority over employment rights are more ambiguous, and the need for effective lateral communications, teamwork, problem solving, negotiations, and conflict resolution has increased. The forces that have produced the opportunities to create new organizational forms are likely to accelerate in the years to come. This will increase the range of choices regarding how to structure and manage employment relationships open to firms and their managers, to employees and their representatives, and to society and its governmental agents. By the beginning of the twenty-first century, the organization men (and women) of the 1950s will be gone, and so, too, will many of the attributes that dominated their corporate lives. Upward mobility within a clearly defined job or function, conformity to the cultural and social norms of the top executives, strict lines of demarcation between work and family activities and obligations, geographic transfer and job choice based on one partner's career needs or demands, and loyalty to the corporation may all be part of corporate history. Hourly workers will no longer be able to count on seniority to produce increased wages, fringe benefits, promotion opportunities, and job security. Unions and collective bargaining will find it more difficult to move those with limited education or training into the middle class.

To do well in the corporation of the future, individual employees will need to enter the labor market with a solid technical and analytic educational foundation, gain access on the job to experiences in decision making, problem solving, and teamwork, commit to a lifelong process of learning and updating of one's skills, and organize into collective networks and organizations capable of bargaining and influencing their employers from the workplace up to the strategic levels of corporate decision making.

To be competitive and prosper in this environment, corporations will need to attract high-quality workers, design work systems that fully utilize their skills, encourage employees to stay long enough to appropriate the benefits of training investments, share power and cooperate with workers and their representatives, and release employees into the external labor markets with marketable skills. For the overall economy and society to prosper in this new environment will require significant reforms of labor and employment policies that provide the education, training, and social insurance foundations needed to promote labor market mobility and effective negotiations, dispute resolution, and cooperation among stakeholders within and across organizations.

Unfortunately, there is little chance these changes will be realized as long as government labor policy remains in a stalemate and American employees remain passive. It is, however, reasonable to wonder if, or more likely when, American employees will react to the long-term stagnation in earnings, increased inequality, reduced job security, and the vacuum in representation that they have experienced over the past decades. Ultimately, it will be up to the American workforce and electorate to decide what priority these issues get on the American agenda.

Meanwhile, corporations in other societies have access to the same technologies, capital, and opportunities to develop their human resources and to learn from each other's experiences as do American firms, employees, and policy makers. Thus, there is now an active global market for ideas and alternative organizational arrangements, with corresponding differences in human resource practices. How American leaders respond to these human resource challenges, international experiences, and opportunities will affect the nature of the American corporation of the twenty-first century.

Notes

Support for this work was provided by the Alfred P. Sloan Foundation. The views expressed are solely those of the author.

1. Richard E. Walton and Robert B. McKersie, *A Behavioral Theory of Labor Negotiations* (New York: McGraw-Hill, 1965).

2. John Kenneth Galbraith, *The New Industrial State* (Boston: Houghton Mifflin, 1971).

3. William H. Whyte, *The Organization Man* (New York: Simon and Schuster, 1956).

4. The data in this section are reported in more detail in *The Report on the American Workforce* (Washington, D.C.: U.S. Department of Labor, 1994).

5. See, e.g., Thomas A. Kochan, "How American Workers' View Unions," *Monthly Labor Review* 102 (1979) 23–33; and Richard B. Freeman and Joel Rogers, "Worker Representation and Participation Survey," Princeton Survey Research Corporation, 1994.

6. Thomas A. Kochan, Harry C. Katz , and Robert B. McKersie, *The Transformation of American Industrial Relations.* (New York: Basic Books, 1986); Freeman and Rogers, "Worker Representation and Participation Survey.

7. *Fact Finding Report of the Commission on the Future of Worker*

Management Relations (Washington, D.C.: U.S. Departments of Labor and Commerce, 1994).

8. For a discussion of the growth in regulation, see chap. 4 of the *Fact Finding Report of the Commission on the Future of Worker Management Relations.*

9. *Final Report and Recommendations of the Commission on the Future of Worker Management Relations* (Washington, D.C.: U.S. Departments of Labor and Commerce, 1995). See also Edward E. Potter and Judith A. Youngman, *Keeping America Competitive: Employment Relations for the 21st Century* (Lakewood, Colo.: Glendridge Publishing, 1995).

10. Edward E. Lawler, Susan A. Mohrman, and Gerald E. Ledford, *Employee Involvement and Total Quality Management* (San Francisco: Jossey-Bass, 1992); Paul Osterman, "How Common Is Workplace Transformation and How Can We Explain Who Adopts It?" *Industrial and Labor Relations Review* 4 (1994): 177–85.

11. See Harry C. Katz, Jeffrey Keefe, and Thomas A. Kochan, "Industrial Relations and Productivity in the U.S. Automobile Industry," *Brookings Papers on Economic Activity* 3 (1987): 685–715; Kim Clark, W. Bruce Chew, and Takahiro Fujimoto, "Product Development in the World Auto Industry," *Brookings Papers on Economic Activity* 3 (1987): 729–71; and Deborah Ancona, "Outward Bound: Strategies for Team Survival in the Organization," *Academy of Management Journal* 33 (1991): 334–65.

12. Thomas A. Kochan, John C. Wells, Michal Smith, and James Rebitzer, "Human Resource Management and Contingent Workers," *Human Resource Management* 33 (1994): 55–78.

13. Annalee Saxsenian, *Regional Advantage: Culture and Competition in Silicon Valley and Route 128* (Cambridge, Mass.: Harvard University Press, 1994).

14. The full data are reported in the record of the Silicon Valley Hearing of the Commission on the Future of Worker Management Relations, U.S. Department of Labor, January 27, 1994. See also Douglas Henton, *Blueprint for a 21st Century* (Menlo Park, Calif.: Joint Ventures for Silicon Valley, 1994).

15. Eleanor Westney, *Imitation and Innovation* (Cambridge, Mass.: Harvard University Press, 1987).

16. John Paul MacDuffie and John Krafcik, "Integrating Technology and Human Resources for High Performance Manufacturing," in *Transforming Organizations*, ed. Thomas A. Kochan (New York: Oxford University Press, 1992) 209–26.

17. See Kochan, Katz, and McKersie, *The Transformation of American Industrial Relations*, pp. 178–205.

18. The evidence on the role and power of human resource executives is reviewed in Thomas A. Kochan and Paul Osterman, *The Mutual Gains Enterprise* (Boston: Harvard Business School Press, 1994) pp. 118–22.

19. Masahiko Aoki, *Information, Incentives, and Bargaining in the Japanese Economy* (New York: Cambridge University Press, 1988).

20. Kirsten Wever, *Negotiating Competitiveness: Employment Relations and*

Industrial Adjustment in the United States and Germany (Boston: Harvard Business School Press, 1995).

21. See the *Final Report and Recommendations of the Commission on the Future of Worker Management Relations*, 1994.

22. A summary of the employment law changes favored by business groups and Republican leaders in Congress is contained in Potter and Youngman, *Keeping America Competitive*, pp. 166–84.

References

Aoki, Masahiko. *Information, Incentives, and Bargaining in the Japanese Economy.* New York: Cambridge University Press, 1988.

Appelbaum, Eileen, and Rosemary Batt. *The New American Workplace.* Ithaca, N.Y.: ILR Press, 1994.

Blinder, Alan, ed. *Paying for Productivity.* Washington, D.C.: Brookings Institution, 1990.

Bluestone, Irving, and Barry Bluestone. *Negotiating the Future.* New York: Basic Books, 1992.

Cole, Robert E. *Strategies for Learning: Small Group Activities in American, Japanese, and Swedish Industries.* Berkeley: University of California Press, 1989.

Commission on the Future of Worker Management Relations. *Fact Finding Report,* and *Final Report and Recommendations.* Washington, D.C.: U.S. Departments of Labor and Commerce, 1994.

Freeman, Richard B. *Working Under Different Rules.* New York: Russell Sage, 1994.

Freeman, Richard B., and James L. Medoff. *What Do Unions Do?* New York: Basic Books, 1985.

Kochan, Thomas A., Harry C. Katz, and Robert B. McKersie. *The Transformation of American Industrial Relations.* New York: Basic Books, 1986.

Kochan, Thomas A., and Paul Osterman. *The Mutual Gains Enterprise.* Boston: Harvard Business School Press, 1994.

Lawler, Edward E. *The Ultimate Advantage.* San Francisco: Jossey-Bass, 1993.

Piore, Michael, and Charles Sabel. The Second Industrial Divide. New York: Basic Books, 1984.

Potter, Edward E., and Judith A. Youngman. *Keeping America Competitive: Employment Relations for the 21st Century.* Lakewood Colo.: Glenridge Publishing, 1995.

Schor, Juliet B. *The Overworked American.* New York: Basic Books, 1991.

Thomas, Robert. *What Machines Can't Do.* Berkeley: University of California Press, 1993.

Wever, Kirsten. *Negotiating Competitiveness: Employment Relations and Industrial*

Adjustment in the United States and Germany. Boston: Harvard Business School Press, 1995.

Womack, James, Daniel Jones, and Daniel Roos. *The Machine That Changed the World.* New York: Macmillan, 1990.

Zuboff, Shoshanna. *The Age of the Smart Machine.* New York: Basic Books, 1988.

8

The Corporation Faces Issues
of Race and Gender

✦

BARBARA R. BERGMANN

The employment policies of American corporations—their handling of matters of race, ethnicity, and gender—are bound to have a profound effect on the American economy and American society. These policies will affect the corporation's mode and efficiency of operation, its costs, and its flexibility. More than any other factors, they will determine whether large numbers of African-American and Hispanic American citizens will continue to have incomes and identities that set them apart from and distinctly below mainstream Americans. These policies will also play a big part in determining the position of women in our society.

The Increase in Workforce Diversity

It is by now a commonplace that the American workforce is highly diverse and getting more so. When business people discuss "workforce diversity," they are thinking principally of the decline in the proportion of the labor force that is non-Hispanic white male. One sentence in the Hudson Institute's *Workforce 2000* has apparently caught and held the attention of many corporate managers: "White males, thought of only a generation ago as the mainstays of the economy, will comprise only 15 percent of the net additions to the labor force between 1985 and 2000."[1]

The statement does not, of course, mean that by the year 2000 only fifteen out of one hundred people in the labor force will be white men. Nor, since it speaks of "net additions," as opposed to simply "additions," does it mean that only fifteen percent of the new young workers coming out of school and onto the labor market will be white men. Of those who have been startled and energized by the Hudson Institute statement, no doubt some have interpreted it in one of these erroneous ways.

Properly interpreted, the statement means that the number of white men is currently growing, and that in the year 2000 there will actually be more of them available than there were in 1985. However, the growth of the white male group will be slower than the labor force growth of other population groups. As a result, the share of white non-Hispanic males in the labor force will be declining below what it currently is. The Hudson Institute statement, whether interpreted correctly or incorrectly, has focused managers' attention on this process. It has heightened their concern with the need to "manage" the increased workforce diversity that has so forcibly been brought to their attention.

While the conscious and widespread concern with workforce diversity among corporate executives is relatively new, this country has always had a workforce that was considerably diverse. Prior to the 1960s, a decade that saw the culmination of the movement for the civil rights of black Americans and also the beginnings of a new phase of the movement for women's equality, that diversity was for the most part downplayed or ignored. There were, everybody knew, some black faces in menial jobs down in the basement or out in the kitchen, or working as hired laborers or sharecroppers on the land in the Old South. There were immigrants who didn't speak much English laboring in small-scale sweatshops in the big cities. There were quite substantial numbers of women working in low-paying jobs, supposedly just for pin money, supposedly just to fill in the time between school and marriage. And there were a small number of low-paid professional occupations, such as elementary teaching and nursing, mostly outside of the corporate ambit, marked off for women, and women alone.

But these workers, when they were thought of at all, were viewed as offering no serious competition to white native-born men for most jobs, especially most good corporate jobs. They were thought of as distinctly marginal. The "real" workforce, as white middle-class Americans viewed matters, was composed of white native-born adult males. White males occupied virtually all the crafts, technical, professional, supervisory, and managerial jobs, and virtually all of the jobs that involved driving or operating movable mechanical equipment.

Yet throughout the entire period of 1900 to 1950, when, as the Hudson Institute put it, white native-born males were considered to be the "mainstay of the economy," they were far short of an overwhelming majority—their share of the labor force in that period was never much above 60 percent.[2] In 1950 native-born white males had about the same share as they had had half a century earlier. In that year white women constituted 24 percent of the labor force, and black women and men together another 10 percent. Foreign-born men were about 6 percent. After 1950 the share of white men lost its stability and started on a decline that continues today.

The main source of the decline since 1950 in the share of white men was the mass entry into the labor force of women. During the fifties the number of women in the labor force increased by 29 percent. In the sixties, seventies, and eighties their numbers rose by 39 percent, 44 percent, and 24 percent, respectively. In 1994 women constituted 46 percent of the labor force. They are continuing to increase their labor force participation rate, while that of men continues to decline.

A second, but much smaller, source of the decline of the native-born white male share has been the influx of Hispanic workers. The Bureau of Labor Statistics began to gather data on Hispanic workers in the 1970s. By 1980 it counted 6.1 million Hispanic workers of both sexes, putting them at 5.7 percent of the labor force. In 1994 there were 11.7 million, or 9.0 percent of the labor force.[3]

By 1980 white non-Hispanic males were no longer an absolute majority of the labor force; in that year they constituted only 48 percent. By 1994 their share was down to 41 percent. Bureau of Labor Statistics projections place their share in the year 2005 at 38 percent (see Table 8.1).

Is There a Problem?

Until relatively recently, American corporations, like virtually all employers both large and small, have been content to allow the replication within corporate walls of the social hierarchy of American society at large, with distinctly different and distinctly subordinate roles for women and for minority people. Having occupations marked out as "belonging" exclusively to one sex or other, or to one race or other, and having the occupations for women and minorities marked out as dead ends has seemed quite natural to everybody, even including those disadvantaged by it. It continues to seem natural to large numbers. A quite obvious example is the informal rule maintained by many firms that "once a secretary always a secretary," despite the presence in the secretarial ranks of many intelligent women with considerable knowledge of the company's operations. These rules are rarely challenged.

Table 8.1. The U.S. Labor Force by Race and Sex in 1994, with Projections for 2005

	1994			
	Millions of workers		Percent of total labor force	
	Male	Female	Male	Female
Non-Hispanic white	53.4	45.5	41.2%	35.1%
Non-Hispanic black	6.5	7.1	5.1	5.5
Hispanic	7.1	4.6	5.5	3.5
Other	3.0	2.4	2.3	1.9
Total	70.0	59.6	54.0	46.0
	2005			
	Millions of workers		Percent of total labor force	
	Male	Female	Male	Female
Non-Hispanic white	57.4	52.3	38.1%	34.7%
Non-Hispanic black	8.2	8.8	5.4	5.8
Hispanic	9.9	6.9	6.6	4.6
Other	3.8	3.4	2.5	2.3
Total	79.3	71.4	52.6	47.4

Sources: For 1994, U.S. Department of Labor, Bureau of Labor Statistics, *Employment and Earnings*, April 1994, p. 145; data refer to first quarter. Projections for 2005 by U.S. Bureau of Labor Statistics, from *Statistical Abstract of the United States, 1992*, p. 393. Of Hispanics, 95 percent declare themselves to be white, and 5 percent black in BLS surveys. However, see note 3.

Until recently, most managers have not seen the traditional confinement of minorities and women to certain jobs as a major problem for their businesses or for the business community as a whole. It is not necessary to postulate animus or malevolence in most of them to account for the origin and continuance of such practices. Most people feel comfortable in following familiar patterns. Managers have certainly felt comfortable filling vacancies for good jobs with white men. We may speculate that there was little conscious thought in doing that, or even in setting up the jobs they allowed to women and blacks as low-paying and dead-end. They were comfortable with those details of the personnel procedures that ensured the automatic continuance of the status quo. Such details include a requirement for geographic rotation for promotable managers, and the recruitment of the pool of candidates mostly by word of mouth. The procedures for judg-ing candidates were highly subjective, giving those opposed to any change full rein to undermine any candidates of unconventional race or sex.

Appointing unconventional candidates for jobs that have been white male monopolies has the potential for creating major and minor difficulties in the workplace both before and after the appointment. Since smooth per-sonal relations are in most cases a necessity if productivity is to be main-tained, managers who sought to make unconventional appointments were asking for trouble. Thus, in the absence of organized and vigorous company policy promoting such appointments, very little change tends to occur.

Most people tend to rationalize the very differing roles of women and men in the workplace by reference to the wishes of women themselves for time and energy to devote to family duties. They rationalize the differences in the positions of blacks and whites by reference to blacks' relatively poorer education and to the poverty-stricken environment that many blacks have had to endure while growing up. While differences among workers in moti-vation and background certainly do exist and do legitimately affect the jobs people get and the wages they earn, they cannot explain the degree of seg-regation by occupation or the degree of the differences in average pay.[4] To return to the example of the dead-ended secretaries, many or even most sec-retaries might not want the added responsibilities that go with a promotion to managerial ranks, yet it is unlikely that 100 percent of them would be un-interested.[5]

In a famous study, sociologists William T. Bielby and James N. Barron looked at records compiled in 1979 by the U.S. Employment Service for 393 workplaces and scored each workplace by the extent of the sex segre-gation in its jobs. A workplace in which all the men worked in jobs without having a single woman colleague, in which there was not a single job title that had both men and women in it, was given a score of 100. A workplace where men and women shared each job title in accordance with their share in the establishment's total workforce was given a segregation score of zero. The average segregation score in the workplaces studied was found to be 93.4. Of the 393 workplaces, 232 had scores of 100—their job categories were perfectly segregated by sex. Later research by Erica Groshen found that sex segregation by occupation within firms continues to be prevalent.[6] Race segregation also continues.

Bielby and Barron found that those few job categories that firms had in-tegrated by sex tended to be those in which the workers did not work to-gether as colleagues at the same work site but were widely scattered geo-graphically. The most striking example they give of a sex-integrated crew was one firm's group of 147 building managers who worked in 147 separate buildings. The tendency to keep crews that work together in the same job segregated by race and sex seems to be weakening slightly in recent years. One now observes an occasional restaurant that has both male and female waiters performing identical functions on the same shift, something virtually unknown fifteen years ago. Airline ticket agents work in groups that are integrated by both race and sex. But single-sex and single-race crews are still the rule rather than the exception.

One front on which progress has been made is the entry of women into jobs that are classed as "executive, administrative, and managerial"; women occupy 43.4 percent of these jobs, as of March 1994, close to their 45.8 percent share of total employment. In 1972 they held only 19.7 percent of these jobs. Blacks occupy only 6.5 percent of the managerial jobs, although they constitute 10.3 percent of the employed. The highest jobs in management continue to be the almost exclusive province of white males, a phenomenon that has been dubbed "the glass ceiling." At Citicorp, for example, 41 percent of managerial jobs were occupied by women in 1992. However, a recent report on the so-called feudal lords of Citicorp showed fifteen out of sixteen of the top executives to be white males. The one exception was a Japanese male. Citicorp is typical in this respect as can be seen from the photos of top executives in corporate annual reports.

One important set of well-paying blue-collar jobs in which black men have made gains are the "precision production, craft and repair" categories, in which 18.7 percent of white men are employed. Of such jobs 8.1 percent are held by blacks. However, jobs of these types have not been integrated by sex; women have only 3 percent of the jobs as mechanics and repairers, and less than 2 percent of the jobs in the construction trades. In effect this means that women who do not have a college education have a far poorer chance than do men to have access to a job with a salary that could support a family above the poverty line. This has obvious consequences for the standard of living of the increasing proportion of children in mother-only families.

A number of recent events illustrate that corporate problems with discrimination by race and gender still persist. Lucky Stores, a West Coast grocery chain, agreed in 1993 to pay nearly seventy-five million dollars in damages to women who were denied promotion opportunities, and another twenty million dollars to set up and run affirmative action programs. The women had been denied full-tme slots, and the relatively small group of women in management jobs had been segregated into certain departments—bakery and delicatessen—which were marked off as dead-end. The managers of these departments were assigned lower pay than other managers. Suits alleging similar behavior have been filed against Safeway Stores and several other grocery chains.

The facts of the Lucky case were strikingly similar to those in a 1972 suit against Giant Foods, a Washington-area grocery chain. That suit had been settled, with the company under order until the late 1980s to remedy the problems. However, a 1994 telephone survey to ascertain the sex of managers by department showed that in the twenty years since the suit very little integration of managerial positions had been accomplished.[7] Meat cutting, a skilled trade requiring apprenticeship, was maintained as an all-male specialty. Bakery managers, still overwhelmingly female, continued to get salaries that were on the lowest level of those paid to department managers. The cost of remedying the bakery managers' relatively low pay would amount to a few dollars an hour per store; the fact that their pay was not raised suggests that their low pay has symbolic significance designating low status, and that preserving that symbol is of importance to those in control.[8] The history of the situation at Giant Foods illustrates the stubbornness of these problems, and how difficult they are to fix when the management is indifferent or opposed to change. A successful lawsuit may give the particular complainants a recompense but leave the underlying situation unchanged. The supermarket cases also show the complicity of some unions in the process of maintaining both segregation by sex and women's lower pay. The supermarket unions negotiated contracts that year after year picked out the female bakery managers for low pay and maintained a segregated meat-cutting department.

One remarkable experimental study, conducted by the Urban Institute, gives direct evidence of differential treatment of blacks and whites by employers. Pairs of male undergraduates, one white and one black, who had been selected and trained to be as like as possible in manner and ostensible qualifications, were sent out to apply for low-level jobs advertised as vacant in several metropolitan areas. Both members of a pair would apply for the same job, and refuse it if offered so the other could have a chance at an offer. The whites got 50 percent more offers than their black counterparts.[9] This kind of differential leads to longer spells of unemployment for blacks who change jobs, and gives an incentive for a black to take and stay in more disadvantageous jobs than a white counterpart would be likely to.

A number of cases have recently come to light in which corporations acted unfairly toward black customers. The large Denny's Restaurant chain recently settled a multi-million-dollar claim by many black customers that they were not served when whites were being served. Company policy apparently required refusing service to blacks in its restaurants when the proportion of black customers rose above some level. Banks have also recently been shown to discriminate against their black customers. What the *Wall Street Journal* called "damning studies" by the Federal Reserve Board showed that at many banks blacks were twice as likely as whites with similar incomes to be turned down for mortgages.[10] Unfairness to black customers is not, of course, the same thing as unfairness to blacks in hiring, placement, and promotion. However, firms that won't deal fairly with blacks as customers are unlikely to deal with them fairly as employees or potential employees.

Information is available on employment by race, sex, and occupation for those corporations that are government contractors from the reports that they must make to the federal government.[11] Table 8.2 gives the share of women and black employees in managerial and crafts occupations for selected corporations in a number of industries. These data show that the extent of women's participation in management jobs varies widely from one industry to another, and also varies considerably within industry. Within the oil business, for example, the share of women in Atlantic Richfield's management jobs is twice as large as their share in the management jobs at Union Oil. Among food manufacturers, a corporation that allows women only a 4 percent share in management jobs coexists with a corporation that allows them a 36 percent share. It would seem that these disparities are unlikely to be the result of women's desires to work at one firm and avoid another for "family" reasons. Rather, these data strongly suggest that these firms differ considerably in what is commonly called their "corporate culture," and that some are far more open than others to hiring women for management jobs. The idea common among economists that discrimination is not an important factor in the differing labor market experience of women and men is contradicted by these data.

Table 8.2 also shows wide differences in corporate representation of blacks in management. Some of the differences may be due to location, since labor markets differ by the size of their black populations. However, it is unlikely that the difference between Nynex's 4.9 share of management jobs for blacks and Southern New England Telegraph's share of 12.8 percent can be accounted for in this way, since both serve regions where the proportion of black workers in the labor force is similar. It must also be realized that corporations can decide whether to locate in areas that are difficult for black workers to reach. Deciding to put a facility in an area deep in all-white suburbia, with poor public transportation, is effectively a decision to have few black workers.

There is also wide variation among these corporations in their allocation of skilled crafts jobs, which include the jobs of first-line supervisors.

Table 8.2. Employment of Women and Blacks in Selected Large
Corporations, 1992

Company name	Total employment	Women's % share		Blacks' % share	
		Managers	Crafts	Managers	Crafts
Oil:					
ATLANTIC RICHFIELD CO	19941	18.9	4.0	3.7	7.2
EXXON CORP	42012	10.7	6.4	6.0	14.7
MOBIL CORP	39709	15.2	4.7	5.9	14.5
UNION OIL CO DBA UNOCAL	9683	8.3	2.7	3.8	9.4
Food manufactures:					
CONAGRA	80466	17.0	10.5	4.0	9.0
GEO A HORMEL & CO	8304	4.1	6.4	1.1	9.1
TYSON FOODS INC	45999	16.4	17.3	7.8	11.6
BORDEN INC	25047	12.1	13.6	3.5	16.6
CAMPBELL SOUP	25967	19.3	12.4	3.3	10.4
GERBER PRODUCTS CO	10455	27.3	5.8	2.3	3.2
H J HEINZ COMPANY	16737	27.6	12.3	2.3	5.7
PET INC PET PLAZA	7333	20.0	12.7	4.2	5.8
RJR NABISCO INC	42130	18.6	10.5	7.9	22.1
KELLOGG CO & KELLOGG SALES CO	6583	22.1	2.6	8.3	5.1
QUAKER OATS COMPANY	11553	25.7	3.3	5.4	4.9
SARA LEE	64575	36.2	12.7	7.7	16.7
Auto manufactures:					
CHRYSLER CORP	88614	7.8	2.3	8.6	11.3
FORD MOTOR CO	140780	4.4	1.6	8.5	9.1
GENERAL MOTORS CORP	380222	11.6	3.2	10.2	8.1
Communications:					
AMERICAN TELE & TELEGRAPH	136176	45.2	7.7	10.6	5.6
AMERITECH CORP	11355	42.3	2.2	10.7	2.8
CENTEL CORP	8844	43.7	10.3	7.6	6.6
MCI COMMUNICATIONS	24516	33.5	40.5	9.0	10.8
NYNEX CORP	22711	40.0	7.6	4.9	2.7
PACIFIC TELESIS GROUP	3101	32.7	—	3.6	—
SOUTHERN NEW ENGLAND TEL CO	11125	63.3	12.0	12.8	5.4
SOUTHWESTERN BELL TELEPHONE CO	52537	40.9	13.2	11.1	8.6
US WEST	10311	51.7	7.9	4.6	2.3
UNITED TELECOMMUNICATIONS INC	42515	31.1	5.4	5.9	4.5
Retail:					
MARRIOTT CORP	185943	41.0	26.9	8.0	18.4
MCDONALDS CORP	93990	46.0	20.0	16.6	5.0
PEPSICO INC	284588	31.8	22.8	14.7	10.7
SUPER VALU STORES INC	26992	22.3	13.3	3.9	3.9
WALGREEN DRUG STORES	52304	26.6	6.8	9.0	4.5
TOYS R US INC	35262	43.7	—	7.5	—

continued

Table 8.2. *continued*

Company name	Total employment	Women's % share		Blacks' % share	
		Managers	Crafts	Managers	Crafts
Banking and finance:					
BANC ONE CORP	31503	48.5	0.0	4.4	7.7
BANK AMERICA CORP	93402	61.2	4.8	5.6	3.0
BANK OF BOSTON	12381	48.6	0.0	4.8	11.5
BANK OF NEW YORK	14576	38.1	—	8.8	—
BANKERS TRUST CO	7890	35.4	0.0	7.3	0.0
BARNETT BANKS OF FLORIDA INC	1113	38.8	0.0	2.5	0.0
BOATMEN'S BANCSHARES INC	13271	48.6	16.7	6.5	8.3
CHASE MANHATTAN BANK NA	27271	42.5	1.7	7.8	6.6
CHEMICAL BANKING CORP	38357	44.4	16.1	10.3	22.6
CITICORP	42709	41.5	5.1	7.1	6.8
COMERICA INC	7597	49.0	0.0	8.0	0.0
FIFTH THIRD BANK	4856	47.4	0.0	3.3	0.0
FIRST BANK SYSTEM INC	9056	51.0	—	1.6	—
FIRST CHICAGO CORP	16048	45.4	0.0	12.5	9.1
FIRST INTERSTATE BANCORP	30320	56.7	0.0	3.5	0.0
FIRST UNION CORP	23748	53.2	9.5	6.7	19.0
FIRSTSTAR CORP	8834	46.9	23.1	1.6	0.0
HUNTINGTON NATIONAL BANK	7089	49.2	0.0	4.2	6.3
KEYCORP	13573	51.9	—	2.0	—
MANUFACTURERS NATIONAL CORP	5758	44.9	—	10.2	—
MELLON NATIONAL CORP	17155	39.7	—	4.4	—
NBD BANCORP	14682	49.8	51.5	11.4	8.2
NORTHERN TRUST CO	6026	45.6	0.0	8.9	18.2
NORWEST CORP	28446	41.7	22.2	1.8	5.6
SALOMON INC	6501	20.5	0.0	3.6	5.2
SOCIETY CORP	13260	31.1	—	3.5	—
STATE ST BOSTON CORP	7813	40.5	—	3.0	—
US BANCORP	12997	57.7	8.0	1.7	0.0
WACHOVIA CORP	17289	48.0	3.2	10.1	34.9
WELLS FARGO BANK	31253	66.1	0.0	7.5	16.7

Source: Tabulations by the author from information made available by the Office of Federal Contract Compliance Programs

There seems to be little correlation between the advancement of women as managers and their occupancy of crafts jobs. For example, AT&T has a far higher proportion of women in managerial jobs than does MCI, but women have a far smaller share of crafts jobs at AT&T. With respect to race, most of the corporations listed in Table 8.2 have a higher proportion of their crafts jobs than their managerial jobs occupied by blacks, the opposite of the case with women.

Business Motives for Reducing Occupational Segregation by Race and Sex

When corporate managers in the human resources field speak of "managing workforce diversity," they are not speaking merely of having on their rosters women and members of minority groups in numbers that reflect their share in the labor force, although of course that is of concern. They are talking about the process of opening up to members of these groups the roles within the corporate workforce that have been, by design or by default, restricted to white men. They are also interested in taking steps to make workers who are assigned to roles not traditional for their race or gender welcome, comfortable on the job, able to learn, and maximally productive.

Giving the Business Freedom of Choice

One motive that businesses have for operating affirmative action plans that gradually do away with occupational segregation by race and sex is their desire to have access to a reasonably large pool of labor for each kind of job. As noted, business executives have become increasingly conscious of the fact that white men now account for less than half the workforce, and that they will have an even smaller share in the labor market of the future, especially among young workers. If employers continued to allow white men to maintain their traditional monopolies over large segments of the job market, they would be forced to recruit important elements of their workforce from a smaller and smaller share of all workers.

As total employment grows, the number of managers and skilled blue-collar crafts workers that are needed also grows, and these are the occupations white males have traditionally dominated. The continuation of that dominance would mean greater competition among employers for an increasingly limited pool of white male workers. It would also result in having a greater proportion of the managerial and crafts jobs filled by the less talented white males, thus degrading productivity. At least some Caucasian and minority women and some minority males do have talents and qualifications that are superior to those of the white males who would have to be hired if the former were excluded.

A restriction by race and sex in those allowed to compete for the better jobs has always meant eliminating good candidates who do not meet those specifications, although many of those countenancing or enforcing the elimination might think otherwise. However, restricting the field of candidates to native-born white men might be tolerated when they constituted 60 percent of the labor force; that restriction might look less tolerable as the share of conventional candidates sinks below 40 percent.

A continued reliance on white males to play their traditional roles could be expected to force business to pay a higher wage premium for white males. In 1994 it cost on average 39 percent more to hire a white male than it did to hire another kind of worker. Some of that differential is due to the better preparation of white males in school and on the job for well-paying roles. (The better preparation on the job is due, in part, to the restriction to white males of jobs in which training occurs.) Another part of the differential is due to the restriction of certain high-responsibility jobs that do not take rare skill to white males. Still another part is the social convention that a white male is disgraced by being forced to accept a salary for which a black person or a white woman can be hired.

In the short run, putting nontraditional workers into previously white male roles does little to reduce wage cost. Unless some new occupational category is invented, and the new workforce is formally separated from the existing workforce, the new workers will have to be hired at the previous scale for the job. However, as time goes on, the reduction in scarcity of eligible workers for these positions should reduce the growth of their wages relative to others'.

It must be recognized, however, that the relatively reduced availability of white men will not guarantee a reduction in occupational segregation by sex and race. There will be more than enough white men to go around for the top jobs, if there is a bit of redefinition as to who is "white" and what the "top jobs" are. In twenty years, many young men of Asian and Hispanic origin will probably be acceptable for those "top jobs" to a far greater extent than their fathers were. Further, and unprecedented, changes in attitudes toward exclusion on the basis of race and sex would be required if African-Americans and women are also to become acceptable.

The Legal Requirements to Integrate Workforces

Title VII of the Civil Rights Act, passed in 1964, made it illegal for employers to act so as to disadvantage people by discriminating against them on account of their race, sex, religion, or national origin. The only penalty that violators could suffer under the Act was the payment to those injured of recompense for economic damage that had been incurred due to the prohibited behavior. (The Civil Rights Restoration Act, passed in 1991, allows the award of punitive damages.) Whether discrimination has actually occurred in any particular case, and the extent of the damages suffered, has to be determined through a lawsuit filed in a federal court. The lawsuit can be brought by the injured workers or by the Equal Employment Opportunity Commission (EEOC), which was set up by the act.

In practice, the EEOC has had the resources to pursue in court only a tiny fraction of the thousands of complaints that are filed with it each year. During the years of the Reagan and Bush presidencies, the EEOC further limited its effectiveness by concentrating on suits on behalf of single individuals. It generally avoided filing class action suits, in which the claims of discrimination by groups of employees could be addressed in a single suit. Class action suits are the only ones that have the had the potential to cause employers adjudged to have discriminated under the act to suffer substantial financial loss. They generate more publicity, lend themselves to statistical evidence, and also make it difficult for the employer to base a defense on the plaintiffs' alleged bad behavior, or incompetence, or peculiarities, as is easily done in cases brought on behalf of one employee or a small number of individuals.

It is unlikely that the threat of lawsuits under Title VII, filed either by employees or by EEOC, has been or will be a serious deterrent to discrimination by corporations, or can provide much of an impetus to the hiring of women and minorities and their integration into jobs in which they have been excluded. Most of the people injured by discrimination are not in a position to sue, or even to complain. Applicants who are not hired cannot effectively judge whether the persons who were hired had superior qualifications. Those who have been hired but assigned to dead-end segregated positions, or passed over for promotion on account of their race or sex, are unlikely to pursue complaints unless they have some superior position outside the company to go to. Many employees are not even aware that segregation by race or sex on the job is wrong or illegal.

A second federal program, based on executive order signed by President Lyndon Johnson in 1965, required nondiscrimination of all firms doing more than fifty thousand dollars worth of business with the federal government, established the obligation of such firms to provide information to the government relating to their compliance, and established contract termination as a penalty for noncompliance. By 1978 the program was requiring federal contractors to engage in an analysis of their utilization of women and minority workers by major occupational group, and to compare that utilization with the availability of such workers. Contractors were required to draft affirmative action programs containing numerical goals and timetables for moving utilization of these workers into line with their availability. They were required to submit these affirmative action plans to the U.S. Department of Labor's Office of Federal Contract Compliance Programs (OFCCP). The OFCCP is supposed to supervise units within the cabinet-level departments, each of which maintains a corps of investigators in contact with the corporations.[12]

The OFCCP program presents the possibility of more vigorous and targeted enforcement activities by the government than those allowed by Title VII. The OFCCP is not limited to responding to the filing of complaints; it can take on a proactive role. It could choose to concentrate on the most egregious offenders among the large corporations, where the most impact might be made. For these reasons, the OFCCP has considerable potential in promoting integration of all job categories by race and sex.

That potential has largely been unrealized. While its activities have probably been more influential in changing corporate practices than those of the EEOC, or those of individual plaintiffs bringing lawsuits, the OFCCP has been of distinctively limited effectiveness. Its only sanction—the decertification of a corporation from the approved list of federal contractors—is too severe to happen very often. In the case of defense contractors, a corporation may be the only source of a product that the Pentagon wants. One can easily believe that the decertification of a corporation that has performed poorly, for example, one with a performance like that of the Ford Motor Company, as revealed in Table 8.2, would exact considerable political costs.

In practice, very few corporations have been subject to decertification; those decertified have been ones that refused to turn in an affirmative action plan. The officials of the OFCCP have devoted a great deal of attention to the details of affirmative action plans that it has considered deficient but very little attention to whether corporations were meeting their goals and timetables under these plans.

All told, the verdict must be that government enforcement of prohibitions against discrimination and encouragement of integration has not been sufficiently vigorous to make much of a difference in corporate behavior. Probably the major impact of government activity in this area has been to familiarize corporate management employees, if not the population at large, with the idea that no race or sex group has a legitimate monopoly on any set of jobs, and that a corporation that allows any set of jobs to be monopolized by white males looks bad.

Corporate Concerns With the Social Health
of the United States

In addition to the issues of access to a larger pool of workers and government compulsion, which, I have argued, have not had major influence, more long-range considerations having to do with the social and political environment of this country also have influenced business managers. In larger corporations, the higher executives are likely to feel some responsibility for the stewardship of this country, both because of the influence they wield and because they understand that the social and political condition of the country affects the climate in which they operate. The more thoughtful among them, especially those with international standing and contacts, feel ashamed about the unsolved problems of race and poverty in this country, and the attendant crime, urban decay, unwed motherhood, drug addiction, and demoralization. They worry that the antisocial behavior of those feeling left out of mainstream America is detrimental, even dangerous, to the society that constitutes the corporation's environment, and they know that this behavior has consequences that are expensive to deal with. They see that these problems cause the United States to lose standing in the world, and they understand that American business loses, too, in an important way from them.

Some business executives undoubtedly would take the point of view that the solution to our problems with race and the underclass lie in sternness, denial of welfare programs, and strict assignment of jobs according to merit, with merit being assessed by those who have been assessing it all along. Others, however, see blacks' problems in the job market as a major cause of America's racial problem, and they see special programs to help put blacks into more and better jobs as a necessary major part of the solution. They worry that America's racial problems, if allowed to continue and if further exacerbated, can put the stability of the country and its institutions into jeopardy. The larger the corporation, the more likely it is that its leadership will feel some responsibility to conduct its personnel policy in a way that is conducive to a healthy, socially unified United States.

Neither left-wing nor right-wing movements have had lasting success in this country in the past. However, increasing tensions between the races, and the crime problems and resentments that such tensions bring, conceivably could fuel political movements that might pose dangers to business as usual.

Business leaders are also sensitive to the striving of women for greater respect and for improved access to the better jobs. It is difficult for anyone who wants to appear to be progressive and modern to continue to advocate traditional attitudes on sex roles. It is difficult for business organizations that confine women to traditional jobs to have an image that is up-to-date and progressive, an image that most business leaders want for their organizations. If business executives have families typical of white married men, almost one-third of those executives with children have only daughters. Many of these sonless men have proven to be advocates for equality for women, at least in managerial and professional jobs.

Affirmative Action Within the Corporation

During the presidencies of Nixon, Reagan, and Bush, conservative administration officials attempted to abolish the affirmative action requirements that the OFCCP imposes on business. Quite remarkably, it was the business community that protested the abolition of affirmative action and succeeded in quashing the move each time it was attempted. The lobbying that went on in favor of keeping the federal government's requirement that each contracting company have an affirmative action program was led by two groups financed by large corporations. One was the Equal Opportunity Advisory Council, which describes itself as "a nonprofit association composed of more than 270 companies dedicated to the establishment of nondiscriminatory employment practices."[13] The other was the National Association of Manufacturers. The U.S. Chamber of Commerce, much of whose support comes from smaller businesses, lobbied on the side of getting rid of government requirements of affirmative action.

Those corporation officials who would like to see integration by race and sex in jobs that previously have been the exclusive province of white males have pushed the implementation of formal affirmative action plans, for which the term "managing diversity" has recently become a euphemism. They have not found it credible to rely solely on the announcement of a mandate to be fair regardless of race or sex. Such integration cannot come easily; race and sex integration are likely to arouse both passive and active opposition from people within the organization. Some of the people who will do nothing to forward integration, or who will actively oppose whatever unconventional candidates may appear, are people who may be highly valuable to the organization, and therefore have considerable power to behave independently.

Corporations whose top leadership wants to break up exclusionary practices are faced with the fact that personnel decisions have been among the most decentralized of corporate functions. Formally or informally, traditional procedures governing which person to hire or promote allow a single blackball to sink the chances of a candidate, which means that the person involved in a decision who is most opposed to change can decide the outcome. Competing ideas of "fairness," and "meritocracy" complicate the administration of an affirmative action plan, and such plans are easily sabotaged, or rendered dead letters under flaccid support from top levels of corporate management.

Judging Merit

No affirmative action plan requires placing in a job someone whose prognosis in performing the job is poor. One of the most crucial tasks under affirmative action is the assembling of a pool of candidates, unconventional by race and/or sex, who are judged capable of performing well in each particular job being recruited for. In the case of some jobs that historically have been segregated by race or sex, the talents and training required for the job are quite modest (over-the-road truck driver is an example). In such cases, finding plausible unconventional candidates is not very difficult. Even in the case of jobs requiring rare talents and preparation (full professor of economics at Harvard), a careful search may well turn up an excellent black or female candidate, who might not have been considered without the spur of an affirmative action plan.

When it comes to choosing from the pool of candidates, even a well-meaning group of decision makers may be using bias-laden methods. Psychologist Faye Crosby has done important experimental work that shows how those making personnel decisions can use a biased process, while convincing themselves that only merit is being examined. She has shown through experiments that when personnel decisions are made one at a time, there is a quite strong tendency on the part of all concerned to favor a man over a woman, as long as the man involved is superior to the woman on at least one of the factors used to come to a decision about their relative merit. For example, if man A has a lower efficiency rating than woman B, and lower education but more experience, A's greater experience will be considered decisive in showing that he is the more meritorious of the two. In the next decision that has to be made, where man C has a higher efficiency rating than woman D but she has more education and more experience, C's better efficiency rating will be cited to show that he has greater merit than D. A series of such decisions will result in the man being judged more meritorious than the woman almost all the time. For a woman to win out, she must be superior on all counts, which will happen in few if any cases.[14]

When all these cases are examined together, it is obvious that the process is biased. The weighting of the various factors supposedly contributing to the decision is being changed from one case to another to give greater weight to the factor in which the particular man being judged excels. In a sense, an affirmative action plan that is rigorously enforced can serve the purpose of forcing the decision makers to make the overall pattern of hirings or promotions conform to the availability of good candidates, rather than allowing each decision to be made in isolation.

The Quota Issue

The aspect of affirmative action that has drawn the most opposition has been the use of numerical goals and timetables for integration of the workforce. These goals have been labeled "quotas," a word that apparently has strong negative connotations for most people. Most of those favoring affirmative action have denied that the label is apt. However, if paying attention to the race and sex of those being hired or promoted, and making sure that some unconventional candidates are successful implies that a quota system is being used, then it must be acknowledged that an affirmative action plan with goals and timetables has quotalike aspects. In fact, it is just these aspects that are necessary to enable a corporation to move forward toward integration. Without them very little change is likely.

The use of numerical goals is, of course, common in all aspects of modern management, not just in affirmative action. These days a modern business uses numerical goals in managing production, productivity, sales, investment, and costs, and in setting aspirations for market share. People in an organization work best if they understand what is expected of them, and the announcement of goals is part of the process of setting up explicit standards for performance. In the absence of numerical goals and of timetables for meeting them, it is difficult to pin down whether anyone has done a good job or to hold anyone responsible for failures. When people don't think they will be held responsible, significant efforts are less likely to be forthcoming.

Goals are particularly important when the things to be accomplished are difficult and possibly distasteful to those who have to bring them about. In affirmative action, managers are asked to do things that are unfamiliar, that may seem to them risky in terms of productivity, and that are very possibly distasteful to them. To cooperate with an affirmative action program, managers have to take a chance on a kind of person they have never previously hired. They have to face and brave resistance that may arise from their peers, from the employees they supervise, and from their customers. They many have to overcome their own biases. In the absence of goals, and a system of rewards for meeting goals, it is natural to let difficult things like affirmative action hiring and promotion slide, to be delayed into the indefinite future.

If a sizable number of hires or promotions are going to be done all at one time, it may be possible to make progress in the absence of formal goals, just on the basis of exhortations to fairness and diversity. These days, the people responsible will say to themselves, "We are going to announce twenty promotions next month. It won't look good if they are all white males. There might even be an outcry." But in the more usual case where hires and promotions are done one by one, the use of incentives to meet goals is indispensable. When a single decision is made, the cost of raising the fuss that may be needed to install an unconventional candidate is high. The cost of letting one more opportunity to make progress slip by is viewed as small or nonexistent. Moreover, the candidate chosen is sure to be better in at least one characteristic than the one not chosen, so, as we have seen, there is always a rationale that can be given for the way things turned out.

Goals and timetables in a plan in somebody's file cabinet are by themselves not sufficient. Affirmative action works best if managers up and down the organization—all of those in a position of influence in the hiring and promotion process—understand that a judgment of how well they have performed in furthering the integration of the workplace will be an important ingredient in the evaluation of their own job performance, and that the success of their own careers with the organization will be affected.

The Xerox Affirmative Action Program

A number of large corporations have the reputation of vigorously pursuing affirmative action programs, among them Procter and Gamble, Xerox, Digital, and Corning. The affirmative action program used by the Xerox Corporation is noteworthy; it features central monitoring of results, attention to managerial incentives, and mechanisms that disarm envy and resentment.[15]

At Xerox, the affirmative action officer sitting at company headquarters has an up-to-the-minute computerized count by race and sex of the incumbents of each type of job. Managers are told that their success in affirmative action will be used as an important criterion in evaluating their overall performance.

The promotion process at Xerox is structured so as to avoid problems with the availability of unconventional candidates. Employees are formally designated as being on a list of "promotable" people when they are judged ready for advancement. Care is taken to see that the promotable group is representative of the capable people of all ethnic groups and both genders, and special help may be given to individuals to allow them to qualify. It is understood that everyone on the list of promotable people is meritorious and will be advanced in a reasonable time. When an opening for promotion occurs, a person is chosen from the list of people considered promotable to such jobs. Since those not chosen have a good reason to anticipate that their turn will come reasonably soon, the resentment at seeing an unconventional candidate advanced, possibly for reasons of race or sex balance, is avoided.

Some painful history at Xerox shows that a hiring program has to be supplemented by vigilance to ensure that the minority and female employees are treated fairly in terms of opportunities for performance on the job. The blacks whom Xerox hired for its sales force in the 1970s turned out to be an outstanding group. Yet within the company, especially in California, they were treated in a discriminatory way. Black sales representatives were systematically assigned to accounts where the opportunities for commissions were far lower than those accounts assigned to whites. When they realized that this was being done to them, the black sales representatives in California organized, stood up for themselves, and demanded that top management correct the discriminatory situation. The head of the company responded to them with a personal visit. He agreed that their complaints were justified, and he ordered the system of account allocation changed.[16]

Xerox appears to have concentrated on integrating workers by race: over 10 percent of its managers and crafts jobs are filled by African-Americans. It has done less well with women, who fill only 27 percent of the managerial jobs, a mark far below that achieved by other major corporations. However, 15.9 percent of Xerox's skilled crafts and first-line supervisor jobs are held by women, an unusually high percentage for a manufacturing company.[17]

Workplace Issues Resulting from Increased Diversity

Many aspects of corporate personnel policies in the past have been based on the assumption that the vast majority of employees were males, each served by a full-time homemaker. Such features of corporate life as the revolving shift, compulsory overtime, and a requirement that aspiring managers make frequent moves from one geographic area to another are left over from the era in which that assumption was largely true. The integration of women into managerial hierarchies and the decrease in the number of families with a full-time homemaker have led to a demand for corporate policies that make it easier for both women and men who are employed to carry on their family lives and duties.

Corporate employees who are part of two-earner couples and who have young children face major problems. It is difficult for such workers to compete with rival employees who are childless, or who have a traditional family with the wife staying home, and who are therefore free to adopt a workaholic lifestyle, or to adapt themselves to whatever the corporation demands of them in terms of geographic moves and heavy work hours. The employees who want to devote time to parenting their children present the corporation with a choice. The corporation can force these employees to conform to the old-fashioned mores of total devotion to work duties, possibly losing the services of some of the most talented. Or it can respond by making arrangements that accommodate the needs of such employees: parental leave on the birth or illness of a child, curtailed work hours, helping with finding child care, or actually providing child care. The corporation may find itself to have an interest in the public provision of child care.

Will the American Corporation Respond Adequately to Workplace Diversity?

The most forward-looking element in U.S. corporate management appears to have set itself a task that is unprecedented, in the United States or anywhere else in the world, for that matter: to erase within the workplace the social caste marks of race and sex. The legal foundation for this great piece of social engineering was laid down three decades ago in the Civil Rights Act. While the promise of the Act has gone unfulfilled in most workplaces, including most corporate workplaces, it does remain on the agenda of some corporate leadership, and support for it appears to be gaining.

The success of this venture is by no means assured, especially with respect to race. There are large elements of the public that take the view that African-Americans have exactly the place in our economy and society that they deserve, and if anything have been unfairly favored over whites by employers. The willingness of conservative politicians, including Presidents Reagan and Bush, to fan this sentiment by demonizing quotas has certainly made its achievement more difficult. It is not inconceivable that the country could reverse course, and wipe out the substantial gains that have been made by affirmative action in some quarters. Such a reversal of progress happened once before in our history, during the administration of President Woodrow Wilson, which swept blacks out of government jobs and resegregated theaters and restaurants in the nation's capital.

To bring all elements in the diverse workforce to full participation, corporate management has to fight powerful inertial forces, as well as outright covert and overt opposition. It has to risk making mistakes and disrupting workplace amity. What progress is being made is going on without significant pressure by the organizations that ostensibly represent the interests of the groups who will benefit. That the venture is going forward, and appears to be gaining adherents, is a tribute to those in the corporate sector with a vision of what the country could be.

Notes

1. William B. Johnston and Arnold E. Packer, *Workforce 2000: Work and Workers for the Twenty-first Century* (Indianapolis: Hudson Institute, 1987), p. 95.

2. U.S. Bureau of the Census, *Historical Statistics of the United States, Colonial Times to 1957* (Washington, D.C., 1960).

3. The U.S. statistical agencies treat racial identity and Hispanic identity as two separate characteristics. When Hispanics respond to the monthly Current Population Survey of the Bureau of Labor Statistics and are asked their race, 95 percent of them declare themselves to be white. In the decennial census, 52 percent of Hispanics declare themselves white, 3 percent black, 1 percent American Indian, 1 percent Asian or Pacific Islander, and 43 percent "other race."

4. Many studies suggest that only about half of wage differences between white males and other groups can be accounted for by education, experience, and family commitments. For a review of some of the literature on evidence for the extent of discrimination see Barbara R. Bergmann, *In Defense of Affirmative Action* (New York: Basic Books, 1996).

5. Research under way by my students suggests that as many as 50 percent of secretaries would welcome promotion to nonsecretarial jobs.

6. William T. Bielby and James N. Barron, "A Woman's Place Is with Other Women: Sex Segregation Within Organizations," in *Sex Segregation in the Workplace: Trends, Explanations, Remedies,* ed. Barbara F. Reskin (Washington, D.C.: National Academy Press, 1984). See also Erica L. Groshen "The Structure of the Female/Male Wage Differential," *Journal of Human Resources* 26 (Summer 1991): 457–72.

7. Unpublished papers by Akiki Naono (1993) and Jacqueline Chu (1994), Economics Department, American University, Washington, D.C.

8. See Paula England, *Comparable Worth: Theories and Evidence* (New York: Aldine de Gruyter, 1992).

9. Michael Fix and Raymond J. Struyk, eds., *Clear and Convincing Evidence: Measurement of Discrimination in America* (Washington, D.C.: Urban Institute, 1993), p. 195.

10. The validity of these studies has come under fire, largely based on the purely theoretical ground that businesses, being profit-making organizations, would not turn away black customers who offered the same or better opportunities for profit as the least desirable white customers they accommodated.

11. The source is tabulations by the author of material obtained from the OFCCP.

12. For a compendium of all of the texts of the relevant executive orders, see Jeffry A. Norris and Salvador T. Perkins, *Developing Effective Affirmative Action Plans,* 4th ed. (Washington, D.C.: Employment Policy Foundation, 1993).

13. Ibid., p. 10.

14. This research is described in Susan D. Clayton and Faye J. Crosby, *Affirmative Action in Perspective* (Ann Arbor: University of Michigan Press, 1992), pp. 73–78.

15. The information about the Xerox Corporation's affirmative action plan is derived from an interview the author had with the manager in charge of the plan in 1992.

16. Raymond A. Friedman, 1991. "The Balanced Workforce at Xerox Corporation." Harvard Business School, case 9-491-049, pp. 6–7.

17. The source is tabulations by the author of material obtained from the EEOC and the OFCCP.

9

Corporate Education
and Training

✦

MICHAEL USEEM

The American corporation gives daily shaping to the lives of the more than 20 million people who seek their livelihood there. Political values, career aspirations, and personal networks are made or remade. So, too, are many of the human skills and work experience that make for productive enterprise. Like any large organization, the business firm is simultaneously drawing upon existing talents and molding new abilities among those who dwell therein. Intended or not, the corporation is one of the nation's preeminent educational consumers and producers.

For employees who arrive on the company doorstep well prepared, an elaborate apparatus for application of their talents is at the ready. Many companies deploy sophisticated systems for ensuring proper match between their human capital and work positions. For employees who enter less prepared, a parallel apparatus for enhancing their talents is usually at the ready as well. Many companies employ complex systems for training new entrants whose human capital does not measure up to the work process. Later, the skills of both groups are likely to be further upgraded in response to changing technologies and advancing careers.

Until recently, the corporation's simultaneous consumption and production of employee work capacities have been so naturally a part of the company's operation, so implicitly a part of the corporate experience, that it largely escaped notice. The virtual absence of even allusion to education and training in *The Corporation in Modern Society*, edited by Edward Mason, was symptomatic of that earlier era's untroubled waters. The companies of the 1950s surely sought well-trained employees, and trained others for what they could not already do. Yet of the fourteen contributors to the Mason volume, only Lloyd Warner worried enough to address the question at any length, and then just the changing university backgrounds of business leaders. Otherwise it would seem that education and training were an established, unremarkable feature of the corporate landscape. Companies had presumably found the skills supply adequate and the costs acceptable for engendering the skills still missing.

Whether precisely descriptive or not, the unspoken image was of a firm facing few talent shortages and little mismatch between old skill sets and new workplace demands. To the eyes of company managers in the 1990s, the seeming unconcern of their 1950s counterparts must seem an enviable, albeit irretrievable, condition. The 1990s executives found themselves facing instead a workplace of uncommon skills, a workforce of uneven quality, and a work future of uncertain needs. The educational quality of the workforce and its fit with a changing corporate form had barely registered on the 1950s radar screen. Now it appeared with sharp definition, an object that could not escape management's eye.

The emergence of education and training as a vexing corporate issue can be traced, above all, to a reconfiguration of the ways in which large corporations are designed and operated. Dating to the early 1980s, restructuring led many companies to place greater stress on strategic business units, new information technologies, and performance accountability. A driving principle had been to decentralize decision making and enlarge employee responsibilities. The emergent architectures called for employees with new skill sets. If employees were to adapt to the more engaging and more demanding work environment of the restructured firm, their education and training would constitute a vital instrument for doing so. It would become all the more so in an era in which employee demography was itself radically changing. As women and minorities entered the workforce in unprecedented numbers, the company's training function acquired the additional function of assisting the management of diversity.

These developments inspired a closer look at education and training, both for and within the company workplace. So central were education and training to productivity and performance that they came to be seen by some as a potent wedge for revitalizing American competitiveness. The U.S. Office of Technology Assessment reported in a 1991 study that the "quality of the U.S. workforce matters now more than ever." Workforce education had become a corporate sine qua non: "Training goes hand-in-hand," the study concluded, "with productivity, quality, flexibility, and automation in the best performing firms." Examination of U.S. manufacturing by an academic commission in 1989 reached much the same conclusion. On examining job training in Japan, Germany, the United States and elsewhere, the commission concluded that company programs that engendered broadly based skills and workforce flexibility were an essential infrastructure for improving American corporate performance. Drawing on both practical experience and research studies in companies that restructured their organizations during the early 1990s, several researchers arrived at a similar summary: "If information and power are moved downward, it is vital that the knowledge and skills to use them be moved downward as well."[1]

The account begins with a brief tour of the restructured firm. The observed corporate redesigns have been largely responsible for placing company education and training on the radar screen. The chapter next focuses on the decentralization of authority and accountability. Here we see a devolution of power and responsibility not only through the managerial cadres but also into the blue-collar ranks. The account then examines the impact of corporate decentralization on employee development. Enlarging the responsibilities of the lesser ranks is observed to bring an enlarged corporate investment in education and training. The chapter next focuses on the question of whether further expansion of company education and training can be expected. It would appear that the company training glass is both half empty and half full. The account, finally, turns to three related developments: (1) the expanding company involvement in school reform; (2) the flattening of employee careers and a consequent narrowing of employee interest in corporate training; and (3) the rising presence of diversity training. The focus is on large companies, and our evidence is primarily drawn from them. Much relevant research, however, is based on cross sections of American employees working in firms large and small, and evidence is utilized from these as well.

The Restructured Corporation

The corporate restructuring of the 1980s and early 1990s had profound impact on both company form and American life. Hostile acquisitions, leveraged buyouts, and wholesale downsizings decimated communities and shortened work careers. At the same time, process reengineering, flexible work methods, and streamlined hierarchies improved employee productivity and product quality. The two faces of restructuring, the devastation and the renewal, reshaped virtually all company investments and programs, including education and training.

To appreciate the altered place of company education and training in a restructured environment, it is useful to consider the somewhat idealized image of the large corporation before the deluge. Take the moment of its employment zenith near the conclusion of the 1970s, a moment when the company was still coasting on a dominant form so well characterized in *The Corporation in Modern Society*. During the final year of the 1970s, the *Fortune* 500, the preeminent roster of the nation's largest manufacturers, had created employment for 16.2 million workers. The economies of scale had served large firms well, giving them a privileged place in a world where manufacturing clout, marketing reach, and vertical integration were still the formula. The nation's five hundred great industrials had more than doubled their employment rolls in just twenty-five years. America's growth engine showed no sign of weakening, corporate concentration no evidence of slowing. A 1976 article speculated on what the editors of *Fortune* magazine would do when, in the year 1998, they could find no more than 479 companies to constitute their famous list. Would the editors allow the cover of the annual "*Fortune* 500" issue the literary license of preserving a trademark whose numbers no longer added up?[2]

If a classic form could be characterized, it was of a functionally defined hierarchy, with managers arrayed in tall lines of authority presiding over narrow spans of control. The central tendency was a seven-by-seven: seven layers of managers, each responsible for seven subordinates. No firm precisely fit any model, but many of the largest tended toward this one. Though the company had been a creature of the market, it had also learned how to tame the vagaries of the market. It would, for instance, create steady growth and stability by drawing a host of unrelated products under one tent. Such diversification allowed the peaks of momentarily prosperous products to fill in the valleys of others. With the vagaries of the marketplace controlled, or at least buffered through sectoral diversity, company employment systems could achieve a stability unknown outside the public sector. Assured employment in American firms rarely reached the legendary standards of the Japanese lifetime employment model. Yet for the some 25 million employees with the good fortune to find themselves inside the walls of the *Fortune* 1,000—the five hundred largest manufacturing and five hundred service firms—it would be a comfortable career of respectable income, solid benefits, and job security.[3]

While the Weberian ideal type found near incarnation during the 1950s, its half-life proved surprisingly brief. Companies that had given rise to William Whyte's *Organization Man* and David Riesman's "other-directed" manager would also give rise three decades later to corporate raider Carl Icahn and buyout specialist Henry Kravis. Whether the market's fleeting infatuation with hostile takeovers and leveraged acquisitions reached their purported objectives of unleashing company value remained a matter of academic dispute. What is more certain is that their actions to reengineer firms financially catalyzed a far more widespread effort to remake them organizationally.[4]

A wave of reengineering would sweep through the *Fortune* 1,000 during the 1980s and '90s, leaving flattened hierarchies and shattered employment systems in their wake. Firms such as Xerox, Motorola, and General Electric had begun early, some efforts dating to the early 1980s or even before. But most major companies would follow in due course, some belatedly as in the case of IBM and General Motors. A 1992 survey of 531 companies revealed how far the restructuring had spread: three-quarters had downsized during just the past year, nearly the same had reorganized, and one-quarter had divested, merged, or acquired. Similarly, a 1991 study of 406 large companies found that one-third had significantly reduced management staff; half had laid off a substantial number of workers; half had sold a business unit; and two-thirds had shut down some company operations.[5]

The aggregate impact of year upon year of such actions is evident in a comparison of the *Fortune* 500 firms of 1980 and 1990. A third of the 1980 companies no longer appeared a decade later because of takeovers, contractions, or bankruptcies. The number of distinct product areas in which they operated declined by half. Their aggregate employment dropped a fifth. After cresting in 1979, the *Fortune* 500 employment totals declined annually over the next fifteen years. Some 16.2 million found work there in 1979, but only 11.5 million did so by 1993. This was only modestly higher than the 9.2 million employed by the *Fortune* 500 in 1960, a third of a century ear-

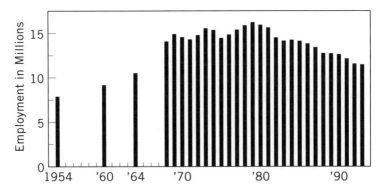

Figure 9.1. Total employment of *Fortune* 500 largest manufacturing firms: 1964–1993. *Source: Fortune.*

lier and just after publication of *The Corporation in Modern Society* (Figure 9.1). During the early 1970s the *Fortune* 500 employed one of every five Americans in the nonagricultural workforce; by the early 1990s they employed only one of every ten. With a nadir still not clearly in sight, the compilers of the *Fortune* 500 in 1998 are still sure to find their five hundred.[6]

Decentralization of Authority and Accountability

A central thrust of the corporate restructuring was to devolve authority and accountability into relatively autonomous operating divisions. Companies typically formed the divisions around the delivery of a distinct set of products or services to internal or external customers. American Cyanamid created 4, Aetna formed 15, AT&T some 22, and Johnson & Johnson nearly 150. Whether known as "strategic business units," "lines of business," "strategic planning groups," or by other rubrics, they shared a long—but taut—leash from headquarters. They were expected to make their own decisions, but they were also held more accountable for their results.

The business units in turn devolved their own authority further down, inscribing unit within unit until the final operating group comprised as few as a hundred employees. ABB Asea Brown Boveri, a global enterprise with an American presence through Combustion Engineering and other U.S. subsidiaries, had carried the model to a widely watched extreme. With 240,000 employees worldwide, ABB operated through no fewer than 4,500 profit-and-loss centers, averaging but 50 employees each. This was the low end of a size distribution whose average was closer to several hundred or even a thousand. Whatever the size, these front-line operating units often functioned as microenterprises. They exercised far more discretion and were held far more accountable than had comparable organizational levels before. And the lines of business into which they were knit displayed scant resemblance to the corporate divisions of old.[7]

The decentralization of company operations meant that numerous lower-level managers now performed many higher-level functions. The operating units had assumed responsibility for most of the functions that had formerly been performed by headquarters or specialist divisions. Planning, financing, marketing, and hiring were delegated downward, leaving a contracted headquarters whose remaining duties were more strategic and financial, less directive and instructional. IBM's belated entry into this migratory stream, following the board's 1993 ouster of its chief executive, is illustrative. The company reduced its corporate staff from 5,100 to 3,900, considered selling its headquarters building, and gave divisions far more autonomy than before (e.g., its personal computer division was no longer obliged to use processors produced by another company division). "Our view of corporate headquarters," offered IBM's senior vice president for human resources and administration, "is that there should be as little of it as possible."[8]

Corporate decentralization reached hourly employees as well. Here its manifestation was in the form of self-directed work teams, quality circles, and related empowerment measures. A study of the *Fortune* 1,000 found that by 1990 about half of the companies had introduced quality circles and self-managed work teams. Another survey of 1,200 large companies in 1992 revealed that two- to three-fifths had introduced work teams, quality circles, or empowerment programs.[9]

Though decentralization had achieved a corporate beachhead by the early 1990s, securing the company interior would require more time. Of companies in the 1990 *Fortune* 1,000 survey that had adopted quality circles or self-managed work teams, the coverage was still typically less than one worker in five. Similar results emerge from a 1992 survey of 875 work establishments. This study revealed that about half the plants and offices had by then adopted self-directed work teams, job rotation, employee problem-solving groups, and total-quality-management programs. But in only a third of the establishments had each device reached half or more of the workforce. Still, the logic of decentralization continued to press such measures downward. More employees found themselves called upon to perform functions formerly the preserve of their bosses.[10]

Decentralization and Development

With the devolution of authority and accountability, employees required enhanced skills with which to do their jobs. Midlevel managers and frontline supervisors needed more general management skills to perform the more demanding tasks placed upon them. Hourly employees needed more diverse workplace skills to perform the more varied tasks expected of them. As one of restructuring's cardinal corollaries, decentralization dictated more education and training. Restructured companies could cope without it, and some did out of fiscal necessity. But others found they could do better with it. General Electric had pursued a restructuring strategy for more than a decade, and education and training had come to constitute an essential foundation. "We had to educate our entire workforce to give them the tools to become meaningfully involved in all aspects of work," observed an executive vice president. "Empowerment . . . is a disorderly and almost meaningless gesture unless people doing the actual work are given the tools and knowledge that self-direction demands."[11]

At the managerial level, one company's experience illustrates the dynamic followed by many. Bell Atlantic Corporation, one of the nation's seven regional telephone operating companies, had initially faced little competition in the early years after its divestiture from AT&T in 1984. But its privileged position as a regulated utility rapidly eroded during the early 1990s due to the rise of a host of new communication technologies and lower-cost providers. To face the far more competitive fray, the company introduced a new architecture. Its traditional divisions, organized around the six states it had been required to serve, were scrapped in favor of eight lines of business focused around distinct classes of customers it sought to better serve (e.g., large businesses, small businesses, and private consumers). To ensure that each line of business could understand its own customers, headquarters granted the lines considerable autonomy, and the business heads in turn pressed their own authority farther down their hierarchies. Repeated decentralization of authority and accountability, in short, was the driving agenda.

For mastering the new, more competitive fray, Bell Atlantic's chief executive urged that every manager act like an "owner" of the company, embracing all of the diverse concerns that are required to run a business. But to do so would require familiarity with matters ranging from finance and strategy to marketing and personnel. To this end, Bell Atlantic did what it had not done before. Over a several-year period during the mid-1990s, it dispatched its middle-to-senior-level managers to a university-based program on general management principles. Despite layoffs and other cost reductions to become more competitive, the company invested more in its management education and development.[12]

At the nonmanagerial level, GTE's restructuring investments are illustrative as well. GTE carried more than 230,000 on its employment rosters at its peak during the early 1970s. Through a series of divestments, plant closings, and workforce downsizings, GTE had consolidated to a third of that by the early 1990s. Integral to its prolonged restructuring was a redesign of the work process. And for this, said GTE's senior vice president for human resources and administration, "you have to give people the tools to work in the new environment." During one round of restructuring during the mid-1990s, the company invested more than fifty million dollars, some eleven hundred dollars per employee, in retraining its workforce for that new environment.[13]

The restructured work environment placed a premium on team products rather than individual achievements, on coaching rather than directing others, on serving customers rather than conforming to rules. The underlying concept was that organizations create a better product or service when employees collaborate on the work, share information widely, and reach collective decisions. To do so, however, required a skill set that many managers and wageworkers did not possess. Restructured companies, accordingly, invested more in employee development, searched for better-educated recruits, or both.

The 1992 study of 875 work establishments, for instance, revealed that restructured work environments were associated with larger investments in employee development. Many of the establishments had invested in off-the-job training and cross training, training in skills not directly related to one's current job. Plants or offices that had introduced empowering work practices were found to give off-the-job and cross training to two-thirds more of their main workers than had other establishments. The 1991 study of 406 large companies revealed much the same. A third or more of the companies reported that they had invested a significant amount of time and money during the past decade to create substantial changes in the work process, job involvement, and quality management. Compared with companies that had not, the restructured companies invested substantially more in entry-level training for new employees and retraining for continuing employees. An early 1990s study of large, unionized firms similarly shows that companies that had reorganized their work systems also had higher levels of employee training.[14]

Companies also expected more of their fresh recruits. Starting credentials for white-collar workers had long since been upgraded to college or more. AT&T recruited two-fifths of its managers during the 1950s from among those without a college degree; by the 1970s, those without a bachelor's degree were not to be found among new, white-collar recruits. More generally, virtually all of those entering the management ranks of large corporations by the 1980s came with a college education, and a large fraction moved up with postgraduate MBA or engineering degrees as well. Educational credentials for hourly workers, by contrast, had long been more diverse. The nonmanagerial ranks at AT&T and other large corporations included many for whom the absence of a high school diploma proved no impediment to either initial hiring or later promotion. The ladder of work opportunity for those earlier denied educational opportunity, however, was withdrawn above the reach of many. The new work environment demanded more than limited education could provide.[15]

Ford Motor Company's evolving recruitment policies illustrate this trend. Ford had extensively restructured its workplace, and the door closed almost fully on those with limited credentials. During the early 1990s, about a fifth of Ford's veteran hourly workers did not hold a high school diploma. By contrast, virtually all—97 percent—of the new hourly workers that Ford recruited during the early 1990s were high school graduates. Similarly, while one in six of its veteran hourly workers had attended at least some college, one in three of its fresh recruits had done so. As the Chrysler Corporation also moved toward a flatter, more decentralized scheme, the same outcome would be expected. In its more self-managed work world, fewer managers were required to manage. "I'm going to pull my [supervisory] people out," offered Chrysler's manufacturing manager, "and turn that assembly line over to an empowered workforce."[16] The ratio of salaried to hourly employees at Chrysler reflected the change. In 1991 the ratio stood at 1 to 25. By 1994 it reached 1 to 48. By the end of the decade, the company expected a stretch to 1 to 100. Wageworkers in Chrysler's evolving environment would increasingly have to have the knowledge and the skills to do their work with little instruction and minimal oversight.

Restructuring not only generated greater demand for education and training but often created better conditions for learning in the firm. In moving away from traditional hierarchies, many companies stressed autonomous work teams in their place, environments known to facilitate learning. An array of studies confirm that individuals acquire greater knowledge and proficiency when they learn through groups rather than individually. Moreover, team training is found to have greater impact than does individual training on work-team productivity. Though rarely introduced for this purpose, the teamwork that was often a central component of corporate decentralization had the effect of helping firms realize more from their training investments.[17]

Operating on Half Empty or Half Full?

Executives presided over the corporation of the 1990s with a far better educated workforce than had their domestic counterparts of the 1950s. At the same time, they invested less in training of their workforce than did their international counterparts of the 1990s. While the historical comparison suggests the training vessel should be seen as more than half full, the interna-

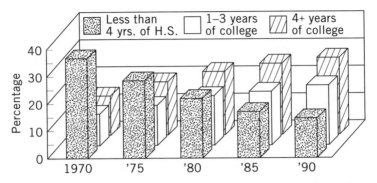

Figure 9.2. Percentage of U.S. employees with at least some college education: 1970–1990. *Source:* Eck (1993).

tional comparison suggests that it should still be viewed as more than half empty.

Corporate management drew on a workforce far more extensively educated in 1990 then in 1970. In 1970 more than one in three workers had completed less than four years of high school; by 1990 only one in eight was so limited. In 1970 one in four workers had completed at least some college; by 1990 nearly one in two had received some higher education (Figure 9.2). Corporate management also provided training to more of the workforce during the early 1990s than a decade earlier. Between 1983 and 1991, while the workforce expanded by 19 percent, the number of workers reporting they had taken training to improve their job skills rose by 39 percent. The number of employees who had received formal company training more than doubled, rising from 7.3 million to 18.0 million. The length of formal company training programs also expanded: in 1983 only one in four required twelve weeks or more, but by 1991 two in three required such length. The breadth of personnel inclusion in formal company skill-improvement programs grew more rapidly than skills training in school programs, on-the-job training, or any other major source. By the late 1980s, U.S. corporations invested in worker training programs the equivalent of some 1 to 2 percent of their payrolls.[18]

Companies focused their expanded training agendas, however, on more experienced and better-educated employees. Between 1983 and 1991, the likelihood of obtaining formal company training or informal on-the-job training to improve one's job skills displayed greatest increase among college graduates with ten to twenty years of work experience. Conversely, the likelihood of receiving formal or informal company training among high school graduates with less than ten years of experience actually declined. Though not a cause, this widening training gap was consistent with a widening wages gap observed between educated and experienced workers and those with little education or experience. The ratio of earnings of college graduates to high school graduates, the "college premium," had sharply increased during the 1980s and early 1990s. This reflected in part the spread of complex production and information technologies, both placing a premium on strong educational foundations and flexible learning.[19]

Direct surveys of employees confirmed the widespread importance of company training and its linkage to work performance. In a 1991 population cross section, for instance, two out of three workers reported that specific training or skills were needed to obtain their current job or that they had taken training to improve their skills. Those who had taken formal company training programs were rewarded with higher earnings within the firms of the training.[20]

While corporate investment in education and training had increased and the investment yielded positive returns, international comparison suggests room for further expansion and higher returns. The magnitude of the gap between achieved and potential levels can be seen in a comparison of the training investments made by American and Japanese automakers in their U.S. plants during the 1980s. Compared with the Japanese use of more flexible and lean work systems, American makers then still relied on the more traditional hierarchical model. General Motors' Saturn and New United Motors Manufacturing, Inc. (NUMMI) plants remained the exception, the "horizontal corporation" still an indistinct vision of the future. The Japanese "transplants," by contrast, already relied on a decentralized model, with small, self-directed production teams and quality circles well informed and empowered to produce.

A late 1980s study of American and Japanese assembly plants in the United States illustrates the difference that organizational form can make for company training. The assembly-line workers in the American plants annually received about 30 hours of training, while the American workers in the Japanese transplants received more than 50 hours. The contrast was even starker for entry-level training of newly hired auto assembly workers. For those coming into the American-owned plants, 48 hours of training on average sufficed. For those entering the Japanese-operated plants, 280 hours of training was the norm. The labor markets and prior employee skills were much the same. The organizational structures into which the assembly workers entered were not. As U.S. companies increasingly embraced the kinds of high-performance work systems already in place among the

Japanese transplants, more education and training could be anticipated. Studies of establishments and enterprises in the United States that have adopted elements of high-performance work systems find that greater stress on education and training is usually a strong correlate.[21]

Cross-national comparisons of private sector training expenditures also suggest that the U.S. glass is still half empty. At the start of the 1990s, for instance, companies in the United Kingdom, Germany, and France invested in training programs amounts equivalent to about a quarter of 1 percent of their respective GNPs (ranging from 0.22 percent in the United Kingdom to 0.28 in France). By contrast, American corporations invested at about a fifth that rate, some 0.05 percent. Data on dollars per participant in company training programs reveal much the same. British companies averaged $5,000 per training program participant, and German companies $7,200. American companies allocated a scant $1,800. Still other indicators point in the same direction. Using 1991 national data on the fraction of new employees receiving formal company training within the first year of employment, one estimate placed the U.S. figure at 8 percent, European rates around 20 percent, and the Japanese fraction at 79 percent.[22]

For many American corporations, the historic figures show that the education and training glass is far more full than several decades earlier. At the same time, the comparative figures suggest that the glass is still far from fully full. Seeking to fill the container further, however, is contingent on further restructuring.

To expand skills training without prior design changes requiring the new skills is akin to expanding job training without the employment market demanding the new graduates. Training strategies therefore generally follow organizational strategies, not the other way around. The dependent role of corporate training can be seen in the results of an early 1990s comparative study of productivity in the United States, Japan, and Germany.[23] Using intensive case analysis, the study focused on nine industries, including food, steel, automobiles, soaps and detergents, consumer electronics, and computers. The study found that many of the national differences in productivity could be traced to differences in the companies' manufacturing and organizational design. Manufacturing design included the extent to which companies used standardized components, minimized parts, and streamlined process. Organizational design included the degree of decentralization in authority, distribution of information, and incentivization of performance. By contrast, differences in workforce skills and other factors played little role in explaining the productivity differences. Many of the differences in the organizational systems were traced in turn to international competition. Companies that faced highly productive international transplants in their home market, for instance, were far more likely to adopt the improved organizational designs pioneered by the transplants.[24]

This study thus confirmed that organizational changes made a driving difference, while educational differences did not. That is not to imply that educational change should not follow organizational change. The research record ought to and often confirms that it does. It is to suggest, however, that education should be seen less as an independent driver and more as a critical corollary of other changes in corporate form. Filling the glass depended on first changing its shape.

One of the changes in shape, however, threatened to drain rather than fill the training tumbler. When company managers were asked during the late 1980s and early 1990s why they had embarked on restructuring, competitive pressures and cost reductions invariably topped the list. Institutional investors, emboldened during the 1980s by their increasing ownership stakes in large corporations, added to the pressures for reduced expenditures. Cutting expenses, whether through process reengineering or budget slashing, would be one way to do so. The education and training budget, with its long-term payoffs but near-term expenses, could appear a prime candidate for trimming. While decentralization enhanced the role of education and training, its common cousin, downsizing, might concurrently undermine it. Moreover, its second cousins, product and service outsourcing and the hiring of part-time, irregular, and temporary workers, could also diminish the number of people reached by corporate education and training. Smaller enterprises generally invested less than did large corporations, and as firms contracted out more of their work and contracted down more of their workforce, they were likely to concentrate the education and training pie on fewer recipients.[25]

The turbulence and notoriety that often followed major layoffs by large companies, however, generated contrary currents that reinforced rather than undermined company investments in education and training. In the aftermath of a publicized downsizing, entry-level recruitment often became more difficult. This in turn led companies to invest more, not less, in entry-level training. They also became more, not less, interested in apprenticeship programs. The lowest training investments are thus reported among firms whose employment is neither growing nor shrinking. While short-term shareholder demands and widespread downsizing pressures might be seen as undermining corporate investments in education and training, they in fact did not.[26]

In several industries, restructuring led to innovative training alliances between companies and unions. The automobile and telecommunications sectors led the way. With prolonged downsizing experienced by both industries during the 1980s and early 1990s, company and union leaders created joint enterprises that provided training not only in job-related skills development but also in skills for transferring within the company, skills for securing outside jobs, career development, financial management, and preretirement planning. Under collective bargaining agreements, the companies funded the enterprises, but both management and labor directed them. The United Auto Workers (UAW) and Ford formed the National Education, Development and Training Corporation in 1982; the UAW and General Motors created the Human Resource Center in 1982; and the UAW and Chrysler established their National Training Center in 1985. The Communication Workers of America and the International Brotherhood of Electrical Workers formed similar ventures with U.S. West in 1984 and AT&T in 1986.[27]

Some programs also provided tuition assistance for current or displaced workers. NYNEX Corporation, whose employment had peaked near one hundred thousand in 1988 but had dropped to eighty thousand by 1994 and was targeted for sixty thousand by 1996, agreed in 1994 to send interested workers back to college. A union agreement provided for the funding of a two-year associate degree through the State University of New York in telecommunications technology.[28]

Making the School Connection

While internal education and training programs have been integral components of conventional corporate practice for decades, during the 1980s and early 1990s many firms also expanded their external relations with public schools as a complementary strategy for workforce development. The more direct involvement in the schools stemmed from two considerations. The first was management's heightened concern over the quality of schooling, particularly in distressed areas of large cities. The second was management's greater interest in exporting its restructuring experience to other institutions with which it has contact.

The building of formal and informal alliances between companies and schools also benefited from a more general expansion of strategic cooperation among corporations during this period. IBM and Apple formed an alliance to develop a microprocessor to rival Intel's personal computer chips; telephone and cable companies joined forces to complement their respective services. Working relations between companies and schools could be seen as a natural extension of the network webs already well developed and understood within the private sector.

Some companies invested directly in schools, while others built joint apprenticeship programs with schools. Initiatives by RJR Nabisco illustrate the first, Sears, Roebuck the second. In the wake of its widely publicized leveraged buyout in 1988, RJR Nabisco's charitable foundation allocated $30 million to schools through a grants competition for school-based initiatives promising "bold reforms." Its Next Century Schools Program offered some $750,000 to each of forty-five schools that offered "radical but sustainable improvements in America's schools." The company also arranged for third-party evaluations of the innovative school programs, and in 1992 it launched a new funding program to support the export of successful initiatives to other schools. "We are looking for programs," asserted the company's CEO, "that will impact the real bottom line—student performance."[29]

Sears, Roebuck & Co. pursued an alternative strategy, choosing instead to build direct ties with area schools through an apprenticeship program. A select group of high school students received two semesters of training in appliance repair and related skills, including report writing, computer research, and customer relations. Sears furnished trainers, appliances, overhead, and part-time employment for all students. For select graduates, it subsequently provided full-time employment as well.[30]

Companies experimented with a range of other involvements in or alliances with school systems. U.S. West mounted a program to encourage average students to remain in school and seek productive employment when they finished. General Mills supported programs to reduce student-teacher ratios. Coopers & Lybrand arranged for employees to mentor high school students. Eastman Kodak led an alliance of corporations with its headquarters' school district to improve the local education system. Security Pacific offered training on bank-related technologies to facilitate transition from school to the workplace. Rockwell International retained its retirees to serve as school science teachers. Polaroid operated an inner-city production facility that trained and then placed minorities with area businesses.[31]

Corporate interest in such direct support for public schools rose sharply during the early 1990s. In 1990, for instance, about a quarter of the companies in a large firm survey contributed money to elementary and to junior high schools; by 1992, more than half did so. In 1990 about a third of the companies reported that their top management was very involved in

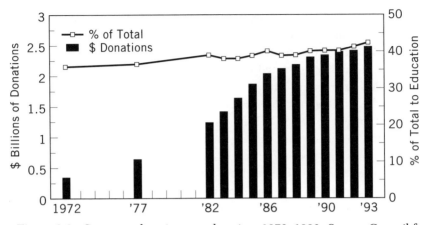

Figure 9.3. Corporate donations to education: 1972–1993. *Source:* Council for Aid to Education.

education issues; by 1992 the fraction was closer to half. Driving the enlarged involvement was concern over the readiness of the workforce. A 1991 survey of 176 large firms revealed that the single most salient factor behind their interest in education reform was the quality of their own personnel, especially wageworkers. When asked which of six goals for educational change announced by the National Governors' Association in 1990 were most important, companies overwhelmingly selected the goal of making U.S. students "first in the world in mathematics and science achievement." They also placed great stress on knowledge of English, history, and geography.[32]

Long-term trend statistics in corporate giving to education reveal much the same. Most company charitable donations to education had been directed at colleges and universities, but the proportions and absolute amounts going to public schools rose sharply during the late 1980s and early 1990s. In 1982, 40 percent of the corporate donations budget went to education, but only a twentieth was allocated to precollege support (Figure 9.3). By 1993 the fraction of the corporate donations budget slated for education remained much the same, but a seventh was now earmarked for precollege programs. In 1982 large companies gave some $50 million to precollege schooling. By 1993 their annual giving had risen more than sevenfold to $380 million (Figure 9.4).[33]

Despite the enhanced corporate interest in schools, the bridge between schooling and work, especially for those not pursuing postsecondary education, remained shaky at best. In Germany, Japan, and some other countries,

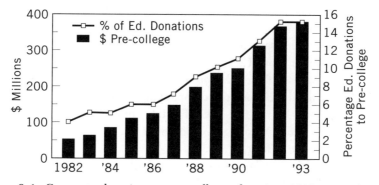

Figure 9.4. Corporate donations to pre-college education: 1982–1993. *Source:* Council for Aid to Education.

major employers had created extensive contacts with schools to ensure a steady draw of well-trained graduates to their payrolls. Apprenticeships were an important element of the relationship. So, too, were the signals that companies sent to prospective graduates when they based their hiring in part on academic performance. Some companies even arranged with secondary schools to hire a set number of graduates and delegated nominating authority to their teachers. The work-to-school transition in the United States, by contrast, remained far less extensively formalized than in Japan and Germany.[34]

The corporate restructuring of the 1980s and early 1990s stimulated greater interest in American schooling and better bridges to it. Restructured firms expressed heightened concern about the educational quality of the workforce and more often forged links with public education. RJR Nabisco's experience is again instructive, especially when contrasted with that of Philip Morris, a company of comparable size and similar product lines in the tobacco and food industries. While RJR Nabisco undertook a number of organizational changes during the five years after its 1988 leveraged buyout, Philip Morris experienced little organizational restructuring during that period.

RJR Nabisco veered onto a different charitable course following its buyout. In keeping with the management culture that emerged in the company's post-LBO restructuring, the giving program became more focused on tangible results, and RJR Nabisco concentrated its giving almost entirely on education, primarily public schools. It stressed accountability and replicability. Seeking program "ideas that will genuinely transform education," RJR Nabisco overhauled its own giving program in seeking to overhaul public education. The company replaced some 1,400 grants annually distributed across an array of recipients with a far smaller number of much larger and far more targeted gifts. By contrast, Philip Morris more than doubled its grants, from 1,219 in 1987 to 3,273 in 1991. Just prior to the buyout, RJR Nabisco directed about one in three of its charitable dollars to education. After the buyout the company inverted the distributive allocation, giving nearly four in five of its charitable dollars to education. By contrast, in 1987 Philip Morris gave one dollar in seven to education and in 1991 still only one in four.[35]

Analysis of the 406 large firms surveyed in 1991 reveals more generally that companies that had downsized were also those most likely to direct donations to public schools, to excuse employees to teach in public schools, and to value apprenticeship programs with public schools. Similarly, companies that had introduced innovative work systems fostering employee empowerment were more likely to have made donations to schools and built direct contact between company employees and school systems.[36]

With the expanded flow of resources also came a more directive message: if corporations can revitalize their own organizations, so too can schools. Executives who had engineered the overhaul of their own firms were often eager to see the strategy applied elsewhere. Organizational decentralization, workforce empowerment, and results accountability were, they suggested, generic concepts that should improve the performance of any large organization, whether for-profit or nonprofit. Corporate managers volunteered more than dollars and time. They proffered models and advice as well.

Efforts by IBM's chief executive to foster educational change offer a case in point. During the early 1990s, CEO John Akers proselytized IBM's way to the school world. "Business employees are constantly measured, trained and retrained," Akers argued, "and it makes no sense to exempt education from this worthy principle." Accordingly, he urged, schools should adopt higher standards of accountability, create stronger means of assessment, face greater market competition, and devolve greater authority to teachers and principals.[37]

IBM joined forces with American Express, Ford Motor Company, Motorola, Proctor & Gamble, and Xerox to urge that colleges and universities also reform their organizations. In an open letter to higher education, chief executives of the six companies asserted that "companies and institutions of higher education *must* accelerate the application of total quality management on our campuses if our education system and economy are to maintain and enhance global positions." If these companies could restructure and streamline their own operations, then surely, too, could other organizations on which business depends.[38]

The transference was effected not only through explicit exhortation but also through implicit pressures on educational institutions that worked with, depended upon, or supplied the restructured firms. This was probably nowhere more evident than in the employment market for new managers and professionals seeking to enter careers in large firms. As managers acquired more responsibility, accountability, and flexibility, a premium was placed on the capacities of entry-level managers to work in settings requiring greater self-direction and adaptability. Colleges and universities, the source of the next generation of managers, received an array of market signals to this effect from corporate recruiters and executive advisers.[39]

Adding teeth to its calls for educational reform, IBM initiated a twenty-four-million-dollar grant program in 1991 in which gifts to colleges and universities were tied to demonstrated efforts to improve their own management. The program was intended, the company announced, to "encourage" a college or university to "apply TQM [total quality management] to the operation of the institution itself and to propagate TQM to other college and universities." If responsive to the call, institutions could receive as much as three million dollars in cash and equipment. Responsiveness was defined by IBM to include a commitment to implement TQM concepts in areas ranging from finance and admissions to instruction and research "to achieve improvements in customer satisfaction." Atlantic Richfield, Honeywell, and other corporations joined with advice giving and grant making of their own to improve school management.[40]

The Uncertain Career

During the 1980s and early 1990s, flatter structures and tougher competition led many companies to abandon personnel policies that had evolved into de facto employment security. For the millions of employees who had pursued their livelihoods in large corporations, restructuring gave more uncertain form to their work careers. Delayered hierarchies meant less upward mobility. Decentralized operations brought more lateral movement. Downsized workforces resulted in early retirement.

The careers of a substantial fraction of the workforce felt the impact. A national cross section of 2,958 employees in 1992 reported that two in five had experienced a downsizing of their firm or a permanent cutback of the workforce. A fifth to a quarter had experienced a merger or acquisition, a reduction in the number of managers at their firm, or turnover in the organization's leadership. Similarly, a national probability sample of full-time employees revealed that two-fifths reported that their firms had experienced a downsizing in 1993.[41]

The flattened work careers can be seen in a comparison of the likelihood that cross sections of employees would remain with their firms over a four-year period. Whether white- or-blue-collar, manufacturing or service, all employee groups displayed less employer stability than in the past. For managers working in 1983, 68 percent were still with the same employer four years later. But for managers working in 1987, only 62 percent remained four years later. The corresponding percentages for blue-collar workers stood at 57 and 49 percent; for manufacturing firms, 64 and 59 percent; and for service firms, 51 and 33 percent. Though these figures may somewhat overstate longer-term trends due to technical issues in the way they are estimated, they generally point toward less work-career stability.[42]

A career foreshortening is also evident in follow-up studies of those who have been laid off in the aftermath of an office downsizing or plant closing. Displaced workers are defined as those with at least three years of job tenure who lost their positions during the previous five years because of a plant closing or move, slack work, or termination of their positions. In a 1990 cross section of the U.S. workforce so affected, a fifth of the displaced workers aged twenty-five to fifty-four remained unemployed or had left the labor force. Among those aged fifty-five to sixty-four, half had not yet found their way back onto the employment rolls.[43]

From the standpoint of many employees, the career flattening and insecurity led to heightened interest in company-underwritten education and training. The devolved responsibility meant they required more diverse skills for work within the firm. The lateral and, in many cases, foreshortened tenure prospects meant they also required more diverse, more generic skills for movement among company divisions or outplacement from them.

At the same time, the career foreshortening constituted a disincentive for the corporation to provide the training. With companies and employees less committed and less loyal to one another, it also made less sense for a corporation to invest in long-term employee development. Consistent with this point, cross sectional studies of firms find that higher employee turnover and shorter employee tenure are generally associated with smaller training investments.[44]

Since employees are likely to seek additional education both to master the more demanding work environment and as a hedge against having to seek work elsewhere, the clashing interests of companies and employees are likely to intensify. Study of company training programs reveals that they generally enhanced employee skills for the firms in which they are obtained but offered relatively little in the way of transferable skills. Wages are higher for trained employees working in the same firm, but not for employees who have moved to other firms. Companies would presumably prefer to keep it that way, while employees would not.[45]

Both employers and employees thus came to view company education and training in more self-interested terms. Since their mutual commitments had become more divergent, their respective self-interests had become less convergent. While both of restructuring's cousins—decentralization and downsizing—concentrated attention on education and training, they did so with contrary impulses. Decentralization placed a premium on education and training programs, downsizing the opposite.

A Diversified Workforce

The diversification of the corporate workforce added further impetus and still different direction to company education and training. The diversification story is developed elsewhere in this volume, and the essence is that the company's employment ranks contain far more minorities and women than when the predecessor volume appeared in 1959. Between 1975 and 1990, for instance, the workforce as a whole grew by 33 percent, while the number of African-Americans in the workforce grew by 46 percent and the number of women by 51 percent. Their growth in the workforce was expected to continue to outstrip overall workforce growth into the twenty-first century. Expansion in the number of older workers, those aged fifty-five or older, was expected to outstrip that of even women and minorities (Table 9.1). Of

Table 9.1. Past and Forecast Growth of the U.S. Workforce, 1975, 1990, and 2005

	Percentage increase	
Group	1975–1990	1990–2005
Total	33.1	20.8
Women	50.9	26.2
African-Americans	45.7	31.7
Aged 55+	7.6	43.7

Source: U.S. Bureau of Labor Statistics (1992b).

course, if the *The Corporation in Modern Society* had instead been published back at the turn of the century as the corporation was first taking form, workforce diversity would surely have also appeared in its pages. Employers struggled to mold a modernized workforce on factory floors swirling with a welter of languages and national backgrounds, and company concerns then were akin to those now confronted a century later.

By some idealized model, the personal demographics of company personnel should have no bearing on their performance. Yet we know from a host of studies that women and minorities can sometimes be isolated from the informal company networks that are a critical source of information, power, and promotion. They may also be insufficiently protected from sexual or racial harassment.[46]

The underlying behavioral problems may be seen as societal failures since they reflect enduring cleavages in the nation at large. Discrimination and harassment are nonetheless problems that companies have addressed through education and training. This is partly because gender and racial conflict within the workplace undercut communication and cooperation, and in part because company polices inadvertently—and sometimes advertently—exacerbated such problems. Federal and state laws, in any case, require corporations to conform with accepted equal employment opportunity practices. Diversity training in the workplace, an effort that would no doubt have seemed absurd to the corporate denizens of the 1950s, became commonplace by the 1990s.

The social cleavages of American society also structured the allocation of training within the firm. Younger male and female employees are about equally likely to benefit from company training, but men are more likely to receive on-the-job training, women to receive off-the-job training. Nonwhites are less likely to receive either. Managerial, professional, and technical occupations are more likely to get both, and it is here that women and minorities are most underrepresented. Nonunionized employees tend to receive less of each. Older workers also tend to be on the short end: a 1985 survey of employees found older workers were less likely to report receiving either on-the-job or off-site employer-sponsored training. The 1991 survey of 406 companies confirmed the same. Three in ten companies reported substantial investments in the training of workers aged fifty or younger while fewer than two in ten so spent on those over fifty.[47]

Confronted with a changing demography that it could not control but must somehow manage, the 1990s corporation trained employees to work with the more diverse workforce and within state and federal law. Training investments in general were still disproportionately bestowed on higher occupational ranks and established demographic groups. Decentralization of decision making and restructuring of the workplace, however, can be expected to diminish such prerogatives. One corollary of flatter company pyramids was more egalitarian access to company training.

Education and training for diversification acquired additional meaning as American companies expanded abroad. Compared with the 1950s, U.S. firms were far more active during the 1990s in selling, producing, and forming alliances across national boundaries. To facilitate the cross-cultural contact that this globalization necessitated, companies enhanced their training of managers for work in diverse national settings, and many such programs have been found in research studies to improve managerial effectiveness in moving across boundaries. The continuing expansion of U.S. corporations abroad, developed elsewhere in this volume, was sure to further stimulate diversity learning. At the same time, as Asian, Latin, and European corporations became more active in the United States and other economies, they, too, invested more in training their employees to understand diverse national settings.[48]

Conclusion

While education and training drew little management attention during the 1950s, it could not escape attention by the 1990s. Looking to manage a far more diverse workforce amid a far more complex work environment, corporate executives today might gaze with some wonder and envy on their predecessors' less turbulent era. Whatever the past, decentralization, empowerment, and related developments have made the education quality of the workforce a priority for many managements. While historical data point toward greater corporate investment in education and training, comparative evidence suggests considerable room for even greater investment. Expanding company programs to further fill the training vessel will first depend, however, on further redesign of the company.

If company structure follows corporate strategy, company training follows corporate organization. Refashioning corporate organization thus requires concurrent refashioning of its educational enterprise. During the 1980s and '90s, companies displayed great variety in their restructuring paths, yet most pointed to more education and training as a base with which employees could shoulder their broadened responsibilities. Companies invested more in skills that could be applied across a range of positions and used to perform a variety of functions within the corporation.

At the same time, the diversification of the workforce dictated new education and training strategies, emphasizing intergroup communication
and cooperation. The flattening of career structures advised new strategies
as well, with employees stressing learning portability and employers stressing proprietary learning. The rising importance of education also counseled
direct involvement of corporations in school programs and reform, with
employers contributing more money and forging more alliances.

The rise of corporate attention to education and training since publication of *The Corporation in Modern Society* could be seen as implying that
education and training programs have worked. Such programs have justified their expenses, it would seem, by making for better corporate managers, more productive employees, higher-quality products, and lower
worker turnover. Studies of management training programs generally confirm this assumption, as do analyses of employee productivity. One analysis
revealed, for instance, that companies that had introduced formal training
programs in the early 1980s had achieved productivity gains 19 percent
greater within three years than firms that had not. Another confirmed that
educated workers are better at implementing new technologies since they
learn and adapt more effectively.[49]

Yet company education and training programs do not always yield the
expected productivity improvements. Gauged by narrowly defined rates of
return, some programs proved more costly than beneficial. They were
nonetheless maintained or even expanded. In these instances the decision
to work with local school districts or train poorly prepared entry-level employees often reflected more a strategic social agenda than a calculating human resource strategy. During the 1980s and early 1990s, investments in
education and training often came to constitute a sign of responsible management, akin to the way charitable donations are often justified.[50]

Even when companies invested in education and training programs for
the express purpose of improving productivity, not all programs delivered.
This was to be expected, however, since education and training programs
designed apart from the redesign of company work and organizational systems are likely to generate skills that would not find ready application or reward. A comparative study of automobile assembly plants around the world
in 1989–1990 illustrates the point. Training programs had little impact on
performance except where the training fit the specific production strategies. Stated differently, company education and training programs can be
expected to enhance results when they are aligned with the company's organizational design, and not when they are not.[51]

Intensified investments in education and training offer an appealing solution to a host of challenges confronting the large corporation and American society. Yet corporate and social systems are far too complex to yield much ground to singular approaches. We know from numerous studies of organizational change that isolated alterations in company culture, decision making, employee compensation, or worker training without simultaneous change in the others often yield no change at all.[52] The enhanced company emphasis on education and training should therefore be seen as both a product of corporate reorganization and a wedge—but only a limited one—for further change. Education and training of the corporate workforce are neither the problem nor the solution. They are, nonetheless, intimately related to both.

Notes

For helpful guidance and support the author would like to thank Peter Cappelli, Jerry Jacobs, Carl Kaysen, Robert Zemsky, other volume authors, and members of the Board of Senior Scholars of the National Center on the Educational Quality of the Workforce.

1. U.S. Office of Technology Assessment (1990, p. 3), Dertouzos, Lester, and Solow (1989); Galbraith, Lawler et al. (1993, p. 188). Similar findings and arguments also appear in National Academy of Engineering (1992); Competitiveness Policy Council (1992); Cohen and Zysman (1987); Cappelli (1993, 1995); and Stone (1991).

2. Tobias(1976).

3. Janger (1989); *Fortune* magazine, various annual issues reporting the *Fortune* 500 and *Fortune* Service 500.

4. Bowman and Singh (1990, 1993).

5. Wyatt Company (1993); Johnson and Linden (1992); Useem (1993a).

6. Davis, Diekman, and Tinsley, (1994); *Fortune* magazine, various annual issues reporting the *Fortune* 500 and *Fortune* Service 500.

7. Lawler (1992), and Katzenbach and Smith (1993); Taylor (1991).

8. Lohr (1994).

9. Lawler, Mohrman, and Ledford (1992); Applebaum and Batt (1994, pp. 60–68).

10. Lawler, Mohrman, and Ledford (1992); Osterman (1994); Applebaum and Batt (1994).

11. Frank Doyle, quoted in Gore (1993, p. 78).

12. Smith (1991).

13. GTE's Bruce Carswell, presentation at a meeting of the National Planning Association, Washington, D.C., March 25, 1994.

14. Osterman (1994); Useem (1993b); Katz and Keefe (1993).

15. Howard and Bray (1988); Useem and Karabel (1986); Useem (1989).

16. Templin (1994).

17. Druckman and Bjork (1994, pp. 159–60).

18. Eck (1993); Amirault (1992); Lynch (1994a).

19. Constantine and Neumark (1994); Freeman and Katz (1994); Murphy and Welch (1993); Scott Morton (1991).

20. Eck (1993); Lynch (1992).

21. U.S. Office of Technology Assessment (1990, p. 15); Womack, Jones, and Roos (1992); Womack and Jones (1994); Kalleberg and Moody (1994); Applebaum and Batt (1994, p. 85); Hashimoto (1994); MacDuffie and Kochan (1995); MacDuffie and Krafcik (1992); MacDuffie (1995).

22. Organization for Economic Cooperation and Development (1991); U.S. Office of Technology Assessment (1990); Lynch (1994a, 1994b); Organization for Economic Cooperation and Development (1993, p. 68).

23. McKinsey & Co. (1993).

24. Lewis et al. (1993); McKinsey & Co. (1993).

25. Wyatt Company (1993); American Management Association (1993); Useem (1993a, 1994); Knoke and Kalleberg (1994).

26. Useem (1993b); Knoke (1996); Knoke and Kalleberg (1994).

27. U.S. Office of Technology Assessment (1990, pp. 242–49); see also Hodson, Hooks, and Rieble (1992); and Kellam (1994).

28. Ramirez (1994); U.S. Department of Labor, Office of the American Workplace (1994 pp. 14–15).

29. RJR Nabisco Foundation (1992); Jehl and Payzant (1992); Bailey (1992b); Gerstner (1994).

30. Wartzman (1992); Hamilton and Hamilton (1992); Rosenbaum et al. (1992).

31. Berenbeim (1991a); Lund (1992); Wild (1993).

32. Ramsey (1992); Berenbeim (1991b).

33. Council for Aid to Education (various years).

34. Rosenbaum and Kariya (1989); Rosenbaum et al. (1990); Nothdurft (1989), General Accounting Office (1991); Soskice (1994).

35. Useem and Subramanian (1994).

36. Useem (1993b).

37. Akers (1991)

38. Robinson et al. (1991).

39. Porter and McKibbin (1988); Johnston et al. (1986); Useem (1989).

40. International Business Machines (1991); Bailey (1992).

41. Galinsky, Bond, and Friedman (1993).

42. Swinnerton and Wial (1995); Organization for Economic Cooperation and Development (1993, pp. 66–69); Constantine and Neumark (1994); Diebold, Neumark, and Polsky (1996).

43. U.S. Senate Special Committee on Aging (1991).

44. Bishop (1994b).

45. Lynch (1992).

46. Kanter (1977).

47. Altonji and Spletzer (1991); Lynch (1991); Meier 1985; Knoke and Ishio (1994); Useem (1994).

48. Kobrin (1984); Black and Mendenhall (1990); Weeks (1992).

49. Burke and Day (1986); Sten and Ritzen (1991); Lynch (1994b); Bishop (1994a, 1994b); Bartel (1994); Bartel and Lichtenberg (1987); Druckman and Bjork (1994).

50. Useem (1988, 1991).

51. MacDuffie (1991); MacDuffie and Kochan (1995).

52. Scott Morton (1991); MacDuffie and Krafcik (1992); Conte and Svejnar (1990); Macy and Izumi (1993); Berger and Sikora (1994); Nadler and Tushman (1988); Nadler et al. (1992).

References

Akers, John F. 1991. "Let's Go to Work on Education." *Wall Street Journal*, March 20, p. A22.

Altonji, Joseph G., and James R. Spletzer. 1991. "Worker Characteristics, Job Characteristics, and Receipt of On-the-Job Training." *Industrial and Labor Relations Review* 45:58–79.

American Managment Association. 1993. "1993 AMA Survey on Downsizing." New York: American Management Association.

Amirault, Thomas. 1992. "Training to Qualify for Jobs and Improve Skills, 1991." *Monthly Labor Review* 115 (September): 31–36.

Applebaum, Eileen, and Rose Batt. 1994. *Transforming Work Systems in the United States*. Ithaca, N.Y.: ILR Press.

Bailey, Anne Lowrey. 1992. "Corporations' New Social Advocacy." *Chronicle of Philanthropy*, April 7, pp. 6–7, 10.

Bartel, Ann. 1994. "Productivity Gains from the Implementation of Employee Training Programs." *Industrial Relations* 33 (October): 411–25.

Bartel, Ann, and Frank R. Lichtenberg. 1987. "The Comparative Advantage of Educated Workers in Implementing New Technology." *Review of Economics and Statistics* 69:1-11.

Berenbeim, Ronald E. 1991a. *Corporate Strategies for Improving Public Education*. New York: Conference Board.

———. 1991b. *Corporate Support of National Education Goals*. New York: Conference Board.

Berger, Lance A., and Martin J. Sikora, eds. 1994. *The Change Management Handbook*. New York: Irwin Professional Publishing.

Bishop, John H. 1994a. "The Impact of Previous Training on Productivity and

Wages." In *Training and the Private Sector: International Comparisons*, edited by Lisa M. Lynch. Chicago: University of Chicago Press.

———. 1994b. "The Incidence and Payoff to Employer Training: A Review of the Literature." Philadelphia: National Center on the Educational Quality of the Workforce.

Black, J. Stewart, and Mark Mendenhall. 1990. "Cross-Cultural Training Effectiveness: A Review and a Theoretical Framework for Future Research." *Academy of Management Review* 15:113–36.

Bowman, Edward H., and Harbir Singh. 1990. "Overview of Corporate Restructuring: Trends and Consequences." In *Corporate Restructuring*, edited by Milton L. Rock and Robert H. Rock. New York: McGraw-Hill.

———. 1993. "Corporate Restructuring: Reconfiguring the Firm." *Strategic Management Journal* 14:5–14.

Brown, C. 1990. "Empirical Evidence on Private Training." In *Research in Labor Economics*, vol. 11, edited by Laurie J. Bassi and David L. Crawford. Greenwich, Conn.: JAI Press.

Burke, Michael J., and Russell R. Day. 1986. "A Cumulative Study of the Effectiveness of Managerial Training." *Journal of Applied Psychology* 71:232–45.

Cappelli, Peter. 1993. "Are Skill Requirements Rising? Evidence from Production and Clerical Jobs." *Industrial and Labor Relations Review* 46: 515–30.

———. 1994, "Introduction." In *Training and Development in Public and Private Policy*, edited by Peter Cappelli. Brookfield, Vt.: Dartmouth Publishing.

———. 1995. "Is The 'Skills Gap' Really About Attitudes?" *California Management Review* 37 (Summer): 108–24.

Caves, Richard E., and Matthew B. Krepps. 1993. "Fat: The Displacement of Nonproduction Workers from U.S. Manufacturing Industries." *Brookings Papers: Microeconomics* 2:227–88.

Cohen, S., and J. Zysman. 1987. *Manufacturing Matters: The Myth of the Post-Industrial Economy*. New York: Basic Books.

Competitiveness Policy Council. 1992. *Building a Competitive America: First Annual Report to the President and Congress*. Washington, D.C.: Competitiveness Policy Council.

Constantine, Jill M., and David Neumark. 1994. "Training and the Growth of Wage Inequality." Cambridge, Mass.: National Bureau of Economic Research.

Conte, Michael A., and Jan Svejnar. 1990. "The Performance Effects of Employee Ownership Plans." In *Paying for Productivity: A Look at the Evidence*, edited by Alan S. Blinder. Washington, D.C.: Brookings Institution.

Council for Aid to Education. Various years. *Corporate Support of Education*. New York: Council for Aid to Education.

Davis, Gerald F., Kristina A. Diekman, and Catherine H. Tinsley. 1994. "The Decline and Fall of the Conglomerate Firm in the 1980s: The De-Institutionalization of an Organizational Form." *American Sociological Review* 59: 547–70.

Dertouzos, M., R. K. Lester, and R. M. Solow. 1989. *Made in America: Regaining the Competitive Edge.* Cambridge, Mass.: MIT Press.

Diebold, Francis X., David Neumark, and Daniel Polsky. 1996. "Comment on 'Is Job Stability Declining in the U.S. Economy.'" *Industrial and Labor Relations Review* 49: 348–52.

Doeringer, Peter B., Kathleen Christensen, Patricia M. Flynn, Douglas T. Hall, Harry C. Katz, Jeffrey H. Keefe, Christopher J. Ruhm, Andrew M. Sum, and Michael Useem. 1991. *Turbulence in the American Workplace.* New York: Oxford University Press.

Doeringer, Peter B., and Michael J. Piore. 1971. *Internal Labor Markets and Manpower Analysis.* Lexington, Mass.: Heath.

Donaldson, Gordon. 1994. *Corporate Restructuring: Managing the Change Process from Within.* Boston: Harvard Business School Press.

Druckman, Daniel, and Robert A. Bjork, eds. 1994. *Learning, Remembering, Believing: Enhancing Human Performance.* Washington, D.C.: National Academy Press.

Eck, Alan. 1993. "Job-Related Education and Training." *Monthly Labor Review* 116 (October): 21–38.

Eurich, Nell P. 1985. *Corporate Classrooms: The Learning Business.* Princeton, N.J.: Carnegie Foundation for the Advancement of Teaching.

Freeman, Richard B., and Lawrence F. Katz. 1994. "Rising Wage Inequality: The United States vs. Other Advanced Countries." In *Working Under Different Rules,* edited by Richard B. Freeman. New York: Russell Sage Foundation.

Galbraith, Jay R., Edward E. Lawler III, and Associates. 1993. *Organizing for the Future.* San Francisco: Jossey-Bass.

Galinsky, Ellen, James T. Bond, and Dana E. Friedman. 1993. *The Changing Workforce.* New York: Families and Work Institute.

General Accounting Office. 1991. *Transition from School to Work: Linking Education and Worksite Training.* Washington, D.C.: General Accounting Office.

Gerstner, Louis V., Jr. 1994. *Reinventing Education: Entrepreneurship in America's Public Schools.* New York: Dutton, 1994.

Gore, Albert. 1993. *Creating a Government That Works Better and Costs Less.* New York: Random House.

Hamilton, Stephen F., and Mary Agnes Hamilton. 1992. "A Progress Report on Apprenticeships." *Educational Leadership* 49 (March): 44–47.

Hashimoto, Masanori. 1994. "Employment-Based Training in Japanese Firms in Japan and the United States: Experiences of Automobile Manufacturers." In *Training and the Private Sector: International Comparisons,* edited by Lisa M. Lynch. Chicago: University of Chicago Press.

Hodson, Randy, Gregory Hooks, and Sabine Rieble. 1992. "Customized Training in the Workplace." *Work and Occupations* 19:27–2.

Howard, Ann, and Douglas W. Bray. 1988. *Managerial Careers in Transition: Advancing Age and Changing Times.* New York: Guilford Publications.

International Business Machines. 1991. "An IBM Total Quality Management (TQM) Competition for Colleges and Universities in the USA." Stamford, Conn.: International Business Machines.

Janger, Allen. 1989. *Measuring Managerial Layers and Spans.* New York: Conference Board.

Jehl, J., and T. W. Payzant. 1992. "Philanthropy and Public School Reform: A View from San Diego." *Teachers College Record* 93:472–87.

Johnson, Arlene S., and Fabian Linden. 1992. *Availability of a Quality Workforce.* New York: Conference Board.

Johnston, Joseph S., Jr., Stanley T. Burns, David W. Butler, Marcie Schorr Hirsch, Thomas B. Jones, Alan M. Kantrow, Kathryn Mohrman, Roger B. Smith, and Michael Useem. 1986. *Educating Managers: Executive Effectiveness Through Liberal Learning.* San Francisco: Jossey-Bass.

Kalleberg, Arne L., and James W. Moody. 1994. "Human Resource Management and Organizational Performance." *American Behavioral Scientist* 37:948–62.

Kanter, Rosabeth Moss. 1977. *Men and Women of the Corporation.* New York: Basic Books.

Katz, Harry C., and Jeffrey H. Keefe. 1993. "Final Report on a Survey of Training and Restructuring of Work in Large Unionized Firms." Philadelphia: National Center on the Educational Quality of the Workforce, University of Pennsylvania.

Katzenbach, Jon R., and Douglas K. Smith. 1993. *The Wisdom of Teams: Creating the High-Performance Organization.* Boston: Harvard Business School Press.

Kellam, Susan. 1994. "Worker Retraining." *CQ Researcher* 4:49–72.

Knoke, David. 1996. "Company Job Training Programs and Practices." In *Change at Work,* edited by Peter Cappelli. New York: Oxford University Press.

Knoke, David, and Yoshito Ishio. 1994. "Occupational Training, Unions, and Internal Labor Markets." *American Behavioral Scientist* 37:922–1016.

Knoke, David, and Arne L. Kalleberg. 1994. "Job Training in U.S. Organizations." *American Sociological Review* 59:537–46.

Kobrin, Stephen J. 1984. *International Expertise in American Business.* New York: Institute of International Education.

Kochan, Thomas, Harry C. Katz, and Robert B. McKersie. (1986). *The Transformation of American Industrial Relations.* New York: Basic Books.

Lawler, Edward E., III. 1992. *The Ultimate Advantage: Creating the High-Involvement Organization.* San Francisco: Jossey-Bass, 1992.

Lawler, Edward E., III, Susan Mohrman, and Gerald Ledford. 1992. *Employee Involvement and Total Quality Management: Practices and Results in Fortune 500 Companies.* San Francisco: Jossey-Bass.

Lewis, William W., Hans Gersbach, Tom Jansen, and Koji Sakate. 1993. "The Secret to Competitiveness—Competition." *McKinsey Quarterly,* no. 4:29–44.

Lohr, Steve. 1994. "I.B.M. May Quit Hilltop Headquarters." *New York Times,* January 13, pp. A1, D3.

Lund, Leonard. 1992. *Corporate Mentoring in U.S. Schools: The Outstretched Hand.* New York: Conference Board.

Lusterman, Seymour. 1985. *Trends in Corporate Education and Training.* New York: Conference Board.

Lynch, Lisa M. 1991. "The Private Sector and Skill Formation in the United States." *Advances in the Study of Entrepreneurship, Innovation, and Economic Growth* 5:115–44.

———. 1992. "Private-Sector Training and the Earnings of Young Workers." *American Economic Review* 82:299–312.

———. 1994a. "Introduction." In *Training and the Private Sector: International Comparisons,* edited by Lisa M. Lynch. Chicago: University of Chicago Press.

———. 1994b. "Payoffs to Alternative Training Strategies at Work." In *Working Under Different Rules,* edited by Richard B. Freeman. New York: Russell Sage Foundation.

MacDuffie, John Paul. 1991. "Beyond Mass Production: Flexible Production Systems and Manufacturing Performance in the World Auto Industry." Ph.D. diss., MIT, Sloan School of Management.

———. 1995. "Human Resource Bundles and Manufacturing Performance: Organizational Logic and Flexible Production in the World Auto Industry." *Industrial and Labor Relations Reivew* 48:192–221.

MacDuffie, John Paul, and Thomas A. Kochan. 1995. "Do U.S. Firms Invest Less in Human Resources? Training in the World Auto Industry." *Industrial Relations* 34:147–68.

MacDuffie, John Paul, and John Krafcik. 1992. "Integrating Technology and Human Resources for High Performance Manufacturing: Evidence from the International Auto Industry." In *Transforming Organizations,* edited by Thomas Kochan and Michael Useem. New York: Oxford University Press.

Macy, Barry A., and Hiroaki Izumi. 1993. "Organizational Change, Design, and Work Innovation: A Meta-Analysis of 131 North American Field Studies— 1961–1991." In *Research in Organizational Change and Development*, edited by Richard W. Woodman and William A. Pasmore. Greenwich, Conn.: JAI Press.

McKinsey & Company. 1993. *Manufacturing Productivity.* Washington, D.C.: McKinsey Global Institute.

Meier, Elizabeth L. 1985. "Managing an Older Workforce." In *The Older Worker,* edited by Michael E. Borus, Herbert S. Parnes, Steven H. Sandell, and Bert Seidman. Madison, Wis.: Industrial Relations Research Association.

Murphy, Kevin M., and Finis Welch. 1993. "Industrial Change and the Rising Importance of Skills." In *Uneven Tides: Rising Inequality in America*, edited by Sheldon Danzinger and Peter Gottschalk. New York: Russell Sage Foundation.

Nadler, David A., Marc S. Gerstein, Robert B. Shaw, and Associates. 1992. *Organizational Architecture: Designs for Changing Organizations.* San Francisco: Jossey-Bass.

Nadler, David A., and Michael Tushman. 1988. *Strategic Organization Design.* Glenview, Ill.: Scott, Foresman.

National Academy of Engineering, Committee on Time Horizons and Technology Investments. 1992. *Time Horizons and Technology Investments.* Washington, D.C.: National Academy of Engineering.

National Education Goals Panel. 1991. *Building a Nation of Learners.* Washington, D.C.: National Education Goals Panel.

National Leadership Network Study Group on Restructuring Schools. 1993. *Toward Quality in Education: The Leader's Odyssey.* Washington, D.C.: U.S. Government Printing Office.

Nothdurft, William E. 1989. *School Works: Reinventing Public Schools to Create the Workforce of the Future.* Washington, D.C.: Brookings Institution.

O'Looney, John. 1993. "Redesigning the Work of Education." *Phi Delta Kappan* 74 (January): 375–81.

Organization for Economic Cooperation and Development. 1991. *Labor Market Policies for the 1990s.* Paris: Organization for Economic Cooperation and Development.

———. 1993. *Enterprise Tenure and the Churning of a Country's Workforce.* Paris: Organization for Economic Cooperation and Development.

Osterman, Paul. 1994. "How Common Is Workplace Transformation and How Can We Explain Who Adopts It?" *Industrial and Labor Relations Review* 47:173–88.

Porter, Lyman W., and Lawrence E. McKibbin. 1988. *Management Education and Development.* New York: McGraw-Hill.

Ramirez, Anthony. 1994. "NYNEX to Cut 22% of Work Force." *New York Times,* January 25, pp. D1, 17.

Ramsey, Nancy. 1992. "How Business Can Help the Schools." *Fortune,* November 16, pp. 147ff.

Riesman, David. 1950. *The Lonely Crowd: A Study of the Changing American Character.* New Haven, Conn.: Yale University Press.

RJR Nabisco Foundation. 1992. "Next Century Schools Program." Washington, D.C.: RJR Nabisco Foundation.

Robinson, James D., John F. Akers, Edwin L. Artzt, Harold A. Poling, Robert W. Galvin, and Paul Allaire. 1991. "An Open Letter: TQM on the Campus." *Harvard Busines Review* 69 (November–December): 94–95.

Rosenbaum, James E., and Takehiko Kariya. 1989. "From High School to Work: Market and Institutional Mechanism in Japan." *American Journal of Sociology* 94 (May):1334–65.

Rosenbaum, James E., Takehiko Kariya, R. Settersten, and T. Maier. 1990. "Market and Network Theories of the Transition from High School to Work." *Annual Review of Sociology* 16:263–99.

Rosenbaum, James E., David Stern, Mary Agnes Hamilton, Stephen F. Hamilton, Sue E. Berryman, and Richard Kazis. 1992. *Youth Apprenticeship in America:*

Guidelines for Building an Effective System. Washington, D.C.: William T. Grant Foundation Commission on Youth and America's Future.

Scott Morton, Michael S., ed. 1991. *The Corporation of the 1990s: Information Technology and Organizational Transformation.* New York: Oxford University Press.

Smith, Raymond. 1991. "Championship Change: An Interview with Bell Atlantic's CEO Raymond Smith." *Harvard Business Review* 69 (January–February): 119–30.

Soskice, David. 1994. "Reconciling Markets and Institutions: The German Apprenticeship System." In *Training and the Private Sector: International Comparisons,* edited by Lisa M. Lynch. Chicago: University of Chicago Press.

Stern, David, and Jozef M. M. Ritzen, eds. 1991. *Market Failure in Training? New Economic Analysis and Evidence on Training of Adult Employees.* Berlin: Springer-Verlag.

Stone, Nan. 1991. "Does Business Have Any Business in Education?" *Harvard Business Review* 69 (March–April): 46–62.

Swinnerton, Kenneth, and Howard Wial. 1995. "Is Job Stability Declining in the U.S. Economy?" *Industrial and Labor Relations Review* 48: 293–304.

Taylor, William. 1991. "The Logic of Global Business: An Interview with ABB's Percy Barnevik." *Harvard Business Review* 69 (March–April): 91–105.

Templin, Neal. 1994. "Auto Plants, Hiring Again, Are Demanding Higher-Skilled Labor." *Wall Street Journal,* March 11, pp. A1, A4.

Tobias, Andrew. 1976. "The Merging of the 'Fortune 500.'" *New York Magazine,* December 20, pp. 23–25, 49, 67.

U.S. Bureau of Labor Statistics. 1985. *How Workers Get Their Training.* Washington, D.C.: U.S. Bureau of Labor Statistics.

———. 1992a. *How Workers Get Their Training: A 1991 Update.* Washington, D.C.: U.S. Bureau of Labor Statistics.

———. 1992b. *Outlook: 1990–2005.* Washington, D.C.: U.S. Bureau of Labor Statistics.

U.S. Department of Labor. 1993. "High-Performance Work Practices and Firm Performance." Washington, D.C.: U.S. Department of Labor.

U.S. Department of Labor, Office of the American Workplace. 1994. *Road to High-Performance Workplaces.* Washington, D.C.: U.S. Department of Labor.

U.S. Department of Labor, Secretary's Commission on Achieving Necessary Skills. 1991. *What Work Requires of Schools: A SCANS Report for America 2000.* Washington, D.C.: U.S. Department of Labor.

U.S. Office of Technology Assessment. 1990. *Worker Training: Competing in the New International Economy.* Washington, D.C.: U.S. Government Printing Office.

U.S. Senate Special Committee on Aging. 1991. *Aging America: Trends and Projections.* Washington, D.C.: U.S. Department of Health and Human Services.

Useem, Michael. 1988. "Market and Institutional Factors in Corporate Contributions." *California Management Review* 30 (winter):77–88.

———. 1989. *Liberal Education and the Corporation: The Hiring and Advancement of College Graduates.* Hawthorne, N.Y.: Aldine de Gruyter.

———. 1991. "Organizational and Managerial Factors in the Shaping of Corporate Social and Political Action." In *Research in Corporate Social Performance and Policy,* vol. 12, edited by James E. Post. Greenwich, Conn.: JAI Press.

———. 1993a. *Executive Defense: Shareholder Power and Corporate Reorganization.* Cambridge, Mass.: Harvard University Press.

———. 1993b. "Management Commitment and Company Policies on Education and Training." *Human Resource Management Journal* 32:411–34.

———. 1994. "The Restructuring of American Business and the Aging Workforce." In *Aging and Competition: Rebuilding the U.S. Workforce,* edited by James A. Auerbach and Joyce C. Welsh. Washington, D.C.: National Council on Aging and the National Planning Association.

———. 1996. *Investor Capitalism: How Money Managers Are Changing the Face of Corporate America.* New York: Basic Books.

Useem Michael, and Jerome Karabel. 1986. "Pathways to Top Corporate Management." *American Sociological Review* 51 (April 1986): 184-200.

Useem, Michael, and Saskia Subramanian. 1994. "Leveraged Buyouts and Corporate Political Action." *Social Science Quarterly* 75 (1994): 475–93.

Wartzman, R. 1992. "Apprenticeship Plans Spring Up for Students Not Heading to College." *Wall Street Jounral,* May 19, pp. 1ff.

Weeks, David A. 1992. *Recruiting and Selecting International Managers.* New York: Conference Board.

Wild, Cathleen. 1993. *Corporate Volunteer Programs: Benefits to Business.* New York: Conference Board.

Whyte, William H. 1956. *The Organization Man.* New York: Simon and Schuster.

Womack, James P., and Daniel T. Jones. 1994. "From Lean Production to Lean Enterprise." *Harvard Business Review* 72 (March–April): 93–103.

Womack, James P., Daniel T. Jones, and Daniel Roos. 1991. *The Machine That Changed the World: The Story of Lean Production.* New York: HarperCollins.

Wyatt Company. 1993. *Best Practices in Corporate Restructuring.* New York: Wyatt Company.

10

The Modern Corporation as an Efficiency Instrument: The Comparative Contracting Perspective

◆

OLIVER E. WILLIAMSON

JANET BERCOVITZ

As James Q. Wilson reports, those who view the modern corporation from a power perspective regard it as a deeply problematic form of organization.[1] We examine the modern corporation from a different perspective and reach different results. As set out herein, both the key legal features of the corporation—perpetuity, contracting rights, and limited liability—and the main contractual regularities that link the firm with each of its constituencies are examined with reference to efficiency (or the lack thereof).

The efficiencies to which we refer are principally of a transaction cost rather than a production cost economizing kind. Such efficiencies are ascertained by examining the firm not in orthodox terms (as a production function, which is a technological construction) but in organizational terms (as a governance structure). This involves us in a microanalytical exercise in which the contractual relation between the corporation and each of its constituencies is examined in terms of the attributes of the transaction. The main obstacles to efficiency that we identify have their origins in information asymmetries.

The general efficiency approach, including a discussion of what we refer to as the "remediableness standard," is set out in section 1. The legal structure of the corporation, managerial discretion, and information impactedness conditions are examined and interpreted in section 2. The comparative contractual relations between the corporation and each constituency are sketched in section 3. The attributes of a board of overseers are briefly discussed in section 4. Concluding remarks follow.

1. Efficiency Analysis

An efficiency purpose is usually thought of as a normative goal: this is what firms "ought to do," even though we know—or believe that we know—they are doing other things. Efficiency and profit maximization are often regarded as equivalent.

We eschew the notion of profit maximization for two reasons: first, we agree with Herbert Simon (1957b) that human agents, managers included, often lack the wits to maximize; second, we believe that the action resides in the details. Jon Elster, we think, got it right when he counseled, "Explanations in the social sciences should be organized around (partial) *mechanisms* rather than (general) *theories*" (Elster 1994, p. 75; emphasis in original).

We examine the mechanisms of organization and contract not because we want to advise firms what they ought to do but because we want to understand complex economic organization. As against rival main case candidates—power, technology, monopoly, adventitiousness, and so on—we contend that efficiency is the most robust alternative.[2] Because, however, that view can be contested, other focused points of view are invited to enter a contest: let each main case candidate "show its hand," whereupon all explanations and predictions will be submitted to the data.[3] Once we have settled on the main case, allowance for other factors can be made—if and as warranted.

One of the reasons we are more sanguine than many others about the efficacy of efficiency is because we combine "realistic" behavioral assumptions with the remediableness standard. This will be evident as we progress, but we think it important to state our assumptions and procedures at the outset.

1.1. Behavioral Assumptions

The twin behavioral assumptions that inform our approach to economic organization are bounded rationality and opportunism. Whereas many economists are cavalier about behavioral assumptions, we are persuaded by Simon that "nothing is more fundamental in setting our research agenda and informing our research methods than our view of the nature of the human beings whose behavior we are studying" (1985, p. 303).

Bounded rationality has been defined as behavior that is "intendedly rational, *but* only limitedly so" (Simon 1957a, p. xxiv). The main ramification of bounded rationality for economic organization is that all complex contracts will be unavoidably incomplete. This is a recurrent argument in transaction cost economics (Williamson 1975, 1985, 1991a), and we will not repeat it here. It plays a central role, however, in the simple contractual schema described in the appendix and in 1.2.

A second ramification of bounded rationality for economic organization—less fully developed but also discussed elsewhere (Williamson 1975, 1994)—is that much of the information relevant to an exchange is impacted, which is to say not only that there are initial information asymmetries between the parties but that these asymmetries are very costly (sometimes impossible) to eliminate. As developed in section 3, information impactedness can and sometimes does give rise to antisocial strategic behavior by the corporation, in that less informed parties are unwittingly exposed to hazard. Customers, especially in final goods markets, and labor are sometimes disadvantaged in this respect.

Whether the adverse consequences of such asymmetries can be corrected with net gains, however, is another matter. The criterion of remediableness (as discussed in 1.3) is pertinent in this connection.

Some students of economic organization take exception with transaction cost economics because opportunism—defined as self-interest seeking with guile—is an unattractive behavioral assumption. Simon, for example, eschews opportunism and describes self-interest seeking as "frailties of motive" (1985, p. 303), which is a much more benign construction. Others favor more affirmative constructions such as "trust." Sometimes the objection to opportunism is that it is too much concerned with description and too little concerned with design: in our "loftier moments" we ought to be concerned with reshaping rather than merely describing economic organization.

We concede merit in normative analysis but believe that this should be informed by an understanding of how things work. Considering the hazards of premature prescriptiveness and our primitive understanding of economic organization, we think that there is no loftier purpose for social scientists than to ask and answer the question, What's going on here?

We would furthermore urge that the choice of frailty of motive over opportunism (or the reverse) will vary with the circumstances. If we ask which of these two best describes *day-to-day* activity most of the time, we believe that frailty of motive is descriptively more accurate. Most people will do what they say (and some will do more) without self-consciously asking whether incremental net gains will accrue to each and every action. Social conditioning and an active conscience in combination with standard procedures and routines help to explain why conscious calculativeness is subliminal in most day-to-day exercises.

Suppose, however, that we ask another questions: As between frailty of motive and opportunism, which better takes us into the *deep structure of economic organization?* Specifically, if our concern is not with day-to-day operating affairs but with the architecture of economic organization, how should we proceed?

The object of the latter is to look ahead, perceive hazards, and fold these back into the organizational design—in all significant contractual contexts whatsoever (intermediate product market, labor market, capital market, etc.). Robert Michels's concluding remarks about oligarchy are pertinent: "Nothing but a serene and frank examination of the oligarchical dangers of democracy will enable us to minimize these dangers" (1962, p. 370). If a serene and frank reference to opportunism alerts us to avoidable contractual dangers which the more benign reference to frailties of motive and reason would not, then there are real hazards in adopting the more benevolent construction.

We contend that a calculative approach that makes express allowance for opportunism helps to unpack issues such as the following: When should we expect the firm to produce for its own needs rather than purchase a good or service (the make-or-buy decision)? When will the firm issue debt rather than equity (i.e., when and why is debt the low-cost form of finance)? When will the firm integrate forward into distribution? How and why do weaknesses in property rights influence ownership and contracting? When do informal sanctions work well and poorly (with what organizational ramifications)? The hazards of opportunism, as these vary with the attributes of transactions, are pertinent to these questions and help to explain contractual and organizational variety that frailty of motive does not. User-friendly words and concepts that signal "all clear" when caution is needed come at a high cost.

1.2. Efficient Contracting

Transaction cost economics maintains that all complex contracts are unavoidably incomplete by reason of bounded rationality. All of the relevant contracting action cannot therefore be concentrated in the ex ante incentive alignment, but some spills over into ex post governance. A comparative assessment of alternative modes of governance—markets, hybrids, public and private bureaus—in terms of their discrete structural attributes is thereupon warranted. Transaction cost economics thus parts way with the orthodox economics conception of the firm-as-production function (which is a technological construction) in favor of the firm-as-governance structure (which is an organizational construction).

But transaction cost economics then makes a second move, which brings economic reasoning (if not economic orthodoxy) back in: it describes the contracting process as one of "incomplete contracting in its entirety." But for incompleteness, the previously described significance of ex post governance would vanish. But for farsightedness, transaction cost economics would be denied access to one of the most important "tricks" in the economist's bag—namely, the assumption that economic actors have the ability to look ahead, discern problems and prospects, and factor these back into the organizational or contractual design. "Plausible farsightedness,"as against hyperrationality, will often suffice.

Consider, for example, the issue of threats. Threats are easy to make, but which threats are to be believed? If A says that it will do X if B does Y, but if after B does Y, A's best response is to do Z, then the threat will not be perceived to be credible to a farsighted B. Credible threats are thus those for which a farsighted B perceives that A's ex post incentives comport with its claims—because, for example, A has made the requisite kind and amount of investment to support its threats (Dixit 1980).

Or consider the matter of breach of contract. Because Machiavelli worked out of a myopic logic, he advised his prince to reply to opportunism in kind (get them before they get you). By contrast, transaction cost economics advises the prince to look ahead and, if he discerns potential hazards, to take the hazards into account by redesigning the contractual relation—often by devising ex ante safeguards that will deter ex post opportunism. Accordingly, the farsighted prince is advised to give and receive "credible commitments."

Although the study of contract in terms of credible commitments is a recent construction, John R. Commons perceived what was a stake sixty years ago. As he put it, "The ultimate unit of activity…must contain in itself the three principles of conflict, mutuality, and order. This unit is a transaction" (1932, p. 4). Not only does transaction cost economics concur that the transaction is the basic unit of analysis, but governance is the means by which *order* is accomplished between parties to a contract, where otherwise *conflict* would undo or upset opportunities to realize *mutual* gains.

To be sure, it is more convenient to think of a contract as a simple exchange mediated by price rather than as a triple (p, k, s)—where p refers to the price at which the trade takes place, k refers to the hazards that are associated with the exchange, s denotes the safeguards within which the exchange is embedded, and price, hazards, and safeguards are all determined simultaneously. To repeat, however, the object is to understand complex economic organization. Hazards are therefore recognized rather than suppressed; and organization is viewed as an instrument to effect hazard mitigation. The matter of remediableness also arises in this connection.

1.3. Remediableness

It is easy to show that markets fail in relation to a hypothetical ideal, and that is what the market failure literature was content to do for many years (Coase 1964). It is likewise easy to show that the modern corporation is a failed form of organization in relation to a hypothetical ideal, as so many critics of the corporation have correctly argued for many years. Similar statements can be made about regulation/regulatory failure and public bureaucracy/bureaucratic failure. Indeed, it is a verity that all feasible forms of organization "fail" in relation to a hypothetical ideal.

The comparative institutional approach to economic organization eschews hypothetical analysis and asks instead that alternative *feasible* forms be compared with each other. It maintains that much mischief and little useful purpose is served by pronouncing failure if no superior alternative can be described.

The remediableness standard (Williamson 1996) is designed to avoid lapses into ideal but operationally irrelevant reasoning by (1) recognizing that it is impossible to do better than one's best, (2) insisting that all of the finalists in the competition among organization forms meet the test of feasibility, (3) symmetrically exposing the weaknesses as well as the strengths of all proposed feasible forms, and (4) describing and costing out the mechanisms of any proposed reorganization. Not only are the relevant comparisons restricted to alternative feasible forms, but allowance is made for incumbency advantages. Thus even if mode A is judged to be inefficient in relation to mode B on a simple side-by-side comparison, if mode A is in place and mode B incurs setup costs, then mode A may prevail. Also, and related, it may not be possible to implement mode B for lack of political support.

Some might object that the remediableness standards exchanges utopian reasoning for Dr. Pangloss, and it is certainly true that the remediableness standard is more deferential to "what is." For example, claims of inefficiency due to path dependency frequently turn out to be irremediable—hence not inefficient at all. Also, various forms of "inefficiency by design"—such as constraints imposed by franchisors on franchisees (Klein and Leffler 1981), efforts to relieve weak intellectual property rights through vertical integration (Teece 1986), and efforts by manufacturers' agents to buttress marketing channels (Heide and John 1988, 1990)—turn out to be efficient under the remediableness standard.

Although remediable inefficiency invites its own demise, there are several qualifications: (1) remediable inefficiency is not always obvious, whence the display by social scientists and other policy analysts that extant programs incur large deadweight losses in relation to a hypothetical ideal may usefully call attention to (potentially) remediable conditions;[4] (2) projects that are not remediable at one point in time, because of differential setup costs, may be remediable at a later point in time, when investment renewal decisions come up for consideration; and (3) a judgment of inefficiency may be withheld from some programs because of perceived breakdowns of organization and/or politics. The qualified version of the remediableness standard thus reduces to the following: except as rebutted by exceptions of the kinds referred to earlier and elaborated elsewhere (Williamson 1996), outcomes for which no feasible superior alternative can be described and implemented with net gains are presumed to be efficient.[5]

2. The Corporation, General

Most of the refutable implications of the efficiency analysis out of which we work accrue to repeated applications of the simple contractual schema to various constituencies (in section 3). It is instructive first, however, to offer general efficiency interpretations of the corporate form and of the Berle-Means concern with managerial discretion.

2.1. The Legal Form

Raymond Vernon puts the issues well in chapter 3 in this volume:

> As numerous scholars have observed, governments have endowed the corporation with some extraordinary attributes: its claim to immortality; its right in most circumstances to make commitments in its own name, without direct participation in such decisions by its owners; and its capacity in most situations to

shield its owners from financial liability. In return, governments usually expect that the corporation's operations will be compatible with the national interests of the country that provides for its creation.

That expectation . . . is not always realized. The managers of large corporations are frequently accused of serving their own interests or those of their stockholders at the cost of the rest of the national economy that authorized their existence. But large enterprises that preside over a multinational network are recognized as being exposed to a very distinctive set of added pressures, namely the pressures applied by foreign governments and other interests operating in the countries in which the foreign subsidiaries of the multinationals are located.

We interpret all of the preceding in efficiency terms. We furthermore aver that citizens have a general interest in having all of their institutions—corporations, partnerships, nonprofits, public bureaus, contracting practices, and so on—efficiently organized and supported by efficient rules of the game (as prescribed by customs and their government). Because, however, history matters and politics trumps economics, rather than the reverse (Stigler 1992), efficiency sometimes takes convoluted forms.

It will facilitate our analysis of the modern corporation to set the redistributional purposes of politics aside and focus on the three structural features to which Vernon refers: perpetuity, autonomous contracting, and limited liability. The advantages of creating an organization form that lasts in perpetuity are that this mitigates the asset valuation problems of partnerships and avoids the endgame problems (and attendant unraveling) that are associated with finite play.[6] Perpetuity is not, therefore, a favor that the corporation extracts from a compliant polity but an efficiency gain that accrues to society.

We interpret contracting similarly. The ability of the corporation to contract in its own name permits the firm to decide the make-or-buy issue on the merits and to avoid costly consultation with the ownership. Were the firm granted only limited contractual autonomy—for example, to contract only in spot markets—there would be much less hybrid contracting, as a consequence of which economic organization would be of a much more bimodal kind: transactions would tend to be of either a generic/spot market or a highly specific/internal kind. That would sacrifice economies of a hybrid kind (Williamson 1991a). As students of Japanese economic organization emphasize (Dore 1983; Aoki 1990; Gerlach 1992), society would be the poorer for it.

The separation of ownership from control in the modern corporation is commonly taken as a given and is often denounced. In fact, however, the separation of ownership from control is *derived* and the resulting "distortions" in the conduct of the corporation may be irremediable—in that it is impossible to implement a superior organizational alternative and realize net gains. Since the hypothetical ideal of costless control is unattainable, more control entails a tradeoff.

Thus, although some investors may be insistent on control—and will be observed to invest in small, local firms in which they have deep knowledge—not all investors are so constituted. It is hardly reprehensible if other investors are observed to invest in large firms in which they have only limited knowledge and cannot meaningfully exercise ongoing control (presumably because the perceived advantages of large size and specialization of decision making exceed the associated costs of separating ownership from control).

There is, however, a serious deterrent to investments of the latter kind *unless* investors who lack detailed, firsthand knowledge are relieved of unlimited financial liability. Limited liability is an obvious efficiency response to investor ignorance.

To be sure, the foregoing efficiency explanations for the "privileged legal forms" of the corporation are merely suggestive and could be dismissed as ex post rationalizations. We nevertheless observe that we know of no more plausible interpretation of the perpetuity, contracting, and limited liability features to which Vernon refers. Awaiting a more compelling interpretation, we contend that these features of the corporation are not special political favors but are efficiency responses to underlying societal/organizational needs.[7] Thus, although it is common to regard the corporation as the creature of the state to which it owes some return duty, we would urge that the corporation is merely an instrument and that—both directly (through resource savings) and indirectly (through Schumpeterian "handing on" (see section 3.3.6)—the entire society benefits when more efficient instruments are devised.

2.2. *Managerial Discretion*

Because we hold that managers are described by the same behavioral attributes as everyone else—bounded rationality and opportunism—we project that managers will not behave as unfailing stewards but will tilt things in favor of their own interests. The answer, therefore, to the query posed by Adolf Berle and Gardiner Means in 1932—"Have we any justification for assuming that those in control of the modern corporation will also choose to operate it in the interests of the shareholders?" (Berle and Means 1932, p. 121)—is decidedly negative, both then and now.

Answering the Berle-Means query in the negative gave rise to the managerial discretion literature of the late 1950s and early 1960s (Baumol 1959; Marris 1964; Williamson 1964). Two issues arise: What types of managerial distortions arise in the modern corporation? Are they remediable?

The types of distortions that arise because managers enjoy information and decision advantages in relation to shareholders (and other constituencies) are legion. William Baumol (1959) emphasized that profits would be sacrificed in favor of sales (size); Robin Marris (1964) formulated this in terms of constrained growth maximization; and Williamson's (1964) model of managerial discretion emphasized distortions in favor of managerial staff and emoluments. Alfred Chandler's (1962) examination of organizational practices in the modern corporation disclosed that subgoal pursuit and politicking in the corporation were common; work on *A Behavioral Theory of the Firm* also featured those attributes (Cyert and March 1963).

Hardworking and conscientious though many managers are, it is hardly unnatural they will tilt matters at the margin in their favor. Albeit in a different context, the so-called dollar-a-year men in the Office of Production Management, of which there were 250 at the beginning of World War II, were of concern to the Senate Special Committee to Investigate the National Defense Program for a similar reason:

> Such corporate executives in high official roles were too inclined to make decisions for the benefit of their corporations. "They have their own business at heart," [Senator] Truman remarked. The report called them lobbyists "in very real sense," because their presence inevitably meant favoritism, "human nature being what it is." (McCullough 1992, p. 265)

Michel Crozier's treatment of bureaucracy presumes an "active tendency of the human agent to take advantage, in any circumstances, of all available means to further his own privileges" (Crozier 1964, p. 194). This last is an uncommonly strong version of opportunism and contemplates managerial discretion in all of its forms. Distortions in size, growth, employment, slack, risk assessments (in which career opportunities and hazards are featured), on-the-job consumption (emoluments), politics, influence costs, and compensation are all to be expected.

One reaction to managerial discretion is to regard it as inefficient and reprehensible. Managerial discretion, however, should surprise no one. It is the *predictable* result of large size (whence bureaucracy) and is compounded by the separation of ownership from control.

To be sure, if large size is unneeded (for technological or contracting reasons), then smaller firms with concentrated ownership will do better. If, however, large size is needed to realize economies of production and organization, then managerial discretion will appear and the question is one of cost-effective measures to bring it under control.

The reorganization of "troubled firms" can be interpreted as one such control effort (Schleifer and Vishny 1991); takeover is another (Gilson and Kraakman 1984); main bank financing is a third (Aoki 1990). Also, managers—especially in firms that are experiencing strain, such as General Motors and Du Pont in the 1920s—have incentives to invent more efficient forms. As indicated, the transformation of the modern corporation from a centralized, functionally organized firm to a divisionalized structure can be interpreted in that fashion (Chandler 1962; Williamson 1970).[8]

There is, moreover, a role for public policy. Antitrust authorities, for example, have no reason to share managerial preferences for growth and may therefore assess the merits of proposed mergers differently. And securities regulators may similarly have a different assessment of poison pills and other defensive tactics. Also, structural rules, on the composition of the compensation committee, for example, can have modest effects. More major reforms—such as allowing banks to be more involved in ownership and oversight respects (Roe 1990)—can be implemented only through the political process, which poses an additional hurdle but is also properly included within the remediableness calculus (Stigler 1992; Williamson 1994).

2.3. Information Disparities

Our concern here is with information disparities where managers have deeper knowledge of contract-relevant information and display it in strategic ways.

Managers, of course, have a lot of knowledge about the firm that is not known to outsiders. Even, moreover, if outsiders would be interested in some of that information, it may not be cost-effective to display it. This brings us to contract-relevant information, by which we mean information that if displayed would be cost-effective—in that its display would yield superior contracts with net gains. Strategic refusals by the management to disclose the truth, the whole truth, and nothing but the truth (subject to the cost-effectiveness proviso) are responsible for much of the more problematic behavior in corporations.

3. Constituency Analysis

We contend that the main relation between the corporation and each constituency is explained by an efficiency logic. Specifically, we examine the contractual relation between the corporation and each of its constituencies—managers, workers, suppliers of product and services, finance, customers—with reference to efficiency (or the lack thereof). This is to be contrasted with those who appeal to power to address these same matters.

These rival logics are examined in section 3.1 and in the simple contractual schema in the appendix. One of the differences between the power logic and the contractual logic is that the former identifies more failures of "social responsibility." A common remedy for such failures is to make a place for all stakeholders on the board of directors.

3.1 Stakeholder Logic

Clyde Summers (1982), Katherine Stone (1993), and Marleen O'Connor (1993) all counsel for the inclusion of labor participation in corporate governance. Thus Summers contends:

> If the corporation is conceived . . . as an operating institution combining all factors of production to conduct an ongoing business, then the employees who provide the labor are as much members of that enterprise as the shareholders who provide capital. Indeed, the employees may have made a much greater investment in the enterprise by their years of service, may have much less ability to withdraw, and may have a greater stake in the future of the enterprise than many of the stockholders. In a corporation, so conceived, employee directors have no more conflict of interest than shareholder directors. (1982, p. 70)

And Marleen O'Connor urges that "legal reform requiring labor participation in corporate governance is necessary not only to achieve social goals concerning industrial democracy but also to promote efficient corporate behavior" (1993, p. 902). What Robert Dahl has referred to as "interest group management" would expressly apportion seats on the board of directors to employees, consumer representatives, and delegates of government (1970, p. 20); and Denis Collins adds environmentalists to this list (1994, p. 122). Still more expansively, R. E. Freeman and W. M. Evan urge that, in order to protect themselves from the opportunistic actions of other constituencies, all "stakeholders [should] be accorded voting rights with respect to deciding how to manage the affairs of the corporation" (1990, p. 338).

More generally, the stakeholder view of the corporation appears to be that all who have significant dealings with the corporation, be these direct (as with labor) or indirect (environmentalists), have a stake and ought to be invited to participate in board deliberations.

As discussed in section 4, we distinguish between a board of directors and a board of overseers and urge that the former be reserved for those who have made equity investments in the firm. Provided that it is strictly advisory, expansive membership on a board of overseers could be a source of net gains.

3.2. Contractual Logic

We contend that a common contractual framework applies to all constituencies—labor, capital, intermediate product markets, and so on. The simple contractual schema on which we rely and that applies to all is set out in the appendix.

As heretofore indicated, we describe contract as a triple (p, k, s), where p is the price, k is a measure of contractual hazard, and s denotes safeguards. The main contractual hazard with which we are concerned is the degree to which a constituency is specialized to a firm. Generic assets pose few hazards, since these can be redeployed to alternative uses and users with little sacrifice of productive value. Firm-specific assets, by contrast, lack easy redeployability (but give rise instead to a condition of dependency). Unless the firm provides security features for firm-specific assets, such assets will carry a hazard premium (which will show up in the price at which the asset is made available to the firm). Because hazards are priced out, it is in the firm's interest to provide safeguards in cost-effective degree. Farsighted contracting by both parties brings about this result.

The key regularities on which we rely to explain the main contracting relation between the corporation and each of its constituencies are these:

1. Constituencies that bear no specialized investment relation to the firm—the assets in question are easily redeployable, hence nonspecific—will contract in a spot contracting (or nearly spot contracting) fashion. This corresponds to Node A in the schema (see appendix), where there are no contractual hazards ($k = 0$) or safeguards ($s = 0$) and price is set competitively.

2. Constituencies that make specialized investments in support of a

transaction are exposed to hazards ($k > 0$). These hazards will be recognized and will be priced out. Buyers, therefore, that refuse or are unable to offer a safeguard will be charged a higher price at Node B ($s = 0$) than will those that do safeguard the transaction and operate at Node C ($s > 0$).

3. If cost-effective safeguards can be devised, it is in the corporation's interest to offer them (Jensen and Meckling 1976).

3.3. *Applications*

We maintain that the main contractual relation between the corporation and each constituency can be ascertained by repeated application of this same contractual schema. As against our earlier *interpretation* of the overarching attributes of the corporation (in 2.1), our purpose here is to *predict* contractual regularities for each constituency. These predictions can then be examined in relation to the data.

Because, however, the schema works out of the strong assumption that each constituency contracts in a knowledgeable way, deviations from the main case can and will occur. Information asymmetries—which go both ways, but we assume preponderantly favor the corporation in relation to its constituencies—can lead to contractual inefficiencies.

Identifying all of those inefficiencies and their remediableness is beyond the scope of this paper. We nevertheless describe what we believe to be the most important or representative of these information-based contractual failures. We successively examine suppliers, investors, customers, employees, and the general public.

3.3.1. INTERMEDIATE PRODUCT MARKETS

The assumption that both parties to a contract are well informed is probably best satisfied in intermediate product markets. The simple contractual schema thus applies with little qualification to these circumstances.

Our first prediction is that contracts between the corporation and suppliers that are supported by generic assets will be of a Node A kind and will require no added safeguards. Each firm will simply go its own way if things do not work out. Disputes will be litigated in court, and relief will take the form of money damages.

Matters change drastically when nontrivial investments in transaction-specific durable assets are involved. Each party in these circumstances has an interest in a continuing relation. Safeguards will thus be introduced to deter inefficient breach and to resolve differences (disputes) through private ordering. These include take-or-pay clauses, penalty clauses, reciprocal trading arrangements, and special information disclosure and dispute-settling arrangements, of which arbitration is an example. Indeed, as assets become more highly specific and the disturbances to which adaptations are needed become great, interfirm contracting may be supplanted by internal organization. Markets give way to hierarchies.

Whether the resulting organization of intermediate product market transactions is actually efficient could be upset by monopoly power and/or information asymmetries. We concur. We would observe, however, that all claims of inefficiency need to be expressed in terms of a remediableness standard, which is a much more demanding test than the more common reference to a hypothetical (but unattainable) ideal. We would further observe that while large buyers sometimes enjoy information advantages over smaller suppliers, many suppliers are also large and informed. Also, many small suppliers often have deep knowledge about the nature of the transaction and/or can hire specialists to overcome the major informational disparities. We believe that most claims of "arbitrary termination" of small suppliers by industrial buyers can be explained either in terms of generic assets (there are no ties that bind) or the hazards have been taken into account in the risk calculus (were reflected in a risk premium); we know of no evidence to the contrary.

3.3.2. FINANCE

The project financing approach to corporate finance supports the following array of contractual relationships: (1) generic but mobile durable assets (autos, trucks, planes, rolling stock) can be procured through lease; (2) general-purpose inventories can be financed with short-term loans; (3) general-purpose durable assets can be financed through debt, to which the asset in question is pledged as security; and (4) special-purpose durable assets pose the most difficult problems and require a more intrusive control structure (Williamson 1988).

Of course, not all firms require significant investment in durable, nonredeployable physical assets. Among those that do not, some can be efficiently organized as professional partnerships (such as law firms) and worker-managed service and manufacturing firms (Hansmann 1988). Firms, however, that make substantial investments in durable, physical, firm-specific assets need to turn to another form of finance: equity.

Debt is "poorly suited" to finance durable, firm-specific assets for two reasons: such assets provide poor security (because their value in their next best use or by their next best user is so much lower); and debt financing is a relatively inflexible and unforgiving form of finance (being rule-bound by interest and principal repayment schedules and by related covenants). Given these disabilities, can a superior form of finance—one that moves the transaction from Node B to Node C—for assets of a nonredeployable kind be devised?

Suppose that a financial instrument called equity is devised that has the following governance properties: (1) it bears a residual claimant status to the firm in both earnings and asset liquidation respects; (2) it contracts for the duration of the life of the firm; and (3) a board of directors is created and awarded to equity that (a) is elected by the pro rata votes of those who hold tradable shares, (b) has the power to replace the management, (c) decides on management compensation, (d) has access to internal performance measures on a timely basis, (e) can authorize audits in depth for special follow-up purposes, (f) is apprised of important investment and operating proposals before they are implemented, and (g) in other respects bears a decision review and monitoring relation to the firm's management.

An *endogenous response* to the governance needs of suppliers of finance who are asked to invest in nonredeployable projects has thereby resulted. These suppliers bear a residual claimant status to the firm and are awarded "control" over the board of directors in exchange.

Also note that it is simply not possible to secure equity finance *on the same terms* if, as John Bonin and Louis Putterman stipulate in the worker-managed firm, "decision-making rights are vested in the workers, and only the workers" (1987, p. 2). Such a stipulation poses added hazards to equity investors, on which account the terms of finance will change accordingly (move back from Node C to Node B). If, therefore, what workers and other constituencies need are protections against information asymmetries, insistence on membership on the board of directors is an extreme and costly solution.[9] As discussed in section 4, a board of overseers, which is given information but not decision rights and has no vote on the board of directors, is potentially responsive to these information needs.

Note further that the ability to concentrate the ownership and shares and take over the board of directors, thereafter to change the management, plays an important background role in the control of the corporation. As compared with a political contest (one-person, one-vote), or a proxy/beauty contest (vote your shares for me because . . .), the takeover agent pays a premium to secure control and exercises that control directly. To be sure, a good deal of managerial discretion survives contests of all kinds. The object, however, is not to annihilate managerial discretion but to reduce it in cost-effective degree. The remediableness test applies.

3.3.3. Customers

Many transactions between firms and final customers are for mundane goods and are transacted in spot markets. Among transactions of a more relational kind, most enjoy the (sometimes weak) protections of reputation effects—in that these are repeat purchase items and/or purchase experience is shared with others. Often, moreover, firms undertake practices to intensify these reputation effects through branding and warranties, authorized service, and the like, thereby to provide added safeguards for consumer durables.[10] Also, groups of consumers can and sometimes do create their own specialized agents to contract on their behalf. The question then is whether best private efforts of buyers and suppliers to concentrate costs and benefits can be further improved with net gains (remediableness).

Laws prescribing "truth in advertising" are one suggestion, but implementing these in a cost-effective way is extremely problematic. Focusing on egregious conditions—such as fraud and health hazards—is one way of delimiting the issues. Elaborating on this is beyond the scope of this paper. Suffice it to observe here that (1) fraud has long been a concern of the law, (2) health hazards are matters to which a net benefit calculus can be usefully applied (Williamson 1981), and (3) the determined opposition of an industry—of which tobacco is an illustration—can frustrate health-corrective efforts by obfuscating data and false reporting.

3.3.4. Labor

We take it as good business practice that all labor is entitled to respect and that termination at will should be exercised judiciously. Because, however, good business practice is not always observed, efforts to assure threshold levels of respect and threshold criteria for termination for even the most generic types of labor have merit. Even, therefore, in firms where firm-specific investments in human capital are negligible, firms will be observed to invest in human relations training for supervisors and will afford workers with due-process remedies so that offending supervisors can be identified and removed or otherwise disciplined. The benefits of these investments to the firm are that the firm will get better work from better workers on better terms.

The following questions concern us here: (1) How will the contractual relation between the firm and its workers vary with changes in firm-specific human assets? (2) How should we think about labor unions? (3) What lapses arise because of information asymmetries?

The answer to the first of these questions is that the simple contractual schema applies to contracts of all kinds, human assets included. Thus, just as it is useful to distinguish between leasing, renting, debt-financed, and equity-financed physical assets—where these vary from least to most in terms of physical asset specificity—so likewise is it useful to identify workers who are fungible among firms, those who have a continuing association but make limited specialized investments, those who acquire deep knowledge, and those who become part of a deep knowledge team. These likewise vary from least to most in terms of human asset specificity, and the degree of added contractual support varies accordingly.

Examples of nonspecific labor are temporary workers (e.g., temporary clericals) and periodic professionals (e.g., outside accountants, auditors, consultants). Although such workers may develop firm-specific skills with their employer (the firm that hires them out), their skills are largely fungible across assignments. Accordingly, the firm to which they are currently assigned does not provide these workers with added employment safeguards or support. Like a leased physical asset, these temporary workers are "out on loan," and the governance relation between them and the borrower (current user) is strictly attenuated.

Workers for whom the employer and place of employment are the same, by contrast, will be afforded with added safeguards at their place of employment. Such added safeguards will not, however, be uniform. Rather, contractual safeguards will be introduced in the degree to which that is cost-effective, which will vary with the degree to which firm-specific assets are built up (a measure of bilateral dependency) and the costs of providing safeguards. The contractual theory on which we rely predicts that ex ante efforts to anticipate and forestall disputes, by developing procedures that respect "zone of acceptance" of the employment agreement,[11] and ex post efforts to deal with misunderstandings and/or disputes, by developing governance machinery in which information is disclosed and disputes are decided on the merits—for example, through arbitration,[12] will increase as firm-specific human assets build up, ceteris paribus.

Rival interpretations of the Wagner Act between Katherine Stone and the "industrial pluralists"—Harry Schulman, Archibald Cox, Arthur Goldberg, and Justice Douglas—are pertinent to an understanding of unions. The latter adopted what, in effect, was an efficiency view: the purpose of the act was to harmonize labor relations, promote cooperation, and please the parties. So regarded, and appropriately applied, unions could serve as a Node C safeguard. By contrast, Stone (1981) advanced an adversarial interpretation, according to which the purpose of the act was to equalize power. Thus, whereas the pluralists viewed arbitration as a means by which to resolve disputes in favor of the continuity interests of the parties, Stone recommended a legalistic approach in which the National Labor Relations Board is directed to "interpret the language of the written agreement, *not please the parties*" (Stone 1981, p. 1552 n. 238; emphasis in original).

Although a legalistic approach to contract is understandably recommended by those who prefer confrontation, that can be a costly way to organize society. For better or worse (depending on one's preferences), the efficiency view has mainly prevailed. Interestingly, Japanese economic organization can be interpreted as an effort to move to a higher degree of contracting perfection (Aoki 1990; Williamson 1991b). Although this last is beyond the scope of this paper, we observe that the study of contracting in the Japanese firm requires that the employment relation, subcontracting, and the main bank be interpreted as an interdependent network (or system).

The efficiency approach explains and justifies a lot of what's going on in the labor arena, but this does not imply that all is well. Troublesome issues of information asymmetry can and do arise. For example, Robert Howse and Michael Trebilcock express concerns about "employers who strategically conceal information about management strategy and the firm's health during bargaining" (1993, p. 756), and Stone (1993, p. 371) observes that reputation effects do not work as a safeguard in end-game situations, such as plant closings. To this we would add that job attributes may not be objectively disclosed.

Two issues arise: How serious are these concerns? And what can be done about them? Regarding the first, we would urge that the recurrent contracting relation between management and labor encourages candid disclosure of job attributes and economic conditions. That is because true economic and job conditions will become common knowledge soon and there are efficiency advantages if management establishes a reputation for candor with labor (or, put differently, there are efficiency disadvantages if management is disbelieved and contested at every turn). In the degree, moreover, to which biased disclosure is observed, ex ante counterbiasing during negotiations can be projected.

For firms, therefore, that plan to be in business on a continuing basis, strategic concealment of the firm's health does not seem to us to be a serious concern. By contrast, end games and employee health hazards with long latency effects are both troublesome.[13]

To be sure, the endgame problem is mixed. If, for example, management does not disclose its plant closure plans, then workers will not have adequate notice to seek other employment. But workers who are given early notice may also decide not to expend their accustomed degree of effort, whence productivity will suffer. Creating a board of overseers to whom business plans are disclosed would overcome the first of these but at the expense of the second. Requiring firms to incur "appropriate" job resettlement and reemployment costs for workers who have acquired large firm-specific skills has attractions but may be difficult to enforce.

Arguably the most troublesome problem is that of undisclosed health hazards that have long latency periods. Especially in industries where physical assets are nonredeployable, postponement of the reckoning by the corporation (and then, possibly, escaping through bankruptcy) is a serious concern. A board of overseers, in such an industry, could well be a useful corrective.

The asbestos experience, which is an extreme case, is illustrative. Undisclosed health hazards in this industry have been described as "a fifty year history of corporate malfeasance and inhumanity to man which is unparalleled in the annals of the private-enterprise system" (Brodeur 1985a, p. 50). The details are related elsewhere (Brodeur 1985a–1985d), but two incidents are especially instructive. The first is a medical study by Dr. Kenneth W. Smith, who retired as medical director of the Johns-Manville Corporation in 1966. The second is a speech by the president of that firm, A. R. Fisher. As reported by Brodeur:

> [Smith made a] survey in 1948 and sent his report to Johns-Manville's New York headquarters early in 1949. The report said that out of the seven hundred and eight workers only four—all of whom had had four years of exposure or less—had X-rays that showed normal, healthy lungs. On page 3, Smith described his policy toward seven workers who showed signs of early asbestosis. "It must be remembered that although these men have the X-ray evidence of asbestosis, they are working today and definitely are not disabled from asbestosis . . . They have not been told of this diagnosis for it is felt that as long as the man feels well, is happy at home and at work, and his physical condition remains good, nothing should be said. When he becomes disabled and sick, then the diagnosis should be made and the claim submitted by the company. The fibrosis of this disease is irreversible and permanent so that eventually compensation will be paid to each of these men. But as long as the man is not disabled it is felt that he should not be told of his condition so that he can live and work in peace and the company can benefit by his many years of experience. Should

the man be told his condition today there is a very definite possibility that he would become mentally and physically ill, simply through the knowledge that he has asbestosis." (1985b, p. 67)

Six years later, A. R. Fisher, who had received a copy of the Smith report and was president of Johns-Manville, delivered a talk on the economics of industrial health to the Industrial Hygiene Foundation of America. The audience was advised, "We in industry realize that as good citizens it is part of our obligation to society to help improve the health of the nation as well as the community" (Brodeur 1985b, p. 67). Surely good health, like charity, begins at home. On the possibility that some firms will see it otherwise, the board of overseers to which we refer in section 4 could have a useful role to play.

3.3.5. MANAGERS

Our basic argument that added safeguards will arise in the degree to which assets take on firm-specific values applies to managers as well to other constituencies. If managers in firms in mature industries that are competitively organized have easier redeployment opportunities than do managers whose employment is of a more idiosyncratic kind in industries where the number of firms is few, then penalties to deter unwanted quits (e.g., nonvested rights), penalties for involuntary termination (e.g., severance pay), and career planning supports should be greater for managers in firms of the latter kind. Those are the main predictions.

Those similarities notwithstanding, managerial contracting is also different. The most striking thing about managerial contracting is that this involves managers contracting with managers. Thus, although it is useful to view the firm as a "nexus of contract" (Jensen and Meckling 1976), that nexus is not entirely neutral: the management—because it contracts with everyone, itself included—is a privileged constituency.

This recalls the concerns of Berle-Means with managerial discretion. As heretofore indicated, the privileged status of managers is a foreseeable consequence of the separation of ownership from control. On our interpretation, this separation is not adventitious but is the cost-effective way to organize large firms with passive owners. Greater scope for the benefits of managerial discretion (informed judgment) is accompanied by greater scope for costly self-seeking by the managers (unwanted managerial discretion)—where the latter affords managers with opportunities to tilt things in their favor. That is the basic tradeoff, and the relevant comparative institutional question is what cost-effective safeguards should be introduced to mitigate unwanted managerial discretion.

Such issues are beyond the scope of this paper.[14] We merely observe (1) that although competition in product and capital markets induces managers to perfect their contracting relation with the firm, there is always a horizon problem (in that the relevant horizon for incumbent managers is normally shorter than is that of the firm); (2) that the recommendations by the American Law Institute that outside directors should dominate the membership of the audit, compensation, and nominating committees on the board of directors are potentially responsive to this condition;[15] and (3) that because the conditions of information asymmetry between capital and management vary among firms, the ownership and organization of firms ought to vary accordingly.[16]

3.3.6. THE GENERAL PUBLIC

The interests of the general public are served by (1) corporate efficiency, (2) competition, (3) environmental safety and preservation, (4) a competent judiciary, and (5) a well-working political process. The first of these is the central thrust of the paper, and we take the fourth item to be obvious. We briefly discuss competition, the environment, and politics.

Efficiency purposes can be frustrated by managerial preferences for a quiet life. Competition in product and capital markets limits those managerial propensities. In industries, moreover, where domestic competition is limited, global competition is an increasingly important check.

More generally, we expect that Schumpeterian "handing on" operates in the long run, where this always works "through a fall in the price to the new level of costs" (Schumpeter 1947, p. 155) whenever rivals are alert to new opportunities and are not prevented by purposive restrictions from adopting them. Efficiency gains not only support lower prices and larger output, but such gains release resources to be used for other productive social purposes. Vigilant antitrust thus has a continuing role to play.

Undisclosed environmental hazards, like undisclosed health hazards, are a concern. One can counsel corporations to be socially responsible in this respect, but such counsel then needs to be implemented. Unintended undervaluations of health hazards or of environmental hazards could lead even the socially responsible corporation to take inadequate measures. And the socially insensitive corporation will be unconcerned with adverse spillover effects.

Such failures will not be corrected by invoking costless regulation, assigning the job to a benign agency, and/or relying on an omniscient court—because none of these is a feasible alternative. This brings us to Realpolitik, which is the (sometimes unseemly) process through which sausage is made. Interest groups thus organize and contest the issues through the political process, the compromise results of which are then implemented through defective regulatory agencies and courts. Sometimes that will be the best that can be achieved (Moe 1990a, 1990b).

Unseemliness notwithstanding, we assume that the political process is working acceptably well—which is to say that while there may be occasion for specific reform, there is no overall case for general reform. In that event, if politics trumps economics rather than the reverse, then even if interest group politics lead to what appear to be large inefficiency losses (as revealed by applying the standard deadweight loss calculus), those losses may be irremediable. That is because "Maximum national income . . . is not the only goal of our nation as judged by policies adopted by our government—and government's goals as revealed by actual practice are more authoritative than those pronounced by professors of law or economics" (Stigler 1992, p. 459).

4. The Board of Overseers

"Good ideas" for reforming the modern corporation proliferate. Although many believe it would be a good idea to award all stakeholders voting rights on the board of directors, that idea does not survive careful comparative institutional analysis.

Whether the creation of a board of overseers is a much better idea is not demonstrated herein. It is motivated, however, by the fact that so many of the contractual "problems" that we identify have information asymmetries at their source. It further has the advantage that it leaves the owners of equity securely in control of the board of directors—which, we contend, is as it should be (see section 3.3.2).

We briefly describe and then assess the merits of a board of overseers.

4.1. Description

As shown in Table 10.1, we distinguish four types of boards: the board of directors, the board of trustees, the board of workers, and the board of overseers. We also distinguish five types of functions: information, operating

Table 10.1. Board Types and Purposes

Board type	Information	Board purposes		Management appointment and pay	Takeover
		Decision review			
		Operating	Strategic		
Directors	x		x	x	x
Trustees	x		x	x	
Workers	x	x			
Overseers	x				

decision review, strategic decision review, the appointment and compensation of managers, and the marketability of ownership.

All boards serve information disclosure purposes, but the board of directors and the board of trustees go beyond this to include the review of strategic decision making and to decide on the appointments and compensation of top managers. Also, whereas boards of trustees are used for nonprofit organizations (universities, foundations, charities, etc.), the board of directors is used in for-profit organizations (the corporation).[17] Because the charter of nonprofits prohibits them from distributing profits, seats on the board of trustees cannot be monetized (Hansmann 1980; Ben-Ner and van Hoomissen 1991)—at least not in the sense of creating salable shares and concentrating votes. This feature is reserved for boards of directors and elicits added control, in the event of serious underperformance, from competition in the capital market.

The board of workers corresponds, approximately, to the two-tier board of "codetermination." Workers have considerable knowledge about operating affairs and can often make useful contributions to those decisions. By contrast, worker participation at strategic and management levels is problematic: not only do most workers lack deep knowledge of strategic and management kinds, but worker participation at these levels would pose hazards for (hence would increase the cost of capital for) equity.

The board of overseers is the least ambitious board. Its purpose is to promote the disclosure of contract-relevant information, thereby permitting each constituency to make more informed (explicit or implicit) contracts.

4.2. Assessment

If the board of overseers is really an efficient solution to the legitimate needs of stakeholders, why hasn't it already been adopted? That is a good question for which we do not have a confident answer. One possibility is that managers view added oversight as a job hazard. Thus, even though the board of overseers does not have the right to review operating and strategic decisions and make management changes, the bright light of publicity can be discomfiting and have adverse career effects. Why run that risk?

A second possibility is that the board of overseers does not yield expected net gains—at least not in most corporations.[18] For one thing, managers whose decisions are subject to disclosure will have incentives to preposition defensively. That can lead to undue precaution. Also, defining the limits of disclosure will not be easy. Who decides, and on what criteria? Finally, disclosure can be frustrated. If regulatory commissions with specialized staff and a legal mandate cannot get to the bottom of things, why should we expect that a part-time board of overseers with disparate interests can do better?

We nonetheless repeat that most of the contractual problems that we identify in 3.3 are due to the strategic use of asymmetrical information in which the management of the corporation enjoys the advantage. What to do? Maybe the very modest constraints on the committee structure of the board of directors, as proposed by the Corporate Governance Project of the American Law Institute, are as much as can be done. (The net gains associated with even these very modest reforms, moreover, could be disputed.)

Conclusions

Many critics of the modern corporation approach it from a normative point of view in which a hypothetical ideal is used as the standard. Albeit interesting, many such criticisms lack operationality, in that they fail the remediableness criterion.

Other critics of the corporation approach the issues from the standpoint of power, but whether power disparities can be relieved with net gains is rarely addressed, much less displayed. As James March has put it, "Power has proven to be a disappointing concept. It tends to become a tautological label for the unexplained variance in a decision situation, or as a somewhat more political way of referring to differences in resources (endowments) in a system of bargaining and exchange" (1988, p. 6).

The intriguing concept of transaction cost was similarly disappointing and likewise tautological for a long time as well. The propensity to invoke transaction costs for purposes of ex post rationalization was overcome only upon (1) making the transaction the basic unit of analysis, (2) identifying and explicating the dimensions of transactions to which comparative contracting ramifications accrue, (3) predicting which transactions would be organized how (by working through the logic of efficient alignment), and (4) examining the data. As developed elsewhere, the efficient alignment hypothesis yields a predictive theory of organization that is broadly congruent with the data (Joskow 1988; Klein and Shelanski 1995).

Although our application of contractual reasoning to the modern corporation is mainly an exercise in positive economics, we do raise the possibility that information asymmetries (in which the management of the firm enjoys the advantage) can be relieved with net gains by introducing a "board of overseers." We do not, however, demonstrate that such a board would assuredly achieve cost-effective relief and we identify a series of obstacles.

We nevertheless aver that it would be superior to the solution favored by stakehold advocates, which is to invite everyone in and democratize the board of directors. Our arguments here are that (1) the principal needs of each constituency are best addressed in a specific way by perfecting the contractual interface between the corporation and each constituency, (2) the board of directors represents an efficiency response to the needs of equity investors, (3) awarding votes and vetoes to nonshareholders will result in an increase in the cost of capital, and (4) the main unmet need of each constituency appears to take the form of information asymmetry (whence the board of overseers).

We conclude by inviting rival main case frameworks to offer their explanations for the leading regularities of the modern corporation. Not only will a contest between rival theories deepen our understanding of the issues, but ours and rival predictions can be examined in relation to the data.

Appendix

It will facilitate the argument to examine transactions in intermediate product markets, but this is merely to give the argument concreteness. The same generic approach applies to all constituencies. Figure A displays the alternatives.

Assume that a firm has decided not to make but to buy a component, and assume further that suppliers are (1) knowledgeable about the hazards, if any, (2) competitively organized, and (3) risk-neutral. The prices at which product will be supplied therefore reflect expected break-even conditions. The break-even price that is associated with Node A is p_1. There being no

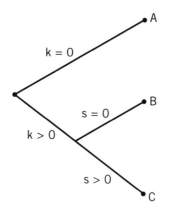

	p	k	p
Node A	p_1	0	0
Node B	$\bar{p}$	$\bar{k}$	0
Node C	$\hat{p}$	$\bar{k}$	$\hat{s}$

Figure A. Simple contractual schema.

hazards, $k = 0$. And since safeguards are unneeded, $s = 0$. (Each party can go its own way with little cost to the other.)

Node B is more interesting. The contractual hazard here is k. If the buyer is unable or unwilling to provide a safeguard, then $s = 0$. The corresponding break-even price is $\bar{p}$.

Node C poses the same contractual hazard, namely k. In this case, however, a safeguard in amount s is provided. The break-even price that is projected under these conditions is $\hat{p}$. It is elementary that $\hat{p} < \bar{p}$.

Note that Jeffrey Bradach and Robert Eccles contend that "mutual dependence [i.e., $k > 0$] between exchange partners . . . promotes] trust, [which] contrasts sharply with the argument central to transaction cost economics that . . . dependence . . . fosters opportunistic behavior" (1989, p. 111). What transaction cost economics says, however, is that because opportunistic agents will not self-enforce open-ended promises to behave responsibly, efficient exchange will be realized only if dependencies are *supported* by credible commitments. Wherein is trust implicated if parties to an exchange are farsighted and reflect the relevant hazards in terms of the exchange? (A better price $(\hat{p} < \bar{p})$ will be offered if the hazards $(k > 0)$ are mitigated by cost-effective contractual safeguards $(s > 0)$.)

Notes

1. See Wilson's contribution to this volume, "The Corporation as a Political Actor" (Chapter 13).

2. The main reason that we put so much stock in efficiency is that remediable inefficiency invites its own demise. Not only does efficiency operate as a carrot (immediate benefits accrue to those who realize private efficiency gains), but efficiency is a stick to which rivals are responsive. In the long run, the fitter (to be distinguished from the fittest) have better survival prospects (Simon 1983, p. 69).

3. Note in this connection that we concur with Nicholas Georgescu-Roegen that "the purpose of science in general is not prediction, but knowledge for its own sake" (1971, p. 37). Because, however, plausible explanations and ex post rationalizations in the social sciences are often easy to come by, Georgescu-Roegen goes on to insist that prediction is "the touchstone of scientific knowledge" (1971, p. 37). Prediction thus plays a vital role in helping to sort the wheat from the chaff.

4. Discussions with officials in the antitrust division of the U.S. Department of Justice convince me that the paper "Economies as an Antitrust Defense" (Williamson 1968), which displayed the large dead-weight losses that attended the prevailing inhospitality view of mergers, had a salutary effect on turning that policy around. (The basic model on which the paper was grounded was first set out in a memorandum to the then assistant attorney general and his deputy, Donald Turner and Edwin Zimmerman, respectively.)

5. The Panglossian form of the remediableness standard is this: All that is is efficient.

6. The unraveling issue is discussed by David Kreps (1990); the valuation problems in any firm, partnership included, are especially severe as assets become highly specific and firms take on large size (Williamson 1976). In the degree, therefore, to which large size and specific assets yield productivity gains, creating an organizational form that lives in perpetuity has advantages.

7. Our interpretation of these three conditions appeals to comparative analysis of a contractual kind. Harold Demsetz (1967) has advanced a property rights interpretation of the modern corporation.

8. Of course, very large and once-successful firms (such as General Motors and IBM in the 1980s) may be able to defer the reckoning for very long periods of time. Caution in authorizing growth—because there may be deferred costs—is simply part of an intelligent tradeoff. To be successful at one period of time (e.g., when computing is done on mainframes, customers are unfamiliar with their needs, and

sales and service capabilities are valued greatly) may require size that is nonviable in the face of later developments (e.g., personal computers and the growing sophistication of customers). If resources are deep and capital market controls apply weakly to very large firms, then change will often await natural managerial succession, when incumbents retire, and/or a crisis. That is not very satisfactory, but—awaiting new controls—may be unimprovable (irremediable) under the circumstances.

9. There are three main costs associated with expanding the franchise. First, presentation of partisan constituencies on the board invites opportunism. Regardless of having negotiated bilateral bargains with the firm, each individual constituency will attempt to extract additional concessions from the corporation in the course of board-level decision making.

Second, "unwarranted" participation on the board of directors by constituents that have struck Node C bargains will lead to contractual instability and inefficiency. Whereas prior to attaining board membership, parties to bilateral contracts relied on judicial or private ordering to fill contract gaps, access to the board increases the parties' reliance on fiduciary "intervention" (Macey and Miller 1993). The expectation of such intervention can lead to the deflection, distortion, and dissipation of corporate assets, and subsequently reduces the value of all existing bilateral contracts.

Third, extending representation or fiduciary considerations to numerous constituencies may result in a loss of managerial accountability and, thus, an attendant increase in managerial discretion. Attempts to balance the diverse interest of many stakeholders can produce policy ambiguities and give managers an "excuse" to pursue their own agenda.

10. Unlike firms, consumers are rarely able to integrate backward, thereby to relieve troublesome transactions by combining the ownership of both stages. Consumer co-ops accomplish this in some degree; backward integration into day care facilities is also observed (Ben-Ner and van Hoomissen 1919).

11. On the zone of acceptance in the employment contract, see Simon (1957a).

12. For a discussion of arbitration as a governance mechanism, see Lon Fuller (1963).

13. Another strategic concern (which may be mainly hypothetical), is the "inconsistent contracting strategy," according to which managers play a "heads I win, tails you lose" game with labor (Williamson 1985, pp. 318–19). To be sure, that game cannot be repeated indefinitely—because labor learns. Successor managements may ask to be excused, however, from the sins of their predecessors, which may be hard to refuse. Full disclosure of all major contracting hazards has obvious advantages.

14. For a thoughtful survey and discussion of the issues, see Roberta Romano (1993).

15. These recommendations are elaborated in the American Law Institute's *Principles of Corporate Governance: Analysis and Recommendations* (1994).

16. Ceteris paribus, high-tech firms will be more specialized and will have more concentrated ownership.

17. The partnership, which is also a for-profit form of organization, has still another type of board: the managing partners. A discussion is beyond the scope of this paper.

18. Industries where spillover hazards are obvious and potentially great may be an exception. Otherwise, the need for oversight may be obvious only after the fact.

References

American Law Institute. 1994. *Principles of Corporate Governance: Analysis and Recommendations*. St. Paul, Minn.: American Law Institute Press.

Aoki, Masahiko. 1990. "Toward an Economic Model of the Japanese Firm." *Journal of Economic Literature* 28 (March): 1–27.

Baumol, W. J. 1959. *Business Behavior, Value and Growth*. New York: Macmillan.

Ben-Ner, Avner, and Theresa van Hoomissen. 1991. "Nonprofit Organizations in the Mixed Economy." *Annuals of Public and Cooperative Economics* 62:521–50.

Berle, Adolf A., and Gardiner C. Means Jr. 1932. *The Modern Corporation and Private Property*. New York: Macmillan.

Bonin, John, and Louis Putterman. 1987. *Economics of Cooperation and Labor Managed Economies*. New York: Cambridge University Press.

Bradach, Jeffrey, and Robert Eccles. 1989. "Price, Authority, and Trust." *American Review of Sociology* 15:97–118.

Brodeur, Paul. 1985a. "Annals of Law: The Asbestos Industry on Trial: I—A Failure to Warn." *New Yorker*, June 10, pp. 49–101.

———. 1985b. "Annals of Law: The Asbestos Industry on Trial: II—Discovery." *New Yorker*, June 17, pp. 45–111.

———. 1985c. "Annals of Law: The Asbestos Industry on Trial: III—Judgement." *New Yorker*, June 24, pp. 37–77.

———. 1985d. "Annals of Law: The Asbestos Industry on Trial; IV—Bankruptcy." *New Yorker*, July 1, pp. 36–80.

Chandler, Alfred D., Jr. 1962. *Strategy and Structure*. Cambridge, Mass.: MIT Press.

Coase, Ronald H. 1964. "The Regulated Industries: Discussion." *American Economic Review* 54 (May): 194–97.

Collins, Denis. 1994. "The Toronto Conference: Reflections on Stakeholder Theory." *Business and Society* 33, no. 1 (April): 82–131.

Commons, John R. 1932. "The Problem of Correlating Law, Economics, and Ethics." *Wisconsin Law Review* 8:3–26.

Crozier, Michel. 1964. *The Bureaucratic Phenomenon*. Chicago: University of Chicago Press.

Cyert, Richard M., and James G. March. 1963. *A Behavioral Theory of the Firm*. Englewood Cliffs, N.J.: Prentice-Hall.

Dahl, R. A. 1970. "Power to Workers?" *New York Review of Books*. November 19, pp. 20–24.

Demsetz, Harold. 1967. "Toward a Theory of Property Rights." *American Economic Review* 57 (May): 347–59.

Dixit, A. 1980. "The Role of Investment in Entry Deterrence." *Economic Journal* 90 (March): 95–106.

Dore, Ronald. 1983. "Goodwill and the Spirit of Market Capitalism." *British Journal of Sociology* 34 (December): 459–82.

Elster, Jon. 1994. "Arguing and Bargaining in Two Constituent Assemblies." Unpublished manuscript, remarks given at the University of California, Berkeley.

Freeman, R. E., and W. M. Evan. 1990. "Corporate Governance: A Stakeholder Interpretation." *Journal of Behavioral Economics* 19, no. 4:337–59.

Fuller, Lon L. 1963. "Collective Bargaining and the Arbitrator." *Wisconsin Law Review* 39 (January): 3–46.

Georgescu-Roegen, Nicholas. 1971. *The Entropy Law and Economic Process*. Cambridge, Mass.: Harvard University Press.

Gerlach, Michael. 1992. *Alliance Capitalism*. Berkeley: University of California Press.

Gilson, Ronald, and Reinier Kraakman. 1984. "The Mechanisms of Market Efficiency." *Virginia Law Review* 70, no. 4:549–644.

Hansmann, Henry. 1980. "The Role of Nonprofit Enterprise." *Yale Law Journal* 89 (April): 835–901.

———. 1988. "The Ownership of the Firm." *Journal of Law, Economics, and Organization* 4 (fall): 267–303.

Heide, Jan, and George John. 1988. "The Role of Dependence Balancing in Safeguarding Transaction-Specific Assets in Conventional Channels." *Journal of Marketing* 52 (January): 20–35.

———. 1990. "Alliances in Industrial Purchasing: The Determinants of Joint Action in Buyer-Supplier Relationships." *Journal of Marketing Research* 27:24–36.

Howse, Robert, and Michael Trebilcock. 1993. "Protecting the Employment Bargain." *University of Toronto Law Journal* 43:751–92.

Jensen, Michael, and William Meckling. 1976. "Theory of the Firm: Managerial Behavior, Agency Costs, and Capital Structure." *Journal of Financial Economics* 3 (October): 305–60.

Joskow, Paul L. 1988. "Asset Specificity and the Structure of Vertical Relationships: Empirical Evidence." *Journal of Law, Economics, and Organization* 4 (spring): 95–117.

Klein, Benjamin, and K. B. Leffler. 1981. "The Role of Market Forces in Assuring Contractual Performance." *Journal of Political Economy* 89 (August): 615–41.

Kreps, David M. 1990. "Corporate Culture and Economic Theory." In *Perspectives on Positive Political Economy*, edited by James Alt and Kenneth Shepsle. New York: Cambridge University Press, pp 90–143.

Macey, Jonathan, and Geoffrey Miller. 1993. "Corporate Stakeholders: A Contractual Perspective." *University of Toronto Law Journal* 43:401–23.

March, James G. 1988. *Decisions and Organizations*. Oxford: Basil Blackwell.

Marris, Robin. 1964. *The Economic Theory of Managerial Capitalism*. New York: Free Press.

McCullough, David. 1992. *Truman*. New York: Simon and Schuster.

Michels, Robert. 1962. Political Parties. Glencoe, Ill.: Free Press.

Moe, Terry. 1990a. "Political Institutions: The Neglected Side of the Story." *Journal of Law, Economics, and Organization* 6 (special issue): 213–53.

———. 1990b. "The Politics of Structural Choice: Toward a Theory of Public Bureaucracy." In *Organization Theory*, edited by Oliver Williamson. New York: Oxford University Press, pp. 116–53.

O'Connor, Marleen A. 1993. "The Human Capital Era: Reconceptualizing Corporate Law to Facilitate Labor-Management Cooperation." *Cornell Law Review* 78:899–965.

Roe, Mark. 1990. "Political and Legal Restraints on Ownership and Control of Public Companies." *Journal of Financial Economics* 27:7–41.

Romano, Roberta. 1993. *Foundations of Corporate Law*. New York: Oxford University Press.

Schleifer, Andrei, and Robert Vishny. 1991. "Asset Sales and Debt Capacity." Unpublished manuscript.

Schumpeter, Joseph A. 1947. "The Creative Response in Economic History." *Journal of Economic History* 7 (November): 149–59.

Shelanski, Howard, and Peter Klein. 1995. "Empirical Work in Transaction Cost Economics." *Journal of Law, Economics, and Organization* 11 (October): 335–61.

Simon, Herbert. 1957a. *Administrative Behavior*. 2d ed. New York: Macmillan.

———. 1957b. *Models of Man*. New York: Wiley.

———. 1983. *Reason in Human Affairs*. Stanford, Calif.: Stanford University Press.

———. 1985. "Human Nature in Politics: The Dialogue of Psychology with Political Science." *American Political Science Review* 79:293–304.

Stigler, George J. 1992. "Law of Economics?" *Journal of Law and Economics* 35 (October): 455–68.

Stone, Katherine. 1981. "The Postwar Paradigm in American Labor Law." *Yale Law Journal* 90 (June): 1509–80.

Stone, Katherine. 1993. "Policing Employment Contracts Within the Nexus-of-Contracts Firm." *University of Toronto Law Journal* 43:353–78.

Summers, Clyde. 1982. "Codetermination in the United States: A Projection of

Problems and Potentials." *Journal of Comparative Corporate Law and Security Regulation* 4:155–83.

Teece, David J. 1986. "Profiting from Technological Innovation." *Research Policy* 15 (December): 285–305.

Williamson, Oliver E. 1964. *The Economics of Discretionary Behavior: Managerial Objectives in a Theory of the Firm.* Englewood Cliffs, N.J.: Prentice-Hall.

———. 1968. "Economies as an Antitrust Defense: The Welfare Tradeoffs." *American Economic Review* 58 (March): 18–35.

———. 1970. *Corporate Control and Business Behavior.* Englewood Cliffs, N.J.: Prentice-Hall.

———. 1975. *Markets and Hierarchies: Analysis and Antitrust Implications.* New York: Free Press.

———. 1976. "Franchise Bidding for Natural Monopolies—In General and with Respect to CATV." *Bell Journal of Economics* 7 (spring): 73–104.

———. 1981. "Saccharin: An Economist's View." In *The Scientific Basis of Health and Safety Regulation,* edited by Robert Crandall and Lester Lave. Washington, D.C.: Brookings Institution, 131–151.

———. 1985. *The Economic Institutions of Capitalism.* New York: Free Press.

———. 1988. "Corporate Finance and Corporate Governance." *Journal of Finance* 43 (July): 567–91.

———. 1991a. "Comparative Economic Organization: The Analysis of Discrete Structural Alternatives." *Administrative Science Quarterly* 36 (June): 269–96.

———. 1991b. "Strategizing, Economizing, and Economic Organization." *Strategic Management Journal* 12:75–94.

———. 1996. "The Politics and Economics of Redistribution and Inefficiency." In *The Mechanisms of Governance.* New York: Oxford University Press, Chapter 8.

11

The Corporation as a Dispenser
of Welfare and Security

✦

GREGORY ACS

EUGENE STEUERLE

The Multiple Roles of the Modern Corporation

The image of the modern corporation, run by managers trying to maximize shareholders' profits, belies the vital role today's corporations play in promoting the commonweal. Indeed, today's corporations promote social welfare directly by serving as an agent for the employee in purchasing pension, health, and other welfare benefit plans and for the government in collecting records and revenue and partially administering related public programs like social security. Governments also enhance the corporation's natural agency role by providing both public mandates and private incentives for it to perform a variety of social welfare functions.

In this chapter we trace the development of the corporation's agency roles by focusing on how the government has come to use the corporation to promote and administer social welfare programs like social security and on how the corporation has become the primary vehicle for providing health and retirement benefits for the majority of Americans. Although this social welfare role is not entirely new, it is only in recent decades that it has received much scholarly attention. Indeed, Mason's classic 1959 volume *The Corporation in Modern Society* failed to devote even a chapter to this issue.

The corporation's role in social welfare is a direct consequence of its natural structural and economic capabilities. Both government and employees take advantage of the modern corporation's size and accounting sophistication, as well as its communication and contact with large employee pools and various suppliers of goods and services. The government relies on, and often requires, corporations to operate and administer parts of its social welfare programs. At a minimum, it engages the corporation as collector of premiums or taxes and as the initial record keeper of data that determine eligibility for receipt of benefits from many public social welfare programs. Of particular importance here are those programs where benefits are related to earnings from employment.

Employees, in turn, look to the corporation to be an agent or intermediary on their behalf and to purchase many private welfare goods and services, such as group insurance services, more efficiently and cheaply than if purchased individually. From the corporation's perspective, if it can purchase goods and services for employees at bargain prices (whether because of bargaining power or favorable tax treatment), it can effectively increase employee pay at no cost to itself, attain goodwill with labor, and/or capture all or part of the excess of employee value over employer cost.

Federal tax policy in the United States adds additional incentives to those natural market forces leading corporations to provide their workers with social goods like private health insurance and pensions. This special tax relief usually is not available if funds flow through other institutional agents or intermediaries such as churches or clubs or if no intermediary is used, as when health or pension coverage is purchased directly by a private individual from a private insurer. Hence, the employers' natural role as an agent is converted into a primary role by tax inducements that encourage employees both to buy welfare benefits and to buy them almost solely through their own employer.

Employer-provided welfare benefits for the most part have been complements to, rather than substitutes for, public social welfare benefits. Supplements to wages and salaries have grown from about one-half of 1 percent of GDP in 1929 to over 10 percent in 1992—with amounts divided about equally between private pension and welfare funds and employer contributions to public social insurance such as Old Age and Survivors Insurance in Social Security (U.S. Bureau of Economic Analysis 1993). The private growth rate has been influenced considerably both by tax rate increases (and, hence, larger incentives) and by expansions in private demand for more health and retirement services as the economy has grown.

While coverage rates for pensions and health insurance rose almost steadily for decades after their introduction, in recent years they appear to have either stabilized or actually dropped (U.S. Department of Labor

1994). Differences in size of benefits remain quite significant across industries. In addition, recent increases in inequality of cash wages do not appear to have been offset by greater equality in private welfare benefits; health benefits, in particular, became more unequal in the 1980s due to drops in percentages of employees covered (Acs and Steuerle 1993). At the end of the twentieth century, these concerns have led to considerable legislative debate and activity over how to insure some level of minium benefits for those uninsured for health and those likely to have little in the way of future pension income. Almost all proposed legislation requires the corporation to expand its role either as provider of private benefits or as partial administrator of public programs.

In the remainder of this paper we examine these issues in more depth. First, we discuss the nature of the corporation's role as agent for the government and the worker. Next, we examine in more detail the historical evolution of the corporation's agency role on behalf of workers, in particular, through provision of health insurance and pensions. This natural agency role is enhanced by government tax incentives, as well as other economic forces such as the rise in demand for health insurance and in the cost of supporting many more years in retirement. Finally, we will discuss more recent trends in the provision of nonwage benefits and their possible implications for the corporation in its unavoidable role as a primary social welfare agent for the workers and governments of tomorrow.

The Corporation as Agent

The Corporation and Universal Government Programs

It is the very essence of government to promote the common good. A conventional method is to provide public goods and services directly and to finance them through general, rather than earmarked, revenues. Over the past century, however, the government has increasingly turned to the corporation as an agent who serves as a principal enforcer and administrator of many earmarked social insurance programs. Although our focus in this paper is primarily on private social welfare benefits provided by the corporation, they cannot be understood apart from direct social insurance programs such as social security and unemployment insurance. These public programs have grown hand in hand with private social welfare programs, partly in response to a similar set of demands. Direct public programs are even more dominant in most industrial countries outside of the United States, where a larger percentage of both health benefits and pension benefits are received directly from the government.[1] Regardless of mix and country, however, the modern corporation plays a major role in financing and organizing both private and public programs.

To understand why the corporation's role has become so vital to the government, we must briefly examine why the government has moved beyond strict welfare program programs for the poor toward programs that involve more universal participation. While health insurance and pension coverage began as essentially private goods, they became a matter of public concern as richer societies became more loathe to let the sick go untreated and the elderly go hungry.

For a variety of reasons, poor-only programs were usually considered inadequate, and governments tried to extend coverage to much larger pools of participants, mainly employees, starting first with larger firms. One argument is political: some believe that the public is more likely to support universal programs in which they are participants, not simply taxpayers.[2] In our view, however, the issue is much more complex.

As an administrative and budgetary matter, higher participation rates—whether through social security–type schemes or private coverage—reduce the need for stricter, means-tested welfare transfers. Means tests are usually more inaccurate and degrading and require more interaction between citizen and bureaucracy over issues such as eligibility.

As an issue of equity, those who fail to prefund their own pensions and health insurance are more likely than others to fall back upon the government for assistance when they become old or ill. Universality, therefore, is as much a requirement on everyone to pay as it is an entitlement for everyone to receive.

As an issue of efficiency, the existence of minimum public benefits in a means-tested program creates disincentives to pay for one's own health and pension in absence of a mandate or countervailing incentives. For programs providing means-tested insurance in old age, for instance, there are powerful incentives for individuals to spend down their wealth in years before retirement or to transfer assets to children as a means of qualifying for the government programs.

Thus, there is an important social insurance argument for encouraging or mandating participation in social welfare programs, either private or public. Essentially, those who are young and healthy are urged or compelled to contribute to a system while they can—before they lose their earnings due to retirement or face the costs associated with bad health.[3]

It is not our purpose here to determine whether each particular type of government intervention turned out to be appropriate, met objectives well, or displaced other useful activities. It is crucial, however, to understand the implications of societal decisions to provide even minimum levels of well-being to everyone. That decision inevitably forces further decisions about requirements or inducements toward more universal coverage. If more universal participation is sought, and it often is, the next step is to find those agents who can help bring about or enforce that participation. It is here that the corporation's role becomes vital.

Note that the corporation seldom turns out to be an agent for stricter, means-tested, welfare programs; after all, it would be a relatively inefficient intermediary since its working employees usually earn too much to qualify for such programs. Governments, however, *do* require or induce corporations to become agents or instruments in the next rung—that broader social welfare policy that seeks to limit the number of individuals who will need to fall back on purer welfare programs.

In practice, the demand for more universal participation in insurance and pension programs has led worldwide to laws mandating participation in public programs, mandating participation in private programs, or subsidizing participation in private programs. In the latter two cases, the programs are usually employer-sponsored. Interestingly, in the pension area, most governments have been more reluctant to go the middle route of requiring contributions to private retirement plans.[4] All three approaches by government, however, are motivated essentially by the same rationales for more universal coverage.

The Corporation as Government Administrator and Accountant

But why does the government turn to the corporation? The size of many corporations, particularly their employment pool, makes them perhaps the best private contacts and administrators for more universal programs. The only other private social institutions of large size and widespread membership are the churches and unions, but their weaker administrative capabilities have never made them viable alternatives as primary administrators. Some unions, however, do operate as sponsors of insurance plans and serve as an additional layer of intermediation between employer payments and insurance companies.[5]

With size, the corporation also developed elaborate accounting systems. The investor or manager, separated by several bureaucratic layers from the work being performed, required an accounting system to determine which activities, plants, investments, and groups were profitable and which were not. Along with these accounting systems came modestly accurate statements of the earnings of individuals. Although designed mainly to help the corporation in its own internal decision making, these earnings statements became the means by which taxes on workers could be assessed and earnings-related benefits, such as pensions and workers compensation, could be determined.

Indeed, the accounting capabilities of the corporation far exceed those of small businesses and farms, the dominant form of employment until a few decades ago. Moreover, because there are fewer formal relationships between payers and payees in small-scale enterprises, the government has limited ability to enforce accurate reporting: when the payor and payee are one, there are no separate ledgers to check.[6]

The government has found multiple uses for the corporations' accounting capacity. The corporation has become the primary collector of revenues from income taxes, social insurance taxes, and, outside the United States, value-added taxes. In industrial countries these taxes are by far the principal sources of financing for government.

In many government social insurance programs, benefit payments from the government are related directly to the amount of wages subject to tax. The corporation turns over to the government or to quasi-government agencies, first, the taxes, "contributions," or "premiums" collected under those programs and, second, the earnings levels from which eligibility for benefits is calculated. For example, in Social Security Old Age Assistance or in unemployment compensation, the employer collects taxes on earnings and turns over to the government a precise statement of the earnings on which tax has been based. These earnings statements are then maintained by the government and used in formulas that determine final levels of benefits to be paid in case of retirement or unemployment.

Many government social welfare programs are employment-based and provide no benefits to individuals without a past nexus to the corporation or employer. Thus, an unemployed entrant into the workforce cannot receive unemployment compensation, nor can a disabled person without past earnings collect Social Security Disability Insurance. In many cases the corporation establishes a relationship with the government social insurance agency that on both the contribution and the benefit side has many similarities to its relationship with private insurance companies.

When the government subsidizes employee benefits, rather than providing them directly, it still turns to the corporation as its agent. It should not be surprising that government involvement here is also extensive, as it regulates that which it subsidizes. For example, the government first requires that corporations allocate the value of tax-favored purchases correctly when measuring both their own and their employees' taxable income, and it sets a variety of limits on the extent to which compensation can be paid in the form of tax-free pension benefits.

Other regulations require the corporation (both as payor of benefits and as the employee's agent) to ensure that subsidized benefits are distributed according to various social standards. For example, the tax laws contain numerous "antidiscrimination rules" to ensure that tax benefits of privately provided pension and health plans are fairly distributed. Thus, health or pension benefits cannot be paid only to highly compensated members of firms. Pension plans must also meet certain funding and fiduciary standards: money must be set aside today to cover benefits promised for tomorrow, and assets should not be held in a form that is unduly risky.

All of these rules, of course, add to the complexity of administration. While smaller organizations often find the associated costs of regulation high relative to the benefits provided, larger corporations possess the accounting and administrative capacity to provide these benefits relatively more efficiently.

The Corporation as Employee Bargaining Agent

Totally independent from any government mandate or incentive, the large scale of the modern corporation allows it to be an efficient bargaining agent for benefits sought by employees. As will be seen, the corporation offered private pensions and health insurance long before significant government incentives were provided. The corporation can purchase many items at lower cost than if purchased directly by the individual, in part because transactions costs are often much less when one purchaser buys for many individuals. Largely because the employer can purchase social goods like group insurance at lower per capita cost than individuals, employee valuation of compensation is often in excess of employer cost (Smeeding 1983).

In the case of pension and health insurance, moreover, larger employers also provide convenient risk pools. Adverse selection becomes less likely in larger groups. It occurs when low-risk purchasers try to opt out of plans containing high-risk individuals who raise average costs. High-risk individuals congregated together, in turn, face higher average costs and often are unable to bear the full cost of their insurance.

The purchaser always has more information about health status than can be observed by the insurer. Hence, individuals and small groups are more likely to seek insurance when they have a higher probability of incurring the event that generates insurance benefits. Insurance companies, therefore, often charge a small employer higher-than-average premiums for health and disability insurance. When individuals purchase insurance through a larger employer-provided pool, on the other hand, the risks to the insurance company are reduced. Once again, employees of larger organizations and corporations typically can buy insurance more cheaply than can individuals acting alone or in small groups.

The role of the corporation in providing social welfare benefits, therefore, is a natural role. Government incentives only enhance that role. It is often difficult to separate the impact of natural and government incentives when examining changes in the corporation's role in providing private, but subsidized, social welfare benefits.

The Evolution of Nonwage Compensation

Figure 11.1 displays the complementary growth in both public and private nonwage compensation since 1929. Supplements to wages and salaries have grown from around one-half of 1 percent of U.S. gross domestic product (GDP) in 1929 to over 10 percent by 1992. Employer contributions to

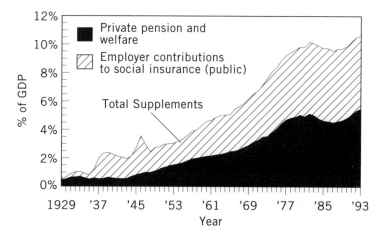

Figure 11.1. Supplements to wages and salaries as a percent of GDP: 1929–1993 (excludes directors' fees from 1948 to 1993). *Source*: Bureau of Economic Analysis, *National Income and Product Accounts.*

public social insurance occupy about half of the total, while private pension and welfare funds occupy the other half (U.S. Bureau of Economic Analysis 1993).

Private pension and welfare funds can be broken down further. In 1948, for instance, employer contributions to these funds were still only at a level of about 1 percent of GDP but rose to over 5 percent by 1992 (see Figure 11.2). Pensions and group health insurance were by far the dominant items; the remainder of this section focuses in more detail on some of the history and rationale behind the growth of these two items.

Employer-Sponsored Health Insurance

The growth of employer-sponsored health insurance is related directly to individual demand for health insurance coverage. In industrial countries this demand has been met by both public and private provision of health care. Countries that have relied less on public provision have tended to place much greater reliance on private care.

In contrast to all other industrialized nations except South Africa, the United States relies on the private sector—especially corporations—to provide health insurance for the lion's share of its population. This unique system evolved out of over a century of often conflicting economic and sociopolitical forces.

The groundwork for the U.S. system of employer-sponsored insurance was laid down as the country moved from being an agrarian to an industrial economy. During the Industrial Revolution, however, corporations tended to provide health care rather than health insurance. Indeed, firms in several industries in which industrial accidents were relatively common, such as railroads, mining, and lumber, saw it in their interest to provide some medical care to their workers. Logging, laying track, and mining all took place outside of population centers, and employers hired doctors and established hospitals in order to keep their workers healthy and productive. One railroad company began to employ doctors as early as 1860. Steelmakers and other manufacturers followed suit in the 1880s (Starr 1982).

Company-provided health care served several purposes: (1) it provided a healthier workforce; (2) it helped the companies control their workers by disallowing disability claims and the like; and (3) it helped bond the worker to the corporation and sometimes took leverage away from the unions. Most employers, however, found it unnecessary to provide any health benefits, and many workers found medical care to be sufficiently inexpensive that they did not feel an acute need for health insurance.

At the turn of the century, the Progressive movement embraced the idea of universal health care coverage (Starr 1982). The idea, however, met strong opposition from three diverse but powerful interest groups: doctors, corporations, and unions. The American Medical Association (AMA) not only opposed universal coverage but initially opposed all efforts to provide health insurance, fearing that third-party payers or administrators might exert undue influence on their practices and profits. Corporations opposed national insurance because they believed it would allow their employees to miss work. And initially, even unions opposed universal public insurance because they feared that government-provided benefits would erode the solidarity of their membership. This early failure to establish government-sponsored universal health care left the door open for an expanded role for private-sector, employer-sponsored insurance.

Private insurance plans themselves began to take hold in the United States prior to the Great Depression. During the 1920s, however, medical costs began to rise relative to income—again, due partly to expanded demand for these services. Insurance became more important to workers: higher levels of demand led to an increase in the probability of incurring high or catastrophic costs, which, in turn, raised the probability that the individual would not have the money to buy the service.

To health care providers, especially hospitals, insurance also became more appealing because it meant that bills more likely would be paid. Against this backdrop, the first Blue Cross plan was established in Dallas, Texas, in 1929. The Dallas public school employees entered into an agreement with Baylor University Hospital to provide services as needed in exchange for a regular premium payment. Other community hospitals soon followed with similar arrangements. In 1932, community hospitals in Sacramento jointly entered into contracts for hospital services with employed persons, offering "free choice" of physicians and hospitals within their "network."

At the same time, groups of physicians entered into contracts with various employee groups. For example, in 1929 Los Angeles city government employees entered into an agreement with two physicians, Donald Ross, and H. Clifford Loos, who would provide medical services for the employees and their families. This plan is often cited as the first prepaid group practice (Field and Shapiro 1993). The mutual benefit association of railway workers in Dallas serves as another example. The association contracted with a private clinic for medical services, while workers and company each contributed monthly premiums. By 1930 the plans covered 1.2 million employees and 1 to 2 million dependents (Somers and Somers 1961).

Medical costs continued to rise over the 1930s, and Blue Cross plans became more prevalent. While the AMA continued to oppose universal insurance, it softened its stance toward the idea of prepaid or contracted health care and accepted insurance for hospital services. By the end of the decade, insurance for physicians services took hold in the form of Blue Shield plans. Yet wide-scale, private health insurance was still in its infancy.

With the onset of U.S. involvement in World War II, employer-sponsored health insurance took firmer root. One temporary enticement came about because of wage and price controls. Employers competing for scarce labor resources during the war found they could avoid such controls by compensating workers in the form of nonwage benefits like health insurance. Linking insurance to employment also made sense for insurers because (1) it provided a natural way to pool risks, diminishing the problem of adverse selection[7] and (2) it reduced administrative costs since insurers could market to employers rather than individuals.

After the war, government policy encouraged the link even further. In 1947 the Taft-Hartley Act stated that nonwage compensation could be included in union contract negotiations. In 1949 the National Labor Relations Board ruled that health benefits could be included in the total compensation package. The 1954 Tax Code cemented this relationship by codifying the previous practice of allowing insurance premiums to be taken as nontaxable compensation by individuals. By this time 60 percent of all workers had insurance for hospital services.

By 1991, seventy million workers received employer-sponsored health insurance from their own employers, and another seventy million were covered as dependents under employer-group plans. Overall, two-thirds of all nonelderly Americans received health coverage through this voluntary system.

Although institutions and government policy were evolving rapidly over this time, the increase in employer-provided insurance cannot be separated from consumer demand. Over much of the twentieth century, both health care and health care insurance appear to have been income-elastic services, that is, services that were demanded in increasing proportions as real income rose. As demand for other goods and services—adequate food, running water, shelter, and so forth—became more satiated, the demand for health care absorbed increasing proportions of gains in real income over time. One needs to be careful, therefore, about historical interpretations that imply that institutional changes among employers and government were somehow independent of these economic forces; more likely, the institutions themselves responded to the changes in individual demand.

Pension Benefits

Pension plans began to emerge in the last quarter of the nineteenth century in response to various social and demographic trends. Increasing urbanization and the associated dislocation of extended families reduced the human and financial resources available to take care of the elderly within the family. This problem was compounded by the fact that the average life span was increasing—indeed, most individuals did not survive to age sixty-five until the current century. Finally, elderly workers were simply less productive than younger workers, and, unlike farms that were integrated with the home, corporations needed a socially acceptable way to replace the old with the young. Providing retirement benefits was one way of addressing these needs.

In the late 1800s a few corporations initiated mutual benefit systems known as "establishment funds" to cover employees of the company. As recorded by the Bureau of Labor Statistics, only 5 were set up before 1871. Over 120 more were created in the next two decades. Benefits were paid out as pensions, as well as death and disability benefits. These relief funds generally were financed by voluntary employee dues. In some cases a form of profit sharing or a company welfare plan was funded by the employer's contribution (Henderson 1908).

The earliest known industrial pension plan in the United States was established by the American Express Company in 1875; the Baltimore and Ohio Railroad followed in 1880. Over the next half century, pension plans were adopted in all the major industries except agriculture. By 1930 virtually all railroads had pensions covering most of their 1.5 million workers, while 168 manufacturing companies covered about 1.3 million employees with their plans (Latimer 1932).

Changes in the tax system contributed to this early growth in pension plans. In 1913 the United States adopted the individual income tax, and in 1916 corporations were allowed to deduct, as "ordinary and necessary expenses," the actual payments to retired workers. A new regulation in 1919 allowed the deduction of corporate donations to an employee pension trust as if they went to a charitable institution. The Revenue Act of 1926 deferred the taxation of employee benefits until the payments were actually distributed (Graebner 1980). That favorable tax treatment did not induce faster growth should not be surprising given the very low marginal tax rates prevailing at the time. With only 5 percent of the population paying any income taxes, no one paying social security taxes, and a top personal individual rate of only 8 percent, the tax advantage for pensions was quite small.[8]

Corporate retirement programs still were far from comprehensive. As of 1932 only 15 percent of American workers were potentially covered under pension plans, and these were more likely to be workers with above-average wages. The systems usually required fifteen to thirty years service, and only 10 percent of the plans legally committed the firm to paying benefits (Graebner 1980).

Pension plan development in the 1930s was significantly affected by two events: the Great Depression and the passage of the Social Security Act of 1935 (Seburn 1991). Prior to the Great Depression, Americans were reluctant to turn to the social security-type schemes that had been adopted in many European countries several years earlier. One reason may have been the development of a larger and more robust life insurance market and the availability of private retirement annuities (Weaver 1983). In the depression, however, some employer pension plans went bankrupt and growth was temporarily halted. According to the Department of Commerce, employers' charges to operating expenses for pension purposes dropped from $128 million in 1929 to $97 million in 1933. After this drop, the operating costs rose to $162 million in 1936 (Dearing 1954).

Private pensions obviously were not abandoned even with a depression under way. Pension and health insurance programs were seldom totally canceled despite the unsteady economy; according to one source, only 7 percent of the existing programs were canceled since the onset of the Great Depression (Dobbin 1992), although modifications and cutbacks could have been quite significant and workers often had only moderate rights vested in the plans. To cut back costs, many businesses that maintained their plans began requiring employees to contribute to pension plans (Seburn 1991).

The advent of social security, interestingly enough, did not halt the growth in demand for private pension coverage. After the depression, the growth in private pension benefits was positively correlated with growth in social security benefits, which were first paid out in 1940.

Social security might even have induced demand for private pensions. Plans for retirement often became centered around the social security normal retirement age of sixty-five and, lately, the early retirement age of sixty-two, as well as earnings tests that appeared to take away benefits if one worked. People began to retire much earlier at the same time that they were living much longer and were becoming healthier. Not only did expected retirement spans eventually begin to approach two decades, but many more people began to live to retirement. Hence, the required amount of funding necessary to support life in retirement became much larger, and the demand for private pensions may have grown as a consequence.

In the wake of World War II, tax incentives also increased significantly. By 1948 over half of the population had income tax liabilities,[9] and the social security taxes on earnings had also been established (although its rates initially were modest, reaching a combined employer-employee rate of 3.0 percent in 1950). In 1950, 9.8 million workers, representing 25.0 percent of private wage and salary workers, participated in pension plans. By 1980, 45.0 percent of private wage and salary workers, or 35.9 million workers, were covered by some type of plan (Turner and Beller 1992).

Over the 1970s and '80s, government regulation of pension plans increased. In 1974 Congress passed the Employee Retirement Income Security Act (ERISA), which increased the equity and stability of private pensions by imposing standards for minimum funding and for fiduciary conduct.[10] The legislation also established tighter vesting standards; that is, the time schedule under which individuals can lay claim to an increasing share of their pension benefits. ERISA requirements were tightened under the Tax Reform Act of 1986 and the Omnibus Budget Reconciliation Act (OBRA) of 1987.

In recent years corporations have increasingly offered pension coverage through defined contribution plans—plans under which the employer puts aside for individual workers a set amount of money at designated intervals but carries no liability for insuring some level of payment in the future. The worker essentially is responsible for managing his or her own retirement account.

The many reasons for this development include increasing regulation of defined benefit plans; taxes on defined benefit plans (through the Pension Benefit Guarantee Corporation) that tend to subsidize underfunded pension plans and penalize those that are fully funded; further development of employee stock ownership, stock bonus, and profit-sharing plans; and the demand for portable pension rights (inflation typically plays havoc with the value of defined benefit plans and makes benefits much less valuable to employees who leave an employer before age fifty).[11]

Between 1975 and 1989, active participation in defined benefit plans remained stable at twenty-seven million, while active participation in defined contribution plans grew from four to fifteen million—although much of the latter figure includes participation in multiple plans by the same individual (Pemberton and Holmes 1995). There is also an increasing tendency to withdraw monies from these defined contribution plans before retirement.

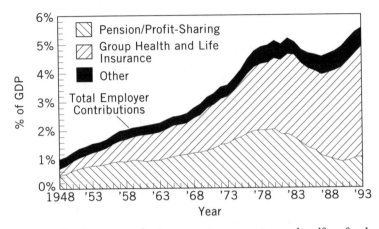

Figure 11.2. Employer contributions to private pension and welfare funds as a percent of GDP: 1948–1993. *Source*: Bureau of Economic Analysis, *National Income and Product Accounts*, and *Survey of Current Business*.

The Changing Shape of Employee Compensation

Today, the modern corporation is entrenched in its role as agent for its employees, purchasing and administering health and pension benefits. Recent trends, however, suggest this role is changing. Indeed, changes in the distribution of wages and benefits over the past twenty-five years have forced corporations and workers to reexamine their compensation packages. After two decades of strong growth following World War II, cash wages for full-time male workers stagnated in the 1970s and '80s.

At the same time, but especially in the 1980s, many nonwage benefits became much more costly. For example, payroll taxes to finance mandatory benefits like social security continued to rise (the combined employer-employee tax rate itself rose from 9.6 percent in 1970 to 15.3 percent in 1990).[12] Corporate pension fund liabilities also increased in the 1970s as federal pension funding requirements became more stringent. The stock market boom of the 1980s provided only temporary relief from requirements for large additional contributions (see Figure 11.2). Meanwhile, the cost of health care and health insurance accelerated at twice the rate of inflation (Economic Report of the President 1995). Indeed, employer payments for health insurance are now in excess of payments to pension plans because of the increase in health care costs (see Figure 11.2).

The increase in the cost of benefits required changes in the modern corporation's agency role. The corporation had to do more than provide convenient risk pools and serve as accounting agent. With higher costs of health care, its bargaining role became increasingly important. This is not surprising; if one accepts the economic argument that employees really pay for most or all benefits through lower cash wages, then their demand for intermediation services would rise with the cost of insurance. Note that the demand may be asserted indirectly: in bargaining for higher total compensation, the employee effectively pushes corporations to try to provide those benefits at lowest cost.

While its administrative role expanded, the corporation also began to retract or recast benefits. The long expansion phases of growth in employee benefits may now be over—or at least beginning to level out. Table 11.1 shows that the share of compensation accounted for by benefits grew from 7.85 to 12.0 percent in manufacturing and transportation between 1969 and 1979. Between 1979 and 1989, benefits' share of compensation in the industry fell slightly from 12.0 to 11.6 percent. In service industries, benefit shares rose from 3.3 percent in 1969 to 6.5 percent in 1979. By 1989 the benefit share slipped back to 6.4 percent.

The incidence of nonwage benefits has been declining most precipitously for those least able to bear the cost of purchasing these benefits privately—low wage workers. Table 11.2 presents the incidence and trend in health benefits by earnings quintile for twenty-five- to fifty-four-year-old full-time, full-year workers. Less than half the workers in the lowest earnings quintile have employer-paid health insurance, an 8.5 percentage point decline over the decade. And while nearly nine out of ten workers in the top earnings quintile enjoy health benefits through their employers, the share fell by 3.2 percentage points between 1979 and 1989.

Table 11.1. Share of Total Compensation Accounted for by Benefits in Selected Industries

Year	Percent manufacturing and transportation	Percent service and retail
1969	7.85	3.30
1979	12.04	6.50
1989	11.55	6.43
1992	12.90	7.29

Source: Bureau of Economic Analysis, *National Income and Product Accounts.*

Table 11.2. Distribution of Health Benefits* Through the Earnings Distribution of 25- to 54-Year-Old Full-Time, Full-Year Workers, 1979 and 1989

	1979	1989	Change
Bottom quintile	56.6%	48.1%	−8.5
2nd quintile	76.5	70.8	−5.7
3rd quintile	84.7	80.3	−4.4
4th quintile	88.9	85.8	−3.1
Top quintile	91.6	88.4	−3.2

*Share of workers whose employers pay all or part of worker's health insurance premiums.

Source: Tabulations from the March 1980 and March 1990 *Current Population Surveys.*

Table 11.3 presents pension participation rates for prime-age, full-time, full-year workers. Fewer than one in three of the workers in the lowest income quintile participate in pension plans, while four out of five workers in the top quintile participate. Coverage decreased in all quintiles, with larger declines among lower earners.

Bloom and Freeman (1992) and Even and Macpherson (1995) also find that the decline in pension coverage over the 1980s disproportionately affected the least skilled and most vulnerable workers. According to Bloom and Freeman, pension coverage of workers aged twenty-five to sixty-four fell from 63 to 57 percent between 1979 and 1988; coverage for workers

Table 11.3. Pension Plan Participation Through the Earnings Distribution of 25- to 54-Year-Old Full-Time, Full-Year Workers, 1979 and 1989

	1979	1989	Change
Bottom quintile	38.4%	31.1%	−7.3
2nd quintile	62.7	52.6	−10.1
3rd quintile	72.6	64.6	−8.0
4th quintile	80.5	74.5	−6.0
Top quintile	82.4	79.0	−3.4

Source:Tabulations from the March 1980 and March 1990 *Current Population Surveys.*

without high school degrees, however, fell by 17 percentage points over the period. Even and Macpherson (1995) show that coverage rates for workers aged twenty-one to sixty-five without high school degrees continued to fall between 1988 and 1993. Over this period the coverage rate for men in this group fell by 17 percentage points.

From a social perspective, these trends in nonwage benefits are disturbing. While nonwage benefits traditionally reduced the level of inequality in earnings and income, they have failed to offset the growth in inequality over the 1980s. In fact, growing inequality in the distribution of health benefits recently has contributed to the growth in the inequality of compensation (Acs and Steuerle 1993).

Implications for the Future

The modern corporation and social welfare are inextricably linked. The corporation will continue to serve as an agent for the government, keeping records of its workers' earnings, collecting revenues to finance social insurance programs, and furnishing these records and revenues to the government. From the Industrial Revolution through much of the twentieth century, the corporation increasingly functioned as an agent for the individual worker, using its size and administrative capabilities to purchase and allocate health and pension benefits. Over the last two decades or so, there have been two changes in the corporation's agency vis-à-vis its workers: corporations have increased their administrative involvement to control health costs and have leveled off their contributions to nonwage benefits relative to total compensation.

These recent trends call into question whether, under current arrangements alone, the corporation will ever be able to provide adequate health and retirement insurance to most or all workers. With health insurance, approximately thirty-seven million Americans, twenty-seven million of whom either work or are dependent on an employed person, were uninsured in 1991 (Winterbottom 1993). In the case of pensions, it appears that only about one-half of the retired population will ever have significant private pension retirement income. As a consequence, the nation has begun serious debate over the design of its health and pension systems, both public and private—a debate that we believe will extend for years to come.

There are three general approaches that could be followed to extend these social goods, health and pension coverage, to more citizens. Each has different implications for the modern corporation. First, responsibility for these goods may fall back on the individual as with government mandates to purchase health insurance or the need to direct the investments of one's pension. Second, the government could take over responsibility for these goods. And third, the government could mandate that corporations take on these responsibilities.

Most proposed solutions to the problems of coverage involve combinations of these three approaches, and most, one way or another, involve the corporation more than ever as agent for the government and the worker. In the area of pensions, for example, the trend seems to be toward more individual responsibility—witness the growth of 401k-type plans—with corporations providing record-keeping services for employees to direct their own plans.

In the area of health, recent debates over reforms to the U.S. health care and health insurance system have focused on all three disparate approaches: employer mandates, individual mandates, and direct government provision (single-payer system). Many proposals would add layers of regulation that are believed to be most enforceable at the business level. For example, the government could have required that within the corporation certain types of plans be offered, that premiums be collected, that penalties be collected from employees who do not buy insurance, or that the employer directly provide insurance. Almost all of these proposals place continued and increased reliance on the corporation to perform its accounting and enforcement functions.

While this partially public and partially regulated private social welfare system may be sustainable, clearly it is cumbersome and falls far short of providing universal health and old age security. We are hard-pressed, however, to suggest a scheme that would rely almost entirely either on government to intervene or on individuals to provide for their own welfare. But the current system must evolve to satisfy the unmet needs of many U.S. families.

If workers are more likely to be mobile, to come from two-earner families, and to change jobs and careers often, then social benefits offered by businesses need to be more portable, vested, and insured against arbitrary loss from inflation or other forces. At the same time, withdrawals of monies from plans in lump sums may be curtailed. In the area of pension benefits, the increased use of defined contribution plans including 401k plans represents a step toward increased portability and flexibility. The Consolidated Omnibus Budget Reconciliation Act of 1986 requiring employers to allow former workers to purchase health insurance through the employer's group plan represents a small step toward increased portability of health benefits

(Flynn 1994). As our semipublic, semiprivate social welfare system evolves, it is clear that the corporation will have a major and probably expanded role to play.

Notes

Support for this research was provided by a grant from the Sloan Foundation. The authors would like to thank Deborah Chien and Gordon Melmin for their capable research assistance. We would also like to thank the editor and other authors in this volume for their helpful comments. All opinions expressed are those of at least one of the authors and do not necessarily reflect the views of the Urban Institute or the Sloan Foundation. All errors are the responsibility of the authors alone.

1. In 1985 public health spending was, on average, about 5.6 percent of GDP for the twenty-four OECD countries, compared with 4.6 percent in the United States. By contrast, private health expenditures were 1.7 percent of GDP in the OECD countries and 6.6 percent in the United States (OECD 1990). Also in 1985, public pension expenditures averaged 9.3 percent of GDP in the big seven OECD countries, while they were 7.2 percent in the United States (OECD 1988). Mean private pension assets of six selected European Community countries, meanwhile, were 32 percent of GDP; in the United States, the pension assets were 64 percent of GDP (OECD 1994; Federal Reserve Board 1994).

2. Wilbur Cohen, for instance, argues, "I am convinced that, in the United States, a program that deals only with the poor will end up being a poor program....Ever since the Elizabethan Poor Law of 1601, programs only for the poor have been lousy, no good, poor programs. And a program that is only for the poor— that has nothing in it for the middle income and upper income—is, in the long run, a program the American people won't support. That is why I think one must find a way to link the interests of all classes in these programs." (Cohen and Friedman 1972, p. 55).

3. See Steuerle and Bakija (1994, chap. 2) for a further discussion of the arguments surrounding the debate over social insurance.

4. Examples of the mandated public participation include social security and unemployment compensation; for subsidized private participation, employer-provided pensions and health insurance are the most obvious. Mandated automobile insurance is perhaps the only major example of mandated private coverage in the United States, but note that this mandate does not require the use of employers as agents.

5. So-called multiemployer plans, for instance, allow workers to carry benefits from one company to another within the same union. Construction workers, for instance, often work for a variety of firms over short periods of time, and the porta-

bility of health and pension coverage afforded them by their union enhances their well-being.

6. Indeed, estimates by the IRS to this day indicate that small businesses and farms continue to underreport their income by substantial amounts on federal income tax returns. Excluding informal suppliers—those individuals who declare no place of business or work from house to house and job to job—about two-fifths of the total compliance gap is estimated to come from noncorporate businesses, rental real estate, farms, and partnerships. One program detects a 32.0 percent understatement of net income for businesses of the self-employed, and this figure excludes much cheating that cannot be detected through examination. See Steuerle (1986, p. 17).

7. As discussed earlier, relatively sick individuals want to buy insurance at average costs for everyone, but then healthy individuals find premiums that subsidize the sick to be too high relative to the benefits they receive.

8. The top corporate rate was 18 percent, but tax policy principles have always held that in accounting for income of the corporation, all compensation payments should be deductible. In any case, cash wages are deductible, so the corporation per se is neutral between two types of deductible payments. The effective incentive for health insurance is a function of the exclusion at the individual level, not the deduction at the corporate level.

9. Taxable income tax returns reported personal exemptions of some 81.8 million (IRS, Statistics of Income 1948, p. 40), as compared with a resident population of 146.7 million (U.S. Bureau of the Census 1993, p.8).

10. To meet their fiduciary obligations, pension fund managers had to seek relatively secure investments. Ironically, this may have worked against the short-term interest of workers in declining industries as their pension funds would not have been invested in their own companies, depriving their employers of capital needed for retooling. Thus, responsible pension fund management to protect a worker's future may have increased the likelihood of unemployment in the present.

11. For example, most defined benefit plans base final payments on wages during years of work. For the younger employee who leaves an employer, inflation so erodes the value of the base that the pension benefits are often quite minimal.

12. Effective taxable payroll was approximately 35 percent of GDP in 1951, compared with 42 percent in 1993 (U.S. Social Security Administration 1994).

References

Acs, Gregory, and Eugene Steuerle. 1993. "Trends in the Distribution of Nonwage Benefits and Total Compensation." Urban Institute research paper prepared for the U.S. Department of Labor, Pension and Welfare Administration.

Bloom, David, and Richard Freeman. 1992. "The Fall in Pension Coverage in the United States." *American Economic Review* 82, no. 2: 539–45.

Cohen, Wilbur J., and Milton Friedman. 1972. *Social Security: Universal or Selective?* Washington, D.C.: American Enterprise Institute.

Dearing, Charles L. 1954. *Industrial Pensions.* Washington, D.C.: Brookings Institution.

Dobbin, Frank R. 1992. "The Origins of Private Social Insurance: Public Policy and Fringe Benefits in America, 1920–1950." *American Journal of Sociology* 97 (March): 1416–50.

Economic Report of the President. 1995. Washington, D.C.: U.S. Government Printing Office.

Even, William, and David Macpherson. 1995. "Why Has the Loss in Pension Coverage Accelerated Among Less Educated Workers?" Paper presented at the Allied Social Sciences Association Annual Meeting, Washington, D.C., January.

Federal Reserve Board. 1994. *Balance Sheets for the U.S. Economy: 1945–1933.* Washington, D.C.: Federal Reserve Board.

Field, Marilyn J., and Harold T. Shapiro, eds. 1993. *Employment and Health Benefits: A Connection at Risk.* Washington, D.C.: National Academy Press.

Flynn, Patrice. 1994. "COBRA Qualifying Events and Elections, 1987–1991." *Inquiry* 31, no. 2: 215–20.

Graebner, William. 1980. *A History of Retirement.* New Haven, Conn.: Yale University Press.

Henderson, Charles. 1908. *Industrial Insurance.* Chicago: University of Chicago Press.

IRS, Statistics of Income 1948. *Individual Income Tax Returns.* Washington, D.C.: Internal Revenue Service.

Latimer, Murray Webb. 1932. *Industrial Pension Systems in the United States and Canada.* New York: Industrial Relations Counselors.

OECD (Organisation for Economic Co-operation and Development). 1988. *Reforming Public Pensions.* Paris: OECD.

———. 1990. *Health Care Systems in Transitions: The Search for Efficiency.* Paris: OECD.

———. 1994. *Private Pensions in OECD Countries: Ireland.* Paris: OECD.

Pemberton, Carolyn, and Deborah Holmes, eds. 1995. *EBRI Databook on Employee Benefits.* 3d. ed. Washington, D.C.: Employee Benefit Research Institute.

Seburn, Patrick W. 1991. "Evolution of Employer-Provided Defined Benefit Pensions." *Monthly Labor Review* 114 (December): 16–23.

Smeeding, Timothy. 1983. "The Size Distribution of Wage and Nonwage Compensation: Employer Cost versus Employee Value." In *The Measurement of Labor Cost,* edited by Jack Triplett. Chicago: University of Chicago Press.

Starr, P. 1982. *The Social Transformation of American Medicine.* New York: Basic Books.

Steuerle, C. Eugene. 1986. *Who Should Pay for Collecting Taxes? Financing the IRS.* Washington, D.C.: American Enterprise Institute.

Steuerle, C. Eugene, and Jon M. Bakija. 1994. *Retooling Social Security for the 21st Century.* Washington, D.C.: Urban Institute Press.

Turner, John A., and Daniel J. Beller, eds. 1992. *Trends in Pensions 1992.* Washington, D.C.: U.S. Department of Labor, Pension and Welfare Benefits Administration.

U.S. Bureau of the Census. 1993. *Statistical Abstract of the United States: 1993.* Washington, D.C.: U.S. Government Printing Office.

U.S. Bureau of Economic Analysis. 1992. *National Income and Product Accounts. Vol. 2, 1959–1988.* Washington, D.C.: U.S. Government Printing Office.

———. 1993. *National Income and Product Accounts. Vol. 1, 1929–1958.* Washington, D.C.: U.S. Government Printing Office.

———. Various years. *Survey of Current Business.* Washington, D.C.: U.S. Government Printing Office.

U.S. Department of Labor, Pension and Welfare Benefits Administration. 1994. *Pension and Health Benefits of American Workers.* Washington, D.C.: U.S. Government Printing Office.

U.S. Social Security Administration. 1994. *Annual Statistical Supplement to the Social Security Bulletin.* Washington, D.C.: U.S. Government Printing Office.

U.S. Social Security Administration, Office of the Actuary. 1994. "Table 13: GDP, Effective Taxable Payroll, and Their Linkages." Unpublished data.

Weaver, Carolyn L. 1983. "On the Lack of a Political Market for Compulsory Old-Age Insurance Prior to the Great Depression: Insights from Economic Theories of Government." *Explorations in Economic History* 2, no. 3: 294–328.

Winterbottom, Colin. 1993. *Trends in Health Insurance Coverage 1988–1991.* Washington, D.C.: The Urban Institute.

12

Almost Everywhere: Surging Inequality and Falling Real Wages

✦

LESTER THUROW

The rapid and widespread increase in inequality in income in the United States over the past two decades has traditionally been the province of countries experiencing a revolution or a military defeat followed by occupation. Indeed, this is first time since the collection of income data began that the median real wages of American males have consistently fallen over a twenty-year period. And never before have a majority of American workers suffered real wage reductions while the real per capita gross domestic product (GDP) was increasing.[1]

As we shall see, the facts are indisputable; moreover, some of these facts fly in the face of conventional economic theory. The reasons why these trends that so adversely impact the American worker—and increasingly all workers—have taken place are disputable, as are the long-term effects and remedies.

Presenting the Evidence

President John F. Kennedy talked about a "rising tide raising all boats" in his 1961 inaugural address, but by the early 1970s, what had traditionally been true in the United States was no longer true. The tides could rise yet most boats could sink. Indeed, in May 1993 *Newsweek* headlined a story about the growing gap: "A Rising Tide Lifts the Yachts." The facts bear this out: from 1973 to 1993, America's real per capita GDP rose 29 percent, yet real hourly wages fell 13 percent and real weekly wages 19 percent for non-supervisory workers.[2] These patterns, which are not related to phases of business cycles, have continued for more than two decades. (In any cyclical peak-to-peak or trough-to-trough comparison over these two decades, the same patterns emerge.) While the real per capita GDP has risen in seventeen out of the past twenty years, real weekly wages have fallen relentlessly in sixteen out of those same twenty years.[3]

In fact, the income inequality that began to increase in the late 1960s spread and intensified so that by 1992, it was increasing both between and within every industrial, occupational, educational, demographic (age, sex, race), and geographic group.[4] In 1993 an all-time record was set: the top quintile of households had 13.4 times as much income as the bottom quintile.[5] Moreover, the most detailed earnings breakdowns available for each of these groups show that the increase in income variance within even the most detailed subclassifications accounts for at least 70 percent of the total increase in variance, with shifts in the industrial mix, the occupational mix, the educational mix, the demographic mix, or the regional mix explaining the rest.[6] In other words, the increase in income differentials between individuals in any single category is more dramatic than income variance across whole categories.

A few years after this increase in inequality began (1973, to be precise), inflation-corrected real wages started to fall for males. As with inequality, real wage reduction gradually spread across the workforce so that, by 1992, real wages for males were falling for all age groups, for all industrial and oc-cupational classifications, and for all educational groups, including those with five or more years of university education.[7] Surprisingly, even the real wages of male college graduates fell 4.9 percent from 1987 to 1992.[8] And the wages of those in their prime working years (ages forty-five to fifty-four) took an even bigger fall—17 percent from 1987 to 1992.[9] If one were to look at earnings by age group, workers in their early careers are simply not getting the wage increases today that they could have expected in the past: real wages both start lower and rise more slowly. And, although real wage reductions started later for women than for men, by 1992 real wages were falling for all female workers except those with four or more years of university education.[10]

At first these falling average real wages were attributed to the employment of many more part-time workers, females, and ethnic minorities, who traditionally have had lower earnings. But from 1973 to 1992, the median

Table 12.1. Changes in Real Wages and Incomes 1973–1992 (In Percent)

Quintile	Full-time year round male workers (wages)	Household (incomes)
First	−23.0	−3.0
Second	−21.0	−3.0
Third	−15.0	−0.5
Fourth	−10.0	+6.0
Fifth	+10.0	+16.0

Source: U.S. Bureau of the Census, *Current Population Reports, Consumer Income*, 1973 and 1992, pp. 133, 148.

earnings for year-round, full-time white male workers also fell 9.5 percent.[11] Whatever is happening is occurring at the core and not just at the periphery of the labor force. Real wages for year-round, full-time male workers have been falling for all but the top (fifth) quintile of the workforce, with the largest declines coming at the bottom (first) quintile of the workforce (see Table 12.1).

Among younger workers, the declines in earning capacity have been particularly sharp.[12] For year-round, full-time male workers eighteen to twenty-four years of age (mostly high school graduates), the percentage earning less than $12,195 (in 1990 dollars) rose from 18 percent in 1979 to 40 percent in 1989. For females, the same percentages rose from 29 to 48 percent. Adjusted for population size, from 1973 to 1992 the earnings share of workers fifteen to thirty-five years of age has fallen 20 percent.[13]

The deeper one digs into the data, the sharper the increases in inequality. In the decade of the 1980s, 64 percent of the wage gains that did occur went to the top 1 percent of the workforce.[14] Looking at incomes rather than wages, the top 1 percent of the workforce got even more—90 percent of the income gains.[15] From 1974 to 1990 the average pay for a *Fortune* 500 CEO went from 35 to 150 times that of the average production worker.[16]

As can be seen in household income data (see Table 12.1), in the 1970s and '80s, the American female came to the rescue of the American male.[17] While male earnings were falling substantially, family incomes fell only slightly. From 1973 to 1992, female real annual earnings rose 33 percent. About one-third of this was due to higher wage rates and two-thirds to more hours of work per year. As far as the average family was concerned,

the wife's increased earnings essentially compensated for the husband's reduction in earnings.[18]

Although female real wages were rising for much of the period, inequality rose sharply for women in the 1970s and '80s. In 1970 the distribution of female earnings was much more equal than that of men. The earnings of women with a college education, for example, were not much higher
than those of women who only graduated from high school. Women simply
did not have access to the high-wage jobs open to men. By the 1990s at least
some of those jobs were open to women, and the female distribution of
earnings was starting to look like the more unequal male distribution of
earnings.

Looking forward, it is unlikely that wives will be able to continue to offset their husbands' falling real earnings since wives, especially those married to husbands in the bottom 60 percent of the earnings distribution, are
most likely already working full-time and have little extra time to use to increase work effort.[19] In addition, in recent years the female real wage rate
has also been falling for all but college-educated women. In the future, rises
in individual inequality are apt to be mirrored in household inequality.

While it has not yet happened, at some point female earnings will start
to make the distribution of household income more unequal since the
women who now work the least and have the most potential free time to devote to increasing their annual hours of paid work are those married to men
with the most earnings.[20] If one believes in selective mating (those men
making high incomes are married to women who could potentially earn
high incomes in a world of equal opportunity), and all of the data point to
its existence, the effects could be large.

More Shocks to the System:
Corporate Downsizing

In the early 1990s, two waves of corporate downsizing started to sweep
across the economy. Announced major corporate downsizings rose from
300,000 jobs cut in 1990 to 550,000 in 1991, and then fell back to 400,000
in 1992. Then a second wave struck in 1993 that clearly had nothing to do
with the 1991–1992 recession.[21] Announced downsizings in that year rose
to 600,000; then, in January 1994, they set a one-month, all-time record of
104,000.[22]

The first wave of downsizings, which took place in unprofitable firms,
brought a permanent reduction in force affecting mostly blue-collar workers—those who in the past had only been laid off temporarily by big firms

during recessions or economic slowdowns. The second wave, which has been sweeping through middle-management and white-collar workers (groups not traditionally laid off during recessions), has been dominated by profitable firms.[23]

Since the second wave was not necessitated by the dictates of economics, what triggered the wave and why it is continuing need to be examined. An additional part of the problem is how can profitable and therefore presumably efficient firms continue to serve existing customers while reducing their workforces by 10 to 30 percent in a short period of time? And given how competitive markets are, could these profitable firms have become inefficient while maintaining profitability?

Some have argued that the reductions that came with the second wave were made possible (or even forced) by a sudden shift in technology, presumably involving modern telecommunications and new computer technologies that allow firms to operate with very different workforce structures than in the past. But these new technologies did not suddenly just appear; they have been gradually permeating the workplace for thirty years. It is difficult to believe that their effects are first being realized now.

More likely, firms have suddenly discovered that there are large, unexploited, soft sources of productivity. It seems that corporate reorganizations that break down walls between research, design, manufacturing, and sales can dramatically lower both labor and time to market. By getting rid of traditional hierarchy, pushing decisions down to the lowest possible level, and working in teams, big gains in productivity can be achieved. Reports of such breakthroughs are many, with the dramatic changes at the Chrysler Corporation being perhaps the best example.

The second wave of downsizings can also be interpreted as the result of the sudden introduction of a new social contract between labor and management. The social contract developed in the post–World War II era had cyclical layoffs, but they were both temporary and limited to blue-collar workers (in the 1980–1981 recession, 90 percent of those laid off were blue-collar workers). Meanwhile, white-collar workers and managers could expect lifetime employment if their firms remained profitable and if their individual performances were satisfactory. As long as the firm grew and remained profitable, real wages would rise for everyone over time.

Under the new social contract, some workers and managers will end up having lifetime employment, but very few managers or workers will be given such a guarantee when they first join a company. With this contract, whenever work can be done by laborers willing to accept lower wages, wages will be lowered—or high-wage workers fired and production shifted to outside suppliers who can produce the same work with lower costs because they offer lower wages. If suppliers' workforces are included in the downsizing statistics, for example, the real reductions in the size of larger firms' labor forces are much smaller than announced reductions.

For employees, downsizing has been devastating. Those workers who were downsized in the first wave received a major economic blow. Twelve percent ended up exiting the labor force entirely, and 17 percent remained unemployed two years later. Of the 71 percent who were reemployed, 31 percent had to take a wage reduction of 25 percent or more, 32 percent had their wages reduced by from 1 percent to as much as 25 percent, and only 37 percent found employment at no loss in wages.[24]

Systematic studies of the second wave of downsizings are not yet available, but individual cases indicate that the reductions in wages were probably even larger. In the recent RJR Nabisco layoffs, 72 percent eventually found work, but at wages averaging only 47 percent of what they had previously been paid.[25]

In addition, in the process of downsizing, firms are developing a contingent workforce in which wages are lower and fringe benefits nonexistent. This contingent workforce is composed of involuntary part-timers, temporary workers, limited-term contract workers, and previously laid-off "self-employed" consultants who now work for wages far below what they had previously been receiving. With this arrangement, companies enjoy lower labor costs and greater deployment flexibility, while contingent workers receive lower wages, no fringes, and much greater economic risks and uncertainty. Contingent workers now total thirty to thirty-seven million, or 25 to 30 percent of the workforce. Even in a premium company such as Hewlett Packard, 8 percent of laborers are employed on a contingency basis.[26]

Because of this trend toward contingent workers, the total labor compensation going to active workers (rather than just wages) is falling, making it clear that inequalities have been rising even faster and real income reductions are even larger than those seen in wages. From 1979 to 1989 the percentage of the workforce with private pensions declined from 50 to 43 percent and the percentage with health insurance declined from 69 to 61 percent.[27]

The Trends Spread

While the pattern of rising inequality and falling real wages appeared first in United States, it is now spreading to the rest of the industrial world. In the early 1980s the United Kingdom started to experience what had begun ten years earlier in the United States. And in the early 1990s, the same trends started to emerge on the European continent[28]—the wage gap between the top and bottom deciles of the labor force was rising in twelve of the seventeen member countries of the Organization for Economic Cooperation and Development (OECD) that kept such records.[29] While the pattern is not endemic—it is not yet clearly visible in Japan—there is a lot of discussion internationally in the business press about the need to reduce wages to remain competitive, and many firms in OECD countries have, for the first time, moved to offshore production to lower their wage costs. Whatever is happening is not limited to the United States alone.[30]

Throughout the 1950s and '60s, European economies operated with unemployment rates substantially below (about half) those found in the United States. But starting at about the same time that inequality started to rise and real wages started to fall in the United States, unemployment started to rise in Europe. By the mid-1990s, Europe's unemployment rate was twice as high as that found in the United States—and in some countries such as Spain, Ireland, or Finland, it was almost four times as high.[31]

While some in southern Europe argue that unemployment rates there are not really as bad as reported, since many part-time workers in the black economy are reporting themselves as unemployed in the regular economy, unemployment rates in northern Europe are clearly worse than reported. Many of these countries, such as the Netherlands, have very generous disability systems, and so enormous numbers of potential workers (about 15 percent) are officially outside of the labor force because they receive government disability payments.[32] If they were counted as unemployed, measured unemployment would be much higher.[33]

Europe's unemployed also remained unemployed for long periods of time—so long, in fact, that they might be better seen as permanent castoffs from the production process rather than unemployed. In France, 39 percent of the unemployed have been unemployed for more than one year; in Germany, the long-term unemployed account for 46 percent of total unemployment; and in Ireland, this number soars to 60 percent.[34] (In contrast, less than 10 percent of unemployed Americans remain unemployed for more than one year.)[35]

Instead of spreading real wage reductions across the workforce, continental Europe essentially managed to protect the wages of those who remained employed at an enormous cost in both unemployment and lost job creation: wages were reduced to zero for the unemployed, and social welfare benefits were used as a replacement for earnings. With wages essentially held above equilibrium levels in this manner, no one was willing to make the investments necessary to create new jobs. In the two decades from 1973 to 1993, while the United States was creating 38.6 million new jobs, Western Europe was creating none.[36] If one averages European wages across the employed and the unemployed, European real wages start to fall at about the same time as those in the United States.

By the early 1990s, the American pattern was apparent in Europe. Wage inequalities started to rise, and real wages started to fall.[37] The changes thus far have been small—in 1993 real German wages fell for the first time, by 1 percent.[38] But the lesson has not been lost. As a symbol of this new reality, right after Christmas in 1994 the French division of IBM announced that 95 percent of its fourteen thousand affected employees had voted to accept a 7.7 percent wage cut. Their labor union had not been consulted.[39]

The realization that change is necessary is growing. The European Commission now regularly issues reports urging changes in the European system of social welfare payments, minimum wages, part-time work, unemployment insurance, and union regulations to permit greater labor force "flexibility." Flexibility is simply a code word for "falling wages."[40] With flexibility, there is every reason to believe that the European wage structure will rapidly move toward the American pattern.

The downsizing that started in the United States also has reached Europe (and is threatening Japan). In the first four months of 1994, 180,000 announced downsizings occurred in Germany—an economy one-quarter as large as that of the United States.[41] France's biggest tire maker cut its workforce at its major French factory in half in a three-year period—while making more tires than ever.[42]

In the more communitarian form of capitalism practiced in Japan, neither the falling real wages seen in America nor the rising unemployment seen in Europe is visible yet. But Japanese companies have built up enormous numbers of idle workers on their private payrolls who even the Japanese admit would be fired if Japanese corporations operated as their American counterparts do. Japan, with its culture of lifetime employment, essentially has a system of private unemployment insurance. If those workers supported on this system of private unemployment insurance were added to those officially recognized as unemployed, about 10 percent of the Japanese labor force would be unemployed—a number not far below that for the European Economic Community as a whole.[43]

Until recently, the Japanese social system has essentially protected its workers from the forces at play elsewhere in the industrial world, but at a steep price. Japanese firms traditionally have made much lower profits than firms elsewhere. In the past four years, however, the Japanese have essentially run an economy without capitalistic profits, something even a strong economy such as Japan's cannot continue to do for long.

The Exiles

Another development has enormous implications for the future of the most advanced industrial economies—the development of what Marx would recognize as a lumpen proletariat, those whose potential productivity is so low that they are not wanted by the private economy at anything close to a living wage. Many of these people are now among the homeless—a floating group that is now estimated to involve about six hundred thousand people on any given night, and seven million over a five-year period in the United States.[44] The rate of homelessness began to rise in the United States in the late 1970s. Initially perceived by the rest of the industrial world as a phenomenon peculiar to America and its inadequate social safety net, homelessness has now spread through most of the industrial world—including Japan.[45] France now estimates that it has six to eight hundred thousand homeless.[46]

This group—the lumpen proletariat—includes people who are the right age to be in the workforce; people who in the past used to be in the workforce; people not in school; people not old enough to have retired; people who today are reported as out of the workforce—neither employed nor unemployed; people who have no obvious means of economic support. In the United States, 5.8 million working-age males have either been dropped from, or have dropped out of, the normal working economy.[47]

As data from the rest of the world indicate, the falling wages and increasing inequality in the United States are rapidly spreading. The reasons behind these trends cannot, therefore, be sui generis to the United States; they must also fit the facts found elsewhere in the industrial world. Unfortunately, the classical explanations do not provide the answers.

Not So Clear Causes

While there is no one magic explanation as to why inequality has risen and wages have fallen, and while at this point no one can say exactly how much of the observed changes in earnings can be traced to any one factor, clearly there exists a constellation of factors that can adequately explain surging inequality almost everywhere and falling real wages for many. A careful examination of the forces at work indicates that the explanation can be found at the conjunction of classic economic effects, such as factor price equalization and skill-intensive shifts in technology, and a number of specific sociological and political occurrences.

Factor Price Equalization

In the past, when national economies were relatively isolated, first world workforces were able to earn wages far higher than those of workers of equal skills in the third world, since they had greater access to raw materials, capital, and superior technologies. But advances in transportation and communications have permitted the development of a global economy: raw materials can be bought by anyone at similar prices and cheaply transported to wherever they are needed (witness Japan, a country with no iron ore and no coal that has the world's dominant steel industry); everyone can effectively borrow capital on an equal-access basis on world capital markets in New York, London, or Tokyo (when it comes to investment, today there are no rich or poor countries); and the art of reverse engineering allows technologies, especially product technologies, to move around the world rapidly (Korea is now one of the world's leading RAM semiconductor manufacturers).

Even if the complementarities between skilled and unskilled labor that in the past have led to higher wages for the unskilled who lived in first world countries and could work with the skilled of the first world still existed, today the skill-intensive portions of the production process can be done in first world countries and the unskilled parts of the production process can be done in third world countries. Essentially, the unskilled in first-world countries are losers, receiving fewer complementary wage benefits.

What economists know as *factor price equalization* (all factors of production are paid equally) must exist if a truly global economy exists.[48] That is, in a global economy, equally skilled workers should earn equal wages regardless of whether they live in developed or underdeveloped countries. Production simply moves from high-wage to low-wage areas until skill-adjusted wages have equalized. Of course, instead of moving production from high-wage to low-wage areas, with immigration, low-wage workers move to high-wage areas until wages equalize. And indeed, from 1980 to 1993, 7.9 million legal immigrants entered the United States.[49] Another 2 million probably entered illegally. The arrival of those 10 million new low-wage, low-skill workers would have had to lower the wages of existing native-born workers, or the laws of supply and demand would have had to have been repealed.

Certain events, such as the changes in wages, occurred at exactly the right time to allow the trend to be tied to factor price equalization. Inequalities started to rise and real wages fell just when imports (as a fraction of GDP) started to rise in the late 1960s and early 1970s. But what is currently in operation is not the classical factor price equalization taught in textbooks.

In classical factor price equalization, the development of a global economy leads to rising exports of low-skill, labor-intensive products from low-wage, low-skill, third world countries. Relative prices fall for these low-skill, labor-intensive products, driving the equivalent import-competing industries in high-wage, first world countries out of business. As import-competing firms exit their industries, they lay off their workers, who are relatively unskilled. Simple supply and demand states that the wages of the unskilled must then fall relative to those of the skilled. More unskilled than skilled workers have to be reabsorbed as import penetration rises.

In the classical model, moreover, the real returns to capital rise (since the supply of labor has risen relative to that of capital) and wage differentials widen. It is also possible for the real wages of both the skilled and unskilled to fall. Effectively, the replacement of relatively isolated first world national economies with a global economy has created a world with more labor (skilled and unskilled) relative to capital than previously existed in first world countries alone.

While classical factor price equalization explains some of the trends noted, there are many that it does not explain and many that are directly contrary to what the theory would predict. Factor price equalization predicts that the wages of the skilled should rise relative to those of the unskilled. This has happened, but only relatively. Among males, the real wages of both skilled and unskilled have fallen—the real wages of the unskilled have simply fallen farther and faster than those of the skilled. But with this relative increase in wages for the skilled, the proportion of skilled workers employed in domestic and exporting industries should have fallen, with the unskilled being substituted for the skilled since they are now cheaper. This hasn't happened: using education as a measure of skills, the proportion of skilled workers has universally risen in U.S. industry. Many analysts therefore maintain that factor price equalization cannot be the cause of declining real wages, a point that was made in the 1994 Economic Report of the President. These observers argue that the widening wage disparities must therefore be found elsewhere,[50] suggesting that a skill-intensive shift in technology has led to less demand for the unskilled relative to the skilled.

The Role of Skill-Intensive Shifts

Because of new knowledge-intensive production processes, such as statistical quality control or just-in-time inventories, it is clear that many industries need workers with higher skills, especially math skills, than were needed in the past. Just as there must be some truth to the factor price equalization explanation, so must there be some truth to a skill-intensive shift in technology explanation.

But the explanation that these trends are the result of a skill-intensive technological shift explains neither why real wages have fallen for skilled male workers (if there has been a skill-intensive shift they should have risen) nor why the variance in wages has dramatically increased within each skill class. There is, of course, no reason why factor price equalization and a skill-intensive shift in technology cannot both be at work along with other factors that have usually not been folded into the equation.

The source of rapidly rising imports over the past twenty years has not been low-wage, third world countries but imports from other first world countries. Exports to other OECD countries have risen from 38 percent of exports in 1953 to 76 percent in 1990.[51] Those wanting to downgrade the importance of factor price equalization are right to point out that imports from third world countries don't seem large enough to explain the huge changes in earnings that have been observed. But imports from other OECD countries are large enough to have produced the observed wage effects.

In the 1970s and early 1980s, factor price equalization was occurring within the countries of the OECD.[52] Having the highest wages within the OECD in the early 1970s, the United States was the first to experience falling wages. But by the late 1980s and early 1990s, the entire OECD was experiencing factor price equalization flowing from the rapidly industrializing economies of the third world. Within the OECD wages have converged substantially.

By the 1990s, some of the OECD countries, such as Japan, on average paid higher wages, especially when fringe benefits are included, than were paid in the United States. But these countries started with much lower wages and even more importantly, they had a very different skill and pay mix. Typically, America's most advanced first world competitors employ many fewer university graduates in their labor forces. And those who have had substantial education are typically paid wages closer to those of lesser-skilled workers.

The very top of the U.S. workforce is both the most skilled and by far the highest-paid workforce in the world. However, if one looks at the skill set of U.S. high school graduates who have not completed any university program (midskill workers), they have far lower skills than similarly employed workers in countries such as Germany or Japan. Those workers' achievement levels at the end of high school are higher, and they receive better postsecondary skill training (such as apprenticeships in Germany and elaborate company training in Japan). Before the wage changes of the past two decades (reductions in the United States; increases for our principal industrial competitors), these midskill workers in other first world countries had both more skills and lower wages.

Given this reality, it is not surprising that the greatest loss of American market share from imports occurred precisely in those industries (autos, machine tools, steel) that were the biggest employers of midskill workers. It is precisely this midskill group in the United States that also saw its wages reduced the most. By the early 1990s, midskill American workers had lower wages than the equivalent workers in the most advanced industrial countries, and their relative wages more closely corresponded to their relative skills.[53]

At the bottom of the workforce, the United States has many more unskilled people (those who would not meet the performance standards of a European or Japanese high school graduate), and it pays them less. As a result, it is not possible to say unambiguously whether the United States is more skilled or less skilled, is higher paid or lower paid, than its principle international first world competitors. Depending on where you look, it is both.

The reason lies in the way U.S. corporations operate. U.S. firms essentially use more managers (11.5 percent of the workforce in the United States versus 5.7 percent in West Germany) to de-skill the production process, which allows them to use fewer midskill workers with fewer skills than are used by firms on the European continent or in Japan.[54]

The more unequal distribution of skills in the United States has led to a more unequal distribution of earnings. If one looks at male heads of households twenty-five to fifty-four years of age working year-round and full-time, the differences between the United States and other industrial countries are sharp. In America the top decile earns more relative to the bottom decile than in other countries, and the middle decile earns less relative to the top, and more relative to the bottom, than occurs elsewhere (see Table 12.2).

Table 12.2. Ratio Relative Earnings for Male Heads of Households 25 to 54 Years of Age Working Year-Round Full-Time (mid-1980s)

Country	Top to bottom decile	Fifth to bottom decile	Top to fifth decile
United States	7.8	2.8	2.8
Canada	6.1	2.6	2.4
Australia	4.3	2.0	2.1
Germany	3.5	1.6	2.2
Sweden	3.3	1.5	2.2

Source: Lawrence Mishel and Jared Bernstein, *The State of Working America 1992–1993* (Armonk, N.Y.: M. E. Sharpe, 1993), p. 429.

The Imports Surprise

Relative prices also haven't changed in the ways that classical factor price equalization would predict. From 1973 to 1992 the price of exports has risen 152 percent, but the price of imports has risen 245 percent.[55] Instead of going down, import prices have gone up relative to other prices. Changes in relative prices would have led one to predict that imports would fall relative to exports and GDP—not the reverse. Given that money wages have risen slower than import prices (there was a 201 percent rise in wages over the same time period) and given that import prices have risen relative to both the GDP and exports, a massive loss of competitiveness in relatively high-wage midskill industries in the United States would seem likely.

One interpretation of the rise in import prices is that after World War II, the United States enjoyed substantial economic rents in midskill industries that were not justified by the basic skills (of management or labor) or unique technologies. Having fully recovered from World War II by the early 1970s, competition with the rest of the industrial world simply eliminated the economic rents that the United States had been enjoying.

In the United States, import-competing industries pay above, and not below, average U.S. wages. Using input-output analysis, it is possible to calculate the total (direct and indirect) distribution of wages for the exporting sector and the import-competing sector. Compared with the wage distributions of the entire economy (Table 12.3), in 1983 the import-competing sector had both higher median wages (21 percent) and more equal wages (while 20.4 percent of the entire workforce earned less than five thousand dollars in 1983, only 12.4 percent of the workforce in import-competing in-

Table 12.3. Distribution of Earnings for Export- and Import-Competing Industries, 1983 (Percent)

Annual earnings	Total workforce	Export industries	Import-competing
0–5,000	20.4	13.1	12.4
5,000–10,000	12.7	10.5	10.4
10,000–15,000	13.6	13.5	13.4
15,000–20,000	13.2	14.8	14.9
20,000–25,000	11.6	14.1	14.2
25,000–30,000	9.1	11.2	11.3
30,000–40,000	10.6	13.0	13.2
40,000–50,000	4.0	2.2	2.2
60,000–75,000	1.2	1.2	1.3
75,000 plus	1.5	1.4	1.4
Median:	$16,168	$18,637	$19,583

Source: Calculated by the author from the Department of Commerce input-output tables.

dustries did so) than those of the entire economy, but import-competing industries also generated slightly higher wages than those found in the exporting sector (5 percent higher in 1983). If one thinks of the industries in the import-competing sector (autos, machine tools, steel, consumer electronics) and the industries in the export sector (agriculture, tourist services), this result is not as surprising as it first seems.

Similar input-output calculations can be made for 1969, revealing that export industries and import-competing industries both had median earnings of $7,550, while the entire economy generated annual earnings of $6,902 (only a 9 percent difference). Considering the industries in which imports have grown in the 1980s and early 1990s (autos, machine tools, and electronics), it is likely that a 1995 input-output table would show an even greater wage premium for the import-competing sector than that which existed in 1983.

Judging by wages, the import-competing sector is slightly more skilled than the export sector. Therefore, contraction of the import-competing industries would not result in a layoff of proportionally more unskilled workers. More midskilled workers would be laid off than either very skilled or unskilled workers. The case for factor price equalization occurring at the midskill level is strong if one looks at the wage structure relative to male high school graduates. Between 1973 and 1992, the premium paid to college graduates soared from 35 percent to 93 percent. But looking downward, the wage premium that high school graduates used to enjoy relative to high school dropouts has actually shrunk. The wages of high school dropouts have risen from 74 to 81 percent of high school graduate wages, and the wages of those with less than an eighth-grade education have held their own—up from 58 to 60 percent of high school wages.[56] This is exactly what one would expect if the pressure for factor price equalization was taking effect in the midskill range rather than at the very bottom of the skill pyramid.

In addition, while the aggregate U.S. trade deficit may be small relative to GDP (3 percent in early 1994), it is very large in midskill industries. With very inelastic labor supply curves, a moderate fall in the demand curve for midskill labor can have a large impact on wages. What looks like a small tail on a very big dog can in fact wag the dog.

The Education Factor

Although the trends of increasing inequality within educational and occupational categories is not fully explained by factor price equalization or a skill-intensive shift in technology, recalling two peculiarities of the labor market makes for a better fit. First, the elasticity of substitution is not symmetrical between skilled and unskilled labor. Unskilled workers are less than perfect substitutes for skilled workers, but skilled workers are perfect substitutes for unskilled workers. Skilled workers can do anything that unskilled workers can do, but unskilled workers cannot do many things that skilled workers can do. This has to be true unless there is something in the educational process of the skilled that makes them psychologically incapable of doing unskilled work.

Second, if one looks at observationally equivalent workers (for whom one has adjusted for hours of work, education, occupation, industry, and years of experience), there is not an equilibrium wage, but rather a wide dispersion of wages. For most classifications, the within-cell variance is almost as large as the variance found in the population at large.[57]

In the real world, wages are attached to jobs, not workers, and workers with equivalent skill levels are spread across a distribution of jobs that use different amounts of their skills and, as a consequence, pay different wages. What matters is not the distribution of bone-hunting skills among the dogs but rather the distribution of bones.[58] Some of the observed differentials reflect the fact that wages have a team component as well as an individual one. Those fortunate enough to work for a high-productivity team (a good firm) are paid more than those with identical skills who work on a low-productivity team (a poor firm). The lucky ones collect rents.

In the real world, equilibrium wages adjust only slowly, while entry hiring skills are quickly adjusted up or down depending on the tightness of labor markets. This is in contrast to classical microeconomics in which wages adjust to clear labor markets in the short run and wage-induced changes in labor supplies clear labor markets in the long run.

The dispersion of wages within skill levels is furthered by "job competition," in which the short-run adjustment process is best seen as a job-filtering system.[59] When unemployment exists or when new supplies of labor come into the system, thus displacing some workers, the most skilled of the displaced workers essentially take the best jobs from those immediately below them in the skill distribution. Thus, if more college-educated labor comes into the system, as has happened, new college entrants will be forced to take what used to be best, highest-wage, high school jobs. The observed wage distribution for college graduates spreads out, and the observed skill level in what used to be post–high school jobs rises—a college graduate now works where a high school graduate used to work. Average high school wages fall as high school graduates are squeezed down the job distribution and out of their best jobs.

In the 1970s and '80s, downward wage pressures coming from massive immigration, the loss of international competitiveness in midskill industries, and a skill-intensive shift in technology were exacerbated by large increases in the supply of college-educated labor. Midskill jobs were becoming scarcer, and college-educated workers were taking more and more of what had been good jobs for high school graduates. An auto industry that used to hire high school graduates for production jobs, for example, would now hire college-educated workers for those jobs. Wages haven't changed, but those who get the high wages in the auto industry have changed.

When skilled labor is released due to rising imports or augmented labor supplies, the asymmetrical elasticities of substitution mean that skilled workers simply bump down the job distribution, knocking those with lesser skills and lower wages out of their jobs. The lowest-paid in each skill class move down to take what had been the best-paid jobs in the skill class below them. The dispersion in the distribution of earnings within each skill class increases as each skill class loses what had been its best jobs and gains more of what had been its worst jobs. Average earnings fall for everyone.

Since homogeneous wages do not in fact exist for what are supposed to be homogeneous skill classes, changes in relative wages depend on the densities of the distributions over which this bumping occurs.The exact change in relative earnings depends on the densities of the different distributions that are being affected.

In the 1970s a glut of college-educated workers forced the earnings of college graduates to fall relative to high school graduate earnings as college graduates moved down into what had been the best high school jobs. Thus, the dispersion of earnings increased among college graduates. High school graduates retreated economically into a denser part of their earnings distribution, so that the decline in their average earnings was smaller than that for college graduates.

In the 1980s the growth in the supply of new college graduates and new high school graduates both slowed due to demographics, but immigration soared and midskill, high-wage industries such as automaking lost market share to imports. These economic pressures lowered the central density of the high school male earnings distribution so fast that relative college male earnings rose even though real college wages were falling faster than they had in the 1970s.

Other Forces at Work

In addition to factor price equalization and a skill-intensive shift in technology, there exist at least ten other factors that have probably contributed to the fall of wages and the rise in income inequality:

1. The new social contract between labor and capital—less favorable toward labor—is partly a product of the firm's new ability to bypass its first world workforce and move to offshore production sites, but it is also partly in response to the collapse of communism and socialism as viable political alternatives to capitalism. Without a political threat to their existence (nationalization), firms can simply be tougher on their labor forces than they could be during the cold war when communist and socialist parties commanded widespread political support. The post–World War II social contract was partially negotiated out of the fear of communism and socialism. That fear no longer exists. Fear of being fired replaces the wage premiums that used to be paid to prevent shirking and turnover.[60]

2. Observed reductions in wages appear worse than they really are if skill inflation has led workers to be recorded as having higher skills than they really have. Employers know the real skill levels by experience and pay wages appropriate to those real skills rather than the formally reported higher skill levels. A major textile manufacturer, for

example, recently tested its high school–educated labor force and discovered that this workforce in fact operated at a ninth-grade equivalency level. What shows up as a reduction in wages for high school graduates may really reflect what are effectively high school dropouts who get coded in government statistics as high school graduates. Real wages fall because average real skills are falling.

3. While the literature is inconclusive as to whether unions affect average wages (equally productive companies, with or without unions, tend to pay the same wages), there is no doubt that they affect the distribution of wages—making wage distributions much more equal than they are where unions do not exist.[61] High school–college wage differentials, for example, have always been smaller in the union sector than in the nonunion sector. With the demise of unions as a force in the American economy, one would expect wage differentials to rise since these differentials have always been higher in the nonunion sector.

In the United States (but not abroad) there has been a dramatic reduction in union membership in the private sector of the economy to only slightly more than 10 percent of the workforce. And even where unions do exist, they have lost much of their power to control wages or negotiate working conditions. This has not happened by accident. In much of American industry a deliberate strategy of deunionization has been employed (see below). Without unions, that new social contract has been much easier to impose.

4. Deregulation has also led to wage reductions. In some of the regulated industries such as trucking and airlines, it is clear that union labor collected some of the rents that accrued from regulation. Truck driver wages and the wages of some airline employees fell dramatically with deregulation. The rents that had been built into their wages were transferred either to the consumers or to the owners of capital.[62]

5. In addition to losing market share to imports, midskill industries such as autos, steel, and machine tools have seen rates of growth of productivity that are much faster than the rates of growth of demand for their products. This leads to additional dismissals of midskill labor.

6. In contrast with its low and even negative levels of productivity growth, service industry employment has boomed. On a net basis all of the growth in employment since 1980 has occurred in the service sector. While a few service industries such as finance pay high wages, on average service wages are 30 percent below those found in manufacturing—about one-third of this differential is due to lower wage rates and about two-thirds is due to the greater prevalence of involun-

tary part-time work. Increasing the mix of service workers automatically lowers average wages.[63]

7. Macroeconomic policies undoubtedly played a role in lowering wages and increasing inequality. The inflationary pressures of the 1970s and early 1980s led governments to adopt monetary and fiscal policies that tolerated much higher levels of unemployment than those recorded in the 1960s. If a lengthy period of high unemployment leads to the need for ever higher rates of unemployment to stop inflation (the long-term unemployed lose skills and serve as less and less of an anti-inflationary weapon, thereby necessitating ever higher levels of unemployment to control inflation), a lengthy period of ever higher unemployment should lead to both lower wages and an increase in the dispersion of wages.

As the unemployed bid for jobs, they lower wages on average, but the biggest impacts will always come on the wages of the least skilled. The unemployed, by the very virtue of their being unemployed, are less trained than those who have remained employed. When layoffs occur, the less skilled are the first to be fired (others with better skills but paid the same wages then are assigned the less skilled jobs) and, being unemployed, they do not get the on-the-job training that those with jobs are getting.

8. In the 1970s, as the baby boom generation entered the labor force, capital-labor ratios rose more slowly, or even fell, as the supply of labor rose faster than the supply of capital. In such a situation wages must fall since every worker is working with less capital. In the 1980s this process should have automatically reversed itself since demographics caused the labor force to grow much more slowly than it had in the 1970s. But the 1980s became a decade of booming immigration and the expected slowdown in labor force growth did not occur, and hence the expected rise in capital-labor ratios did not occur.

9. There has been a shift of resources, from wages to other forms of worker compensation. If one looks at the share of GDP going to labor over the nineteen years from 1973 to 1992, it remains approximately constant. There seems to have been no shift in the coefficients of the production function describing how capital and labor generate output. The returns to capital do not seem to have risen. But the share going to wages is down substantially (5 percentage points), while the share going to pensions is up substantially. Fully funded pension programs are simply wages being shifted from today to tomorrow, but less than fully funded pension programs or health insurance programs in

which benefits go to current retirees (the usual case) are effectively wage reductions for those currently employed. What shows up in the statistics as fringe benefits is really a private social welfare payment from the young to the old.

10. Within the public sector, spending on investments such as infrastructure are down, while income transfers to the elderly are up. Since infrastructure is not imported and some of the elderly's consumption goods are imported, much less of government spending ends up producing the relatively stable, high-wage, first world jobs that are not subject to import competition.

Looking Forward

The effects of the current trend toward income inequality will reverberate for a long time to come. Many issues have yet to be resolved, and others are still on the horizon. The impacts of these issues must be taken into account by our political and corporate leaders in their planning for the future.

The Cascade of Changes Will Continue

During the 1970s and '80s, rising blue-collar productivity, often spurred by information technologies such as robotics, and rapidly rising imports in mid-skill manufacturing industries reduced the need for factory workers. In contrast, white-collar productivity stagnated or even declined and white-collar employment soared despite the uses of massive amounts of information technologies in areas such as accounting and finance. By the mid-1990s, however, it seems clear that firms have learned how to use information technologies to reduce the number of white-collar and middle-management jobs. Technological pressures to reduce employment are moving up the earnings distribution and are afflicting ever higher-earnings groups. How far wages can be reduced for these groups remains to be seen. The limits are sociological: When does a sullen, noncooperative workforce, especially in the management cadres, raise costs more than what can be gained from wage reductions?

Since midskill wages in many advanced industrial countries are now above those in the United States, most of the factor price equalization flowing from other first world countries is probably now behind us. But in front of us lies the integration of the second world into the first world, and a very different third world.

While communist countries did not run effective civilian economies, they ran excellent education systems. The Soviet Union was a high science society, with more engineers and scientists than any nation other than the United States, and China is capable of quickly marshaling hundreds of millions of midskill workers. The end of communism and the success of the little tigers on the Pacific Rim have led the third world to junk import substitution as a route to economic development and become export-oriented. Exports from low-wage, third world countries are apt to be much larger in the years ahead than they were in the years behind. While, in the past, a few tens of millions of workers in several countries (Singapore, Hong Kong, Taiwan, and South Korea) used to be export-oriented, now third world countries containing billions of people want to be export-oriented (Indonesia, India, Pakistan, and Mexico). Whatever one believes about the proportion of the observed real wage declines and increases in wage dispersion that can be blamed on factor price equalization in the past, the proportion is going to be larger in the future.

In the 1970s and '80s, the United States prided itself on creating tens of millions of jobs. All of these jobs were in the service sector, but most of these jobs reflect a onetime adjustment that is now behind us. Ninety percent of the jobs created in the 1970s and '80s were in producer services (finance and the real estate necessary to house the millions of newly hired white-collar workers), retail trade, and health care.[64] The shift to a global capital market is now complete, and new information technologies are reducing the number of white-collar workers in finance. As their numbers are reduced, additional office space will not be needed. In retailing, there was a onetime shift to twenty-four-hours-a-day, seven-days-a-week shopping, and a onetime shift to part-time workers to reduce fringe benefits. Both changes are now essentially complete. Restaurant employment boomed as women entered the paid labor force and did not have time to cook, but here too the shift to eating away from home is essentially now complete.

If President Clinton's health care reform had gone through and all firms had been required to put 8 percent of payroll into health insurance regardless of whether their employees are full-timers or part-timers, retailing would have eliminated many of its part-time jobs and gone back to full-time workers. However dead the Clinton program might be, given that the United States already spends 15 percent of GDP on health care, at some point (and somehow) the United States will have to stop health care costs from rising. When it does, health employment will quit booming.

Looking forward, jobs, if they are created, will be created in a much more balanced mix between services and other sectors of the economy. If the Europeans move to wage flexibility, they will probably get some of the service job creation in the late 1990s and early twenty-first century that the United States got in the 1970s and '80s. As a result, patterns of wages and employment in Europe will follow those already evident in America: falling real wages for many, rising inequality almost everywhere. Unfortunately there is every reason to suspect that more of the same lies ahead. No slow-down in any of the current trends is evident.

The Capitalistic Corporation

The dramatic shift in the distribution of earnings raises three important questions:

1. How much of the observed shift in the distribution of wages can be attributed to deliberate corporate decisions—as opposed to actions forced upon corporations by the external economic environment?
2. How will the shift in the distribution of wages, and hence disposable income, affect corporate behavior?
3. What political forces might be directed at corporations if unhappy voters with falling real wages and corporations facing global competition cannot forge a new social contract?

First, while corporate decisions (such as moving to offshore production sites, creating wage gaps) are central in producing what has been observed, most of those decisions are clearly endogenous reactions to market forces rather than exogenous causes. The one great exception is the deliberate actions undertaken by American corporations to drive unions out of the American economy (the hiring of consultants who specialize in getting rid of unions, decertification elections, efforts to alter labor laws so that unions are harder to establish and easier to eliminate, and a willingness to ignore legal requirements, simply paying the small fines that labor law violations bring). This has not happened elsewhere and did not have to happen in the United States. And when these actions are considered in light of the fact that corporate compensation committees have escalated CEO salaries from 35 to 150 times that of entry-level workers in the past twenty-five years, one could argue that capitalists have declared class warfare on labor—and are winning.[65]

However, in countries where unions are still important, where no efforts have been made to defeat labor, and where CEO salaries have not exploded, the same patterns of falling wages and rising inequality are now emerging. Deliberate corporate actions to eliminate unions may have speeded up the observed process in the United States, but there is no reason to believe that they have led to long-term results fundamentally different than those found elsewhere.

Corporate threats to go abroad to lower wage costs certainly play a role in lowering wages at home. There are those in Germany who think that the decisions of BMW and Mercedes to build plants in the United States have more to do with negotiating with German trade unions than with servicing the U.S. auto market. But the same pressures exist even when firms have no offshore production sites and no plans to establish them. In today's economy, everyone has to meet global competition from those abroad who have lower wages. If higher wages are not sustained by higher productivity, they cannot be defended, whatever the capitalist would like to do.

In the end, there is little or no evidence that the observed changes in the wage distribution reflect deliberate corporate decisions. While firms clearly have some freedom to choose among different technological possibilities and operate those technologies with different distributions of skills and hence wages, changes of the magnitude that have been occurring in the past twenty years could not have been caused by deliberate corporate decisions to shift to a more unequal skill mix. At the very least, the set from which technologies are picked must have changed to permit the use of a wider distribution of skills, and hence wages, within the production process.

In answer to the second question, within the corporation, the observed changes in wages are going to have two big effects. First, because changes in wages lead to changes in disposable income, marketing efforts and product development will have to be refocused on the groups that have been gaining income and away from those that have been losing income. Second, a new social contract will have to be developed with the workforce (for labor and management), if corporations are to have the high-quality workforces they need in order to be productive.

Corporate marketing and product development have already responded to the shift in the distribution of income. In retailing, the middle-class stores (Sears, Macy's, Gimbels, and so on) have all had economic problems in the past fifteen years, while the upscale stores (Bloomingdales) and the downscale stores (Walmart) have all been doing very well. This shift has occurred not because there just happened to be idiots managing all of the middle-class stores and geniuses managing at either end of the spectrum. Customers with middle-class incomes were becoming fewer in number—

some moving upscale as their incomes rose and others moving downscale as their incomes fell. Those well positioned to take advantage of these shifts in the distribution of spending power won in the world of retailing in the 1980s and early 1990s.

Similarly, the shift in purchasing power toward the elderly (their share of consumer income has essentially doubled in the past twenty-five years) lies behind the great economic success of the cruise line industry. Cruising is a perfect vacation for those whose mobility is impaired or who may have days when they don't feel well while on vacation. As cruise lines illustrate, the focus of new product development will shift from the young, whose income has fallen, to the old, whose income has risen.

As discretionary income moves from the young to the old, advertising will follow it, and the television programming that is now focused on the young will gradually shift to focus on the old. The young may have more malleable consumer preferences, but it does no good to alter those preferences if the young have little discretionary income. Shifts in the distribution of wages, and hence purchasing power, will play a large role in selecting those corporations that make money in the years ahead.

The answer to the third question involves the current replacement for the old post–World War II social contract, which simply forces workers to accept that they must live in a world of "survival of the fittest" capitalism. In the long run, this approach will not work, politically or sociologically. Capitalism has a current advantage in that with the death of communism and socialism, it has no plausible social system as an active competitor. It is difficult to have a revolution against capitalism without an alternative ideology. But capitalism cannot survive long unless it delivers rising living standards to a majority of its participants—something will arise to replace it even if that something is not yet visible.

Currently, the old social contract is being replaced by fear—fear of losing one's job and having to take an even bigger cut in real wages to get reemployed. But motivation through fear only works in the short run. In the long run every business firm needs an enthusiastic workforce willing to voluntarily participate in the production process—not a sullen workforce that does the minimum necessary to avoid being fired. To get that enthusiastic workforce, corporate America will have to offer a new social contract.

In the mid-1990s that new social contract has yet to be developed. In the 1980s and early 1990s some firms experimented with a social contract in which a core group of permanent workers enjoyed the old social contract and a peripheral group of temporary workers enjoyed no social contract (the General Motors pattern at Saturn). But this pattern only works if the group outside of the social contract is relatively small. Rising inequality and falling real wages now afflict a majority, not a minority, of the American workforce. Something else will have to be developed.

One possibility is a social contract based on the proposition that no firm can offer its workers lifetime employment in the new global economy but that it will invest in the lifetime careers of its workforce while they are employed by the firm. But a workable, acceptable version of that contract has yet to be developed.

Political Ramifications

If corporate America cannot come up with an acceptable social contract, the resulting dissatisfaction with the economic system is apt to show up in the political process. To some extent it may already have done so. If one looks at voting behavior in the 1994 election, two groups swung heavily toward the Republicans—fundamentalist, born-again Christians and white, high school–educated, blue-collar males. The latter, a traditionally Democratic voting group, of course, has suffered the largest real wage reductions in the past two decades. Since the Democrats had no answers to the problems of workers, they voted Republican to experiment with something else. Republican economic policies may not solve their problems, but from the perspective of white male high school graduates, trying anything different is better than doing nothing. The political danger is, of course, that Republican policies will not restore rising real wages nor eliminate rising inequalities. If that is the case, in a short time these voters will become unhappy with Republican policies and chase after whatever demagogue happens to be around at the time. The fury that was directed at the Democrats in late 1994 could easily be directed back at the business community in the years ahead.

American capitalism has a strength and a weakness when it comes to dealing with these likely political pressures. Its strength is that it has more fundamental political support than does capitalism in Europe. The fact that socialist parties never developed as an important American political force says something. Faith in capitalism's ability to deliver rising standards of living will probably die slower in the United States than in Europe. Its weakness is that it is the major deliverer of what elsewhere would be social welfare benefits (medical care, disability benefits, etc.) to the working middle-class who are below retirement age. As these benefits are cut back, the anger of this middle-class group is apt to rise rapidly. Economically, to

lose one's job and one's company-provided fringe benefits is much less serious in Europe than it is in the United States.

Democracy is like capitalism. In the long run, it is appreciated only if it
delivers. If capitalism does not deliver rising real wages for a majority in a
period when the total economic pie is expanding, it will not for long hold
the political allegiance of a majority of the population. If the democratic
political process cannot remedy whatever is causing that reality to occur
within capitalism, democracy will also eventually be discredited.

In democratic societies, governments exist to ensure that a majority of
their citizens are included in the benefits generated by their economies.
Inclusion is a central goal. When inclusion is absent for any length of time,
democracy and government are in trouble. A large group of voters with free-
floating hostility, not benefiting from the economic system, is not a recipe
for a good, or a stable, society.

Notes

1. Lynn A. Karoly, *The Trend in Inequality Among Families, Individuals, and
Workers in the United States* (Los Angeles: Rand Corporation), 1992, pp. 44, 66.

2. Council of Economic Advisers, *Economic Report of the President 1994*
(Washington D.C.: Government Printing Office, 1994), p. 320.

3. Ibid., pp. 277, 320.

4. U.S. Department of Commerce, Bureau of the Census, *Current Population
Reports, Consumer Income, 1992* (Washington, D.C.: Government Printing Office,
1992), series P-60, p. VI; Sheldon Danziger and Peter Gottschalk, eds., *Uneven
Tides* (New York: Russell Sage Foundation, 1993), p. 7.

5. U.S. Department of Commerce, Bureau of the Census, *Current Population
Reports, Consumer Income, 1993* (Washington, D.C.: Government Printing Office,
1993), series P-60, p. 21.

6. Danziger and Gottschalk, *Uneven Tides*, pp. 69, 85, 102, 129; Steven J
Davis, "Cross-Country Patterns of Changes in Relative Wages," *Brookings Papers
on Economic Activity* 2 (Washington, D.C.: Brookings Institution, 1993), p. 273;
Lynn A. Karoly, "Changes in the Distribution of Individual Earnings in the United
States 1967–1986," *Review of Economics and Statistics* (February 1992): 107, 113;
Frank Levy and Richard J. Murnane, "U.S. Earnings Levels and Earnings
Inequality," *Journal of Economic Literature* (September 1992): 1333.

7. Barry Bluestone, "Economic Inequality and the Macro-Structuralist
Debate" (paper presented at the Eastern Economics Association Meeting, Boston,
February 1994), p. 8.

8. Lawrence Mishel and Jared Bernstein, *The State of Working America
1992–1993* (Armonk, N.Y.: M. E. Sharpe, 1993), p. 14.

9. "Male Educated in a Pay Bind," *New York Times,* February 11, 1994, p. D1; Richard D. Reeves, "Cheer Up, Downsizing is Good for Some," *International Herald Tribune,* December 29, 1994, p. 4.

10. Steven Greenhouse, "Clinton Seeks to Narrow a Growing Wage Gap," *New York Times,* December 13, 1993, p. D1.

11. Ibid., p. 304.

12. Mishel and Bernstein, *The State of Working America,* p. 36.

13. Ibid., p. 88.

14. Daniel R. Feenberg and James M. Poterba, "Income Inequality and the Incomes of Very High Income Taxpayers," Working Paper no. 4229, (Cambridge, Mass.: National Bureau of Economic Research, 1992), p. 31.

15. Ibid., p. 5.

16. Robert H. Frank, "Talent and the Winner-Take-All Society," *The American Prospect* (Spring 1994): 99.

17. Peter Kilborn, "More Women Take Low-Wage Jobs Just So Their Families Can Get By," *New York Times,* March 13, 1994, p. 24; Wallace C. Peterson, *Silent Depression* (New York: Norton, 1994), p. 87.

18. Mishel and Bernstein, *The State of Working America,* p. 72.

19. Danziger and Gottschalk, *Uneven Tides,* p. 195.

20. Ibid., p. 210.

21. Stephen S. Roach, "Announced Staff Cuts of U.S. Corporations," *The Perils of America's Productivity-Led Recovery: Morgan Stanley Special Economic Study,* (New York: Morgan Stanley, 1994), p. 1.

22. John A. Byrne, "The Pain of Downsizing," *Business Week,* May 9, 1994, p. 61.

23. George Church, "The White Collar Layoffs That We're Seeing Are Permanent and Structural," *Time,* November 22, 1993, p. 35; Bruce Butterfield, "Working but Worried," *Boston Globe,* October 10, 1993, p. 1; Gail Lem, "Dofasco Steel Works," *Toronto Globe and Mail,* October 28, 1993, p. B-1; John Holusha, "A Profitable Xerox Plans to Cut Staff by 10,000," *New York Times,* December 9, 1993, p. D1.

24. Mishel and Bernstein, *The State of Working America,* p. 174.

25. Church, "White Collar Layoffs," p. 35.

26. Bennett Harrison, *Lean and Mean* (New York: Basic Books, 1994), p. 201; Poly Callaghan and Heidi Hartmann, *Contingent Work: A Chart Book on Part-Time and Temporary Employment* (Washington, D.C.: Economic Policy Institute, 1994), p. 1.

27. David E. Bloom and Richard B. Freeman, "The Fall of Private Pension Coverage in the United States," *American Economic Review* 82, no. 2 (May 1992): 539–45; Virginia L. DuRivage, ed., *New Policies for the Part-time and Contingent Work Force* (Armonk, N.Y.: M. E. Sharpe, 1992), p. 22; The Urban Institute, *Inequality and Benefits* (Winter/Spring 1994): 21.

28. Steven Davis, "Cross Country Patterns of Change in Relative Wages,"

Brookings Papers on Economic Activity 3 (Washington, D.C.: Brookings Institution, 1993), p. 273.

29. "Rich Man, Poor Man," *The Economist,* July 24, 1994, p. 71.

30. "Inequality," *The Economist,* November 4, 1994, p. 19.

31. "Labour Pains," *The Economist,* February 12, 1994, p. 74.

32. Heino Fassbender and Susan Cooper Hedegaard, "The Ticking Bomb at the Core of Europe," *McKinsey Quarterly* 3 (Summer 1993): 132.

33. Frank Riboud, "Army of Invalids," *Worldlink* (May/June 1994): 5.

34. Richard Donkin, "World Outlook for Jobs Gloomy," *Financial Times,* April 27, 1994, p. 4.

35. Council of Economic Advisers, *Economic Report of the President 1994,* p. 320.

36. Ibid., p. 306.

37. Ariane Benillard, "Cost Savings of Relocation Lure German Companies," *Financial Times,* November 9, 1993, p. 1.

38. "Real Earnings Down for Western German Workers, Up in East," *This Week in Germany,* March 11, 1994, p. 4.

39. "French Staff Takes IBM Wage Cut," *International Herald Tribune,* December 27, 1994, p. 10.

40. "New Law Allows Private Employment Agencies," *This Week in Germany,* April 22, 1994, p. 4.

41. Martin Orth and Rudiger Edelmann, "Flexible Working Times: Only a Trendy Concept?" *Deutschland* 1 (February 1994): 1.

42. Marlise Simons, "In French Factory Town, Culprit Is Automation," *New York Times,* May 12, 1994, p. A3.

43. Takeuchi Hireoshi, "Reforming Management," *Journal of Japanese Trade and Industry* 2 (1994): 12.

44. Jason DeParle, "Report to Clinton Sees Vast Extent of Homelessness," *New York Times,* February 17, 1994, p. 1; Christopher Jencks, "The Homeless," *New York Review of Books,* April 21, 1994, p. 20.

45. "Europe and the Underclass," *The Economist,* July 30, 1994, p. 19.

46. "Homeless in France," *International Herald Tribune,* December 20, 1994, p. 1.

47. Sylvia Nasar, "More Men in Prime of Life Spend Less Time Working," *New York Times,* December 1, 1994, p. 1.

48. *Economic Policy Institute,* "Declining American Income and Living Standards," (Washington, D.C., 1994).

49. George J. Borjas, "The Economics of Migration," *Journal of Economic Literature* (December 1994): 1668.

50. Robert Z. Lawrence and Matthew J. Slaughter, "Trade and U.S. Wages: Great Sucking Sound or Small Hiccup" (paper presented at *Micro-BPEA meetings,* Washington, D.C., June 1993); Paul Krugman and Robert Lawrence, "Trade, Jobs, and Wages," MIT working paper no. 21, Cambridge, 1994.

51. Paul Krugman, *Peddling Prosperity* (New York: Norton, 1994), p. 231.

52. Manouchehr Mokhtari and Farhad Rassekh, "The Tendency Toward Factor Price Equalization Among OECD Countries," *Review of Economics and Statistics* (November 1989): 636; Dan Ben-David, "Equalizing Exchange, Trade, Liberalization and Convergence," *Quarterly Journal of Economics* (August 1993): 653.

53. Farhad Rassekh, "The Role of International Trade in the Convergence of per Capita GDP in 1950–1985," *International Economic Journal* 6, no. 4 (Winter 1992): 1.

54. Derek Bok, *The Cost of Talent* (New York: Free Press, 1993), p. 223.

55. Council of Economic Advisers, *Economic Report of the President 1994*, p. 273.

56. U.S. Department of Commerce, Bureau of the Census, *Current Population Reports, Consumer Income, 1973*, p. 119 and *Current Population Reports, Consumer Income, 1993* (Washington, D.C.: U.S. Government Printing Office), p.114.

57. The concept of equilibrium wages can be rescued by postulating that within each measurable skill class, there exist other unmeasurable skills such as the ability to learn new skills or the ability to implement new technologies that explain the observed differentials. But this is to rescue the theory with a tautology and to make it empty. It explains everything and anything, but by doing so it explains nothing.

58. Michael Sattinger, "Assignment Models of the Distribution of Earnings," *Journal of Economic Literature* (June 1993): 833.

59. Lester C. Thurow, *Generating Inequality* (New York: Basic Books, 1974).

60. Laura D'Andrea Tyson, William T. Dickens, and John Zysman, *The Dynamics of Trade and Employment* (Cambridge, Mass.: Ballinger, 1988), p. 94.

61. Lawrence M. Kahn and Michael Curme, "Unions and Nonunion Wage Dispersion," *Review of Economics and Statistics* (November 1987): 600.

62. *Paying the Toll* (Washington, D.C.: Economic Policy Institute, 1994), p. 1.

63. Lester C. Thurow, *Toward a High Wage High Productivity Service Sector* (Washington, D.C.: Economic Policy Institute, 1988), p. 1.

64. Ibid.

65. Robert H. Frank, "Talent and the Winner Take All Society," *The American Prospect* (Spring 1994): 99.

13

The Corporation
as a Political Actor

✦

JAMES Q. WILSON

In the quarter century between the early 1950s and the mid-1970s, the American corporation changed dramatically the manner in which it engaged the political process. Most of these changes were born of necessity: declining success in Congress with respect to matters of fundamental importance to corporate management, a profound alteration in the ways in which money and information could be converted into political resources, the resurgence of intellectual opinion favorable to markets with respect to some transactions and unfavorable to them with respect to others, and a steady erosion in the prestige of business executives and the legitimacy of the large corporation.

After the end of World War II, the status of American business was high and its prospects bright. The corporation had fully recovered from the criticisms spawned by the Great Depression. And even these criticisms had never taken the form of a fully developed, popularly supported attack on the legitimacy of capitalism or a market economy. Though there were Marxist parties in this country, they never had the electoral appeal of their counterparts in France and Italy. The legendary feats of wartime production coupled with the rapid economic growth experienced by a nation spending to compensate for years of deferred consumption made the business executive a popular figure and photographs of belching smokestacks a symbol of progress. This is not to say that business interests always prevailed in Washington. Business won decisively on some important matters and lost on others. It scored a major victory with the passage of the Taft-Hartley

413

Labor Act in 1947, but it had to accept an increase in the corporate tax rate to 51 percent, an extension of rent control, and the passage of a housing act that the U.S. Chamber of Commerce denounced as "creeping socialism." There were fights over amendments to the antitrust laws, with business prevailing on some details and not on others.

The key political issues of the postwar period did not, however, seriously threaten the status, governance, or management of the corporation. Business leaders argued with politicians over the distribution of corporate earnings as between shareholders and tax collectors, about the rules governing unfair trade practices, and over the desirability of allowing the government to enter certain industries (such as the production of low-cost housing). But these issues were external to the management of the enterprise: with one exception, they did not directly affect how the factors of production—labor, capital, land, technology—were combined. The important exception was labor relations. Since 1935 firms had been required to bargain collectively with and grant union-shop status to unions that had won representational elections among employees. This was a major reduction in managerial authority, and accordingly efforts to reverse its impact acquired the highest political priority. With the passage of the Taft-Hartley Act in 1947 and the Landrum-Griffin Act in 1959, business was able to roll back some of the gains unions had won in 1935. These laws made illegal certain union tactics, gave employers the right to sue unions for damages, and placed a number of legal constraints on union leaders.

Thirty years later, matters had changed dramatically. The fiscal burden on corporations had lessened but the managerial burden had increased. By 1986 the corporate tax rate had fallen from 51 to 34 percent and the corporate share of federal tax revenues had declined from over 37 percent in 1957 to less than 18 percent in 1988. In 1955, when business enjoyed great popular legitimacy and unparalleled access to the Eisenhower administration, corporate income taxes amounted to 4.6 percent of the gross national product. By 1980, when the White House was occupied by a man, Jimmy Carter, widely perceived to be antibusiness, corporate income taxes only consumed 2.4 percent of GNP. From a balance sheet perspective, corporate America had improved its political position.

But that was not how business leaders saw the matter, and the reason was the dramatic reduction in managerial autonomy. Beginning in the mid-1960s and continuing through most of the 1970s, dozens of consumer, environmental, and civil rights laws had been passed that by design or effect powerfully constrained the freedom of corporate managers to direct their productive processes. In addition to these laws, the courts had developed new, more restrictive doctrines governing a firm's liability for injuries caused by its products and services and affecting its freedom to fire employees at will. These rules of strict liability and wrongful termination not only put the firm's assets at risk, they generated profound new uncertainties that would affect product development and manufacturing, service delivery, and employee relations. Firms, like individuals, prefer certainty: over a rather wide range of variation, humans can adapt to rules provided the rules are known and relatively stable. Uncertainty produces anxiety and increases transaction costs. Since the mid-1960s, corporate uncertainty increased.

These new developments were accompanied by and in large measure caused important changes in how corporations behaved in the political arena. For the first time, they had to become more or less full-time political actors.

Scholars studying politics in the 1950s or the 1920s might be pardoned for assuming the corporations were already fully engaged in politics: how else could one explain the political success business enjoyed on so many matters? And in fact, *for certain kinds of issues* firms did have effective political representation. The authors of the Smoot-Hawley Tariff of 1930 certainly did not need to guess at what firms wanted: the latter's demands for favorable tariff rates on individual products were clearly and persuasively conveyed.[1] The members of Congress who voted for the Taft-Hartley Act were not in doubt about the interest their business constituents had in this matter. The countless grants, loans, subsidies, deductions, and exemptions with which the history of federal legislation is littered are ample testimony to the ability of firms under certain circumstances to convey an effective political message.

But the political skills and resources suitable for obtaining firm-specific benefits (such as individual tariffs or tax deductions) or for defeating common enemies (such as organized labor) in an era in which business enjoys high prestige are not the same as those appropriate for coping with general legislation that will apply with uneven or unknown effect across a wide variety of firms or for advancing business interests when business itself (and especially big business) has suffered a serious loss of popular confidence.

From the 1930s down to the 1960s, scholars wrote knowingly about business lobbies, such as the National Association of Manufacturers (NAM) or the U.S. Chamber of Commerce and imputed to them, often correctly, considerable influence. But the reality behind these assumptions of general business power, at least when business had to confront proposals that would confer on an administrative agency the authority to determine internal management procedures or set in unknown ways the rules for corporate conduct, was graphically revealed by what was indisputably the best single study of business-government relations in postwar America. In 1963 Raymond Bauer, Ithiel de Sola Pool, and Lewis Anthony Dexter published their account of the domestic politics of foreign trade from roughly 1953 through 1960. The bills being debated were designed to enlarge or limit the authority of the president and his agents to set trade policy across a variety of industries. Here is the authors' summary of the lobbying activity surrounding these measures:

> The lobbies were on the whole poorly financed, ill-managed, out of contact with Congress, and at best only marginally effective in supporting tendencies and measures which already had behind them considerable Congressional impetus from other sources . . . When we look at a typical lobby, we find that its opportunities for maneuver are sharply limited, its staff mediocre, and its major problem not the influencing of Congressional votes but the finding of clients and contributors to enable it to survive at all.[2]

There were, to be sure, exceptions: the American Cotton Manufacturers Institute and the Foreign Oil Policy Committee were generally successful in getting restrictions placed on the importation of foreign textiles and oil. But most trade associations, and certainly the large peak associations—the NAM and the Chamber—were divided, uncertain, or ineffective.

This was the status of corporate political representation in the early 1960s on the eve of the most powerful wave of antibusiness legislation to come out of Congress since the first Roosevelt administration. It is hardly surprising that business lobbying proved ineffective in so many cases. When the representatives of the American automobile industry were not only defeated but humiliated during debates over passage of the National Traffic and Motor Vehicle Safety Act of 1966, it may have struck some observers as an isolated case of powerful firms being caught off guard by an unexpected wave of regulatory sentiment. (One journalist was to refer to the auto industry as the "paper hippopotamus."[3]) But it was not an isolated case at all: when members of Congress discovered how easily they could defeat three of the largest industrial corporations in the world, they were emboldened to pass laws regulating air and water pollution, toxic wastes, pharmaceuticals, and occupational safety and health, and to make it clear that they would not object to government attorneys interpreting the civil rights laws as authorizing a requirement for affirmative action hiring plans in the private sector.

As their political weakness became clear, American corporations set about devising ways to get back into the game. In the ensuing decade, the political strategy and tactics of large American corporations were reinvented. The new system is unlike the old in several significant respects.

From Market Regulation to Process Regulation

Until the 1960s, the characteristic government-business issue involved *market regulation,* by which I mean rules specifying the conditions under which a firm could enter or remain in an industry. These rules took many forms. Some required licenses to practice a profession (say, as a securities broker) or to enter an industry (say, a broadcast license or a domestic aviation certificate). Others placed limits on the freedom of firms in an industry to combine (the antitrust laws). Still others specified the prices that could be charged (as with utility rate regulation) or the benefits that could be paid (as with ceilings on interest payments on bank deposits). And others, perhaps the most numerous, allocated to particular industries taxes (and tax deductions and exemptions), subsidies, tariffs, and quotas that set bounds on, or floors under, the profitability of firms in those industries.

Market regulations imposed both burdens and benefits: the burdens were taxes and restrictions on anticompetitive practices, the benefits were subsidies and restrictions on entry that reduced competition and hence made possible setting prices at above-market levels. The net benefit (or burden) varied from industry to industry and from time to time. Airlines, for example, resented the slowness or seeming unfairness with which the Civil Aeronautics Board (CAB) allowed fare increases or service on new routes, especially at times when costs were rising. But these same airlines would defend the CAB's reluctance to allow new carriers to enter the industry or to permit prices to fall to market levels.

Whenever the benefits exceed the burdens, market regulation is the province of client politics. Client politics exists when the benefits of a program are concentrated on a small group or sector and the costs are diffused across a large population. For example, government support of milk prices benefits dairymen and distributes the cost over the entire milk-buying public at a very low per capita rate.[4] When these circumstances exist, the beneficiaries—the clients—of the policy have a strong incentive to organize and campaign to obtain the benefit, and those who pay the costs have very few incentives to organize and campaign against it. It is harder to mobilize many people than a few, especially when the per capita benefits of success are low for the former and high for the latter. In a famous essay, George Stigler explained why producer interests would always dominate consumer interests; though his theory was marred by its overgenerality (it predicted that neither market deregulation nor pro-consumer regulation would occur), it was an accurate analysis of much, if not all, of market regulation.[5]

By the mid-1960s, *process regulation* had become the dominant mode of new governmental actions directed at American corporations. Process regulation specifies the ways in which the factors of production may be acquired or combined within a given firm. There had been some process regulation before the 1960s. Meat packers had been subject to government standards, enforced by meat inspectors, since 1906. Pharmaceutical manufacturers had been required to test their products for safety since 1938. But these early examples of process regulation were not only not burdensome, they were in fact advantageous to the dominant firms in those industries. Many meat packers had supported federal regulation because the government inspection constituted a stamp of approval that aided sales and discouraged new, low-cost producers. The major drug manufacturers—the so-called ethical drug industry—had supported many of the laws enforced by the Food and Drug Administration because they drove out of business competitors who made patent medicines that could not pass safety (and later efficacy) standards.[6]

The early forms of process regulation that were opposed by business because they placed unwelcome burdens on corporate management involve labor legislation and in particular the Wagner Act of 1935. Labor law that required collective bargaining reduced managerial prerogatives, redistributed authority over employment decisions, and generated uncertainty. By contrast, labor law that mandated minimum wages and maximum hours, while often resisted by business, did not redistribute managerial authority or generate much uncertainty beyond the question whether higher wage costs would create a competitive disadvantage. If the laws were applied across all firms in an industry, the costs could be passed on to the consumer. Union representation, by contrast, would affect different firms differently, with some having to cope with labor stoppages that their competitors could avoid.

Until the 1960s there were few other examples of burdensome process regulation. Then the floodgates opened. Most of the new forms of consumer, environmental, and worker health legislation was resisted by many, if not all, firms, but to little avail. Tough clean air and clean water laws were passed, an Occupational Safety and Health Administration and a Consumer Product Safety Commission were created, and many existing laws—on meat inspection and drug safety—were strengthened. Not only did most of this happen over business opposition, many of these laws became tougher as they worked their way through Congress. Moreover, some forms of deregulation worsened the economic position of firms that had once benefited from the regulations. Most of the major domestic carriers opposed the deregulation of civil aviation, but they lost and the industry—once protected by government—was thrown open to competition starting in 1978. The fears of many of the established carriers were realized when new low-cost entrants and competitive pressures drove marginal prices below average prices for existing high-cost airlines, forcing many into mergers or bankruptcy.

It might be argued that the new regulations, such as those pertaining to auto safety or worker health, imposed costs that could easily be passed on to the consumer or that served to restrict entry into, and thus reduce competition in, certain industries. In some cases this turned out to be the case. But that was not how business perceived these issues. There is little evidence that business conspired in the passage of these laws or offered merely pro forma or self-serving opposition. Rightly or wrongly, corporate America thought it had been beaten, and beaten decisively.

The Changing Political Environment

In the 1950s the dominant form of corporate political representation was the trade association (such as the American Petroleum Institute or the National Coal Association) and the peak association (such as the NAM and the Chamber of Commerce). The former were highly pragmatic, the latter distinctively ideological. A trade association spoke for a particular industry on matters that affected most or all firms in that industry in more or less the same way, such as most market regulation. A peak association represented business on those matters that affected most businesses in the same way, such as much labor and tax legislation. Only a few firms maintained individual Washington representatives, and coalitions among firms, though they were occasionally formed, were relatively rare.

The rise of process regulation revealed the weakness of the older system of representation. Process regulations often affected different firms within the same industry differently. For example, rules governing pollution emitted from power generators had different technological and cost implications depending on whether the utility burned gas, oil, or coal and, if the latter, whether low-sulfur or high-sulfur coal. Utilities located in the East near abundant sources of high-sulfur coal had interests that differed from those located in the Southwest close to mines producing low-sulfur coal.

The cost of retrofitting existing blast furnaces to bring them into compliance with health and safety standards might well be greater than building new and technologically more advanced furnaces; thus, safety and health rules might penalize old steel mills and advantage new ones.

Moreover, process regulations created markets for firms that sold equipment used to make manufacturing processes conform to the regulations. As a result, firms seeking to overturn such regulations no longer had only diffuse, unorganized opponents to contend with; they also had organized industries that stood to gain from the enforcement of these regulations. Utilities might not like to install smokestack scrubbers, but the makers of these scrubbers saw matters differently.

But there was a deeper problem with the old system of corporate representation—its inability to shape mass or elite opinion that supported, if it did not initiate, many of the new process regulations. The politics of market regulation was insider politics, that is, it involved making low-visibility, personal appeals to key legislators and administrators. The politics of process regulation was, to a much greater degree, outsider politics: it required a firm to counter adverse publicity; make arguments to a wide audience of reporters, editors, and public-interest lobbyists; and generate (where possible) grassroots support for its position. Insider politics involves networking; outsider politics involves mobilization.[7]

There had always been some amount of outsider politics in the business repertoire: industrial opposition to much of the New Deal (and in particular to labor legislation) and to government plans for publicly financed housing or medical care led to advertising campaigns stressing the theme that the Constitution did not authorize nor did economic prudence warrant these initiatives. The slogans used in these campaigns tended to be simple, not to say simplistic: the proposals were "un-American," "socialistic," or "unconstitutional." Such messages had some effect but only under circumstances that, by the late 1960s, no longer obtained. Two conditions in particular were important. First, for an ideological argument against a proposal to carry any weight, the proposal had to constitute a new departure, even a radically new one, in existing practice, such that one could plausibly argue that it lacked constitutional warrant or historical precedence. By the late 1960s that argument no longer had much force: there was scarcely any aspect of American life into which the government had not already intruded with the consent of the Supreme Court.

Second, if a pro-business advertising campaign were to be received sympathetically, the business community had to enjoy broad popular support, such that its pronouncements would be given great weight and its opponents would seem to represent a political fringe. Beginning in the early

1960s, however, the very high public confidence in business leaders (and, indeed, in most institutional leaders) had begun to wane. Whereas in 1968 70 percent of the public said they thought business tries to strike a fair balance between profits and the public interest, by 1976 only 15 percent had these views.[8] By the late 1960s the "legitimacy barrier" that could have kept many forms of regulation off the national agenda had collapsed; now, almost any proposal was politically legitimate.[9] But at the very time when business had to fight to control the political agenda, its capacity for doing so had been weakened by a popular loss of confidence in business leaders. Some of this loss could be ascribed to particular crises or scandals, such as the Unocal oil spill on the Santa Barbara beaches in 1969 and the birth defects caused by thalidomide in 1961.[10] Another part could be attributed to public concern over high oil prices following the Arab oil embargo in the early 1970s. But these production scandals and commodity shocks were not the main cause of the loss of confidence in business leadership. Corporations, along with labor unions and government officials, were experiencing a general, long-term public reevaluation that might best be explained as the evaporation of the artificially high esteem corporations and the government had enjoyed as a consequence of World War II and the postwar euphoria associated with the Eisenhower administration.[11]

The need for business to adopt an outsider or mobilization strategy was intensified by changes in Congress that began in the late 1960s and reached fruition in the early 1970s. An insider strategy fit comfortably with a Congress dominated by a few powerful committee chairmen who controlled the agenda by quietly killing bills they did not like. Owing to changes brought about by members of the House Democratic caucus in the early 1970s, the old Congress had been replaced by a new Congress. In the new one power was vastly more decentralized, individual members greatly empowered, the staffs much enlarged, and committee meetings far more open to public scrutiny. These changes created strong incentives for individual members, even the most junior ones, to become associated with high-profile issues that would have substantial publicity value and to introduce bills regarding these issues without deferring to the House leadership. Coalitions still had to be formed to secure the passage of these bills, but now the coalitions tended to be more ad hoc and issue-specific and less regularly party-oriented. One revealing measure of the newfound importance of ad hoc coalitions was the emergence of issue caucuses as a feature of congressional organization. These caucuses reflected ethnic, regional, economic, and ideological alignments among like-minded members. In 1959 there were only four; by the late 1980s there were over one hundred.

Corporations had to develop a political strategy that was adapted to a more decentralized, individualistic, and entrepreneurial Congress. This strategy would have to be based on the assumption that key congressional leaders could no longer be counted on to block or pass any given bill; instead, a host of individual members would have to be cultivated. To reach individual members who were increasingly elected and reelected without the aid of local party organizations, corporations would have to mobilize individual voters in each member's district. To shape the kinds of coalitions that would form around any given bill, corporations would have to provide timely, detailed, and politically useful facts about the bill and its alternatives. To cope with the reliance of these coalitions on powerful symbols ("CLEAN WATER!" "HEALTHY BABIES!" "PREVENT CANCER!") as a way of maintaining unity and overcoming opposition, corporations would have to develop an equally powerful imagery of their own ("SAVE JOBS!" "COMPETE WITH THE JAPANESE!" "FIND NEW LIFESAVING DRUGS!").

To execute this strategy, firms would have to gather information about threats and opportunities quickly and mobilize employees and managers promptly. No firm could assume that its interests were identical to those of every other firm in its industry. No firm could assume that it could afford to rely on ideological slogans to keep government at arm's length. These facts implied a new pattern of corporate representation, one that gave the individual firm direct and particular representation in Washington and relied more on ad hoc coalitions among like-minded firms than on the presumed unity of a trade association or the pro-business stance of a peak association.

The New Corporate Political Actor

David Vogel has cataloged how these considerations were put into practice. Between 1968 and 1978 the number of firms with their own public affairs office in Washington increased from one hundred to more than five hundred. By 1980 more than 80 percent of the *Fortune* 500 companies had their own Washington office, over half of which had been created since 1970. Nearly a third were staffed by more than ten persons. Between 1974 and 1979, three-fourths of the *Fortune* 500 companies had promoted their public affairs officers to the rank of corporate vice president. Firms that did not find it cost-effective to have their own Washington office retained representation from among the lawyers and lobbyists for hire there; by 1982, 2,445 firms had some form of representation in the nation's capital. In 1978 a survey showed that the chief executive officers of the *Fortune* 1,000 were spending about 40 percent of their time on public and governmental issues, twice the amount of time spent only two years earlier. Boards of directors were increasingly selecting as their firms' CEOs people with backgrounds in law and experience in representation. The top job in chemical companies was once reserved for scientists, that in electric utilities for engineers; now both kinds of firms were increasingly choosing lawyers as their CEOs.[12]

When different firms experienced a common policy problem, they increasingly formed ad hoc coalitions rather than relying on trade or peak associations. The effort to change product liability law was an important example. The Product Liability Alliance, formed in the 1980s, was itself an assemblage of earlier coalitions dedicated to this issue. Under the leadership of Robert Malott, CEO of FMC Corporation, it eventually embraced over two hundred corporations, organizations, and industry associations. It was active for the better part of a decade without achieving anything like a victory. Despite making only glacial progress, it persisted, with its leaders and members acquiring greater skill and a deeper understanding of Washington politics. In particular, it learned the lessons of the new era of congressional policy-making—the need for constant public education, the importance of having the tenacious commitment and direct involvement of CEOs, and the difficult art of building broad alliances within a decentralized Congress.[13] This and other efforts like it exemplified a vast increase in the level of corporate commitment and sophistication compared with the struggle, thirty years earlier, over reciprocal trade.

Though single-firm representation and ad hoc coalitions gained in importance, the traditional trade and peak associations continued to operate. But they had to make adjustments as well. The semiconductor industry proved to be one of the most skilled at adapting to the new circumstances. For the first twenty years of its existence, the industry had no representation in Washington. Some firms belonged to various electronics trade associations, but these groups were too large and diverse to be especially helpful. In 1977 the big chip manufacturers, such as Intel and Motorola, formed the Semiconductor Industry Association. Slowly it recruited allies among related firms. Its approach to Washington was to enlist key executives to make frequent personal calls, supply data, generate press releases, and capitalize on the glamour associated with a high-tech business. It downplayed ideology and partisan politics and emphasized cooperation and national goals. As a result it obtained much more government aid in the industry's trade wars with Japan than did comparable industries facing comparable rivals in the 1950s.[14]

Though the advent of process regulation affected almost all corporations, they had an especially dramatic effect on small ones. Before the passage of such laws as the Occupational Safety and Health Act (OSHA) and the Employment Retirement Income Security Act (ERISA), many small firms had never experienced federal regulations involving anything more complicated than collecting income and Social Security taxes from their employees. When OSHA and ERISA hit, small companies were galvanized. Few could afford to have their own representatives in Washington, and so they enrolled in large numbers in trade and peak associations that specialized in representing small business. The result was a dramatic increase in the membership of the National Federation of Independent Business (NFIB) and the National Small Business Association.[15]

Some of the older associations did not adapt as easily. The NAM lost members (its peak year was 1957) and influence. In an effort to rebuild itself, it began to moderate its ideological positions and to offer alternatives to government policies that it once opposed outright. By contrast, the Chamber of Commerce gained members during the 1970s and the early 1980s, largely as a result of an intensive recruiting campaign. As a result of its efforts, the Chamber enhanced its ability to generate grassroots (i.e., local, small business) support for its congressional lobbying efforts. And it, like the NAM, began to become more accommodationist. But the NAM and the Chamber, in trying to reposition themselves for the new political era, faced a quandary: if they wanted to grow, they had to recruit small firms; big firms were not much interested in working through peak associations. But small firms were unhappy with an accommodationist stance: feeling deeply threatened by unfamiliar and burdensome regulations, they wanted representatives who would fight hard. NFIB was prepared to do just that, and to be critical of the Chamber in the process. Soon the Chamber found itself being shunned by some large firms that found it too diverse and cumbersome and by many small firms that thought it too soft and yielding. As a result, the success of its earlier membership recruitment efforts suffered some reversals. Between 1989 and 1991 the Chamber's annual revenues fell from $72 to $66 million.[16] Both organizations, but especially the Chamber, remain important, but their ability to influence complex legislation continues to be hampered by their size, diversity, and governance structures. They can be useful as generators of mail and calls to Washington and as sources of pro-business testimony before Congress, but many corporate leaders, especially big-firm CEOs, find other avenues of political access more useful.[17]

Notable among these are the elite business groups such as the Business Roundtable, an exclusive fraternity of top executives that relies on status to

THE CORPORATION AS A POLITICAL ACTOR

win access to the White House and that does not delegate its representational function to a paid staff. The Roundtable, limited to about two hundred CEOs, conducts its work through member-run task forces (the Product Liability Alliance began as a Roundtable task force). Its style is pragmatic, its language nonideological, its key resource prestige. Begun in 1972, its existence is organizational testimony to the fact that most of the top corporate leaders of America have abandoned the effort to maintain a boundary around government power in favor of an effort to direct the use of that power. In an earlier period, when business viewed government as either an adversary to be overcome or an ally to be exploited, something like the Roundtable would either not have existed or, if it existed, would have enjoyed its greatest success when an antigovernment, pro-business president such as Ronald Reagan was in office. In fact, the Roundtable had more influence in the Carter than in the Reagan administration.[18] Government today, in the view of many top corporate leaders, is not a force that can either be contained or directed; rather, it is one that responds to its own powerful incentives, that will regulate business whether business wants that or not, and with which one must negotiate the best available deal. Business defenders of the Roundtable's accommodationist strategy point to the failures of the NAM's more adversarial stance; business critics of the Roundtable worry that it often sells out economic principles (as evidenced by its willingness to endorse President Carter's wage and price guidelines).

Trade associations have proliferated as industry has specialized and government has grown. But there are signs that corporate leaders are increasingly suspicious that trade association staffs may not be the best representatives of vital firm interests.[19] This suspicion may have been sharpened by the recent increase in the salaries of trade association executives at a time when the combined impact of an economic downturn and a wave of corporate mergers led to declining revenues and mergers among many trade associations. The American Council of Life Insurance merged with the National Association of Life Companies, the Association of Bank Holding Companies with the Association of Reserve City Bankers, the Industrial Biotechnology Association with the Association of Biotechnology Companies, and the American Paper Institute with the National Forest Products Association and the Forest Industry Council on Taxation. The Health Insurance Association of America lost four of its biggest corporate members.[20]

Amid the restructuring of the system of business representation that occurred during the 1970s and '80s, corporate America won some victories and sustained some losses. It prevailed in many fights over labor law (such as the ban on common situs picketing), it made progress but with no clear victories on other issues (such as product liability reform), and it began to have an impact on the way some kinds of environmental laws were written (such as the authorization of tradable emission rights in the 1990 amendments to the Clean Air Act). In the 1986 Tax Reform Act it obtained reductions in corporate rates (which it liked) but at the price of losing many exemptions and deductions (which it did not like). But there was no massive rollback in regulatory burdens; on the contrary, new crises were now quickly followed by new regulations.

The new system of corporate representation was, in effect, based on the assumption that there would be fewer opportunities for drawing a line in the sand against an unwanted expansion of government authority and more opportunities for negotiating how that expansion would occur. A telling example is the position of much of big business on President Clinton's health care reform proposal. In 1953, business would have simply opposed it root and branch; in 1993, by contrast, it opposed the Clinton version but endorsed, provisionally, the more moderate (but still costly and complex) version offered by Representative Jim Cooper. This was a tactic; most firms probably wanted no comprehensive federal plan at all. But it was a sign of the times that such a tactic seemed prudent. In 1953, business could afford to be seen as opposed to federal ("socialized") health plans; in 1993, it could not afford to be seen in that light.

Similarly, the chemical industry once viewed itself as the proud product of American science and technology. The idea that its processes should be regulated in any detail would have been dismissed by the scientists and engineers who ran Dow, Du Pont, or Union Carbide as the scheme of an (at best) uninformed or (at worst) malicious nonscientist. "Better Living Through Chemistry" was more than one firm's slogan, it was an idea genuinely embraced by the entire industry. Then came Bhopal and the death of hundreds of Indians when a Union Carbide plant experienced a catastrophic failure. The result was the development of a major program of industry self-regulation designed to either head off or at least moderate additional governmental regulations.[21]

Client politics remained important in the new era, but the chances of any firm or industry getting a benefit unobserved and unopposed by other interests were now much reduced. Even the once-powerful lobby that had obtained government subsidies for tobacco growers had to settle, in the face of antismoking campaigns, for a system of government-administered but industry-funded subsidies.

Not all of the growth in firm-specific representation was driven by regulatory pressures. As the federal government grew, it not only imposed more costs, it offered more benefits. Many of these benefits took the form of government contracts to buy everything from military hardware to office desks and to acquire services ranging from consulting work to telecommunications. Indeed, the demand voiced by business leaders for greater efficiency in government has often led, via contracting out, to greater business for business.[22] There is evidence that a significant part of the increases in firm representation in Washington has been caused by the need to acquire and monitor these contractual relationships.[23]

Corporate Tactics

The proactive, firm-specific style of contemporary corporate political representation combines new and old lobbying tactics. The old insider tactics are familiar enough: drafting bills, supplying information, buttonholing members of Congress and White House aides, and hosting receptions and meetings. These have not changed, except to enlarge the definition of who constitutes an insider. Business has discovered that it must pay more attention to anonymous congressional staffers and lower-level bureaucrats and work with rank-and-file members of Congress as well as congressional leaders.

The new outsider tactics include telephone, letter-writing, and FAX-message campaigns in which employees, managers, customers, and suppliers are stimulated, where possible, to support a firm's or industry's position. Among the best-known examples of these were the mobilization by the banking industry of popular opposition to a proposal to withhold taxes on savings deposits and by the soft-drink industry of public hostility to a regulation that would have banned certain artificial sweeteners.

Business also makes more artful use of television advertisements to carry its message. The campaign by the Health Insurance Association of America against the Clinton health plan was an especially effective example: it portrayed a scene in a home with actors portraying a couple worried about a health plan they did not understand. It suggested, without declaiming slogans, that the plan was arcane, complex, expensive, and perhaps unworkable. In the past, an announcer would have labeled the plan socialistic, but business has learned that talking heads delivering heavy-handed slogans are no longer very effective.

The most controversial and least well understood corporate political tactic has been the use of money to finance election campaigns, especially the money given through political action committees (PACs). For many decades it has been illegal for corporations to make campaign contributions, but not until the passage of the 1971 campaign finance reform act (and its later amendments) was it possible to enforce that rule. The 1971 law authorized firms (along with unions, trade associations, and other groups) to form a PAC that could raise and distribute campaign contributions subject to the following rules: the PAC must have at least fifty members and give to at least five candidates; contributions must be voluntary; no one person can give more than five thousand dollars to a PAC, and no PAC may give more than five thousand dollars to any single candidate in any given election. (Since a candidate may run in both a primary and a general election, the maximum contribution in a single "election cycle" is ten thousand dollars.) A PAC can also give up to fifteen thousand dollars to a political party and make unlimited "independent expenditures" on behalf of candidates. An "independent expenditure" is one made without the cooperation or consent of, and not in consultation with, a candidate or his or her agents. (In practice, independent expenditures are usually made to purchase ads attacking disliked candidates.) A firm can use corporate funds to pay the administrative costs of its PAC (no firm can have more than one) but not to make contributions to candidates. Foreign corporations may not form PACs, but the U.S. subsidiaries of foreign companies may if the PAC officers and contributors are U.S. citizens.

There were virtually no corporate PACs when the law was passed in 1971; by 1992 there were over seventeen hundred. In that election they gave a total of sixty-four million dollars to congressional candidates. This amount of money has conjured up images of business-related money flooding the electoral process, producing what some critics call "the best Congress money can buy."

The reality is a good deal different. There is great variation in the size and tactics of corporate PACs, but the typical one is a rather modest effort. In 1980 only about half of the *Fortune* 500 companies had a PAC at all, and the average dollar contribution per candidate of those that did was only about five hundred dollars.[24] Over the succeeding decade, the average contribution drifted slightly higher, but it remains the case that it is typically much less than one thousand dollars. Of the ten PACs that gave the most money in the 1992 election, none was sponsored by a corporation (most of the Big Ten were the creatures of professional associations, such as realtors and physicians, or of labor unions). The contributions of NEPAC, the Northrop Corporation PAC, are typical of most big corporate PACs: in the 1986 election, it gave small amounts to over one hundred House candidates and over thirty Senate candidates. Most of the contributions were between three to five hundred dollars; there were only twenty-one House contributions that amounted to one thousand dollars or more and only one that exceeded three thousand dollars. Corporate PACs make almost no independent expenditures.

Not only do corporate PACs tend to write small checks, they tend to send them to incumbents. In 1992 nearly 80 percent of corporate PAC contributions went to incumbents; since most incumbents were then Democrats, this meant that Democrats, including very liberal ones, got about half of all the campaign money raised by corporations.[25] (Labor unions, by contrast, gave almost no money to Republicans.)

These averages hide some important differences, differences that appear to be associated with the strategic needs of particular industries. The firms in most industries follow what might be called an accommodationist strategy: they give many small contributions to a large number of incumbents with little regard to party or ideology. Firms in these industries are trying to maintain access—the opportunity to get their phone calls returned and to arrange occasional meetings with key legislators. To the extent there are large contributions, they tend to go to legislators occupying key committee posts. Industries following an accommodationist strategy tend to be ones that have large government contracts (such as aerospace), that obtain important government subsidies (such as tobacco), or that have a long history of market regulation to which they have made a more or less comfortable adjustment (such as broadcasting).[26]

By contrast, the firms in some industries follow a more adversarial strategy. They are more likely than accommodationist firms to fund challengers, Republicans, and conservatives. In this group one finds industries that have recently been subjected to particularly intense process regulation (such as mining, chemical manufacture, petroleum refining, and metal products) or that face particularly acute foreign competition (such as textiles and shipbuilding) or both (such as paper and wood products). There is also a tendency for adversarial firms to give somewhat larger amounts than do accommodationist firms: those in mining, chemical, petroleum, and paper were (at least in 1980) twice as likely to write checks in amounts between one and five thousand dollars than were those in drugs, broadcasting, or automobiles.[27]

It is beyond the scope of this essay to analyze with any care the result of these corporate spending patterns. A fair summary of the existing studies would, I think, be this: there is no consistent and systematic evidence showing that PAC contributions, independent of other factors (such as constituency pressures, legislator ideology, and party affiliation), have a significant impact on voting in Congress. Some studies find some effects in some issue areas, others find no effects in other areas.[28]

The uncertainty in the data is not hard to explain. It is very difficult, even with the most advanced statistical techniques, to sort out the independent effect of money on a legislator's voting decision, especially since the causal connection between money and voting is unclear. A PAC may give money to a representative to induce him or her to act in a certain way, as a reward for already (and on other grounds) having acted in that way, or simply to maintain access to someone without regard to how he or she acts.

Even if these analytic problems did not exist, it would be astonishing for one to find a strong relationship between campaign money and policy outcomes. Most legislators operate most of the time in an environment in which scores of interests contribute small (and occasionally large) sums of money on all sides of almost every issue. Under these circumstances, the legislator is free to choose a course of action without risking the loss of large sums from any big donor. Sometimes, of course, a legislator may have to decide how to act on an issue supported by large sums with no equivalent sums on the other side, but in these cases it is quite likely that every other feature of the situation—the constituents' expressed preferences, personal ideology, and obvious reelection needs—would incline him or her to make the same decision as the one endorsed by the money givers.

There are ways whereby corporate (and other) PACs can send a stronger message. The most important is "bundling": combining checks from several like-minded PACs into one bundle and delivering the contribution all at once to an undecided legislator. We have no good data on how often bundling occurs or with what effect.

It is probably because corporate PACs have such a weak or uncertain effect on policy outcomes that so few firms, including nearly half of the *Fortune* 500, have taken the trouble to organize them. Here, as in all aspects of a corporation's life, the market speaks: money and effort that are spent without obvious advantage are money and effort on which firms will economize.

Corporate Hegemony

The United States is a capitalist nation, one of the few in which capitalism is not controversial. Except during economic crises, and to a surprising extent even then, Americans endorse (or at least accept) most of the major features of a capitalist economy—competition, private property, market exchanges, and (within very broad limits) income inequality.[29] Some writers, especially those on the Left, argue that the legitimacy enjoyed by capitalism (though not by corporate executives) in this country cannot be natural or the product of free choice. Instead, they suggest, this legitimacy must have been acquired by some combination of political manipulation and cultural conditioning.

This was the thesis of Charles E. Lindblom's influential book, *Politics and Markets*.[30] To Lindblom, the privileged position enjoyed by business in this country arises from the fact that a weak state cannot compel economic performance, it can only induce it. To induce it, government must not challenge business prerogatives on any fundamental matters. It may tax and regulate, but only up to a point. This deference that politics pays to markets is reinforced by business conditioning of the popular mind through its influence on schooling, the mass media, and university and cultural life.

It is odd that Lindblom published these views in 1977, since it was at that very time that corporate America had undergone its most severe political challenge since the 1930s. At the very moment when all manner of process regulations were being imposed and unfriendly legal doctrines being enunciated, business firms were portrayed as enjoying a "privileged position." His response, of course, was that these challenges affected only the secondary interests of business, not their primary ones. Property, markets, and privately directed investment were the primary or grand interests of business, and these were not seriously challenged. Corporate hegemony remained intact.

One can quarrel with the extent to which these fundamental interests were in fact immune to government interference. Process regulation by its very nature alters property rights just as market regulation alters market position. Surely few corporate executives felt, in the early 1970s, that they enjoyed anything faintly resembling a privileged position. But in a deeper sense there is an element of truth in Lindblom's position: Americans still support both regulation and competition, government and markets. Capitalism is legitimate.

That it is, however, is hardly the result of corporate conditioning. The claim that business induces people to embrace business values by shaping the textbooks we study, the newspapers we read, and the television we view is so much at odds with both common experience and scholarly research as to be ludicrous. The antibusiness values of the entertainment industry, the editors and journalists of the national press, and the professors at our most prestigious universities have been frequently documented.[31] But it is scarcely necessary to consult these documents: try to recall the last time one watched a motion picture or television program in which corporations and their executives were not portrayed as (at best) hopelessly stuffy or (at worst) scheming villains. Anyone who thinks that public school textbooks are friendly to business has not read many; if they are friendly to anything, it is to the plight of various oppressed groups. And anyone who teaches in a university and thinks it defends pro-business values must not have an appointment in the social sciences or humanities.

What, then, can explain the willingness of Americans to support the key elements of a capitalist system? The answer, though difficult to specify with any exactitude, must be found in the nation's history and a popular culture that is much older than capitalism, corporations, or industrialization. Tocqueville noticed this in the early 1830s, when we were still an agrarian society: Americans were committed to individual self-reliance, limited government, and private property. Immigration did not change this culture, in large part because it was so congruent with the motives—a fear of persecution and a desire for material advancement—that had led immigrants to America. When large corporations finally emerged, they were the object of mixed reviews: admiration for their accomplishments in building railroads, generating power, and supplying consumer wants, and suspicion because they constituted an undesirable and even threatening concentration of power.

Unlike in Europe, big national government arose in America, as Thomas McCraw has argued, after big corporations were already in place.[32] The result was a struggle for power, with corporations defending their position and government seeking to reduce it. The result was a unique pattern of quasi-cooperative, quasi-adversarial business-government relations, an uneasy tension between bargaining and fighting, respect and hostility, that cannot be found in another industrialized nation. Elsewhere, big government preceded big business, and so business grew up under the tutelage and often at the direction of the political authorities. Small wonder that abroad, antitrust laws are weak, economic regulations are designed by neo-corporatist alliances between government ministers and business executives, and investment decisions are heavily influenced by national industrial policies.

In Europe, where corporations experience the greatest government support, the political system is most deeply divided between parties of the far Right and far Left. In the United States, where corporations are often in an adversarial relationship with government, party politics is moderate and radical parties almost nonexistent. Americans do not ordinarily debate the grand political and economic alternatives or flirt much with Marxist, absolutist, or social democratic parties. The reason has little to do with corporate cultural hegemony and everything to do with history, institutions, and an individualist culture. One might almost turn the Lindblom argument on its head: in those nations, such as Germany or Japan, where business enjoys the greatest political privileges, it has the least legitimacy; in the United States, where it enjoys the fewest privileges, it has the greatest legitimacy.

Business executives might take some small comfort from this fact. They profess not to like a government that is slow, cumbersome, conflict-ridden, suspicious of many ordinary business activities, and sometimes animated by a desire to impose what they view as the most unreasonable regulations. They may yearn for an older time when the federal government was small and (ordinarily) not threatening. Whatever the merit—and there is much— in the business desire for a government policy that is reasonable, pre-dictable, and sympathetic, the price attached to having such a government may be very high. In a strong state with well-established coordinating mech-anisms for managing government-business relations, the conflicts *within* the government—a fractious Congress, an inconsistent bureaucracy, an ag-gressive judiciary—would be pushed *outside* the government into the arena of political parties and social movements. Marxist, populist, and "green" parties, reflective of deep cleavages in public opinion, are found precisely in those nations that have such formal or informal coordinating mechanisms. The benefits to business of our fragmented, uncoordinated, adversarial sys-tem may be precisely its tendency to maintain public confidence that "no one is getting away with anything" and thus to reduce the chances of mass disaffection from either democracy or capitalism.

Notes

1. For the classic account, see E. E. Schattschneider, *Politics, Pressures, and the Tariff* (New York: Prentice-Hall, 1935).

2. Raymond A. Bauer, Ithiel de Sola Pool, and Lewis Anthony Dexter, *American Business and Public Policy* (New York: Atherton Press, 1963), p. 324.

3. Elizabeth Drew, as quoted in Mark V. Nadel, *The Politics of Consumer Protection* (Indianapolis, Ind.: Bobbs-Merrill, 1971), p. 143.

4. Client politics is distinguished from other kinds of political transactions in James Q. Wilson, ed., *The Politics of Regulation* (New York: Basic Books, 1980), chap. 10.

5. George Stigler, "The Theory of Economic Regulation," *Bell Journal of Economics and Management Science* 2 (1971): 1–21.

6. See Paul Quirk, "Food and Drug Administration," in *The Politics of Regulation*, ed. James Q.Wilson (New York: Basic Books, 1980), esp. pp. 191–97.

7. The distinction between insider and outsider politics is adapted from

Hedrick Smith, *The Power Game* (New York: Random House, 1988), chap. 9. Smith uses the terms "old-breed" and "new-breed" lobbying.

8. Seymour Martin Lispet and William Schneider, *The Confidence Gap* (New York: Free Press, 1983).

9. I explore the significance of the legitimacy barrier in James Q. Wilson, "American Politics, Then and Now," *Commentary,* February 1979, pp. 39–46.

10. Thalidomide was never marketed in the United States; the birth defects occurred among European or Canadian babies or among some American babies whose mothers had taken thalidomide while traveling abroad. But the shock of learning of deformed infants was skillfully exploited by then-Senator Estes Kefauver to aid in the passage of the 1962 drug amendments.

11. This argument is developed in James Q. Wilson, "The Contradictions of the Advanced Capitalist State," *Forbes,* September 14, 1992.

12. David Vogel, *Fluctuating Fortunes: The Political Power of Business in America* (New York: Basic Books, 1989), chap. 8, esp. pp. 195–99. See also Graham K. Wilson, *Business and Politics: A Comparative Introduction,* 2d ed. (Chatham, N.J.: Chatham House, 1990), chap. 2; and Kay Lehman Schlozman and John T. Tierney, *Organized Interests and American Democracy* (New York: Harper and Row, 1986), pp. 74–82.

13. Martha Wagner Weinberg, "The Political Education of Bob Malott, CEO," *Harvard Business Review* (May–June 1988): 74–81.

14. David B. Yoffie, "How an Industry Builds Political Advantage," *Harvard Business Review* (May–June 1988): 82–89.

15. Vogel, *Fluctuating Fortunes,* p. 199.

16. The problems of the Chamber of Commerce are discussed in Kirk Victor, "Deal Us In," *National Journal,* April 3, 1993, pp. 805–9.

17. Sar A. Levitan and Martha R. Cooper, *Business Lobbies* (Baltimore, Md.: Johns Hopkins University Press, 1984), chap. 2.

18. Ibid., p. 38.

19. Graham K. Wilson, "The Political Behavior of Large Corporations" (unpublished paper, Department of Political Science, University of Wisconsin, n.d).

20. Peter H. Stone, "Still Flying High," *National Journal,* January 23, 1993, pp. 176–88.

21. I am indebted to the research of Peter Kappas at UCLA for this example; his extensive analysis of chemical self-regulation is forthcoming.

22. For one account of this growth, see Donald F. Kettl, *Sharing Power: Public Governance and PrivateMarkets* (Washington, D.C.: Brookings Institution, 1993).

23. Graham K. Wilson, "Corporate Political Strategies," *British Journal of Political Science* 20 (April 1990): 281–88.

24. Mike H. Ryan, Carl L. Swanson, and Rogene A. Buchholz, *Corporate Strategy, Public Policy and the Fortune 500* (Oxford: Basil Blackwell, 1987), p. 128. See also Larry J. Sabato, *PAC Power* (New York: Norton, 1985), pp. 84–86.

25. Press release, Federal Election Commission, April 29, 1993, pp. 1–3.

26. Ryan, Swanson and Buchholz, *Corporate Strategy*, pp. 145–49. See also Theodore J. Eismeir and Philip H. Pollock, "The Retreat from Partisanship: Why the Dog Didn't Bark in the 1984 Election," in *Business Strategy and Public Policy,* ed. Alfred Marcus, Allan Kaufman, and David R. Beam (New York: Quorum Books, 1987), pp. 137–47.

27. Ibid. See also J. David Gopoian, "What Makes PACs Tick? An Analysis of the Allocation Patterns of Economic Interest Groups," *American Journal of Political Science* 28 (1984): pp. 259–81.

28. See the summary in M. Margaret Conway, "PACs in the Political Process," in *Interest Group Politics*, 3d ed., ed. Allan J. Cigler and Burdett A. Loomis (Washington, D.C.: CQ Press, 1991), p. 211.

29. Herbert McCloskey and John Zaller, *The American Ethos* (Cambridge, Mass.: Harvard University Press, 1984), chap. 5. See also Andrew Schonfield, *Modern Capitalism* (Oxford: Oxford University Press, 1969), and G. K. Wilson, *Business and Politics*, pp. 39–42.

30. Charles E. Lindblom, *Politics and Markets* (New York: Basic Books, 1977).

31. See, e.g., S. Robert Lichter, Stanley Rothman, and Linda S. Lichter, *The Media Elite* (New York: Hastings House, 1986); William Schneider and I. A. Lewis, "Views on the News," *Public Opinion*, August–September 1985, p. 7; Everett Carll Ladd Jr. and Seymour Martin Lipset, *The Divided Academy: Professors and Politics* (New York: Norton, 1976); Seymour Martin Lipset, "The Academic Mind at the Top: The Political Behavior and Values of Faculty Elites," *Public Opinion Quarterly* 46 (summer 1982): 143–68.

32. Thomas K. McCraw, "Business and Government: The Origins of the Adversary Relationship," *California Management Review* 26 (winter 1984): 33–52.

14

Architecture and the
Business Corporation

✦

NEIL HARRIS

In the modern era, four great categories of clients have divided support for
architecture among themselves: churches; rulers and governments; private
builders erecting domestic structures; and corporate enterprises, seeking
places within which to train, produce, store, display, sell, or manage. For
one reason or another, each of these customer groups has dominated specific moments of architectural invention. A stroll through the highlights of
post-Renaissance architecture in Europe quickly reveals their shifting status, as sources of both wealth and professional honor.

In the United States the patterns of patronage have been closely related
to social and political experience. Until recently governmental support, on
a national level, was much limited by both tradition and constitutional interpretation. Churches, in all their numbers, have been competitive and
nonofficial, only rarely supplied with the capital required by impressive ec-
clesiastical commissions. Thus two great sources of potential architectural
employment operated under conditions that might be called constrained,
and the challenge of capitalizing a high proportion of significant American
architecture was placed on the shoulders of private clients, building for either domestic or institutional purposes.

The domestic story has been surveyed often, among others, in broader
architectural histories, treatments of pattern books, and studies of evolving
gender cultures and philosophies of family living.[1] These narratives have
been further enlivened by the presence of extravagant private clients, whose

ambitions and egos encouraged architects to produce structures simultaneously expensive and original.

The history of corporate patronage, on the other hand, has been examined more intermittently. Its very diversity discourages analysis. Despite the
fact that many industrial and mercantile settings have come to symbolize
national genius, technological mastery, and modernity itself, and despite
the fact that business construction has often dominated total annual building expenditures, corporate architecture has rarely enjoyed an integrated
analysis.[2] Indeed, when *The Corporation in Modern Society* was published,
no contributor even mentioned the role of the corporation as a patron of architecture or indeed as the patron of any other art form. Nor did any hint
appear that many large American corporations were just about to enter, in
a massive way, the arena of cultural philanthropy, and had already, for a variety of reasons, linked their reputations to an endorsement of design modernism. The claims, ambitions, and responsibilities of corporations as fun-
ders of culture would swell during the sixties, seventies, and eighties. But
they were not entirely without precedent, particularly within architecture,
as a review of the previous century reveals.

A mapping strategy may suggest just how more recent activities built
upon—and differed from—what came before. After invoking some historical background, this paper will confine itself to three moments of corporate
activity—in the 1920s, during the 1950s and '60s, and during the 1970s
and '80s. To provide at least some minimal focus, only structures designed
to house profit-seeking firms, along with their administrative, research, service, or manufacturing employees, will be considered. Stores, showrooms,
and storage and transmission structures all are excluded, partly for reasons
of space and coherence, and partly because of the many other variables
their appearance invoked. Forceful and ingenious as many of these building
types have been, they probably represent less of a national contribution
than the headquarters complexes, the major areas to be considered, and
they will be joined, to a lesser extent, by factories and banks, other corporate arenas that occupied the extended attention of American architects.

In the years before World War I, many types of business were already investing in self-consciously conceived and symbolically rich structures.
Notable among these were banks.[3] In the nineteenth century American
banks were notoriously unstable, and in a country where wide distrust and
bitter debate surrounded the issuance of paper money and the allocation of
credit, banks and bankers often acquired sinister and unsavory reputations.
Partly acknowledging a need to project strength and stability, partly in-

dulging their personal taste, partly as slaves to fashion, and partly to associate themselves with civic goals and official authority, bankers became energetic adapters of neoclassicism and employers of notable American architects, including Thomas U. Walter (who helped design the Capitol in Washington), William Strickland, Benjamin Latrobe, and Robert Mills, dominant figures in the antebellum profession.[4]

After the Civil War, greater diversity seemed possible and local variations flourished. In Philadelphia, Frank Furness produced a series of idiosyncratically picturesque and richly ornamented banks, attracting wide attention and some controversy. Other architects, like Russell Sturgis, Joseph Lyman Silsbee, and Horatio N. White, building in upstate New York, flirted with Ruskinian Gothic, French Empire, and Louis XII versions.[5] But Greco-Roman dress for banking never entirely disappeared, and by the late 1890s, despite some growing competition from Louis Sullivan and a series of Prairie School buildings, it had reasserted itself. Most bankers believed that dignified opulence was the best way to impress potential customers and allay potential critics.[6]

Privately owned though they were, banks projected an air of public authority, and were instantly identifiable, either on village streets or on urban boulevards, their templelike features providing a distinctive livery. At the turn of the century, major firms like McKim, Mead and White, George B. Post, and D. H. Burnham outdid one another with the splendor of their marbles, the height of their domes, the glitter of murals and stained glass, and the elaborateness of their ironwork. Bankers encountered (and commissioned) extensive apologias for spending money on their financial houses, written by specialists in planning and design. Conservative though they might have seemed as a professional group, bankers discovered advantages in hiring well-known architects with a demonstrated capacity for planning efficiency, and knowledge of an ornamental vocabulary that was simultaneously expensive and restrained.

Other nineteenth-century business enterprises courting public favor and goodwill also considered architectural finish and massive scale worthwhile investments. Notable among these were telegraph companies, newspapers, wholesale and retail houses, and, most emphatically, insurance companies.[7] These last, again like banks, seeking both to stimulate public confidence and to divert attention away from visible scandals, governmental investigations, and spectacular failures, commissioned headquarters of palatial magnificence in major cities, their height and expense making them local landmarks. With the capital available to afford the best contemporary architects, occasionally sponsoring competitions among them, and often national in its advertising focus, the insurance industry clearly intended its buildings to be part of a larger marketing strategy, reproducing their facades on the pamphlets, brochures, and other promotional materials its printing plants turned out in huge numbers.

But the real breakthrough demonstrations of architectural advertising came outside the insurance industry, summed up by two early twentieth century Manhattan skyscrapers. The first of these was the 1902 commission given Ernest Flagg by Frederick Bourne, president of the Singer Sewing Machine Company, to expand his New York business center.[8] This commission produced, just a few years later, the tallest inhabited structure on earth, the "Eighth Wonder of the World," Singer advertising literature crowed.

The Singer Building demonstrated the advantages of an ambitious commission and emphasized the value of setting a record, in this case for height. It brought instant and international celebrity to the client. Sixty years later, as the Sears Tower in Chicago demonstrated, this remained an important element in commercial patronage patterns.

Like many corporate commissions in this era, the job rested almost entirely on personal connections. Ernest Flagg's circle of friends and relations included Vanderbilts and Scribners, who, as his career was in the course of development, peppered him with orders for homes and office buildings. Bourne was not a blood relation, but friends had told him about Flagg and he came to the architect directly with his proposal; he did not simply invite him to enter a competition, nor set up a corporate committee to make the choice.

The demands the crowded site made on Flagg were complex and challenging. After designing a series of smaller buildings he produced the needlelike tower that helped set the fashion for local skyscrapers. The building furthered its advertising functions by flaunting (in terra-cotta) the company colors of orange and green; a triumphant Flagg went on to design several European showrooms for the firm. The Singer Company, a symbol of American salesmanship and technology through much of the world, eagerly publicized the accomplishment in pamphlets, postcards, and advertisements. Its headquarters had become an international landmark, demonstrating the rewards that a showy building by an accomplished architect could provide.

No one followed the Singer success story more closely than Frank W. Woolworth, who just before World War I would build on it, literally and metaphorically, with his own entry into the "world's tallest" sweepstakes.[9] Woolworth's architect, Cass Gilbert, who was already known for major civic pieces like the Minnesota capitol in St. Paul, produced what traditionalist critics and many of the general public believed to be the most beautiful of the country's skyscrapers. Its gothic terra-cotta ornament, mosaic-encrusted interiors, and soaring tower produced an orgy of spiritual reference making; the phrase uttered by a local clergyman at the dedication, the "Cathedral of Commerce," epitomized the rapture it excited. Officially opened (through remote control) by the president of the United States, the Woolworth Building immediately became, as its owner confidently anticipated, a giant signboard for the five-and-ten-cent empire he ruled. While most of its floors were rented out to individual tenants (at premium prices), the Woolworth name (along with his well-publicized suite of offices near the tower's summit, decorated in Napoleonic manner) gave it clear identity. The combination of great height, vast expense, clear visibility, and a highly esteemed architectural style summarized the ingredients that promised to reward major business builders in this era.

Certainly, remaining just within the office building category, there were other, far less glittering alternatives. A group of Chicago architects had been at work, since the 1880s, on a highly distinctive set of speculative office buildings—among them the Rookery, the Old Colony, the Manhattan, and the Monadnock—that emphasized neither the owner's name nor his logo. Instead they epitomized massiveness, efficiency, convenience, and economy.[10] These qualities, far from being purely utilitarian, were, in the hands of gifted professionals like John Wellborn Root, Daniel Burnham, Holabird and Roche, and William Lebaron Jenney, expressive dreams. Plunked down in the heart of a major city, their brick facades eschewed the elaborate ornamentation and historic quotations favored by many eastern skyscrapers, although, as the twentieth century moved forward, even Chicago's towers increasingly bore neoclassical and Gothic Revival touches and, in their marbled lobbies and extraordinary light courts, indulged some taste for luxury.[11] Investors in these midwestern ventures were content, in many instances, to let the rational organization of the structures speak for themselves. In any case, the imposition of height restrictions in Chicago, which came in the 1890s, effectively prevented the kind of skyscraper competition in the nation's second city that was taking place in its first.

Industrial buildings, horizontally rather than vertically extended, encouraged midwestern architects to even more impressive efforts. While some industries, like steelmaking and meatpacking, discouraged creation of impressive, closed-in structures, the mail-order houses, particularly Montgomery Ward and Sears, Roebuck, with their immense roster of clerks

and their huge stocks of goods, did commission extensive and carefully designed central headquarters. In Buffalo the Larkin Company, also engaged
in mail-order promotions, got from Frank Lloyd Wright what some considered the most innovative office building in the country.[12] It was soon featured in company advertising, and its great motto-encrusted light court and
specially designed furniture, along with many other novelties, made it a
classic exercise in industrial bureaucracy. Printing firms, food packagers,
railroad car builders, carriage makers, and, in other parts of the country,
textile mills, shoe manufacturers, machine tool makers, and a host of other
specialized industries also required immense industrial structures.[13]

But these factories, while they adorned the letterheads and business
forms of great companies, rarely played a major part in their advertising or
image making before the early twentieth century. Great size obviously
meant something, reassuring investors and impressing customers, but industrial building materials, locations, and functions removed them from
conventionally formed lists of popular buildings. Specialists, engineers and
architects alike, could admire the inventiveness of these huge plants; professional journals occasionally featured a particularly adventuresome or
technically innovative establishment.[14] And visitors, ever since the middle
decades of the previous century when the Lowell and Manchester mills had
collectively captured the status of national tourist attractions, found much
to praise, either in the symbols of domesticity and traditional refinement
which some factories sported with their domes, cupolas, colonnades, por-
ticoes, or in the plain, uncompromising, even austere commitment to the
work ethic they expressed.[15]

But admiration for industrial buildings in America, at least before the
teens, was largely confined to professional circles and articulated by specialists. Many factories remained securely in the hands of mill doctors, as
they were called, who formed their plans on the basis of precise insurance
company calculations. Slow burning was a more significant issue for their
industrial clients than elegance of conception or detail. The exceptions
came with several larger planned complexes, like the Georgian-style industrial park known as Nela Park built for General Electric in Cleveland, or,
somewhat earlier, with creation of the town of Pullman, Illinois.[16] The industrialist George Pullman turned to a young local architect, Solon Beman,
seeking designs for an entire community, a factory for making Pullman cars
surrounded by houses, a church, hotel, schools, shopping arcades, and
other amenities. The experiment that was Pullman ended in disaster for the
firm and many of its workers with a violent strike and forced sale. "An experiment in feudalism" was the label affixed by one contemporary econo-

mist. But Beman's work was widely admired and the architect obtained a series of commissions from the Pullman Company, including its Chicago
headquarters building on Michigan Avenue.[17]

Pullman in the 1880s and Nela Park in the teens were exceptional in
the attention they attracted, although there were quite a few company
towns scattered across the country.[18] During the twenties things would
change, for both office and industrial buildings in America. In this decade,
for various reasons, both the role business could play in shaping design
ideals and the range of available options expanded.[19] Underlying this were
several things. First, the triumphant status accorded American businessmen in a decade apparently filled with limitless expansion. Large pockets of
poverty and the determined sniping of a series of artists and writers did not
seriously dent the accents of praise offered by journalists, politicians, and
clergymen to the commercial and material dreams of American traders and
manufacturers. A rising stock market, penetration into world markets, and
a range of novel products and technologies made heroic figures of a series
of American chief executives. New industries, particularly in entertainment
and communications, sought expressive outlets, and philosophies of selling
became simultaneously more precise in their advice and more comprehensive in their ambitions.[20]

Second, American production methods, typified by but not confined to
the automobile industry, achieved international reputation and, among
artists and architects alike, provided a fertile source of imagery and reflec-
tion. The River Rouge complex developed by Henry Ford, the plants of
Chrysler, Kelvinator, General Motors, Westinghouse, General Mills, and
others were not only enormous; they had, by the twenties and thirties, begun to enter the architectural lexicon as models of rational simplicity and
engineering brilliance.[21] And the engineer, in the twenties, shared honors
with the business executive. If one president could declare that "the business of America is business," another was actually an engineer himself, the
first to enter the White House. The engineering aesthetic began to be identified with corporate management, and efficiency themes appeared to deserve aesthetic recognition.

This was related to a third massive trend in the twenties that would
have much to do with new possibilities for business architecture: the emergence of modern vocabularies which sought to transcend eclectic formats
and traditional decoration in favor of materials and formal motifs that
seemed more appropriate to the twentieth century.[22] Steel, glass, and concrete now attained symbolic priority, along with machine-inspired references and exotically derived ornament.[23] Business corporations increasingly found it in their interest to identify themselves, in their structures,

packaging, showrooms, and advertisements, with a spirit of novelty and innovation.

Thus the notion of America as a business civilization whose cultural achievements could be traced to the pervasive power of commercial and industrial experiences fascinated a series of commentators, foreign and domestic.[24] They looked for evidence of the role business played in American culture in the structures that it commissioned for its own use. Factories and skyscrapers in modernistic modes became signature images for the decade as a whole, climaxed by the greatest single corporate architectural achievement sponsored by any American business group: the creation, during the 1930s, of Rockefeller Center.[25] This essentially speculative venture brought together many themes. For one, in its ambitious intellectual and artistic goals, an academically inspired thematic program that linked muralists, sculptors, ceramicists, metalworkers, and other artists, fine and applied, it associated corporate power with culture, suggesting linkages with art patronage that would be fulfilled decades later. For another, in its creation of what was essentially a new city, it caught the utopian objectives that business leaders occasionally betrayed in speaking of a social order that would match the efficiency of their commercial ideals. And third, in the Radio City theaters and the entertainment complex developed around the Rockefeller complex, the interest of business in associating itself with personalities and activities that were popular, dynamic, and contemporary became absolutely clear. Sixty years after its construction had begun, Rockefeller Center remained what was probably the most successful, if the most expensive, corporate investment in architecture, city planning, and environmental management.

The development of design motifs in the interests of corporate personality actually had been better established, earlier, in some other countries. The electrical trust, AEG, in Germany had turned to artist-architect Peter Behrens before World War I to design for it posters, ads, factory buildings, and products.[26] In the twenties Frank Pick of London Transport enlisted a series of talented artists and architects to plan the signage, the graphics, the stations, and, above all, the posters favored by the London Underground.[27] About the same time, also in Britain, Jack Beddington, of Shell-Mex, hired artists to design ads and maps for the company.[28] And, slightly later, in Chicago, the Container Corporation of America, after a conversion to modernism stimulated by the enthusiasm of its chief executive officer, Walter Paepcke, commissioned packaging, showrooms, logos, and designs from accomplished artists like Herbert Bayer and turned to a coordinated approach to promotion that brought it considerable celebrity.[29]

There were business enterprises in the twenties that reveled in more traditional displays of corporate power and dignity, or, if dignity was not their aim, happily exploited the cachet of well-known monuments. Thus the Wrigley Corporation in Chicago turned to Daniel Burnham's successor firm, Graham, Anderson, Probst, and White, for a Michigan Avenue head-quarters building.[30] This firm, skilled in creating office and institutional structures of great scale throughout the United States, produced, despite continuing height restrictions in Chicago, a brilliantly fantastic structure in white terra-cotta, with a tower modeled on La Giralda in Seville. Its obser-vation floor, 398 feet high, was for a while the highest point in the city. The landmark status of the building was emphasized by nighttime illumination, with almost two hundred projectors providing what *Architectural Forum* termed "the most striking form of advertising" for the company.[31] Wrigley Chewing Gum had already created a truly extraordinary neon sign in Times Square, perhaps the most spectacular electric sign in the country. And while much of the building was rented to individual tenants, and the image was rarely employed in company ads, it advertised the corporation exten-sively and brought to its mundane product a level of dignity that would oth-erwise have been unattainable. It also may have expressed William Wrigley's own interest in city beautification, which he demonstrated as a member of the Chicago Plan Commission.

The status architectural patronage brought individual corporations in the twenties was shown still more dramatically in a contemporary structure just across Michigan Avenue, whose commission was awarded only after it hosted what was probably the best-publicized and most influential archi-tectural competition in American history. This was Colonel Robert R. McCormick's Chicago Tribune building, a fixture in Chicago for genera-tions before it decided to move all its operations to this site along the Chicago River.[32]

None of the earlier buildings put up by the *Tribune* had required a com-petition, although several were large and lavishly appointed. The competi-tion was presented by the newspaper as an act of public largesse. "There is no precedent for this contest," it asserted, insisting that this was the first time that any corporation—business, religious, or civic—had recognized "the importance of a commercial building as a force for beauty and inspira-tion" in the lives of ordinary Americans.[33] The claim, given earlier rhetoric and a series of competitions, was certainly exaggerated. But the publicity that followed upon the several hundred submissions was indeed unprece-dented.

In this skirmish between modernism and traditionalism, traditionalism won out. There were many, then and now, who lionized the second-prize entry by Eliel Saarinen. But the Gothic tower by Raymond Hood that would soon face the Wrigley Building across the street quickly became an admired part of the Chicago scene, and an effective symbol for the newspaper to use in its promotional campaigns. As an act of corporate self-interest, the competition and the choice could hardly have been bettered, the tower's ornamentation pleasing public sentiment in a city that had developed its characteristic architecture in a spirit of decorative restraint.

Proclaiming similar civic intentions, other corporations in the United States proceeded, some of them more quietly and more traditionally, to construct monuments to themselves. But they did so now in a language that was self-consciously intended to redeem business from charges of philistine niggardliness, and to make claims for public gratitude and esteem. Ignoring the great insurance towers and newspaper buildings that had been constructed decades before World War I, architects, critics, and businessmen alike contrasted the twenties with all past eras, arguing that never before had commerce so openly embraced the possibilities afforded by artistic design. Writing in 1924 in *Architectural Forum*, John Taylor Boyd Jr. commended businessmen for acknowledging the value of handsome interiors. Two decades earlier, a Spartan period "when American civilization was narrower," such attitudes were hard to find. "Today the more progressive leaders of the commercial world hold no prejudice against art," he happily observed, "and are as willing to make use of it as of anything else."[34] "There is no reason why our industrial buildings should be ugly," the architect Cass Gilbert, now designing warehouses and factories, wrote about the same time. "It is not necessary for a building to be ugly in order to be useful."[35] A colleague, Harvey Wiley Corbett, who had worked on some of New York City's most dramatic twenties skyscrapers, agreed with this point of view. We have begun to realize "that beauty and utility are not, and never have been strangers," Corbett wrote, enthusiastically endorsing a commercial modernism that paid little heed to precedents.[36] Whereas a few years ago a monumental structure "was almost surely a public building, serving the municipality or state," wrote the *Architectural Forum*, observing the opening of a Kansas City life insurance building, "the field has been broadened to afford greater scope." "Great financial organizations" realized the benefits of "a beautiful architectural setting."[37] Similar views were accompanied in other architectural journals by illustrations of some of the decade's notable business structures: the Cunard, the Barclay-Vesey, New York Life, and American Radiator Buildings in New York, the Straus and Pittsfield Buildings in Chicago; Pacific Telephone and Telegraph and Pacific Gas and Electric, both in San Francisco; Philadelphia's Provident Bank, and telephone buildings all over the United States.[38] During these years hardly a month passed without the opening of some major office building in a large American city. While many, even most of these structures retained the motifs that had adorned the neoclassical, beaux arts towers of earlier years, an increasing number associated themselves with the colors, materials, and machine ornament that now seemed identical with modernism. In their exuberance and boldness, several became almost iconic in their capacity to typify the spirit of the entire postwar era, image makers for a generation and a culture. And because they were, simultaneously, often associated with some great business enterprise, they further cemented the relationship between the twenties and American business.

One such was New York's Chrysler Building, whose height, sumptuousness, and decorative references to hubcaps and radiator ornaments, tires and mudguards, called further attention to the products made by its owner. The Chrysler Building was pure advertisement, one historian has argued, referring to those characteristic motifs that so quickly recalled the automobile.[39] Its architect, William Van Alen, who altered the building's program when it was sold, before completion, to Walter Chrysler, was labeled the Ziegfeld of his profession by a critic who found his commercialism to be too assertive.[40] That did not prevent the building from serving Chrysler as effectively as an earlier building had served Woolworth. And corporate clients found architects like Van Alen, Raymond Hood, Ely Jacques Kahn, and many others, eager to combine their own aesthetic vocabulary with the promotional ambitions of products and services.[41] Hood's American Radiator Building on West Fortieth Street, with its glowing golden top and color gradations, served as a spectacular metaphor for the stove-making company; his McGraw-Hill Building emblazoned the publisher's name in bold neon letters that ran across the top of the spectacularly modern structure.[42]

Advertising, however, was not the only justification advocates for architectural patronage urged upon business leadership. The teens and twenties witnessed a considerable development of what has been labeled "welfare capitalism"—programs designed to cement worker loyalty to corporations by providing a variety of amenities, from sports teams and financial advising to scholarships for children and attractive cafeterias.[43] Creating a working environment that was appealing as well as efficient began to emerge as an important reason for spending time and money on architectural planning. Here the emphasis lay less on impressing potential customers and more on the value of enhanced physical surroundings to morale and, ultimately, to profitability. The two apologias, at this point, were not in tension, although in later decades they would occasionally seem to indicate alternative strategies.

Typical of the new line of argument was John Taylor Boyd Jr.'s asking, in 1924, whether it was profitable for management to force employees to labor in "bleak, cheerless, badly proportioned offices with bare walls and clumsy furniture," when they were growing accustomed, at home or at play, to more beautiful settings.[44] A generation earlier, he admitted, businessmen would have responded that workers should keep their minds on the job. But the growth of mechanization and standardization, he continued, produced the realization that business must be made more human, more hygienic, and ultimately more beautiful. Modern structures, like Albert Kahn's Detroit Daily News, well furnished and well planned, were not foolishly luxurious but simply restored the human scale and individuality that business had enjoyed in the days of much smaller units.

In his 1928 study of American commercial buildings, R. W. Sexton was even stronger. Without personality, he argued, there was no privacy, and without privacy no true efficiency. "In a sympathetic environment a business man will go about his work in an entirely different spirit, for the thing that formerly made his business life tedious and monotonous has been eliminated." Treated like a prisoner, a man worked as a prisoner, and his employer would suffer the consequences.[45]

The theme of worker efficiency was also sounded by visitors to the new factory complexes. In some ways the distance between conditions in the old and the new industrial settings was even more dramatic than the contrast between the two generations of office buildings. Before World War I a number of companies, like General Electric in Cleveland, Curtis Publishing in Philadelphia, and Heinz in Pittsburgh, had, in their planning, indicated some concern for safety and welfare.[46] They devoted attention, among other things, to factory landscaping, exercise facilities, or specially commissioned art. But they were exceptional. The newer factories attracted most attention by reason of their scale and shape rather than their specific amenities. They became, in the twenties and thirties, favored subjects for photographers interested in developing symbols for American industrial strength, or indeed offering clues to national character itself.[47] These valorized landscapes of concentrated power were soon associated with their sponsoring corporations—Ford, General Motors, U.S. Steel—as intimately as the office headquarters towers were with their owners. But they were also somewhat more abstractly viewed as well, visited, on a daily basis, by fewer outsiders and less connected to corporate promotion and public relations.

Public relations, to be sure, was a specialty developing alongside the new architecture, and its growth as a profession suggests the concern of business corporations with developing more positive reputations.[48] Beginning frequently as publicity departments concerned with responding to some specific crisis—Du Pont established a publicity bureau in 1916 to deal with explosion rumors while American railroads employed a publicity bureau in 1908 to service their regulatory positions—public relations departments literally stemmed from a 1907 establishment by American Telephone and Telegraph, seeking to combat the threat of a government takeover. The onset of the Great Depression stimulated other firms—including General Motors and U.S. Steel—to create their own departments.

In keeping with this trend, architectural apologists in the twenties retained an emphasis, in supporting elaborate building schemes, not on employee welfare but on company reputation, the impact that design could have on customers and the public. As Charles Loring remarked, reviewing the immense, elaborately detailed, and richly appointed banking hall that York and Sawyer had constructed for the Bowery Savings Bank opposite Grand Central Station, "There are nearly two hundred thousand depositors . . . and each one as he enters can say: 'This was built for me; herein am I privileged.'"[49] Almost twenty years earlier, in promulgating his great Chicago Plan in 1909, Daniel Burnham insisted to an audience of businessmen that "beauty has always paid better than any other commodity," and, he went on, "it always will."[50] This theme was given its full due during the 1920s.

After the crash of 1929, however, most American businesses were hard put to invest money or rhetoric in the creation of buildings and work settings. It was all they could do to keep a labor force operative under any conditions. Massive commercial and industrial construction practically ceased. The one exception came in the popular world's fairs of the thirties. In New York and Chicago, particularly, dozens of American corporations turned to architects and industrial designers for pavilions that would advertise their products and their personalities, frequently doing so with structures that literally reproduced their commodities.[51] Walter Dorwin Teague created a giant cash register for the National Cash Register Company in Chicago in 1933; the Skidmore and Owings building for RCA in New York six years later resembled a radio tube; the Carrier Corporation, just breaking into the air-conditioning market, built an igloo; Swift and Company had a giant hot dog; Haviland, a towering thermometer; American Tobacco, a carton of Lucky Strike Greens. Ford, Westinghouse, General Motors, Chrysler, General Electric, General Cigar, Sealtest, Beech-Nut, Johns-Manville,

Heinz Foods, and dozens of others, while eschewing such literal reproduction, employed the cream of designing talent (it came cheap in the thirties) to produce their spectacular displays. But the structures designed by Henry Dreyfus, Norman Bel Geddes, Raymond Loewy, Ely Jacques Kahn, Shreve, Lamb, and Harmon, William Lescaze, Donald Deskey, Gordon Bunshaft, and Harvey Wiley Corbett, however memorable, were temporary, living on in postcards, brochures, and popular memories. They anticipated future roadside structures and influenced exhibition planning, but as enduring contributions to American architecture they suffered in comparison with the twenties headquarter towers and massive factories.

And the corporate architecture famine would continue for another ten or fifteen years after the New York fair closed in 1940. During the years surrounding World War II, despite the intensified industrial output that the conflict stimulated, wartime production needs and material shortages constrained extensive corporate investment in construction. There were large American cities that did not experience the opening of a single major structure for some twenty-five years. Chicago paused betwen 1934 and 1954; Atlanta's five-story Fulton National Bank Building, of 1955, was the first downtown project completed since 1930; Phoenix's First National Bank of Arizona, completed about the same time, was its first since 1932. St. Louis experienced a similar pattern.[52]

By the 1950s, however, American corporations were ready to launch more ambitious building programs; pent-up demand, changing architectural styles, novel building and environmental technologies, and new conceptions of the social, economic, and legal implications of enhanced expenditures joined the older justifications in what amounted to an era of lavish expectations and heroic achievements. The evolving structure of American society—demographic and geographic—and transforming patterns of work and residence would stamp their own character on the new corporate landscape. In what could be termed a mood of triumphant modernism, American business embraced an internationally oriented, stylistically sophisticated, highly repetitive, and historically transcendent approach to the design of both their headquarters buildings and their workplaces.[53] Their continuing interest in reputation, along with unprecedented levels of corporate wealth, stimulated a new level of participation in an age of business patronage.

By the 1950s an internationally sanctioned modernism had achieved unrivaled symbolic dominance as the style most appropriate to the efficiency-oriented business corporation. Its relative uniformity, avoidance of color and decoration, and boxlike outlines contrasted with the extravagant indulgences found in skyscraper modernism of the 1920s. Its materials as well as its overall appearance suggested contemporaneity and adaptation to the logic of the existing world. Moreover, the most famous architectural practitioners had, by the fifties, become almost exclusively devotees of modernism. Had a business corporation wished, it would have had to search long and hard to find a reputable architect eager to design structures suggesting the monumental eclecticism that had so well serviced banks and corporations through the twenties.

One additional element nurturing the taste for modernism involved the ideological disputes dominating the cold war. Several historians have argued persuasively that growing acceptance of experimentation in the graphic and building arts was accentuated by the desire to contrast such tolerance with Soviet aesthetic philistinism.[54] The warfare between the Russian government and almost any kind of artistic avant-gardism was startling in the fifties and sixties. Communist states were becoming notorious for their suspicion of anything that departed from the best-established monumental traditions in architecture, or from positive representation in painting and sculpture. Sometimes gingerly, sometimes forcefully, American government and American business sought, in this same time period, whatever their own doubts about the aesthetic character or even the political implications of modernism, to demonstrate the greater tolerance of a capitalist society toward artistic experimentation.[55] And that meant self-conscious as well as self-celebrating patronage of artists and architects who, just decades before, would have seemed far too daring, austere, or, in the case of graphic artists, outlandish for serious consideration.

There seemed a special opportunity for corporations, moreover, in a society where official support for the arts, in the form of direct legislative expenditures, remained unpopular. Demonstrating the cultural vitality of capitalism, and sustaining traditions of governmental restraint in matters of culture, meant that corporate executives had to show what enlightened businessmen could do for the visual arts. Writing in 1956, during the heart of the cold war, Henry Luce, publisher of *Time, Life, Fortune,* and *Architectural Forum,* spoke, in words intended to recall William James's "will to believe," of a "will to beauty." Luce argued that "every director of a business corporation has a chance to make the next office building a little more beautiful, with a little more fun and joy in it." The extra cost, Luce promised, would be a good investment. Mingling Sunday school sermonizing with aesthetic idealism, Luce declared that "we shall not become truly masters of our economy until we have taught it to serve also our ideals of beauty."[56]

Luce had precedents. His arguments had been taken up earlier. Even before World War II several American corporations—Container Corporation, Encyclopaedia Britannica, IBM—had begun systematically to commission or collect artworks, and during the war they were joined by a number of others, including Standard Oil of New Jersey and Pepsi-Cola. In post–New Deal America, with its stringent new tax structure subjecting wealthy individuals to stricter demands, some argued that corporations would have to replace single patrons if the arts were to flourish.[57]

But it was not until after the war that patronage forged links with ideological and patriotic arguments, along with emphases on employee welfare and local responsibility. By the 1950s dozens of companies, from Hallmark and Inland Steel to Chase Manhattan and Reynolds Metals, had become absorbed by modern, American, or folk art. But art collecting was just one part of this cultural intervention. A 1953 New Jersey court decision that acknowledged corporate philanthropy as a legitimate exercise of management, intimately tied to both the preservation of business and the American way of life, constituted an important validating moment.[58] During the next few decades corporations would underwrite museum exhibitions, artist-in-residence programs, television documentaries, and opera productions. By 1961 corporate contributions to American philanthropies were exceeding five hundred million dollars annually—a figure multiplied tenfold twenty-five years later—and corporate collections were being featured in special museum exhibitions, spearheaded by the famous 1960 show at the Whitney Museum of American Art entitled *Business Buys American Art*.[59]

With an expansive vision of their cultural missionary role so widely accepted, it took little to persuade major corporate executives that the headquarters, production, and research buildings they required should be given over to the care of significant architects. In some instances, as in the automobile industry, this was merely continuing a tradition established long before. The Albert Kahn Company, whose founder had built so extensively for General Motors, Ford, Chrysler, Hudson, and Packard, was already handling 20 percent of all American architect-designed industrial building by the late thirties.[60] It, with Lockwood Greene, the Austin Company, and several other specialists, would continue to play major roles, but they were joined by new architectural firms whose simultaneous mastery of modernist idioms and reputations for efficiency in planning large and complex assignments helped them garner commissions.[61]

Personal connections with corporate executives, of course, remained a significant basis for employment, just as it had earlier in the century. The children of executives—of Detroit newspaper tycoon Ralph Booth, of

Pittsburgh department store owner Edgar J. Kaufmann, of H. J. Heinz II, of Herbert Johnson, who owned the wax company bearing his name, and of Samuel Bronfman of Joseph Seagram and Sons—interested in architecture on professional, personal, or purely intellectual grounds, succeeded in steering to celebrated architects like Eliel Saarinen, Gordon Bunshaft, Frank Lloyd Wright, and Mies van der Rohe some of their most significant commercial commissions.[62] In other firms it was the deep commitment of a corporate executive, like William Hewitt of the John Deere company, James M. Willcox of PSFS in Philadelphia, or Horace C. Flanigan of Manufacturers Trust, that proved responsible.[63] Whatever the apologias offered by corporate public relations departments, annual reports, or reviews in architectural journals, corporate patronage was often a matter of a powerful executive's personal encounter with an architect he admired, and the personal chemistry that resulted from some productive meetings.[64]

Nonetheless, in postwar America many corporations deliberately sought out important architects even when no preexisting connections existed. The cachet of an architectural design, particularly one linked to the heroic character of modernism, seemed promising in itself, and was viewed by some as a form of payback to the community that had produced the corporate profits. Nowhere was this more apparent than in the extraordinary array of dozens of structures—churches, schools, library, and firehouse among them—subsidized by the Cummins Engine Company, led by J. Irwin Miller, its chief executive officer, for its hometown of Columbus, Indiana.[65] With the exception of Cummins Engine, however, the expenditure of funds on a building did not merit treatment as a philanthropic activity, like creating an art collection, supporting museum exhibitions, contributing to local institutions, or underwriting community activities. Most corporate executives, building now on generations of experience, treated a memorable or distinctive structure as a merchandising asset or as an aid in hiring and retaining a workforce.

This last issue became of greater importance as corporate headquarters followed factories out of the city. In the fifties and sixties many businesses, facing higher taxes, reduced services, heavier traffic, and longer commutes, began to move out of center cities into suburbs or small towns.[66] Here they faced new problems, among them respecting a natural environment that was cherished and often fiercely guarded by local inhabitants, and providing a stimulating setting for a workforce that had grown used to the concentrated amenities for eating, shopping, and recreation that were part of most central cities. While these same conditions had existed for a long time with blue-collar workers in the suburbs, most factories treated their needs for eating and recreation in a rather minimal and purely utilitarian form, relying on wage scales and benefits as attractions.With secretaries, accountants, engineers, scientists, and managers, accustomed to more exacting standards of diversion, businesses found themselves turning to carefully planned settings. These plants now incorporated elaborate landscaping that simultaneously shielded the workplace and made it more secure. The buildings provided within themselves occasions for visual drama and variety, relieving lunch hours of monotony and spiritlessness. Attention also was paid to planned settings for interaction, particularly necessary in the research and development centers that were now central to corporate expansion.

So architects became important contributors to the larger corporate work ethic, partners in planning the nurturing environment. This had been an interest of some architects since the days when Frank Lloyd Wright had created his innovative Larkin Building in Buffalo, but now designer involvement in the larger business enterprise became a matter of broader discussion. Decisions about color, scale, form, and materials were more than simply a set of aesthetic judgments; when corporations were the clients such choices suggested attitudes toward motivation and attention span. Good architecture was, in short, a business necessity, and no one needed to apologize for calling in the profession's biggest (and most expensive) names.

In the fifties and sixties corporations could reap rewards for urban civic gestures as well.[67] Three modern structures—the Mies van der Rohe–designed building for Seagram's in New York; the Park Avenue tower produced by Skidmore, Owings and Merrill (SOM) for Lever Brothers; and the glass-walled branch bank Gordon Bunshaft of SOM created for Manufacturers Trust—constituted the shock wave of high corporate design in the 1950s. They were not simply triumphs of aesthetic modernism. They were as influential in their generous development of public spaces and their friendliness to urban pedestrians as in their articulation of structural materials and building forms.

The two skyscrapers, Seagram's and Lever House, using different techniques, featured, amid the crowded canyons of Manhattan, large public plazas, until then (with the massive exception of Rockefeller Center) rarely associated with American office buildings. Seagram's had to purchase additional lots to permit the building to avoid the ziggurat-like form which New York zoning ordinances had been mandating for decades; its unencumbered, spacious, soaring mass consumed only one-quarter of its property, permitting the landscaped public area that constituted its plaza.[68] This meant a loss of important rentable space on the ground level, but, as one contemporary architectural journal pointed out, this was not an irrational position, even from an economic standpoint. "The building was expected to sell itself on the basis of the elegance of its spaces and their material appointments . . . thus higher rents . . . would yield an eventual margin of profit."[69] The company was heaped with praise for its civic-mindedness in providing the great plaza. It included furniture by Mies himself, tapestries by Miró and Stuart Davis, a redesigned corporate seal by Herbert Matter, and special lettering throughout the building by Elaine Lustig. The novelty of preparing one wing for a spectacularly designed restaurant brought further éclat to the owner. Seagram's was built, argued *Architectural Forum*, not as an investment intended to produce quick money but "to produce a long-term return in public good will, institutional advertising, and—only incidentally—in cash."[70]

Lever House, opened several years earlier in 1952, represented an even more radical challenge to existing practices. Nathaniel Owings, in his book of reminiscence about the extraordinary firm he had helped to found in the 1930s, argued that the building's genesis went back to 1946 and was part of a revolt against the "Stone Age" values of the country's office building managers, a "tight little group who stood in the way of rebuilding the central city." Debating with one prominent manager, George Bailey, in a 1949 convention, Owings suggested putting up slender office buildings over underground garages (to pay for the extra land), and covering such parcels with parks. While conceding its value to an ambitious tenant, Bailey at once dismissed the idea as utopian.[71] Owings bided his time.[72] In Charles Luckman, the president of Lever Brothers, he found the man to back his vision. Typically, the ego of the executive officer and the prestige of the corporation were tied together. On the twenty-first story of his innovative structure Owings laid out a luxury apartment for the president, complete with exercise room, earning Luckman's gratitude and respect. And he got backing for a series of other costly actions.

Not that they failed to bring the firm favorable publicity. *Time*, admitting that SOM had built in a modernist style some labeled "crackpot," nonetheless described the building as a "park-like complex of garden and patio" and pronounced the "net effect" as "one of jet-propelled urgency held thankfully and restfully at bay."[73] *Newsweek* found it simultaneously a "green sliver of glass, suspended from the sky" and "the very symbol of business efficiency, inside and out."[74] Owings wryly observed that critics declared the building a "monument to American industry," despite the fact that the ownership was English and Dutch. But people were impressed "that we hadn't hung a big sign on the building saying 'Lever House,' and the building became better known than if we had."[75]

The five-story Manufacturers Trust building went still further than Lever House in violating the norms. Probably the most conservative group among architectural clients, bankers apparently remained committed, in the early 1950s, to marble halls, Corinthian columns, and bronze teller cages. There had been one notable exception during the 1930s—the completion in 1932 of the remarkable and innovative skyscraper for the Philadelphia Savings Fund Society, by George Howe and William Lescaze.[76] Widely admired, at home and abroad, for its meticulous craftsmanship, rich materials, and revolutionary approach to its banking hall—reached on the second floor from escalators—PSFS was a totally designed masterpiece, with everything from its floor coverings to desks, inkwells, and clock faces coming from the hands of the firm.

But PSFS spawned no imitators. When Manufacturers Trust opened its doors in 1954, there were collective gasps of astonishment and admiration that ranged across a broad spectrum of mass-circulation journals. Writing in the *New Yorker* in tones of absolutely rapturous delight, Lewis Mumford paid tribute to its crystalline walls, its luxuriant vegetation (a working gardener, two days each week, tended to the bank's rather elaborate tropical plantings), its Harry Bertoia metal screens, and, above all, its functional coherence. Mumford concluded, in words that financiers must have found enticing, that by raising its thirty-ton vault from the cellar to a highly visible window location off Fifth Avenue the bank had "made the most of a natural advertisement. This is what one calls inherent symbolism." It was entirely unnecessary for Manufacturers Trust to do much with any other name plating. The building was "as complete a fusion of rational thinking and humane imagination as we are capable of producing today . . . As a symbol of the modern world, this structure is almost an ideal expression," the natural possession of a culture "that has explored the innermost recesses of the atom, that knows that visible boundaries and solid objects are only figments of the intellect."[77]

Few commentators could match the range of Mumford's historical allusions and critical insights, but *Time*, *Newsweek*, *Business Week*, and *Fortune* were equally admiring of the audaciousness of the bank and the courage of its president, H. C. Flanagan, who had managed to persuade a somewhat reluctant board of trustees that such radical modernism would redound to the bank's advantage.[78] Here again, as with officials at Lever Brothers and at Seagram's, the taste, preferences, and personal views of influential executives were fundamental in shaping innovative aesthetic decisions.

Within a few years, metropolitan avenues throughout the country were lined with variations on the Lever House–Seagram Building–Manufacturers

Trust models, many of them uninspired, repetitious, vastly enlarged, and monotonous versions of these archetypes, but desperately seeking the cachet of
modern sophistication, civic spirit, and design flair that these corporations
had, at least momentarily, captured for themselves.[79] Specialist corporate architects like those working at SOM were soon being called on by executives,
eager to harness some of their design flair and reputation for their own purposes. With glass curtain walls, flat roofs, and sealed interiors, these structures were praised by business and architectural journals alike for their innovative construction techniques and advanced systems.[80]

A number of these skyscrapers did indeed gain attention and prestige
for their corporate clients. In a number of cases—Inland Steel in Chicago,
Crown Zellerbach in San Francisco, CBS in New York—they found critical
acclaim for their design accomplishments as well.[81] There was, moreover,
among architects like I. M. Pei, Edward Durrell Stone, Minoru Yamasaki,
Eero Saarinen, and Gordon Bunshaft, far more variety than later critics
were willing to admit, in form as well as material.[82] Steel and glass did not
exhaust the modernist vocabulary, and within just a short time radical deviations from the modernist canon, like the Transamerica Building in San
Francisco, were on the boards.[83]

While some of the tall city buildings were not commissioned by industrial corporations but by speculative builders, willing to rename them for
major renters and more interested in profitable returns than in prestige,
banks, insurance companies, and utilities companies played a major role in
this early expansion.[84] Fashion and efficiency—central air-conditioning,
newly sophisticated elevator systems, tinted glass to reduce energy costs,
landscaped plazas—were the keynotes.[85] But increasingly their location in
central cities became matters of concern, both to corporations and to city
planners.[86] The landscaped plazas that initially garnered accolades in
highly congested business districts were soon being attacked as breaches in
facade walls and subversions of retail traditions that had given the city
much of its appeal and vitality.[87] What American cities needed was not, apparently, more open space for greenery but functionally attractive and even
compressed settings for marketing goods and services. All that was increasingly less possible in the antiseptic, repetitive, standardized landscapes that
modernist planners produced in the fifties and sixties, when bulldozing
town centers all over the country seemed to be the solution to aging and be-
grimed structures.

By the seventies a confluence of forces, already apparent during the
previous twenty years, was transforming assumptions about the design and
location of office buildings, albeit moving them in different and sometimes

opposed directions. This was opening up a fourth, postmodern moment in the evolution of corporate architectural patronage. Most crucial to this moment was a sense of frustration with urban modernism and a loss of confidence in prevailing assumptions about city planning and contemporary design.

The first (and dominating) expression of this reaction came in the form of corporate relocation, removal from the traditional downtowns of cities like New York, Chicago, and Philadelphia, either to different parts of the country or to suburban and exurban sites, chosen for their ease of automobile access and parking, their proximity to executive residences or the new superhighway system, their climate, their scenery, or their general isolation. Certainly corporate expansion continued within the city; indeed some observers professed astonishment at how long it lasted in the seventies and eighties.[88] Any number of major corporations, Proctor and Gamble in Cincinnati, Transamerica in San Francisco, AT&T in New York, Pittsburgh Plate Glass in Pittsburgh—and there were dozens of others—commissioned downtown headquarters buildings, dominating in size or shape, from important architectural firms in the seventies and eighties. Big corporate clients, Walter McQuade wrote in *Fortune* in 1973, "who could justify the additional construction expense as a part of public relations," favored striking structures.[89] They clearly considered the urban location and advertising value of such buildings an advantage.

But despite such exceptions, the creation of big-city skyscrapers as symbols of company strength and commercial greatness no longer made sense to other corporate giants by the 1970s. Accumulating grievances with urban life—its crime, dirt, congestion, even, some argued, its racial, economic, and ethnic diversity—combined with new ideals of corporate efficiency to argue for very different locational strategies. And even where urban skyscrapers remained a possibility, stylistic choices and building arrangements now became very different.

The origins of this process lay far back in the twentieth century. For various reasons some corporations had long preferred spots outside the central downtown, where land was more available or less expensive, where, for reasons of convenience, sentiment, or principle, a more efficient or handsome headquarters structure could be erected.[90] This followed in the wake of older industrial corporations whose factory land needs were, in general, more voracious and was accompanied by newer, more experimental enterprises, in sectors like electronics, that preferred a place on the urban fringes.

But what had been a muted if unmistakable movement in the first half of the century grew with force in the fifties and sixties, and by the seventies could no longer be ignored.[91] It wasn't only that large factories favored sites beyond the city frontier or that highway rings were hosting strings of young companies. Rather, as *Architectural Record* observed, a bit nervously in 1963, entirely new types of office buildings were appearing in the suburbs, seemingly independent of traditional locational needs.[92]

Some of these were specialized and limited in size. Beneficiaries of revolutions in data processing and communications, committed increasingly to research and development units that required extensive laboratories and libraries, many corporate managers realized they could house their arsenals of computers, Bunsen burners, and Teletypes less expensively in suburbs, where relatively small if highly trained labor forces were required to tend them. Airline companies, with their tremendous data-processing needs, were one example. Relocation into new suburban industrial parks had become an attractive option.[93]

But such migrations paled alongside the spectacular relocation of major enterprises, deliberately abandoning long-standing metropolitan commitments for smaller communities dozens of miles away—in Westchester County, New Jersey, or Connecticut if they had been New York–based; to the northwestern suburbs near Chicago; to Troy, Warren, and Auburn Hills near Detroit; to Plano and Irving near Dallas; or to the suburbs of smaller cities like Cincinnati, Toledo, Detroit, and St. Louis. Some were reluctant to accept the trend. In 1955 *Business Week* could assert that "there was a time, a few years ago, when owners and managers of big downtown buildings grew fairly seriously worried about competition from the suburbs." But, said the journal, such worries had now faded. Suburban relocation was not quite what corporations had expected. Employees, particularly women, didn't want to move there, it explained, so far from convenient shopping.[94] Four years later *Architectural Forum*, commenting on a Chicago-based firm's move to Skokie, fifteen miles away, observed smugly that it ran counter to "the recent trend of major U. S. firms to stay in the city," citing Union Carbide's recent decision to remain in Manhattan.[95]

Just a short time later such comments had the quality of a bad joke. For by 1963 a rising tide of suburban relocations was causing great urban anxiety. Two in particular made both economic and, eventually, architectural news—the decision of IBM to move from New York City to Armonk, New York, and the migration of General Foods, in the midfifties, to White Plains and, some years later, to Rye, New York.[96] Over the next twenty years, hundreds of major corporations would make similar transitions—Union Carbide, despite its 1958 commitment, from Park Avenue to Danbury,

Connecticut; AT&T Long Lines to Fairfax County, Virginia; Johns Manville from New York City to the outskirts of Denver; Pepsico, Norcross, Nabisco, Borden, Uniroyal, General Electric, General Dynamics, American Cyanamid, Shell Oil, Ingersoll Rand, also from New York and often, but not always, to points nearby—while smaller corporations like TRINOVA, of Toledo, left for neighboring communities like Maumee. When Johns-Manville announced its corporate move from Manhattan to Colorado in 1971, it was estimated to be the thirty-fourth major corporation to leave New York City in the previous five years.[97] Between 1960 and 1990 New York City's share of *Fortune* 500 headquarters dropped from 23 to 9 percent; Chicago's numbers were halved.[98] While some cities like Los Angeles, Portland, Oregon, and Houston were less affected by the movement, many others, like Detroit, St. Louis, and Philadelphia, were suffering the same challenges confronting New York.[99] Polls taken in the seventies by the Roper Center found a majority of respondents agreeing with views that the move to the suburbs, while nice for executives who lived nearby, threatened urban tax bases, forced longer travel times on their ordinary employees, and rendered suburban areas noisier and more crowded.[100] Analysts argued that corporate executives, unlike previous generations, were not urban-oriented or dependent on the city's cultural attractions. Their supposed problems attracting high-quality labor forces only reinforced their own prejudices.[101]

In the eighties and nineties entirely new corporate giants—Nike, Apple Computers—wouldn't have to endure the traumatic move from urban centers; they had grown up and would remain entirely outside the metropolis, in places like Beaverton, Oregon, or Cupertino, California.[102] And their philosophy of management and environmental design reflected a more rural orientation. All of this had profound implications for corporate architectural design, a point realized long before Sears in Chicago announced in the 1980s that it would abandon its twenty-year stay in the world's tallest skyscraper for an unknown destination—later settled on as Hoffman Estates, Illinois. It was not that major corporations seemed to be putting less money into environmental amenities or high-priced architectural specialists—in the mid-eighties *U.S. News*, marveling at the expensive new headquarters buildings, urban and suburban, termed them American castles, as "eye-catching in their own right as some of the old palaces built for Europe's nobility"—it was just that for a substantial number of companies, goals had changed along with corporate styles.[103]

The suburban complexes married the specific vocabulary proposed by their architects to an overwhelming emphasis on employee productivity and togetherness. No longer did the corporation invariably seek to capitalize upon its scale and magnificence in promotional literature or in the face it revealed to the public. While some individual structures like Kevin Roche's General Foods complex in Rye retained visible monumentality as a corporate ideal, and others were "image" buildings, meant to create an impact on speeding automobile drivers, many of the most elaborate and expensive corporate headquarters now lay hidden behind elaborate landscaping, all but invisible to legions of commuters, accessible only to accredited employees and business contacts passing through security systems that would have made foreign governments envious.[104]

The reasons for this new tone were multiple. Some companies wished to avoid calling attention to their opulence, or professed hostility to traditional forms of display. Others, desperately seeking zoning variances in suburban communities unhappy about concentrated growth, promised to disguise themselves and interfere as little as possible with the rhythms of daily life. The "elongated, rambling" building Charles Moore designed for TRI-NOVA near Toledo, in 1989, was inspired by "the rolling hills of a Kentucky bluegrass horse farm," blending "comfortably with nearby neighbors." Its farm imagery "provides an alternative to the usual imperial symbols of corporate identity," Susan Bleznick wrote."[105] Still others, selecting spectacular sites in which to locate themselves, chose to respect the natural contours of the landscape and to preserve as much as possible the features that had attracted them there in the first place. Prominent landscape architects were now crucial partners in the creation of these new corporate environments, as well as parking engineers who had to determine the conditions for automobile access. "If great landscapes must be built upon," wrote the *Architectural Record* in its review of the Johns-Manville headquarters near Denver, "it is best to touch them lightly."[106]

Examples of the new sensibility abounded in the architectural press, with the descriptive rhetoric taking on the values these architects and corporate executives wished to project for themselves. Thus the CIGNA Company, which in the mideighties enlarged its office complex in Bloomfield, Connecticut, designed by the Architects Collaborative, chose, in the words of the *Architectural Record*, "environmental richness," "energy consciousness," and "cost effectiveness," in preference to a "jewel-like" "glass box." Its wooded and "rolling" site supported what was described as a "campus," overlooking a "spring-fed" pond. The huge structure, more than half a million square feet of space, had parallel wings built on either side of a two-level atrium meant to serve as a "social hub" for the worker community.[107] Such atria, which blossomed by the dozens, were a hallmark of the corporate headquarters buildings of the seventies and eighties.[108]

Twenty years earlier, a similar sensibility had already evidenced itself. Reviewing Eero Saarinen's impressive building for John Deere's Administrative Center in Moline, Illinois, *Architectural Forum* noted that its 350,000 square feet were "masked by its careful insertion into the rounded landscape." Conceptually its individuality stood aloof, "enriching rather than destroying the landscape by contrast." But the small valley helped to disguise its bulk.[109] And even earlier than this was the move of Connecticut General from its Georgian-styled Hartford center to a "hilltop farm out in the rural beauty of Bloomfield, surrounded by the aura of real age, the English kind of countryside that Constable painted and Thomas Hardy wrote about." The 400,000-square-foot building that SOM designed for the insurance company was visible in its entirety, really, only from the air. And it was significant, *Architectural Forum* noted, that this was an insurance company, "for insurance companies—second only to royalty—are the world's biggest dealers in symbols. They have to be: their product is an intangible security." The traditional way to go about looking strong was through heavy masonry, but in contemporary America, the *Forum* continued, it was through audacious and well-mannered consumption. Security in architecture was no longer symbolized up by a massive arch but "by a long free span," and in an executive headquarters by employees living in luxury "surrounded by art and conveniences," which now included tennis courts, bowling alleys, and superbly designed cafeterias. The only apparent embarrassments to this 1957 masterpiece were the parking lots, filled with the "bulbous" bodies of Detroit's automobiles, flashy incongruities compared to the suave precision of the steel and glass building. "The building's lean gleam will outlast the car's fat shine," promised the architectural journal.[110]

Twenty years later the architects may have changed, along with some specific problems, but the rhetoric of understatement often remained much the same in many places. Commenting on the Roche Dinkeloo–designed new corporate headquarters in Wilton, Connecticut, for Richardson-Merrell Corporation, later Richardson-Vicks Inc., the *Architectural Record* enthused over the decision to screen the building from the outside world. The fifty-seven-acre site, again with the requisite "rolling meadows," offered great opportunities for corporate advertisement, and a "good many companies would have told the architects to plot their building and parking in full views of passers-by," but not Richardson-Merrell and Roche-Dinkeloo. They decided to "get lost together, to go above the meadow, ensconce themselves on a slight rise above a ravine with a creek gurgling through," and nestle among maples, oaks, pine, and cypress. They saved most of the trees on the property, and solved the parking problem by dividing spaces between a below-grade slab and a hidden rooftop section. The architect, Kevin Roche, observed approvingly, "You know, it's really quite unimposing."

Roche's remark caught much of the new spirit.[111] "We didn't want the appearance of grandeur and affluence," an executive of Becton Dickinson declared, happily surveying the new 1987 headquarters built for the firm in Franklin Lakes, New Jersey, by Kallmann, McKinnell and Wood. "We wanted a country house." The architect was asked for lots of natural light and an interesting building to walk through. "And it shouldn't be visible to the public at large."[112] "Once the town bullies," Margaret Gaskie wrote in *Architectural Record*, "the factory and its gang of related facilities are learning that politeness pays."[113] The Union Carbide World Headquarters in Danbury, Connecticut, was "virtually invisible from nearby highways and residential subdivisions," *Architectural Record* assured its readers.[114] Country house or college campus, the corporation spent extravagantly on its landscaping—on man-made lakes, shrubbery, trees, exotic flowers. Who "would have expected to find some of the most carefully conceived and lavishly executed landscapes of our times embedded in the suburban periphery?" Robert Bruegmann asked, examining the McDonald headquarters in Hoffman Estates, Illinois, and TRW near Cleveland, both landscaped by Sasaki Associates. "And who would have expected missile builders and soft-drink manufacturers to be the patrons of these meticulously manicured lawns and clipped hedges?"[115]

Not all of the new suburban corporate buildings needed or desired such understatement. Kevin Roche himself, according to the critic Francesco Dal Co, was absorbed by "the possibility of obtaining instant effects. The image must produce an effect immediately in order to be assimilated immediately. This effect is that which the public demands and fashion conforms." Determined to "satisfy the user's need to identify with the figures of his buildings," Roche emphasized outward appearances, Dal Co insisted, even at the expense of structural coherence.[116] The importance of the new (1981) McDonnell Douglas Company facility in St. Louis by Hellmuth, Obata and Kassabaum needed to be sensed "when viewed at high speeds from adjacent highways and from the nearby municipal airport," said the project designer.[117] And other projects possessed a flashiness that enabled passing motorists to get a sense of their splendor from the nearby highway.

Yet much of the time Roche, with other influential corporate architects of this period like I. M. Pei, Gordon Bunshaft of SOM, and the Architects Collaborative, designed headquarters buildings meant to impress the workforce more than the general public—to soothe executives, encourage staff loyalty and togetherness, and, above all, to cut down on employee turnover. Their language of justification seemed occasionally to echo the high-minded rhetoric of the entrepreneurs of Connecticut and Massachusetts 150 years earlier who created factory villages at Waltham and Lowell, complete with matron-run dormitories, to satisfy the farm girls who staffed the textile mills. Conscious of the need to supply substitutes for downtown diversions—shopping, strolling, eating out—planners turned to gardens, sculpture, changing exhibitions of art and company history, elaborate recreational facilities, and temperature-controlled atria, carefully landscaped and designed to encourage easy, and productive, socializing.[118] When General Electric moved a corporate office from New York City to Fairfield, Connecticut, its architects, SOM, sought to "offset the inconvenience of the site's relative isolation" through creation of a public park and provision of three types of dining facilities, lounges, and a store. All this "contributed towards a high percentage of the 700 empoyees making the move with the company from New York City."[119] "The company and William Pedersen shared a conviction that the building should dignify workers who spend a third of their waking hours in it," *Architectural Record* reported of the AT&T Long Lines Eastern Regional Headquarters in suburban Virginia, whose Long Galleria served as a substitute for a city street.[120] Some architects now enlisted the aid of so-called organizational ecologists, helpful in ensuring that "productivity-enhancing functions" would benefit from building design.[121]

Thus Roche himself, playing down the number of headquarters buildings he had designed, argued that corporations were "tremendous clients" because of the possibility of expressing a sense of social responsibility, which he was able to fulfill through outdoor community spaces for local groups, club rooms, cafeterias, terraces, balconies, and similar amenities. In Conoco he sought to "create a park into which the whole building is placed. It is a campus and will have the same felicitous effect on the occupants as if they were working in a well-planned university campus." Union Carbide was "a more determined effort to design a workplace which people would enjoy and understand and relate to."[122] Such structures were designed only after hundreds of interviews with employees and executives, trying to determine the optimal shape, size, and furnishings of offices. Trade-offs included allowing staff to choose from among a variety of furniture (and art styles), in return for uniform or diminished private spaces. As part of this absorption with environmental efficiency, management often commissioned elaborate interior treatments, either by the architects of record or by specialist interior designers and furniture makers. This tradition, which went back to Frank Lloyd Wright and his memorable structures for the Larkin and Johnson Wax companies, was sustained by master architects like Mies van der Rohe, whose attention to details like hardware and plumbing fixtures was legendary.[123]

While the great suburban estates that were office headquarters formed one kind of pattern, however, architects in the seventies and eighties began to create for corporations differently conceived urban expressions that caught an equally significant part of the larger mood. These also apparently served, more faithfully than ever before, certain environmental needs, but they retained the goal of impressing a larger, anonymous public. One important departure from their predecessors lay in their apparent repudiation of the modernist regularity and austere symmetries that had become so closely identified with the corporate ethos. A number of important architects did not abandon glass boxes, of course, and some companies had always remained with older, eclectic approaches. But architectural firms like Johnson Burgee, Kohn Pedersen and Fox, and Skidmore Owings and Merrill, closely identified with major corporate projects, were soon featuring buildings whose broken rooflines, irregular outlines, historicist references, and applied ornament contrasted dramatically with the modernist classics of the fifties and sixties. There were anticipations, of course, but the Johnson Burgee Chippendale-topped AT&T Building on Madison Avenue in New York was as much a trendsetter in its right as Seagram's and Lever House had been two decades earlier.[124] Johnson Burgee's PPG Center in Pittsburgh and corporate structures from Illinois to Texas and from Delaware to Ohio carried the theme forward.[125]

More than stylistic details seemed at stake, for the indulgence in fantasy, the exploitation of ornament, and the references to local history suggested a broad change of attitude. Angry satirical critiques were quickly launched by modernists, who found the new structures a betrayal of the principles that had been defended so bravely a few years earlier. To some the pastiches of ornament, the delight in traditionally rich marbles and bronze, the dramatic lobbies and atria seemed sinister as well as vulgar, promising to blend categories of the serious and the playful, the political and the cultural, the public and the private, the historic and the contemporary, in ways that threatened to be socially as well as aesthetically regressive. In this latest phase corporate architects appeared simultaneously to flaunt and hide their clients' wealth and power. It was not clear whether the designers were satirizing or promoting the interests of their employers.

Thus the complexes designed, in both Florida and California, for the Walt Disney Company, caught, in their mock heroics, the paradoxes of the colloquially monumental. With Arata Isozaki, Michael Graves, and Robert A. M. Stern employed by this great entertainment powerhouse, Disney was signifying its commitment to high-profile architects who could supply it with celebrity-centered showcase designs. In Lake Buena Vista, Florida, Stern provided for Disney a modern-day Doge's Palace, replete with fifteen-foot-high gold letters, visible from the nearby freeway, spelling the word casting.[126] It was, indeed, a casting center. Inside, heroic statues of memorable Disney creations like Mickey Mouse and Donald Duck adorned a great atrium. Despite its special mixture of spectacle and historic reference, however, the Disney organization was interested in the same thing driving many other corporations: identifying and then inspiring a labor force that would be impressed by and loyal to its corporate employer. The architects happily cooperated, for the route to such loyalty seemed to be buildings elaborately planned and well finished.

In the cities, corporate headquarters buildings took a somewhat different turn in the seventies and eighties. It was not necessary for most of them to provide the special amenities that suburban complexes required, for shopping and recreation were usually available nearby. But in choosing postmodernist architects, redoing historic structures in expensive acts of preservation, or placing themselves within multiuse complexes that incorporated residences, shopping centers, and entertainment halls, corporations, and influential developers of speculative buildings, were apparently determined to emphasize their links with existing institutions and their commitment to local history. In effect, the strategy was now to invoke, through historicist motifs, the immediate environment, the texture of urban life, and even specific existing structures, rather than link the corporation to a transcendental, international, and ultimately decontextualized architectural style. Thus the self-conscious diversity of Battery Park City, "intended to connect with familiar spatial routines and experiences" from the marble lobbies recalling the opulent interwar skyscrapers to the "retrieval of classic New York City park furniture including old-style trash cans."[127]

By the late seventies many corporations found older and sometimes historic structures more appealing (and less expensive) than shiny new ones. Clients had more faith in them, claimed a San Francisco lawyer whose firm took over an old mansion. As battles swirled around the preservation of buildings like Grand Central Station and the Woolworth Building, as the list of noteworthy nonresidential structures in the National Register of Historic Places swelled (in ten years) from one thousand to fourteen thousand, and as tax breaks multiplied for corporate clients willing to spend money on rehabilitation, new attitudes spread, even among former modernists. "Glass buildings don't make us laugh but old buildings make us happy," Philip Johnson noted.[128] Levi Strauss in San Francisco chose to leave ten floors in the new Embarcadero Center for some old waterfront warehouses; an oil drilling firm in Dallas redid the city's oldest elementary school for its headquarters; the Bradbury Building in Los Angeles and the old, mansard-roofed city hall in Boston were renovated and made ready for new offices. Many corporations now seemed comfortable identifying themselves with the past rather than the future, reveling in local rather than transcendental and international aspirations, the spirit of so many of the fifties and sixties structures.[129]

Again, such contextual interest seemed better served by adaptations of traditional styling. "Modern classicism" was the label given to Adrian Smith's NBC tower for Chicago, whose limestone details acknowledged the nearby Chicago Tribune building's Gothicism but whose outline seemed to recall the old RCA building of Rockefeller Center.[130] William LeBaron Jenney would have been pleased, wrote Margaret Gaskie in the *Architectural Record*, by the 303 West Madison Tower erected in Chicago by SOM. With stained glass at its entrance, a two-story loggia at its crown, and broad Chicago windows, it was full of references to the Old Chicago School.[131]

Specificity was not necessarily in the interest of public identification. Corporate building names increasingly were acronyms or verbal logos, better understood by stock purchasers than by customers. IDS, ITT, AT&T, INA, INS, CSAA, PSE&G, and TCF were among these entries. But even more typical of the tall office buildings of the eighties were simple street addresses or development-given names—Two Chatham Center in Pittsburgh; Tampa City Center; Market Place in Seattle; City Center in Fort Worth; First City Center in Dallas; One Liberty Place in Philadelphia; Brickell Center in Miami; Copley Plaza in Boston; Gateway Center in Chicago and in Pittsburgh—a series of made-up addresses that confused even local fire departments. City ordinances were soon on the books insisting that every building possess, aside from any given name or developer plaza, an actual street address.[132]

In fact, structures named by anyone but their developers were becoming increasingly rare in American downtowns by the 1980s. One 1983 inventory of office buildings counted ninety-three of over eight stories completed, that year, in twenty-one major cities. Of them fewer than a dozen bore identifiable corporate names. The others, with street addresses or assumed titles, were owned by Olympia and York, Tishman Speyer, JMB/Metropolitan Structures, Gerald D. Hines, Trammell Crow, Cabot, Cabot and Forbes, and dozens of other developers.[133] Developers, financed by banks and insurance companies, had become the dominant commissioners of urban towers, constructing them as part of their larger speculative strategies. They had always been major players in the commercial landscape, of course, but never to this extent, and several formed close relationships with major architectural firms like Johnson, Burgee. Meanwhile, the corporate landmarks of another era changed hands as their owners sold them for capital needs, moved, were taken over by another company, or were merged into a new name. Corporate identity had become, in many instances, too porous an entity to be attached to anything as permanent as a named building. In a number of instances, the opulently conceived, carefully designed headquarters building became something of an embarrassment to corporations trying to stave off financial disaster and attempting to project an image of austere management and careful cost accounting.[134] New levels of prosperity in Europe and Asia, moreover, were underwriting the construction of dramatic, soaring, innovative corporate structures, challenging the skyscraper monopoly American cities had held for so long and shifting the focus of attention away from domestic developments.

Successful developers, however, naturalized some of the rhetoric that corporate spokesmen had used in decades past, arguing, or at least accepting the argument, that good architecture had good economic consequences, that in speculative developments the hand of a master designer as well as his reputation could help rent space. Sometimes, it was argued, developers took ambitious risks that corporate patrons dared not.[135] According to one Hartford developer, "tenants look to the credibility of a building's architect, and its design, as an extension of their own credibility." Architectural magazines took up the theme with energy. *Architectural Record*, for example, crowed that the Hartford developer was merely saying what "city builders in the 19th and early 20th centuries knew all along: that the fiscal exigencies of the bottom line by no means preclude the time-honored architectural principles of firmness, commodity, and delight." Developers of speculative office buildings, it went on, "have discovered that good design is a marketable commodity among corporations seeking prestige."[136]

The apparent disappearance of great corporate structures in American downtowns, replaced by developer complexes, towers with impenetrable acronyms, and massive governmental centers—state, local, and federal—does not indicate a decline of corporate architectural patronage. Instead, it suggests a process of redistribution in the interest of defining more specific and more segmented audiences for these structures. Designers remain critical to corporate welfare. They are used, particularly in suburban head-quarters buildings, to shape the loyalties and invigorate the energies of the labor force. In cities they provide indications of corporate identity, not always through displays of corporate power but often through gestures of goodwill and voluntarism, providing civic amenities or endorsing local traditions through preservation of popular structures or references to local landmarks. In large-scale developments such designers are called on to create new modes of spatial order, more private and more exclusive, apparently safer and better controlled than the public spaces that have historically hosted free assembly. If Baron Haussmann was alive in the America of the 1980s, he would probably have been working for a private developer rather than a public authority. And he might well have been found in a suburban subdivision rather than a central city.

During the last 150 years American business corporations have commissioned work by dozens of the most celebrated American architects. Since these structures clearly served both instrumental and expressive purposes, they were not the products of disinterested benevolence. Self-aggrandizement and personal taste were as significant as improving community relations, increasing employee job satisfaction, and lowering production costs in leading proprietors, board committees, and chief executive officers to prominent designers. From one standpoint, corporations patronized eminent architects just as they sought out prominent lawyers, reputable accounting firms, competent engineers, and experienced advertising specialists.

But from another angle, the quest for architectural accomplishment suggests something more than sheer economic self-interest or personal egotism. Constructing a building is, in the end, a performance, an action that might successfully identify individual and collective interest. The notion that buildings are part of a civilization's cultural inventory, that they reflect credit or shame upon their investors, and that a commercial civilization stands in particular need of measurement, appraisal, and evaluation from a world-historical standpoint has encouraged some businesspersons to assume the risks associated with great expenditures and ambitious architecture.

Corporate objectives as well as styles have changed over time. Business buildings, like house organs, advertising programs, and marketing strategies, must confront different audiences: consumers, managerial elites, neighbors, workers, stockholders, technicians, and architectural critics. The needs of specific companies and larger economic conditions shift priorities among these constituencies. And buildings contain multiple messages. They are simultaneously instruments of identification, statements of aesthetic commitment, machines for work, and contributions to a local landscape.

Allowing for such variations, however, corporate design has disclosed larger rhythms. From the obsession with stability and hankering for philanthropic dignities which many banks and business houses favored at the turn of the century, to the identification with soaring ambition and machine dreams of downtown skyscraper headquarters in the twenties, to the fixation with transcendent efficiency and modernism in the glass houses of the fifties and sixties, to the affiliations with local history, landscaped understatement, and suburban self-containment of the seventies and eighties, American business has projected far broader trends than specific company needs. Its evolving architectural taste has reflected changes in national living styles and popular preferences. Certainly it has dramatized these shifts, for the large scale of many corporate structures has highlighted those crucial moments when one stage passes into another. But corporations are generally reluctant innovators, acceding to novelty only after protracted and worrisome discussions. The vast majority of business structures reveal that conformity, even when obviously imitative and repetitive, has been more popular than pioneering.

Still, there has probably been no large society whose landscape so fundamentally reflects the needs and ambitions of business corporations as America's does. To honor the hundredth anniversary of the American Institute of Architects, the *Architectural Record* polled a panel of professionals for a list of the most significant American buildings created during the previous century.[137] Of the twenty selected as most outstanding, more than half were banks, stores, and office buildings. If such a poll were undertaken in the midnineties, instead of the midfifties, the proportion would probably be even higher.

Distinction remains a fugitive goal, for buildings as for individuals. Does the business corporation have a better record of achieving it in architectural design than governmental, religious, and domestic clients, or nonprofit institutions? Answering this question is almost impossible. But certainly in terms of popular sentiment and nostalgic memory the collective power of the Chrysler, Woolworth, Empire State, New York Times, Metropolitan Life, and Grand Central Station buildings in New York, John Hancock, Chicago Tribune, and Wrigley in Chicago, Smith Tower in Seattle, Esperson and Gulf in Houston, and Candler in Atlanta, to single out just a handful among many hundreds, is difficult to challenge. A society that measures time by changing commercial jingles and television theme music will not undervalue a building's function as billboard, or insist upon civic and religious structures as the only appropriate collective symbols. Corporate architecture is to our physical landscape what civil religion is to our politics: an instrument of social integration. But even more powerful than its individual triumphs is the assumption it rests upon: that for much of the time market forces and private needs are sufficient conditions for creating monuments of taste. And, while they can also immortalize greed, vulgarity, and self-indulgence, the public and domestic spheres can support such tendencies even more easily.

Apologias and audiences shift; the philanthropic, ecological, self-celebratory, and efficiency themes ebb and swell; specific sites migrate from downtown to suburb and back; but business corporations have remained potent shapers of the national landscape. Will they continue to do so? Amid a surge of home offices, a radical decentralization of the work environment, and a newly tightened scrutiny of balance sheets and philanthropic commitments, corporate design and land use may, in future years, have less impact on American life than in the past. As in other areas, corporate managers and stockholders may grow more wary of heavy investing in their physical settings, however much other parts of the community depend on active corporate engagement with environmental and aesthetic issues.

Whether or not the next several decades will spawn as decisive a support for modern architecture as the past thirty years have witnessed, in one way or another large corporations will pursue their building projects. By executive whim, formal competition, systematic investigation, or committee decision, the planning of office and factory spaces will continue to legitimate trends and, occasionally, to initiate them. Understanding the process as well as the results is fundamental to current debates over landscape form and use. And this means, in the end, understanding its historic evolution and the shifting functions performed by the corporate enterprise in America.

Notes

1. For some sense of the huge literature on American domestic architecture, see, among others, Elizabeth Collins Cromley, *Alone Together: A History of New York's Early Apartments* (Ithaca, N.Y.: Cornell University Press, 1990); David P. Handlin, *The American Home: Architecture and Society, 1815–1915* (Boston: Little, Brown, 1979); Colleen McDannell, *The Christian Home in Victorian America, 1840–1900* (Bloomington: Indiana University Press, 1986); Gwendolyn

Wright, *Building the Dream: A History of American Housing* (New York: Pantheon, 1981); and Gwendolyn Wright, *Moralism and the Model Home: Domestic Architecture and Cultural Conflict in Chicago, 1873–1913* (Chicago: University of Chicago Press, 1980).

2. As will soon be apparent, many individual biographies, local studies, specific building histories, building type studies, and firm histories invoke this larger area. But there are few texts on the history of American corporate patronage, even those brief surveys such as H. A. N. Brockman, *The British Architect in Industry, 1841-1940* (London: George Allen and Unwin, 1974), which exist for other cultures. There are, however, earlier surveys, such as R. W. Sexton, *American Commercial Buildings of Today* (New York: Architectural Book Publishing Co., 1928), and sections of books such as Talbot Hamlin, ed., *Forms and Functions of Twentieth-Century Architecture* (New York: Columbia University Press, 1952), vol. 4, pp. 7–267, covering banks, office buildings, and factories, as well as other commercial and industrial settings, or, on an international scale, Nikolaus Pevsner, *A History of Building Types* (Princeton, N.J.: Princeton University Press, 1976), chaps. 12–13, 15–17. Robert A. M. Stern, Thomas Mellins, and David Fishman, *New York 1960: Architecture and Urbanism between the Second World War and the Bicentennial* (New York: Monacelli Press, 1995), a massive survey, contains a good deal of information about corporate architecture and its patronage, but it appeared too late for me to consult while preparing this essay.

3. Two recent surveys of bank architecture include overviews of the historical evolution of banks: John Booker, *Temples of Mammon: The Architecture of Banking* (Edinburgh: Edinburgh University Press, 1990), which treats mainly British banks; and *Money Matters: A Critical Look at Bank Architecture* (New York: McGraw-Hill, 1990). Booker (pp. 224–29) notes the influence, in the 1920s, of American bank design, notably the monumental American banking hall, on British practices.

4. All of these architects have been treated by biographers and architectural historians. For an early survey of neoclassical architecture in America, see Talbot Hamlin, *Greek Revival Architecture in America: Being an Account of Important Trends in American Architecture Prior to the War Between the States* (New York: Oxford University Press, 1944).

5. The best study of Furness remains James F. O'Gorman, *The Architecture of Frank Furness* (Philadelphia: Philadelphia Museum of Art, 1973). See also George E. Thomas, Michael J. Lewis, and Jeffrey A. Cohen, *Frank Furness: The Complete Works* (New York: Princeton Architectural Press, 1991). For some of the New York State variations, see *Architecture Worth Saving in Onondaga County* (Syracuse: New York State Council on the Arts, 1964), pp. 67–79.

6. For a pictorial survey and brief commentary on some of the more significant neoclassical banks, see "Recent Bank Buildings of the United States, "*Architectural Record* 25 (January, 1909): 1–66. For Sullivan see Lauren S. Weingarden, *Louis Sullivan: The Banks* (Cambridge, Mass.: MIT Press, 1987).

7. The best survey of this interest, and an invaluable history of corporate aspirations in architecture which I have found especially helpful in preparing this essay, is Kenneth Turney Gibbs, *Business Architectural Imagery in America,
1870–1930* (Ann Arbor, Mich.: UMI Press, 1984). Gibbs takes particular care to
analyze the ambitions of the insurance companies, and the massive structures they
constructed in several cities from the late nineteenth century on. Also helpful is Gail
Fenske and Deryck Holdsworth, "Corporate Identity and the New York Office
Building: 1895–1915," in *The Landscape of Modernity,* ed. David Ward and Olivier
Zunz (New York: Russell Sage Foundation, 1992), pp. 129–59.

8. The most comprehensive treatment of Flagg and the Singer commission
can be found in Mardges Bacon, *Ernest Flagg: Beaux-Arts Architect and Urban
Reformer* (Cambridge, Mass.: MIT Press, 1986).

9. The Woolworth Building has been treated by almost every major text on
the history of the skyscraper and indeed the history of New York City itself. For a
particularly helpful summary of the project set against the development of the New
York City skyscraper, see Robert A. M. Stern, Gregory Gilmartin, and John
Montague Massengale, *New York 1900: Metropolitan Architecture and Urbanism
1890–1915* (New York: Rizzoli, 1983), pp. 164–77. For a builder's view of the
episode, see Louis Horowitz and Boyden Sparkes, *The Towers of New York: The
Memoirs of a Master Builder* (New York: Simon and Schuster, 1937), pp. 103–23.
Horowitz was president of the Thompson-Starrett Company, one of the major construction companies in the United States. The discussion in Thomas A. P. van
Leeuwen, *The Skyward Trend of Thought: Five Essays on the Metaphysics of the
American Skyscraper* (The Hague: AHA Books, 1986), pp. 60–68, is particularly
stimulating, as are the author's comments on the relationship between the romance
of tall buildings and the ideology of business. See, particularly, his introduction pp.
1–10.

10. Various books by Carl Condit have long served as the most authoritative
summaries of Chicago office buildings in this period, notably *The Chicago School of
Architecture: A History of Commercial and Public Building in the Chicago Area,
1875–1925* (Chicago: University of Chicago Press, 1964). For a comparison between the Chicago and New York approaches to office buildings, see Gibbs,
Business Architectural Imagery in America, pp. 55–65.

11. Daniel Bluestone, *Constructing Chicago* (New Haven, Conn.: Yale
University Press, 1991), pp. 116–35, establishes that Chicago architects considered
artful embellishment to be crucial to the success of their buildings and the satisfaction of their corporate clients.

12. This is described in detail in Jack Quinan, *Frank Lloyd Wright's Larkin
Building: Myth and Fact* (Cambridge, Mass.: MIT Press, 1987).

13. For more on these early twentieth-century factories, see Reyner Banham,
*A Concrete Atlantis: U.S. Industrial Building and European Modern Architecture
1900–1925* (Cambridge, Mass.: MIT Press,1986), pp. 23–108. Some architects,

such as Nabisco's Albert G. Zimmerman, were employed by corporations to design structures for them in different parts of the country, and these naturally tended to resemble one another. In the case of light industries such as baking, or with warehouses, these could often be found not far from the city center, and were seen by many people on a daily basis. See the centerfold in William Cahn, *Out of the Cracker Barrel: The Nabisco Story from Animal Crackers to Zuzus* (New York: Simon and Schuster, 1969), pp. 136–37.

14. See, e.g., Russell Sturgis, "Factories and Warehouses," *Architectural Record* 19 (May 1906): 368–75; George C. Nimmons and William K. Fellows, "Designing a Great Mercantile Plant," *Architectural Record* 19 (June 1908): 403–12; and Russell Sturgis, "Some Recent Warehouses," *Architectural Record* 23 (May 1908): 373–86.

15. For reactions to American factories and factory towns, see John P. Coolidge, *Mill and Mansion: A Study in Architecture and Society in Lowell, Massachusetts, 1820–1865* (New York: Columbia University Press, 1942); Thomas Dublin, *Women at Work: The Transformation of Work and Community in Lowell, Massachusetts, 1826–1860* (New York: Columbia University Press, 1979); Marvin Fisher, *Workshops in the Wilderness: The European Response to American Industrialization, 1830–1860* (New York: Oxford University Press, 1967), pp. 91–117; and Hannah Josephson, *The Golden Threads: New England's Mill Girls and Magnates* (New York: Duell, Sloan and Pearce, 1949).

16. For Nela Park see Eric Johannesen, *Cleveland Architecture, 1876–1976* (Cleveland: Western Reserve Historical Society, 1979), pp. 110–15. For Pullman see Stanley Buder, *Pullman: An Experiment in Industrial Order and Community Planning, 1880–1930* (New York: Oxford University Press, 1967); and James Gilbert, *Perfect Cities: Chicago's Utopias of 1893* (Chicago: University of Chicago Press, 1991), pp. 131–68.

17. Beman's Chicago work is treated by Thomas J. Schlereth, "Solon Spencer Beman, Pullman, and the European Influence on and Interest in His Chicago Architecture," in *Chicago Architecture, 1872–1922: Birth of a Metropolis*, ed. John Zukowsky (Munich: Prestel-Verlag, 1987), pp. 173–87.

18. The important story of company towns is told in several places, but a good summary of nineteenth century versions can be found in John S. Garner, *The Model Company Town: Urban Design Through Private Enterprise in Nineteenth-Century New England* (Amherst: University of Massachusetts Press, 1984). See also John W. Reps, *The Making of Urban America: A History of City Planning in the United States* (Princeton, N.J.: Princeton University Press, 1965), pp. 414–38; and Leland M. Roth, "Three Industrial Towns by McKim, Mead, and White," *Journal of the Society of Architectural Historians* 38 (December, 1979): 317–47.

19. For connections linking design, machinery, and business ideals in the twenties, see Arthur J. Pulos, *American Design Ethic: A History of Industrial Design to 1940* (Cambridge, Mass.: MIT Press, 1983), pp. 270–333, and, for the following

decade, pp. 336–419; and Richard Guy Wilson, Dianne H. Pilgrim, and Dickran Tashjian, *The Machine Age in America, 1918–1941* (New York: Harry N. Abrams, 1986), pp. 43–90.

20. For a monumental survey of architectural and design practices, covering New York City alone, which pays particular attention to commercial ideals and business traditions, see Robert A. M. Stern, Gregory Gilmartin, and Thomas Mellins, *New York 1930: Architecture and Urbanism Between the Two Wars* (New York: Rizzoli, 1987).

21. For some examinations of just how this industrial landscape was represented within twentieth-century American graphic art and photography, see Marianne Doezema, *American Realism and the Industrial Age* (Cleveland: Cleveland Museum of Art, 1980); Martin Friedman, *Charles Sheeler* (New York: Watson-Guptill, 1975); Mary Jane Jacob and Linda Downs, *The Rouge: The Image of Industry in the Art of Charles Sheeler and Diego Rivera* (Detroit: Detroit Institute of Arts, 1978); and Wilson , Pilgrim, and Tashjian, *The Machine Age in America*, passim.

22. See Norman Bel Geddes, *Horizons* (Boston: Little, Brown, 1932); Sheldon Cheney and Martha Cheney, *Art and the Machine: An Account of Industrial Design in 20th-Century America* (New York: McGraw-Hill, 1936); Paul T. Frankl, *Form and Re-Form, A Practical Handbook of Modern Interiors* (New York: Harper, 1930); Hugh Ferriss, *The Metropolis of Tomorrow* (New York: Ives Washburn, 1929); and Jeffrey L. Meikle, *Twentieth-Century Limited: Industrial Design in America 1925–1939* (Philadelphia: Temple University Press, 1979).

23. Among other surveys of twenties (and thirties) architecture see Barbara Capitman, Michael D. Kinerk, and Dennis W. Wilhelmm, *Rediscovering Art Deco USA* (New York: Viking Studio, 1994); Sheldon Cheney, *The New World Architecture* (New York: Longmans, Green, 1930); Carol Newton Johnson, *Tulsa Art Deco: An Architectural Era, 1925–1941* (Tulsa, Okla.: Junior League, 1980); Cervin Robinson and Rosemarie Haag Bletter, *Skyscraper Style, Art Deco New York* (New York: Oxford University Press, 1975).

24. Among the many foreign architects and artists who came to the United States at this time, drawn, in part by the chance to see some of the striking commercial and industrial accomplishments, were Le Corbusier and Erich Mendelsohn. Mendelsohn photographed skyscrapers, urban scenes, and industrial settings on his visit. Many European modernists emigrated to America in the fifteen or twenty years following World War I, including William Lescaze, Eliel Saarinen, Eugene Schoen, Walter Gropius, Mies van der Rohe, Herbert Bayer, Marcel Breuer, Lucian Bernhard, László Moholy-Nagy, Herbert Matter, Serge Chermayeff, Richard Neutra, and Raymond Loewy. They helped to transform the practice of architecture and commercial design.

25. The creation of Rockefeller Center is described in many places. The two most extended treatments are Alan Balfour, *Rockefeller Center: Architecture as Theatre* (New York: McGraw-Hill, 1978); and Carol Herselle Krinsky, *Rockefeller*

Center (New York: Oxford University Press, 1978). But just as indispensable is the first chapter of William H. Jordy, *American Buildings and Their Architects: The Impact of European Modernism in the Mid-Twentieth Century* (Garden City, N.Y.: Doubleday, 1972), pp. 1–85; and Stern, Gilmartin, and Mellins, *New York 1930,* pp. 617–71.

26. This episode is well described in Tilmann Buddensieg, *Industriekultur: Peter Behrens and the AEG* (Cambridge, Mass.: MIT Press, 1984). The text was originally published in German in 1979.

27. Nikolaus Pevsner, "Patient Progress One: Frank Pick," in *Studies in Art, Architecture, and Design* (New York: Walker, 1968), vol. 2, pp. 190–209, treats Pick's remarkable patronage. For the broader London transport effort, and particularly for the posters, see Oliver Green, *Art for the London Underground* (New York: Rizzoli, 1990).

28. For an overview of corporate interest in modern design, advertising, and art patronage during the interwar years, see Neil Harris, "Designs on Demand: Art and the Modern Corporation," in Neil Harris, *Cultural Excursions: Marketing Appetites and Cultural Tastes in Modern America* (Chicago: University of Chicago Press, 1990), pp. 349–78.

29. Paepcke's remarkable patronage is treated most extensively by James Sloan Allen, *The Romance of Commerce and Culture: Capitalism, Modernism, and the Chicago-Aspen Crusade for Cultural Reform* (Chicago: University of Chicago Press, 1983), chaps. 1–2.

30. For more on the Wrigley building see Sally Chappell, "As If the Lights Were Always Shining: Graham, Anderson, Probst and White's Wrigley Building at the Boulevard Link," in *Chicago Architecture 1872–1922: Birth of a Metropolis,* ed. John Zukowsky (Munich: Prestel-Verlag, 1978), pp. 291-301; and Sally A. Kitt Chappell, *Transforming Tradition: Architecture and Planning of Graham, Anderson, Probst and White, 1922–1936* (Chicago: University of Chicago Press, 1992), pp. 52–55, 123–25.

31. "Architecture and Illumination: A Notable Example in the Wrigley Building, Chicago," *Architectural Forum* 35 (September, 1921): 135.

32. Much has been written on the *Tribune* competition. A history of the competition and the site can be found in John W. Stamper, *Chicago's North Michigan Avenue: Planning and Development, 1900–1930* (Chicago: University of Chicago Press, 1991), pp. 61–88.

33. The *Tribune* was quoted in its editorials in an article, "The Tribune Tower, Chicago," *Architectural Forum* 43 (October, 1925): pp. 185–86. In his report to the newspaper on the competition Alfred Granger, an architect, declared, "Never before has the 'quality of beauty' been recognized as of commercial value by an American corporation, yet all the greatest architecture of the past has been based upon beauty as its fundamental essential" (ibid., p. 186).

34. John Taylor Boyd Jr., "Office Interiors," *Architectural Forum* 41 (September 1924): 143–45.

35. Cass Gilbert, "Industrial Architecture in Concrete," *Architectural Forum* 39 (September 1923): 86. This whole issue was devoted to industrial architecture, and the other contributors expressed sentiments similar to those of Gilbert.

36. Harvey Wiley Corbett, "The Architects' Forum," *Architectural Forum* 46 (February 1927): 176. This was a guest editorial.

37. "Kansas City Life Insurance Company Building," *Architectural Forum* 43 (October 1925): 191–92.

38. For sample comments see Royal Cortissoz, "The Cunard Building," *Architectural Forum* 35 (July 1921): 1–8; Alfred Hopkins, "Some Ideas on Bank Buildings—Artistic and Practical," *Architectural Forum* 36 (January 1922): 1–8; Frederic C. Hirons, "The Architecture of Banks," *Architectural Forum* 38 (June 1923): 253–62; Philip Sawyer, "The Planning of Banks," *Architectural Forum* 38 (June 1923): 263–72; John H. Ely, "Home Office Building for the Mutual Benefit Life Insurance Company, Newark," *Architectural Forum* 49 (October 1928): 497–507; Leo J. Sheridan and W. C. Clark, "The Straus Building, Chicago," *Architectural Forum* 42 (April 1925): 225–28; and William C. Hays, "Some Recent Office Buildings in San Francisco,"*Architectural Forum* 41. (September 1924): 101–4. For the career of one of the period's bank builders, and also for some of his views on the impact of richly designed and substantially proportioned banking halls, see Dennis Sharp, *Alfred C. Bossom's American Architecture 1903–1926* (London: Book Art, 1984), passim.

39. Richard Guy Wilson, "Architecture in the Machine Age," in *The Machine Age in America, 1918–1941,* p. 163.

40. Kenneth Murchison as quoted by Richard Guy Wilson (ibid., p. 165). The original developer of the building was William Reynolds, who sold his lease in 1928 to Walter Chrysler.

41. Stern, Gilmartin, and Mellins, *New York 1930,* pp. 507–615, contains excellent summaries and analyses which focus on the skyscraper work of these and other New York architects.

42. For Hood and his various skyscrapers see Arthur Tappan North, *Contemporary American Architects: Raymond M. Hood* (New York: McGraw-Hill, 1931); and Walter H. Kilham Jr., *Raymond Hood, Architect: Form Through Function in the American Skyscraper* (New York: Architectural Book Publishing Co., 1973).

43. Daniel Nelson, *Managers and Workers: Origins of the New Factory System in the United States, 1880–1920* (Madison: University of Wisconsin Press, 1975), pp. 114–21, treats the years just before World War I. He identified (p. 115) at least forty manufacturing firms that introduced extensive welfare programs in the ten years before the war, with heavy concentrations in textiles, machinery, and iron and steel. Among the firms represented were National Cash Register, Remington Typewriter, International Harvester, Amoskeag Mills, Procter and Gamble, Curtis Publishing, H. J. Heinz, and Firestone Tire and Rubber.

44. Boyd, "Office Interiors," pp. 143–46.

45. Sexton, *American Commercial Buildings of Today,* pp. 111–12.

46. For Heinz see Robert C. Alberts, *The Good Provider: H. J. Heinz and His 57 Varieties* (Boston: Houghton Mifflin, 1973), pp. 181–94. For Curtis Publishing see Edward Bok, *The Americanization of Edward Bok: The Autobiography of a Dutch Boy Fifty Years After* (New York: Scribner's, 1920), chap. 22.

47. In addition to visitors like Erich Mendelsohn, who published photographic texts featuring American factories, and American photographers like Charles Sheeler and other precisionists, the picture journals of the thirties, like *Life* and *Fortune*, were important popularizers of the industrial complexes, as was *Architectural Forum* with its use of important contemporary photographers. This was not an exclusively American phenomenon, of course, as the work of contemporary Russian artists and photographers, or of Carl Grossberg and August Sander in Germany, makes clear. See the catalog *Kunst und Technik in den 20er Jahren: Neue Sachlichkeit und Gegenstandlicher Konstruktivismus* (Munich: Lenbachhaus, 1980).

48. For the history of public relations see Morrell Heald, *The Social Responsibilities of Business: Company and Community, 1900–1960* (Cleveland: Case Western Reserve University Press, 1970); Kenneth Henry, *Defenders and Shapers of the Corporate Image* (New Haven, Conn.: College and University Press, 1972); Alan Raucher, *Public Relations and Business, 1900–1929* (Baltimore, Md.: Johns Hopkins University Press [1968]); and Richard S. Tedlow, *Keeping the Corporate Image: Public Relations and Business, 1900–1950* (Greenwich, Conn.: JAI Press, 1979).

49. Charles G. Loring, "The Bowery Savings Bank," *Architectural Forum* 48 (June 1928): 799.

50. Taken from a speech given to the Merchants' Club, April 13, 1897, reprinted in Charles Moore, *Daniel Burnham, Architect, Planner of Cities* (Boston: Houghton Mifflin, 1921), vol. 2, p. 102.

51. The most extensive recent discussion of these fairs is Robert W. Rydell, *World of Fairs: The Century-of-Progress Expositions* (Chicago: University of Chicago Press, 1993). For an elaborate and well-illustrated treatment of the New York fair see Larry Zim, Mel Lerner, and Herbert Rolfes, *The World of Tomorrow: The 1939 New York World's Fair* (New York: Harper and Row, 1988).

52. When the postwar building boom began, such gaps were noted. See, e.g., "Offices: Building Fast," *Business Week,* July 23, 1955, pp. 31–32; and "Offices: They Can't Catch Up," *Business Week,* December 29, 1956, pp. 25–26.

53. The breathless tone of the new building boom was caught in journals like *Time, Newsweek, Fortune,* and *Business Week* in the mid 50s. See, e.g., "The Builders Keep Right On," *Business Week*, January 12, 1957, pp. 43–48; "Manhattan's New Towers Massive Machines for Work," *Business Week,* January 12, 1957, pp. 50–56; "Real Estate: New Look in Manhattan," *Time,* October 1, 1956, pp. 78–79; "Real Estate: Beauty Treatment," *Time,* December 10, 1956) p. 98.

54. Most elaborately argued in Serge Guilbaut, *How New York Stole the Idea*

of Modern Art: Abstract Expression, Freedom, and the Cold War (Chicago: University of Chicago Press, 1983).

55. There was still, in many places, business resistance to such endorsement of modernism. Thus the Bank of the Southwest in Houston rejected a William Zorach sculpture for its new Kenneth Franzheim building, on the basis of its modernity. See Stephen Fox, *Houston Architectural Guide* (Houston: American Institute of Architects and Herring Press, 1990), p. 39. For the suspicion of modern art which was in place just after World War II, see Margaret Lynne Ausfeld and Virginia M. Mecklenburg, *Advancing American Art: Politics and Aesthetics in the State Department Exhibition, 1946–48* (Montgomery, Ala:, Montgomery Museum of Fine Arts, 1984). For a broader consideration of American attitudes to modern art ,see George H. Roeder Jr., *Forum of Uncertainty: Confrontations with Modern Painting in Twentieth-Century American Thought* (Ann Arbor, Mich.: UMI Press, 1980).

56. Henry R. Luce, "The Place of Art in American Life," *Architectural Forum* 104 (January 1956), p. 133.

57. For more on the history of corporate art collecting in America see Mitchell Douglas Kahan, *Art Inc.: American Paintings from Corporate Collections* (Montgomery, Ala.: Montgomery Museum of Fine Arts, 1979). See also Harris, "Designs on Demand," for a discussion of this issue and for references to discussions of corporate collecting in the 1940s, '50s, and '60s.

58. This landmark case, *A. P. Smith Manufacturing Company v. Barlow*, was decided in the chancery division of the Superior Court of New Jersey. It has been much described. The U.S. Supreme Court dismissed the appeal of stockholders trying to bar the board of directors from making philanthropic donations. Another important moment in the history of corporate philanthropy had come twenty years earlier, with the passage of the Revenue Act of 1935, permitting corporations to deduct up to 5 percent of income as gifts to charities.

59. Note, among others, Oscar Schisgal, "Our Newest Patron of the Arts," *Reader's Digest,* May 1960, 192–98; "Art for Sales' Sake at Reynolds (A Portfolio)," *Fortune,* November 1960, pp. 158–61; "Culture, Inc.," *Time,* February 21, 1964, pp. 85–86; "The Corporate Splurge in Abstract Art," *Fortune,* April, 1960, pp. 138–47; Henry J. Seldis, "Business Buys Art," *Art in America* 52 (February 1964): 131–34; and Charlotte Willard, "The Corporation as Art Collector," *Look,* March 23, 1965, pp. 67–72. For more recent observations on business collecting see Marjory Jacobson, *Art for Work: The New Renaissance in Corporate Collecting* (Boston: Harvard Business School Press, 1993); and Rosanne Martorella, *Corporate Art* (New Brunswick, N.J.: Rutgers University Press, 1990). Martorella points out that by the 1980s the Directory of Corporate Art Collections listed holdings of over seven hundred corporations in North America, Europe, and Japan, almost 80 percent of them begun after 1960.

60. This figure is taken from W. Hawkins Ferry, *The Legacy of Albert Kahn* (Detroit: Detroit Institute of Arts, 1970), p. 75. For Kahn's massive achievement see also *Architecture by Albert Kahn Associated Architects and Engineers, Inc.* (New

York: Architectural Catalog Company, 1948), a photographic survey of the firm's output up to that point; Frederico Bucci, *Albert Kahn: Architect of Ford* (New York: Princeton Architectural Press, 1993); and Grant Hildebrand, *Designing for Industry: The Architecture of Albert Kahn* (Cambridge, Mass.: MIT Press, 1974). Kahn also designed the homes of many of the industrialists who commissioned factory buildings from him, among them James Couzens, Edsel Ford, Henry B. Joy, George C. Booth, Horace E. Dodge, and John S. Newberry. Such a combination of domestic and corporate patronage could be found elsewhere, in Frank Lloyd Wright, for example, and constitutes an interesting subject in its own right.

61. For the Austin company see Martin Greif, *The New Industrial Landscape: The Story of the Austin Company* (Clinton, N.J.: Main Street Press, 1978). For Lockwood Greene see Samuel B. Lincoln, *Lockwood Greene: The History of an Engineering Business, 1832–1958* (Brattleboro, Vt.: Stephen Greene Press, 1960). These other firms included C. F. Murphy Associates, Skidmore, Owings & Merrill, the Architects Collaborative, Kevin Roche, Welton Becket, and John Dinkeloo and Associates, firms which would be major shapers of administrative and headquarters buildings for large corporations. The professional journals of the fifties and sixties demonstrate such penetration, e.g., "Industrial Buildings," *Architectural Record* 125 (January 1959): 147–70.

62. Biographies of the architects, memoirs, and firm histories indicate these relationships. Thus, for Wright's close ties to Herbert Johnson see Bruce Brooks Pfeiffer, ed., *Letters to Clients: Frank Lloyd Wright* (Fresno: California State University Press, 1986), passim. "Give me enough enlightened business men and I can change the face of the nation," Wright declared (p. 133). For Mies and Phyllis Bronfman see Franz Schulze, *Mies van der Rohe: A Critical Biography* (Chicago: University of Chicago Press, 1985), pp. 270–83.

63. Hewitt's role is described in Wayne G. Broehl Jr., *John Deere's Company: A History of Deere & Company and Its Times* (New York: Doubleday, 1984), pp. 636–41.

64. For an analysis of how corporations chose their architects, concluding that selection had become protracted and bureaucratized by committee discussion, see "How Today's Clients Choose Architects," *Architectural Forum* 110 (February 1959): 114–15.

65. Miller was also, for a time, president of the National Council of Churches. Architectural fees were financed, in many cases, through the Cummins Engine Foundation. For more on Columbus see *Columbus, Indiana: A Look at Architecture* (Columbus, Ind.: Visitors Center, 1974). For an early commentary on the program, see "Excellence in Indiana," *Architectural Forum* 117 (August 1962): 120–23, describing an elementary school in the town designed by John Warnecke.

66. For one statement of this philosophy see "Office Center in Suburbs," *Business Week*, March 20, 1954, pp. 138–40. For a consideration of some of the problems involved with relocation, made somewhat later, see Charles Hoyt, "Office Buildings in the Suburbs," *Architectural Record* 156 (October 1974): 125–40.

67. Professional journals heaped praise on structures setting aside space for

public use. "If surrender of one-fourth the plot to trees and pavement, sculpture (forthcoming), pools and fountains was a calculated gift to the city, it surely earned the citizens' affection," declared *Architectural Forum* about the new *Time-Life* tower. See *Architectural Forum* 113 (July 1960): p. 75.

68. For Seagram's see Schulze, *Mies an der Rohe,* pp. 270–83.

69. Ibid., p. 275.

70. "Seagram's Bet on Elegance," *Architectural Forum* 109 (July 1958): 76. This issue of the *Forum* contained two other articles on the new building.

71. For a sense of an important earlier building manager's view, with its emphasis on efficiency and impatience with architectural innovation, see Clarence T. Coley, "Office Buildings, Past, Present and Future," *Architectural Forum* 41 (September 1924): 113–14. "The best investments are made in office buildings that are useful and comfortable," wrote Coley, the manager of the Equitable in New York. "Much money is spent and poorly invested, according to the writer's belief, in an attempt to make office buildings agreeable to look upon, beautiful and artistic, as it has been proved that space in them cannot be sold for any higher price" (Ibid., p. 113).

72. Nathaniel Alexander Owings, *The Spaces in Between: An Architect's Journey* (Boston: Houghton Mifflin, 1973), pp. 104–5.

73. *Time,* April 28, 1952, p. 74.

74. *Newsweek,* May 5, 1952, pp. 82–83.

75. Owings, *The Spaces in Between,* pp. 107, 109.

76. For the history and influence of this project, see William H. Jordy, "PSFS: Its Development and Its Significance in Modern Architecture," *Journal of the Society of Architectural Historians* 21 (May 1962): 47–83; Jordy, *American Buildings and Their Architects,* pp. 87–164; and Robert A. M. Stern, *George Howe: Toward a Modern American Architecture* (New Haven, Conn.: Yale University Press, 1975), pp. 108–32.

77. Lewis Mumford, "Crystal Lantern," *New Yorker,* November 13, 1954, pp. 181–87.

78. "Something to See," *Time,* August 31, 1953, p. 78; "Money Changing in a House of Glass," *Life,* October 25, 1954, p. 62; and "Bank Counts Its Money," *Newsweek,* October 16, 1954, pp. 48–52.

79. For an example of post–Lever House rhetoric, see "More Glass Houses," *Newsweek,* August 31, 1953, p. 77. And for a stimulating discussion of the corporate and institutional turn to modernism, and its association with a rhetoric of progress and imperial destiny, see Alan Gowans, *Styles and Types of North American Architecture: Social Function and Cultural Expression* (New York: HarperCollins, 1992), pp. 271–317.

80. For typical praise see James S. Hornbeck, "Office Buildings 1965," *Architectural Record* 138 (December 1965): 139–62, reviewing a series of structures in Portland, Minneapolis, and Tampa; and "Office Buildings 1967," *Architectural Record* 141 (June 1967): 171–86. This last essay singled out buildings

by Emery Roth, Victor Gruen, and Vincent Kling, arguing that corporations were now insisting on quality in the buildings they leased, and that developers had responded by providing them with upgraded systems and design. For praise of plazas see Allan Temko, *Two Buildings: San Francisco 1959* (San Francisco: San Francisco Museum of Art, 1959), commenting on two new SOM creations, the Crown Zellerbach and John Hancock Buildings. Crown Zellerbach, Temko pointed out, produced "a magnificent gift of urban space, carved out of a rapidly declining waste, to the people of San Francisco" (p. 15). Of all the plaza skyscrapers it was the most generous in its deployment of opening space, Temko asserted, and made the "dry formalism of Lever House and Seagram uninspired by comparison" (p. 17).

81. See, e.g., "A Campus Setting for Research," *Architectural Record* 126 (October 1959): 211–16. "Today's dynamic world of commerce for some time has been acutely aware of the values and virtues of establishing an appropriate corporate image," the writer went on, in an article describing Ulrich Franzen's group of buildings for Philip Morris. "Now more progressive firms are realizing what a tremendous impact an equally knowing sort of architect—and general esthetics—can have in fostering an Image. It is a bold, straightforward method, which creates a singular, and well retained, concept in the public's mind. Witness the durable pictures of Corning, General Motors, Seagram, Lever Brothers" (p. 212).

82. Among these critics, of course, was Tom Wolfe, *From Bauhaus to Our House* (New York: Farrar, Straus and Giroux, 1981). The Wolfe book, along with already apparent changes in the late seventies, helped promote a wider skepticism of modernism as a style and a set of principles.

83. See Alvin Zelver, "Oh San Francisco!" *Architectural Forum* 132 (January–February, 1970): 68–71, describing the controversy William Pereira's plans were arousing. In the early sixties, even while plans were being announced for the World Trade Center and the Prudential Center in Boston, critics were complaining of the monotony of the new landscape and praising buildings which appeared to possess some "romantic" individuality. See, e.g., "Innovation in Chicago," *Architectural Record* 135 (January 1964): 133–38, a commentary on the United States Gypsum Building by Perkins and Will.

84. James W. Pygman and Richard Kateley, *Tall Office Buildings in the United States* (Washington:, D.C.; Urban Land Institute, 1985), analyzes the rhythm and pace of tall office building in twentieth century America, concluding that not "until the early 1970s did the development of major high-rise office towers by other than corporate or institutional owners become an accepted and geographically widespread practice" (p. 20). In New York City, at least, the impression was otherwise. See, e.g., "Offices: Building Fast," *Business Week*, July 23, 1955, pp. 31–32.

85. For the increasing costs of building produced by advanced technologies, see "Manhattan's New Towers Massive Machines for Work," *Business Week*, January 12, 1957, pp. 50–56.

86. Lewis Mumford was a particularly sharp critic of the scale and location of

these buildings, and the growing problems of urban congestion. See, e.g., Lewis Mumford, "The Sky Line: Skin Treatment and New Wrinkles," *New Yorker,* Oct., 23, 1954, pp. 118-24. "As a whole," Mumford wrote of the new buildings, "they are an ironic commentary upon the intelligence of our financiers (vestigial) and the civic foresight of our city planning commission (absent)" (ibid., p. 118).

87. James S. Russell, "Icons of Modernism or Machine-Age Dinosaurs," *Architectural Record* 177 (June 1989): pp. 142–47, expresses more recent disenchantment with the isolated tower and the open plaza. Twenty years earlier such themes surfaced in the writings of several critics such as Jane Jacobs and, with a number of differences, Peter Blake. See Peter Blake, "Slaughter on Sixth Avenue," *Architectural Forum* 122 (June 1965): 122, commenting on the series of structures, including the Equitable Life, J. C. Penney, Sperry-Rand, and Hilton Hotel buildings, erected on the Avenue of the Americas in the previous several years. Blake is quoted in Victoria Newhouse, *Wallace K. Harrison, Architect* (New York: Rizzoli, 1989), p. 160.

88. See, among others, Herbert L. Smith, "Big Scope for Smaller Scale," *Architectural Record* 173 (January 1985): 97–113, although it concentrates on smaller-scale suburban construction; and Grace Anderson, "Five by KPF," *Architectural Record* 175 (February 1987): 126–35, who noted: "Despite the puzzlement of those who wonder how developers will find more tenants and office workers, despite the concern of environmentalists who worry about overcrowding and perpetual shade, despite the head-shaking of the naturally modest who deplore gigantism and hubris, the building type proliferates and evolves" (p. 126).

89. Walter McQuade, "A Daring New Generation of Skyscrapers," *Fortune,* February 1973, p. 81.

90. For this lengthy process in one metropolis, see Robert Bruegmann, "Schaumburg, Oak Brook, Rosemont, and the Recentering of the Chicago Metropolitan Area," in *Chicago Architecture and Design, 1923–1993: Reconfiguration of an American Metropolis,* ed. John Zukowsky (Munich: Prestel-Verlag, 1993), pp. 159–77.

91. For an overview of a related theme, the popularity of small-town and peripheral locations with American corporations in the seventies and eighties, see David A. Heenan, *The New Corporate Frontier: The Big Move to Small Town, U.S.A.* (New York: McGraw-Hill, 1991). A table (p. 30), reflects the decining hold of major cities on corporate headquarters.

92. "Office Building 1963," *Architectural Record* 133 (April 1963): pp. 181–204.

93. See ibid. for examples of these building types.

94. "Offices: Building Fast, Filling Fast," *Business Week,* July 23, 1955, p. 32.

95. "Engineered for Thinking," *Architectural Forum* 110 (February 1959): 116–121.

96. There were other dates considered significant. Thus a writer in the *New York Times* compared the 1970 move of Pepsico from New York City to Purchase,

New York, with the decision, almost twenty years before, of Joseph E. Seagram & Sons to remain in the city. See *New York Times,* June 9, 1972, p. 39.

97. For a review of corporate moves outside New York City, on the occasion of the Johns-Manville announcement, see *New York Times,* May 20, 1971, p. 24. See also *New York Times,* April 28, 1971, p. 1; *New York Times,* March 7, 1971, p. 56; *New York Times,* February 28, 1971, sec. 8, p. 1; *New York Times,* February 5, 1971, p. 33; *New York Times,* July 11, 1971, sec. 8, p. 1; *New York Times,* July 20, 1971, p. 23; and *New York Times,* August 22, 1971, sec. 3, p. 3, for more commentaries on corporate moves out of the city, efforts to counter them, and their social and economic impact.

98. Heenan, *The New Corporate Frontier,* p. 30.

99. See "Cities Where Business Is Still Holding Up," *U.S. News & World Report,* March 31, 1975, p. 60; and *New York Times,* April 28, 1971, p. 1.

100. These polls, released by the Roper Center at the University of Connecticut in the spring of 1974, can be found on *Public Opinion Online,* April 9, 1989.

101. See the charges brought by New York City's economic development administrator, in *New York Times,* February 5, 1971, p. 33.

102. See Mark Alpert, "Office Buildings for the 1990s," *Fortune,* November 18, 1991, pp. 140–50.

103. "When a Company's Home Is Its Castle," *U.S. News & World Report,* April 11, 1983, p. 78.

104. For Roche's General Food Company Headquarters see Francesco Dal Co, *Kevin Roche* (New York: Rizzoli, 1985), pp. 17–18, 51.

105. Susan R. Bleznick, "Midwestern Vernacular: Charles Moore's TRINOVA Headquarters Rephrases Agrarian Form," *Inland Architect* 35 (July–August 1991): 54.

106. "The Johns-Manville World Headquarters Building," *Architectural Record* 162 (September 1977): 93. The Architects Collaborative, designers of the building, won out over several prominent firms in a company-sponsored competition. The building was dedicated in 1976.

107. Margaret Gaskie, "Classic Contemporary," *Architectural Record* 173 (March 1985): 136–43. The company had an earlier building designed by Gordon Bunshaft, in the Lever House manner. The energy crisis, however, discouraged further moves in that direction.

108. For one effort to make up for the loss of downtown amenities with a surrogate city street and social spaces, see Grace Anderson, "A Lofty Gallery Skylights Suburban Offices: AT&T Long Lines Eastern Regional Headquarters," *Architectural Record* 169 (November 1981): 88–95.

109. "John Deere's Sticks of Steel," *Architectural Forum* 121 (July 1964): 76–83.

110. "Insurance Sets a Pattern," *Architectural Forum* 107 (September 1957): 112–27. The question of how to disguise parking soon became more significant. By the early seventies the Western Union corporate headquarters in Saddle River, New

Jersey, placed parked cars in "shelves" screened by trees, to avoid the "supermarket appearance" of a "flat plane of asphalt." See Hoyt,"Office Buildings in the Suburbs," 125–40. Some years later, corporate complexes were spending even more money disguising the presence of cars. See, e.g., John Gallagher, "Making Waves: Landscaping Enriches Ford Regent Court," *Inland Architect* 35 (July–August 1991): 46–49.

111. Will Marlin, "Two Business Buildings," *Architectural Record* 159 (February 1976): 81–90.

112. Mildred F. Schmertz, "Recollection and Invention," *Architectural Record* 176 (January 1988): 62–73.

113. Margaret Gaskie, "Productive Politesse," *Architectural Record* 176 (October 1988): 104.

114. "Restructuring the Corporate Habitat," *Architectural Record* 171 (October 1983): 111.

115. Robert Bruegmann, "The Corporate Landscape," *Inland Architect* 33 (October–November. 1989): 33–42. Bruegmann's essay, aside from incisive commentary on three major suburban complexes, places their landscaping approaches within broader historical traditions. See also Philip Berger, "Natural Connection," *Inland Architect* 36 (September–October 1992): 41–43, on the elaborate landscaping of the Ameritech Center in Hoffman Estates.

116. Dal Co, *Kevin Roche*, pp. 17–18. The part of the interview (pp. 55–85) with Roche that covers his corporate architectural projects—and they include Union Carbide, College Life Insurance Company of America, Richardson-Vicks Inc., Cummins Engine, Exxon, General Foods, and Conoco—contains some of the most interesting and insightful comments by an architect about corporate clients and designing for corporate headquarters in recent times.

117. Charles Hoyt, "Space-Age Imagery," *Architectural Record* 169 (December 1981): 69.

118. See the discussion in Grace Anderson, "Offices Go to the Suburbs," *Architectural Record* 171 (April 1983): 113–29.

119. Hoyt, "Office Buildings in the Suburbs," p. 130.

120. Anderson, "A Lofty Gallery Skylights Suburban Offices," p. 88.

121. Alpert, "Office Buildings for the 1990s," p. 146.

122. Dal Co, *Kevin Roche*, p. 58.

123. For more on the Johnson Wax commissions, see Jonathan Lipman, *Frank Lloyd Wright and the Johnson Wax Buildings* (New York: Rizzoli, 1986).

124. For the significance of this commission see Gregory Gilbert, "AT&T Corporate Headquarters," in *The Critical Edge: Controversy in Recent American Architecture*, ed. Tod A. Marder, (Cambridge, Mass.: MIT Press, 1985), pp. 47–62.

125. For more on these structures and the firms involved, see Carleton Knight III, *Philip Johnson/John Burgee Architecture, 1979–1985* (New York: Rizzoli, 1985); Sonia Chao and Trevor D. Abramson, eds., *Kohn Pedersen Fox: Buildings and Projects, 1976–1986* (New York: Rizzoli, 1987); Paul M. Sachner, Richard

Maschal, and Douglas Gantenbein, "Three Cities, on Spec," *Architectural Record* 176 (July 1988): 98–111; "You Are What You Build," *U.S. News & World Report,* July 11, 1988. p. 44; and Alpert, "Office Buildings for the 1990s." For a summary of some earlier moves away from the classic modernism of the sixties see McQuade, "A Daring New Generation of Skyscrapers."

126. For more on this see Paul M. Sachner, "Entertainment Architecture," *Architectural Record* 177 (September 1989): 66–71.

127. Darrel Crilley, "Architecture as Advertising: Constructing the Image of Redevelopment," in *Selling Places: The City as Cultural Capital, Past and Present,* ed. Gerry Kearns and Chris Philo (Oxford: Pergamon Press, 1993), p. 243.

128. The attorney and Philip Johnson are quoted in "Landmarks That Work," *Newsweek,* June 19, 1978, pp. 63–64.

129. See the special issue of *Progressive Architecture* 60 (November 1979), devoted to historic preservation, as one instance of this broad interest. For a taste of this sensibility applied to hotels see "The Riches in Older Hotels," *Business Week,* November 11, 1976, p. 120. And, for a very recent example, John Handley, "History Lessons Earning 'A' in Economics," *Chicago Tribune,* May 8, 1994, sec. 16, p. c.

130. Paul M. Sachner, "Rich as Rockefeller," *Architectural Record* 178 (April 1990): 68–73.

131. Margaret Gaskie, "Chicago Style 1989," *Architectural Record* 177 (September 1989): 92–95. Architects also spoke a language of greater sensitivity to suburban and exurban downtowns. The headquarters building designed for Pitney Bowles adjoined the downtown of Stamford, Connecticut, and, according to Henry Cobb, the I. M. Pei partner in charge of the design, there was a conscious effort to "minimize the building's impact on the low-rise neighborhood." The firm's strategy, Cobb declared, was "to acknowledge the building's scale but use the inevitable volume to enrich the public realm." Pitney Bowles committed itself to landscaping and maintaining the site, a knoll of land with spectacular views of Long Island Sound. See Paul M. Sachner, "Pillar to Post," *Architectural Record* 176 (June 1988): 122–27.

132. See "Skyscraper Name Games," *Chicago Tribune,* April 4, 1993, Sec. 16, p. c.

133. Pygman and Kateley, *Tall Office Buildings,* pp. 110–14.

134. See, e.g., Steve Lohr, "I.B.M. May Quit Hilltop Headquarters," *New York Times,* January13, 1994, sec. 1, p. C18; and Claudia H. Deutsch, "I.B.M. Sells Its Building in New York," *New York Times,* May 7, 1994, p. 19.

135. See the summary of a 1986 university conference on corporate architecture by Catherine Ingraham, reporting on a Kohn Pedersen Fox designer's view that speculative developers provided more design opportunities for architects than did corporate clients. She might well have singled out for attention Johnson Burgee's Pennzoil Place in Houston and Helmut Jahn's Liberty Place in Philadelphia. Catherine Ingraham, "Icons of Late Capitalism: Corporations and Their Architecture," *Inland Architect* 31 (January–February,1987): 75–79. A more popular notion

found the corporate headquarters—Humana in Louisville, Procter and Gamble in Cincinnati, Hercules in Wilmington, Pittsburgh Plate Glass, Bank of the Southwest in Houston, AT&T in New York—far more interesting and bolder than the speculative developers. See Jayne Merkel, "Corporate vs. Speculative: What a Difference Design Makes," *Inland Architect* 29 (October–November, 1985): 33–36.

136. These comments appear in the same article quoting the Hartford developer (Sachner, Maschal and Gantenbein, "Three Cities on Spec," pp. 98, 104). But Jayne Merkel reported that in interviewing dozens of "tenants, potential tenants, developers, city officials, realtors," regarding new office space in downtown Cincinnati, "not one mentioned design as a factor in rentability." Merkel, "Corporate vs. Speculative," p. 36.

137. "One Hundred Years of Significant Buildings. I: Office Buildings," *Architectural Record* 119 (June 1956): 147–54. Although this essay treated only office buildings, it included the full list of all structures (excluding houses) in order of preference. The first twenty, in preferential order, consisted of the Wainwright Building in St. Louis; Carson Pirie Scott in Chicago; Rockefeller Center and Lever House in New York; Trinity Church in Boston; PSFS in Philadelphia; the General Motors Technical Center in Dearborn; Lake Shore Drive Apartments in Chicago; Johnson and Sons Administrative Center in Racine, Wisconsin; the Monadnock in Chicago; the Daily News Building in New York; the Norris Dam built by the TVA; the Boston Public Library; the Stock Pavilion in Raleigh, North Carolina; the Christian Science Church in Berkeley; the Woolworth Building in New York; the Crow Island School in Winnetka, Illinois; the Nebraska State Capitol in Lincoln; Johnson and Sons Laboratory in Racine; and the United Nations Secretariat in New York City. Fourteen houses, including the Robie House, Falling Water, and Taliesen West, were listed separately.

Index

The American corporation
today